Art and Print Production

SECOND EDITION

N.N. Sarkar
Formerly Associate Professor
Indian Institute of Mass Communication
New Delhi

OXFORD
UNIVERSITY PRESS

Oxford University Press is a department of the University of Oxford.
It furthers the University's objective of excellence in research, scholarship,
and education by publishing worldwide. Oxford is a registered trade mark of
Oxford University Press in the UK and in certain other countries.

Published in India by
Oxford University Press
YMCA Library Building, 1 Jai Singh Road, New Delhi 110001, India

© Oxford University Press 2008, 2013

The moral rights of the author/s have been asserted.

First Edition published in 2008
Second Edition published in 2013

All rights reserved. No part of this publication may be reproduced, stored in
a retrieval system, or transmitted, in any form or by any means, without the
prior permission in writing of Oxford University Press, or as expressly permitted
by law, by licence, or under terms agreed with the appropriate reprographics
rights organization. Enquiries concerning reproduction outside the scope of the
above should be sent to the Rights Department, Oxford University Press, at the
address above.

You must not circulate this work in any other form
and you must impose this same condition on any acquirer.

ISBN-13: 978-0-19-808556-0
ISBN-10: 0-19-808556-7

Typeset in Baskerville
by Anvi Composers, New Delhi 110063
Printed at Repro India Limited

Third-party website addresses mentioned in this book are provided
by Oxford University Press in good faith and for information only.
Oxford University Press disclaims any responsibility for the material contained therein.

Preface to the Second Edition

The first edition of *Art and Print Production* was a complete book in itself that covered the basic concepts of art and design, their production, and important application areas. It provided a working knowledge of most of the processes that students could put to practical use in their professional lives. The second edition of the book takes this approach further by including the latest trends in the world of print production.

My interactions with the students and professionals of different areas of mass communication ever since the book was published kept me active in monitoring the content of the subject in relation to the market trend. There has been a lot of change in the discipline, especially in the area of technology. Today, desktop publishing (DTP) is being widely used, aided by the availability of a variety of related software tools in the market. Going with the trend, most of the changes in this edition are technology driven.

Constant research and development in computer applications for designing and production is visible in printed material across the world. Therefore, features of design software tools are given adequate importance in this edition.

Modern offset presses have now transitioned to computer to plate (CtP) technology as opposed to the conventional computer to film printing process. It produces superior quality by increasing the sharpness of images and reducing the registration defects. It is also very efficient in generating output plates. In addition, we have digital printing that completely removes the need for printing plates. The second edition provides a comparison between film plate and CtP to exhibit a clear idea of cost and quality effectiveness for those who are yet to make up their mind about switching over to the new digital environment.

Billboards as a form of outdoor design have long been a medium to advertise and promote various products and services. The viewers of billboards are usually mobile, a condition that restricts the viewing time. This limited exposure time forces outdoor designers to follow a disciplined creative approach. Till not so long ago, outdoor designing was the domain of skilled painters and fabricators but not any longer; the revolution of print technology has penetrated into this field as well. Keeping in consonance with the demand of the day coupled with the challenges ahead, a completely new chapter on outdoor design has been included in this edition.

The contribution of digital technology is central to this edition; however it has not overshadowed the role of art and aesthetics of the media. I am confident the students will be greatly inspired by the examples which are supplemented with a host of visuals. It will help them develop their entrepreneurial skills. Substrate and other materials for fabrication discussed in Chapter 21 shall serve as reference manual and ready reckoner for the advertisers and users of outdoor design.

Key Features

- Explores and provides technical inputs for various aspects of designing
- Looks at the latest technology and trends in art and print production

- Discusses the Roman script as well as the Devanagari script (an integral part of Indian designs) in a separate chapter on typography
- Includes a chapter on digital prepress
- Encourages self-study, with the concepts discussed in the chapters amply and vividly illustrated with photographs, figures, exhibits, and tables
- Explains various printing techniques and processes through step-by-step photographs captured on camera
- Colour plates to depict the visual effect of various types of images

New to the Second Edition

- New chapter on outdoor design
- New section in Chapter 5 on software tools for designing
- New section in Chapter 8 on handling a print project
- New section in Chapter 9 on computer to technology

Coverage and Structure

The book has 21 chapters that succinctly cover the entire gamut of the concepts and technologies involved in art and print production and their application to some select areas of print communication.

Chapter 1 discusses the concept and theory of art and covers all the issues arising in the planning, execution, and production of printed material. Chapters 2 and 3 discuss the two major components of graphics types and visuals and highlight aspects such as the form, aesthetics, and functions of these components. Chapter 4 discusses the layout planning of graphic components, and Chapter 5 deals with the principles of design, based on which a design is made and evaluated. Chapter 6 discusses the use of colour on a printed page and deals with our perception of and responses to colour, in addition to colour schemes and the production aspects of colour.

After discussing some essential concepts of art and print production in the initial chapters, the book goes on to discuss the technological aspects of print production in Chapters 7 to 12. While Chapter 7 discusses issues arising at the pre-printing stage vis-à-vis text matter, illustrations, and colour, Chapter 8 deals with printing processes and their suitability for various types of projects. Chapter 9 discusses various aspects of digital prepress, such as image assembly, colour separation, and colour proofing. Chapter 10 discusses desktop printing (DTP), which is an efficient printing process for short-run jobs. Chapter 11 deals with various issues related to the use of paper in printing, such as costs, varieties, and standard sizes of paper. Chapter 12 discusses costing and estimating, which are important aspects of the production business.

The applications of the concepts discussed in the book are covered in Chapters 13 to 21. Chapter 13 discusses newspaper make-up and highlights the primary concerns of a newspaper designer—time constraints and the short life of newspapers. Chapter 14 discusses advertising design, which is a challenging task for designers of printed literature. While Chapter 15 discusses identity design, Chapter 16 deals with print material that is issued periodically. The chapter delves into aspects such as the editing, designing, and production of magazines and newsletters.

Chapter 17 discusses poster designing and the strengths and weaknesses of the medium in the Indian context. Chapter 18 deals with the characteristics of packaging and the Indian packaging scenario. All businesses, big or small, send printed pieces directly to their prospective clients and stakeholders. Chapter 19 discusses the designing of these communication pieces. Chapter 20 discusses book design and the role of the designer, author, and publisher in creating a functional and aesthetically pleasing book. Chapter 21, which is a new chapter on outdoor design, provides an overview of the characteristics of outdoor media, their design and production process, the outputting devices and how they work, as well as various substrates and their suitability for different formats of outdoors.

Acknowledgements

I am grateful to the printing unit of Sterling Publishers Pvt. Ltd, Greater Noida, who helped me go through the details of the DTP system. I would also like to thank Anup Kumar Ghosh for his valuable inputs. I also thank Mr Probudha Sircar for his suggestions and feedback.

N.N. Sarkar

Preface to the First Edition

The term 'art' has various connotations. It is a medium of communication and expression, and includes a diverse range of activities such as the performing arts, literature, and visual art. Visual art provides us aesthetic pleasure and acts as a source of information about everyday life, culture, history, etc. in the form of paintings, sculptures, and carvings on ancient caves, temples, and monuments. A blend of design elements, colours, forms, and, in some cases, graphics, are used in various forms of visual art.

The human mind has always been sensitive to art and design. All art forms have been created out of available resources which have been put together by artisans to meet the intrinsic needs of creativity and expression. Today, there are visible changes in the forms and processes of art. With the growing availability of resources, our needs have multiplied and the scope of art forms has spread. Modern technology has facilitated the reproduction of art. Paintings can be captured for posterity in the form of photographs, and performing arts like theatre and dance can be immortalized on CDs and DVDs. Graphic art, which is a form of artwork created for information dissemination, encompasses such forms as drawings, paintings, prints, and photographs, which are manipulated.

Printing is an extension of graphics. It is the process of reproducing an image by pressing an inked surface to a substrate that receives the impression. A print design becomes a 'reality' when a work of art is reproduced and appears in the printed form. Every printing task demands equal attention on the part of the printer as well as the print buyer, who need to consider several variables ranging from the budget to the time schedule, printing process, prepress task, paper stock, and binding and finishing. All of these variables affect the shape of the final product.

Printing technology has evolved over the centuries. Block printing was practised by the Chinese as early as the second century. Since its inception, printing technology has seen four different revolutions. The first revolution was Gutenberg's invention of the movable type system, which mechanized the art of printing. The second revolution came about with the invention of the monotype and linotype processes, which are mechanical systems of composition. The third was phototypesetting, and desktop publishing (DTP) is considered to be the fourth revolution. The catchword in the future of print media is the 'convergence' of various media in the form of online newspapers or e-papers, books accompanied by CDs, encyclopaedias accompanied by e-books, multimedia books, etc.

A large number of mass communication and design institutes offer various courses related to mass media, which is a fast-evolving field. 'Art and print' is an integral part of any such course. Courses such as journalism, advertising, public relations, graphic design, and printing technology impart knowledge on the concepts, printing technologies, and applications of art and design, which helps students put this knowledge to practical use in their professional lives.

For long, the study of 'art' and 'production' has been limited to graphic designers and printing technologists. However, with the growing reach and availability of information technology, the scope, applications, and user base of these subjects have proliferated. One can now find a number of international books on these subjects. On the surface, such books may have a lot of extravagance and glitz, but when applied to the Indian context, most of them are limited in scope and treatment. These books have mostly been written by foreign authors for foreign audiences, and fail to relate to the needs in the Indian context. This book is an attempt to meet this need, keeping in mind the applicability and availability of technology in India as of now or in the foreseeable future.

About the Book

Art and Print Production has been specially designed to meet the needs of undergraduate and postgraduate degree/diploma students of various mass communication, printing, and design courses. Beginning with the concept and theory of 'art', the book discusses all technical issues arising in any pre-printing or post-printing situation and encompasses all the issues arising in layout planning, designing, and graphic technology as a whole. This book helps identify print- and design-related problems, analyses the same, and suggests solutions that can be adapted to the local needs, tastes, and perceptions.

Designed for self-study, the concepts discussed in the chapters are amply and vividly illustrated with photographs, figures, exhibits, and tables. The visual effect of various types of images has been heightened through the use of colour plates. Various printing techniques and processes have been captured on camera and have been explained step-by-step through photographs. The chapter on typography discusses the Roman script in detail and also covers the Devanagari script, which is an integral part of Indian designs. The chapter on digital prepress connects art with print production. Concept review questions at the end of each chapter facilitate the understanding of various subjects discussed in the chapters while the project assignments help the students put their knowledge to practical use.

It has been our endeavour to incorporate all the features of the syllabi of various universities and institutions teaching the subject to enhance the value of this book. The scope of the subject is vast, but this book focuses on print communication and is holistic and exhaustive in its approach and treatment.

Acknowledgements

It is impossible to write a textbook without the help of others. A number of professionals, subject experts, former students, friends, and family members have helped me in their own inimitable ways. They have played a major role in shaping this book and making it more meaningful and relevant. I wish to express my sincere appreciation and gratitude to each of them.

I am grateful to Mr Christu John, Librarian, YMCA, who was the one who first pushed me to OUP to get this book published, and has been my never-failing inspiration throughout the period of writing. I am also indebted to the Indian Institute of Mass Communication (IIMC), New Delhi, for help in various aspects such as the use of the library, printing press, and, of course, for the encouragement and guidance from my former colleagues, Dr Jaishri Jethwaney, Prof. Swapan Brahmachari, Mr Sushabhan

Mandal, and Mr Sudhir Goel. Special thanks are due to Prof. Nawal Singh, who was always approachable and whose critical comments and valuable suggestions have helped in the development of the book's contents. I would also like to thank prepress specialist Mr Sameer Khanuja for his valuable technical inputs.

I would like to thank academic and mass communication experts Dr J. Bhagyalakshmi, Mr Dipankar Banerjee, and Prof. B.D. Mendiratta. I gratefully acknowledge the contributions of Prof. Subhash Sud and Mr Nishant David, who helped me in developing the contents of the chapters in their respective fields of specialization. Thanks are also due to Mr S.K. Khurana, Editor, *All about Newspapers*; Mr Lalit Nadir, Production Manager, *Hindustan Times*; and Mr Sumit Bhattacharjee of NBT. Mr Subrato Das, Laboratory Assistant, and the students of graphics design at the Indo-Canadian School of Advanced Technology, Faridabad, deserve special thanks for creating a number of illustrations for the book. I would also like to thank Mr Kamal Chatterjee and Mr Gurmeet Sapal for helping me with some illustrations.

I am grateful to Ms Amla Singhvi, Managing Director, IPP Press; Mr S.K. Ghai, Managing Director, Sterling Publishers; Mr K. Goswami, Production Manager, Nutech Photolithography; and Mr P. Bapaiah, Registrar, IIMC, for allowing me to photograph various printing operations. I have used some of these in the book. Thanks are due to Sukanya Sarkar for her contribution to the cover design, and to Mr Vikram Kalra for his photography inputs.

The illustration for the parts of a book jacket, used in the chapter on book design, has been taken from the jacket of the book *Popular Indian Art: Raja Ravi Varma and the Printed Gods of India* by Erwin Neumayer and Christine Schelberger (OUP 2003). I would like to thank Lowe and Hidesign for permission to use their advertisements to explain some crucial concepts in this book.

I would like to thank OUP, especially the editorial staff, for giving the book its final shape.

Ideas gathered from various books, publications, and papers—both published and unpublished—and design samples of various advertising agencies and organizations have been used to explain important concepts and to demonstrate their application for the benefit of students. Wherever possible, I have duly acknowledged their contributions and sought permission for their use in the book. Some may have been missed out inadvertently or due to inability to locate the source. I would love to acknowledge the same if these instances are brought to my notice.

I sincerely hope that the book would meet the needs of students, teachers, and professionals. I look forward to receiving suggestions and feedback at my email ID: nnsarkar2000@yahoo.com.

N.N. Sarkar

Brief Contents

Preface to the Second Edition   iii
Preface to the First Edition   vi
Detailed Contents   xi

1.	Art and Production: An Overview	1
2.	Typography	14
3.	Visual Images	50
4.	Layout	75
5.	Principles of Design	90
6.	Colour in Design	110
7.	Copy for Printing	131
8.	Printing Processes	159
9.	Digital Prepress	193
10.	Desktop Publishing	226
11.	Paper and Finishing	248
12.	Costing and Estimating	267
13.	Newspaper Make-up	289
14.	Advertising Design	315
15.	Identity Design	337
16.	Periodicals	367
17.	Poster Design	392
18.	Packaging Design	411
19.	Direct Communication	433
20.	Book Design	459
21.	Outdoor Design	480

Index   508

Detailed Contents

Preface to the Second Edition iii
Preface to the First Edition vi
Brief Contents ix

1. Art and Production: An Overview 1

Introduction *1*
Visual Art *1*
   Visual Aesthetics 2
   Visual Literacy 3
Communication Art *3*
   Creativity in Communication Art 3
Graphic Art *4*
   Components of Graphic Communication 5
   Functions of Graphic Communication 6
   Making the Print Work 7

2. Typography 14

Introduction *14*
Developments in India *15*
Standardization of Letterforms *16*
Types of Letterforms *17*
Typography—Structure, Design, and Function *18*
   Physical Structure 18
Design Style *23*
   Grouping of Typefaces 24
   Type Families 29
Function of Type Composition *31*
   Appropriateness 31
   Readability vs Legibility 32
   Type for Text, Display, and Poster 33

3. Visual Images 50

Introduction *50*
Functions *51*
Categories of Visuals *52*
   Originals 53
   Visuals on Printed Page 61
Editing of Illustrations *68*

4. Layout 75

Introduction *75*
Terms in Layout Planning *76*
Stages of Layout Planning *80*
   Stage I 80
   Stage II 81
   Stage III 84
   Stage IV 85

5. Principles of Design 90

Introduction *90*
Principles of Design *91*
   Vocabulary 91
   Syntax 98
Basic Approach *104*
Design Software *106*

6. Colour in Design 110

Introduction *110*
Functions of Colour *111*
Colour Vision *112*
Our Responses to Colour *114*
Colour Combination *118*
   Colour Schemes 118
   Colour Perspective 121
   Some Guidelines 123
Reproduction of Colour *124*
   Fake Colours 125
   Spot Colours 126
   Process Colour 126

7. Copy for Printing 131

Introduction *131*
Verbal Copy *131*
   Copy Marking 132
   Copy Fitting 133

Typesetting 137
Proofreading 140
Visual Copy 143
　Cropping and Scaling 143
　Sizing and Marking 146
　Reproduction of Illustrations 148
Colour Copy 151
　Colour Separation 151
　When to Use Spot Colour 154
　When to Use Process Colour 154
　*When to Use Spot and
　　Process Colour Together* 154

8. Printing Processes 159

Introduction 159
Trend towards Modernization 161
　Developments in India 162
Printing Processes 163
On-demand Printing 164
　Electrostatic Printing 165
　Digital Printing 165
　Mini Offset Printing 166
Major Printing 167
　Relief Printing 167
　Planography 171
　Intaglio or Gravure 180
　Stencil or Silk-screen Printing 181
Specialized Printing 184
　Thermography 184
　Die Stamping 186
　Hot Foil Stamping 187
　Hologram Printing 187
Handling a Print Project 188

9. Digital Prepress 193

Introduction 193
Basic Concepts 194
　Image Types 194
　Image Resolution 195
　File Formats 196
　File Transportation and Storage 197
Image Input 198
　Input Devices 198
Image Processing 200
　Halftones 200
　Colour Images 201

Image Assembly 205
　Page Layout 206
　Artwork 206
Image Outputting 211
　Handing Over 211
　Proof Checking 212
Computer to Technology 216
　Computer to Film 216
　Computer to Plate 217
　CtP vs Film Plate 221

10. Desktop Publishing 226

Introduction 226
Capabilities 227
Users of Desktop Publishing Systems 228
Equipment Required for Desktop
　Publishing 229
　Hardware 230
　Software 233
Features of Some Specific Software
　Programs 238
　CorelDRAW 238
　Photoshop 239
　PageMaker 240
　QuarkXPress 241
Some Dos and Don'ts while Working 242
　Software-specific Guidelines 243

11. Paper and Finishing 248

Introduction 248
Paper Characteristics 249
　Physical Characteristics 249
　Surface Characteristics 250
Paper Varieties 251
Paper Sizes 253
　Traditional British Sizes 253
　International Sizes (ISO) 255
Weight and Quantity 255
　Calculation of Paper Requirement 256
Paper Selection 257
Folding, Binding, and Finishing 258

12. Costing and Estimating 267

Introduction 267
Costing 268

Detailed Contents **xiii**

Estimating *269*
   Relationship between Costing
     and Estimating 269
   Stages of Estimation 270
   Principal Printing Operations 277
Graphic Design Business *281*

13. Newspaper Make-up   289

Introduction *289*
Newspaper Designing *290*
   Effect of Television and New Media 291
Design Approach *292*
   Design Principles 293
Newspaper Form *296*
Newspaper Format *297*
Design Elements *299*
   Advertisements 299
   Text Matter 301
   Headlines 302
   Pictures 304
Page Make-up *306*
   Front Page 306
   Editorial Page 309
   Section Pages 309
   Colour Pages 311

14. Advertising Design   315

Introduction *315*
Advertising Communication *315*
   Graphic Design 316
Design Approach *322*
   Attracting the Target Audience 322
   Holding the Audience's Interest 324
   Developing a Desire 324
   Facilitating Action 325
Visualization *326*
Design Execution *327*
   Identifying Design Elements 327
   Selecting Effective Illustrations 328
   Creating Harmony in
     Headlines and Copy 329
   Developing a Layout Style 330
   Making the Layout Presentable 331
   Fitting the Layout within the
     Production Limitations 333

15. Identity Design   337

Introduction *337*
Identity Marks *338*
   Sign 338
   Symbol 338
   Trademark 339
   Trade Name 339
   Logo 339
   Brand Name 340
   Other Identity Marks 340
Symbolism in India *342*
   Colour Symbolism 344
   Effect of Language and Culture 345
Basic Symbols Used in Identity Marks *347*
   Shapes 347
   Letterforms 348
   Images 349
Creating an Identity Mark *351*
   Research 351
   Design Brief 351
   Creative Concept 352
   Presenting a Solution 358
   Implementing the Chosen Solution 359
   Change and Redesign 359

16. Periodicals   367

Introduction *367*
Magazines and Journals *368*
   Functions 368
   Physical Characteristics 368
   Editorial Planning 374
   Design Planning 375
   Production Planning 384
Newsletters *385*
   Newsletter Formats 386
   Newsletter Designing 387
   Newsletter Production 388

17. Poster Design   392

Introduction *392*
Indian Context *393*
   Reach of Posters 393
   Quality of Posters 394
   Current Scenario 394
Strengths of the Poster Medium *396*

xiv *Detailed Contents*

Limitations of the Poster Medium *398*
Rules for Poster Designing *399*
   Select as Few Design Elements as Possible 399
   Restrict the Number of Words 400
   Try to Create the Maximum Impact through Visuals 400
   Never Think of the Visual and the Caption Separately 400
   Treat All the Elements of Design as One Unit 401
   Develop a Distinctive Style 401
   Make Use of the Full Value of Colour 402
Steps in Poster Designing *404*
Poster Production *405*
   Production Methods 405
   Processing Techniques and New Technology 406

18. Packaging Design   411

Introduction *411*
Indian Packaging Industry *413*
Packaging Media *413*
   Flexible Packaging 414
   Folding Cartons 415
   Containers 416
Design Brief *418*
Problem-solving Steps *419*
   Concept 419
   Complexity 421
   Compromise 421
   Choices 421
Design Approach *422*
   Shape and Proportion 422
   Types 422
   Logos 423
   Illustrations 423
   Colour 425
Packaging Technology *426*
Legal Issues *428*

19. Direct Communication   433

Introduction *433*
Business Correspondence Material *434*
   Letterheads 434
   Business Cards 437
   Envelopes 439
Promotional Literature *440*

Brochures 442
Leaflets 446
Booklets 447
Souvenir Items *449*
   Calendars 450
   Diaries 452
Distribution *454*

20. Book Design   459

Introduction *459*
Book Anatomy *461*
Prerequisites for Book Designing *462*
   Well-organized Manuscript 462
   Information about the Project 463
   Guidelines for Page Make-up 463
Stages in Book Design *465*
   Typographical Matter 465
   Pictorial Matter 467
   Page Layout 470
   Cover Design 471
   Paper for Book 475
   Book Binding 476

21. Outdoor Design   480

Introduction *480*
Outdoor Media *481*
   Forms of Outdoor Media 481
   Advantages of Outdoor Media 484
   Disadvantages of Outdoor Media 484
Creative Factors *484*
   Scope and Challenge 485
   Basic Design Rules 485
   Scope of Innovation 488
Outdoor Design as Public Art *492*
Digital Environment *496*
   Imaging 496
   Resolution 496
   File Format 496
   Digital Colour 497
Outputting Devices *498*
   Inkjet Printers 498
   Image and Print Quality 499
   Cutting Plotter 500
Print Consumables *501*
   Ink 501
   Substrates 502

Index 508

List of Colour Plates

Plate 1
- Duotone effect (*Chapter 3, p. 67*)
- Fake duotone (*Chapter 3, p. 67*)
- Posterization effect (*Chapter 3, p. 63*)
- Colour wheel (*Chapter 6, p. 119*)
- Additive and subtractive colours (*Chapter 6, p. 114*)

Plate 2
- Colour schemes (*Chapter 6, p. 122*)

Plate 3
- Colour perspective (*Chapter 6, p. 123*)
- Spot colour using screen tint and overprinting (*Chapter 6, p. 126*)
- Image manipulation in billboards (*Chapter 21, p. 486*)
- Innovative OOH using regional languages (*Chapter 21, p. 491*)

Plate 4
- Four-colour separation and combination of three and four colours (*Chapter 9, p. 205*)
- Standard screen angles for colour separation (*Chapter 9, p. 207*)

CHAPTER

1 Art and Production: An Overview

Learning Objectives

After reading this chapter, you should be able to
- understand the concept and philosophy of art
- define visual art and understand the meaning of visual literacy
- categorize visual art on the basis of aesthetic and functional considerations
- describe communication art in visual form and understand the importance of creativity in communication art
- gain insight into how communication art can be made effective
- discuss the concept of graphic art, define it, and understand the difference between graphic and non-graphic images
- delineate the various components of graphics
- discuss the application of graphics in different media formats and look at the processes involved in the planning, execution, and production of print work

INTRODUCTION

Art means different things to different people. In Indian philosophy, art is *satyam shivam sundaram*. *Satyam* is truth; *shivam* is that which does good to all; and *sundaram* is beauty. Art is much more than music, dance, drama, and the objects to be found inside museums and galleries. When we think of art, we usually mean something more than mere skill.

There are many activities that require skill, but art is special. Great art has universal appeal, because it has a message that moves us deeply or awakens us to new insights into human nature. Art touches us everyday and everywhere—at home, at school, in the office, and on the street. Art is both the process and product of man's creativity; it is an experience. Exhibit 1.1 presents various views on art.

Let us now briefly look at various types of art. The categories described here are not mutually exclusive, but they have been segregated for ease in understanding.

VISUAL ART

The meaning of art differs from person to person, depending upon one's capabilities. However, we all respond to art emotionally. Physiologically, it reaches us through our

> **Exhibit 1.1 What is art?**
>
> 'The sensation and emotion derived from pleasure, vision and ecstasy are the most powerful human motive forces in creation of art.'
> —Upanisada
>
> 'Cold exactitude is not art; ingenious artifice, when it pleases or when it expresses, is art itself.'
> —Eugene Delacroix
>
> 'Art is the lie that makes us realize the truth.'
> —Pablo Picasso
>
> 'A man climbs a mountain, because it is there. A man makes art, because it is not there.'
> —Cart Andre
>
> 'To reduce art and speak of it exclusively in terms of sensation is to do violence to the inner man.'
> —Ananda Coomaraswamy
>
> 'Subjects of study primarily concerned with human culture (as contrasted with scientific or technical subjects).'
> —Concise Oxford English Dictionary
>
> All of these concepts can be expressed in a single statement:
>
> 'Science is rational objective analysis; art is emotional subjective synthesis.'

sensory receptors. The art that reaches through our eyes is visual art. Defined thus, almost all forms of art (inclusive of the performing arts of drama and dance) are, in fact, visual. Visual art, which is a non-verbal form of communication, is also a language because visual expression is used to communicate or interpret the artist's message.

Visual Aesthetics

Aesthetics is a branch of philosophy called value theory or axiology, which is the study of sensory or sensori-emotional values, sometimes called judgments of sentiment or taste. Aesthetics is an oft-used synonym of art, although many thinkers feel that these two closely related fields need to be distinguished. Aesthetic consideration within visual art is usually associated with the sense of vision.

In simplistic form, visual art has broadly two categories: fine art and applied art.

Fine art It is basically concerned with aesthetic pleasure; it may or may not have much of utilitarian value. The term 'fine' implies beauty, skill, superiority, elegance, exclusiveness, and perfection. Therefore, fine art, in its simplest form, would be a piece of work that embodies some of these qualities. It may include drawing, painting, sculpture, and architecture. Fine art is purely a product of an artist's search for self-expression.

Applied art Applied art is art for a purpose. Fabrics, ceramics, furniture, etc. have gained a specific value, which sets them apart from fine art. One cannot, however, really draw a sharp line between fine art and applied art. Some fine arts such as architecture have utilitarian value. Thanks to mechanical reproduction, many fine arts have today been brought to the domain of applied art as well. Applied art can, thus, be defined as a product of an artist's search for a visual solution to problems of man's basic needs such as food, clothing, and shelter. Both functionality and aesthetics are measures of creativity in applied art.

Visual Literacy

'Beauty lies in the eyes of the beholder', goes the popular adage. The subjectivity of an individual viewer's response to visual communication is largely altered by visual literacy. To understand visual language or to communicate visually, a certain degree of intellectual ability, called visual literacy, is required. Here, 'intellectual ability' refers to one's ability to know, perceive, or conceive of an act or faculty that is distinct from emotion. Visual literacy goes beyond understanding the literal content of an image, which comes from one's involvement in the world of visuals. Visual literacy, as defined by the International Visual Literacy Association, is 'a group of vision competencies a human being can develop by seeing and at the same time having and integrating other sensory experiences. The development of these competencies is fundamental to normal human learning. When developed, they enable a visually literate person to discriminate and interpret the visual actions, objects, and/or symbols, natural or man-made, that are encountered in (the) environment. Through the creative use of these competencies (we are) able to communicate with others. Through the appreciative use of these competencies, (we are) able to comprehend and enjoy the masterworks of visual communications'.

COMMUNICATION ART

Communication art is art with a message. Here, we are referring to the visual communication of an optically stimulating message that is understood by the viewer. Communication art is a field that overlaps some areas of fine and applied art. It is historically rooted in the fine arts of drawing, painting, and writing, yet it is an applied art in the sense that it has a very clear purpose—communication.

In the world today, thousands of messages are reaching us everyday. The first set of messages—brands of soap, toothpaste, and other personal care products—reaches us as we get up in the morning. We get ready for breakfast and the second set of messages reaches us—brands of food and the morning newspaper loaded with the concomitant classified and other advertisements. We then go to work, on the way we are literally bombarded with messages—bus schedules, route maps, posters, hoardings, street signs, names of shops, etc. At work, again, there is no cessation of messages received—correspondence, documents, and advertisements in myriad forms; computer outputs; audio-visual aids; etc. Weary in the evening, we turn our back on the messages of a busy day and relax in our favourite chair. Perhaps unknowingly and all too unwittingly, we then tune in another barrage of messages through the television, magazines, or books.

Communication art is omnipresent—everywhere and at all times, we see it—and yet, rarely do we notice it.

Creativity in Communication Art

Creativity is the primary impulse of all the arts. Defining creativity would be as subjective as defining love or hate. Creativity is an abstraction conceived by the imaginative instincts of an artist's mind and influenced by his/her related environment, past, and present. The dictionary meaning of creativity is 'to create', or to bring into existence or give rise to something that is original in nature. Creativity in communication art, although essentially and significantly related to originality, becomes a tool of mass communication. It has a definite direction and a specific objective.

Communication art should be aesthetic and functional. The three primary players in this balancing act are: the visible object, the creator of the object, and the intended viewer. Therefore, visual art (object) must link the mind of the artist (creator) with the mind of the target audience (viewer) and convey a clear and concise message. In order to create this link, one should be visually literate. If such a link is not established or if the message is misunderstood, visual art is ineffective and hence lacks creativity, even if the artwork is creative in purely aesthetic or functional terms. Thus, the true measure of creativity in communication art is effectiveness.

In order to be effective, a piece of communication art must

- stop the target audience;
- hold the target audience;
- send an absolutely unambiguous message; and
- if the main purpose is advertising, evoke an instinctively positive response—usually brand purchase.

GRAPHIC ART

Graphic art is a subset of visual art. The word 'graphic' is derived from the Greek word *graphiko*, which means writing.

Graphic art, thus, is a medium that conveys a written message. However, there is ambiguity in this definition. A written message is not the only element used in graphic art. More often than not, it is juxtaposed with related pictures that have been manipulated.

Although each category of art has distinctive characteristics, it is not possible to draw a line between these categories. Figure 1.1 illustrates how art can be narrowed down to graphic art. Modern users have simplified the term 'graphic art', christening it 'graphics'. Today, graphic art is not just confined to printing. We find pictures and letters with a spoken message on TV and video. Titles of TV serials and the special effects of advertisements and animation films are all graphics. These are all created by the human hand. Earlier, ink, brush, pen, etc. were used to create a graphic by hand. Now, in tune with the spirit of modern age, sophisticated equipment, including computers, is used to create a graphic.

Take the example of a rectangular photograph in which images are formed by blending different levels

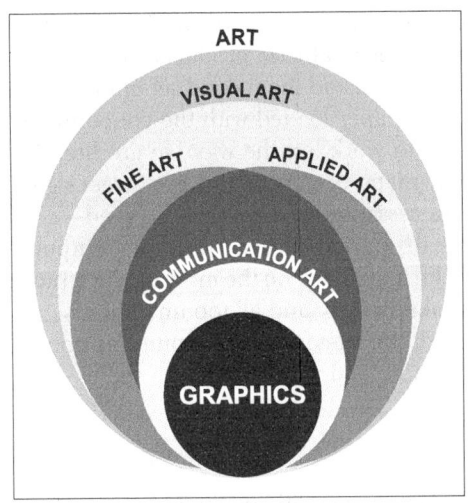

Figure 1.1 Art narrowed down to graphics

of tones. Such a picture is termed a continuous tone picture—it is not a graphic. The moment it is altered by eliminating the unwanted background, it is called a graphic. Notice how the main content is enhanced for this manipulation.

Manipulation is also applied in moving forms such as film or television. Imagine that you are watching a cricket match sitting in your drawing room and enjoying your team's batting. Suddenly, something unusual happens. Your favourite player is declared out, that too by LBW. You, like most other fans, are disappointed and doubtful about the umpire's decision. Now, it is the duty of the communicator or the telecaster to satisfy the millions of cricket fans. Graphics is the tool used by the telecaster to draw lines between the wickets and show the movement of the ball as it hits the leg in front of the leg stump. Will you call it a graphic when the TV camera focuses on the crowd or the advertisement boards in the field? The answer is no, because the pictures coming through the camera are continuous—flow or analogue images like the normal playing action. Images such as the introductory details of a player at the start of his batting or that of a moving duck to make the situation humorous as a player is declared out without scoring are examples of the use of graphics on TV.

Movement is the basic characteristic of electronic media. A road map shown on a video screen may be a graphic, but it will be effective only if the direction arrow is moving. This movement is also part of a graphic. An animation film is also a graphic as all its frames are drawn manually or mechanically.

Graphics is also defined as the process of representing a three dimensional entity on a two dimensional surface, using various tools and techniques. The basic purpose of graphics is to enhance the message.

A painting by M.F. Hussain, the famous Indian painter, may be called a piece of fine art. The moment it is used for a calendar, it will be called graphic communication and the work will be called graphics. This is because the original painting has been reproduced through some system and process. If you carefully observe a reproduced painting, you will notice a number of dots in different sizes. Done mechanically, it is, again, a work of graphics.

Arthur Turnbull, an international authority on graphics, gives us a more academic definition: 'Graphic communication is a process of conveying messages by means of visual images, which are usually on a flat surface.'

Components of Graphic Communication

If we have pictures with a spoken message, as we usually have on TV or video, they are not strictly graphics as they are created by a continuous flow of (analogue) pictures and sounds. Printed messages, of course, are a part of graphic communication. In sum, graphics may be defined as a part of visual communication that is manipulated to enhance the message. Whichever definition we might choose, we find that graphic communication has three basic components: (i) written messages; (ii) visual images—pictures, drawings, paintings, photographs, etc.; and (iii) layout.

All three components are basically pictures. Written messages are formed by letters of the alphabet, which are primarily pictures. We know that man had first started writing by using pictures. When these pictures are arranged graphically to convey a specific meaning, this new arrangement is known as a pictograph.

Although the art of writing has developed greatly over the years, the basic system of arranging pictures has not changed much. The pictures have just been simplified to form graphic symbols. These symbols, in groups, are capable of conveying a message. They are complex symbols. In order to communicate effectively, one needs to learn the symbols and their meaning in combination, which we call language. The idea of the language is understood when these letter symbols are arranged in sequence.

Pictures, like photographs or paintings, are more direct and capable of conveying the message instantly. There is hardly any language or geographical barrier in understanding a picture.

Often, neither written messages nor pictures are capable of conveying the intended message. This is because written messages may be so complex that one fails to grasp the inner meaning of the message even though one may have learnt the language and its word symbols. Here, pictures come to one's rescue. Children's books are usually full of pictures and have scant letter content. An Indian child reading a folk tale of Malaysia will find it difficult to imagine the face and dress of a queen described in the story without an illustration. As the child grows up, the picture content goes down. However, even grown-ups often find language complex and difficult to comprehend without the aid of pictures and diagrams. Language is incapable of explaining a scientific formula without a diagram. Quite often, pictures too pose the same problem. Can you understand a newspaper picture without a caption? Will even the best photograph of an advertisement sell a product without a headline and a copy?

Only a combination of words and pictures is capable of conveying a message effectively. Here, layout has a major role to play. Layout is a plan. We plan to arrange the words and pictures logically with a view to create effectiveness. Both the writer and the designer work together, and both are considered creative people. While the copywriter is more concerned with the message content in terms of language, the graphic designer is more concerned with the message presentation (typography, pictures, layout, etc.).

Functions of Graphic Communication

Let us compare the spoken word and the written word. Just as a person uses gestures and facial expressions to enhance the meaning of the spoken word, one uses type style, size, formatting, colour, etc. to enhance the meaning of the written word.

Graphic design is not a mere decoration of the written message—it is a conscious and meaningful effort to maximize the impact of the written message. It is through a graphic design that a written message acquires the power to stop and hold the target audience. A truly effective graphic communication is the combined result of both message content and message presentation.

According to designer Will Burtin, the main function of graphic design in contemporary communication is translating and condensing ideas or problems in such a way that they pave a shortcut to understanding.

The relative importance of content and presentation varies from situation to situation. Where message content is being actively sought, message presentation may be no more than a succinct headline. For example, job and tender advertisements are often dull in appearance, yet they are among the most read parts of a newspaper. On the other hand, where message content is only passively sought, message presentation may spell the difference between full awareness and stark ignorance. Let us take an example. Glossy magazines are literally packed with four-colour display advertisements of soaps, toothpastes, and thousands of attractive products; yet most of us flip through the pages and continue reading the editorial matter, stopping only at the occasional advertisement that is so unique that it almost jumps out of the page to grab our attention.

Most written matter needs some graphic design to increase its appeal and impact. Headline size and typeface, placement on a page, margins and borders, colour, and a number of other things will determine whether a particular message will hit the target audience or just be thrown into the dustbin without even a casual look at it. It is important to note that well-written words combined with well-conceived designs make the print work.

Making the Print Work

Graphics may be two-dimensional, three-dimensional, moving, or static. Print communication graphics are static in nature. Good graphics require sound planning, effective execution, and proper handling of the production process. Designing skills, good visual perception, and knowledge of technology are essential requirements for giving shape to the final graphic design. The final idea is then reproduced for mass communication by one of the various production methods available. Figure 1.2 illustrates the steps involved in graphic communication.

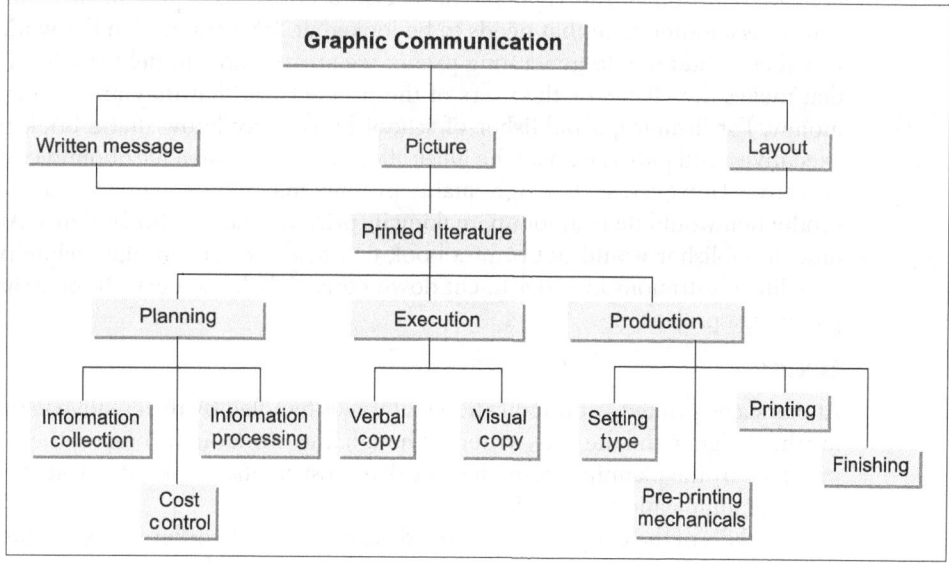

Figure 1.2 Steps of graphic communication

Planning

Every good printed material has good planning behind it. Planning starts from collecting information that provides a clear understanding of the project. The client may be the source of initial information. Mostly, information comes in the form of a design brief. The fact-finding process may include the use of various consulting agencies such as the consumer research bureau or one's own sources.

The ultimate goal of this process is to make sure that one is in complete agreement with the client about the scope of work and the objective reflected in the design brief.

Information should be precise—it should be neither too much nor too little. Too much information confuses the creative mind while too little information is sterile of alternative ideas, killing all chances of creativity. At the planning stage, the basic questions are: Who are we trying to communicate with? What are we trying to tell them? How do we do it?

The answer to the first two questions may be the urban middle class and our trying to promote a new savings scheme. The answer to the third question may be an advertisement, folder, or even an article in a newspaper. The collected information further tells us about the product or the idea that we want to sell or transmit.

How can we reach the target audience? We may just make a simple announcement of the programme or provide information to the target audience through an appropriate medium.

The planning of communication material for printing is usually done by a team of workers. In an advertising agency, the copywriter, visualiser, media planner, and accounts executive work together as a team. In some cases, the planning team depends on the availability of professionals. In some cases, it may even be limited to a single person. Selection of the right media is also a critical component of planning. Cost control is another issue that needs to be looked at. We should plan the work in such a way that, in addition to generating profits, we are also able to deliver a level of service that makes the clients or the users of the product feel that they are getting value for money. For instance, a publisher of school books may know that a book printed on executive bond paper, with all the illustrations in colour and a hardbound cover, will be attractive. However, such a high-quality product may not be viable because the cost of production would then shoot up, making its price prohibitive for students. At the same time, a publisher would not print a book that discusses art on plain white paper with only line illustrations in order to cut down costs. A balance needs to be maintained in planning a project.

Execution

At this stage, printed communication material is handled by the creative team comprising the designer and the copywriter. Although they work on the basis of the information provided by the planning team, their work is most creative as it is the structure on which print communication is based.

The skills of the copywriter and the designer are quite different. A synthesis of their skills creates the most effective communication material. In many situations, however, they work independently. For instance, for publishing a book, the author may provide a complete manuscript to the publisher. The publisher, in turn, may engage a designer to execute the visual and verbal copy for production. In case the illustrations needed for the book are not supplied with the manuscript, the publisher, in consultation with the designer, arranges for the same. Other decisions such as type style, book format, margins, division of chapters, etc. may then be taken independently by the designer.

Similarly, in case of magazines, the contributors of the articles can hardly involve themselves in designing the magazine. In many cases, the editor takes the responsibility of designing and uses his/her visual imagination and graphic skills. The editor might have acquired these skills in his/her journalism education or simply from years of experience. It does not seem, however, that designers can easily be replaced with journalists. Execution of printed material is changing with technological developments. In newspaper designing, paste-up jobs are now a thing of the past. Designers and sub-editors now work out the layout digitally. This has simplified the job considerably, bringing in scope for more creative ideas and enabling designers to complement the verbal copy with visuals to make the message clearer. Until recently, newspapers used to avoid this due to time constraint. Designers now get more time to prepare the magazine supplements of a newspaper. That is why these pages have more visual appeal as compared with the main newspaper.

Creativity in magazine and newspaper layout is somewhat limited. Since the designers have to work within the framework of these publications, the basic format, consisting of aspects such as column grids, type style, margins, etc., is predetermined and remains the same issue after issue.

Print advertising, folder designing, and package designing offer great scope for designers. Designing these is much more challenging than designing a book, magazine, or newspaper. This is because, as ad space is expensive, clients cannot accept a design that would not sell the product or idea, even though it may be a very good piece of art. Thus, while creating print advertisements, folders, and packages, in addition to the aesthetics of the design itself, designers also have to keep various other considerations in mind.

The high cost of advertising space is because of tough competition. The competition is not only between different media but also within a medium. In a newspaper, an advertisement competes with other advertisements and written material for the attention of the reader. Here, team work ensures success in the competitive race. Advertising agencies have come into existence because they ensure success through team work. They are much in demand from elite advertisers.

Success comes to designers who have strong visual perception and a very sound knowledge of human psychology. Designers should update their knowledge of print technology, which is rapidly changing. They should also keep their eyes open for new type designs and their effect in attractive designing.

Copywriters and other professionals must also have some exposure to graphic design. They can then help the designers with positive ideas. They must also have knowledge of the design principles, typesetting complexities, paper qualities, production constraints, and new technology.

Idea generation and printing the same on paper in a visual form is not complete unless prepress work is prepared. Prepress work includes the processes of typesetting, imaging, page make-up, colour management, and trapping. It is a highly technical job.

Until recently, a part of the prepress task was performed by highly skilled artists and the other part by specialized technicians working manually or on expensive proprietary systems. Today, digital prepress technology is increasingly being used. Prepress tasks can now be accomplished by a single person with the help of computers. Designers and copywriters who have the knowledge and access to the relevant technology can complete their own prepress task to a large extent.

Production

The idea of a piece of printed material becomes a reality when it is finally reproduced for mass production. Every printing job requires the sustained effort from the printer and the print buyer, with equal attention to a complex set of variables ranging from the budget to the time schedule, printing process, prepress task, paper stock, binding, and finishing that may affect the final product. The production process may start with an evaluation of the whole job in terms of the tasks that can be performed in-house and the services needed from other prepress service providers.

Sometimes, due to time constraint, separating the prepress task and printing instead of assigning the entire job to a printing outfit that does not have all the facilities under one roof may prove economic in terms of cost and time. Many a time, the production process costs more if the work is not done correctly for lack of expertise and equipment needed to accomplish the job. Errors may surface only after the film output is obtained. At this stage, there is usually no alternative but to discard the job and go through the whole process again. As a result, delays occur in the printing cycle, which translates into higher costs.

Once it has been decided which tasks will be performed in-house and which ones will be contracted, a commercial printer needs to be chosen. From the client's perspective, three things are considered while choosing a printer: price, quality, and service. In addition to considering these factors, the print buyer should check the capability of the printer's plant and his/her service record before considering a printer. The printer should have a good service record in terms of meeting all schedules including final delivery and taking care of the minute details of the job.

The printing job should be satisfactory for both the parties. The printer should accept the job with a proper copy and all the specifications clearly specified therein. In many cases, the print buyer may be a production specialist, but most of the time detailed specifications come from the designer. These details include specifications about making of films for the original, line and half-tone job, their reproduction sizes, percentage of tint, and whether the illustrations should bleed or crossover. Details about the quality of paper to be used, print run, colour sample, and colour instructions in case of colour jobs should also be specified. For binding and finishing, the manner in which the product is to be stitched and trimmed and special requirements such as lamination, perforation, die cutting, etc. may be specified. The elements and steps involved in graphic communication, as discussed here, are presented in Figure 1.2.

To get the best result from a printer, the designer or print buyer should send the final error-free proofs to the printer along with illustrations, if any, duly cropped and scaled. Electronic files may be accompanied by a proof sheet with necessary instructions for colour, type font, dots per line, trapping, cut mark, etc., and also details of the various versions of software used in creating the file. These issues have been discussed in detail in the following chapters, which would help the reader handle production jobs with ease and confidence. In addition to knowledge regarding the printing process, it is important for designers and print buyers to possess good communication skills so that they can build a good relationship with printers they depend on to get their work done.

SUMMARY

The concept and meaning of art differs from person to person, but we all respond to art emotionally. We perceive art through our sensory receptors. The art that we perceive through our eyes is called visual art. Visual art can be broadly categorized into fine art and applied art. Fine art is concerned with aesthetic pleasure, whereas applied art is art that is created to serve a particular purpose. Communication art transcends the borders of fine and applied art. It is an art with a message. A creative message enhances the effectiveness of the communication art.

Communication art can be further streamlined into graphic art. Graphics is defined as the process of presenting visual forms which have been manipulated to enhance the communication message. The three components of graphics are—the written message, visual image, and layout. These three components have a distinctive identity and are used independently or in combination. In some graphics, the layout or picture arrangement is capable of conveying the message effectively.

Graphics may be of two-dimensional, three-dimensional, moving, or static form. Print communication graphics are static in nature. A good print communication has good planning behind it. The planning is handled by creative people. It is then followed by execution. Here, design skill, visual perception, and knowledge of technology work together to give shape to the graphic design. Finally, the idea in the form of the design is duplicated for mass communication by one of the various production methods available.

KEY TERMS

Analogue Image   Physical variables of continuous flow of pictures, such as images on TV, voltage stabilizer, etc.
Applied Art   Aesthetically pleasing design or decoration of functional objects. It is used in distinction to fine art, although there is often no clear dividing line between the two.
Art   A product of human creativity, made with the intention of stimulating our senses through aesthetics or emotional impact.
Commercial Printer   Printers who undertake and deliver printed material in lieu of money.
Communication Art   Anything that adds meaning to a message.
Copywriter   Generally writes copy for advertisement and promotional literature. Copywriters are expected to establish their credibility with editors, designers, and readers through strong research and the use of appropriate sources and citations.
Creativity   A mental process of human activity involving the generation of new ideas or concepts, or new associations between existing ideas or concepts.
Drawing   The act of making an image that involves scribbling of marks on a surface by applying pressure with a wide variety of tools.
Fine Art   Art produced or intended primarily for beauty rather than utility. An art that requires highly developed techniques and skills.
Graphic Art   A visual image that is manipulated to enhance the message.
Graphic Design   A form of visual communication using text and/or images to present information or to promote a message. Graphic design often refers to the process designing in solving the communication problem.
Graphic Symbols   Also referred to as pictographs, pictograms, or pictures, these are symbols that are used

in place of, or as supplements to, written words. The pictures provide non-verbal information about various object and activities.

Painting The act of making an image by applying a pigment suspended in a carrier or medium and a binding agent like glue to a surface such as paper canvas or wall.

Photograph Pictures developed by means of action of light. Light patterns reflected or emitted from objects are recoded onto a sensitive medium or storage chip through timed exposure.

Prepress The process of preparing the copy vis-à-vis technological parameters before it reaches the printing press.

Print Buyer Organizations or persons who get the material printed by paying money.

Verbal Copy Information to be printed in words for communication. Words are the abstract representation of objects in our environment.

Visual Art Works of art, such as paintings, photographs, sculptures, and graphic art, which appeal primarily to our visual sense and typically exist in a permanent form.

Visual Literacy A set of mental skills and competencies in human beings that enables them to discriminate and interpret visual actions, objects, and/or symbols—natural or man-made—that are encountered in the environment.

REFERENCES

Concise Oxford English Dictionary 1999, Tenth Edition, Oxford University Press Inc., New York.

Gorden, Bob and Maggie Gorden 2002, Consultant Editors, Digital Graphic Design, Thames & Hudson Ltd, UK.

Holmes, Charles 1946, *A Grammar of the Arts*, G. Bell and Sons, London.

Industrial Design Centre, IIT 1987, *Indian Symbology*, Proceedings of the Seminar on Indian Symbology, Bombay.

Russell, Stella Pandell 1975, *Art in the World*, Rinehart Press, San Francisco.

Smith, Ken (ed.) 2005, *Handbook of Visual Communication: Theory, Methods and Media*, Lawrence Erlbaum Associates Inc., New Jersey.

Turnbull, Arthur T. and Russell N. Baird 1980, *The Graphics of Communication*, Holt, Rinehart and Winston, USA.

Wikipedia, the free encyclopedia, accessed in December 2006.

REVIEW QUESTIONS

1. Define the following terms: art, visual art, fine art, and applied art.
2. What is visual literacy?
3. What is the meaning of visual aesthetics?
4. Explain how graphic art is a form of communication art.
5. What do you mean by creativity? How does communication art become effective with a touch of creativity?
6. Define graphic art. Identify the graphics of various media formats and describe their characteristics.
7. What are the components of graphics? Explain the characteristics and functions of each component.
8. How can one make the graphic work?

PROJECTS

1. To become a graphic designer, you would need to build your source materials. Collect as much material as possible of printed pages, photographs, drawn or painted images; scan them; and store

them in CDs or folders for each of the following topics:
   (a) Furniture, pottery, and tapestry
   (b) Sculpture—modern and ancient
   (c) Architecture—building, place of worship, and monument
   (d) Folk art of different regions
2. Prepare a project on the history of graphics. The project may be in three parts:
   (a) Prehistoric visual communication;
   (b) Graphics after Gutenberg's invention of the movable type;
   (c) The influence of modern art in graphic designing.
   You will have to visit libraries or browse the Internet to collect the required information.
3. Make a sketch book of size 12" × 10" of ordinary paper. Keep on sketching whatever you find in front of you. As you gain a little confidence, begin sketching moving objects. Use a soft pencil (4B) or sketch pen to draw the images, as far as possible, in a single stroke. Avoid using an eraser for removing shortcomings in your sketches.
4. Buy a cartridge paper sketch book of size 16" × 11"(approx). Title it 'Graphics Appreciation Book'. Every week, collect a printed form of a graphic design and paste it on the left side of a page. Note your appreciation or criticism on the facing page on the right. Cover the following points:
   (a) Kind of printed piece (brochure, advertisement, book cover, etc.)
   (b) Source (published in a magazine/newspaper or collected from ---)
   (c) Target audience (sex, age, education, lifestyle, etc.)
   (d) Communication objectives (generating awareness, selling a product or idea, informing or educating)
   (e) Design quality in terms of form, colour, type, and appropriateness
   (f) Conclusion or suggestions for improvement

Show your appreciation book to your teacher and take his/her comments or judge it yourself in terms of your gradual improvement in quality of appreciation.

CHAPTER

2 Typography

Learning Objectives

After reading this chapter, you should be able to

- trace the historical background of the letterform
- discuss the various types of letterforms used in modern communication
- understand the physical structure of type, including type body, typeface, and type font
- understand the measurement of type
- discuss digital letterforms
- familiarize yourself with various design styles and their appropriateness
- discuss typefaces, type families, and variations in typefaces
- understand the functions of type composition and develop the ability to select the appropriate typeface for a particular design
- gain an insight into the considerations involved in setting styles for newspapers

INTRODUCTION

The earliest writing systems known to man were pictographic. A pictograph simply means picture writing. The symbols used therein stand literally for the objects they depict. The clarity of the message depends, to a large extent, on the writer's graphic ideas. The first people to use pictographs were the Sumerians, who lived in Iraq about 5000 years ago. Pictographic writing was the monopoly of a group of high-class Egyptians about 3,500 years ago. The Egyptian way of picture writing is known as *hieroglyphics*, which means 'carving'. Hieroglyphics are made up of pictures of people, animals, birds, plants, and other everyday things.

The pictographic system evolved into the more sophisticated ideographic system, which could deal with abstract ideas. The symbols became stylized and standardized, so that they were easy to write and translate.

The next advance was the invention of the syllabary. Here, the symbols represent the sounds of speech rather than objects or ideas. As a result, the number of symbols required is far less. The originators of the alphabet belonged to a tribe called the Sumerians. They realized that a picture could stand for a single sound just as well as for a whole word. They chose some of the Egyptian symbols to stand for sounds. This made it faster and easier to write. Finally, they had 22 symbols that could be

Exhibit 2.1 Importance of written language

'Written language has become the vehicle of civilization and so of learning and education. Writing is one of the main aspects of culture which clearly distinguish mankind from the animal world.'

—David Diringer

'The invention of the letterform is regarded as one of the most significant intellectual achievements of man and nobody knows how old it is. From the rock paintings of primitive man to the computerized mechanical writing of space-age man, writing has come a long way. The styles of writing have changed from time to time, from place to place, reflecting the environment of the period and the inward development of man.'

—R.K. Joshi

Figure 2.1 Early Semitic, Phoenician, Greek, Roman, and Indus Valley forms of writing

put together to make a word in their language. At that time, the Phoenicians, who were business people living along the eastern shore of the Mediterranean, borrowed the Semitic alphabet during their trade. Alphabet at that time had no vowel signs.

As Phoenician goods were exported to the other side of the sea, this alphabet also found its way outside the area. Acquiring it about 1000 BC, the literary-minded Greeks refined it by adding vowel signs. This alphabet was then passed on to the Romans, who further developed the form that we use today. Figure 2.1 presents some of the early forms of writing discussed here. The importance of written language in today's world is expressed in the extracts presented in Exhibit 2.1.

DEVELOPMENTS IN INDIA

For hundreds of thousands of years, the only way people could pass on ideas to others was by talking, so they had to do a lot of memorizing. Despite the fact that memorizing is less permanent than writing, some civilizations have been rather slow in taking to writing. The Indian civilization also believed in an oral culture. Many of our *shastras* were passed on from one generation to another for hundreds of years by word of mouth.

The inscriptions of the Indus Valley Civilization (2500 BC) represent the earliest form of writing in India. However, we do not know what language they used for communication. Some schools of thought believe that the Indus Valley ideograms were the origin of the Indian languages, but no scientific proof has so far been adduced in support thereof. Figure 2.1 shows some Indus Valley ideograms.

The earliest decipherable Indian alphabet is the Brahmi script. The shapes of all the letters are modifications of the component parts of the square, circle, and cross symbols (500-300 BC). In the third century BC, Ashoka strived to spread the message of Buddhism by inscribing the wayside rocks and pillars with the Brahmi script. Figure 2.2 shows the letters of the Ashokan Brahmi script. The Buddhist monks wanted to spread their religion, so they used letters. However, there was no systematic development of the Buddhist alphabet.

Figure 2.2 Letters of the Ashokan Brahmi script

STANDARDIZATION OF LETTERFORMS

Though the history of the letterform is more than 5000 years old, its standardization came only with the advent of movable type, the credit for which goes to Johann Gutenberg. The practice of printing from woodblocks existed many years before Gutenberg. It was in the eighth century that China pioneered the process of printing from the relief surface of woodblocks. It was a slow and tedious process. Once the printing was done, re-arrangement of the same page was impossible. Gutenberg solved this tricky problem by means of a system of movable type that allowed type characters to be arranged in any order and used as per need. It is believed that China knew about movable type in the eleventh century. It was invented by Pi Sheng. However, his techniques did not come to be widely used because of the complicated nature of the Chinese ideograms. At that time, there were about 80,000 ideograms.

Besides movable type, Gutenberg found satisfactory solutions for other major problems in printing: (i) a method of making type in large quantities, (ii) holding type in place for printing, (iii) a press for making type impressions on paper, and (iv) printing ink. All these techniques helped shape the modern methods of typography and printing.

Printing came to India with the British. Type development of Indian scripts is less than 200 years old. During the early days of the British rule, Charles Wilkins came to

Figure 2.3 Wilkins's types in Bengali and Devanagari

India to serve the East India Company. During his stay in Malda in Bengal, he showed some interest in the Bengali (Bangla) alphabet and some experiments in casting letters by pouring molten metal on sand. By 1811, Wilkins had produced a complete font of Bengali type. He had also involved himself in designing type in Devanagari and some other Indian scripts. Figure 2.3 shows Wilkins's type in Bengali and Devanagari scripts. Wilkins published his first book, *Hitopadesa*, in Devanagari script in 1810.

TYPES OF LETTERFORMS

We broadly use three types of letterforms for communication: signographic, calligraphic, and typographic.

Signographic These letterforms are drawn, painted, and fabricated. The term 'signographic' is derived from 'sign writing'. Various instruments, such as paints, brushes, scales, and knives, may be used to develop the letters on various surfaces. Efforts are made to make the letters artistic. This style of writing is even chosen for printed letters. Computer generated letters that are manipulated to make a logo can also be called signographic letterforms.

Calligraphic Calligraphic letterforms are free hand written letters. Calligraphy is the art of beautiful writing. Normal pens, brushes, and ink are used to write these letters. Skilled calligraphy lends an artistic touch to the writing and creates a personal touch in communication.

Typographic The word 'type' generally refers to letter characters that have been developed by some mechanical system with the help of a body of metal piece, a negative film, or a string of digits in a computer. Typography refers to the rules and conventions that govern the assembling of the type into pages for printing.

Typeface is the image of a letter we get on paper, which is created by the type body mentioned earlier.

Signographic and calligraphic letterforms are not standardized. Since they are drawn by hand, if a letter appears more than once in a word, it may not exactly be the same. Typographic letterforms are standardized as they are made from moulds, stencils, or grids. These letters appear the same on the page as many times as they are printed. Figure 2.4 shows samples of the three different letterforms.

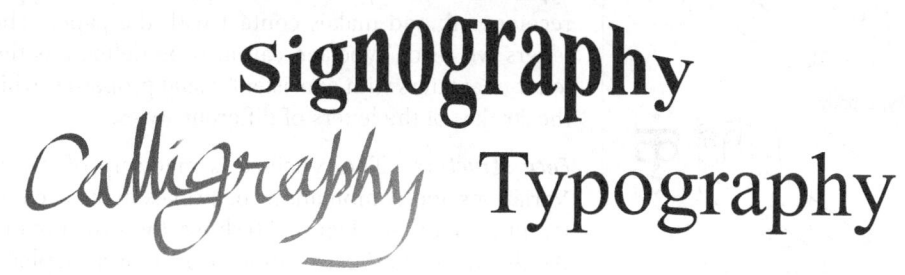

Figure 2.4 Samples of signographic, calligraphic, and typographic letterforms

18 Art and Print Production

Typography is both an art and a science. It is an art because it touches the heart of the reader. Because of the flexible nature of types, a designer can arrange them according to his/her wish to entertain the reader. Reading, in addition to providing knowledge and information, is also a source of enjoyment and involvement. Creative typography can ensure that reading is enjoyable.

Typography is also a science because many technical considerations are involved in type designing and type composition. Different technical rules have been developed through research and testing. These rules must be understood. In order to produce an effective communication message, a designer needs to make use of his/her imagination, creativity, knowledge of human psychology, and technical know-how.

TYPOGRAPHY—STRUCTURE, DESIGN, AND FUNCTION

In this chapter, we have divided the discussion on typography into three parts: (i) physical structure, (ii) aesthetics of typographic composition which comes from various design styles, and (iii) function or readability.

Physical Structure

In this section, we shall discuss the common features of type and the methods used for type measurement. We shall also look at the various digital letterforms available these days.

Type features

In typography, almost all languages have some common features—type body, typeface, and font. We need to understand the basic difference between these terms to avoid confusion in professional handling of typography. Figure 2.5 illustrates the type body and typeface in a block.

Type body The concept of type body comes from the hot metal type in which all the images are in rectangular blocks, different in width but identical in height. If these blocks are arranged side by side, they will make words. The letters on it form a mirror image. In a negative film for phototypesetting, the body is opaque and the image area is transparent. A series of dots create a body in computerized typesetting.

Typeface The typeface is that portion of the type body that receives ink and makes contact with the paper. These are the letters we read. Typeface can also be defined as the design of letter characters with consistent visual properties which relate to the strokes of the letters of different styles.

Face structure The typeface is made up of various strokes. Variations and combinations of strokes make each typeface different from others. Figure 2.6 shows the structure of a typeface. As shown in the figure, some strokes of an alphabet are in a consistent size. This is known as the x-height of the letters. The main design strokes of lowercase letters are within this height.

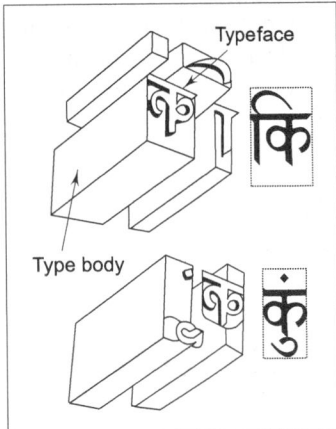

Figure 2.5 Metal type body and its face

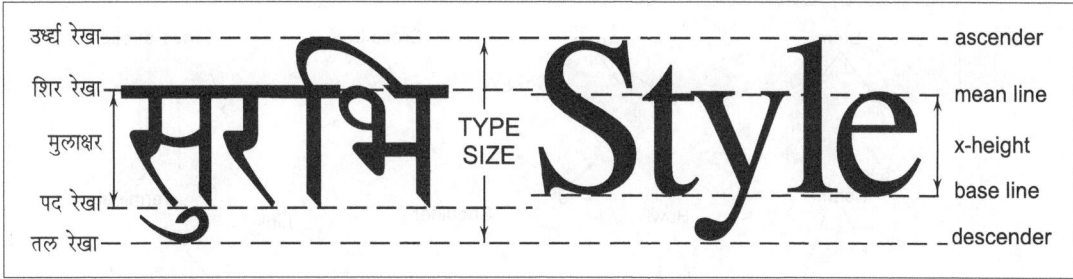

Figure 2.6 Structure of a typeface

Some of the letter strokes extend above the x-height and some strokes drop below the x-height. These are called ascenders and descenders, respectively. The letters b, d, f, h, k, l, and t have ascenders, while the letters g, p, q, and y have descenders. The x-height of the type creates the tonal effect of the type composition. These features—ascenders, descenders, and x-height—are common in Devanagari type also. A careful look at Figure 2.6 will show that the x-height is within the boundaries of two lines. The top line is known as the mean line and the bottom line is known as the base line.

As shown in Figure 2.7, some typefaces are structured in a combined form on the same type body. These are known as *ligatures*. A ligature may be a combination of two to three letters. Generally, ligatures replace characters that occur next to each other when they share common components. Ligatures are not required in Devanagari letterforms as the letters of most of the words are joined by the stroke at the mean line.

Parts of a face The strokes of a face structure comprise of several parts which got their names from familiar objects in our environment. All the parts of a typeface are illustrated in Figure 2.8. These parts may be categorized under three groups for easy recognition—primary strokes, curve strokes, and decorative strokes.

Primary strokes As shown in Figure 2.8, the *stems* that are formed by significant vertical and oblique lines give the letters their basic shape. Short strokes off the stem at the top of stems are called *arms* and those at the bottom are called *legs*.

The horizontal stroke that joins the two stems together is called a cross bar. When a crossbar intersects a stem, it is called a *cross stroke*, as in the letters t and f. The *terminal* is the finishing of a stroke with self-contained treatment without a serif.

Curve strokes The space within a rounded letterform, either fully or partly enclosed, is called a counter, as in the letters 'c' and 'd'. The *bowl* is the rounded form of letter that encloses the counter. The curved stroke of letters like 'h' and 'n' is the *shoulder*. The curved stroke of the letter 'S' is called the *spine* and the short curve of the lowercase letter 'g' is called a *link*. The bowl created in the descenders of lowercase letters such as 'g' in some typefaces is known as a *loop*.

Decorative strokes *Serifs* are the short strokes attached to the stems and arms of letterforms. Serifs may be bracketed, inclined, straight line, or square/slab. An ear is the part of the letter stroke that extends from the main stem, as in the letters 'g' and 'r'. A *swash* is a decorative extension of the arms of a letterform used to make the letter stylish.

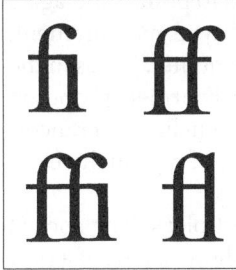

Figure 2.7 Ligatures

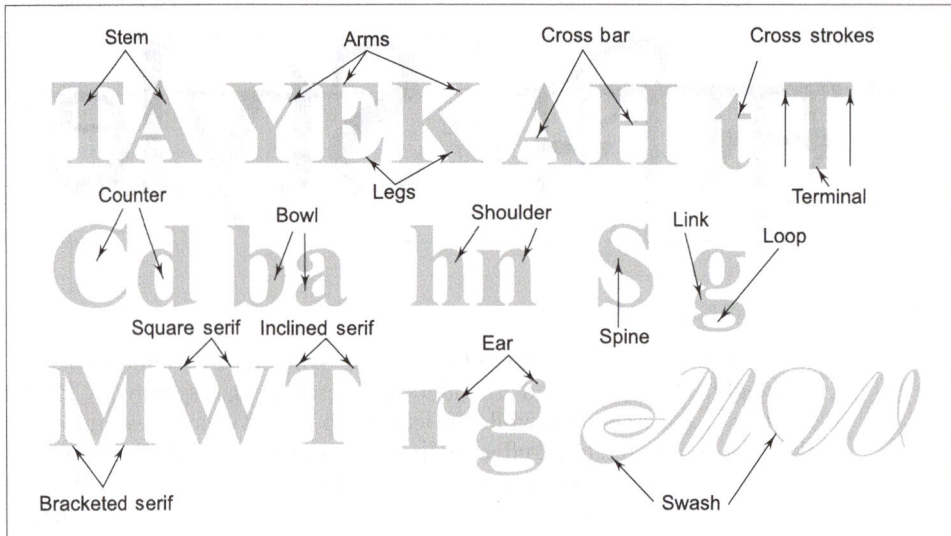

Figure 2.8 Parts of a typeface

Font The meaning of the word 'font' is often confusing because it is understood differently by different people. In simple terms, a font provides for displaying a set of symbols through well-defined shapes for each symbol. The symbol is a generic concept and the font is an instance of specific representation of a set of symbols. Traditionally, the symbols mentioned here have been the letters of the alphabet in a particular language along with punctuation marks and special characters. Fonts were created by craftsmen and artists during the days of printing machines that used movable type faces. Today, fonts are created by artists and designers who work with computer-based tools. In the world of computers, the word 'font' refers to the general shape of a set of characters. A font can contain characters of many sizes and several variations of the basic family shape. Typeface and font are often used synonymously.

Type measurement

For many years, type designing was an inexact technology, especially in the area of type measurement. Different type casters used to produce different sizes of type. The sizes were known by their names, for example, nonpareil (6 point), elite (10 point), and agate (5½ point). No two printers could agree on a standard system of type measurement, which meant that a type cast by one foundry could not be used by another. It was in the mid-eighteenth century that a French typographer, Pierre Simon Fournier, proposed a type measuring unit, which was further developed by another Frenchman, Francois Didot. This type measuring unit was accepted as a uniform measure of type in the USA and the UK in 1888, and thereafter in the entire printing world.

The units developed by Fournier–Didot are termed points and picas. The special scale, which carries these units, is called the pica scale. Figure 2.9 shows a part of a pica scale. This scale is used not only for type sizes but also for other printing dimensions such as line length, rule, and galley depth. A point is the smaller unit of this scale and a pica is the bigger one. There are only two units in this measurement system. Seventy two points or six picas equal one inch. This means that there are 12 points in a pica. Actually, 72 points are slightly less than one inch (0.9963"). Therefore, for all practical purposes, a communicator should use a pica scale.

A type is measured by its body, not by its face. This is so because body height is the only feature of a type that remains constant, the faces being variable. Most of the time, the body of a type is not accessible to the communicator, nor does it leave any impression on paper along with the face. A type specimen catalogue provides the body size along with each face. This may not solve the problem all the time. We know that the type height includes ascenders, descenders, and x-height. If we draw two parallel lines, one from the top of the ascender and another from the bottom of the descender, then we obtain the body height. This can be easily measured by the pica scale.

The type size can be measured on the pica scale in another way. Most pica scales carry a specimen letter of different point sizes. As shown in Figure 2.10, by matching the specimen letter, we can find the required size of type. However, since all the sizes of specimens on a pica scale are not available, the previous method is more reliable. While matching the required size with the specimen letter on the pica scale, it should be kept in mind that uppercase specimen letters should be matched with uppercase letters only. Similarly, if the letters are in lowercase (x-height), they should be matched with lowercase letters only. In case the specimen does not match exactly with the face, the difference may be added or subtracted as per the units of the pica scale. This is not a very accurate method as there is no standard design system for height, ascenders, and descenders, and there is no way the exact difference can be measured. There is no uppercase letter in the Devanagari script, so this type can be measured by using the specimen system on x-height. For comparable bilingual copy, it is important to note that Devanagari face looks slightly smaller than its equivalent Roman face within the same type size. Therefore, the Devanagari type chosen should be slightly bigger than the equivalent Roman face so that they may appear to be visually equal. As shown in Figure 2.11, the x-height of the face is the determining factor for choosing an equivalent type size in the Devanagari script.

Figure 2.9 Type measurement scale

48E Type Size

Figure 2.10 Matching the specimen letter with the type size

Digital letterforms

The advent of digital information technology has opened new vistas in the designing and use of letterforms. Traditionally, letterforms were designed by experienced artisans. Attempts have, however, been made in the last two decades to integrate the design process with the use of computers in order to create digital type fonts. A typeface or letterform that has been stored as digital information is referred to as digital type. This information is created by converting a black-and-white-dots image into a 2D matrix of black and white dots or pixels. This matrix is called raster image or bit map and can be used by phototypesetters, CRT displays, laser typesetters, and other output devices capable of utilizing digitized images. The use of design systems for the creation of these digital forms has led to an analysis of the way type designs are created by type designers. Their methods have been integrated into a variety of systems for creating digital forms.

The widespread use of personal computers since the mid-1980s completely changed the way types are used in design. There has been a change of approach of contemporary designers towards the development of type design and its use in communication with the advent of new digital technology. Designers are now more concerned with experimentation and communication of the message through the aesthetics of the typeface rather than a simple arrangement of letters for readability. The seemingly infinite number of fonts available today many a times makes it difficult for designers and prepress personnel to decide on the appropriate font for their design. Therefore, a few facts about digital fonts need to be understood.

The three font formats commonly in use today are PostScript, TrueType, and OpenType. Of the three formats, PostScript has historically been the preferred format for electronic publishing while TrueType fonts have been btter known for providing

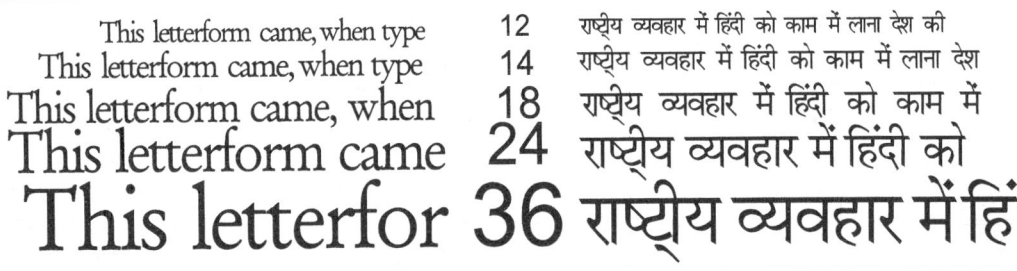

Figure 2.11 Comparison of Devanagari and Roman letterforms

great-looking screen rendering for Web design application. Recent increased support for OpenType fonts makes it a logical choice for reproducing type both on screen and on paper.

PostScript fonts   PostScript fonts are based on the Adobe PostScript language. There are three basic versions of PostScript: Type1, Type2, and Type3. Type1 fonts are widely used in desktop publishing. These fonts use a subset of the PostScript language. Type1 font files consist of two files—a screen font with bitmap information for on-screen display and a file with outline information for printing the font. For commercial printing, both the Type1 font files must be included with the application file. Due to differences in their structure, Mac and Windows PostScript Type1 fonts are not cross-platform compatible.

TrueType fonts   Unlike PostScript Type1 fonts, TrueType fonts include display and output information in a single file. TrueType technology actually involves two parts: the TrueType Rasterizer and TrueType fonts.

The Rasterizer is a piece of software that is embedded in both Windows and Mac operating systems. It gathers information on the size, colour, orientation, and location of all the TrueType fonts displayed and converts that information into a bitmap that can be understood by the graphics card and monitor. It is essentially an interpreter that understands the mathematical data supplied by the font and translates it into a form that the video display can render.

The fonts themselves contain data that describe the outline of each character in the typeface. Higher quality fonts also contain hinting codes. *Hinting* is a process that makes a font that has been scaled down to a small size look its best. Instead of simply relying on the vector outline, the hinting codes ensure that the characters line up well with the pixels so that the font looks as smooth and legible as possible.

OpenType fonts   OpenType is a scalable computer font format developed jointly by Microsoft and Adobe Systems. These cross-platform fonts are so simplified that it is believed to be the latest standard in high-quality digital type for both print and Web application. These are offered in two formats: OpenType PostScript (.otf), which is best suited for publishing, and OpenType TrueType(.ttf), which is ideal for Web application where high qualiy screen output is critical.

DESIGN STYLE

Typefaces are available in thousands of design variations, especially Roman characters. Scores of these are already in existence and still more are being designed. The reason behind the new designs is the desire to see our printed material in a new visual form. The demand for new typefaces has never abated, nor will it ever abate. Technological developments in the printing industry are pushing the demand further. Many type designers, these days, are engaged in designing new faces suitable for new technology. The common users of typefaces find it difficult to remember or recognize so many faces. Even a professional designer cannot remember all the faces. In the case of Indian faces, designers face difficulty in not having many standardized options. In order to facilitate identification and to use these faces suitaby in design, the faces can

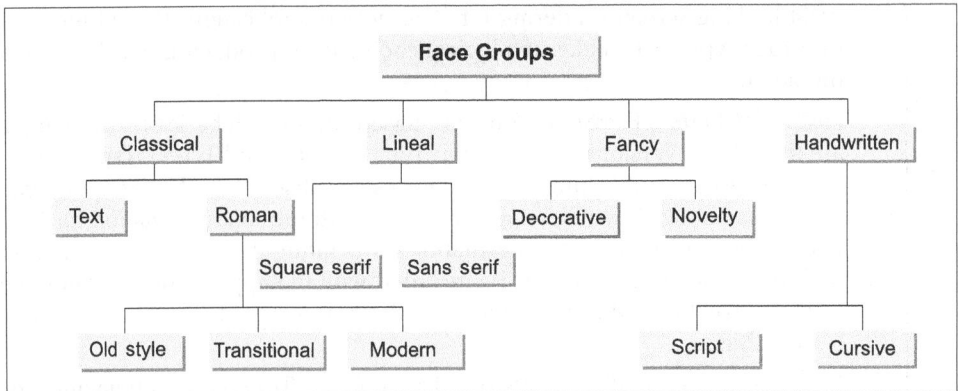

Figure 2.12 Grouping of typefaces

be divided into four groups. These groups are based on the basis of the strokes of characters and gradual development of faces, which evolved into a style.

Grouping of Typefaces

Grouping of typefaces is not easy. That is why typography pundits have never been able to agree on a particular system of grouping. Some of them indicate five; others, as many as eleven. For our purposes, however, we shall divide typefaces into four categories—classical, lineal, fancy, and handwritten. Figure 2.12 illustrates this classification of typefaces.

Classical typefaces

As discussed earlier, typefaces have their roots deep in the past. Early type designers developed their type style by copying from old scripts, which are carved on metal sheets, pillars, or rocks. The first movable type cast by Johannes Gutenberg was developed from the ancient religious manuscripts of Germany. His type was designed with thick strokes created with a reed pen and was a bit fancy, with angular strokes. The thick strokes of Gutenberg's type made the composition appear very dark. Hence, it was also known as 'Black Face'. This was the only face available during that time. It was also known as text. Modified later, it was given the name 'Old English'. Actually, Old English is one of the families of *text* sub-groups. These days, these faces are used only for specific purposes, such as for newspaper mastheads, nameplates, certificates of diplomas or degrees, invitation cards, and for creating an aged effect through typography. Figure 2.13 shows samples of Black Face and Old English.

Roman is the second sub-division in the classical group. Early Roman faces were developed by the Germans, who had perhaps been influenced by Gutenberg. The basic characteristics of Roman faces are thick and thin strokes within a letter with a short crossline attached to the main strokes of the letter, known as a serif.

While studying the development of Roman faces, we find that some of their features varied from period to period. On the basis of the thickness of the serif and letter strokes, we may divide all Roman styles into *old, transitional,* and *modern.* The old and modern

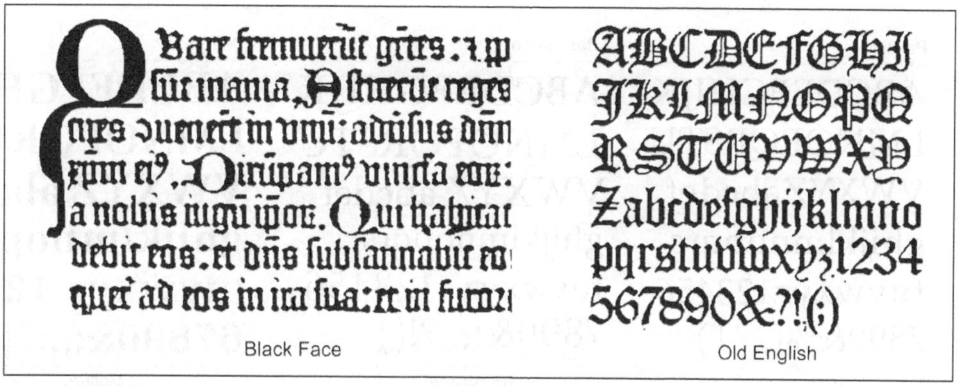

Figure 2.13 Black Face and Old English type

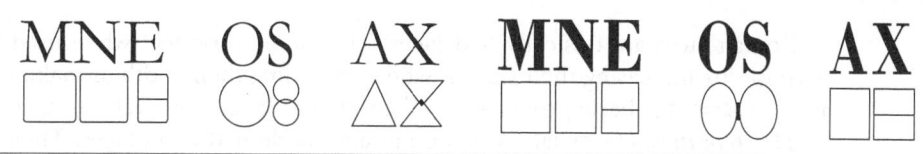

Figure 2.14 Geometrical shapes of letters

letter forms are also based on geometrical shapes—square, triangle, circle, and rectangle. The appearance of the old style is consequently more mechanical than optical. According to Sean Morrison, the uppercase letters M and N fit into a square of the same size. Similarly, the single-story round characters fit into a circle circumscribed by a square. Two-story characters such as E and S, on the other hand, are built on squares or circles stacked one on the other and are, therefore, only half as wide. Figure 2.14 illustrates how these letters are based on geometrical shapes.

Caslon, Palatino, Perpetua, and Garamond are examples of old style Roman faces. Another designing characteristic of the old Roman style is low x-height and long ascenders and descenders. The style was also designed on the basis of the printing surface that was available during that period. As can be seen in Figure 2.15, thin strokes are not in contrast with thick strokes. The serifs are also fairly heavy, which makes it possible to print clearly and constantly on rough surfaces such as that of handmade paper.

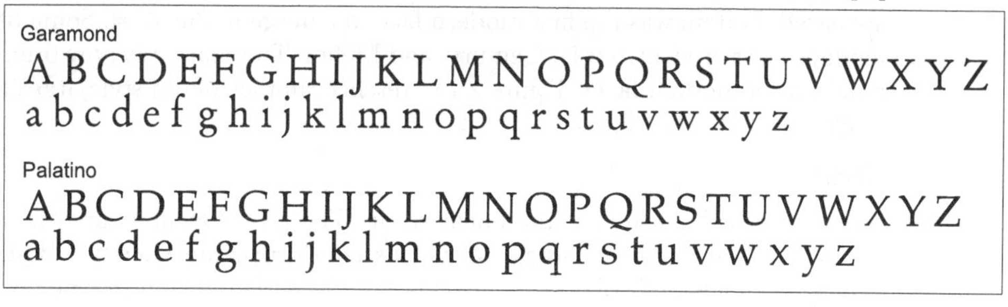

Garamond
ABCDEFGHIJKLMNOPQRSTUVWXYZ
abcdefghijklmnopqrstuvwxyz

Palatino
ABCDEFGHIJKLMNOPQRSTUVWXYZ
abcdefghijklmnopqrstuvwxyz

Figure 2.15 Old Roman faces

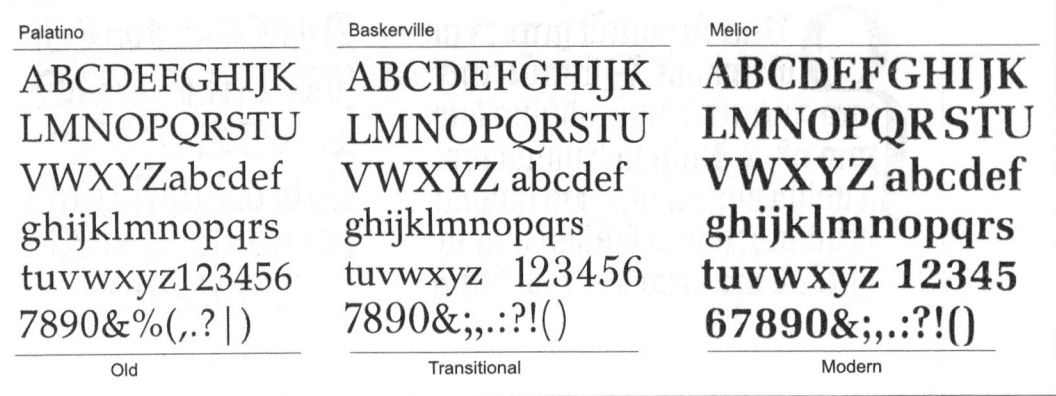

Figure 2.16 Samples of old style, transitional, and modern style Roman faces

Roman faces are basically text faces. They look imperfect when used for display purposes by increasing their size, or when expanding their width or making them bold as this distorts the basic proportion of the square, triangle, or circle, as the case may be.

The *transitional* faces fall between old and modern Roman faces. Their widths are in uneven proportions, and their serifs are bracketed and gradually thinner towards the point. Few transitional face styles are available because they are like a bridge between the old style and the modern one. Baskerville is a typical transitional Roman face. Transitionals are basically old style faces with modifications that move them towards the modern Roman face.

The *modern* style was the first all-purpose face which could be used for both text and display matter. It could be used not only for books but also for packaging, posters, billboards, and other advertising items. In fact, it came to Europe with the industrial revolution, when individual craftwork was giving way to mechanical form to suit mass production. According to Sean Morrison, modern alphabets are rational and based on equal-width ellipses and rectangles, not circles and squares. The strokes of the letters and serifs are simply hair lines, while the thick strokes are fairly heavy and symmetrical. The curved strokes are optically of the same width at their widest point, and narrow into the hair lines. The x-height is reasonably large. This is a pure typographic form. The handwritten forms that had been visible in the earlier faces have completely disappeared. Bodoni was the first modern face to emerge in the West. Some of the other modern faces are Caledonia, Century, and Melior. The market is now brimming with hundreds of modern faces. Figure 2.16 presents samples of old style, transitional, and modern style Roman faces.

Lineal

The next broad category is the lineal group. The term 'lineal' is used for this group because of its even body characteristics. This letterform came when type designers were experimenting with display types. That is why the early lineal form type resembles the Roman style, that is, it has an even body with a serif. One of these sub-groups is square serif. Some typographers refer to this style of typeface as the Egyptian style as it has a striking resemblance to modern Egyptian architecture. The early attempts of square serif faces came from making display faces. The original square serif characters having two weights, that is, thick and thin strokes, were made uniform and light so that they would go well with the modern face. Bookman, Clarendon, and Souvenir are some of the two-weight square serif faces.

Square serif The next attempt on revising the square serif style was to use it for text matter by making the type weight lighter. This was the typeface of the nineteenth century machines and buildings. The typefaces have some mechanical structural effect. The face could not gain much popularity for text matter because of its monotonal effect. A monotonal long copy is too tiring to read. It, however, looks interesting for promotional literature or an advertising copy. When a designer wants to attract the attention of the reader to the design at the cost of type legibility, he/she selects some of the typefaces of this style, such as Rockwell, Serifa, and Cairo.

Sans serif In the early nineteenth century, type designers experimented successfully with face designs by removing the serif from the previous design styles. 'Sans' is a French word, which means 'without'. The term 'sans serif' is thus self-explanatory—a face style without serif. Some typographers call it the Gothic style. In fact, some typography books have taken 'Gothic' as a group. The word 'Gothic' is associated with old style, so it may be better to call this modern face 'sans serif'. Some of the sans serif faces maintain the old style proportions, where the width of the faces is more or less uneven. Futura and Gill Sans are some of the members in this family. In even-width branches, we find Univers, Helvetica, Avant Garde, Antique Olive, etc. Figure 2.17 displays some lineal typefaces.

Today, typography is dominated by the second half of the twentieth century Lineal type group. Experts have yet to come to a conclusion and agree upon which face is more effective in terms of legibility—classical or lineal. However, it has been well established that the lineal group, especially sans serif, is designed for today's purposes. The

Figure 2.17 Samples of lineal typefaces

Figure 2.18 Samples of fancy typefaces

style is also considered modern as its strokes resemble the modern way of writing with ballpoint pens and sketch pens. This typeface is well adapted to digital computers and transfer of images by various printing processes.

Fancy

This category embraces all the faces that do not have any clear-cut characteristics of other groups. It may as well be divided into two sub-groups—novelty and decorative. *Novelty* faces resemble classical faces sometimes and lineal faces at other times. Take the example of Optima faces. They are two-weight alphabets but without serif. These faces are widely used in the composition of contemporary text matter. Eras is another family. It is fancy because of its unusual forward leaning character and some unionized loops in its faces. Friz Quadrata is included in the family of novelty for its minute triangular serif; Eurostile for its unusual rectangular letterform. Novelty faces may be used for text-matter as well as for display purposes.

The other category of the fancy group is *decorative*. The faces in this category have been designed mainly for display purposes, and not for text-matter, because a long copy in decorative faces is too difficult to read. Since these faces are decorated, they attract instant attention. This sometimes tends to reduce the communication value. Extra care should, therefore, be taken in selecting this typeface. Some more well-known families are Ringlet, Arnold, and Gallia. Figure 2.18 displays some samples of decorative and novelty faces.

Handwritten

This group imitates the handwritten form. Sometimes, we confuse faces of this group with calligraphy. Calligraphy is letter design drawn or written carefully by hand, whereas handwritten type means a letter image received on paper through impressions from a type body. Therefore, if a letter appears more than once in a word or passage, it will

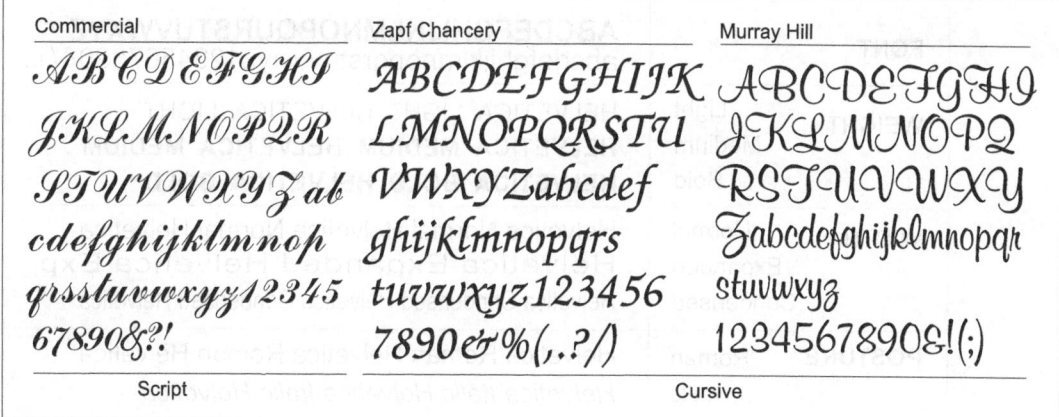

Figure 2.19 Samples of handwritten typefaces

look the same in case of handwritten type whereas, in calligraphy, these letters may differ from each other.

Two categories of faces are visible in the handwritten group. One may be called Script, which is mainly joint letters; the second category is Cursive, which has separate letters. In both cases, faces maintain their basic character, that is, the face is designed by pen or brush or some other instrument. Palace, Freestyle, and Commercial are families of the Script category; Murray Hill, Legend, and Zapf Chancery, are families of the Cursive category. Most letters of this group are slanted to the right. This also gives the impression of handwriting. Figure 2.19 shows some samples of the handwritten group.

These faces are not used much in graphic design. These faces are appropriate for invitation cards and headings of announcements. Handwritten communication adds a personal touch. However, because of low legibility, Script and Cursive faces should not be used for long copy and headings in capital letters.

Type Families

A type family is a group of typefaces bound together by similar visual characteristics in many sizes and variations. Each type family in a group is different from the other, but each member of a particular family has some characteristics in common with the members of that the other families in that group. For example, Caslon, Garamond, and Baskerville are families of the Roman group. They are slightly different from one another in terms of design, but each character is designed in such a way that when they are arranged as a word or a sentence, they look so harmonious that we call them a family.

Some of the families owe their names to the person who first designed the letter character. Others got their names from a country or publication which brought them fame. William Caslon, Claude Garamond, Giambattista Bodoni, and Eric Gill had designed Caslon, Garamond, Bodoni, and Gill Sans respectively. Egyptian Gothic, Americana, and Cairo are based on country names; Century and Times Roman on magazine names.

FONT		ABCDEFGHIJKLMNOPQURSTUVWXYZ abcdefghijklmnopqrstuvwxyz1234567890&()‥
WEIGHT	Light Medium Bold	HELVETICA LIGHT HELVETICA LIGHT **HELVETICA MEDIUM HELVETICA MEDIUM** **HELVETICA BOLD HELVETICA BOLD**
WIDTH	Normal Expanded Condensed	Helvetica Normal Helvetica Normal Helvetica Helvetica Expanded Helvetica Exp Helvetica Condensed Helvetica Condensed Helvetica
POSTURE	Roman Italic	Helvetica Roman Helvetica Roman Helvetica *Helvetica Italic Helvetica Italic Helvetica*

Figure 2.20 Typefaces of the Helvetica family

Gradually, individual names are disappearing and abstract names are being given to new faces. Type design is now not an individual craft. Rather, it is a group effort. Within families, there are a number of variations in terms of width, weight, and posture.

There is no logical system of measuring width or weight. The width of a typeface may be normal, condensed, or expanded. The proportion of normal faces is generally 2:3. If the proportion of a typeface is more than that, the face may be called expanded; if it is less than 2:3, it is called condensed. 'Weight' refers to the relative thickness of the element of a typeface. Weight comparisons should be carried out within typefaces of the same size.

It is very difficult to define the weight of a typeface, which gives a tone to the type composition. Lighter faces tend to look light grey; the slightly thicker ones, dark grey (medium); and the heaviest ones, darkest grey (bold). A typeface will never look black or full tone as there are white spaces (counter, shoulder, letter spacing, etc.) in each type body. 'Posture' refers to how a particular type stands. There are two postures—Roman, where types stand straight; and Italic, where they are slanted to the right. Figure 2.20 shows the font, weight, width, and posture of typefaces of the Helvetica family.

Traditionally, a font consists of letters, figures, and punctuation marks in one size. All the design elements of a face are so harmonious that if any other type appears in the type matter, it is marked as a compositional error (w.f.) in proofreading.

Indian typefaces

A cursory look at our own Indian typefaces will show a marked similarity with Roman faces in terms of groups, weight, width, and posture. In this section, we shall analyse only the Devanagari faces. Designers can exploit the similarity in Devanagari and Roman faces in preparing bilingual designs. Very often, they are baffled by the problem of visually translating designs which have been conceived in Roman. The Indian society has changed beyond recognition in the last two centuries, but in the field of typeface design, we have not made much headway. As mentioned earlier, type design of Indian languages came with printing two hundred years ago, but never has this process been very rational.

At a time when the West has made so much progress, the Indian counterparts have developed few faces which may be taken as models of modern type designing.

The classical Devanagari faces are derived from the style created with a reed pen. We find in them a similar thick and thin stroke of Roman characters. Serif was also used in early type designs, which were suitable for religious books that are much in demand in India. Besides reed pens, steel nibs of different varieties, round or flat lead pencils, brushes, and ball point pens are also used in creating Devanagari faces. Many graceful and easily flowing designs are drawn in a traditional way. New tools such as ball point pens, pencils, and round steel nibs have given birth to Lineal faces. These faces may be used for children's books as they create a style effect that is similar to writings by stone pencils on slates, which is very familiar to children. Lineal faces developed by the National Institute of Design became functional faces with their use in Airport signboards. An attempt has been made by the different type design institutions to put the designs in standardized forms which can create the effect of Sans Serif and Roman faces. Some faces are now available in digitized letters.

In the days of hot metal type, some type foundry had developed display faces that were mainly decorative or fancy in nature. However, no foundry has designed a common family name so far. A type design developed by Gujarat Type Foundry in the family name 'Uma' is almost the same as the one developed by Prakash Type Foundry, Pune, called 'Balakrishna'. Many bookfaces were issued by Nirnaya Sagar Type Foundry in classical styles. Medium and bold weight faces in different sizes, suitable for both text and display copy, were also developed by it.

FUNCTION OF TYPE COMPOSITION

Selection of the right typeface for a design is a complex task. Advises advertising guru David Ogilvy, 'Never use type self-consciously.' Even in the days of hot metal type, various type families were available. However, they were limited in size, weight, width, and posture. Modern technology has created flexible options for choosing a typeface in a design. Today, a designer can create a face in any size with an increment of fraction of a point, and expansion and condensation of width in any percentage. Overlapping, shading, etc. can be done from the same stencil or grid. More flexible kerning facility, that is, the option of placing two adjacent characters so that one is positioned within the space of the other, helps a designer create a more pleasing composition. For a new face, a designer also draws one set of characters and creates variations through computer manipulations, which distort the original face. All this makes correct identification of faces almost impossible.

Appropriateness

Some faces are so versatile that they can be appropriate for any job. Others are more limited in what they can do. They have some special qualities that set them apart. Consciously or unconsciously, these qualities do touch the reader's mind.

For the selection of a typeface, one can no longer rely on old family names alone. It is now essential to study meticulously the type styles available in computer and their flexibility in various software. Some faces offer a number of variations in terms of size, width, weight, and posture, while others offer artistic styles such as 3D, shadow, and texture. Type design is undergoing development for creative use by designers, and the technology available is also changing, affecting the choice of typefaces in a design. However, the aesthetic value of a typeface, its physical characteristics, and personal preferences of the designer are the most important considerations for choosing a typeface.

With increasing progress in education and information dissemination, designers have become more conscious of the need to create moods through written matter. The age, education, and standard of the reader are the parameters for creating such moods. For some languages, hundreds of type designs are available in the market; for some others, very few. Designers are usually in a dilemma while selecting typefaces, for there is no objective formula to guide them on which one to take and which one to reject. Many communication messages fail because of lack of knowledge of typography.

So far, we have discussed the physical form of the type and typefaces. These faces start talking, when they are arranged to make words and sentences. In order to achieve this goal, the writer and designer should work together. A writer might have written an effective communication message, but a poor design may kill the message even before it reaches the prospective reader. Type selection is important not only for the legibility of a message, but also for the creation of a congenial environment for the idea that the communicator wants to transmit. Type composition can create an environment of help, shouting, calmness, age, newness, delicacy, health, sickness, and so on. A shouting message will be more appropriate in sans serif bold type than in Optima (Novelty) medium face. For a booklet on the Steel Authority of India, square serif will be more appropriate than light face Futura. For a computer manual, old face Garamond will definitely look out of place. In the heading of an advertisement that promotes a cream to maintain soft skin, Arial light face will be an appropriate choice for the mood and effect needed for the product.

Readability vs Legibility

Since type is meant to be read, readability should be the decisive factor in choosing a typeface for a design composition. Readability has several aspects. The first is the writer's idea. The second is the language. The third is the construction of sentences. Compound and complex sentences, unfamiliar words, improper punctuation, and long paragraphs reduce readability. The fourth is the reader's interest. The fifth is the legibility of type composition. Designers are mainly involved in this part.

Legibility means clarity of letter character in the type composition. While reading, some words fall within the eye span and the reader absorbs the meaning of the words at a certain speed and moves on to grasp the subsequent words. This movement of the eye depends critically on legibility. Therefore, a type composition that can be read faster should be considered more legible. Often, an individual letterform is beautiful and also identifiable but in a composition, it is not legible. Decorative and script letters are examples of illegible faces. Letterforms that are closer to the fundamental shapes of the alphabet are more legible. Readability and legibility are interrelated and should be considered as such in selecting typefaces for particular applications. In short, legibility describes a font; readability, its function. Most of the type that is set and read is text; the legibility rules, therefore, are basically meant for text matter.

Type for Text, Display, and Poster

For the purpose of design, there are three kinds of type styles—(i) for the text matter or body copy, (ii) display matter, and (iii) posters and big size designs. The text matter or body copy constitutes the main typographic composition. The designer's ultimate goal in each design is to draw the reader into the text matter and involve him/her in the idea of the communicator. Type sizes of 5 to 12 point (8–14 point in the case of Devanagari) are considered appropriate for text matter. These sizes are visually clear and legible at a distance of 10–14″ from the eye. Text types are small because small types enable us to read more words within one eye focus. While reading, our eye works like a lens of a camera. We shoot a photograph after focusing on an object containing a number of elements. In the same way, we read a number of words in a line of a page by concentrating our mind and eye on that area. We first read and understand a group of words. Eye focus is then shifted to another group of words. In the case of Devanagari, faces up to 14 point size can be considered as text faces; for as far as size is concerned, 14 point Devanagari matches with 12 point Roman face in terms of the tonal quality of type composition.

Display faces may vary from 12–14 point up to 72 point. These sizes are used mainly for headings and subheadings as they are highly visible and eye-catching. The function of display faces is to summarize the content and to attract attention. Since the functions of display and text faces are different, they are governed by separate legibility rules.

The typefaces for posters and other big size designs are above 72 points. Poster faces may not follow basic typographic rules. They act as visuals and are often measured by actual faces and not by body, especially when only uppercase letters are used. The main purpose of the typeface in a poster, banner headlines, or advertisement gimmick is to attract attention.

Text matter

The primary condition in choosing a typeface for text matter—the pleasant uniform grey area—is that the reader should read the lines, columns, sentences, paragraphs, and pages with ease. Legibility is thus the main consideration in designing the text matter.

Face style Typographers believe that the right type style may enhance the legibility of the text matter. They give various arguments for this. Type style with thick and thin strokes creates a rhythm in design and moves faster by spotting the rhythm. Therefore, we find that most of the running matter is in Roman or Classical faces. Type experts feel that the serif of the Roman faces accelerates horizontal movement. Roman faces are considered the basic types. Studies have confirmed that a Roman face can be read 10–12 per cent faster than its immediate competitor, the sans serif type. Medium Roman is more legible than light and bold faces. Too little or too much contrast with the background is tiring for the eyes.

Another consideration is the familiarity of the face. Classical Roman faces are much more familiar than Lineal faces. Some believe that it is easier to read text written in Roman face as we have been reading books, magazines, and newspapers in this face since our childhood. This view is challenged by the revolutionary group of type designers. They believe that familiarity can be changed in no time. According to them, Lineal faces are more familiar to modern children as they start writing with a pencil or ball point pens on paper, rather than with reed pens or metallic nibs as in earlier days.

Most people consider sans serif faces slightly unusual because of their monotonal design character. Recognition of letterform basically comes from the shape and dimensions of the counter. This is easy in thick and thin lines and letter spacing. Roman face letters look separate because of the serifs, yet they also look linked, which helps smooth reading. The unusual nature of Lineal faces tempts designers to use them in headings and subheadings, that is, in display compositions.

Sans serif faces are also appropriate for children's books, promotional literature, and in advertising copy when running text matter is limited. Here, designers want to call the attention of the reader to the copy at the cost of legibility of the composition.

Newspapers and magazines use Classical Roman faces. Recently, some Indian newspapers and magazines have started using sans serif faces for regular body setting. *The Hindu* is a good example of this. It had been set earlier in Excelsior (serif face)—a traditional newspaper type which was quite popular in the pre-War era. After independence, *The Hindu* had to switch over to Corona, an elegant type slightly heavier than Excelsior and, therefore, better equipped to cope with coarse-grain government newsprint. With the arrival of photocomposition and facsimile transmission, *The Hindu* adopted a typeface that was free of the vulnerable serifs and thin strokes. The serifs and thin strokes of the traditional faces could not stand up well in a co-axial facsimile transmission system. Thus, it has again started using serif faces for its text matter because of advancements in transmission technology through satellites.

Like Roman faces, the Devanagari Classical faces, which are thick and thin, are popular for running matter. Of course, very few alternative text faces are available in Devanagari. As with Roman faces, the distinct mean line helps in horizontal movement. Mean lines also hold the letters of a word and set the words apart so that the typesetter gets greater control over word spacing. The Devanagari face scores over both Roman and sans serif faces because of this line. Classical faces have maintained their position in text matter. The popularity of some faces has been greatly increased due to their availability for desktop publishing.

From the example of *The Hindu*, we can also see how the selection of a face style also depends on the quality of paper. Thin bracketed serifs of Baskerville face look pleasant on smooth art paper. The legibility of this face will definitely be reduced on coarse paper such as newsprint or maplitho.

Figure 2.21 displays samples of some commonly used face styles and their attributes.

Special style for newspaper The x-height is another criterion in choosing the face style. Body faces are divided into two categories—book and news. The faces which can be used in relatively inexpensive printing in small sizes are called news text faces. They are relatively bold, a bit condensed, and have a large x-height. Since the larger x-height is more pronounced in words, condensed faces can accommodate more words in a shorter line length of a newspaper. Figure 2.22 shows samples of words set in large and small x-height.

The most common faces are book faces, which are used for texts of magazines, books, and other printed literature. These are found in great variety. Magazines and newspapers do not change the type style for body copy with a view to maintaining familiarity. Familiarity enhances legibility. In order to develop a house style, many publishing houses and institutions use a certain type style. Besides making reading easy, this makes for instant identification of their publication.

Tiffany	This nostalgic font is an alternative to the more common—and commonly used—serif faces. But don't let its delicate elegance fool you. **Tiffany Heavy is just that—big, bold, and heavy.**
Bookman	Bookman has a strong, straightforward look, and works particularly well in display or, as the name suggests, in book printing and other publications where long blocks of highly legible text are needed.
Palatino	Palatino combines a distinctly modern flavour with a calligraphic influence from the 16th century heritage. For elegant communication, Palatino is both practical and popular.
Helvetica	Since its release in 1954, Helvetica has become the world's most popular typeface for two reasons—its legibility is superb and its design flawless.
Futura	Futura is the classic example of the geometric sans serif. An all purpose face—when used in text type with normal weight—it communicates objectivity and directness. **It commands authority and attention in headline with bold face.**
Souvenir	Its rounded features soften the traditional formality of serif fonts, but unlike some casual fonts, it is not overwhelming in lengthy blocks of text. In display, it is warm and friendly.
Baskerville	This font has a delicacy and grace that come from the subtle transfer of stroke weight from thick to thin, and its long elegant serif. These features, along with its general light weight, give Baskerville the ability to create copy that is invitingly easy to read.

Figure 2.21 Commonly used face styles and their attributes

> Faces with large x-height are more pronounced in words but can accommodate less letters.
>
> Faces with small x-height require less line spacing and can accommodate more letters.

Figure 2.22 Samples of typefaces with large and small x-height

Other faces Preferences of type style in terms of frequency of use are Roman, Lineal, Novelty, Cursive, Script, and Decorative. We have already discussed Roman and Lineal sans serif faces. Lineal square serif faces (for example, Rockwell) have a mechanical appearance. Even textured, running matter is uncomfortable to read. Therefore, this style has not become popular for books and magazines. However, it looks very elegant in advertising copy and corporate literature.

Souvenir is another square serif, two-weight typeface. It has some of the characteristics of Roman face, such as thick and thin strokes, but, because of its fancy style, it is grouped in Novelty. This face is very popular in magazines and other novelty publications. Among sans serif Novelty faces, Optima is popular for text matter because of its thick and thin strokes.

Some of the Cursive faces are used for running matter but definitely not for long copy, where they impair reading speed and cause eye fatigue. Zapf Chancery is a classic example of this cursive face. Inevitably associated with wedding and greeting cards, it is virtually unreadable for running matter. Decorative faces are hardly ever used for text matter.

Uppercase vs lowercase Words are recognized by their shapes rather than by the individual letters that make them up. The shape of a word is formed by a combination of the external contours of its letters and its internal word pattern. For greater legibility, text matter should be set in mixed uppercase and lowercase faces, and uppercase letters should be used sparingly. In a mixed composition, lowercase has more characters per line. The x-height of the face, which has more design strokes, creates two parallel lines with an occasional break of monotonous uniformity by ascenders and descenders. The texture created by lowercase letters is so pleasing to the reader that it enhances legibility. In contrast, text matter that is typeset in uppercase (all caps) creates a uniform parallel and almost uniform white space between lines, impairing legibility, as shown in Figure 2.23. Sometimes, because of lack of letter spacing, words in uppercase are confusing. For example, two or more vertical lines coming together (NIL), or two round characters such as G and/or Q and O may be difficult to read. For text matter

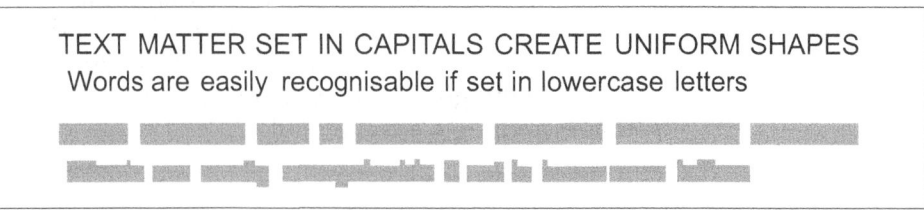

Figure 2.23 Shapes created by uppercase and lowercase letters

> LINE IN ALL CAPITAL LETTER IS DIFFICULT TO READ
> LINE IN ALL CAPITAL LETTER IS DIFFICULT TO READ
> LINE IN ALL CAPITAL LETTER IS DIFFICULT TO READ

Figure 2.24 Text matter set in all caps

that is set in all caps, the matter should be limited to two or three at a time with enough space between lines, as lines of matter set in all caps are strenuous for the reader. All caps should never be used for fancy and hand written styles for text matter, irrespective of length of copy. Figure 2.24 illustrates the fact that such matter is difficult to read. One's main purpose in designing text matter is to highlight or contrast the shapes.

The above-mentioned rules are not applicable to Devanagari types as they do not have uppercase letters. Setting text copy in uppercase is also uneconomical as it occupies almost 50 per cent more space than the equivalent size lowercase type.

Size Various rules govern the selection of the proper type size. The size of a type refers to its body, and not its face. A face with a bigger x-height, such as Times Roman, appears to be larger than one with a smaller x-height, such as Garamond. Bigger size faces are more legible than smaller faces because they show clarity of type design. However, the consideration of clarity alone should not dictate the use of bigger size faces. Larger size type occupies more space. Fewer words come within the eye span, requiring more time to read the copy. Very small faces too are difficult to read. They lack an invitation, much less a warm one, to the copy. The decision about size, therefore, should be coordinated with other legibility factors such as line width, space between the lines, and readers' educational level and age. Figure 2.25 displays the effect created by large and very small type size.

In general, newspapers use 7 to 8 point size while other long copy publications use 9 to 12 point type size. Newspapers in Devanagari use 8 to 10 point size and other publications in Devanagari use 12 to 14 point. Larger line length demands a bigger face. Designers often exploit readers. Where the reading matter is very interesting, small size type is used for economy of space. Tender notices and income tax forms are examples where this is practised.

Size will also depend on the surface on which the impression is to be made. Coarse grain and coloured paper demand bigger sizes. Reverse letters and fancy and handwritten faces should be set in bigger sizes. A condensed face in small size is difficult to read. Normal width types are acceptable faces for text matter at all times.

> Few words of large text faces fall within the focus area of our eyes, and very small faces strain the eyes. Both make reading difficult.
>
> Few words of large text faces come within an eye focus. Very small faces are strainious to eyes. Both make reading difficult.

Figure 2.25 Effect created by large and very small type sizes

Spacing There are four types of spacing in type composition—letter spacing, word spacing, line spacing, and paragraph spacing.

Letter spacing The type designer takes care of natural letter spacing while creating a letterform. This letter spacing is quite adequate for most of the running text. There are several options to achieve various moods in type composition. Spacing of type composition can be obtained mechanically and optically. Optical spacing is more pleasing than the mechanical one. The type body itself determines the letter spacing. This was especially true in the days of hot metal composition, which was basically mechanical. Efforts were made to avoid this rigidity by cutting the metal body to bring the wide-shoulder letters closer and by manufacturing some of the letters jointly, such as ae, fl, fi, and fie. They look apart, if set individually. These joint faces are known as *ligatures*. Today, digital typesetters can control the letter spacing as normal, loose, or tight by increasing or decreasing the spacing by half a unit. Figure 2.26 shows samples of matter where the spacing is normal, tight, and loose. The facility of kerning, whereby two adjacent characters can be placed in such a way that one is positioned within the space of the other, offers a more pleasing composition. Based on their dominant strokes, Roman letters can be categorized into vertical, curved, a combination of vertical and curved, and oblique. Letters within each group have similar characteristics and are more likely to be confused with each other. Therefore, more space should be kept between two vertical strokes, and less space is required between two curved and oblique letters. In case of the Devanagari script, designers should be more careful in spacing the letters. Loose spacing sets apart the letters because of the distinct white space between mean lines. Tight spacing causes some confusion in recognizing letters such as र followed by व. It may be identified as ख. Some letters such as प, ष, म, भ, and य, थ, घ, ध look similar in a group. Setting these faces tightly will obviously be at the expense of legibility.

Normal
Proper letter spacing depends on many factors such as the typeface you use, the amount of copy, line spacing, type size and weight, nature of the design, audience and viewing situation, and your own taste.

Tight
Proper letter spacing depends on many factors such as the typeface you use, the amount of copy, line spacing, type size and weight, nature of the design, audience and viewing situation, and your own taste.

Loose
Proper letter spacing depends on many factors such as the typeface you use, the amount of copy, line spacing, type size and weight, nature of the design, audience and viewing situation, and your own taste.

Figure 2.26 Matter with normal, tight, and loose letter spacing

Word spacing Word spacing is always influenced by letter spacing. Tight spaced letters need tight word spacing while loose and normally spaced letters require loose and normal word spacing. A traditional practice for word spacing is to use the width of a lowercase face, for example, the letter 'e' in Roman or म in Devanagari. Sometimes, the word spacing used is too much. Figure 2.27 shows how too much word spacing may break the line into separate elements. Thus, it is important for designers to specify word space according to the purpose of the composition and type design. For example, Fournier is a narrow set type, whereas Baskerville is a wide set type. They need narrow and wide word spacing respectively. Since the mean line (शिर रेखा) of Devanagari holds letters together in a word, narrow word spacing is often sufficient for a text copy. Bold faces and medium sans serifs are easier to read if set with slightly loose word spacing.

We should be a little flexible in word spacing for justified composition. The word space is reduced or increased to accommodate the last word (without breaking) in a line or to take this word to the next line. Sometimes, this may lead to an undesirable white gap in the page. This occurs when word spaces come one above the other for a number of lines. To eliminate this white space, it is necessary to adjust the space between the words. In general, spaces should be optically even within the words. Too much uneven space reduces legibility.

Line spacing Like letter spacing, type designers also take care of line spacing. Most of the time, the natural line spacing is not adequate for type composition. If set naturally, the composition looks very tight and most people may skip a line or read the same line again, reducing the reading speed. Therefore, we need to decide how much space to use between the lines of text matter.

The space between lines is termed as *leading* in the printing trade. This term originated in the hot metal era, when a thin strip of lead was used by composers to space out type lines. This term continues to be used in the digital era and is an essential element determining the appearance of a type composition. Figure 2.28 demonstrates the effect of normal, tight, and loose line spacing on readability.

Line spacing decisions come from the size of the type being used, style of the face, line length, and setting of the composition. Smaller size type in long line length needs more leading. A type style with small x-height needs less leading as its ascenders and descenders naturally take care of the white space between the lines. Word spacing also has an influence on line spacing. Wide-set word spacing needs more line spacing. In general, white space between the x-height of the two lines should be more than the word spacing, so that the texture formed by the words in a line is easily identifiabe.

Too   much   word   spacing   breaks   the   line   into
separate   elements,   disturbing   the   unity   among   words.

Figure 2.27 Text with excessive word spacing

> **Normal**
> Too little line spacing creates dark, uninviting 'colour' that may cause the eye to skip a line when scanning to find the text one. Too much line spacing causes the eye to jump from line to line and is disruptive to reading.
>
> **Tight**
> Too little line spacing creates dark, uninviting 'colour' that may cause the eye to skip a line when scanning to find the text one. Too much line spacing causes the eye to jump from line to line and is disruptive to reading.
>
> **Loose**
> Too little line spacing creates dark, uninviting 'colour' that may cause the eye to skip a line when scanning to find the text one. Too much line spacing causes the eye to jump from line to line and is disruptive to reading.

Figure 2.28 Effect of normal, tight, and loose line spacing

This helps the eye traverse the line smoothly. Longer line length needs more leading. Typographers recommend 1 to 3 point leading for 8 to 10 point size type with up to 22 pica line length, and 2 to 4 point leading for 11 and 12 point size type with up to 30 pica line length. Justified setting needs more leading than single side aligned or centered copy. These line spacing rules apply to Devanagari type as well.

Paragraph spacing A paragraph is the writer's concept. The designer cannot tamper with it. Paragraph spacing is, however, the designer's area, through which he/she can increase the legibility of type composition. There are several ways to separate a group of lines from the other group, maintaining the harmony of each group. According to the traditional separation practice, the initial line is indented and no additional space is provided between the paragraphs. This may sometimes look uncomfortable, especially when the last line of a paragraph fills almost the complete measure.

When line spacing is 2 to 5 point, 6 point paragraph spacing is acceptable. A paragraph with a sub-head needs at least a one-line space at the top. A separate section in the running text may also be offset by a one-line space. In an advertising or a magazine copy, using oversized initial letters known as drop letters also sometimes fulfils this purpose.

Line length While discussing line spacing, we have already touched upon the concept of line length. It, however, needs a little elaboration as the length of a line influences legibility to a great extent. Several rules and formulae are available for determining the line size. The most common is that the line size (in picas) should be twice the type size (in points) being used, that is, 8 point size and 10 point size type should have 16 and 20 pica line length, respectively. Small sized type requires short line length; bigger type requires a longer line.

The argument for the rule discussed above is that, while reading, at least four inches (24 picas) are within the eye span of the reader. One can read a line of this length without changing the focus of the eye. These rules may vary from type style to type style. A large x-height face needs more line spacing and longer line length. A line may contain 12 to 14 words on an average. In Devanagari, it may contain 14 to 16 words as Devanagari uses long words sparingly.

Italic, light, and bold faces have low legibility. The line measure should be shorter to compensate for this. Justified setting may have longer line size than unjustified setting. Line size should not be shorter than 11 picas, as the flow of reading would be constantly interrupted by breaks and hyphenated words. A line set in condensed letters can be of short measure as it may contain an adequate number of words.

Setting format The format of typesetting refers to the manipulation of space by type. The most common setting format is *justified*, where the type composition is aligned both on the left and the right. It is considered the most legible format because of uniform line length. The reader's eye moves from left to right and in between uniformly.

The justified format has some drawbacks as well. Often, word spacing is squeezed or stretched to accommodate the last word or to take it to the next line. However, the reader hardly notices this and it has little, if any, impact on the total grey tone of the composition. Therefore, for a serious-looking, conventional page, a justified setting is preferred.

The next most legible format is the *left flushed* (or *left aligned*) and *right ragged*. Here, the reader's eye movement is almost as uniform as in the justified format. An additional advantage of this format is that there are few hyphenated words at the end of a line. Even so, this format should be used with caution, as white space between columns looks quite wide and irregular. If it is used for a long copy, the reader may even skip the message. For a short copy, however, this format looks dynamic and more contemporary in style.

Two other setting formats are *left ragged* and *right aligned*, and *centred*. These formats are best avoided for long copy, because they impede reading speed. The reader takes time to find the beginning of the next line because of the uneven starting point. There is, however, no bar on their use for special purposes. For example, a right aligned short copy creates unity with a rectangular illustration. A centred format for an invitation card and a poetry book will be more appropriate than any other format.

Figure 2.29 illustrates the formats discussed in this section. The selection of a setting format depends greatly on the type of layout and other elements being used in the layout. Books, magazines, and newspapers follow the traditional justified setting. Glossy magazines and Sunday supplements of newspapers occasionally use a right ragged format, which goes well with other visual elements. Art directors of advertising layout and promotional literature play with the setting format to achieve their communication goals by creating unity between the content and the format.

Weight Types come in various weights—bold, medium, light, etc. The weight of a type creates the tone and texture of the type composition. There is no set standard for the weight of a typeface and weight varies from manufacturer to manufacturer. We identify type weight by the relative lightness and darkness of the face. This is very subjective, there being no instrument or formula to measure this weight. A long copy set in light and bold is tiring for the reader's eye. Both these faces are common for a

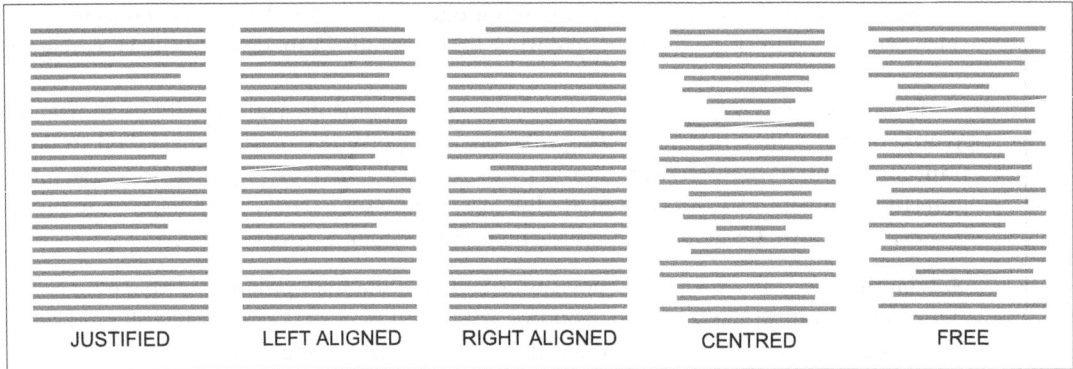

Figure 2.29 Setting formats

short copy, especially where emphasis and variations are needed. Medium weight faces are most legible, so they are in use in almost all publications. Figure 2.30 presents samples of text set in bold and medium-weight font. Selection of the face weight depends greatly on the layout of the visual element. Designers develop a layout by laying a tint (parallel lines or specimen copy block) and then decide which weight or face is the best.

Like light and bold faces, italic (slanted) faces are also used for variations or emphasis. These are normally not used for long copy as they are not quite as easy to read as normal (upright) faces. Italic faces are also available in various weights. While using these faces in a running copy, their style and weight should be harmonized with their counterpart upright faces, else the harmony of the composition will be disturbed, impairing legibility.

Mix type style This style is not used in a typographic design, especially for text matter. Modern typographers call this the rule of typographic harmony. This harmony is achieved by using one family of type throughout a design. Contrast and variations can be obtained by using type from different series of the same family. In extremely unavoidable cases, a slight mixing might be acceptable, but one should be very cautious in mixing different type styles. Mixing different families from the same race (group) may cause confusion, unless they are of a strongly contrasting design.

Reverse type The term 'reverse type' refers to matter set in white (or light) letters against a dark background. This arrangement of type has less legibility, because white letters on a dark background shrink optically. If reverse letters are used in a design,

Black strokes and white space in and around the faces of medium-weight type create a grey mass which is pleasing to the eyes.	**Long copy in bold face is tiring for the eyes. It can, however, be used for short copy when emphasis and variation are needed.**

Figure 2.30 Text set in bold and medium-weight fonts

Figure 2.31 Reverse type against dark and tint backgrounds

they should be slightly bigger in size. As can be seen in Figure 2.31, reverse type on tints or colours is even less legible because of the lack of contrast. A long copy should not be set in reverse or on tint or colour.

Type in colour Type set in colour also appears to sink into the page, losing much legibility. Since contrast and clarity are the main factors of legibility, care should be taken to print the type composition. A long copy should never be set in colour. If colour is used for a heading, subheading, or a blurb, a bigger and bolder type should be chosen. Black type on white reads 40 per cent more rapidly than type reversed out from black and grey. The poorest legibility is seen in the case of matter set in black on red or red on black. The best legibility is seen in matter set in black on white or yellow.

Display faces

When we see the text matter, we see words; when we see the headings, we see letters. Therefore, the type style is the main consideration in selecting display faces. The purpose of a heading is to invite the reader into the design and to tell him/her the message in a very short and subtle form. Here also, the designer's role is as important as the copywriter's.

There is no set type style rule for headings. The harmony rule may not always work as the design may look very passive and monotonous. Lineal and traditional faces are widely accepted heading type styles. A slightly fancy style is not undesirable at appropriate places. Some decorative styles may, however, even sabotage the message. For example, Old English or Script faces set in uppercase are too difficult to read.

Every display word must be thought of as an individual shape in its particular context, as it offers a slightly different problem according to the relationship of the curves and straight lines of which it is composed. One should be sensitive in creating shapes from every word in display by increasing letter spacing or selecting upper and lowercase letters. If matter in all caps is typeset in a spaced out manner, it may appear as if there is too much space between each letter, especially in the case of letters which have wide shoulders (TA). Solid curved lines that come one after another should be spaced out, but two vertical strokes should be set together. When set solid, lowercase faces look more pleasing than the loosely spaced ones. Again, spaced out headlines are not uncommon in special circumstances. Spaced out uppercase letters should be preferred over lowercase faces as two imaginary parallel lines hold the letters together to make the word legible. Long headlines should not be set in uppercase as lowercase letters can be accommodated better than uppercase ones and are hence less likely to be confused.

In display, irregular line length should be chosen over justified formats. The format may be centred, left aligned, right aligned, or free set according to the nature of the job and the designer's task. Centred settings are very formal and go well with formal design and justified body copy. The left aligned style is an all-purpose display setting. It looks less formal and creates contrast even when set in the same family of text copy. Ragged left settings are comparatively dull. They are often used to balance with other elements. Free setting is the most dynamic composition, used mainly in advertising or type format, which serves the purpose of advertising. The heading should be aligned optically, and not be left to the typesetter to be aligned mechanically. The physical appearance of the headline composition is quite often a function of the arrangement of lines and the division of phrases. With a view to accentuating and enhancing the meaning of the composition, words should be grouped logically.

White space around a headline is another creative task. Headlines with wide white space are more legible than those surrounded by other visual elements. Short lines need more white space to read sentences downwards. Comparatively less surrounding space is needed for horizontal lines as the eye moves horizontally. The length of a line should be visually related to the space around it and other elements that may be present in the design.

In display, the space between lines can also be handled freely. Optical spacing is often used for a pleasing composition. The general rule for type is that uppercase faces need more spacing than type set in lowercase faces. Sometimes, to create a compact and more pleasing composition, the designer reduces the line spacing so much that the descender of one line comes within the area of the ascender of the next line. The white spaces between ascenders and descenders are reduced in this way. It should be ensured that line spacing is more than word spacing when uppercase letters are used with other letters.

The weight of display faces is an important factor. The eye moves from dark to light, big to small, and unusual to usual. The reader can be attracted to the headline by using a bigger size type. The size and thickness of type will also depend on the seriousness of the message and the designer's wish or preference. Sharp contrasts result if the typeface is large in size and heavy in weight. It looks less formal and opens up the design. This effect can be avoided by using tint or colour for the oversize head. Otherwise, the heads are likely to overpower the text.

Slanted or vertical displays are unusual. In case they are to be used, the character should be oriented normally. Vertically or horizontally stacked upright letters create an unusual margin that is difficult to read, so, for unusual settings, bold faces are preferred to light ones and upright to rotating at desired angle. The more desirable solution is to rotate the head at 90° and place it on the left margin if it is to be read from the bottom to the top. When it is against the right margin, it can be oriented so that it reads from top to bottom. Headlines in the outline are not uncommon, but less legible in comparison with traditional solid black. Headlines can be made slightly more legible by filling them with tint or colour. It should be ensured that the stroke of the letters have the harmonious dark colour that is being filled. For example, red stroke can be used for orange fill, blue stroke can be used for pink fill.

Tiffani Bold	Caslon Black	ओंकार बोल्ड
Windsor Bold	Cheltenhan	प्रज्ञा बोल्ड
Antique Olive Com	Pump	मित्र बोल्ड
Avant Garde Gothic	News Gothic	योगेश बोल्ड
Cable Heavy	Univers	विजय बोल्ड
Helvetica Medium	Venus Bold	शक्ति लाईट
GillExtraBold	Optima Bold	अर्जुन
Grotesque	Futura Demi	बकुल मिडियम
Futura Black	Folio Bold	चक्र मिडियम
Futura Display	eurostile	चक्र बोल्ड
Broadway	Murray Hill	अरावली
Arnold Bocklin	Palace Script	अक्षरधारा
Manuscript	Brush Script	देवनागरी
DAVIDA	Le Griffe	मनोहर बोल्ड

Figure 2.32 Samples of display faces

Figure 2.32 shows some examples of display faces. Various combinations of mixed faces make the headline interesting and inviting. Modern typesetting equipment and graphics software have opened opportunities for designers to type in various artistic ways. Creating a heading in a spiral form, curve, or in some other form has now become a matter of a few computer commands.

SUMMARY

The history of letterform can be traced back to 5000 years, when the Sumerians, who lived in Iraq, made use of pictographs for written communication. The revolution in writing came about with Gutenberg's invention of standardized movable type. From the rock paintings of primitive man to the computerized writing of modern man, writing has come a long way over the years.

Irrespective of the history of development of type, we use broadly three types of letterforms for communication. These are: (i) signographic, where letters are drawn, painted, and fabricated; (ii) calligraphic, where free hand written letters are used; and (iii) typographic, where mechanical, standardized letterforms are used.

Typographical letterform is designed to get the message across and make reading an enjoyable and involving experience. The use of type requires skill and imagination. In order to understand this graphic component, one should study the physical structure, aesthetics, and function of type.

The physical structure consists of type body, body structure, typeface, and font. Points—units of a special scale known as pica scale—are used to measure type. Typefaces are available in thousands of design variations. Each one has its own style to contribute to the aesthetic aspect of type composition. Since they are so many type faces, all the faces have been divided into four groups to facilitate identification and to use them suitably in design.

The most commonly used group is classical Roman. The face style of this group is thick and thin strokes with serif—a short line attached to the main stroke. Caslon, Palation, and Times Roman are some of the families in this group. The next broad category is the Lineal group. The term 'lineal' is used for this group because of its even body characteristics. Lineal style with uniform serif (short stroke) is called square serif while that without serif is called sans serif type. Families of this group are Serifa, Rockwell (square serif), Helvetia, and Avant Garde (sans serif).

Fancy is the third type group. As the name suggests, the strokes of the letterform are decorated. Some families of this group, such as Eras and Fritz Quadrata, are less decorated and called novelty style. Faces such as Ringlet and Gallia are called decorative. The type style of the handwritten group resembles calligraphy. Common fonts in the handwritten group are Murray Hill, Legend, and Zapf Chancery.

The main function of the type composition is to enhance readability. Faces can be categorized into three types: text matter, display matter, and poster. For text matter, the type size ranges from 5 to 12 point. This constitutes the main typographical composition. Faces for display matter range from 12 point up to 72 point, used mainly for headings and subheadings. Text for posters are designed in type sizes above 72 points. These are designed to attract attention.

Legibility is a factor that affects the readability of the text matter. 'Legibility' refers to clarity of letter characters in a type composition. There are some rules of legibility, which are used in handling type composition. Rules help the designer to choose a type style, its appropriate size, line length, weight, and setting format in such a way that the reader can read the lines, columns, sentences, paragraphs, and pages with ease. There are some rules for display faces as well. As the display faces are meant for attracting attention and to summaries the content, type style and size weight are the main considerations in selecting the display type.

KEY TERMS

Ascenders (see x-height) Letter strokes that extend above the x-height of the letter. The letters, b, d, f, h, k, 1, and t, have ascenders.

Brahmi Script Letterform in geometric shapes belonging to the ancient civilization of India (500–300 BC) and considered the origin of most Indian scripts.

Calligraphy Free hand-drawn letters or the art of beautiful writing.

Classical Roman Type Style with thick and thin letter strokes with short cross lines attached to the main strokes, known as serifs.

Classical Style The style developed from old manuscripts, having thick and thin strokes created with reed pens.

Descenders (see x-height) Letter strokes that drop below the x-height of the letter. The letters, g, j, p, and y have descenders.

Devanagari An alphabetical script of India used for writing some of the Indian languages, including Hindi and Sanskrit. It is also called 'Nagari'. According to Sanskrit literature, 'Nagari' stands for the alphabet of India and 'Deva' stands for God.

Display Faces Type size ranging from 13 to 72 points used mainly for headings and sub-headings.

Fancy Decorative Highly decorated style, not legible in text composition, but creates fancy mood and attracts attention.

Fancy Novelty Slightly decorated faces not having any clear characteristics, may be used for both text and display purposes.

Greek Alphabet The Phoenician alphabet acquired by the Greeks about 1000 BC, to which they added five vowels to make it phonetic.

Handwritten Style Type style that resembles calligraphy, but the letter image is received on paper through impression on the type body.

Hieroglyphics The Egyptian system of picture writing in which pictures were carved on various surfaces.

Hot Metal Type Types that were cast by melting metal, which required heat.

Ideogram Simple drawings that symbolize ideas or concepts rather than concrete objects.

Indus Valley Ideograms The earliest forms of writing in India (2500 BC). The language used for communication has not yet been deciphered.

Justified Format Arrangement of lines of type so that they are aligned on both sides.

Kerning The practice of adjusting space between two adjacent letters so that one part is positioned within the other.

Leading Spacing between lines of type, measured in points.

Legibility Clarity of letter characters in the type composition that helps the movement of the reader's eye on a design.

Lineal Style Letters having uniform strokes.

Movable Type Original method of setting type in which individual letter characters were hand-picked for moving each letter and then arranged in sequence to form words or sentences.

Phoenician Alphabet The Semitic alphabet borrowed and modified by the Phoenicians—a group of business people living along the eastern shore of the Mediterranean—during trade.

Pica Scale A special scale for type measurement which carries the units in points and picas.

Pica The pica is a bigger unit on the type measurement scale. One pica is equal to 12 points.

Pictograph Picture writing used for communication by early man.

Points Units on the type measurement scale. One point is almost an equivalent of one-sixth of an inch.

Poster Type Type size over 72 points, highly visible and eye-catching from a distance, used mainly for posters and big-sized designs.

Reverse Type White or light coloured letters against a dark background.

Roman Alphabet The alphabet that we use today, the Roman alphabet was borrowed from the Greek and refined to meet the communication needs during that time.

Sans Serif Uniform stroke letters without serifs, considered the modern style because of its look that resembles the modern way of writing.

Semitic Alphabet The alphabet developed by Semitic tribes who lived in Iraq about 5000 years ago.

Signography Drawn, painted, manipulated, or fabricated unstandardized letterform.

Square Serif Lineal faces having even strokes with serifs, resembling the Classical Roman style.

Syllabary Symbolic writing system that represented the sound of speech rather than objects or ideas.

Text Faces These faces are small in size, ranging from 5.5 to 12 points, used to develop the main reading text.

Type Body Rectangular shapes of letters with faces that receive the ink and transfer it onto paper.

Typeface Particular style of letters that we read on printed page.

Type Family All the letter characters in a type family are designed in such a way that when they are arranged as a word or sentence, they look so harmonious that we call them a family.

Art and Print Production

Type Font A set of symbols, with well-defined shapes for each symbol, that includes letters of the alphabet in a particular language along with punctuation marks, figures, special characters, etc.
Typography Standardized letterform made from a mould, stencil, or grid.

Width, Weight, and Posture of a Family Relative expansion, thickness, and standing style of letters within a particular family.
X-height The part of lowercase letters excluding ascenders and descenders.

REFERENCES

Clair, Kate and Cynthia Busic-Snyder 2005, *A Typographic Workbook*, Second Edition, John Wiley & Sons, Inc., New Jersey.

Conover, Theodore E. 1990, *Graphic Communication Today*, West Publishing Company, St. Paul.

George, T.J.S. 1989, *Editing — A Handbook for Journalists*, Indian Institute of Mass Communication, New Delhi.

Ghosh, P.K., 'Software Package for Generating Digital Letterform', paper submitted to the Calligraphic Seminar held at Bombay in February 1986.

Industrial Design Centre, IIT 1987, *Indian Symbology*, Proceedings of the Seminar on Indian Symbology Bombay.

Joshi, R.K., 'Calligraphy—The Art of Writing', *CALTIS-84 Souvenir*, Institute of Typographical Research, Pune.

Kane, John 2003, *A Type Primer*, Prentice Hall Inc., New Jersey.

Meggs, Philip 1998, *A History of Graphic Design,* Third Edition, John A. Wiley & Sons, New York.

Michael Adams, J. and Penny Ann Dolin 2002, *Printing Technology* 5E , Delmer Thomson Learning, USA.

Morrison, Sean 1986, A Guide to *Type Design*, Prentice-Hall, New Jersey.

Naik, Baburao S., *Typography of Devanagari*, Directorate of Languages, Govt. of Maharashtra, Bombay.

Swam, Cal 1969, *Typography*, Lund Humphries,London.

Turnbull, Arthur T. and Russell N. Baird 1980, *The Graphics of Communication*, Holt, Rinehart and Winston, USA.

REVIEW QUESTIONS

1. Trace the historical background of the letterform.
2. Discuss the earliest development of the Indian alphabet.
3. What do you understand by 'standardization of the letterform'?
4. Define signographic, calligraphic, and typographic letterform.
5. Explain the physical structure of type.
6. Describe the concepts of font and families in typography.
7. How are types measured? Describe the pica scale.
8. What is the difference between text type, display type, and poster type?
9. How are typefaces identified? Describe the characteristics of different face style groups?
10. What is the basic function of type composition?
11. Compare the concepts of readability and legibility.
12. What are the points to be considered while choosing type style for text and display text composition?
13. What are the legibility rules for text and display type composition?

PROJECTS

1. Collect examples/samples of signographic, calligraphic, and typographic letterforms. Paste them on a sheet of paper and explain why signographic and calligraphic letterforms are considered to be unstandardized letterforms, whereas typographic letterforms, are standardized letterforms.

2. Obtain a photocopy of the pica scale from the page printed on this book, preferably on a transparent sheet. Identify the units of the scale and the specimen capital letters along with their sizes on the scale. Cut and paste a display word has uppercase letters as well as ascenders and descenders of some lowercase letters. Explain the use of the pica scale in measuring this word.
3. Take the front page of a newspaper. Identify the headings used on this page. Write the size in points against each of the headings.
4. Draw a table on an A4 size paper with five columns and five rows, with the headings shown in the table below. Let the first column occupy half the page. Identify words in each face style group and paste them in their respective rows in the table.

Specimen	Size (point)	Width	Weight	Posture
Classical				
Roman				
Lineal				
Fancy				
Handwritten				

Indicate their size, width, weight, and posture in their respective column. Try to obtain specimen words in display type, having one or more letters in uppercase or letters in lowercase with an ascender or descender.
5. Type a paragraph containing about 100 words on your computer screen. Copy and paste the paragraph five times on the same page. Manipulate them as per the following instructions and evaluate the legibility of each composition.
   (a) 12 point × 24 pica justified Times Roman
   (b) 10 point × 30 pica left-aligned Helvetica Bold
   (c) 10/13 point × 14 pica justified Bookman
   (d) 11/13 point × 26 pica right-aligned Arial Narrow
   (e) 9/12 point × 20 pica justified Lucida
   (f) 8/14 point × 18 pica centre-format Commercial Script
6. Select display type faces from the font menu of any draw programme in your computer. Create the mood of the following words by manipulating them.
   (a) Rainy season
   (b) A hundred-year-old university
   (c) Chocolate I love
   (d) Tour and travel operator
   (e) Men's summer shirt
   (f) Health-care centre

CHAPTER

3 Visual Images

Learning Objectives

After reading this chapter, you should be able to
- understand the basic functions of visual images
- identify the broad categories of visual images and their various physical forms
- understand how hand-drawn, painted, photographed, and computer generated visuals are developed
- discuss the various types of visuals on a printed page created by combining and manipulating images
- acquire basic knowledge of the process of editing an illustration

INTRODUCTION

Graphic communication has three components—the written message, visual images, and layout. Visual images are the second component of graphics. Images used for visual communication may be hand-drawn, painted, photographed, or generated digitally on the computer. These images can thus be referred to as sketches, paintings, photographs, or illustrations.

Some forms of visual images have been in use from time immemorial. Pictures have been found on the walls of caves, rocks, and weapons used by early man. They had been in use long before man could read or write. The illustrations used in the early days of printing were mainly wood engravings, which played an important role in the development of mass communication. The intaglio process was the method used for illustration reproduction in printing in the old times. Many illustrations in early publications were produced by sketch artists and engravers. The times have changed drastically since then, and many new devices of communication have now been developed. The developments in photography and the advent of digital information technology have now brought us to the age where we can manipulate any image to the required size or dimensions and create moving images (animation) out of a single image.

Today, we encounter visual images every day on TV and in books, magazines, and newspapers. Posters, billboards, and other displays in striking colours; big-sized pictures; and images in various other physical forms in our environments reflect the importance of visuals in communication in the modern age. Today, visuals are not merely aimed at decorating the communication message. They serve the function of enhancing the communication and creating an impact on the target audience. They perform the important tasks of explaining, instructing, entertaining, and creating the mood for the message.

FUNCTIONS

The primary function of visual communication is to attract attention and to provide additional information that has not been communicated in the text. Today, illustrations do all this and more; they explain, instruct, entertain, and create the mood of the message.

Attract attention Large photographs, unusual or stylized illustrations, and images designed in appropriate colours are always the key sources of attraction in any communication material. Newspapers, which are largely textual, now routinely use blow-ups of natural disasters, terrorist attacks, or developments in society to generate initial interest. Human-interest photographs of winter mornings, flying birds against sunsets, or boats waiting for customers are used in newspapers in a bid to attract the reader. Such images can appeal to our emotions more powerfully than words. Figure 3.1 illustrates one such image. Images are used in advertisements as well. An advertisement would fail to stand out in the competitive environment without a visual—such is the impact created by graphics.

Figure 3.1 Human-interest photograph

Provide information Illustrations take the form of charts when the communicator wants to convey complicated statistics. Not many of us read the long budget speech delivered by the finance minister every year. However, we do take a quick look at the charts provided alongside the reports. Reports about increased income tax rates, election results and party positions in comparison to past performance, and comparative export–import figures can be presented in a visual form as pie charts and trend graphs. Such visual presentations help provide information in such a way that the data can be comprehended at a glance.

Explain and instruct Magazines and newspapers use visuals in the form of information graphics to explain important ideas and events. They often rely on visuals created by illustrators when it is not possible for their reporters to capture important events on camera.

Illustrations are an effective medium for providing usage instructions for consumer products. For example, when we purchase a computer, the manual provided with it illustrates the steps to install the system and load various software with the help of detailed diagrams of the computer and its parts and programs.

Maps are another acceptable tool for visual communication. They guide the reader to a place and help him/her locate places of particular interest on the map of the region, country, or world. Visuals are especially appropriate in a country like ours, where a large section of the population cannot read.

Entertain Visuals such as cartoons are a source of entertainment. Some artists have specialized in this area of visual communication. Comic strips are often children's favourite reading material. Even grown-ups enjoy browsing through them. Cartoons can be effectively used to provide comic relief in long-running texts and to draw the attention of young readers.

Figure 3.2 Op art

Figure 3.3 Pop art

Set the mood of the message Artists specializing in illustrations can develop several styles and moods, depending on the need of the particular project. Folk art, abstract art, realistic art, silhouettes, collages, woodcuts, wash paintings, and pastels are some popular styles. The mood created by an illustration may be delicate, bold, light, or strong.

Indicate the period of the artwork Visuals give us an idea about the period in which they were made. Some visual forms are dominant during specific time periods. Wood-cut illustrations were popular during the nineteenth and twentieth centuries. Near-photograph drawings, which had been quite popular in the 1950s, are now almost out of date. Similarly, optical and popular art, commonly known as op art and pop art, respectively, were the popular visual forms in the 1960s. Figures 3.2 and 3.3 show an op art and a pop art. Computer graphics are the visual forms of this age.

CATEGORIES OF VISUALS

A visual image may be developed with the help of various tools and techniques, in various ways—manually, photographically, digitally, or mechanically. These images may be in either two-dimensional (2D) or three-dimensional (3D) form. As our discussion is limited to the area of print communication, we shall discuss only 2D image in this chapter. These days, various types of images can be created and manipulated through computer applications, so more and more images will be created entirely digitally. Many illustrators, however, still prefer drawing their sketches on paper and using a scanner to convert these into digital files. Colour and finish is then applied digitally. Unique visuals can be created through a manual and digital combination of images according to the function that these visuals need to perform. The designer's imagination and skill in handling the tools are important factors determining the physical form of the visual. Since there is no limit to imagination, the physical form of a visual is unlimited. In this section, we shall discuss some commonly used visual forms, which are the bases on which innumerable forms can be created. The physical forms of visual images can be categorized in many different ways. For our purposes, we shall discuss physical form under two groups—originals and visuals on a printed page.

Originals

An original image is required for creating a design before it goes for printing. The original can be in the physical form of a drawing, painting, photograph, or digitized image. One can draw or paint an illustration with a pencil, paint and brush, or in ink. We may call these *hand-drawn* illustrations. Originals may also be obtained in the form of photographic images, instant images, or computer-generated ones. *Photographs* may be taken through a photography camera and further developed by using various chemicals and tools used in altering the physical form of pictures. *Instant images* are readymade copyright-free illustrations available in books, catalogues, or on the website. *Computer-generated* illustrations are drawn and painted using computer tools. Illustrations that are drawn and painted conventionally or photographed and then enhanced digitally are also called computer-generated illustrations.

Hand-drawn images

Illustrations created with the help of traditional media such as pencil, pen, watercolour, etc. are called hand-drawn illustrations. These can be split into two major groups—line and continuous tone images. Line images are formed by solid colours or without gradation of tones whereas continuous tone images are formed by blending one colour into others, as in pencil sketches and watercolour paintings.

Line images The most common line images are pen and ink or brush and ink drawings on a white background. The images are drawn in black ink, creating the maximum contrast against white paper. Pen strokes can be used to create images of different shapes, thickness, position, style, and texture while brush strokes can create images in thick and thin free style, non-uniform texture. These are also called *line illustrations* because they do not have any colour gradation.

Each variation in the line stroke contributes to the mood of the visual communication. Horizontal straight lines give a feeling of calmness and speed—the calm of the sea, the speed of the arrow. Vertical bold lines suggest strength—the strength of a pillar or that of the stem of a tree. Curved lines suggest the beauty of a flower and the grace of a creeper. Wavy lines create the rhythm of dance and movement of water. A thin line creates a delicate soft effect; a bold line creates a strong, confident, and controlled effect. A free hand-drawn line looks casual and informal; a scaled line looks mechanical and rigid. Lines can add texture to an illustration and lend visual interest to it. The texture created depends on the type of line chosen—rough or smooth, curving or jagged. These choices help to convey the artist's message to the audience.

Images drawn in white paint or light colour on a dark background are called *reverse images*. When the image is identified by outlines without details of its content, the style is known as a *silhouette*. Woodcut style is the old technique of making illustrations, and hence an old style. Many interesting forms such as *scratching* and *dry-brushing* can be created with a wide variety of tools.

Continuous tone images Drawings that are made on a medium in which the value of the pigment is diluted by adding water or white or light pigment are known as continuous tone drawings. Artists specializing in illustrations can create several styles and

Figure 3.4 Folk style painting

moods with their brush and watercolour, depending on the need of the particular assignment. A painting with transparent watercolour, in which values of colours are diluted by adding water, is called *wash painting*. *Pencil sketches* are also continuous tone images. As pencils cannot create the effect produced by colour on paper, continuous tone images are produced by shading the drawn picture. Images created with crayons are called *pastel texture* style. Although this style also has a contrast effect similar to line drawings in pencil, it is a continuous tone image because the colours used are smudged, thus line reproduction is not possible. Most of the *folk style* paintings are also continuous tone images despite the fact that these are drawn in sharp lines. A look at the sample of folk painting presented in Figure 3.4 shows that, at many places, the lines are blurred, especially where colour wash is rendered. Some other continuous tone image styles are modern, such as contemporary paintings made in oil or acrylic media; traditional, such as flat tempera paintings in Indian style; and paintings with flowery and ornamental motifs or graphic shapes.

Continuous tone images can also be created without conventional tools such as brush and paint. For example, *collages* are continuous tone pictures or designs created by gluing various flat elements cut or torn irregularly from printed pages or other flat objects such as cloth and photographs to a flat surface that forms a composite picture. The word 'collage' is derived from the French word 'collar', meaning 'to paste'.

Photographic images

An original photograph is also a continuous tone image. We get an image of a three-dimensional object on a two-dimensional surface by means of photographic tones. Tones of different levels blend with each other or continue, thus forming an illusion of three dimension.

For the purpose of illustrating a message, photograph is the primary choice of a designer. Photographs represent real life. People tend to believe photographs more than any other form of illustration. The popular sayings 'seeing is believing' and 'the camera never lies' reinforce these beliefs. A photograph of an event or happening is much more effective than hand-drawn images. News editors choose photographs of some aspects of an event, excluding others, to put across their point of view.

Advertisers create completely imaginary situations with the help of photographic images to fabricate a dream for which they would like us to aspire. Corporate houses select only certain photographs for display in their house journals, visitor's rooms, and other common areas so that the company is perceived as a happy and united one.

Photographs perform different functions in a design. Some are used for precise information, some for mood and meaning, and some others may be used simply for achieving the desired look. Cut-out images are used when we wish to select only the required content. Text copy or other visual elements can be accommodated very close to the cut-out picture. These effects are very popular in advertising design. Photographs in a brownish tinge create a mood of the past, bluish and reddish duotones lend coolness and warmth, respectively, while the vignette effect creates the effect of blending with others and distortion for humour.

Photographs used as illustrations and intended for reproduction should be sharply focused and well lighted. Although it is believed that the quality of photo-tone can be improved through computer manipulations, it is seen that most photographs printed by halftone process retain their shortcomings. In fact, the image quality is further reduced during the printing process. Halftone dots compress the value range of the original. Thus, some amount of details is lost. Photographic originals have two broad physical forms—(i) black and white and (ii) colour.

Colour Photographs that have sufficient details should be chosen for printing. Normally, details of the contents are seen in the mid-tone value areas of a photograph. A good photograph, however, contains details of objects in the highlighted and shadow areas as well. Here, lighting plays an important role in bringing out the details of an object.

Three types of lighting are used in photography—flat, side, and balance. *Flat lighting*, where light is flashed from the front side, creates large tonal masses that are too dark or too light, resulting in the loss of details. *Side lighting*, where light is flashed on the object from one side, makes the photograph lose details of objects in the lighter area. Both flat light and side light create contrasting colours. The best result is obtained by *balanced lighting*, where indirect light falls on the object, reflecting light from all sides, as in a natural environment. Balanced lighting produces photographs containing full tonal value. In other words, light and dark areas are properly blended by middle value with sufficient details of the content. The terms 'value' here refers to the lightness and darkness of colour. Middle value is about 50 per cent of colour value or tone.

Most types of colour prints tend to lose some of the colour quality and fidelity of the original. Thus, reproduction films for process printing are preferably made directly from the original transparency or digital photograph. Digital photo processing requires less processing time. Resolution is the main criteria for choosing original digital photographs. This concept has been discussed in detail in Chapter 9. Digital photographs can be modified on the computer and directly outputted either on film for offset printing or on special photosensitive paper (not bromide). The digital photo process provides good quality colour prints with vivid colours.

Black and white Photographs in black and white have almost become a thing of the past. Most commercial photo labs do not provide this service these days. Developing black and white photographs is costlier than developing colour ones, if at all this facility is available. Since black and white images are unique for some communication messages, its use has not been eliminated altogether.

Like colour photographs, balanced lighting yields the best results in black and white photographs.

Flat and side lighted photographs are also useful for reproduction where these are used to develop various forms by photo alteration techniques such as duotone, quartertone, posterization, etc., which are now carried out through computer manipulation.

Sometimes, when a design requires a black and white image but a negative film is not available, black and white prints are made from colour bromide or transparencies. This does not yield as good a photograph as an original. It will be too dark or too light and the contents may lose the details. Such losses are known as *generation* loss.

Black and white photographs can be developed on a digital camera and scanner through the grayscale command option. The quality requirement can be met by selecting the right resolution.

Photographs—black and white as well as coloured ones—are easily available online and in CDs. Such photographs, which can be used for specific purposes on payment and with permission, are referred to as stock photographs. Exhibit 3.1 provides a list of sources of stock photographs. The prices of stock photographs may range from nominal

---

Exhibit 3.1 Some sources of stock photos

Getty Images is a stock photo agency, based in Seattle, Washington, with distribution offices in various parts of the world, including India. It is the leading supplier of stock images for businesses and individuals. It has an archive of 70 million still images and illustrations and more than 30,000 hours of stock film footage. It targets three markets—creative professionals (advertising and graphic design), the media (print and online publishing), and corporate communication departments for other businesses. Getty images continues to capitalize on the Internet and CD-ROM collections for distribution. The company has also begun offering custom photo services for corporate clients.

India Picture presents a diaspora of photographic images to be used by professionals worldwide. Their user-friendly site provides much needed aid to people as diverse as advertising professionals and the home users wanting a photo bank to prepare a project. Among the vast range of images, they endeavour to cover a plethora of sections ranging from abstract concepts to human emotions.

Photo Division is the biggest production unit of its kind in the field of photography in India. The Division provides photographs to the media units of the Ministry of Information and Broadcasting and other central and state government bodies. It also supplies on-payment photographs and transparencies to the general public. The Division has its headquarters in New Delhi, with well-equipped laboratories and equipment for handling different kinds of photographs stored in the photo library for easy retrieval of data. Photo Division has now switched over to digital mode of photo transmission. It has well-equipped laboratories and equipment for handling different kinds of jobs and assignments in black-and-white and in colour at its headquarters in Delhi. News Photo Network has also been installed at its Head Office. The network for linking with all regional offices is in progress. The process of digitally storing photographs on current events in the News Photo Network is currently on. It also feeds photographs to the Press Information Bureau, which makes available these photographs in their home page on the Internet. The Division has four regional offices at Mumbai, Chennai, Calcutta, and Guwahati.

India Image Library is a gallery of colour transparencies and black and white photographs shot by Australian photographer Robert Watson on several trips to India. This site exhibits a sample range of some of the thousands of images in the India Image Library, many from specific regions of India and other more general images of people and situations that are really the essence of a fascinating country.

PhotoIndia.com has the expertise and experience to undertake large-scale turnkey projects, assignments, research and editing, archival and scanning, and digital asset management for companies. It has recently launched its Collector Print Series, which exemplifies the best in photographic craftsmanship and aesthetics from India's leading photographers. PhotoIndia.com is specialized in creating unique, affordable, distinct, and remarkable photo intensive solutions that are both focused and compelling at the same time. Whether the client's first priority

Contd

Exhibit 3.1 *Contd*

is affordability, high-end state of the art media, or cost-effective technology, they have the ability, flexibility, and diversity to fulfil their requirements.

They also help in enhancing the client's corporate image and promote their products and services.

---

to exorbitant, depending on the purpose of use and source. For example, the cost of procuring a photo from Photo Division for public service publication by a government organization is very nominal. However, for obtaining a photograph for commercial use from the same source, one has to pass through several formalities and pay a higher price.

Where to obtain photographs It is often difficult for the designer to find the right photograph. The designer can take the photograph or commission a professional photographer who can meet his/her requirements. Lack of professional skill and time required for the first option are often a setback to one's work. The effort required to find a professional photographer and the costs involved in paying for his/her services may also force the designer to look for an alternative. Despite the fact that a large number of copyright-free photographs are available on the Internet and in CDs, many graphic designers are still largely dependent on various other sources. Stock photographs may be the right source of material for communication purposes. Together with the images generated by the designer, they can be a good source of images required for the design.

Stock photos consist of existing photographs that can be licensed for specific uses. Book publishers, speciality publishers, magazines, advertising agencies, filmmakers, web designers, graphic artists, interior decor firms, corporate creative groups, and other entities utilize stock photography to fulfil the needs of their creative assignments. By using stock photography instead of hiring a photographer to shoot pictures on location, customers can save valuable time and stay within the budget. With a wealth of images, stock photography databases that may be browsed online save photo researchers valuable time. With today's digital delivery methods, images may be purchased online and delivered via e-mail or downloaded right away.

Stock photos are sometimes called photo archives. The term photo archive often refers to the website or physical location where the photographs are stored. Photo archives are also referred to as image banks. As modern stock photography distributors often carry stills, videos, and illustrations, none of the existing terminology provides a perfect match for the state of the industry.

Instant images

Instant images are copyright-free visual images available in books, CDs, and on the Internet. Artists and communicators use instant images for projects with tight schedules. These images are also helpful for people who lack the skill to draw and paint.

Visual symbols Instructional graphics, presentation graphics, charts, and logos of brands are some common images that are used in our communication material. Their physical appearance has some obvious reference to some activity or thought. Their use has become so common that they are termed as 'symbols'. For example, the image of a pigeon with an olive branch symbolizes peace; an anchor symbolizes stability, security, and hope; a rose stands for beauty and romance; glass symbolizes something that is fragile, breakable, or transparent; and the image of an umbrella symbolizes shelter and protection. While using such images, one should be sure of their visual impact.

A large number of books and catalogues with instant images are available. Birds, animals, human faces, day-to-day use materials, borders, motifs, etc. are easily available in different styles and shapes. Figure 3.5 shows a motif. Instant images can be used in logo or brand name designs, pictorial charts, or for illustrating various communication materials. Usually, copyright permission is not required for the use of such images. There are literally thousands of such images and motifs that can effectively used for illustrations and designing. Such images may be drawn by hand, traced, photocopied, or scanned from the original.

Clip art It is a term used for non-photographic graphic images that can be cut-out from a book, CD, or the Web. Today, many computer software programs come with also have some copyright-free visual images known as *clip art*. Figure 3.6 illustrates some clip art images. Such images can be easily downloaded and manipulated as per the designer's requirement. However, if the images are not used creatively, the design will be deficient in quality and originality.

Digital images

Today, computers have made a lot of facilities available to illustrators. A person who has ideas for a design can create an effective illustration even if he/she does not possess the skill to draw and is not fully trained in the use of computers. Graphic software with myriad tools of drawing and painting are available today. These tools are displayed on the computer screen in the form of minute icons. They work in the same manner as conventional tools such as pens, brushes, and colour palettes needed in developing an illustra-

Figure 3.5   Motif   **Figure 3.6**   Clip art

tion. One can easily generate the illustration with free-hand tools or create innumerable shape patterns with shape tools. It is also possible to scan photographs and hand-drawn illustrations to generate a digital image, since the computer understands only digital language.

Scanned images are very flexible and can be easily manipulated. They can be inverted to obtain negatives, flipped to form a mirror image, and copied or cropped to focus attention on a particular detail. They can also be distorted to produce a humorous effect. A poorly printed photograph can be improved by contrasting its content or by restoring its lost edges. The same picture can instantly be tried in different sizes and styles and be moved to a new layout. The most exciting aspect of a scanned image is experimenting with several possibilities, which would have taken several hours to accomplish by traditional methods. Computer-generated illustrations are handled in two ways—vector and raster.

Vector images The mathematically defined curves and lines segments of computer images are called vectors. Since vector images create objects such as rectangles and circles, they are also called object-oriented graphics. An illustration drawn in a vector program occupies a fraction of space in the computer memory and can be scaled to virtually any size without any loss of details. Thus, a particular thickness of line created on a screen can be reproduced accurately on a high-resolution laser printer. Some of the programs that create vector images are Illustrator, FreeHand, MacDRAW, and CorelDRAW. Figure 3.7 shows a vector image, where the image is sharp.

Raster images Also known as bitmap images, these images are made up of several tiny dots known as pixels. Here, a painting-like illusion of continuous tone is created by pixels. These images are thus called paint-oriented graphics. As in the case of halftone images, the more the number of pixels, the sharper is the image on the computer screen. To understand this concept, we can think of a sheet of graph paper. Each square in a graph paper represents one pixel. If we take two graph papers—one made up of small squares and another made up of bigger squares—and make a circle on each paper by filling the squares on the edges of the circle in black, the image created on the graph paper with the smaller squares will be sharper.

In a computer, raster images are stored by recording the exact placement and colour of each pixel. The computer identifies the image in terms of a collection of little squares. The drawback of raster images is that, when we try to enlarge a raster image, the resultant image is jagged or pixellated. This is because, when we scale the image, in reality, we are just enlarging the pixels, which results in a jagged image. Figure 3.8 shows a bitmap image, where the edges of the image are jagged as the pixels are visible.

One can create one's own illustration in raster image with programmes such as Photoshop, Corel Paint, Pixel-Paint, Photo-Suit, etc.

In general, working with vector graphics requires less artistic skill than working with bitmapped graphics. One can not create realistic pictures such as human faces or landscapes on vector graphics. To use a bitmapped graphics application, one needs to use the mouse and other pointing devices just as an artist uses a pencil, pen, or brush. Difficulties may be faced in combining a hand-drawn scanned image with a bitmapped one.

Figure 3.7 Vector image

Figure 3.8 Bitmap image

Visuals on Printed Page

A second way to categorize visuals is to classify them on the basis of how they appear on a printed page. For the purpose of mechanical reproduction, there are two basic types of visuals—line images and halftones—but in combination and manipulation, a number of physical forms can be obtained on a printed page.

Line image

An original line image when reproduced remains a line image. A look at Figure 3.9 shows hardly any dots in the illustration. This illustration has been printed without any gradation.

Line illustrations with flat tones of a single colour or combined colours are called *line and tone images*. Figure 3.10 shows a line and tone image. If such an image is combined with a continuous tone image such as a photograph or painting, it will take the form of a *line and halftone* on a printed page because, during reproduction, line will remain line whereas continuous tone will be converted into halftone.

Figure 3.9 Line image

Figure 3.10 Line and tone image

Figure 3.11 Line and halftone image

Figure 3.11 illustrates a line and halftone image. If the combined images are created on a computer, the line portion will retain its sharpness when printed. If, however, the line image is scanned, it will produce a jagged image.

Many physical forms of line images can be obtained by changing the photographic tone. The *solarization* effect in a photograph is achieved by eliminating the middle and light tones, which will look white and the rest of the area will be dense black, thus forming a line image. Figure 3.12 shows a photograph created through solarization.

Colour or monochrome continuous tone originals can be given a false rendition, which can be either subtle or graphically striking. Single or multiple bandwidths of colour and tone can be selected on the original and changed in tone to any chosen colour. The absence of gradation produces a poster-like effect created by separating the continuous tone to sharply defined areas of white, black, and grey or other flat tones of colours. This effect is called *posterization*, which simulates line and tint image. Figure 3.13 (*see also Colour Plate 1*) shows a line and tint image created through posterization.

Quartertone is another form of line image, created by converting continuous tones of a photograph into precise dots or lines. It is conventionally done by blowing up a halftone negative. Figure 3.14 shows a conventional quartertone image. Traditionally, quartertones were produced mechanically. Figure 3.15 shows the effect created in mechanical quartertones. Now, with the advent of sophisticated Dainippon scanners, there has been tremendous improvement in this technique. Advertising designers use the quartertone effect not only for its look but also for its good printed results. Images developed in quartertone may also be used to print a continuous one image by silk-screen process.

Figure 3.12 Line drawing by solarization effect

Figure 3.13 Posterization by flat tones (see also Colour Plate 1)

Figure 3.14 Conventional quartertone

In *reverse line illustrations*, the physical form of the image is changed mechanically, that is, the image area is taken in white and the background in dark, as shown in Figure 3.16. This effect can be obtained on the computer or by instructing the processor to print the illustration in reverse.

A *silhouette image* is identified by its outline, without details of the content, as shown in Figure 3.17. It can be of solid colour or reverse.

Instant art images that have been copied from a book, scanned from an original drawing, or downloaded from clip arts on the computer are meant for the printed page. They may be simple line images or images in different combinations.

Most charts and graphs on printed pages are either line images or line and tint images. If a chart or graph is combined with a picture, it is called a *pictograph*. A chart is a tool used to represent a table containing numerical data visually. Data displayed in a well-conceived chart can make it more understandable, and often helps the instructor to present his/her point more quickly. Charts are particularly useful for presenting a lengthy series of numbers and their relationships in a visual form.

Figure 3.15 Mechanical quartertone

Until recently, charts and graphs were mostly made by hand, using drawing tools such as set square, 'D' scale, etc. on graph sheets. Understanding of statistical information was necessary to develop a chart by hand. Today, most charts are generated on the computer. The software used for this purpose is Microsoft Excel. This

Figure 3.16 Reverse line illustration

Figure 3.17 Silhouette image

software provides various options for converting statistical data into charts with the help of the ChartWizard or sample chart. Computer charts are based on numbers that appear in a worksheet, as shown in Figure 3.18. Converting a range of numbers into a chart is quite easy, and many people find this aspect of Excel rather fun. One can experiment with different chart types to choose one that suits his/her purpose. Regardless of which chart-type option is chosen, one has complete control over the chart's appearance. Depending on his/her requirements, one can change the colour, move the legend, format the numbers on the scales, add gridlines, and so on.

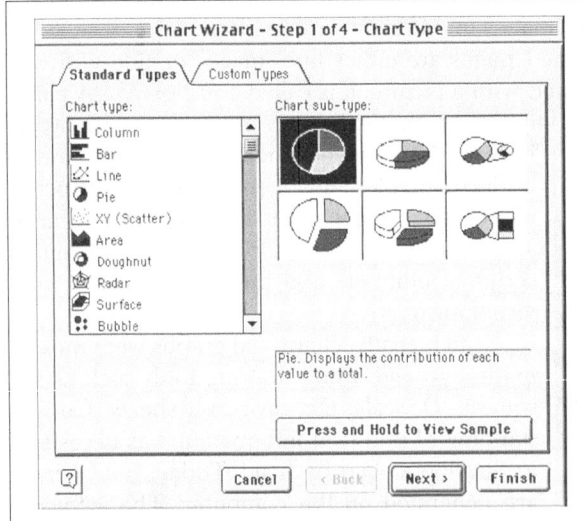

Figure 3.18 Chart wizard

There are many chart types, the most common ones being column, bar, line, and pie charts. There are several subtypes associated with each. Column or bar charts are useful for displaying discrete data. They can represent any number of data series and the columns can be stacked on top of each other. The advantage in using a bar chart is that the category labels may be easier to read. Bar charts can consist of any number of data series. In addition, the bars can be stacked from left to right, as shown in Figure 3.19 (a). Line charts are frequently used to plot data that is continuous rather than discrete. For example, plotting daily sales as a line chart may enable us to spot

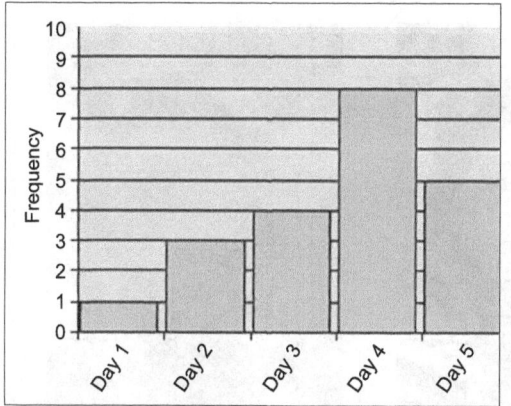

Figure 3.19 (a) Bar chart

Figure 3.19 (b) Line chart

Figure 3.19 (c) Pie chart

trends over time. Figure 3.19 (b) shows a sample line chart. Pie charts are useful when we want to show relative proportions or contributions to a whole, as shown in Figure 3.19 (c).

The placement of a chart or graph in a page is as important as making the chart. The chart must relate to the other material but not overpower it. Charts and graphs are usually more readable when separated from surrounding text.

Normally, all the charts and graphs should carry a heading or caption that summarizes the whole content. Labeling, which represents the information within, is another important consideration. It helps the reader find the less obvious information with ease. Some charts and graphs need a grid in the background. This element often enhances the communication power of charts and graphs and helps the readers relate the visuals to the number involved. There is no fixed rule for determining the most appropriate chart type for a set of data. The rule of thumb is to use the chart type that gets the message across in the simplest way.

Halftones

Continuous tone illustrations such as photographs, wash paintings, and pencil drawings should be reproduced by breaking them into dots. The original is called a continuous tone, because the image is formed by various tones that blend with each other. Such illustrations cannot really be transferred to another surface from a printing plate, unless they are separated as image and non-image surfaces.

Each of the tiny dots of the image surface will carry ink, which creates an impression on paper. As an optical illusion, small and widely spaced dots will appear light whereas big and closely spaced dots will appear dark.

66 *Art and Print Production*

Figure 3.20 Special effects—half-line, circle, and mezzotint

Traditionally, images were photographed through a screen (glass or film) to obtain a half-tone. These days, most of the halftones are created digitally. If the image is printed by simple dots, we may identify it as a *halftone*. When the dots of the halftone are very small, we may feel that we are seeing continuous tones from a certain viewing distance. Dots are clearly visible when we observe the image very closely or through magnifying glass. We shall learn more about halftones in Chapter 7.

Figure 3.21 Pixelization and crystallization

Screened images are termed according to their physical alteration. The image is called a *half-line* when the original tone is a broken line. One can obtain several special effects such as *circle, steel etch, wavy screening,* and *mezzotint* by using the special screen of the printer or from the computer filter menu. *Mezzotint* is a form of visual which is created using irregular dots. Figure 3.20 shows some of these effects, namely, half-line, circle, and mezzotint.

A continuous tone image in a computer is formed by pixels which are normally too small to be visible to the naked eye. Sometimes, pixels are deliberately created in an effect called *pixelization*. On a printed page, each pixel is formed by a number of halftone dots. Pixels are rectangular in shape. A picture can be modified by making the pixels *crystallized*. Figure 3.21 shows the modification of images by *pixelization* and *crystallization*.

Figure 3.22 Embossing effect

Physically changing a continuous tone image with a photo editing application can be an interesting process. It can be used to turn a photograph into an imitation of a painting utilizing mixed media and also by stylizing the image through filters such as *texturizing, pointilizing,* and *embossing*. Figure 3.22 shows the embossing effect.

The *duotone effect* is obtained by printing a black and white photograph in two colours, normally one in black and other in colour. Duotone can be achieved in two ways—by printing both the colours in halftone, as shown in Figure 3.23, or by printing a halftone in black on a light solid colour, termed as a *fake duotone*. Readers can refer to Colour Plate 1 to see the duotone effect and the fake duotone effect. Duotones can lend a unique effect of warmth to a design and create an artistic look that is different from either a black and white or a four colour reproduced image. Moreover, they can be reproduced at a much lower cost as compared to full colour images. A duotone print can lend depth to a black and white photo, besides adding colour to it. A black and white photo may also be printed in single colour or in three colours. Accordingly, it can be termed as a monochrome or a triotone, respectively. These effects are usually not used on a printed page. Triotone images do not look very different from duotone images, and they usually cost more than duotones. Monochrome images are dull and fail to standout because of a lack of contrast.

Figure 3.23 Duotone (*see also Colour Plate 1*)

Cut-out halftones can be obtained on a printed page in several ways—by eliminating all the dots in the background, by converting the shape of the image into a non-rectangular one, and by placing the cut-out content on a tint background or another halftone image.

68 *Art and Print Production*

Figure 3.24 Vignette, feathering, and cut-out effects

Vignette effect created on a printed page is also in halftone, but creates an illusory effect of the original continuous tone image. Here, a bleeding effect is created with the help of gradually receding dot sizes.

Feathering is another blending effect, but its physical form is slightly different from a vignette. Here, blending in colour is at the back of the content whereas, in vignette, the content blends with the background. The feathering effect gives lift to the content. Figure 3.24 shows the cut-out, vignette, and feathering effects.

A *collage* is a style of pictorial composition in which several distinct pictures are cut or torn and combined into a composite one. It is an image in continuous tone. A collage on a printed page is known by the same term. Figure 3.25 shows a collage on a printed page. A collage created on the computer or by manipulating photo negatives, however, is known as a *montage*. Sometimes, the term *collage* is confused with the term *montage* because both visual styles use several sources to create a single image. In a collage, all the materials used are hard, inflexible, and can be touched and handled by hand whereas, in a montage, the materials used are soft and flexible and need to be manipulated photographically, through computer commands, or by combining separate bits of film in motion pictures.

EDITING OF ILLUSTRATIONS

Like a verbal copy, an illustrated copy also needs to be edited. This is because pictures rarely come to the designer in the required size, content, and quality needed to illustrate a message. Visual editing refers to the process of deciding on the required content, eliminating the unwanted elements, compensating for technical defects, and scaling and cropping to fit the pictures in a design. It is necessary for all line and continuous tone illustrations.

Figure 3.25 Collage

Large pictures are better than small ones for the purpose of reproduction. When a small picture is enlarged to cover a big area, it looks crude and many of its shortcomings are amplified. On the other hand, when a big picture is reduced, the opposite happens. In other words, there is a definite improvement in quality. Scanned coloured transparency images and digital photographs should be edited on the computer screen. The resolution of the image should be considered in relation to the percentage of enlargement.

In the case of hard copy illustrations, the best way is to select the content by two 1½″ wide L-shaped scales (Ls) cuts of paperboard. These two Ls can be placed on the illustration opposite to each other and moved around. As shown in Figure 3.26, they serve as a frame and one can see the centre of interest in the picture separated from other elements. The 'L' scale also helps the editor to select the content horizontally or vertically, as per the demand of the layout. These scales can be used to edit different mug shots (pictures of head and shoulder of a person) which are to be used in a single layout. This is particularly necessary when we receive photographs with the head of each person in different sizes. The contents of non-rectangular shapes may also be decided first within the rectangle using 'L' scale.

Figure 3.26 Content selection with 'L' shaped scales

The layout of an image may sometimes demand a change in the direction or motion of the photo content. Instructions to the printer for the same can be given by marking 'flip' beside the image that needs to be reversed. The photo editor should exercise caution while carrying out such instructions because, if the photograph content shows letters or someone dressed in a sari, for instance, the reversed image will be flawed.

For eliminating unwanted elements from a photograph, the physical form of the photograph may be altered. Editing is not complete unless an illustration is in correct proportion to the size in which it has to be reproduced. In most cases, especially rectangular continuous tone illustrations, to make the size of the image proportionate, trimming some part of the illustration is absolutely necessary. This is called *cropping*. While cropping, we need to be careful about the content. For example, to convert a picture of several people into a picture showing only their faces, we may often cut some person's body, head, or hand in the image. This makes the resultant image look imbalanced and may annoy the person whose picture is being used. Precise artistic judgement needs to be exercised in this operation.

If a cut-out or a vignette has no frame, it can be enlarged or reduced at will to fit within the desired area. A rectangular photo that has definite edges is often aligned with other elements of the layout. If the proportions of the original are not conducive to such alignment, they must be altered. The determination of the proportion that will result from a predetermined enlargement or reduction is known as *scaling*.

Since proportional alteration is dictated by the nature of the illustration, understanding the visual scaling and cropping methods is desirable. Some of these techniques have been discussed in Chapter 7. These techniques not only help us to enhance the visual content but also enable us to reduce the processing problem of the printer.

The following are some essential guidelines about editing pictures:
- A human face should not be surrounded by too much blank space. Otherwise, the face will sink into the background.
- In case two or more faces are appearing side by side on the same page, they should appear to be similar in order to maintain visual harmony.
- Cutting of pictures should be avoided so that they can be reused with different croppings.
- The cropped area and scaling should be marked with a pencil or a soft-point pen on the backside of the picture or on the overlay placed on the picture.
- Ballpoint pen should be avoided for marking or writing captions on the backside of a photograph, as it may spoil the image side of the picture with embossed marks.
- In the case of bleed photographs (content running to the edges of a page), an extra allowance should be made at the time of scaling. It should be ensured that no important content falls within or near the bleed area.
- Photographs that are well composed or surrounded by a border/frame should not be cropped. An alternative layout should be considered in such cases.
- The use of photographs which have been printed or downloaded from a website should be avoided. During reproduction, the screen of the printed photo will be further broken, and a low-resolution website photo will reduce the quality on the printed page.
- Illustrations in unusual shapes should be avoided unless it is a strong demand of the design. It will occupy some unnecessary white space in the design.
- Outlines should be used around the photograph when the background of the photo is very light. Otherwise, the lighter area of the photo may merge into the page it is printed on.
- Only those photographs which have enough details and clearly visible content in both highlight and shadow areas should be selected for printing.
- Colour transparencies and digital photographs are good for reproduction. Their quality and resolution should be ascertained on the basis of their expected enlargement.
- In case the size of the content of a visual is to be understood in a layout, a familiar living object—preferably a human figure—should be placed near the content for comparison.
- A happy mood visual should never be placed in a layout with a story of disaster or death, just as a sad visual should not be placed next to a story of happiness and joy.

SUMMARY

Visual images are a component of graphics. Images may also be referred to as pictures, illustrations, or photographs. Visual images have been in use for ages. However, their physical forms and characteristics keep changing with developments in tools and techniques.

The primary function of visuals is to attract attention and to provide additional information which has not been communicated in the text. Today, visuals are also used to explain, instruct, entertain, and to create the mood of the message.

An illustration or visual is developed in various ways—manually, photographically, digitally, and mechanically, in either moving or static form. Print media visual is of a two-dimensional, static form. They can be categorized into—(i) originals and (ii) visuals on a printed page.

An original picture can be a drawing, painting, or digitized image. Hand-drawn images may be continuous tone images such as paintings and pencil sketches, or line drawings with its full value of colour. An original photograph is also a continuous tone image—it may be in colour or in black and white. The quality of a photograph is judged from the details of content in both light and shadow areas. Copyright-free instant images are also used as originals. Plenty of them are available in books and catalogues or in compute software as clip art. Original images may also be created on the computer screen or obtained by scanning a visual that has been drawn or photographed. Computer generated visuals are of two types—vector or object-oriented images and raster or paint-oriented images. Raster images are also known as bitmap images.

Visuals on printed page are of two basic types—line images and halftones. In combination and manipulation, however, a number of physical forms can be obtained. Some of the visual forms of line and line image combinations are line and tone, line and halftone, solarization, posterization, reverse line, silhouette, etc. The illusion of continuous tone on a printed page is formed by a number of tiny dots and is called halftone. The various physical forms of halftone images are cutouts, vignettes, feathering, collage, etc.

Most illustrations received for design and printing are not properly organized. They need editing to fit into a good layout and design. Here, editing refers to the process of deciding on the right content, elimination of unwanted elements, compensation of technical defects, and scaling and cropping. Software such as Photoshop are available for the purpose of visual editing. Some manual methods, such as the 'L' scale, are also used for deciding on the visual content.

KEY TERMS

Bitmap Images These images are formed by rectangular grids of small squares known as pixels. Each pixel contains data that describes whether it is black, white, or a level of colour.

Bleed Picture The practice of running an art to the edge of a page. The effect is produced by printing the image beyond the desired dimension and then trimming the sheet to obtain the bleed.

Bromide Photography papers that are coated with a light sensitive emulsion of silver bromide in gelatin.

Clip Art Graphics, photographs, and sometimes other media (sound and video) clips published in collections for convenient use in creating webpages and other publications.

Collage A style of pictorial composition in which several distinct pictures are cut or torn and combined into a composite one.

Comic Strip A short strip or sequence of drawings that tells a story, usually drawn by a cartoonist or an artist.

Continuous Tone Image An illustration or photograph—whether black and white or colour—that consists of many shades between the lightest and the darkest tones, and is not broken up into dots.

Cut-out Image The process of obtaining a non-rectangular image by cutting out the unwanted content or background that highlights the image.

Duotone A technique of two-colour halftone printing made from two identical plates of a single-colour photograph.

Folk Art A wide range of objects that reflect the craft traditions and social values of various social groups. Folk art is generally produced by people who have little or no academic artistic training and use established techniques and styles of a particular region or culture.

Halftone Image A continuous tone image such as a photograph, broken up into a pattern of dots of varying sizes, from which a printing plate is made. When printed, the dots create varying greys to give an illusion of continuous tone.

Instant Images Copyright-free visuals available in books, catalogues, and CD-ROMs that can be used instantly in design.

Intaglio Process A printing process that uses an etched or engraved plate which is smeared with ink and wiped clean. Then, the ink left in the recesses forms the print.

Information Graphics Also known as info graphics, information graphics are visual representations of information in the form of signs, maps, graphs, charts, etc. These are used when information needs to be explained quickly or simply.

Montage A composite photograph made by exposing and manipulating two or more photonegatives.

A computer image created by manipulating several digitized pictures or a motion picture created by combining separate bits of film to portray a single event through multiple views is also known as a montage.

Mug Shot A photographic portrait with shoulders. The term derives from the term *mug*, an English slang term for *face*. Originally, mug shots were used to keep a photographic record of all arrested individuals.

Op Art A form of abstract art characterized by the use of geometric shapes and brilliant colours to create optical illusions, as of motion, and free the art of all but visual associations.

Pictographs Pictures juxtaposed with charts and graphs.

Pointilizing An effect of computer filter that simulates the technique of impressionist painting in which the image is developed with tiny dots of pure colour with the help of a pen or brush.

Pop Art A style of painting that emerged in Britain and the US in the late 1950s and early 1960s. Pop art was based on the imagery of objects of everyday use, and imitated the styles of popular culture and techniques of commercial art.

Quartertone Enlarged halftone illustration whose dot size to tonal scale becomes 50 per cent and is visible to the naked eye.

Silhouette An image that is identified by its outline without details of its inside content, such as a dark shadow against a lighter background.

Stock Photographs Also called photo archives or image banks, stock photographs consist of existing photographs that are stored and then licensed for specific uses.

Transparency In photography, a transparency is a still, positive image created on a transparent base using photochemical means.

Vector Graphics Also called object-oriented graphics, these are images that are made up of mathematically defined curves and line segments called vectors.

Wash Paintings A painting with transparent watercolour, in which values of colours are diluted by adding water. The diluted colours blend with each other and form the various levels of tones.

Wood Engraving One of the early methods of creating visuals by cutting a wood block by knife or chisels.

REFERENCES

Adler, Elizabeth W. 1991, *Print That Works*, Bull Publishing Company, California.

Caplin, Steve 2005, *How to Cheat in Photoshop*, Focal Press.

Conover, Theodore E. 1990, *Graphic Communication Today*, West Publishing Company, St. Paul, Minnesota.

Galer, Mark 2004, *Photography Foundation on Art and Design*, Focal Press, p. 128.

Parker, Roger C. 1990, *The Makeover Book*, Galgotia Publications Pvt. Ltd, New Delhi.

Schlemmer, Richard M. 1990, *Handbook of Advertising Art and Production*, Prentice Hall, New Jersey.

Turnbull, Arthur T. and Russell N. Baird 1980, *The Graphics of Communication*, Holt, Rinehart and Winston, USA.

www.wikipedia.org, free encyclopedia.

http://www.ackland.org/tours/classes/glossary.html

Jethwaney, Jaishri and Shruti Jain 2006, *Advertising Management*, Oxford University Press, New Delhi.

REVIEW QUESTIONS

1. What are the basic functions of visuals? Illustrate your answer with examples.
2. What are the tools and techniques used to create illustrations in two-dimensional format?
3. What are the physical forms of images in the original form and those on a printed page? Briefly discuss each of these.
4. What is a stock photograph? Where can you obtain stock photographs and how?
5. What are the physical characteristics of silhouette, wash painting, collage, cut-out, duotone, and quartertone images?
6. Distinguish between vector images and raster images.

74 Art and Print Production

7. Write notes on line images, halftones, posterization, solarization, reverse line images, and vignette effect.
8. List the various types of charts and their physical characteristics.
9. Explain visual editing. Elaborate the visual editing technique with the help of 'L' scale.
10. Explain the process of editing pictures in photo editing software.

PROJECTS

1. As a project on physical forms of visuals:
   (a) Collect or make five samples of original visuals.
   (b) Collect five samples of printed visuals.
   (c) Collect five samples of readymade visuals.
   (d) Paste all the visuals on A4 size sheets, label them, and write the definition of each. Make sure that the definition matches with the visuals you have pasted.
   (e) Staple the pages along with a blank sheet on the top as the cover of your project.
2. Scan a coloured photograph which has enough details in both highlight and shadow areas and apply the following effects on it using a photoediting software: duotone, posterization, pointilization, line screen, and pixelization.
3. Scan a photograph that has several shortcomings. List these on a sheet of paper. Enhance the image in a photo editing software. Observe both the images on the computer screen and evaluate the improvement.
4. Take a typographical two-page spread of a magazine. Collect three cut-out visuals from a printed page. Cut them along the edges with a six-point white outline. Paste them on the magazine's text matter as per your aesthetic judgment. Evaluate the page on the following points:
   (a) Have the visuals improved the look of the page?
   (b) Are they obstructing the reading flow of the text?
   (c) Do you feel that the visuals have overpowered the text?
   (d) What alternatives would you suggest?
5. Prepare three alternative types on charts using Microsoft Excel based on the data in the following table and select the appropriate one to be published in a newspaper. Give reasons for your choice.

Media reach in India								
	Press		TV		Cinema		Radio	
	NRS 02	NRS 05	NRS 02	NRS 05	NRS 02	NRS 05	NRS 02	NRS 05
All India	26.4	27.2	53	56	9.9	6.5	23.4	23.4
Urban	48.1	45.4	45.8	52.6	13.1	9.8	20.4	23.2
Rural	17.1	19.1	8.8	14.5	8.6	5.10	24.6	23.5

Figures in percentage

6. Take a printed photograph that you feel was not edited properly in terms of its content selection. Edit the photocopy of the photograph with the help of an 'L's scale and show how it is now improved.
7. Collect photographs of four individuals with a different focus, composition, and background. Print these on a page with equal importance. Scan the pictures and make them visually equal.

CHAPTER

4 Layout

Learning Objectives

After reading this chapter, you should be able to
- understand the need for layout planning in graphic design
- look at the common terms used in layout planning for different visual communication media
- discuss the key stages of layout planning
- gain insight into the characteristics required in a layout person
- develop an understanding of the use of new technology in developing layout

INTRODUCTION

Let us assume that we need to make a poster for a cultural function at the local club. We have collected some photographs depicting dance and music and placed them on a sheet of paper. We have done the lettering and club logo by hand. The required poster size is 20″ × 30″, so it has taken a considerable amount of time to make the poster. However, in the end, we find, to our chagrin, that the poster is not up to the mark although the design elements were arranged by us to our satisfaction.

What should we do in such a situation? Accept the bad design or discard the whole thing? We choose to do the whole thing again. This time, we are satisfied and some of the club members also like it. We take this poster design to a printer. The printer is willing to print the poster, provided he gets the artwork for the same, as the design prepared by us is not fit for production. This chapter discusses how we can deal with all such problems.

As in the case of a building, a plan is needed for a graphic design. This is because, like a building, a graphic design is also a structure. A graphic design plan is known as a layout. Several people work on the layout to make a graphic design. To prepare an advertisement design, we may need a photographer or illustrator to provide the visuals, a composer to provide the typesetting for the advertisement copy-block and headline, a finishing artist to paste all the elements together or a computer operator to assemble and manipulate images from different software files, and a printer to reproduce the advertisement. The person responsible for designing the layout of the graphic design plan is the architect of the plan. Both imagination and skill are needed to develop a layout.

TERMS IN LAYOUT PLANNING

Different terms are used for layout planning in different visual communication media.

Press layout These are layouts for advertisements to be published in newspapers or magazines. Press layouts are different from others in that the layout person needs to adhere to certain norms due to size, colour, and time constraints. Media space is bought to publish a layout in these media. For newspaper display, advertisement sizes are measured in column centimetre or square centimetre. There may be restrictions on border and bleed for such advertisements, especially in magazines. Layout planners also need to consider the page on which the advertisement is to be published. Some newspapers and magazines also have restrictions on the font used, mode of artwork, etc. and accept only those designs that conform to their style. Figure 4.1 shows a press layout for an advertisement.

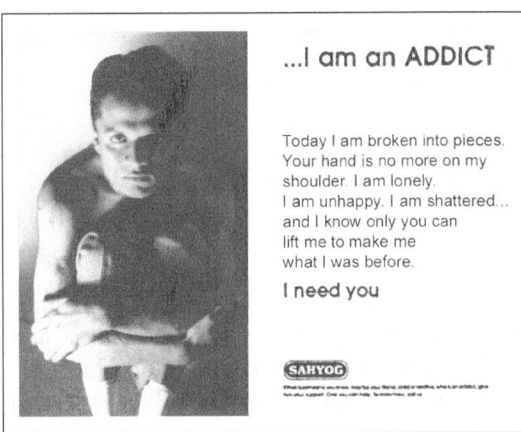

Figure 4.1 Press layout

Most media organizations accept the artwork in soft copies, preferably in a PDF format. Layouts with film output or laser printout (camera-ready copy) are also accepted by many regional newspapers and magazines. In many cases, press layouts are not accepted directly by the media organization concerned. In such cases, the advertisers send the layout to them through an accredited advertising agency or media buying firm which takes care of all the norms needed to publish the advertisement.

Page layout Page layout refers to the page plan for any multi-page publication, be it for a magazine, brochure, annual report, book, booklet, or a diary. Page layouts for many publications are planned for two pages together. This is because, as we open the book, we see both the pages together. Therefore, they are one unit of design and the elements placed on the left page are coordinated with the elements on the right facing page in terms of visual syntax.

A page layout application is required for planning the layout of a multi-page publication digitally. The application allows us to see the facing pages on the screen in the form of a grid which establishes the overall appearance of the pages. The grid is a non-printable guideline for the layout person. It indicates the top, bottom, left, and right margins for the main content of each page. It also sets positions for items such as headers and footers. Most publications predominantly contain text. Everything that pertains to text is normally consistent throughout the publication and is positioned according to the grid. Grids are also used to position the visual and other graphic elements on the page that give the page a comprehensive look. Figure 4.2 shows a page layout.

Dummy A dummy is an imitation used to represent the real product. In publications, proof prints are taken for all the laid out pages separately and compiled to develop a

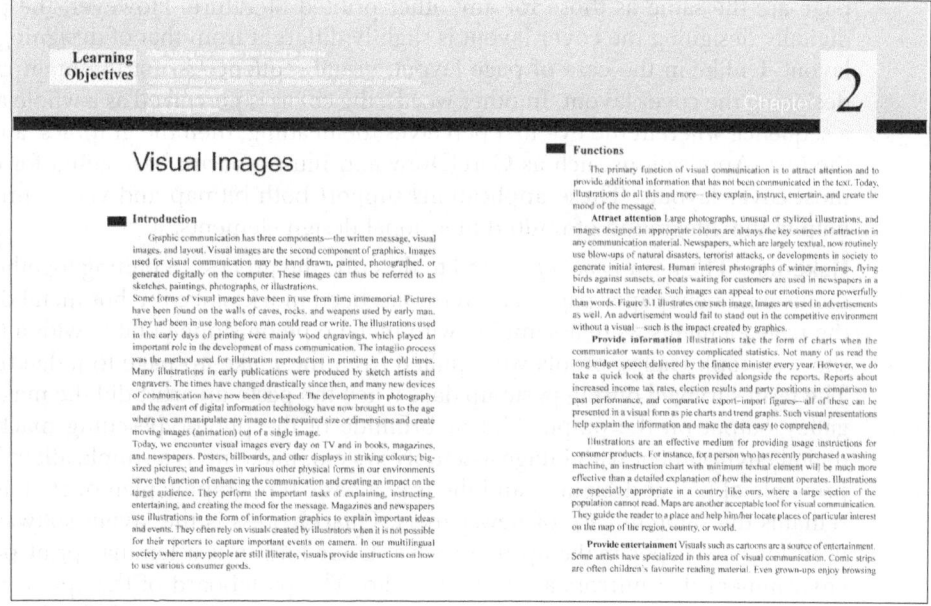

Figure 4.2 Page layout

prototype of the publication. A dummy of a publication is practically a three-dimensional finished rough that gives the feel of a printed product.

Generally, two single pages are pasted back to back and then all are stapled together to get a rough idea of what the product will look like. In case of a folded brochure, individual page prints are pasted on both sides of a big sheet in sequence. The sheet is then folded to obtain a dummy. Blank sheets of paper folded in the same manner as the final product with page numbers and heads duly marked, when unfolded, can be used to show page and copy positions for paste-up or imposition. These are also called dummies.

In book production, a dummy helps to plan the cover or jacket and the inner pages. Here, a dummy refers to a prototype for the book with the estimated blank pages bound in case, without any printing. The dummy gives the layout artist the trim size of the pages, size of the cover, and the width of the spine, which help him/her plan the text margin and the design on the covers and spine. This facilitates the book binder to cut the pages, paste the cover, and fold the jacket in the exact position, so that no part of the design goes out of its respective position.

Cover layout The cover of a printed publication is a form of visual expression. It gives the potential customer an idea about the content. People often base their purchase decision on what they see and read on the cover of the publication. A book cover comprises information bearing, decorative, and background elements that are presented in a two-dimensional graphic form. The masthead, title, blurb, and picture on the cover carry information about the contents of the publication, while the borders and graphics serve as decorative and background elements. Colour and blank space on the cover are also examples of background elements. These elements are the language in which the publisher communicates with the target readers. The rules for designing a cover page are the same as those for any other printed literature. However, the process of digitally designing the cover layout is slightly different from that of designing the page layout. Unlike in the case of page layout, visual sequence is not the main criteria for designing the cover layout. In other words, the cover is perceived as a whole and not in a sequence wherein the eye first perceives the heading, then the graphics, and, finally, the text. Applications such as CorelDraw and Illustrator are best suited for designing most cover layouts. These applications support both bitmap and vector images, and help in the integration of multi-dimensional design elements.

Make-up The term *make-up* is used to describe the process of putting together the elements on a newspaper page. This term has been in use since the hot metal days when the page elements were assembled with metal type on stone (a table with a thick steel sheet on top). Galley proofs were pulled from the make-up page to judge the layout. The term survived during paste-up days when the paste-up artist did the make-up with galley output on the output film or bromide of the phototypesetting machine. In a digital environment with image assembly system, make-up is a simple affair. The basic principle of layout designing and the way a basic typographic plan or style is adopted remains the same in case of newspapers. QuarkXpress is the layout software mainly used for newspaper make-up these days. Users find in it a familiar print production environment that mirrors a paste-up studio. The pasteboard of the application fulfils the same function as work surfaces such as paste-up tables and desks. Because of its box-based interface with subtle grids and varied column widths, newspaper make-up is now more interesting and flexible.

Mock-up In common usage, a *mock-up* is a scale, model, or device used to get a basic idea about the aesthetics and physical and functional form of a product. In graphic design, a mock-up may be a package, window display, or exhibition stall. In software, architecture, and engineering, the mock-up comes from the idea of making a *prototype*. Even though mock-up is often confused with the word prototype, it actually refers to a graphic, image, paper illustration, or simple configuration of the product being made. Mock-ups are used for systems, games, etc. to describe the screen and user interaction. Mock-ups are also used in the consumer goods industry, as part of the product development process, when the size, impression, and/or artworks have to be tested and approved.

Model Mock-ups and models work in almost the same way in planning and designing. A proportionate layout of a window display would be a mock-up, while the prototypes of the products displayed in the layout would be models. A physical model is used in various contexts to represent the physical form of an object. The object may be a single item (e.g., a bottle) or a large system (e.g., the solar system). Figure 4.3 illustrates a model.

The dimensions of the model and the object it represents are often similar in the sense that one is a rescaling of the other. In such cases, the scale is an important characteristic. However, in many cases, the similarity is only approximate or, sometimes, even intentionally distorted. Sometimes the distortion is systematic, as in the case of a model of the topography of a large area (as opposed to a model of a smaller mountain region, which may well use the same scale horizontally and vertically, and show the true slopes), where a fixed horizontal scale is used, but the vertical scale is taken in a larger scale.

Figure 4.3 A model

Physical models in science and technology allow us to simulate or visualize something about the thing they represent. A model in this sense is a physical object such as an architectural model of a projected building or an existing one. An architectural model may be used to facilitate the visualization of internal relationships within the structure or external relationships of the structure to the environment. Models can also be used as toys.

Storyboard Layouts are not necessarily only for printed material or product designs. In any medium where ideas must be presented or simulated visually, such as film, TV, or webpage, visual presentations begin in the form of layouts known as storyboards. A storyboard is a series of related pictures depicting what the action might be in the actual film when it is finally produced or on the website when it is launched. Storyboarding is a very simple yet intuitive technique in the layout process. It involves visualizing the sequence of the concept and drawing sketches or developing images on various frames and exhibiting the same roughly on paper, as shown in Figure 4.4. Storyboards may range from very rough ones to highly detailed ones. Some of the details may be in the

Figure 4.4 Storyboard for a film on mobile phone

written form. The more the details, the easier the work for the production team in case of film, video, or animation production. In case of websites, storyboarding helps to plan and visualize the layout of each page and gives an idea about the three-dimensional navigation and relations throughout the site.

Storyboards can be drawn or developed on a computer screen with the help of various storyboard software available. Some of them are Storyboard Quick, Storyboard Artists, Storyboard Artist's Studio, and Auto Actuals. These software are designed for media savvy professionals who want to create amazing storyboards for film, video, multimedia, or any other type of media development. With an intuitive, easy-to-use interface, several pre-drawn props, and customizable characters and locations, these programs are a perfect combination of creativity and automation.

STAGES OF LAYOUT PLANNING

From idea generation to the final product, layout designing passes through various stages. Different degrees of finish are associated with each stage. To understand the various stages of layout planning, let us again take the example of the poster design we had prepared after spending a lot of time and money.

Stage I

Consider the poster-making example discussed in the beginning of the chapter. Dissatisfaction with the final product could have been avoided, if we had first developed our idea and put on paper a quick sketch in small size, indicating the basic compositional arrangement. The photograph could have been represented by a rectangle or any other shape; the headline or other typographic matter, by parallel lines and colour strips. The first sketch may not have satisfied us, but as it takes very little time and skill to draw such a plan, we could have tried several alternative approaches.

Known as a *thumbnail sketch*, this raw sketch is the first stage of layout designing. Figure 4.5 shows a thumbnail sketch. There are several advantages of a thumbnail sketch. As discussed earlier, it can be done quickly. Time-saving is thus the major advantage of using a thumbnail sketch. It is also economical, because one does not need to waste much colour, paper, etc. at this stage. At least half a dozen trial layouts can be prepared on one

Figure 4.5 Thumbnail sketches

A4 sized sheet of paper. There will then be several arrangements to choose from. Each trial provides new ideas. All these ideas are recorded in a visual form and one can then judge one's own ideas in terms of effectiveness. Therefore, thumbnail sketches are meant for the person who is developing the idea, and not for the client or anybody else.

Thumbnail sketches should be drawn to proportion, because the selected thumbnail is redrawn in a full-size layout. A horizontal thumbnail sketch cannot be enlarged to a vertical rough layout.

To draw a thumbnail sketch, one does not necessarily need to be an artist. Creativity is one of the most essential requirements for layout planning. Many successful layout persons come from an arts background. Persons with a degree in public relations or journalism may also become successful layout planners because of their knowledge of information collection and the general rules of layout design, typography, and production. Layout persons may also be people with a marketing and management background, who have experience in sales and marketing. A fourth category of layout people are printers. We often depend on printers for layout designing. Most small enterprises pass on their advertising materials to a printer without thinking of layout and design. Here, the printer works as a layout person.

Stage II

The second stage of layout planning is that of developing a rough layout. The rough layout may be of different degrees of finish, ranging from very rough to well-finished. This type of layout is mainly used for presentation to the client or to the senior authorities of the institution, who evaluate and discuss the proposed idea in the form of a visual. The degree of finish is dependent on the client's demand, availability of time and information with the designer, and the designer's skill in translating an idea into a visual form.

This stage should be handled by a skilled artist. Usually, this stage is a part of the procedures followed by advertising agencies, so that an idea for an advertisement campaign, folder, or TV commercial can be visualized better by the client. The rough layout of the campaign is presented to the client. The client then evaluates the idea prior to incurring the expense of producing the final work. Rough layouts can save a great deal of money as well as time and effort. It is much cheaper to produce a rough layout than produce an actual advertisement or TV commercial. This is the *raison d'etre* for this phase of the business.

Retail advertisers may find it expensive to get an advertisement designed by an advertising agency. In such a case, they can get a rough layout prepared by freelance artists. There is no fixed rate for the preparation of a rough layout. Charges depend on the type of work required and the artist's skill and experience. Recognizing the importance of the growing demand for graphic communication, many institutions have developed their own in-house design studios along with their publications or public relations departments.

Rough layouts are, broadly speaking, of two types—working rough and finished rough. The *working rough* serves simply as a rapid guide for the back-shop. The designer's back shops are the DTP operator, photographer, printer, etc. In case of rough layouts, the designer works as his/her own client. He/she prepares a working rough, approves it, and then prepares a finished rough. For this, the designer may need a photograph and typesetting resources from the back-shop to make a presentable rough layout. Sometimes, though, the designer may directly send the working rough to the printing press, especially if there is a paucity of time. To understand how a working rough is developed, let us take the example of the DANLEP Leprosy advertisement. DANLEP, a social service wing of the Danish Embassy in India, had decided to publish an advertisement on Leprosy in memory of Mahatma Gandhi on 30 January. They had booked the newspaper space for this advertisement earlier, but had to come up with the layout plan within a very short span of time. On 28 January, they quickly decided to draw up a working rough of the required advertisement. They consulted the photo library and selected a suitable photograph. Two symbols were then chosen and cut off from a printed publication. A communication consultant quickly wrote the copy. A layout artist prepared the working rough. Instructions for the printer were given on the layout itself. Figure 4.6 shows the rough layout of this leprosy advertisement and the final printed advertisement. Often, this type of layout needs to be made due to time constraints. Working roughs, however, do not always conform to requirements and, consequently, reduce the effectiveness of the communication.

Many editors, proud of the aesthetic quality of their journals, prepare working roughs for the advertisements they receive from retailers. Most of the time, they send the advertisement copy in a format similar to that of the leprosy advertisement discussed earlier. Conscientious editors sometimes even rewrite the copy.

The second type of rough layout is the *finished rough*. The client is always an important and busy person—*important*, because he/she is going to pay for the design; *busy*, because he/she may not have the time to listen to the layout planner's account of how the idea will be sold, which can scarcely be shown in the visual layout. The design should speak for itself, leaving nothing for the designer to explain. So, the design should be presented as it will look after printing. The layout should be of the

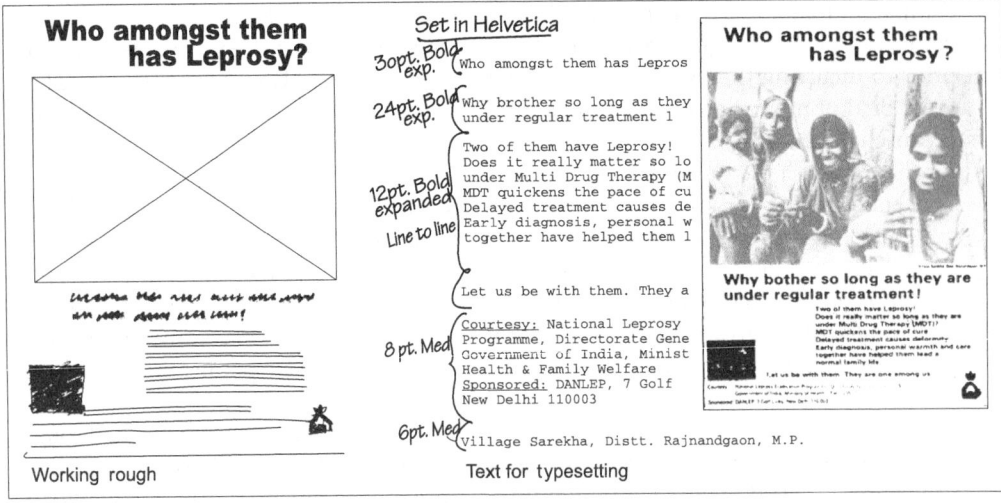

Figure 4.6 Rough layout and final printed advertisement

actual size of the finished advertisement. All elements should be presented clearly and accurately with regard to size, style, spacing, placement, etc. Figure 4.7 shows a working rough and a finished rough of an advertisement to promote literacy.

Until recently, most layout tasks—such as display type for headline, format for running text matter, creation of original art, graphic shapes, colour, etc.—were performed exclusively by skilled specialists working manually. The only mechanical help available was photography and a cumbersome typesetting system. Now, most of the tasks can be accomplished digitally.

Computers present a creative graphic environment that allows us to use the relevant software in much the same way that we work at our desk or drawing board. Applications allow the display of text and graphics very close to the way they look when printed. Typefaces are shown in their actual sizes and styles, and scanned images can be combined with art of other graphic applications in a variety of ways for a wide range of creative results.

A rough layout can be presented to the client in the form of a low-resolution printout from an inkjet printer, or the information of the layout can be stored in a CD or pen drive which can be displayed on a computer for the client's approval. Here also, a low-resolution image or a compressed file should be used so that it can be handled efficiently in terms of storing, transporting, and opening the soft-copy contents of the design.

Rough layouts are not only meant for gaining clients' approval but also act as a guide for professionals involved in making the artwork and in the prepress task for reproduction. They also serve as an instructional copy for the printer. Instructions should be marked on the layout itself or on the margin of the layout. In order to prevent the layout from getting dirty, instructions may be marked on a protective flap. Layouts in a CD may carry the instructions on a separate sheet or on its labels.

Figure 4.7 Working and finished rough of literacy advertisement

84 *Art and Print Production*

Stage III

In general terms, if the rough layout is further finished, it is called a *comprehensive layout*. The design process of a comprehensive layout involves the making of a dummy layout of the page to be reproduced, showing the exact placement of page elements such as text, graphics, colours, etc., in a form that is comparable to the printed sheet. In a digital layout, the finish looks exactly as it will after printing. Figure 4.8 shows the making of a comprehensive layout.

A comprehensive layout should be made with utmost care. The illustration should be drawn by a trained illustrator and pasted on the layout. If the size is not in proportion to the layout, a bromide print or a photocopy of the required size should be taken. The selected photograph to be pasted on the layout should be finished. There are a number of techniques for handling photographs for a comprehensive layout. The different techniques of photo finish are cut-out, vignette, quarter-tone, etc. These are discussed in detail in Chapter 20.

In case of digital comprehensives, the illustrative matter is scanned and finished through software such as Photoshop, CorelDraw, and Illustrator. Before scanning an image, the quality requirement for the layout should be determined and the correct resolution should be chosen. High resolution scanning of graphics is time consuming and occupies a lot of computer memory space. Line art, text, and flat colours occupy less memory space, thus reducing the time required for image manipulation.

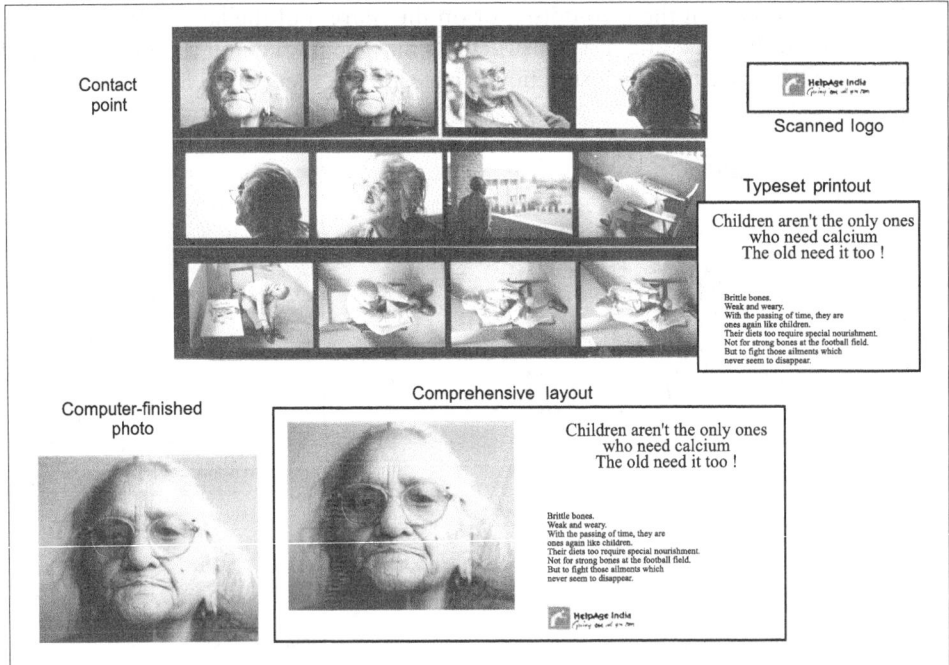

Figure 4.8 Comprehensive layout

Once the image has been scanned, it can be modified using various filters and brushes available in Photoshop. This software allows us to turn the visual work into a good imitation of an oil painting, watercolour painting, or a drawing. The sharpen filters can restore the apparent focus in out-of-focus photographs. Blur filters are available for smoothening the hard edges. The artistic filters can, when carefully and thoughtfully applied, elevate an ordinary picture to something quite extraordinary. The eyedropper tool enables us to select a colour and apply it on any of our painting images. The rubber stamp colours selected parts of the picture and places it wherever we want it. These techniques and other features of Photoshop can be used for making effective comprehensives. The manipulated pictures should be stored in a computer hard disk in EPS or TIFF format for further use in other applications.

For comprehensive layouts, typefaces that display and print correctly should be chosen. PostScript and TrueType fonts are the two industry standards for imaging that can be scaled to any size, and still remain sharp and smooth in any object-oriented program such as PageMaker and Illustrator. They, however, lose the sharpness in a paint-oriented program such as Photoshop because they are pixilated in it.

In a multi-page publication, a comprehensive dummy can be prepared by importing graphics and text on a page layout program. The program allows to set up master pages with elements that repeat on every page. Simple lines, boxes, and shapes can be added besides imported graphics. The imported image can be positioned on the page at will by sizing, masking, and rotating. The formatting of the text is so flexible that it can be wrapped around any shape of illustration or can follow the pattern we develop.

The use of colour in a comprehensive layout is unlimited. In the digitized form, as many as sixteen million colours can be used in such a layout. Any range of colours can be created on the screen with different proportions of primary colours. Care should, however, be taken when colour is used in a comprehensive or on a printed page as it may not exactly match the colour we see on the screen. Today, there is an increasing number of colour printers that offer a wide range of resolution and colour quality. The quality of colour depends on the quality of the paper on which the matter is printed. A laminated effect can be obtained on a certain quality of paper, which can match the high quality offset printing.

Stage IV

This stage of layout planning involves artwork, and is known as the mechanical. Conventionally, the printer produces a black and white image or a black image on a white page of a camera-ready copy used to make a film positive or negative for the purpose of printing. Mechanicals too are increasingly being generated digitally. This stage of layout development should be handled by a trained artist with considerable knowledge of printing and prepress work.

All the elements of the page, such as area for illustration, graphic shape, and colour, must be indicated in the form of outlines. The typed matter will be in the form of line art, without any gradation of tones. Photographs will be treated as continuous tone art that need to be converted into a halftone image by breaking the continuous tone into small dots. The artwork should carry the necessary instructions about the use of colours

Figure 4.9 Conventional artwork

for different elements. The instructions can be written in pencil on the artwork or on a tissue overlay, as shown in Figure 4.9.

These days, most of the artwork is handled digitally. The images of the layout are scanned and their information is stored in a computer hard disk in digital form and then used to create a complete page. Digital page planning offers tremendous flexibility to the designers and printers and allows multiple options in positioning the scanned images, laying of tints, colour correction, trapping, and even changing typefaces and type sizes just before getting the output on film or paper. Whatever may be the form of a layout, the printer needs a rough layout or a comprehensive layout and the artwork to accomplish the prepress task. The rough layout is all the more necessary for the printer to match the colours and exact position of the design elements with the layout for the printing form.

SUMMARY

Letters and pictures, when arranged logically, form a graphic design. A plan is necessary to create a graphic design. Such a plan is known as a layout. Anyone who can think visually can be a layout person. Press layout, page layout, dummy make-up, mock-up, model, and storyboard are some of the terms used in layout planning in different visual communication media.

From idea generation to the finally produced design, layout passes through various stages. The first stage of layout planning is that of generating a thumbnail or rough sketch of the idea. This stage of layout planning can be handled by any creative person. The advantage of thumbnails is that they are economical, save us time, and help us in getting more ideas.

A developed thumbnail sketch is called a rough layout. Skilled professionals handle this stage of layout planning. Rough layouts are normally used for presentations to the client and as a positional guide for other professionals such as printers. A rough layout may be a very rough layout—known as a working rough—or a finished rough layout—called a finished rough. The first one is a hurried guide for professionals involved in the layout process and the latter accurately indicates image position, colour, etc. When a rough layout is further finished, it is called a comprehensive layout. It is complete in all respects and looks exactly as it will after printing.

The fourth and final stage of layout planning involves the mechanical or the artwork. Conventionally, it is a black line image on a white paper for making film for printing. These days, most of the artwork is handled digitally and the film output is obtained through a computerized outputting device. An artwork should be accompanied by a rough layout or comprehensive to accomplish the prepress task of the printer.

KEY TERMS

Artwork Line drawings, photographs, or continuous-tone or halftone illustrations for the purpose of reproduction.
Camera-ready Copy Also called CRCs, these refer to the complete pages of a publication assembled with text and graphics and ready to be photographed as the first step in the process of making plates for offset printing.
Comprehensive Layout A layout that is finished in all respects and is ready for making film or plate.
Design Studio The working place of artists or creative people.
Dummy A three-dimensional prototype layout that has the simulation look of an actual publication.
Finished Rough A layout that presents the complete visual look in terms of the physical characteristics of elements and their placement.
Galley A three-sided metal tray used to hold type. The term 'galley proofs' refers to long strips of printed photographic or cold type ready to be proofread and used for paste-up jobs.
Imposition An arrangement of pages for printing so that they will appear in proper order for folding.
Inkjet Printer A printer that operates by firing jets or spots of ink on to paper.
Line Art Black and white original illustrations which can be reproduced without breaking the image into dots.
Make-up The process of putting together the elements of a newspaper page.
Mechanical A final layout in the form of paste-up or camera-ready copy which holds all the elements of composition that can go for film outputting.

Mock-up   A scale model or device used to get a basic idea about the aesthetics and physical and functional form of the final product.

Page Layout   A page plan for multi-page publications such as magazines, brochures, annual reports, books, or booklets.

Prepress Task   The set of tasks needed to prepare print documents conventionally or digitally.

Press Layout   Advertisements meant for publishing in newspapers or magazines.

Resolution   Clarity of the graphic image, as determined by the number of pixels per inch.

Rough Layout   A sketchy two- or three-dimensional plan to show the placement of elements.

Storyboard   A storyboard is a series of related pictures depicting what the action might be in the actual film or website.

Thumbnail Sketch   A small preliminary sketch of ideas with a possible arrangement of elements.

Trapping   In colour printing, it is the method of minute expanding or shrinking one adjacent colour area into another to compensate for the creation of gaps between colours.

Working Rough   Simple sketch used as a rapid guide for the designer's back-shops, such as the DTP operator, photographer, and printer.

REFERENCES

Adler, Elizabeth W. 1991, *Print That Works*, Bull Publishing Company, California.

Book, Albert C., and C. Dennis Schick 1997, *Fundamentals of Copy & Layout*, National Textbook Company, USA.

Conover, Theodore E. 1990, *Graphic Communication Today*, West Publishing Company, St. Paul.

Jute, Andre 1994, *Graphic Design in the Computer Age Publication for Professional Communicators*, B.T. Batsford Ltd., London.

Stevenson, George A. 1968, *Graphic Arts Encyclopedia*, McGraw-Hill, New York.

Turnbull, Arthur T. and Russell N. Baird 1980, *The Graphics of Communication*, Holt, Rinehart and Winston, USA.

http://en.wikipedia.org.

REVIEW QUESTIONS

1. Why do we need a layout for developing a graphic design?
2. List the terms used in layout planning in various media formats.
3. What are the qualities needed in a layout person and why?
4. What are the stages of layout planning? Discuss the functions of each stage in brief.
5. Define thumbnail sketch. Elaborate its importance in developing an idea.
6. Compare rough layout with comprehensive layout.
7. In what kinds of situations is a working rough used?
8. Write a detailed note on both conventional and digital artwork.
9. Why must the rough layout be sent to the printer along with the artwork?
10. Explain, with examples, the use of computers in creating, presenting, and producing a product.

PROJECTS

1. Select an advertisement from a printed page of a newspaper or magazine. Prepare four thumbnail sketches of the advertisement with different arrangements of its elements. Write comments on each sketch you have prepared and the one you consider the best.

2. Prepare a working rough for two facing pages of a magazine with necessary typographical instructions. Who are the professionals who should work on your layout? Write about each one's involvement in developing a finished rough.
3. Prepare a finished rough poster layout on any one of the following social issues: AIDS, dowry, environment, terrorism, child marriage, literacy, and drug abuse. Write five alternative slogans/captions on the topic you have chosen. Select the best for your layout. Your mechanical limitations are—size: 18″ × 23″, colour: three, printing: offset process. The layout may be drawn/painted or computer-generated. It should be pasted on stiff board for presentation.
4. Write a story for a 40-second TV commercial on eye donation. Make a storyboard of nine frames. Write the actions to be taken against each frame. The story of the eye donation campaign is as given: A middle-aged tourist is seen in front of the Taj Mahal, Great Wall of China, Niagara Falls, Leaning Tower of Pisa, and London Bridge. He desires to see all the beautiful places in the world—is it possible? It is possible—only if he donates his eyes to someone. (A story by M. Rehman)
5. Develop a rough digital layout for a package for a folding carton in which a digital phone with its accessories will be packed. Make a dummy box by cutting, creasing, and folding a piece of cardboard. Now make a mock-up of the package by pasting the printout of the layout you have prepared on the computer.
6. Prepare a conventional or digital artwork for the poster you have created for Question no. 3. What action will you have to take while handing over the artwork to the printer?

CHAPTER 5

Principles of Design

Learning Objectives

After reading this chapter, you should be able to
- appreciate the importance of designing in our everyday lives
- understand the principles of design in order to create effective designs and develop the ability to critically evaluate designs
- discuss the vocabulary and syntax used in designing
- identify the elements in a design and understand how they can be used to create a design that is visually pleasing as well as informative
- discuss a basic approach to creating a graphic design

INTRODUCTION

The environment that surrounds us may be either natural or man-made. Both kinds of environments have some visual characteristics which influence us directly or indirectly. Man-made environment may be thought of as a structure. A graphic design is also a structure that fulfils one of the most important human needs—that of information exchange. Most of us do not notice the visual qualities of a design that impart information; we simply consider it a pattern. A design, however, is much more than an ornamental or decorative *pattern*. It is a *structure* that has a well-conceived plan behind it. A design is an arrangement of elements based on some principles, known as design principles. We, therefore, must understand design principles not only to exchange information but also to develop our ability for critical appreciation of designs.

Knowingly or unknowingly, all of us are involved in designing. We design when we dress ourselves up. We make a conscious effort to select our shoes so that they match the colour of our dress and are in harmony with our clothes. We design when we arrange the furniture in our living room. We keep values such as aesthetics and functionality in mind while rearranging the room. We arrange the sofa set and the telephone table in such a way that they do not obstruct free movement in the room. At the same time, we also try to ensure that the arrangement looks aesthetically pleasing.

We are involved in designing even while carrying out everyday actions such as taking notes in class. A look at our notebooks will show that we indicate the important points in capital letters, with occasional underlined sentences. We leave white space for easy access to running notes. We may also make crude small sketches to support our notes. These are all part of a planned design. Graphic designers also plan their designs in a similar way. Their design elements are photographs, types, logo, colours, etc. Handling this job demands professional skills and, of course, imagination.

PRINCIPLES OF DESIGN

Planning for contemporary printed material is such a variable creative process that only general procedures can be laid down for applying the basic design requisites. In such a scenario, it would be helpful to understand the basic purpose of each design requisite in a given situation and how the principles of design can be applied to create an effective visual.

A design message aims at transferring meaning from one mind to another. Meaning is born partly from the message content and partly from the message presentation. The message content partly comes from a copywriter; the message presentation largely from the graphic designer. From the designer's point of view, the message that needs to be communicated has two levels of meaning. The first is the *primary meaning*, which is the direct message of a word, sign, or image. The *secondary meaning* is what is conveyed or suggested by the overall design.

The principles of design suggest effective and pleasing ways to arrange text and graphics on the page. The ability to position the elements in a design logically and regulate their size, shape, and tone effectively depends on an understanding of diversified design vocabulary and syntax. Designers use the vocabulary of point, line, shape, and tone, along with the syntax of proportion, balance, rhythm, harmony, contrast, and unity, to communicate with the target audience. The design vocabulary helps choose and shape the design elements while the syntax helps in the orderly presentation of design elements.

Once they have gained some experience and expertise, designers do not make any conscious effort to follow vocabulary and syntax rules while working on a design. It comes to them spontaneously.

Vocabulary

Design is a language. We respond to designs emotionally. Being a language, a design has a vocabulary through which the designer communicates his/her intended message. Point, line, shape, and tone are some examples of the vocabulary used by designers. These concepts are discussed in this section.

Point

In Geometry, the term 'point' refers to an element that has position but no extension. In design, it refers to an element that can be seen clearly either as a structure or an action in a visual design.

Visual progression starts with a point, whether we are viewing or making a design. A point in a design is something that is visually simple and, as we proceed, starts gaining complexity. A point can be tangible and real, or intangible and imaginary.

An *imaginary point* is one that can be felt but not seen. The optical centre of a blank space is an example of an imaginary point. When we look at a blank space, we do not

Figure 5.1 Point, geometrical centre, and optical centre

see the entire space at a glance. The eye normally hits a spot known as the *optical centre* of the space. This is an imaginary point slightly above the *geometrical centre* of the space. To be specific, if we divide the space horizontally into five equal parts and vertically into two equal parts, the optical centre is the point located at the intersection of the vertical division and the horizontal division, which is two units from the top and three units from the bottom of the space. Figure 5.1 shows how the geometrical centre and optical centre of a space can be located. In conventional cover designs, the main element (usually, the title of the book) is placed at the optical centre.

Margins are an important element of page design. The four margins are never equal. The bottom margin occupies more space so that the centre of the typographic elements is placed slightly above the middle of the page. If we frame a photograph to decorate our room, the white margin at the bottom will be wider than the other three white

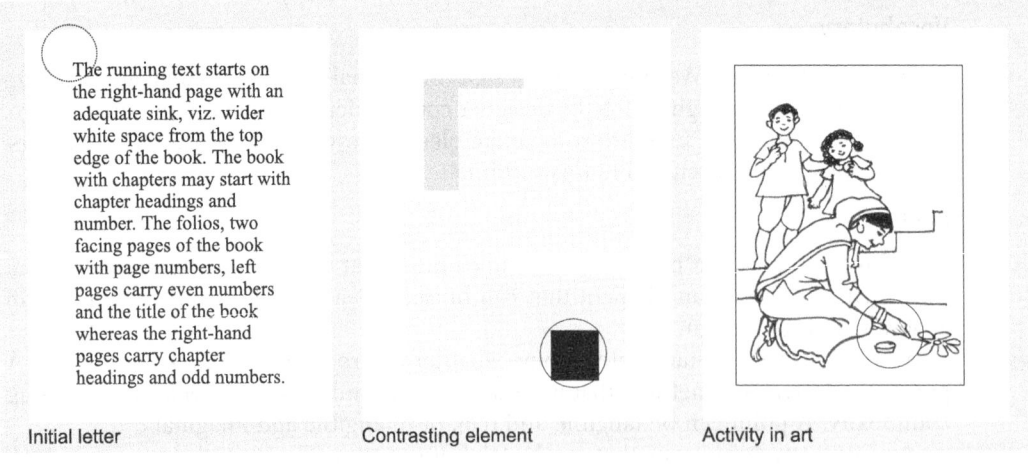

Figure 5.2 Real or structural points

margins. These are a few of the many situations that use the idea of the optical centre. To locate the optical centre, rather than using a scale every time one makes a layout, one should depend on one's visual judgement.

A *real or structural point* is a position in space which holds a strong attraction for the eye. The initial letter of a printed page, a contrasting element of a design, and an action part of a visual are examples of real points. Some of these are shown in Figure 5.2.

Line

When we extend a point we get a line. Lines too may be real or imaginary. *Real or structural lines* are visible in every element of a design, including space. The edges of the elements are nothing but lines. A group of letters can form a line. A white space around the text block of a book may be considered as a structural line. An *imaginary line* can be felt when two or more elements are in alignment. No lines are visible between the elements, but one can feel that one element is held to another by an imaginary line. A look at Figure 5.3 (a) shows the horizontal imaginary line holding the word 'chapter' and the chapter number. Figure 5.3 (b) shows the central imaginary line passing through all the elements of the page, thus holding them together. In Figure 5.3 (c), the vertical imaginary lines create a link between the three left-aligned elements and the two right-aligned elements. The line as a visual is more complicated than the point. We see lines in almost every object we encounter.

Lines can be straight or curved, heavy or light, smooth or rough, continuous or broken, and real or imaginary. Each line can create a mood and a meaning in a design. If horizontal, a feeling of calm and speed—the calm of the sea, the speed of an arrow—is created. A vertical line, on the other hand, suggests strength—the strength of a pillar or that of the branch of a tree.

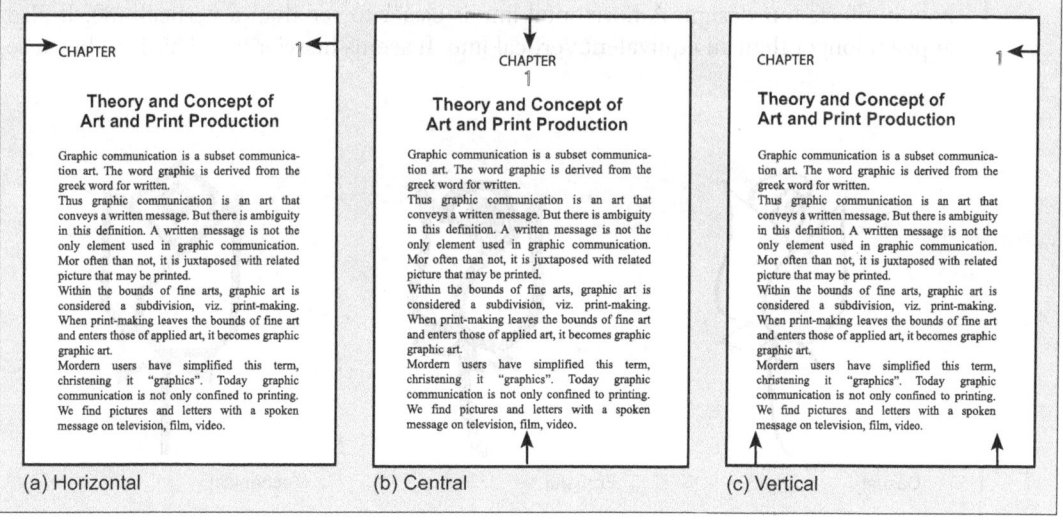

Figure 5.3 Imaginary lines

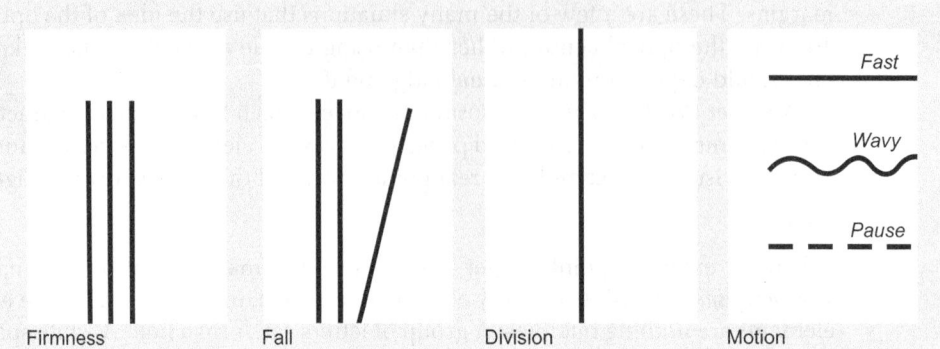

Figure 5.4 Meaning and mood created by lines

Straight lines give a sense of direction. Broken lines give the feeling of low speed or pause in movement. Straight horizontal lines lead the eye from left to right, whereas vertical rules take the eye downwards. As shown in Figure 5.4, straight vertical lines give the feeling of firmness, but if a line is slanted, it loses its strength and gives the feeling of a fall. Curved lines suggest the grace of the creeper, the movement of water, the growth of a plant which rises from the ground in the form of vertical curved lines and of opposition—a line divides space into two parts which come in opposition to each other. Lines are used forcefully, casually, or mechanically to create a mood or express character or personality. This is so because they are abstractions of objects and figures that create the mood and the personality. Figure 5.5 shows how lines can be used in a casual, forceful, or mechanical manner.

Sometimes, lines say things the designer did not mean to say as optical illusion may be at play. As designers, we need to understand the complexities of optical illusion and how it affects our design. A horizontal line is easier to see than a vertical one. It also appears longer than an equivalent vertical line. It seems heavier too. This is so because

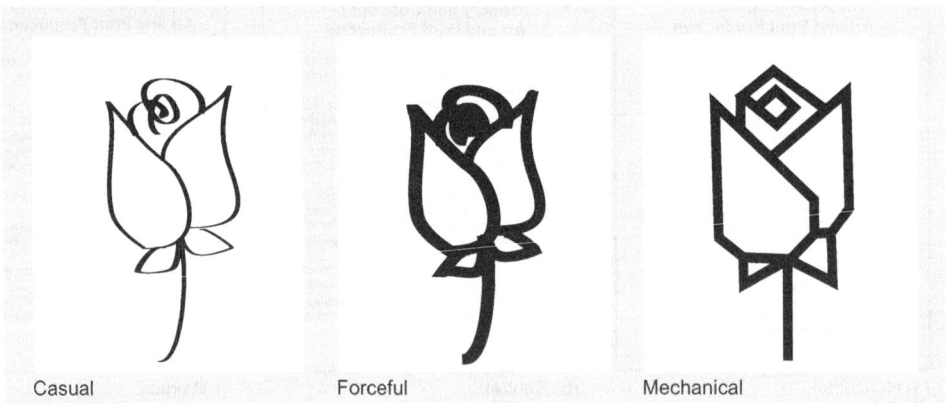

Figure 5.5 Casual, forceful, and mechanical lines

the natural movement of the eye is horizontal. To neutralize this optical illusion, if we want a vertical line to appear exactly as long and as heavy as a horizontal one, we need to lengthen the vertical line slightly and make it slightly heavier. Lines or stripes running in a single direction tend to lengthen that direction. This is why a short woman wearing a sari with vertical stripes looks a little taller than she really is.

We see lines in almost every object we encounter. For example, doors have vertical lines, side walls have horizontal lines. The real world is also full of shapes. Lines differ from the other visual components because the lines that we perceive may not exist in reality. Such lines exist only because of tone or colour contrast. We often perceive lines where none exist—edges, counters (boundary of a three-dimensional object), and intersections of a plane appear to be lines. An object is reduced to lines when we see it from a distance.

Shape

An area enclosed by lines is usually perceived as a whole entity or shape. A line is obtained by extending a point. By pulling down a line, we get a plane or two-dimensional shape. As shown in Figure 5.6, the two-dimensional shape can be further extended in different directions to obtain a cube, which is a more complex shape with volume. A visual can thus progress from point to line to plane to volume, that is, from simple to complex.

We tend to impose three basic shapes on what we see—square, circle, and triangle. There are innumerable variations and combinations of these shapes. Each shape has a certain weight, which cannot be measured by any instrument. It is an optical weight that can be felt emotionally. Bigger, darker-toned, and ragged-edged shapes carry more weight than smaller, lighter-toned, and smooth-edged shapes. Figure 5.7 illustrates the relative weights of squares, circles, triangles, and other shapes in various sizes, tones, and textures.

Like lines, shapes suggest some mood or meaning. The circle suggests peace and protection. It is also the symbol of the universe. In the Indian context, it suggests the cosmos and beyond in the phenomenal world—a circle of existence. The square is a dull shape because of its uniform size. It is also a symbol of the earth because of its stable shape. The triangle is the symbol of safety and also tension. It resembles an arrow, which creates the mood of *rudra*—lightning and storms. It also symbolizes fertility and the healing rain. Different meanings of shapes have extensively been used in the *Tantra* art.

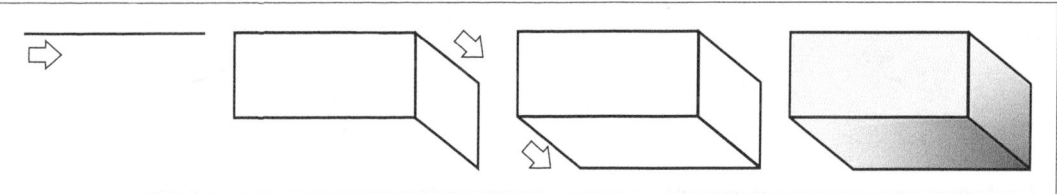

Figure 5.6 Line extended to form complex shapes

96　*Art and Print Production*

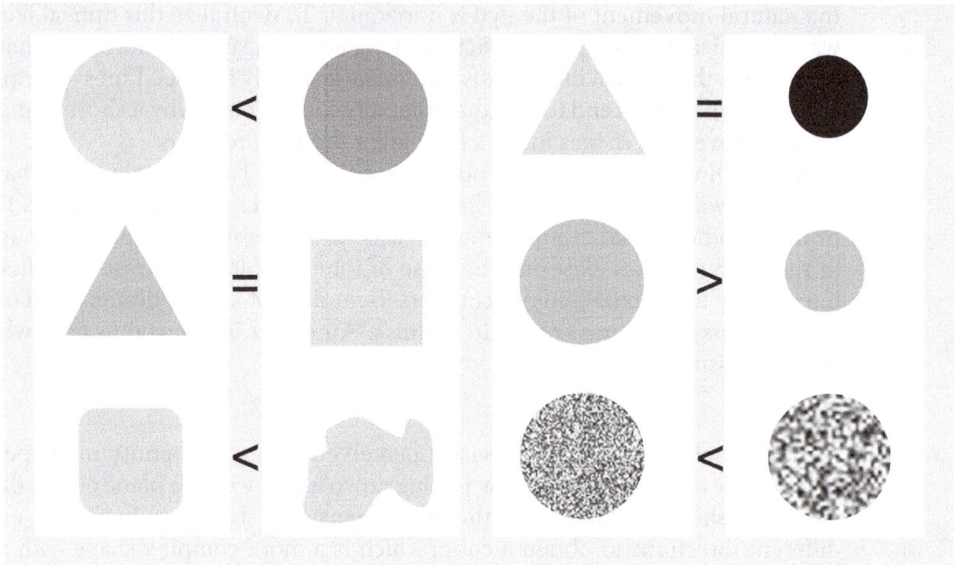

Figure 5.7　Relative weight of various shapes

While planning a design, each shape should be considered as an element of design. The shape may be very distinct or vague. Distinct shapes are easily separable but the vague ones are merged with each other or there are no distinct edges. If one or more shapes are placed within a big shape, they lose their identity. As shown in Figure 5.8, all the shapes can be made identifiable by placing them in such a way that parts of their edges are visible out of the edge of the other shapes.

Shapes have a proportional relationship in terms of size. If we take two shapes of the same size, the one filled with various elements will look smaller than the one sparingly filled. A comparatively big shape looks even bigger when surrounded by smaller shapes, and a small shape looks smaller when surrounded by bigger shapes. A shape can also

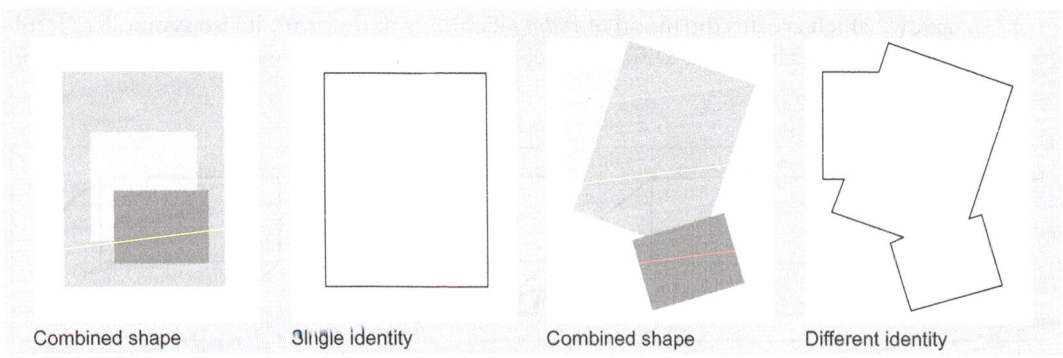

Figure 5.8　Combined shapes with single and distinct identity

Principles of Design 97

be made to stand out from surrounding shapes by strong colour or value contrast or by using different textures.

Some shapes carry information while others are just used for decoration. Photographs, copy-blocks, and headlines are information-bearing elements. Margins, white spaces, borders, and colours, however, are decorative ones.

Tone

The term 'tone' refers to the relative lightness or darkness of a surface quality, which can be felt by our eyes. Our visual systems are set up to sense colour as we see everything in colour with our naked eyes. The degree of lightness and darkness of colour helps us to perceive an object in three-dimensional form even on a two-dimensional surface. These qualities of colour are called values of colour hue. An image retains its characteristics even when the different values of colour hue are converted into tones of a single hue, as shown in Figure 5.9. A black and white photograph is a good

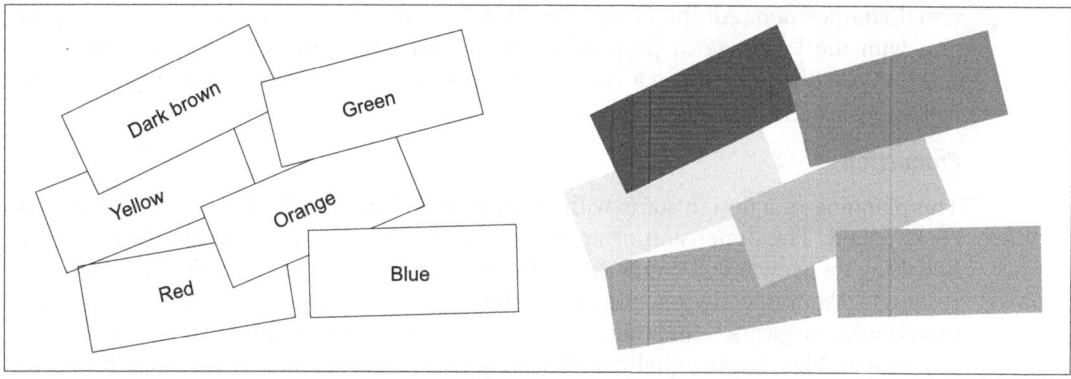

Figure 5.9 Different values of colour hue converted to tones of a single hue

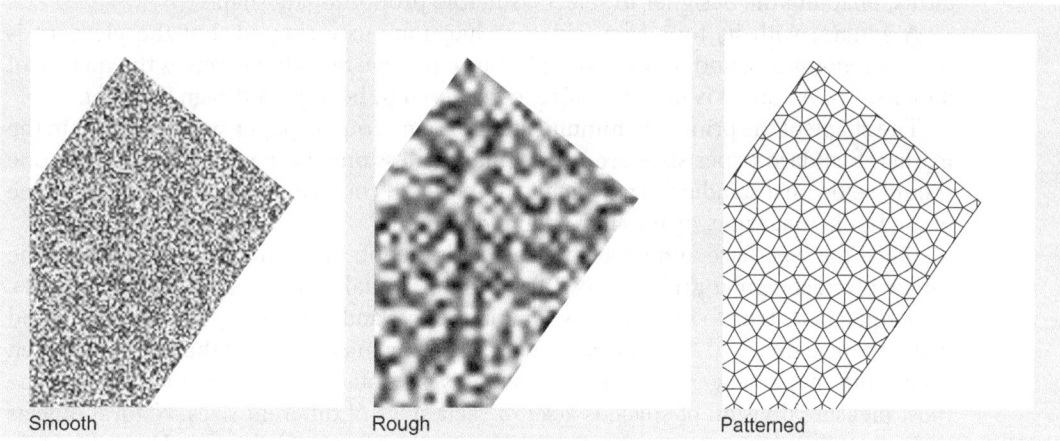

Figure 5.10 Smooth, rough, and patterned texture

example—one can change a colour TV picture into black and white. What we see then are only the tonal differences. Tones are of various degrees—shining to dull and smooth to rough. A rough surface can be sensed visually as having texture. Texture can also vary from smooth to rough, hard to soft, and plain to patterned, as shown in Figure 5.10. The designer can create the illusion of texture on a flat surface. For example, a drawing on hand-made paper by crayon suggests the roughness of a ploughed field.

The tone of a composition created by a light typeface will look light in comparison with an equivalent-sized composition using a heavy typeface. The tone and texture influence the weight of the shape.

Syntax

Syntax is the orderly presentation of the visual elements that form a design. Design is a language. Artists and designers use this language to express their ideas and create a visual composition. All the design vocabularies discussed so far can form a composition with the language of proportion, balance, rhythm and contrast, and harmony and unity. While working on a visual composition, we try to create an arrangement that will appeal to the emotions of the audience.

Proportion

The planning of a design starts with settling on a shape in which design elements will be arranged. The dimension or area of a layout is an important design decision. The first thing the viewer will notice is the shape of the design. The most pleasing shape is a rectangle. We frequently encounter this shape in our daily lives. Houses, rooms, furniture, books, magazines, and many other objects in our environment are in the shape of a rectangle. The pleasing qualities of rectangles were recognized by the ancient Greeks. The ideal shape was known as a golden rectangle. In a golden rectangle, the ratio of the sides is $1:\varphi$ or $1:1.618$. The ideal shape notwithstanding, a rectangle offers a variety of forms, enabling the designer to select a suitable proportionate shape.

A square, with its four even sides, is harmoniously shaped, but the element is static, monotonous, and uninteresting because the eye quickly perceives the quality of dimensions. A square is not, therefore, considered to be a good design element.

The shape of the printed communication depends on the paper sizes available in the market. Standard paper sizes are rectangular. Unless one has a very good budget, one should settle on a standard size which, when folded, conforms to the rectangular shape of the book, magazine, or brochure being designed.

Once the basic size and shape are selected, the job of the designer is to divide the shape into rectangular grids and vertical and horizontal guidelines for making layouts. Four equal parts tend to make the layout unattractive and unexciting because of the rigid mathematical division. A layout can be improved by making one of the divisions larger. Many different arrangements of elements may be obtained from such a division. The most pleasing division of space is a set of rectangles of different sizes. Natural objects are not uniform in nature—therein lies the secret of nature's beauty. Had mountain peaks all been uniform in size, trees equal in height, and wave movements equal in

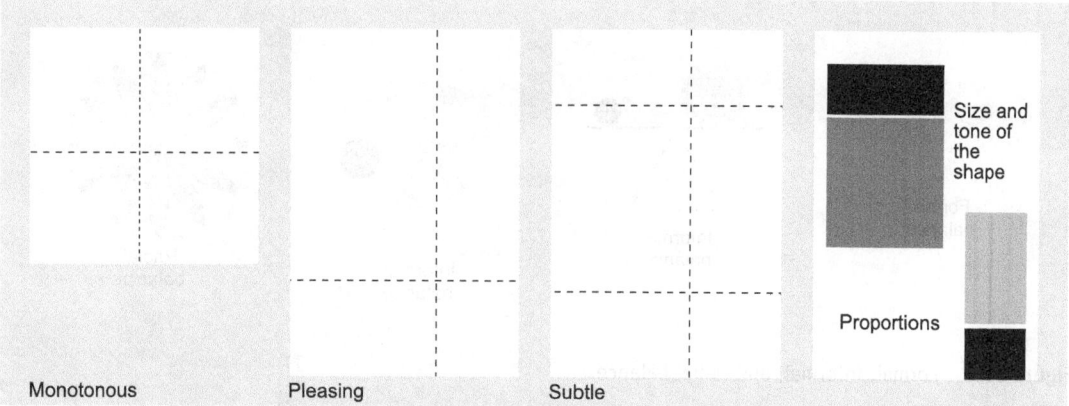

Figure 5.11 Space division using various proportions

space, we would not go to hill stations or the seaside to spend our holidays there. Like nature, design elements should be subtle in form. A photograph should be chosen as a design element in such a way that its tonal qualities and size are different from those of other elements such as another photograph, copy-block, or headline. The space around the elements separates one element from another. There may be a few sub-elements in one element.

When we put two or more elements together, we make a composition. We place them in some order on a space. These compositional forces are measured by proportion. One is larger than another, one is darker than another, and one's texture is smoother than another's, and so on. On the basis of the proportion, the reader decides which one to read first. Proportion develops a relationship of size and strength between one element and other elements or the design as a whole. Figure 5.11 shows some possible compositions using various proportions.

Balance

Design elements should be put together not only in proportion but also in balance. The balance principle is like the principle of gravity. When two objects of equal weight and volume are put on a balance, they seem to be equally far away from the centre of gravity. Balance in design is defined as 'a state of rest due to the action of forces that counteract each other'. In a design, balance should be from left to right and not from top to bottom, although we may wish to have a top- or bottom-heavy design sometimes. We must place elements on the page in such a way as to make them look comfortable in a particular space.

There are three kinds of balance in design—formal or symmetrical, informal or asymmetrical, and radial. There are times when a formal balance is just what is needed. A *formal balance* places all elements in a precise relationship to each another. It gives us the feeling of formality, exactness, carefulness, and stiffness. It is used for a target audience that believes in formality and considers such designs dignified and reserved. Book covers, company report covers, specialized booklets, etc. are often designed formally.

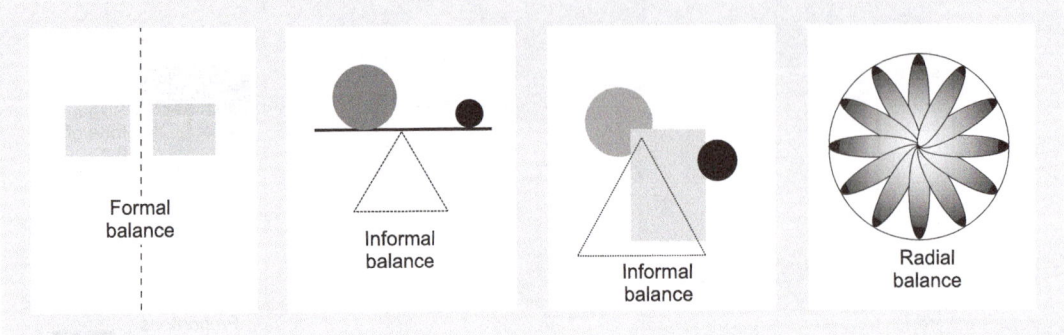

Figure 5.12 Formal, informal, and radial balance

In a formal design, space is divided equally from left to right, and elements of equal weight are placed equidistant from the central line. If a single element is to be balanced, that element should be placed at the centre of the space so that the imaginary centre line can divide the element down the middle. In comparison to informal balance, formal balance is easier to achieve. Although this kind of balance has its place in design work in many situations, it is uninteresting and stiff.

In most layout work, balance is achieved informally. Elements of similar but not precisely the same weight are placed in relationship to one another so that there is weight at the bottom of the layout as well as at the top, and to the left as well as to the right, so as to balance the whole. Here, the optical centre acts as a pivot of a weighing machine or as the centre of gravity. If a heavy element is placed near the optical centre on the right side of the space, the lighter element should be kept away from the optical centre on the left side, to counterbalance the bigger element. If another element is placed with the left side element, one should visually estimate the total weight of these two elements and then decide where to place them, so that they look stable. Handling two or three elements in informal balance is easy. It is more difficult where the number of elements and sub-elements is more.

Radial balance is a symmetrical balance. It is, however, different from other symmetrical designs because, here, elements are arranged within a radius. The centre point of the radius plays a major role in holding the elements together. Examples of these types of designs are *rangoli* and *alpana*, designs in temple ceilings, etc. Many formal designs can be made interesting by using the principle of balance. Most flowers are balanced in radial form. Figure 5.12 shows sample designs created by using formal, informal, and radial balance.

Rhythm

Rhythm is a word we often hear in relation to music. What is rhythm? In music when a *tala* (sound) or a string of words is repeated, we say that the music is in rhythm. Our life also moves in rhythm—we follow a repeated pattern of sleeping, eating, dressing up, and so on in our daily lives. Nature also follows a rhythm—seasons change, flowers bloom, crops ripen, rivers flow, and waves reach the seashore. The basic element of

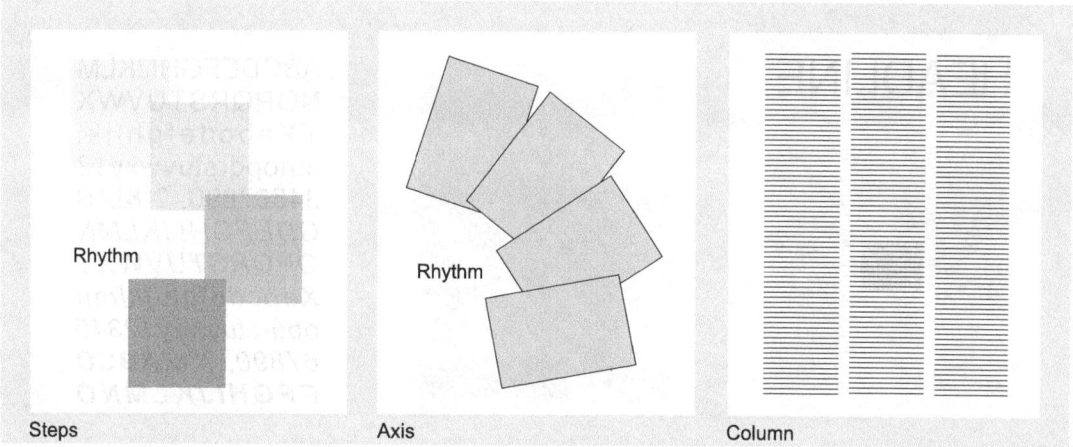

Figure 5.13 Rhythm created by repitition of elements

rhythm is *repetition*. In design too, rhythm is produced by the regular repetition of similar lines, shapes, and tones or colours. A newspaper page is an example of rhythm in graphic design. Its column grids form a repeating pattern on the page. Same-sized shapes with different tonal variations that are arranged in repeated steps can create rhythm. Same-sized shapes with equal visual qualities will also produce a rhythmic look if they are placed on an axis in progression, as shown in Figure 5.13. The reader's eye spots the rhythm and moves smoothly over the page.

Designs in complete rhythm are monotonous. Our life becomes monotonous as we engage in almost the same activities daily or periodically. To break the monotony of our lives, we go to a hill station or the seashore. Design monotony too needs to be broken. Subtle placement of headlines or other graphics break the monotony of a newspaper page. If we want to see for ourselves how artists make effective use of rhythm, we can place a piece of tracing paper over the design and trace some of the repeated shapes or lines. The tracing will reveal to us patterns that had not been apparent before.

Harmony

The design elements of a page should be harmonious. One element should go with another element in terms of tone, shape, and design characteristics. *Shape harmony* refers to the general structure of the elements, which are by nature the same. For example, if the illustration, body copy, and headline in an advertisement design are in a rectangular shape, design elements are in harmony. The design elements will fail to deliver the message to the reader if they are in conflict with each other.

The same principle applies in case of tone and texture. *Colour harmony* is achieved by choosing colours that have one common hue. For example, red, red orange, and orange, in which red is the common hue; or blue, green, and yellow green, in which blue is the common hue, may be chosen for a design.

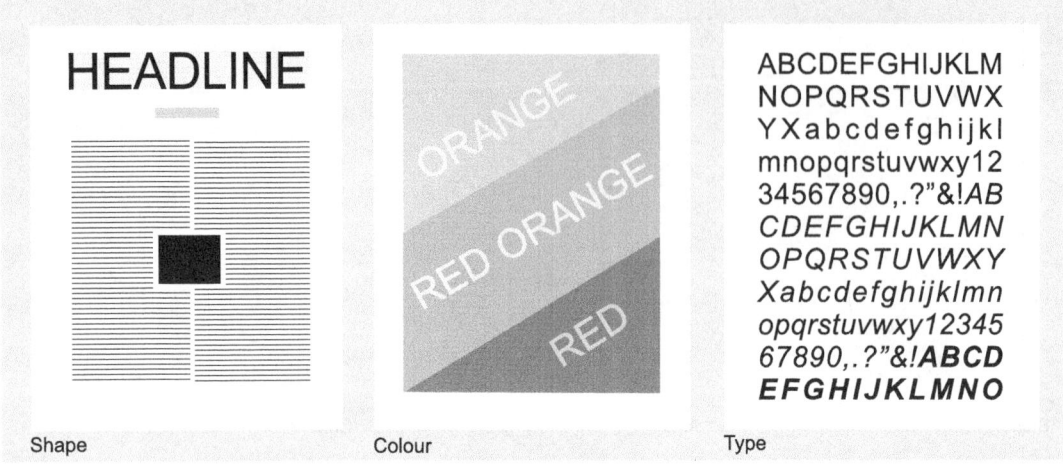

Figure 5.14 Shape, colour, and type harmony

Typographical harmony is more apparent than shape and tone harmony. Typographical harmony means that the individual characters, including figures, signs, and punctuation are of the same type style, and are designed in such a way that they look homogeneous and blend together. In a typographical design, to achieve harmony, we can select one type family and, for variation, use different sizes of the same family, including bold and italic faces. We should not use condensed or expanded types for the purpose of harmony, for they are used for the purpose of contrast. Figure 5.14 illustrates shape, colour, and type harmony.

Complete harmony is often boring. The monotony can be broken by using variety. It will not only awake the target audience from passiveness but also make them take interest in the composition. There are many ways to achieve variety—by using different sizes, shapes, colours, textures, and subject matter. For example, a magazine designed in the same type will be tedious for the reader if the pages are not broken by bold headlines of a different family and occasional blurbs which not only break the monotony of the page but also summarize the story.

The challenge is in using enough variety to generate interest without losing the sense of harmony in the design. For this, the designer may need to experiment with a lot of elements for the design, but needs to have enough sense to know when he/she has gone too far.

Tone harmony refers to the weights of the design elements. A bold illustration goes well with bold lettering. Ornamental borders and ornamental types harmonize. A straight tone goes well with a uniform lineal type design.

Contrast

Roy Paul Nelson rightly said, 'Expressed negatively, the principle is contrast; put positively, it is emphasis.' Either way, some element should stand out in a design. When graphic emphasis is given to several items, they all compete for attention, frustrating the reader and negating one another in effect.

Figure 5.15 Ways of creating contrast

In any form of communication, some points or ideas must be stressed more than others. Their selection is, of course, a matter of planning and visualization. As shown in Figure 5.15, contrast can be achieved by making one of the items bigger in size or by tilting one of the uniform shapes. An unusual shape can create contrast with usual shapes. A darker-toned element will stand out from lighter-toned elements. A rough texture has more contrast value than a smooth texture. When some lines in a design run horizontally and suddenly a small vertical line appears on them, it can create contrast. On a page designed in black and white, a small coloured element can give contrast to the page. Some other ways of achieving contrast include varying the widths of copy-block, using a drop-letter, that is, initial big letter in a text block, and occasional blurbs or brief descriptions of the content on a page.

Unity

Individual elements of a design must relate to each other and to the total design. When we see a loosely printed communication, our eyes cannot find a centre of interest and shift from one point to another. If the visual elements fight against each other, they can cancel each other's effectiveness or split the composition into several parts. It is important that all of the parts of a composition work together to make a united whole. Another way of saying this is—the whole is more important than the sum of its parts. A design should be so constructed that its elements are harmoniously combined and comprehended at the first glance as a unified composition. It is often necessary to adjust, even compromise, the details to harmonize the total composition.

Unity can be achieved in various ways. Some are obvious, such as enclosing everything in a border; and grouping some elements by pushing out the white space and using the same basic shape, tone, typography, colour, or mood throughout. Some of the non-obvious ways are—uniting the elements by imaginary lines, arranging elements on an axis, and inserting lines through the elements. Figure 5.16 illustrates some way of creating unity in the elements of a design. Some basic rules are required for bringing about unity in combined pictures and types. The most important of these are

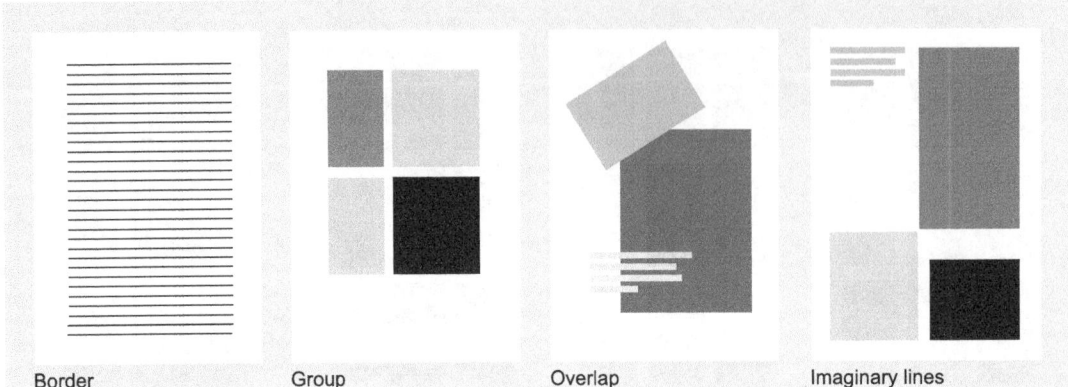

Figure 5.16 Creating unity in design elements

grouping together individual display units that have a common interest and are of equal importance, and evaluating the design importance of the collective group as a unit.

BASIC APPROACH

Having discussed the principles of design and the elements that govern the design process, we shall now look at a basic approach for creating a graphic design. We can start our design with thumbnail sketches or miniature layouts. These layouts bring forth ideas, save time, prove economical, and even help try several approaches. The best thumbnail may be selected for developing a rough layout, and then, the final design.

Grid and guidelines To create grids and guidelines for the design, we can divide the space in subtle forms of rectangles, which will allow us to allocate the visual elements in unity with endless possibilities. Some of the elements may be placed within the rectangular grid; one or two in other shapes. That makes for dynamism and liveliness. The grid lines can then be drawn on the layout sheet in pencil. As these lines are very light, they will not disturb the elements of the design being arranged. In case we want to develop the layout digitally, we can use the guidelines from the software options on the computer. These lines can be removed once we have completed the layout, or they can be retained for further alteration. In case a proof print is required, these lines will not appear on the printed page. Rectangular grids can be created by column options in the software command. The column width, number, space between the columns, and the margins around the column box can then be chosen. The text should then be allowed to fill the column grids. Libraries of grids can be created and applied to the master pages of the multi-page layout.

Elements of design Photographs, drawings, paintings, headlines, text block, graphic shapes, logos, etc. are the elements of design. Each one has different visual qualities in terms of its size, tone, texture, and edges. Some are very distinctive and separated from other elements, some are subdued or vague. A combination of many elements sometimes creates a major element. A predominant display element should be chosen and placed along with other subordinate elements. This should be done logically, by maintaining the proper visual sequence. The picture should be selected skilfully by sizing, shaping, and toning in subtle proportions. In case the design involves handling of type, the copy should be broken down into forceful display units and text masses that will emphasize the important points of the message in a logical sequence.

Simplicity Although ornamental and intricate designs have their own place in graphic communication, simplicity transmits an idea more quickly than ornamentation. As designers, we need to ask ourselves—'How communicative is the design?' and not 'How beautiful is it?'. The design can be made effective by using less non-information-bearing elements, few type styles, and equally few shapes and sizes of art. White space border, margins, and graphic shapes are the non-information-bearing elements of a design. Type composition, photographs, etc. are the information-bearing elements.

Attraction and curiousity We need to ask ourselves again and again—'Does the design attract attention? Does it arouse curiosity?'. We need to emphasize design element or activity of the art or the word content. Initial fixation being not enough, we should make an attempt to bring the reader's attention to the rest of the design elements. We should have a deliberate placement of elements to create opposition by abrupt transition rather than gradual tones. This can be done by using the occasional bold typeface, varying the width of the copy block, and by superimposing lines on continuous tone art. Pictures can be made gimmicky by using various photo alteration techniques. They can be used in big sizes wherever possible. Due importance should be given to colour. Bright and complementary colours have more attraction value. Curiosity can be aroused by selecting and manipulating the information-bearing elements in the design properly. These should be allowed to come out of the design by using subdued backgrounds or contrasting colours. White space around these elements may help us to achieve this.

Movement and progression While designing, we need to take care of the movement of the reader's eye on the design in a deliberate manner. We can lend motion or direction to a composition through variety, orderly repetition of some elements, and long horizontal or vertical elements. Increasing and decreasing one or more qualities of visual elements produces a sequence or transition. In general, the eye moves from left to right and top to bottom, big to small, unusual to usual, colour to non-colour, and unfamiliar to familiar. The various curved forms of elements can enhance optical movement. Multiple overlapping images give the impression of motion. Fuzzy edges are also perceived as movement. This is because, when a figure moves past at a very high speed, it becomes somewhat blurry. This experience leads us to interpret motion.

Comprehensibility Harmonious type style, necessary content, appropriate colour scheme, and subtle placement of elements make the design comprehensible. In order to ensure that the design can be comprehended easily, we need to select an appropriate number of design elements. The number of elements in the design should neither be too little nor too much. In creative work, it is important to know when one should stop working on the design. We can check our composition by placing a sheet of tracing paper on the design and drawing an outline around the main design elements or by making a silhouette of these elements. If the tracing shows the outline of each of the elements either partly or fully, the design can be accepted. If, however, the outlines of one or more elements cannot be traced at all, we need to think of a rearrangement of the elements. We may also try another method—we can block out one of the main elements of the design or hide the layer on our computer screen. If the hidden element is not missed by us, we should realize that the arrangement was not right.

Readability Comprehension and readability should be our final approach to the design. Our design should give the flavour of the key communication message, making for effortless understanding. Proper types along with other visual elements should be selected to enhance the effectiveness and readability of the design. Both the visual and the verbal elements should be handled together. One should not cancel the other. Clarity of type image, details of illustrative content, judicious white space, and appropriate colour scheme make the design readable.

Production The layout should be fixed according to the production needs. The content should be adaptable to the outputting device, printing machine, and substrate on which the design will be printed. The artwork should be prepared on paper as camera-ready copy. The computer file should be checked before handing over the digitized layout to the prepress service provider for imaging. The files should be checked for missing fonts, material not indented for printing, and any components that may prevent proper imaging. The printer or prepress service provider should be consulted while handling this part of the design.

DESIGN SOFTWARE

Adobe InDesign has most of the features needed to make a complete design for print communication. The newer versions can do more than creating text, graphics, and layouts. These versions are used in creating web page and e-book, can add interactivity, motion, sound, video to documents, and has facility to navigate to complex layouts. Some noteworthy features are as follows:

Work area of the programme InDesign work area consists of the document window, pasteboard, toolbox, and the floating palettes. One should navigate these to get the best use of extensive drawing, layout, and editing capabilities of the programme.

Setting up the document In order to get a consistent page layout, set up the document by creating master pages, specify the number of pages, page size, and number of columns.

Using frames Framers are the containers for the text and other objects. Working with the frames provides greater flexibility and control over the design.

Applying colours and tints The swatches palette allows creating the colour, either spot or process, makes it easy to apply, and modify in tints and gradients in the document.

Working with text The tools of the programme can precisely control the typographies of the documents such as change of fonts, font style, text alignment, tabs for tables, and indent.

Importing and editing text Text created in other documents can be imported and threaded through frames. Imported text can be edited within the frame.

Importing and linking Besides creating graphic in its own programme, InDesign allows import of graphics from other programmes. It can enhance the document by linking it with graphics and tables created in other programmes.

Principles of Design 107

Working with graphcs The toolbar lets one make not only various shapes but also makes your page design slick and interesting in combination with the imported graphics.
Master page Multi-page documents need master pages to save time. These are used to insert layout elements on various pages automatically.
Image format InDesign supports any image format; some are acceptable in preparing a file for print with CMYK colour mode and appropriate resolution too.
Preflight check It enables one to take a good look at the artwork before printing to ensure that all images with resolution, missing fonts, specific colour, etc. are accurately placed.
Printing It can be performed on the desktop printer as a draft of the work or on a commercial press using its required steps. The quality and colour of the final output depends on the necessary care taken to prepare a document for print.

SUMMARY

Graphic design is a visual structure that fulfils our need for information exchange. In order for a design to communicate the intended message effectively, it should be based on a well-conceived plan. In a graphic design, the visual elements are arranged on the basis of some rules, known as design principles. A graphic designer uses design vocabulary and syntax to communicate with the target audience. The vocabulary of point, line, shape, and tone, along with the syntax of proportion, rhythm, harmony, balance, and unity, help the designer to select appropriate visual arrangements and arrange them in the design.

A point may be imaginary or real. A real point is a position on a space which holds strong attraction for the eye. An imaginary point can be felt but not seen. It is an optical centre on blank space, very important in planning a design. Lines too may be real or imaginary. These are visible in every element design. An area enclosed by lines is perceived as a shape. Each shape has a certain optical weight, which can be felt by its size, tone, and edges. Tone is the lightness and darkness of a surface quality.

Orderly presentation of shapes is called syntax. All shapes or design elements should be proportionate. These are then put together in balance. Design balance refers to the optical weight of elements placed on the left and right sides of a space to counterbalance each other. Some design elements are arranged in rhythm by the repetition of similar lines, shapes, tones, or colours. Some are also arranged in harmony. Harmony refers to similar characteristics of elements. Both harmony and rhythm are often monotonous if contrast is not appropriately applied. In any form of communication, some points/ideas must be stressed more than others. Individual design elements of a design must relate to each other and to the total design.

KEY TERMS

Asymmetrical Balance A type of balance where the design elements are placed around the optical centre. A heavy-weight element placed near the optical centre is counterbalanced with the smaller element placed away from the optical centre.
Balance In a graphic design, balance refers to the equilibrium and visual weight of a page. Balance is a matter of weight distribution.
Blurb A brief verbal copy written as promotional text for a book jacket or for highlighting the essence of an article or some of its points in a magazine or book.

Contrast A design principle in which some of the design elements are stressed more than others to make them stand out, which gives the page life, sparkle, and emphasis.
Decorative Elements Elements such as line, border, white space, and colour, which are used in a design not only for the purpose of decoration but also to enhance the function of information-bearing elements.
Drop Letter The initial big letter of a copy block that drops into the lines of type below.
Golden Rectangle A rectangle in which the sides are in the golden ratio $1:\varphi$ or $1:1.618$. Golden rectangles

were considered to be the ideal shape by the ancient Greeks.

Harmony A design in which one element goes with other elements in terms of line, shape, and design characteristics.

Imaginary Point An intangible point on a space that can be felt but cannot be pinpointed.

Information-bearing Elements Elements such as photographs, drawings, and paintings, which carry information in a design.

Line An extension of a point.

Optical Centre An imaginary point on a blank page that is slightly above the geometrical centre.

Proportion The relationship between different elements of a design in terms of size, motion, and dimension. Proportion develops a relationship of size and strength between one element and other elements or the design as a whole.

Radial Balance A design principle where elements are arranged within the radius. The centre point of the radius holds the elements together.

Rhythm A design with regular repetition of similar lines, shapes, tones, or colours.

Shape An area enclosed by lines.

Structural Point A real or tangible point in a design that holds strong attraction for the eye.

Symmetrical Balance Also known as formal balance, it is a type of balance in which all the elements are placed on both sides of a space, dividing them by an imaginary line. Both sides have a uniform relationship with each other.

Syntax Orderly presentation of the visual elements that form a design. The elements in a graphic design can be arranged into a visual statement using the syntax of proportion, balance, rhythm, harmony, contrast, and unity.

Tantra Art One of the several art forms in Indian culture that show the paths leading an individual to spiritual elevation.

Tone Relative lightness and darkness of a surface quality, as seen with our eyes.

Unity A design principle which states that all the elements of a design should be so constructed that its elements are harmoniously combined and comprehended at the first glance as a unified composition.

REFERENCES

Adler, Elizabeth W. 1991, *Print That Works*, Bull Publishing Company, California.

Block, Bruce A. 2001, *Visual Story*, Focal Press, USA.

Booth-Clibborn, Edward and Daniele Baronoi 1979, *The Language of Graphics*, Harry N. Abrams Inc. Publishers, New York.

Conover, Theodore E. 1990, *Graphic Communication Today*, West Publishing Company, St. Paul.

Dreyfuss, Henry 1972, *Symbol Sourcebook*, McGraw-Hill, USA.

Nelson, Roy Paul 1991, *Publication Design*, Wm C. Brown Publishers, USA.

Nelson, Roy Paul 1989, *The Design of Advertising*, Wm C. Brown Publishers, USA.

Russell, Stella Pandell 1975, *Art in the World*, Rinehart Press, San Francisco.

Turnbull, Arthur T. and Russell N. Baird 1980, *The Graphics of Communication*, Holt, Rinehart and Winston, USA.

Walsh, Vivien, Robin Roy, Margaret Bruce, and Stephen Potter 1988, *Winning by Design*, Blackwell Publishers, UK.

Stevenson, George A. 1968, *Graphic Arts Encyclopedia*, McGraw-Hill, New York.

REVIEW QUESTIONS

1. Explain the principles of design.
2. What is the vocabulary of a design?
3. How is the shape vocabulary used to identify the elements of design?
4. Explain design syntax.
5. Proportion, rhythm, contrast, harmony, and unity are all used during the design process. Discuss the effect of each in a design.
6. What are the differences between symmetrical and asymmetrical balance? Explain it with the help of diagrams.

7. What should be the basic approach in developing a design?

8. Discuss the importance of the optical centre in arranging the design elements.

PROJECTS

1. (a) Take one-fourth of a drawing sheet (cartridge paper) and draw some rectangles or grids on it with a soft pencil.
   (b) Collect some matt finished coloured paper, cut it into different shapes.
   (c) Place the shapes as far as possible within the grids of the drawing sheet and keep on trying various alternatives.
   (d) Paste them on the sheet once you are satisfied with your arrangement.
2. Repeat activity 'a' above. This time, create a design by cutting out different shapes of head lines, photographs/drawings, text blocks, etc. from a printed page. There may be no relation in terms of meaning between the headline, content of the photo, or the text, but each one should have a different shape, tone, or texture. Now, place the shapes within the grids, consider different arrangements, and paste the arrangement you are most satisfied with.
3. Select an advertisement from a magazine or newspaper. Identify the elements used in the advertisement. Give a critical review of its design principles.
4. Make four thumbnail sketches for a design of two facing pages of a corporate brochure (size: 7.5 × 10 inches). The number of elements to be used are: one headline, four sub-head lines, three coloured photos, and five hundred words of text block. You may use some non-information-bearing elements to enhance the effect of information bearing elements mentioned here. Select the best thumbnail to develop a rough layout.
5. Open a two-page spread of a layout program on your computer. Prepare a rough layout on the basis of the best thumbnail you have developed. Type the headline on the theme of the brochure. Type some sub-headlines, which may or may not be related to the topic. Import some photographs from a picture gallery, which may also not be related to the topic. Place the text matter of 500 words from any word processing file. Keep on shuffling all these elements on the page until they come closer to your thumbnail. At any stage, you may change the font and size of the pictures, add or modify the non-information-bearing elements for a better-looking layout. Save the file and take a printout of your layout through an inkjet printer.

CHAPTER

6 Colour in Design

Learning Objectives

After reading this chapter, you should be able to
- appreciate the importance of colour in graphic designs
- understand the ways in which colours are seen and perceived
- discuss how human beings respond to colours and understand the widely accepted symbolism of a few common colours
- gain an insight into how appropriate colour schemes can be created by combining various colours and familiarize yourself with the concept of colour perspective
- understand the techniques and process of colour reproduction

INTRODUCTION

We see the world around us in myriad colours. Unlike most other animals, we are endowed with the special ability to distinguish between millions of colours in their various shades. Colour, thus, is used as an effective tool of communication by us. We respond to colour emotionally. Its impact on our mind is direct and emotional, unlike that of the written or spoken word, which has an indirect effect on us and is based on cultural differences. This is more so because, so far, no universal system has been developed for distinguishing colour. Hence, it is free from the laws that govern a language.

For effective use of colour as a communication tool, a basic understanding of the way we perceive colour, the meaning that certain colours hold for us, the way various colours can be combined to create an effective message, and the way coloured images can be reproduced in printed material is imperative.

Light is the source of all colours. Objects have a special ability to absorb certain wave lengths of light that fall on them and reflect others to our eyes, which are then processed by our brain. A plant looks green because it reflects mainly green light, and absorbs most other colours. The paper we write on, however, reflects all colours of light, so the eye perceives it as white. The light that falls on objects may also be radiated or transmitted. The images that we see on TV/computer screens and LCD monitors are due to the light that is radiated or transmitted by these screens, respectively.

Artists make use of colour to communicate the intended message effectively. Sometimes, however, an artist or a printer uses colours with limited knowledge of various colours and their multiple shades. It is very important for students of graphic design to familiarize themselves with the various shades and variations of colour. For instance, it is not enough to state that a leaf in an image should be green. One needs to specify *which* shade of green is required in the design—pale green, leaf green, or olive green.

Along with knowledge of the basic colours and colour reproduction processes, the artist should also have an understanding of the impact of different colours on the human mind and the symbolic associations of colour in various cultures and regions. Colours mean different things to different people. In our country, many colours are identified by the objects they represent—*sindur* (red), *kajal* (black), *haldi* (yellow), *jamun* (violet), and *mehendi* (sepia) are a few examples of such objects. It is thus imperative for an artist to ensure that the symbolic use of colour conforms to the cultural background and surroundings of the target audience.

A discussion of the detailed process of colour perception in human beings is beyond the scope of our subject of study. In this chapter, we shall study colour in relation to its effective use in graphic communication.

FUNCTIONS OF COLOUR

The use of only black and white is almost unimaginable in the printing world today. Advertisers and publishers have realized that they can recover their invested money ten times more easily if the matter is in colour, despite the fact that colour printing is approximately three times as expensive as black and white printing.

Amongst all the elements in a design, colour has the maximum attraction value. In any graphic design, the designer has a relatively short span of time to capture the viewers' interest. Although the human eye can scan a wide area, the part of the field of the vision which it focuses on is quite small. As a result, when a large-scale display is combined, it is usually colour that first catches the eye, followed by pictures, formal symbols, trademarks, logos, and words. Colour—in isolation or in combination—can be recognized immediately and from a greater distance than a shape, word, or pattern.

Colour can create the right atmosphere. It represents a product or object with high fidelity. The brain has to exert relatively lesser effort to comprehend a communication which is in colour. The presence of colour results in successful transmission of the communication message. It can provide accent and contrast, where they are wanted, and can help emphasize important points. A dash of colour can add sparkle to the page. It can direct the reader through the message. The colour in a landscape of a green field, a blue river, or a sky with icy and hazy mountains can have a tranquilizing effect on our minds.

Colour can cheer. We feel excited when a friend gives us a gift wrapped in coloured paper and tied with a bright ribbon. *Colour can stimulate.* We may go through a dull magazine article we would otherwise have ignored because of the use of coloured illustrations and photographs. *Colour can provoke.* At times, the provocative colour of a poster forces us to act. *Colour makes one proud.* The blue uniform of the Indian cricket team is a proud badge of identification for the team and its supporters. *Colour can antagonize* when it is 'colour for colour's sake'. *Colour can reflect the mood of the situation.* Subdued and rusty colours can be colours of the past. The jarring colours in a pop concert symbolize the restlessness of the teenage audiences.

Colour is a sensation. The sense of sight functions only when light reaches the eye. Colour sensation produces physical reactions. We feel cool in blue attire or in a shaded room with blue and green curtains. We feel warm in a brightly coloured room with red, orange, or brown curtains. *Colour arm is information.* It is a quicker way of communicating instant information. On the road, we stop at a red light and move on when it changes to green. In a coloured chart, each colour stands for some specific information. *Colour is perception.* We form strong associations with some colours. Our strong likes and dislikes for certain colours notwithstanding, we would hardly associate a dull-coloured dress with a young girl even though it might seem befitting for old people.

Colour is for retention. Colour has a strong memory value. This characteristic of colour is fully known to advertisers and communicators. They use it well in their communication materials in order to bring back to the viewer's mind the product or their own corporate identity. When we think of Néstlé's Maggi noodles, the first thing that comes to our mind is the yellow package. Surf makes us think of blue and Liril brings up images of lemon green.

Despite the undeniable influence of colour on a design, it cannot compensate for a poorly visualized design. If colour is not skilfully used in a design, the communicator may fail to get the message across. Although readers may initially be attracted by the power of colour, their interest may not be sustained unless the design has the strength to build up the readers' interest and persuade them to give time and attention to absorb the message. Here, colour plays a secondary role. Between colour and shape, shape plays the primary role because shape is mandatory for a design while colour is not.

In order to make the best possible use of colour as a communication tool, we need to understand the way we view colour, respond to it, combine colours, and reproduce them.

COLOUR VISION

The colours that we see depend on numerous factors. Depending on the interaction of an object and the way light falls on it, the physical characteristics of the object, etc., we see the object in certain colours. It is, however, difficult to separate what we see from what we know, because, the colours that we see with our eyes are interpreted by our brain. Thus, our perception of colour is dependent on various psychological, emotional, and aesthetic factors.

The colours that we see may be reflected, radiated, or projected. Accordingly, they are known as *reflective, luminous,* or *transmission* colours. Colours reach our eyes mainly from natural sources, paints and dyes, TV and computer screens, and colour films.

The widest variety of colours is the visible spectrum. This spectrum is made up of colours that most people can see. Some of these colours are encountered in nature; other visible colours are entirely man-made. Ink, paint, and dyes, for example, are man-made colours. Colours that are reflected to our eyes when light strikes an object are called *reflective colours.* For instance, the colour of an image on a piece of paper is reflective colour. The colour that reaches our eyes is what is left over after the paper and ink have absorbed a certain wavelength. If green and red are absorbed, we see blue. Similarly, if blue and red are absorbed, we see green. When all the colours are absorbed, we see black.

Some of the colours that we perceive reach us from TV and computer screens. We see as many as 16 million colours on a TV or computer screen. The screen shows colour by emitting red, green, and blue light (RGB), which are added together at different levels. This enables us to see an incredibly wide range of colours. These colours are known as luminous colours because they are radiated by the screen. Digital flat panel and colour neon signs also emit *luminous colours*. As with television screens, traditional cathode-ray-tube (CRT) monitors have 'guns' that shoot electron beams towards the inside of the screen where they strike a phosphor coating. When a beam hits a red phosphor, it gets excited and emits red light. The same thing happens with the green and blue phosphor. As the voltage of the gun changes, so does the intensity of light.

The colours that are seen on the silver screen are projected through positive transparencies or films. Such colours are called *transmission colours*. Colours seen on white flat panels of LCD monitors are also transmission colours, but these colours work in a slightly different manner. In these cases, colours are projected through filters to either block the light or to allow it to pass. There are no electron guns; instead, tiny transistor switches—one each for red, green, and blue—placed in front of each screen spot control the light through polarization.

To sum up our discussion, reflective colours are components of pigments and dyes while luminous and transmission colours are components of electron and electrical light, respectively.

Physical dimensions of colour

Colour has three physical dimensions—hue, value, and chroma. The term *hue* is used to describe a specific colour, such as red, green, or blue. We see a red colour because a red hue is there, a blue colour because of a blue hue, and so on. The quality of the hue can be changed by adding another hue to it. By mixing one hue with another, we change the basic nature of the hue.

Value refers to the lightness or darkness of a hue. Value is more when the hue is light and less when the hue is dark. The scale of value is determined by the amount of light it reflects.

Chroma refers to the purity or intensity of a hue. Chroma too can be changed by making the value light or dark. Both ways, it loses its intensity. Chroma can also be changed without changing the value by mixing a hue of the same value with the original one.

Primary colours

We see a multitude of colours every day, whether they are created from pigments or from light. All colours, however, can be created by using the some basic colours, known as *primary colours*. These basic components of colour, when combined, produce all the remaining hues. Red, green, and blue (RGB) are the primary colours of light. They are

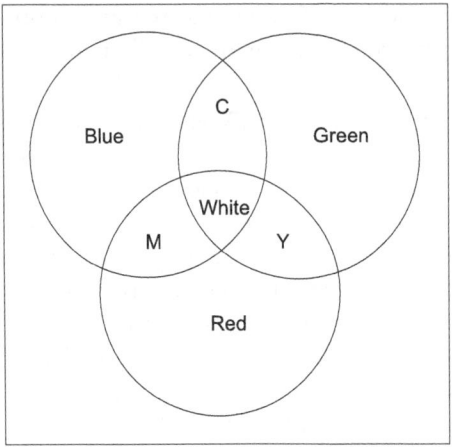

Figure 6.1 Additive colours (*see also Colour Plate 1*)

Figure 6.2 Subtractive colours (*see also Colour Plate 1*)

also called *additive colours* because these three colours can be added to produce white light. The additive colours are shown in Figure 6.1 (*see also Colour Plate 1*).

Secondary colours

We know that the presence of all colours of light (both from the sun and artificial) gives white, and that the absence of all colours gives black. A combination of any two of the primary colours produces the *secondary colours* of light. A combination of red and blue produces magenta; green and blue give cyan; and green and red produce yellow. Magenta, yellow, and cyan are known as *subtractive colours*. These are shown in Figure 6.2 (*see also Colour Plate 1*). These are the primary hues of pigments. They are subtractive because, in contrast to additive primaries, they produce dark colours when mixed. When dyes or pigments are superimposed, the resultant colour is the result of the simultaneous or successive subtraction of various colours of light passing through the combination. They are known as *primaries* because any range of colours can be produced by mixing these together in various proportions.

In the case of pigments, the presence of all colours is black (almost) and the absence of all colours is white (paper). In full-colour printing, the primaries are called *process colours*. Pigment primaries are complements to light primaries and vice versa. This characteristic of colour is used in separation and in printing a continuous tone colour ilustration.

OUR RESPONSES TO COLOUR

The way we respond to colour depends on various biological, socio-cultural, and psychological factors. We shall now explore some of these factors.

Psychophysical response

Colours play a vital role in our emotional life. Colour sensation produces physiological reactions in us. We feel cool in blue-coloured or pre-eminently bluish rooms and warm in red-coloured or pre-eminently reddish rooms. Red tends to raise our blood pressure, pulse rate, respiration, and skin response (perspiration) and excite brain waves. There is noticeable muscular reaction (tension) and greater frequency of eye blinks in response to the colour red. Other warm colours such as orange and yellow produce similar but less pronounced reactions in us. Colours such as blue and green slow down our metabolism and blood pressure. Our response to purple and violet is akin to our response to blue. These colours are, therefore, called cool colours. Cool shades of colours look clean and inviting but passive. The hues from red to yellow, including orange and red-violet, psychologically transmit heat. Warm colours are bright, splashy, and aggressive. They attract attention and stir our emotions. Warm colours tend to make a room smaller while cool colours make it larger. A blue object appears smaller and farther away than a red one of the same size and at the same distance. A box painted in a warm or dark colour gives the feeling of being heavier in comparison to a same-sized box painted in a cool or light colour. A card cut in the shape of a leaf may appear greener than a round disk cut from the same card. The subjective assessment of size, shape, weight, and distance by means of colour influences our responses towards the design.

Socio-cultural response

There is no specific law of colour preference but research findings show that men show a higher preference for plain, deep shades while women have a higher preference for light, delicate tints with designs. Bright colours are preferred by children. Colour preference also varies with geographic, national, cultural, and economic factors.

Collective colour association is more likely to be influenced by cultural convention and established tradition. Associations with and preference for colour can be expected to vary from nation to nation and culture to culture. Graphic designers should, therefore, be aware of the significance of colours in various regions. They need to be cautious while using colour as it symbolizes different things in different regions. Let us look at a few dominant associations of colour in our country. Culturally, green has a special value in Islamic cultures, and is used in the covers of religious texts, flags, etc. The colour blue has a positive connotation in Hinduism as it is the colour of Lord Krishna. Saffron is also considered to be a holy colour in Hindu culture. It is used in most Hindu ceremonies and festivals. Saffron also has special value in Sikhism. This positive association with the colour is evident from the Sikh flag, which is also saffron in colour. Yellow orange has special significance in Buddhism, and is associated with the notion that everything that is born has to die and pass away, just as green leaves turn yellow.

Besides the various associations with colour across religions, regional differences are also very pronounced. Bright colours come to the mind as soon as one tries to picture Rajasthan. Outside India, turquoise blue is a colour that is associated with Iran. Red is of special value in China, as it is considered to bring luck and prosperity. Colour manufacturers have developed different colour shades on the basis of the colour connotations of specific countries—Indian red, Chinese white, and Prussian blue—are some such examples.

Some colours are associated with similar things across cultures. People of many cultures have an automatic negative perception of the colour black. It has been found that blue is universally considered to be the best colour. It has the most positive and the least negative cultural associations across cultures.

Individual response

Different individuals have different preferences for colour. Some people believe that individuals react to different colours in different ways, and that their physiological reaction to colour has a psychological effect as well. Birren (1978), in his book *Color & Human Response*, has noted the following reactions to colour in individuals.

Red, orange, and yellow Colour preference depends on a person's attitude and taste, among other things. Red, orange, and yellow contribute to a person's impulsive attitude. Reds are considered to be active, motivating a person to be more athletic, sensual, and brave. Orange and yellow are cheerful and luminous colours, but they are warm rather than hot like red. Yellow is considered to emphasize mental and spiritual well-being, and signifies intelligence.

Green People who prefer green are considered to be socially adjusted, civilized, and conventional. People who claim to like neither blue nor green, but do like blue-green, are considered to possess great self-love, and are usually sophisticated, charmingly egocentric, sensitive, and refined.

Blue The colour blue is believed to bring in stability. Those who like blue are considered to be people who know how to make money and the right connections in life. They seldom do anything impulsive. They are also considered to be cautious, steady, admirable, and generally quite conscious of their virtues.

Purple and violet Those who choose purple and violet as their favourite colour are usually considered to be sensitive and to have above-average taste. They are fond of arts, music, and other such refined pursuits.

Brown It is the colour of earth, and is usually preferred by homebodies. More persons dislike brown than like it for its dull and boring look.

Black, white, and grey People's attitudes towards these colours are usually conflicting. These colours express different feelings at different times. These are the colours that have largely been found to figure in the responses of disturbed persons. For such individuals, colours are bleak, emotionless, and sterile. Some also attribute preference for such colours to high value, sophistication, and elegance. A preference for grey almost always represents a deliberate and cultivated choice. Grey is sober and indicates a willingness to keep on an even keel, to be responsible, agreeable, and useful in a restrained way.

Symbolic response

Some colours are used as symbols across different colours and regions. Since most people are used to what these colours signify, designers use colour symbolism as a tool for communication. While using colour for its symbolic value, care should be taken to ensure that the colour that predominates in an advertisement or printed piece fits the overall mood and emotions of the message. It should also be noted that a colour that is symbolically very positive for a particular group of people may be negative for some other group. Therefore, it should be ensured that the symbolic use of colour conforms to the cultural background and geographical surroundings of the target audience.

Let us now take a look at the symbolic meaning of some colours across different cultures.

Yellow It is a bright and happy colour like sunshine. It is identified with imagination and enlightenment. Pale yellow is soothing—it makes for a breezy atmosphere. Yellow on food products indicates that the food is delicious. Subdued yellow on pastry, cream, butter, custard, and ice cream makes it look appealing. Yellow is also a warning colour, possibly because insects and snakes tell us with their bright yellow colours that they are poisonous.

Red It is the colour of action, passion, strength, heat, leadership, and stimulation, but negatively, it indicates danger, fire, blood, war, anger, radicalism, aggression, and provocation. The Indian cultural connotation of red is that it is a masculine colour—the colour of the sun. It is the strongest of all the familiar colours. The colour red alters one's body chemistry and puts it into action. Deep red is aristocratic, elegant, and powerful. It goes very well with Indian traditional values. Light red or pink is a feminine colour. It is a fiery, alluring, exotic, daring, and passionate colour.

Orange It represents knowledge, civilization, enthusiasm, luxury, and a flame. Orange is mostly considered to be a positive colour. It is close to the spirit of yellow or red. However, orange may also represent negative qualities such as aggression, arrogance, gaudiness, sentimentality, etc.

Blue It is the colour of the sky and the sea. It has a calming effect on us. It gives a sense of infinity because of the vastness of the sea, sky, and the ocean. It also symbolizes truth, intellect, loyalty, and a spotless reputation. Blue is the colour of security and authority—this is why most banks use it for their corporate identity programmes. Manufacturers sell products associated with cleanliness and hygiene in blue. Cool blue negatively tends to imply distance, detachment, and aloofness in graphic design. It comes next to red in terms of frequency of use. Dark blue connotes industriousness, efficiency, and authority. Negatively, it may represent a stormy sea, the night, or doubt and discouragement.

Green It is tranquil and pastoral—it is the colour of trees and grass, nature, freshness, and vegetation. In Indian culture, green represents femininity. Mother *Vasundhara (earth)* is green. Bright green is for spring and fertility. Green is also the colour of disgrace, greed, envy, poison, and jealousy. The successful campaign of ONIDA TV was based on the slogan 'Neighbour's envy owner's pride'. The use of green in this advertisement symbolized jealousy.

Purple It is a sensual but sophisticated colour, long associated with royalty, pomp, power, and spirituality. It falls near the quality of pink in terms of romantic association. Negatively, purple may connote sublimation, regret, and humility.

Brown It is rich and fertile. It is the colour of earth and earthy products such as clay, brick, and terracotta. Brown is popular in modern home furnishing because of its traditional link to the stability of earth. Dark brown represents rich hardwood, such as teak, and tanned leather. Brown, when associated with food products such as bread, rice, and cereals indicates that they are wholesome, healthy, and organic. Brown is the colour that instantly comes to our mind when we think of chocolate, tea, or coffee. Negatively, brown is sad and wistful, like a grass-less mountain, the dried field of a farmer, or dry, fallen leaves. Brown will always be associated with rustic elements and dirt.

White It represents purity, truth, and peace. It is often associated with a sense of sterility, cleanliness, and innocence. The use of white is prominent in health care centres, medicines, and baby care products. In Indian mythology, white represents water, which, in turn, stands for life. Negatively, white may be thought of as being ghostly, cold, blank, and void. It stands for fearfulness and unimaginativeness. In the Indian culture, it is the colour of mourning.

Black It is the colour of night and death, evil and sin, sickness and negation, witchcraft and occult. It is the colour of infinite and endless space, in which all things lose their distinction just as all colours and all light lose their distinction in black. It is popular among artists for its association with wealth and elegance. Black in advertising denotes beauty, sophistication, and exclusiveness.

Grey It is generally considered a negative colour for its symbolism of neutralization, indifference, grief, old age, dust, and pollution. It can, however, be used positively for maturity, wisdom, patience, reverence, and retrospection.

Gold It is a rich and majestic colour which reflects the majestic aspect of the sun and symbolizes honour and wisdom. It is warm and opulent, valuable and prestigious. Negatively, it is extravagant and expensive.

Silver It stands for purity. It symbolizes a test of truth. It is classic and futuristic. Silver is the colour of the moon. When lavishly used in design, it signifies richness and power. In the ancient Hindu culture, it was the colour of *Agni*, the god of fire. Being close to grey, it may also be perceived as being dull and passive without the support of a strong colour.

Colour planning is a challenging job which requires professional skill and imagination. The designer should constantly keep in view all the objectives of the communication and then use colour logically to the extent that it contributes powerfully to the realization of the objective. Abstract expression of colour may show the designer's skill but it often fails to communicate the basic message.

COLOUR COMBINATION

The colour scheme, or the way we combine colours in a design, should reflect the purpose of our design and take the intended audience into consideration. We have already discussed the physical characteristics of primary and secondary colours. In order to decide on the colour scheme for a design, we need to understand how colour can be further categorized. Colours may be bright and vivid, light and dull, and dark and achromatic.

Colour Schemes

There are twelve colours that stand out because of their distinct characteristics. Graphic designers have divided them into two groups—warm and cool. Red and yellow are

Colour in Design 119

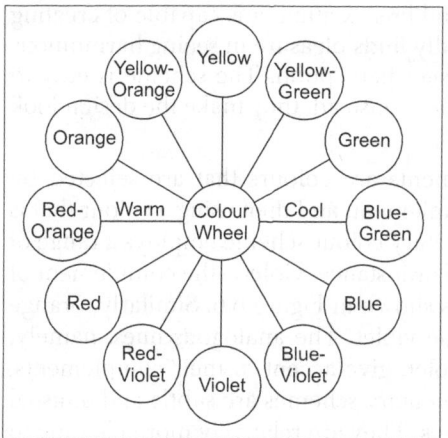

Figure 6.3 Colour wheel (*see also Colour Plate 1*)

warm colours while blue and predominantly blue are cool colours. A *colour wheel* containing all the twelve colours, as shown in Figure 6.3 (*see also Colour Plate 1*), has been created for deciding on a colour scheme.

Complementary scheme Colours opposite to each other on the wheel have nothing in common. When a colour scheme is prepared selecting one or two colours from each side of the wheel, the result is a tremendous contrast which is often successful in attracting attention. The arrangement of colours in this way is termed as a complementary scheme. Figure 6.4 shows complementary colours on the colour wheel. This colour scheme has an important place in design. Complementary colour schemes are often used in sports areas, restaurants, and children's items. It should, however, be noted that bright colours tire the eye if seen for a long time. Bright colours, therefore, should be used with care.

Two complementary colours are even more vivid when they occupy an area in equal proportions, especially when a flickering effect is used. Flickering effects are often used to grab attention in advertising, packaging, and poster and hoarding designs, so that the message may be seen from a long distance. By changing the proportion of the complementary colours, an entirely different visual effect can be achieved. Different proportions of colour help in orderly movement of the eye over the design.

Analogous scheme Colours that are adjacent to each other on the wheel are more harmonious. In a colour scheme of blue, green, and yellow-green, a bit of blue is present in all the colours, leading to loss of contrast. This type of scheme is known as an analogous scheme. Analogous colours on the colour wheel are shown in Figure 6.5.

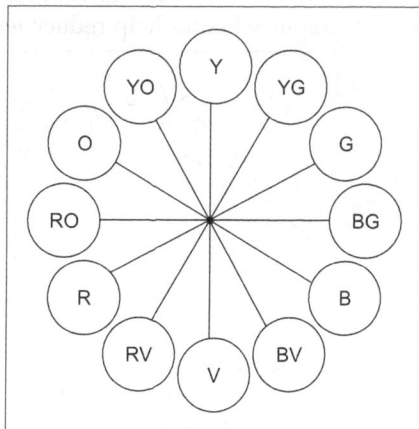

Figure 6.4 Complementary scheme

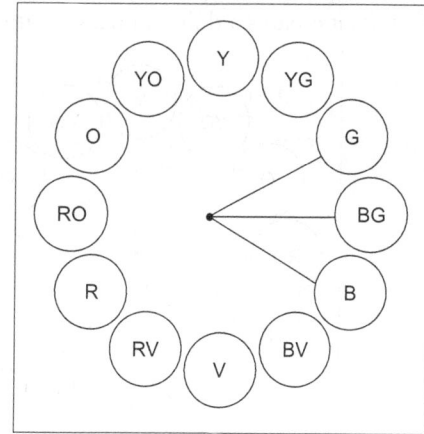

Figure 6.5 Analogous scheme

Although an analogous scheme is passive and less exciting, it is capable of creating an atmosphere of harmony. The eye undoubtedly finds pleasure in seeing harmonious colours. Here again, proportion influences design perception. The scheme is easy to create. The shades do not overshadow each other—instead, they make the design look richer and offer more nuances.

Split complementary scheme Split complements are colours that are selected by choosing a colour on the wheel, finding its complement, and then using a colour that is adjacent to the complement. A split complementary colour scheme employs a range of analogous hues 'split' from a basic key colour. For instance, violet—the complement of yellow—is split to red violet and blue violet, as shown in Figure 6.6. Similarly, orange is the split complement of blue green and blue violet. The analogous hues, namely, red violet–blue violet and blue green–blue violet, give accent to their complements, yellow and orange, respectively. Split complementary schemes are subtle and unusual rather the shocking like complementary schemes. They are relatively more pleasing to the eye, yet, they can be provocative and can attract attention in several circumstances. Split complementary schemes are similar to complementary schemes in many ways, but they offer more variety.

Triad scheme The combination of three colours that are approximately equidistant on the colour wheel is referred to as a triad scheme. To find the triad colours, we can draw an imaginary equilateral rectangle within the colour wheel and make sure each angle of the triangle points to one of the colours on the wheel. In this way, we can obtain sets of three colours as we rotate the triangle. For example, red, blue, and yellow; orange, violet, and green; red orange, red violet, and yellow green are triad colours, as shown in Figure 6.7. Triad schemes are effective when strong visual contrast is needed to retain the balance and richness of colour. If the combination of triad colours in a design looks gaudy, it can be subdued by mixing a little white or grey with the colours.

Soft scheme Colour schemes can be visualized without pure hues or with colours beyond the colour wheel. When grey is added to a pure hue, the characteristics of the colour change. Grey makes the colour soft and muddy. Like a monochromatic scheme, it creates a dull and passive atmosphere. Soft colour schemes help reduce tension and

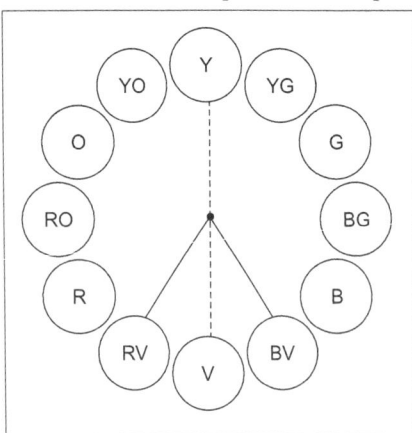

Figure 6.6 Split complementary

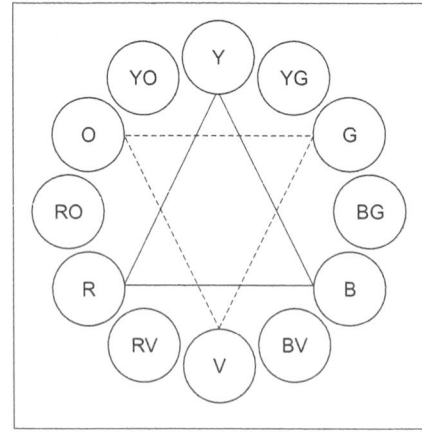

Figure 6.7 Triad scheme

create an almost dreamy mood. Such colour schemes can be effective in their own quiet way, and may, in fact, surpass in effectiveness the aggressive, overconfident colour schemes that surround them.

Dark scheme   A dark colour scheme creates a feeling of heaviness and a serious effect. It represents contrast in nature, such as that of day and night. Dark schemes are created by mixing black or some dark hue with the basic hues. It helps the basic colours retain their identity when it is used as a background. Dark colours are most visible on a light complementary. Therefore, dark colour schemes can be selected in order to give accent to design elements and type.

Monochromatic scheme   A colour scheme that uses different values and strengths of a single hue is called a monochromatic scheme. The eye easily adapts to the sensation of a single hue, and such adaptation affects the perception of other colours seen immediately afterwards. Monochromatic schemes are smooth, but less exciting as they are made of the same hue. Such arrangements are generally dull and weak, but they quietly assist the other elements of the design to come to the forefront. This effect is often achieved on printed pages by screening a colour in different percentages.

When a colour monochromatic design is converted into greyscale, the resulting image is in black and shades of grey. Such an image is also *monochromatic*. Black, for many, is not a colour. Therefore, a scheme of black and its tones is described as a *monotone*. Black on white creates the maximum contrast, and is capable of retaining certain value of colour in the form of tone and shade. In most cases, therefore, it transmits the message successfully.

Figure 6.8 illustrates various colour schemes. To see these schemes in colour, readers are advised to refer to Colour Plate 2. The background chosen for each colour scheme is in a gradient tone of black to white. This is because, all the colours, irrespective of their combinations, get maximum ascent and descent either on black or white. Also, they retain their identity and characteristics on such a background. The effect of a black and/or white background can be clearly seen if a different colour background is used for the colour schemes.

Colour Perspective

In the context of vision and visual perception, *perspective* is the way in which objects appear to the eye based on their spatial attributes or their dimension and the position of the eye relative to the objects. For example, the parallel lines of a railway track are perceived by a standing human being as meeting at a distant point in the horizon. A person standing at the corner of a building at the ground level sees each of the walls recede to an imaginary point on the horizon. The horizon itself is at the level of the viewer's eye. The level of the eye determines what a person is able to see. The size and details of an object are very clear to a person standing close to it. However, as the person moves farther away, the object begins to appear smaller and loses the details. This phenomenon is referred to as perspective.

With changing distance, colours change as much as lines and shapes do. The colours of an object, however, lose their identity much before its shape does. Faraway hills and objects not only appear smaller than similar objects closer to us, but also look bluish and merge into the sky and the hues of the ocean, with the hues deepening towards the horizon. Very bright hues, such as orange and red, seem bright at a distance, but they

122 *Art and Print Production*

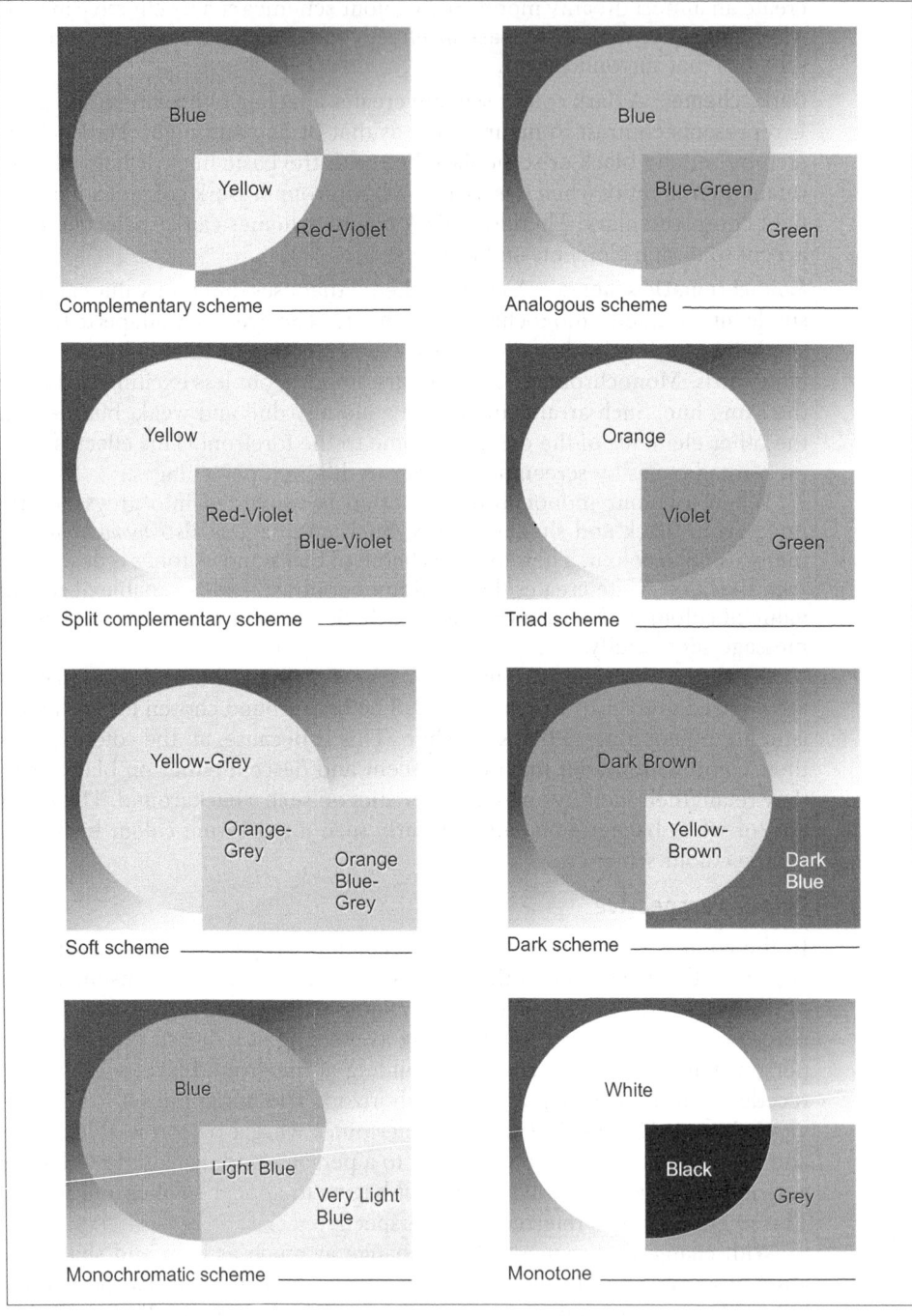

Figure 6.8 Colour schemes (*see also Colour Plate 2*)

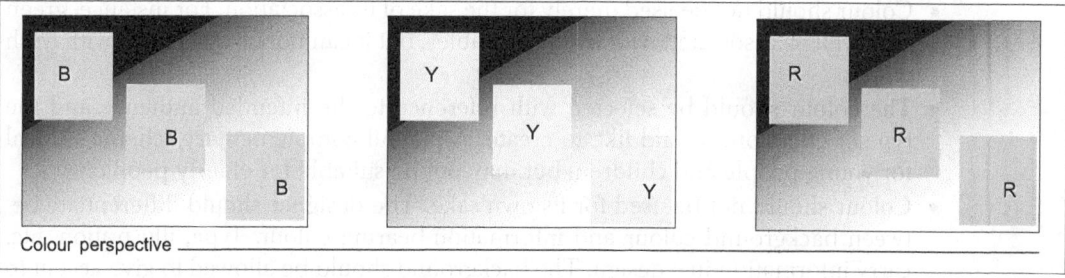

Figure 6.9 Colour perspective (*see also Colour Plate 3*)

too appear invariably lighter and hazier the farther away they are. An object does not change colour in a noticeable manner at a distance of a few feet. Therefore, colour schemes for outdoor designs are made keeping in view the optimum distance from where the design will be seen.

In reality, everything around us is three-dimensional. In graphic design, however, we work on a two-dimensional surface. Here also, the effect of distance and the illusion of three dimensions can be created by selecting the appropriate tonal value of each colour against the background. This can be further understood with the help of an example. In Figure 6.9 (*see also Colour Plate 3*), the red rectangle against the white background appears to be coming close to us. However, as the tonal value of the background is increased and gradually turned into black, the rectangle appears to go farther away from us. Similarly, the blue rectangle also appears closer on a white background and farther on a black background. The yellow rectangle, however, appears closer on a black background. These differences occur due to differences in the tonal value of various colours. Colours can thus be combined in various ways to give a three-dimensional look to a design.

To gain a clearer understanding of colour perspective for graphic designing, we can take a sheet of colour paper with 50 per cent saturation of that colour and keep on pasting same-sized rectangles cut out of vivid colour paper. This will give us a feel of varying distance in each case.

Some Guidelines

While creating a coloured graphic design, we need to keep several considerations in mind. The tools and techniques to be used for the design are the foremost consideration. Then, the mood and feeling we want to create in the design need to be decided upon. Finally, the appropriate shapes need to be selected and the colour rendition needs to be completed.

Some guidelines that should be kept in mind while combining colours for a graphic design are discussed here.

- The graphic designer should know his/her working environment and the physical characteristics of colour. The effect of colour combination may differ from a computer monitor to a printed page, from the natural environment to the photographic print, and from additive to subtractive colours.

- Colour should not be used merely for the sake of its association. For instance, green may well be associated with fresh vegetables, but it can not be associated with fresh pastry.
- The colour should be selected with reference to the intended audience and the type of effect one would like to create. A playful complementary scheme is ideal for young people and children, but may not be suitable for elderly people.
- Colour should not be used for its own sake. The designer should differentiate between background colour and information-bearing colour. Type, illustration, etc. carry information in a design. The background should be allowed to give accent to the information-bearing elements.
- Colour harmony should be maintained by using analogous or monochromatic colour schemes. Emphasis should be placed on one of the hues or tones, otherwise the design will be dull and passive.
- Colour perspective should be used when the design element is to be perceived at a distance. It may also be used to create a three-dimensional object on a two-dimensional surface.
- Too many colours, particularly when they lack common elements, kill the design. The designer should, therefore, limit the number of colours used in a design. One of the colours should be allowed to be dominant for the purpose of contrast.
- Vivid colours should be used consciously in a design. Such colours attract the viewer's attention to the page. Thus, depending on the requirements of the design, the amount of space and proportion occupied by vivid colours on a page should be controlled.
- The designer should use the most familiar colours—for example, the colours of nature—rather than unfamiliar ones to convince a conventional audience. Some audience groups may not accept a tree in pink or a fruit in gold even if these are used for creating a fantasy.
- Brown may individually be dull and boring, but its shades, which give an earthy feel, may be the right choice for background colour in a design. For instance, brown types on natural shade lucky parchment paper create a good design combination.
- Types in gold and silver are illegible on most surfaces. These colours, therefore, should be used in the background lavishly to obtain a rich look.
- While creating the effect of perspective in a design, it should be kept in mind that objects moving away lose their colour before they lose their shape.
- It should be noted that the effectiveness of a particular colour will depend on how and in what combination we use it, for no colour is inherently bad.

REPRODUCTION OF COLOUR

In our daily lives, we regularly see beautiful colours on different paper formats and derive information and enjoyment from them. We shall now try to understand the technicalities involved in reproducing colours on a printed page. Colour printing is a critical part of the design process. It is important to develop a basic understanding of the process of colour reproduction for designs used in printed matter.

In most printing processes, colour images are created on paper by using ink. The term 'colour printing' refers to the use of multiple colours on the same sheet of paper. Printing with more than one colour requires printing plates and impressions as many as the colours to be printed. This involves high costs and time and special skills are required for colour printing. These days, many affordable digital printers are available, which can print coloured matter as easily, and almost as inexpensively, as only in black. Despite the availability of these technologies, colour printing has been practical only for publications that are printed on a large scale as they involve complicated preparatory steps, know as prepress processes. We shall discuss the prepress process in detail in Chapters 8 and 9. Given below is some basic information on the types of colour used for producing printed matter.

There are three types of colours used in the production process—fake, spot, and process.

Fake Colours

Fake colour printing refers to the process of printing black and white images in two or three colours or giving a fake colour rendition to black and white images. The effect achieved by using two colours is called *duotone effect* and that achieved by using three colours is referred to as *triotone effect*. These effects may be created by using sepia and black for a nostalgic or old effect, yellow and red for sunset, and blue and green for freshness and coolness. Fake colour printing is especially useful when one wants the image to be in colour but he/she is short of the required budget.

Two techniques can be used for fake colour printing. The first technique is to print a single-colour halftone on a coloured sheet. Such figures are also known as *fake duotones*. The sheet may be a simple coloured paper. Alternatively, a flat light colour or coloured tint may be printed on a sheet. This technique is comparatively simple as no accurate registration in required at the time of printing. However, the contrast in the image is reduced because the flat background colour reduces the intensity of the highlighted areas.

The second technique is to print a duotone halftone. The duotone halftone is the most popular technique in fake colour printing. Here, two separate screen films are made from a single black and white original photograph (or a colour bitmap image converted to greyscale) by creating screen angles 30° apart. This is done to avoid creating unwanted screen patterns (moiré effect) or overprinting of dots when these images are transferred on to paper. The screened film images are exposed on to plates which are printed in two colours. It is preferable to have one of the colours in black. The second colour may be chosen depending on the mood of the image to be created. The importance of black in duotones is because it gives stronger details to the image, which often helps to enhance the mood. Fake duotone and duotone have been illustrated in Chapter 3. Readers can also refer to Colour Plate 1 to understand these effects.

The triotone effect is generally avoided for two reasons. One, it requires conversion of the black and white original into a processed colour halftone and critical registration at the time of printing. Thus, more costs are involved in printing additional colour.

126 *Art and Print Production*

Figure 6.10 Spot colour with tints (*see also Colour Plate 3*)

Figure 6.11 Spot colour in solid overlapping colours (*see also Colour Plate 3*)

Second, no significant effect can be achieved that is better than the duotone effect. Spending more money and time, in such a scenario, may be needless.

Spot Colours

The inks that printers use or mix for a specific job are called *spot colours*. Spot colours can be selected from a colour matching system or hand mixed to match a colour provided by the designer. The term 'spot colour' is also used to refer to flat colours or line reproductions in colour, which have no gradation of colours on a printed page. However, an illusion of different tones or colour hues can be created with a single spot colour by using a screen tint. Tints break the solid areas into uniform series of dots. The sizing of dots is specified as a percentage of the paper area that is covered with ink. Combining tints of more than one colour can create a number of variations. For example, different red tints create pink while red tints combined with blue make violet. Figure 6.10 (*see also Colour Plate 3*) shows a spot colour image with tints.

Overprinting is another technique to obtain multiple tones of colours by using only a limited number of flat colours. For example, yellow, orange, red, green, blue, and violet can be achieved by mixing only yellow, red, and blue in different proportions. Red overprint on yellow makes orange, blue overprint on yellow makes green, and blue overprint on red makes violet. Figure 6.11 (*see also Colour Plate 3*) shows a spot colour image created with overlapping flat colours.

Process Colour

In printing, process colour refers to the use of four specific translucent pigments—cyan, magenta, yellow, and black. These are also called process blue, process red, process yellow, and process black. Since the colours are translucent, they act as filters and blend to form other colours, creating the illusion of an original coloured continuous tone picture, as shown in Figure 6.12. Any number of colours can be

(a) Process colour in normal dot size (b) Process colour with enlarged dots

Figure 6.12 Process colour printing

achieved by combining and blending one or more of these four colours in different proportions and in different screen angles. Process colours are used to reproduce continuous tone colour images such as colour photographs, colour transparencies, paintings, and pencil drawings.

The various techniques involved in colour printing have been discussed in detail in Chapters 7 and 9. The following production facts should be kept in mind in order to control the cost of colour printing while achieving the desired printing quality.

- Fake duotone or single-colour printing on coloured paper creates a two-colour effect without any extra cost.
- Two or three solid colours with a variation of tints and overlapping give a reasonably good effect of multiple colours.
- Photographs should not be printed in a colour other than black or a very dark colour. Otherwise, the clarity of the photograph will be lost.
- To get a two-colour effect of a photograph, it should be printed in black on a light colour or through the duotone process, where two screened plates are prepared—one is printed in black and the other is printed in colour. It should be ensured that the screen angles of the plates are different.
- Care should be taken when a four-colour process is selected and there is a solid colour appearing in the same forme. It is usually better to print the solid colour separately as a fifth colour.
- Reverse printing is often risky for small type against a halftone coloured illustration. Some of the colours may spill over the type image, reducing its legibility due to misregistration or the blotting factor of the paper.
- Progressive proofs of four-colour separation jobs should be taken, especially if the material is to be printed at a place other than where it has been processed.
- Though it costs more, the results of colour printing are superior if processing is done from a coloured transparency.

- The colour original should be scanned in appropriate resolution. It should be re-touched and modified in a colour electronic prepress system (CEPS) to enhance the quality of the image.
- In order to achieve accuracy and neatness, the montage should be made on the system itself instead of assembling several films.
- Care should be taken while using screens in the case of coloured halftones that are to be printed on a rough-surfaced paper. A slightly coarser screen will work best in such situations.
- Type in colour with very thin strokes and fine serif should be avoided if the message is to be printed on newsprint or other low quality paper.

Digital images are good for reproduction. Moreover, these images do not need to be scanned. Care should, however, be taken to select high-resolution images for good results.

SUMMARY

We perceive the world in a myriad of colours. Light is the source of colour. When light strikes an object, the object may selectively absorb, reflect, or transmit certain frequencies of light. The colours of the objects that we perceive largely depend on the way these objects interact with light and reflect or transmit it to our eyes. The way we perceive colour has been discussed in detail in the chapter.

Colour is an important tool of communication. It serves a variety of functions. It is one of the elements in a design that has the maximum attraction value. The use of appropriate colours can create the right atmosphere, provide ascent and contrast to the design, add sparkle to the page, and direct the reader through the message.

Colour can cheer and bring excitement. It can stimulate, provoke, and also makes one proud. Negatively, it can also antagonize when used as a mark of protest or opposition.

We respond to colour emotionally. Our psychological reactions to colour, such as strong likes or dislikes, affect our physiological reactions, such as blood pressure, pulse rate, skin response, etc. Besides psychological and physiological responses to colour, we also exhibit some collective associations with colour. For instance, red is symbolic of luck and prosperity for people in China, while blue is associated with Lord Krishna by many people in India. Symbolic responses to colour are varied—they differ from culture to culture and from place to place.

In order to use colour efficiently in designs, one should understand the way colours are perceived and the way we respond to images in colour. In addition to this, knowledge of colour schemes and colour production is extremely important. The colour scheme for a design should be chosen in such a way that it reflects the purpose of the design. For ease in handling various colour schemes, designers use the colour wheel, which is made up of twelve identifiable colours. Combinations of various colours on the colour wheel can offer an infinite range of colours. Each one can create a different mood, meaning, and contribute to the final design.

Reproduction of colour can be done by using fake, spot, or process colours. Fake colour printing is the process of giving a fake colour rendition to a black and white image. Spot colours are the colours used or mixed by printers for a specific job. Spot colour also refers to flat colours or line reproductions in colour. Process colour refers to the use of four specific translucent pigments—cyan, magenta, yellow, and black—which can be combined and blended in different proportions to achieve a number of different colours.

A number of production-related facts have been listed at the end of the chapter, which need to be kept in mind in order to ensure that the final design is well-planned and effective.

KEY TERMS

Achromatic Colours Black, white, and grey—the colours devoid of hue.

Additive Colours Red, green, and blue are known as additive colours because these three primary hues of light can be added to obtain white light.

Analogous Scheme A scheme made of colours that are adjacent on the colour wheel. Analogous schemes appear harmonious because of the presence of colours that are close to each other on the colour wheel.

Chroma Purity and intensity of a hue.

Colour Wheel A wheel consisting of twelve distinct colours that acts as a tool that helps graphic designers in selecting or describing a colour scheme.

Complementary Scheme A scheme containing colours that are directly opposite to each other on the colour wheel. Since there is nothing common in their visual quality, they create tremendous contrast in a design.

Fake Colour A production technique that gives a fake colour rendition to a black and white image.

Flat Colours Colours that are painted or printed without gradation of tones.

Hues A synonym of colour, or the quality that distinguishes colours in the visible spectrum.

Luminous Colours Colours that are radiated by illuminated computer and TV screens.

Monochromatic Scheme A colour scheme made up of different values and strengths of a single hue, which makes the scheme soothing but, at the same time, dull.

Pigment Primaries Cyan, magenta, and yellow are the pigment primaries. These are made of natural colouring matter of animal and plant tissues. According to colour theory, they are capable of producing any colour when combined in different proportions.

Process Colours A set of ink for printing consisting of cyan, magenta, yellow, and black. These four translucent-based inks, when overlapped, create many different colours.

Reflective Colours Colours that are reflected to our eyes when light strikes an object are called reflective colours. Objects have a special ability to absorb certain wave lengths of light that fall on them and reflect others to our eyes, based on which we perceive different colours.

Spot Colours The ink used by printers that is obtained by mixing various pigments to get the desired colour.

Subtractive Colours Pigment primaries are known as subtractive colours because they produce dark colours when combined or reduce the light passing through the combination.

Tints Value of white, black, or any colour.

Translucent Pigment Colours made up of white transparent pigments. These are used to reduce the colour strength or overprinting on other colours that are seen through the translucent pigment.

Transmission Colours Colours that are seen on transparent films against light

Value Relative lightness or darkness of different areas of pictures or surface quality.

REFERENCES

Agfa Prepress Education Resources 1992, *An Introduction to Digital Colour Prepress*, USA.

Berry, Susan and Judy Martin 1991, *Designing with Colour*, B.T. Batsford, London.

Birren, Faber 1978, *Color & Human Response*, John Wiley & Sons Inc., New York.

Birren, Faber 1988, *The Symbolism of Color*, Citadel Press, New Jersey.

Chijilwa, Hideaki 1987, *Color Harmony*, Rockport Publishers, Japan.

Conover, Theodore E. 1990, *Graphic Communication Today*, West Publishing Company, St. Paul.

Dreyfuss, Henry 1972, *Symbol Sourcebook*, McGraw-Hill Book Company, New York.

Eiseman, Leatrice 2000, *Pantone Guide to Communicating with Colour*, Grafix Press Ltd, USA.

Johnson, Harold 2003, *Mastering Digital Printing*, Muska and Limpan Publishing, Cincinnati, Ohio, p. 122.

Jute, Andre, *Colors for Professional Communicators*, Batsford, UK.

Padwick, Gordon 1994, *Guide to Color Printing Techniques*, Random House Electronic Publishing, New York.

Varley, Helen (ed) 1980, *Colour*, Marshall Edition Ltd, UK.

Whelan, Bride M. 1997, *Colour Harmony*, Rockport Publishers, USA.

www.wetcanvas.com, *Colour Theory and Mixing Lesson 5*, accessed in February 2007.

REVIEW QUESTIONS

1. How does colour add value to a graphic design?
2. What are the ways in which we normally see colours?
3. Define, hue, value, and chroma.
4. Explain the colour theory of additive and subtractive colours.
5. Explain how millions of colours can be used in a graphic design.
6. Discuss colour sensation, colour preference, and colour symbolism in relation to the psychological effects of colour.
7. Discuss the characteristics of complementary, analogous, split complementary, and monochromatic colour schemes. Mention their negative and positive effects in colour designing.
8. What are the points that should be considered while choosing colours for a design?
9. Explain spot colour, fake colour, and process colour printing.
10. What are the points to be kept in mind while printing coloured images and designs?

PROJECTS

1. Collect examples that depict the following functions of colours and evaluate each sample in terms of whether it serves the intended purpose.

   Colours that: (a) cheer; (b) attract attention; (c) create the right atmosphere; (d) make one proud; (e) represent a product; (f) provide information; (g) provoke into action; and (h) antagonize the viewer.

2. Trace the outlines of the figures of additive and subtractive primaries (Figure 2.1 (a) and (b)) on a drawing sheet. Fill the space as per the colours labelled in the diagrams. Do the same on the computer screen as well and note the percentage colours used to make each primary.

3. Select an effective design in colour. Scan and copy it on your computer. Change the colour mode of one of the designs to greyscale. Now, compare the two designs. Discuss how much effectiveness is lost in the greyscale design.

   Collect samples of complementary, analogous, and monochromatic colour schemes. Write a note on the appropriateness of each sample in relation to the subject and intended target audience.

4. Collect three samples of what you consider effective use of colour symbolism. Write an evaluation of each sample.

5. Select some printed pages containing spot and process colours independently or in combination. Analyse the colours and share your opinion about their use in particular situations. Write a note on the technicalities involved in obtaining these images on paper.

6. Make a colour layout on the computer with headings, text, photos, and some graphic shapes. Prepare an artwork for the same with registration marks on it.

CHAPTER 7
Copy for Printing

Learning Objectives

After reading this chapter, you should be able to
- understand the link between the artistic process and the production process
- acquire knowledge about the three types of copy needed for print production
- handle verbal copy for typesetting and look at various ways of copy fitting and white space management
- gain insight into the development of typesetting methods and current conditions
- familiarize yourself with some common proofreading symbols and their applications
- identify, scale, crop, and mark visuals for reproduction on a printed page
- understanding the procedures involved in reproducing illustrations
- discuss the commonly used types of copy for colour printing
- gain knowledge of colour separation in print production
- decide when to use spot colour, process colour, or a combination of both for an effective print communication

INTRODUCTION

Once the three components of graphic communication—the written message, visual images, and layout—have been decided on, the next stage is that of preparing the copy for printing. This stage is the link between the artistic process and the production process. Professionals such as copy editors, typesetters, and designers are largely involved in this stage.

Three types of copy are required for printing—(i) verbal copy, that is, copy with letters and words; (ii) visual copy, that is, copy with pictures; and (iii) colour copy, or copy with images there to be printed in colour. These are handled independently or in combination to give shape to the final publication as per the requirements of the project.

In this chapter, we shall take a look at the various processes involved in preparing copy for printing.

VERBAL COPY

A manuscript that has been typed out is known as a typescript. Ideally, the original manuscript should be typed or keyed-in on a personal computer, preferably in double space with margins on the left and right sides of the paper. This enables one to mark corrections, if any, above the line concerned or on either side of the margin without diminishing the readability of the script. The idea in doing so is to provide a clean copy to the composer. The composer or typesetter is likely to introduce fresh errors or repeat lines in the case of closely spaced typed matter or an illegibly corrected/edited manuscript. Therefore, care needs to be taken to ensure that the copy marked for the typesetter is neat and legible.

Copy Marking

Once the manuscript or typescript is ready, it should be marked for typesetting. The typesetter requires some basic information pertaining to the type size, font, layout, etc. in order to typeset a document. In the case of a copy that is entered on a word processing system, instructions for display type (above 12 points) should be marked on the line itself, and directions for body copy (up to 12 points) may be marked on the margins. The designer usually marks the copy on the layout design itself. To maintain neatness, it is preferable to mark the instructions on the overlay of the artwork.

Given below is some basic information without which the typesetter will not be able to typeset a single line of copy.

Type size The type size should be marked in points.

Type font/family In case the designer is not aware of the names of the multiple type families that are in use, he/she can take the help of a type specimen catalogue or the font menu on a personal computer.

Space between the lines The space between the lines, referred to as leading, is also to be expressed in points.

Width, weight, and posture Without instructions for the kind of fonts to be used for the body text, display matter, figure captions, etc., the typesetter may typeset the matter in normal, medium, and Roman postures for the entire text.

Mixed letters or all capitals Clear instructions should be given on whether the copy needs to be typeset in all caps or mixed letters such as title case and sentence case in case the text has not been typed in the manner desired.

Line length The required line length should be indicated in picas, drawing a horizontal arrow above the typed copy.

Space formatting The designer needs to mention whether the text should be justified, left aligned, right aligned, or centered. Here again, without instructions, the typesetter might compose the text in the justified format.

Special instructions Instructions such as indenting, drop letters, space between the paragraphs, letter spacing, line to line composing, etc. should be clearly specified.

Copy editors use some standard symbols to provide instructions to typesetters. Some of these are displayed in Exhibit 7.1. These symbols are used in order to mark the copy with fewer written instructions and to avoid confusion. It should be kept in mind that type composition costs both money and time. A copy that is improperly marked and poorly-organized results in the print buyers having to incur high costs.

Exhibit 7.1 Common copyediting symbols

Instruction	Symbolic marks	Instruction	Symbolic marks
1. Set in boldface	Art and Production (wavy underline)	7. Centred	\ Art and Production /
2. Set in italics	Art and Production (underline)	8. Delete	(Art and Production) circled with deletion mark
3. Set in capitals	Art and Production (double underline)	9. Start a new paragraph	¶ Art and Production
4. One em indenting	☐ Art and Production	10. Change to small letter	Art and /production
5. Flush left	⊢Art and Production		
6. Flush right	Art and Production⊣		

Copy Fitting

Copy fitting is the process of ensuring that a block of text is not too long or too short to fit the space allotted for it in a document. Another term used for copy fitting is *text fitting*.

Before sending a copy for typesetting, another point a communicator should bear in mind is the fact that the space occupied by typed copy and printed types is different. He or she thus needs to estimate the space that the typed copy would occupy after composition. Sometimes, the communicator has to restrict the verbal copy within a pre-specified area. This is especially true in case of advertising layouts, where the copy must fit the area provided on the layout.

In light of these considerations, one needs to decide on the word limit for the written message. If one exceeds this limit, he/she may have to change the layout to accommodate the typeset copy or delete some portion of the copy. This would require reconstruction of the copy and re-typesetting of some parts. For this, the typesetter usually levies extra charges. To avoid such extra monetary and time costs, one should engage in copy fitting before the material is sent for typesetting.

Copy may be fitted within a given space either manually or digitally. We shall take a look at both these processes in this section.

Digital copy fitting

Modern typesetting methods allow us to fit copy by enlarging or reducing it to a fraction of the original point size and by controlling the space between words, letters, and lines. Expansion and condensation also help a great deal. While working on Microsoft Word or any other layout software, one may have to deal with overset or underset problems as one proceeds along the document. Various other software are also available, which have special features that help to manage overset or underset text, that is, text that cannot be accommodated within the allotted space and text that leaves a lot of extra space, respectively. To arrive at a satisfactory layout, the designer or typesetter may have to try one or a combination of the various methods of copy fitting that are available.

The verbal copy may be adjusted on the computer to fit the space provided in the layout in several ways. Some of these are discussed in this section.

Shrink the page to fit   Word processing software has a 'shrink to fit' option to compress matter that flows into two pages so that it can be fitted on one page. However, it does not work very well in case the text matter is just slightly less than two pages. The reason is that Microsoft Word accomplishes the shrinking by reducing the size of the font in the document. Since it is limited to half-point reduction, the compressed matter still flows to the second page. This option is thus only useful in case the text is slightly over a page.

Re-word the text   Editing the text is the prerogative of the copywriter or copy editor. To fit the text in the design, one may use his/her discretion and eliminate repetition, use abbreviations, break words, or combine two adjacent paragraphs into one, as the situation demands. As long as readability is not compromised, the text can be edited to fit the layout.

Reduce the font size   Sometimes, reducing the size of the font in the entire text is the easiest and best thing to do. Type faces having a larger x-height can easily be reduced by a point or half without compromising on legibility.

Care should be taken to avoid having the body text in different font sizes in a single document. In other words, it is not a good idea to increase or decrease the font size of a certain section of the body text in order to make the matter fit on a page. This will make the page look imbalanced and awkward.

Space between paragraphs   The space between body text paragraphs rarely needs to be the same as the distance between two lines. A gap of half a line or 6 points can be plenty. The designer does not need to limit himself/herself with the built-in steps for changing the space before or after a paragraph. He/she can type in the increments or reductions up to about one-tenth of a point. Widow or orphan words, that is, single words at the end of a paragraph that appear at the end or beginning of a page can be avoided by adjusting the space between the paragraphs. This can also be done by adjusting character or line spacing.

Space between lines (leading)   Auto line spacing is apt for some fonts and results in a pleasing appearance. However, when the designer has to restrict the text within a given space, auto line spacing may not be the best choice. Instead, he/she can modify the space between the lines as per the requirement. Microsoft Word and most layout software allow the user to adjust line spacing in increments of a tenth of a point, so that he/she has considerable control over the spacing. Line spacing that differs by a fraction of a point in different paragraphs or text blocks are undetectable and help the designer to fit the copy within the given space.

Inter-character spacing   This is one of the most powerful ways to compress text. Here, one has the options of both default condensed setting and control setting of 0.1 point increment. Compression of the latter kind is imperceptible, and can create dramatic differences in line break.

Width of the font   Expansion and condensation of the font used is also a popular technique used for fitting the text within the given area. However, there is a limit to such compression or expansion, beyond which it becomes noticeable. A designer can change the width of the font between 0.10 to 12.70 points without the difference becoming too apparent. Care should, however, be taken to change the font width for the entire document or, at least, for a discrete block of text.

From the present discussion, it may appear that copy fitting is quite a manageable task, especially when one is working on a Word Document. However, it must be kept in mind that we may run into problems in manipulating or altering the text if the word document is used in other layout software. Such a risk is higher in the case of text in a Word file that has been formatted heavily or combined with charts and diagrams. Therefore, it is advisable to use the command of the respective software in fitting the text.

White space management White space management ensures that the matter is appropriately displayed within the given space. Dedicated software with various features are available to manage overset or underset text. These are known as variable data publishing software. Some of them offer the option of setting up the text matter in such a way that it fills up the allotted space. The text can be made big or small enough to occupy the entire area that is reserved for it.

PAGEFLEX design solutions allow sophisticated variable data designs in which elements on a page can be flexed and repositioned on the basis of designer-specified criteria to accommodate varying amounts of personalized content. For example, when the length or size of custom content is different from the size of the box the content is flowing into, the box can expand in either the horizontal or vertical direction (or both), to accommodate the content. Designer-specified rules determine the maximum and minimum dimensions, as well as behaviour of the surrounding elements on the page. The result is the ability to define sophisticated templates that accommodate a wide range of variable content by flexing the page layout.

Traditional method

Many a time, the traditional method of copy fitting can be quite handy. In the traditional method of copy fitting, the space the copy will occupy when it is set in a specific type size and line length is estimated before marking the hand-written or typed copy for typesetting. This way, if the area within which the matter needs to be typeset and the type size, spacing details, etc. are known, the number of words to be written can be estimated. It should, however, be noted that this calculation works in the case of normal type only, and not for expanded or condensed text.

There are several traditional methods of copy fitting. We shall now discuss one of the methods for generating very rough estimates for body copy by word counting for a long copy. This method may be used for copy fitting in books, magazines, promotional literature, or newspapers.

Text matter We already know that 12 points are equal to 1 pica and 72 points or 6 picas are equal to one inch. An em is a square body of type. An average English word inclusive of one after-word space is of 3 ems while an average Devanagari word with one after-word space is of 2.5 ems. Using this information, we can calculate the depth of a copy when the total manuscript pages, type size, and line length are specified. The following steps can be used for such calculations:

1. Count the total number of words in the manuscript.
2. Convert the measure, that is, line length, into ems of the size of type to be composed.

3. Find out the average number of words that can be set in one line by dividing the line length (ems) by 3 or 2.5, as the case may be.
4. Divide the total number of words in the manuscript by the number of words per line to get an estimate of the total number of lines in the composed copy.
5. Multiply the number of lines by the type being composed to obtain the depth of the copy in points. This may be converted into picas or inches by dividing the depth obtained by 12 or 72, respectively.

Example 1 3,040 words are to be set in 9 point type and 18 pica line length with 2 point leading. What will be the galley depth in picas?

Solution Total no. of words in the manuscript = 3,040
Line length in ems $= (18 \times 12) / 9 = 24$ ems of 9 points
Average no. of words $= 24/3 = 8$ words per line
Total no. of lines $= 3,040/8 = 380$
Required depth $= \{380 \times (9 + 2)\}/12 = 348.4$ or 348 pica

In case the area is given, the type size and leading are known, and the number of words to be written for this area is to be estimated, the calculation is carried out backward. An example is provided below.

Example 2 How many words should be written for an area of 21 pica × 260 pica if 11 point type size with 2 point leading of Devanagari type is used?

Solution Depth of the copy = 260 pica
No. of lines that can be accommodated $= (260 \times 12)/(11 + 2) = 240$
Line length in ems $= (21 \times 12)/11 = 22.9$ or 23
Average no. of words per line $= 23/2.5 = 9$
Total no. of words $= 9 \times 240 = 2160$

Display type Display type serves the purpose of a visual. Designers mostly provide accurate instructions for lettering in terms of size, style, etc., keeping in mind the occasion and audience for the printed matter. Instructions for the typesetter need to be marked clearly on the protective flap or in the margin of the layout.

The display type can be decided on in many ways. Some type experts recommend the unit count system for the 26 letters of the Roman script. The communicator must bear in mind the width of each character for both small and capital letters. In the case of the Devanagari type, this method is much more difficult because of half letters, *matras*, and full letters. Therefore, it is better to take the help of a type specimen book. Headlines may be approximately written in freehand. The size of the type can be determined with the help of a pica scale. The letters can be traced if a specimen in the same size is available. Another option is to trace the letters of the headlines in any size and then enlarge or reduce them by photo-copying them to fit in any convenient size. If the headline is written in instant lettering, it will be very accurate because the instant lettering sheet has details such as the display type size, style, etc.

The jargon and calculations involved in copy fitting may give one a feeling that it is a very difficult process. With a little practice, however, one will find it very simple and will feel confident enough to practice copy-fitting of printed material competently. This will not only make the job easy but also save a lot of time and money.

Typesetting

The creative planning of any printed material starts with production planning and solving the problems of time and cost. These are considerably controlled by using various techniques in typesetting. Keeping this in mind, advertising agencies, publishing houses, institutions, and many government and public sector undertakings have started acquiring in-house typesetting instruments such as DTP software, IBM PCs, and electronic typewriters. These days, composing or typesetting is no longer the job of a composer or typesetter alone. Rather, the art director and designer, who prepare the camera-ready copy or computer file for the offset process, also handle the typesetting aspect. Modern typesetting machines are user friendly and can be used with ease by creative people. The speed and sophistication of computer typesetting have brought about momentous changes in the printing world and the information dissemination process. In the last century, the speed of typesetting has increased incredibly from 2,000 characters per hour to two million characters per hour. Computers; modems; and co-axial, facsimile, and satellite transmission have brought about a revolution in typesetting. So fast is the speed of this development that, by the time this book is published, far more advanced typesetting methods might show up in the market.

Until recently, hot metal composing was the predominant typesetting method. Its use is now waning as the letterpress process of printing is becoming obsolete. Cold typesetting has replaced hot metal composing because of its compatibility with offset and other modern printing processes.

With the growing popularity of desktop publishing in recent times, many of the traditional clients of typesetters have begun to produce their own newsletters and advertising and other print material instead of contracting the job to typesetters. Many organizations and businesses, however, still continue to outsource this job to typesetters and other pre-print service providers.

Background and development

Typesetting is the arrangement of individual letters in sequence. Typesetting procedures changed drastically during the last 40 years of the twentieth century. As discussed, for hundreds of years, type was set with metal printing elements. This was called 'hot type' because molten lead was used to manufacture individual letters, which were then set into complete words, sentences, and paragraphs. At first, the molten lead letters were set by hand, one letter or space at a time. The letters were mirror images of actual letters so that, when printed, they would read correctly. The set type was locked into a frame and ink applied to it, and the paper was printed directly from the type.

Intertype was the first mechanical typesetting machine. Commonly known as Linotype, it was first used in commercial printing in 1886. Intertype typesetting was also a hot type method, but it sped up typesetting considerably. Typesetting machines became faster and more sophisticated for the next 80–90 years, but operated on the same principle as the one Johann Gutenberg used in the 1400s when he invented the movable type.

Cold typesetting came into widespread use in the 1970s. Unlike hot type, which is three dimensional, 'cold type' is two dimensional. Cold type may be any of a variety of methods in which photographic principles are used to create an image on specially treated paper. In cold typesetting, as a typesetter keys in the letters, the machine generates photographic images of the letters and reproduces those images on photosensitive paper or film. The images are arranged on a layout sheet and the printer photographs them to make a film negative from which a printing plate is then made. All cold typesetting begins with keying in of the text on a keyboard like that of a typewriter. The data inputting may be done by a typesetter. These days, it is done by authors as they compose the text with word processors.

Cold type has undergone several changes in both data storage and output. The first phototypesetting equipment stored the text on paper tape. The tape was punched using a special keyboard, and this specially-punched encoded tape drove the typesetting equipment, sending instructions about typeface, size, and appearance of the set type.

The next development in phototypesetting brought equipment with powerful software, photo fonts, and magnetic data storage. This was actually the first true photo-typesetting machinery, and in the 1990s, was still in use in many typesetting operations.

The next generation of cold type created characters from digital information instead of a photo negative. The output was produced on photosensitive paper or film. This equipment became the standard in the 1980s. Subsequent generations of equipment employed various laser technologies for outputting. These technologies do not fall under phototypesetting because they do not employ photographic technology and the output is obtained on regular paper rather than photosensitive paper.

Current conditions

The application of electronics and computers has moved the industry to digitized imaging, where material is printed directly from the computer to paper or a printing plate. More typesetting companies are now offering extensive pre-printing services, including digital colour scanning with electronic dot generation, electronic colour page composition, electronic page layout, and off-press colour proofing.

Digitized typesetting opened up a world of possibilities for interface technology—the ability of two computers to communicate with one another. Some experts in the typesetting industry had predicted that, by the early 2000s, 50 to 75 per cent of typesetting would be accomplished via interface technology, and this prediction is proving to be true.

Data interfacing   An interface is a boundary across which two systems communicate. An interface might be a hardware connector used to link to other devices, or a convention used to allow communication between two software systems. Data may be transferred through direct or remote interfacing. Some commonly used modes of digital transmission are discussed in this section.

Direct interfacing A direct interface includes a cable connection with other computers such as word processors or personal computers, optical character recognition systems, or media conversion. Discussed below are some common software for data conversion.

Optical character recognition (OCR) It is basically a high-speed scanning device that converts typewritten and typeset copy into digital information. Once the characters are scanned, these are saved in a word format which can be manipulated like any other direct entry text of the computer. Not long ago, it was a slightly costly device. The software was loaded into a computer to accomplish the job. These days, inbuilt flatbed scanners are available with OCR systems. With the gradually dropping prices of computer hardware with various facilities, this system has become handy for many typesetters, especially for those who have to handle long text.

The OCR system also has some shortcomings. The scanner sometimes introduces fresh errors in the text. It may not recognize the character from an unlearned original typeset copy. As a result, it will produce the output as it has interpreted it, thereby introducing errors in the documents. For instance, the scanner may read an 'i' as an 'l' if the dot of the 'i' is slightly merged into its main stroke.

Adobe InCopy It is a professional word processing software product made by Adobe Systems. It is tightly integrated with Adobe InDesign and the most recent version is Adobe InCopy CS2.

InCopy is primarily used by newspapers and magazines to edit and style copy. The software contains such features as spell check and allows users to change and edit words or paragraphs. Another key feature is the ability to apply style sheet to paragraphs or words. In addition, the software automatically measures the length of a story in column inches.

Unlike consumer word processing products, InCopy is not designed for printing on traditional desktop printers. Instead, it is linked to Adobe's own desktop publishing program—InDesign—which allows the user to design, lay out, and print the copy as part of a finished product.

Adobe FrameMaker It is a desktop publishing application that is popular for large documents. It is produced by Adobe Systems. Although (or perhaps because) FrameMaker has evolved slowly in recent years, it maintains a strong following among professional technical writers. As an all-in-one package optimized for technical writers, FrameMaker remains unrivalled. However, for deployment in high-end technical publication departments, native XML authoring systems are starting to replace it.

Remote interfacing Remote interfacing refers to telecommunication through a modem. A computer's digital signal must be converted to an analogue signal before it can be transmitted over a traditional phone line. This requires the use of a modem, which modulates a digital (converts to analogue) and demodulates a signal (converts to digital).

Many different types of digital transmissions are available today. The most widely used ones are Integrated Service Digital Network (ISDN), Digital Subscriber Line (DSL), and Asymmetric Digital Subscriber Line (ADSL). These services, all offered by telecom companies, provide varying speeds of transmission and are chosen according to the data transfer requirements and budget.

Interfacing, regardless of the method, requires appropriate software for conversion of data from word processing to typesetting equipment. Not all word processing programs and typesetting equipment, however, are compatible, requiring the client and the typesetter to coordinate their work in advance of transmission. Typesetters do not ordinarily have the capability to convert all of the hundreds of word processing programs to their typesetting programs. A third-party service bureau can, however, handle most conversions.

The technological advances in typesetting have enabled publishers to transmit manuscripts to keyboarders or typesetters in other countries where they need to pay lower wages, thereby cutting publishing costs. Use of satellite and other technology is expected to further expand the options available to publishers.

Proofreading

The quality of printed literature largely depends on error-free typesetting. Proofreading plays a major role in ensuring that the proofs are free of errors. The need for proofreading has remained the same despite the technological revolution in print communication.

When the material for printing is typeset or keyed in on a computer, the first impression of this material or rough copy of the printed matter is known as a *proof.* In the letterpress days, this was known as a *galley proof.* The proofreader marks his/her instructions on the margins of these proofs. The instructions pertain to the required corrections in the proofs—letters or words to be deleted, inserted, or transposed; changes in spellings, punctuation, capitalization, word division, etc.

The marked proof goes back to the typesetting room, where the changes marked by the proofreader are entered, and a new proof, called a 'revise', is sent to the proof room along with the marked proof (sent earlier). Comparing the new proof with the old one, the proofreader checks for corrections and for possible new errors. There may be second, third, or even more revised proofs, if deemed necessary for ensuring accuracy.

Proofing of typeset jobs is an extremely vital step in the production process. A poorly proofread job with errors could necessitate a reprint, with the client having to incur the additional costs. All typesetting requires internal as well as client proofing levels. It is the client's responsibility to verify the accuracy of the type, size, and composition. Once the client signs on the proof, any errors that were missed during proofing become the client's responsibility. Any errors made by the printer or typesetter that are deviations from the approved proof will be corrected by them at no charge

Exhibit 7.2 Proofreading marks—a sample

In text	Margin	Meaning	Correction
Corrections			
(Art and Print Production)	U	change to roman	Art and Print Production
Art and Print Production	//	change to italic	*Art and Print Production*
Art and Print Production	~~~	change to boldface	**Art and Print Production**
Art and Print Production	≡	change to caps	ART AND PRINT PRODUCTION
Art and Print Production	/	change to lowercase	art and print production
Art and Print Production	=	change to small caps	ART AND PRINT PRODUCTION
Art/and/Print/Production	#≡	space evenly	Art and Print Production
Art and Print/Production	#	add space	Art and Print Production
Art / and / Print / Production	#	reduce space	Art and Print Production
Art and Print Produ c/t/i/o/n	⌒	close up completely	Art and Print Production
Art and Print[Production	[	turn line here	Art and Print Production
Art and Print Produc tion]	]	take back	Art and Print Production
Art and Print/Production	⌐	start new paragraph	Art and Print Production
Art and Print⌒Production	↶	no paragraph	Art and Print Production
Art and Print Prodcu̯tion	⌢	transpose letters	Art and Print Production
Art and Print(Prod)	○	no abbreviation	Art and Print Production
⌊Art and Print Production	□⌊	indent 1 em	Art and Print Production
\Art and Print/ \Production/	\ /	center	Art and Print Production
Art and Print Production⌋	⌐	move flush left	Art and Print Production
⌊Art and Print Production	⌐	move flush right	Art and Print Production
Art and ~~printing~~ Production	Print ∧	subsitute	Art and Print Production
Deletions			
Art and Print Productions/	ℓ	delete (take out)	Art and Print Production
Art and Print Prod/uction	ℓ	delete and close up	Art and Print Production
Art ~~and~~ Print Production	....	leave as printed	Art and Print Production
Art/and Print Production	ℓ #	delete and leave space	Art and Print Production

Contd

142 *Art and Print Production*

Exhibit 7.2 *Contd*

In text	Margin	Meaning	Correction
Additions			
Art and Print Productin	on/	letter	Art and Print Production
and Print Production	Art/	word	Art and Print Production
Art and Print Production	,/	comma	Art and Print Production,
Art and Print Production	;/	semicolon	Art and Print Production;
Art and Print Production	:/	colon	Art and Print Production:
Art and Print Production	./	full point	Art and Print Production.
Art and Print Productions	'/	apostrophe	Art and Print Production's
Art and Print Production	" / "	quote and unquote	"Art and Print Production"
Production oriented	/-/	hyphen	Production-oriented
Art and Print Production	?/	question mark	Art and Print Production?
Art and Print Production	!/	exclamation point	Art and Print Production!
Art and Print Production	(/)/	parentheses	(Art and Print Production)
Art and Print Production	[/]/	brackets	[Art and Print Production]
Art and Print Production	⊢/	em-dash	Art and Print Production—
Art and Print Production	…/	ellipsis	Art and Print Production…

For proofreading, one needs to memorize the proofreading marks shown in Exhibit 7.2 and remember the following points:

- Proofs that are being corrected should be marked up in the margin as well as in the text.
- The proof page should be divided into two imaginary halves. Mistakes appearing on the left half of the page should be marked on the left margin and those appearing on the right half of the page should be indicated on the right margin.
- Marking should be done in sequence from left to right against the line on which the error occurs and each marking should be followed by a stroke(/).
- In case of extensive corrections, the text should be re-written legibly. Another option is to mark 'see copy' against the concerned passage and cross it out.
- Proofs should be marked in pencil or coloured pens. The queries should be encircled and the instructions should preferably be marked using a different coloured pen.

Exhibit 7.3 shows a sample proofread page with instructions for the typesetter.

> **Exhibit 7.3   Proofread copy—a sample**
>
> COLOUR SYMBOLISM
>
> Blue is the colour of the sky and the sea. It has a calming effect. It gives the sense of infinity because of the vastness of the sea, sky, and ocean. It also symbolizes truth, intellect, loyalty, and spotless reputation. Blue is the colour of security and authority. That's why most banks use it for their corporate identity programms. Manufacturers sell products associated with cleanliness and hygine. Cool blue colour negatively tends to employ distance, detachment, and aloofness in graphic design. It comes next to red in terms of frequency of use. Dark blue connotes industriousness, efficiency, and authority whereas negatively night and the stormy sea, doubt and discouragement.
>
> Black is the colour of night and death, evil and sin, and sickness and negation, witch craft and occult. It is the colour infinite and endless space, in which all thing lose their distinction just as all colours and all light lose their distinction in black. It is popular among artists for its association with wealth and elegance. Black in advertising denotes beauty, sophistication, and exclusiveness.

VISUAL COPY

Visual copy for printing includes photographs, drawings, paintings, borders, graphic shapes, etc. We have learned to improve the idea and content of the visual in Chapter 3. We shall now discuss how a visual is developed from an idea to the final image on a printed page.

These days, visuals for printing are largely processed digitally. However, even now, many images are drawn or painted on paper or photographed by conventional and digital methods. Irrespective of the physical form of the visuals used in a design, the designer needs to learn about some basic processes involved in preparing visuals for printing.

Cropping and Scaling

Illustrations should be altered to make them proportionate to the size in which they need to be reproduced. This can be done by cropping, enlarging, and/or reducing the original image. In most cases, especially in the case of rectangular continuous tone illustrations, trimming some part of the illustration may be necessary to obtain a proportionate image. This is called *cropping*.

Scaling of an illustration refers to the process of enlarging or reducing the original picture to a predetermined proportionate size. If a picture is enlarged in width, it will be proportionately enlarged in depth also. This is done through the printer's camera or through computer image manipulation. The designer or the photo editor can calculate the scaling at the time of preparation of layout and before sending it for processing. Several methods of scaling are available, including digital methods. Some of these are—slide rule, size finders, percentage chart, mathematical calculation, diagonal line, and dragging the software's crop tool. Learning at least two simple methods from the ones discussed in this section may prove handy even for digitized page planning.

Mathematical method

Let us understand the mathematical method of scaling with the help of a few examples.

Example 3 A photograph measuring 16 cm × 20 cm is to be reduced to 10 cm width. Find out the depth.

Solution The calculation is based on a simple equation, as shown below:

$$\frac{16 \text{ (Old Width)}}{20 \text{ (Old Depth)}} = \frac{10 \text{ (New Width)}}{x \text{ (New Depth)}} \text{ or } 16x = 200 \text{ or } x = 200/16 \text{ or } 12.5 \text{ cm}$$

Example 4 If a photograph of 30 cm × 18 cm is to be fitted in an area of 16 cm × 12 cm, what will be the new proportionate size?

Solution The above situation is slightly difficult because the original and new dimensions are not in the same proportion. Therefore, to achieve proportion, the photograph should be cropped from one side. How do we decide which side—width or depth—to crop it from? Since the width is to be made shorter than the depth, we shall have to crop the original width.

$$\frac{x \text{ (Old Width)}}{18 \text{ (Old Depth)}} = \frac{16 \text{ (New Width)}}{12 \text{ (New Depth)}} \text{ or } 12x = 288 \text{ or } x = 24 \text{ cm}$$

Therefore, the cropped area = 30 − 24 cm = 6 cm.

Diagonal line method

The diagonal line method is very simple. It is not, however, very accurate. It is popular among designers because it helps them visualize the area of content that will occupy the space, when enlarged or reduced. The measurement can be done on the back of the photograph or on the overlay sheet.

In order to increase or reduce a rectangular image, one can draw a diagonal line across two corners of the rectangle. The rectangle can then be scaled, that is, a smaller or bigger rectangle can be formed by drawing lines parallel to the adjacent sides of the original rectangle from the diagonal line proportionate to the original, as shown in Figure 7.1.

In case the shape of an illustration is other than a rectangle or is without any precise edge, such as a vignette, a rectangle may be drawn through its extreme lines, as shown in Figure 7.2. The figure can then be made bigger or smaller, as explained in the previous figure. The rectangle determined by this process is adequate for the purpose of the layout. In other words, at the time of preparing the layout, this area can be taken as the exact area that needs to be left for that particular illustration.

If the area for an illustration in the layout is predetermined and the proportions of the illustration are found unsuitable, the shape of the original must be altered by

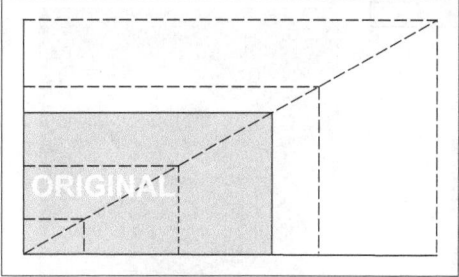
Figure 7.1 Scaling of a rectangle

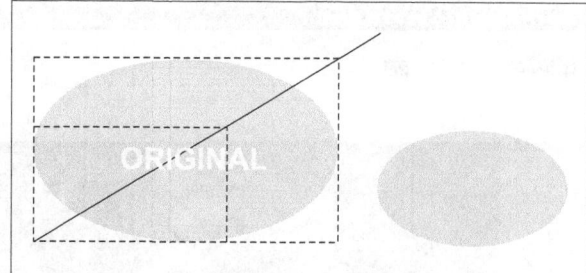
Figure 7.2 Scaling of an irregular-shaped figure

cropping the image to make it proportionate to the required illustration. To determine the amount of space to be cropped, one can draw a rectangle of the required dimensions on the overlay of the original illustration and then draw the diagonal line for that rectangle. This diagonal will intersect the dimensions of the original at a point. A right-angle line can be drawn from that point to form a new rectangle, which is proportionate to the required rectangle. The remaining portion may be cropped from the original, as shown in Figure 7.3. The area to be cropped may be taken from either of the sides, or partly from one side and partly from the other, depending on which side and how much

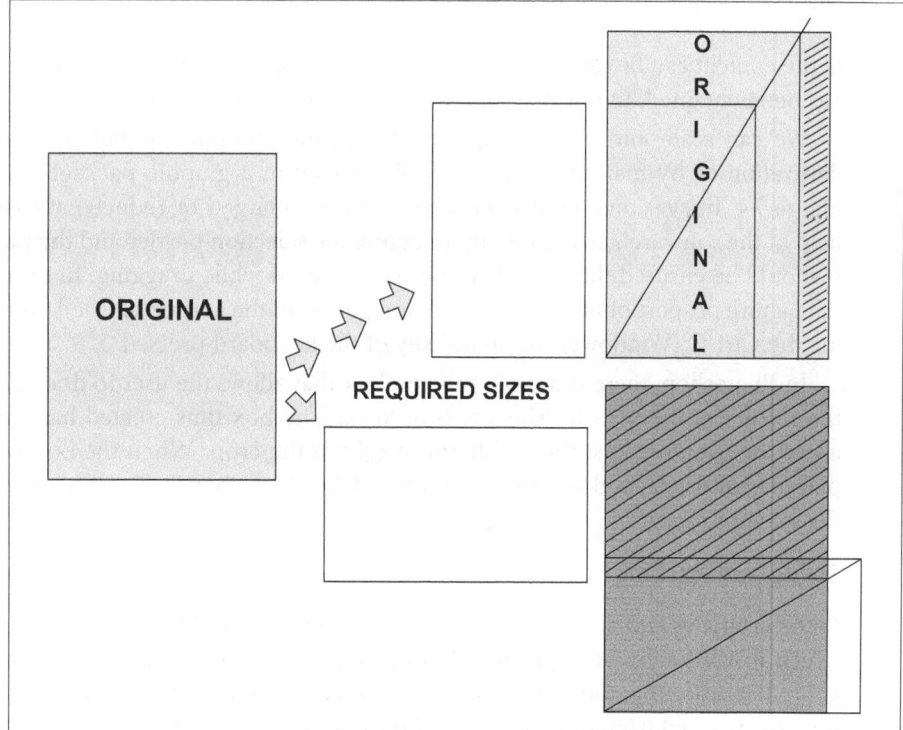
Figure 7.3 Scaling and cropping an original to a predetermined size

146 *Art and Print Production*

Figure 7.4 Digital cropping and enlarged scaling

of the content can be sacrificed. Once a figure that is proportionate to the required size has been obtained, the printer can then reduce it to fit the required area.

We can scale and crop images at will on the computer either by scanning the illustration or by manipulating the outline shape in a graphic package, as shown in Figure 7.4. Images on a computer screen can be enlarged or reduced at ease with the help of the software's sizing tool by dragging the selection border and the picture area. It should be ensured that the picture is not distorted while dragging. In order to make the picture proportionate, it should be dragged from the corner-selected node by keeping the Ctrl/C (Windows) command key of the keyboard pressed.

In Photoshop, there is a tool in the toolbar that allows the user to drag a box across the section of the scan he/she wants to keep. The box thus created has handles that allow the user to adjust the width and height of the crop. When the box is sized and placed over the desired section, a double click inside the box (not on a handle) performs the selected crop.

Sizing and Marking

Once cropping and scaling are over, the illustration should be marked in the size in which it will finally be reproduced. To avoid confusion for the camera operation or computer scanning, the size should be marked in either width or depth. Usually, an arrow is marked from one end of the image to the other end, with the size marked in cm or pica accompanying the word 'enlarge' or 'reduce', as shown in Figure 7.5.

Figure 7.5 Sizing and marking to enlarge/reduce an image

Rectangular continuous tone illustrations should be marked for a slightly bigger size (1 or 2 mm), so that when they are stripped onto the flat, they conveniently occupy the area provided in the artwork. Sometimes, screens and tints are also marked on the illustration. Screens are always specified on the basis of the quality of paper on which the illustration is to be printed and the process of printing being used. Generally, finer screens are required for smooth surface paper and coarse screens are required for coarse surface paper. The printer may be consulted in case one needs advice on these issues.

Illustrations are also marked in percentage. The marking is very simple. If we divide the required width by the original width and multiply this figure by 100, we obtain the percentage of reduction. For example, if the original size of a 10 cm × 14 cm image is to be reduced to 7 cm width, the percentage of reduction will be (7 ÷ 10) × 100 = 70%. In the same way, if an image of size 5 cm × 9 cm is to be enlarged to 12 cm width, the required enlargement will be (12 ÷ 5) × 100 = 240%. Such re-sizing can be done through digital cameras also, as all digital cameras are programmed for enlargements and reductions in percentage.

Scanned images can also be enlarged or reduced in percentage on a computer. Here, the percentage should be specified in either width or depth, so that it will be in exact proportion.

Visuals can be placed within a pre-determined shape (rectangle, ellipse, polygon, etc.) on a layout. The masking command of the layout software hides the content of the picture that falls outside this pre-specified shape, as shown in Figure 7.6.

Computerized scaling and cropping can help a great deal in reducing the problems of processing visual images. The following points should be kept in mind while cropping, scaling, and sizing visual images.

Figure 7.6 Cropping a figure to fit a pre-determined shape

- A picture should be cropped and the extra elements in the application used to create the picture should be deleted before placing it in a page layout program. Anything that is cropped in a page layout program still requires the printer to calculate parts that are no longer visible.
- Excessive scaling down of a bitmapped graphic should be avoided once it has been placed it in a page layout program. A scaled-down bitmapped graphic retains all of its digital information and can cause long print times with no appreciable benefit.
- Bitmapped images should be scaled and simplified and/or manipulated in the program used to create them before the image is placed on the page. A good rule of thumb is to re-size the pictures in the image editing program or while scanning if they need to be scaled up or down by more than 20–25 per cent.

Reproduction of Illustrations

For the purpose of mechanical reproduction, there are two basic types of visual copy—line copy and continuous tone copy. Line copy will remain a line copy when reproduced, but a continuous tone copy will result in a halftone when reproduced.

Line reproduction Illustrations which can be reproduced in flat colours without using any dots are called *line art*. A line art illustration may be an outline drawn with a brush or pen and ink or a solid area that produces strong contrast. The process of reproduction of line illustrations is referred to as *line reproduction*.

Traditionally, for line reproduction, a black and white original is placed on the copy-board of the process camera. A contrast film is placed at the back of the camera behind the lens. A high-contrast negative (opaque and transparent) is made on exposing the film, which is used for the line reproduction plate.

Digitally, line reproductions are created on draw programs such as CorelDraw, Illustrator, etc., which form a vector image. Line images drawn or created on paper are scanned into an application for the purpose of reproduction. The image so obtained is a bitmap image. Vector images are excellent for line reproduction as they retain the sharpness of the original even when it has been resized or manipulated. Care should be taken in case of scanned line images.

Halftone reproduction Continuous tone illustrations such as photographs, wash paintings, and pencil drawings should be reproduced by breaking the image into dots. The original is called continuous tone, because the image is formed by various tones blending with one another. Such illustrations cannot really be carried to another surface from a printing plate unless they are separated as image and non-image surfaces.

Each of the tiny dots of the image surface will carry ink, which makes an impression on paper. As an optical illusion, small and widely spaced dots will appear light whereas big and closely spaced dots will appear dark.

The dot pattern is obtained by placing a 'screen' in the back of the camera between the lens and the film or generated by a computer's film outputting device such as the imagesetter. It is then transferred to the plate. Screens can be coarse or fine, depending on the quality of reproduction required. The finer the screen, the better is the result. The screen value is measured in terms of the number of dots per linear inch (lpi). Up to 85 lpi, line screens can be considered as coarse screens; above that, they can be considered as fine screens. Figure 7.7 shows a halftone image in different screen values.

Standard screens are made up of small squares and circles (opaque and transparent), which break up the light into dots of various sizes, depending on the amount of light reflecting from the subject being photographed or programmed in the computer. In a reproduced copy, there are small dots on the image. These dots are present even on completely white or dark areas. Therefore, the reproduction process reduces the tonal value of the original to half. This is why a reproduced continuous tone image is called a halftone.

Line and halftone The integration of a continuous tone image and a line image for reproduction is called line and halftone copy. Special artwork needs to be prepared for this type of reproduction. The line drawing should be positioned on the photograph or wash painting on a transparent overlay. The line and halftone should be photographed separately and then combined to make a single-piece positive. In case the line and tone originals are on the same sheet, the line as well as toned area will bear a dot pattern, which might destroy the sharpness of the line work. Digital integration is normally done on page layout software programs such as InDesign, PageMaker, and QuarkXpress. Readers are advised to refer to Chapter 9 for further details on the subject.

Line and tint Line illustrations with flat tints and blends are reproduced by this process. For line and tint reproductions, we can draw the line illustration and mark the area desired to be blended or toned. After making the negative or positive of the line illustration, the printer is directed to strip the pre-screened film on the desired area, which is then transferred to the plate for printing. *Tint* is a term used to describe the

Figure 7.7 Halftone image in 45 lpi, 75 lpi, 100 lpi, and 133 lpi

saturation of a colour, or how light a particular colour is. The tint required for a particular colour may be indicated as a percentage value, depending on the desired saturation. Computer-generated blends, referred to as gradations, describe the gradual transition from one colour shape to another with varying degrees of smoothness. Interestingly, when tint and blend shapes are combined with line images in a vector-based computer program, the line images remain as sharp and the tint or blend images remain as smooth as they were in the original. Moreover, combined images occupy very little memory space on a computer, thereby enabling easy handling of visual copy.

COLOUR COPY

There are three types of copy normally used for colour printing—reflective, transmission, and digitized. Two basic factors—line and continuous tone images—are common for all the types of colour copy.

- Reflective copy is the copy that is viewed with the light which is reflected from the original. Coloured photographic prints, drawings, and paintings are some examples of reflective copy.
- Transmission copy is copy that is viewed with light passing through it. Positive colour film transparency is an example of transmission copy.
- Digitized or luminous copy is copy that is created on the computer by digital information and viewed through an illumination of the computer screen. All the colour images seen on the computer either in RGB, CMYK, or grey scale mode are digitized copy.

Whatever may be the types of copy, for the purpose of reproduction, they are treated in two ways—spot colour and process colour. Spot colour is pre-mixed colour which can be created and specified by a colour matching system. Spot colour may also be hand-mixed pigments. Process colour is made up of the three pigment primaries and black. Colour separation is required for both types of colour printing.

Colour Separation

Colour separation involves the extraction of the component hues of a colour image in order that each of these hues can be recorded on photographic emulsion. This emulsion is ultimately capable of producing a positive image, either by spot or process colour printing process.

A common method of colour copy preparation (artwork) is the key-drawing technique. All the areas of colour are drawn on a sheet of paper using a thin outline by placing an overlay on the main part of the drawing with registration marks on it. A registration mark is a positional guide for colour printing. The marks are needed for all multi-colour printing to maintain accuracy with which separated colours are superimposed on each other when reproduced.

Spot colour

Colour separation for spot colour printing is done photographically as well as digitally. More than one negative is taken from the original, depending on the number of colours to be printed. Each negative is then cut out and the part that is not to be printed is blocked out.

In the case of three-colour photographic separation, three identical negatives are made from the original artwork, as shown in Figure 7.8. On the first negative, everything that is not to be printed is opaqued out by hand. In the same way, the second and third negatives are also prepared as per their respective colour. Thus, the design is separated into three components. The non-opaque parts represent an individual colour for making

152 *Art and Print Production*

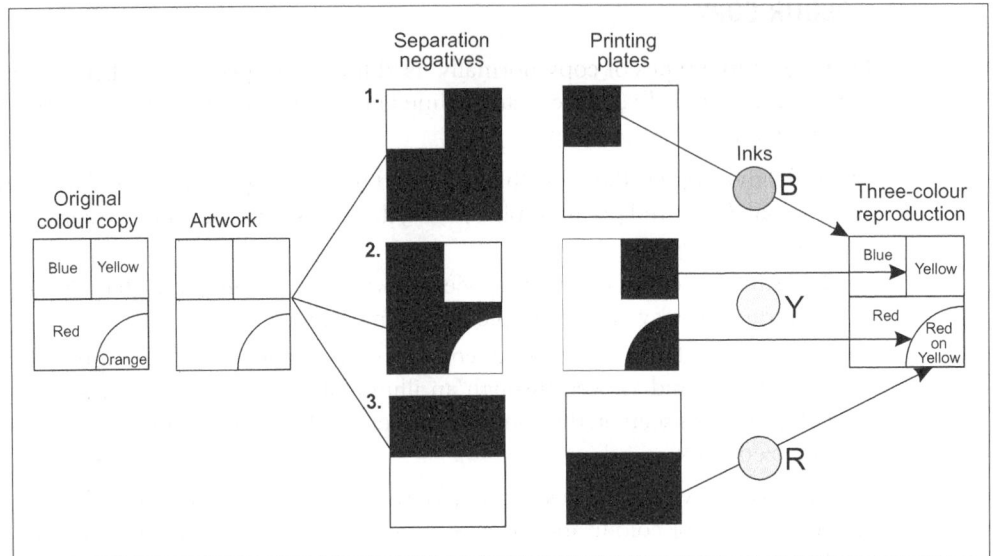

Figure 7.8 Colour separation for spot colour printing

a plate. It is important to understand that the separated films are not in colour, they are in black or opaque, that is, they are almost identical in appearance. In digital spot colour separation, non-printing areas are filled by vector images of computer programs.

Process colour

In process colour work, continuous tone colour copy is produced by three pigment primaries and black, that is, CMYK. Here, C stands for cyan, M for magenta, Y for yellow, and K for black. Although the three primaries are capable of printing any colour job, black is added for depth in the dark areas and more details, creating a more realistic effect.

Conventionally, a process camera is used for making a negative for each of the process colours or subtractive primaries, with the help of a filter of the respective additive primaries. To make a negative for the yellow colour of the original, a blue filter is placed in front of the lens of the camera. The purpose is to absorb all the wave lengths of light reflecting only the yellow components of the original. As a result, all the colours of the light that have been absorbed will pass through the lens and be recorded on the photographic emulsion, thus making the area all dark or opaque and leaving only the yellow areas transparent. The filters are analogous to the light primaries (RGB) and complementary to the pigment primaries.

A green filter will absorb blue and yellow and produce a negative of magenta, and a red filter will absorb red and yellow and produce a negative of cyan. To make a negative of black, either all the filters or a single amber (yellow-orange) filter is used. Since the negative image area is transparent, it will be dense on the plate after exposing. The area carries the ink to the plate. When the four plates are printed one by one on paper with their respective pigment, the result will be a range of colours of the original copy. Figure 7.9 shows the traditional process colour printing.

These days, most colour separation is done by electronic scanners. This computerized equipment can produce four-colour positives simultaneously with much high speed and superior quality. The basic principle of the colour separation by scanning is the same as that of the conventional process.

Modern colour scanning equipment is attached to a VDT and colour separation is carried out in a desktop environment. A scanner 'reads' slides, transparencies, or photographs electronically and converts them into bitmapped images (rectangular grid of pixels). The operator can see the scanned image on the terminal and make precise colour corrections and adjustments to match the artwork and create a wide range of special effects. We have discussed more about spot and process colour printing in Chapter 9.

Design, typesetting, and page layout can be created at the same place by one person or a group. This saves time and minimizes the amount of material handling. Last-minute change, quite expensive in traditional methods, is less expensive and often much easier to accomplish.

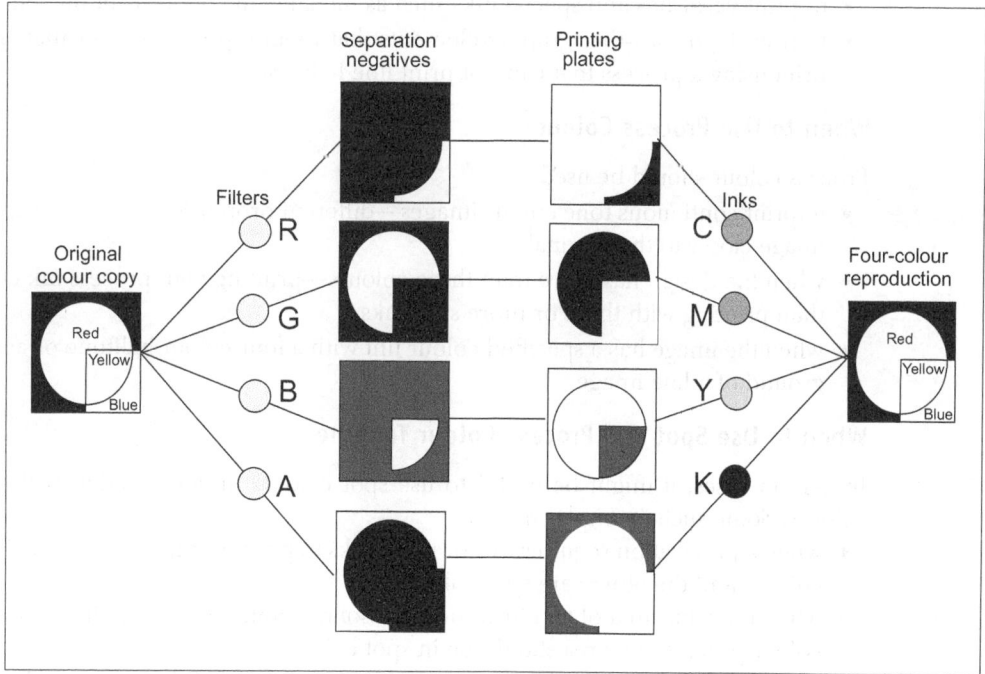

Figure 7.9 Traditional process colour printing

For combined process and spot colour printing, copies are shot separately for line and halftone and then stripped on flats, which hold the film positives or negatives in position for exposing on to the plates. Flats are made of opaque paper or transparent sheet. Making a flat requires considerable skill. This stage of colour processing is termed 'planning'. Printers often charge an extra amount from the print buyer, depending upon the complexity of colour separation.

We use either spot colours or process colours for most colour print projects. Budget plays a large role in the decision regarding spot or process colours, the printing method, and the specific design elements used in the layout. In general, a couple of spot colours cost less than 4-colour or process colour printing, but when we use full colour photos, process colours may be the only feasible option. Some situations also call for both process colours and spot colours in the same print job.

In order to control the cost of colour and, at the same time, achieve the desired printing quality, the following points should be kept in mind while preparing a copy.

When to Use Spot Colour

Spot colour should be used
- to print the typographical content to maintain legibility.
- to create a multi-colour effect by using a limited number of colours—overlapping and tinting give reasonably good variations.
- to print varnishes and special inks such as metallic ink, fluorescent ink, etc.
- to print logos or other graphic elements that require precise colour matching. To print using a process that can not print fine halftones.

When to Use Process Colour

Process colour should be used
- to print continuous tone colour images—different proportions of colours make the image closer to the original.
- when the design has more than three colours—printing with process ink costs less than printing with three or more spot inks.
- when the image has a specified colour tint with a four-colour halftone or as a background of a line image.

When to Use Spot and Process Colour Together

In certain cases, it might be useful to use spot colours in combination with process colours. Some such examples may be
- when a publication requires five or more inks to print. In this case, four are process colours and the others are spot colours.
- when the wide area of an illustration is a solid colour and the small area is in four colour process, the area should be in spot colour.
- when portions of a full colour publication are coated with a clear varnish (the varnish is specified as a spot colour).

SUMMARY

In print production, the stage when the copy for printing is prepared is the link between the artistic process and the production process. Normally, three types of copy are used in print production—verbal, visual, and colour.

The verbal copy is the copy with written or typed words, which forms the original manuscript or typescript. The manuscript is marked and sent to the typesetter or printer for typesetting. The instructions marked for the typesetter may include compulsory specifications such as type size, font, and line length, and optional specifications such as space between lines, family variations, setting format, etc., which can be set automatically by the typesetter.

Copy fitting is another requirement of verbal copy preparation. It is the process of ensuring that a block of text is neither too long nor too short to fit the space allotted for it. There are various methods of copy fitting available. These include digital methods of copy fitting and traditional word/character counting calculations.

Typesetting is the arrangement of letter characters in sequence. Originally, molten lead letters were arranged by hand to typeset a text. Today, most of typesetting is done using digital technology, which is fast, cost effective, and offers several quality options.

In order to ensure that the typeset proofs are error-free, the copy should be proofread. Familiarity with the standard proofreading marks and their use are very essential for all those who are involved in the production process.

Visual copy is commonly termed as art in the print trade. As visual images are not found in the actual size and proportion in which they are to be printed, scaling, cropping, and marking of visuals are mandatory. Although all these processes can be carried out digitally, using a computer or a process camera, mathematical and diagonal methods of cropping and scaling help in visualization and layout making.

For the purpose of production, there are two types of visuals—line and continuous tone. Various visual effects are obtained on a printed page by combining these two types of visuals and their tints.

Special attention should be given to colour copy as colour is used in most printed material. Three types of colour copy are usually used in colour printing—reflectitove copy, transmission copy, and digitized copy. These, along with the process of colour separation, have been discussed in the section on colour copy in the chapter.

KEY TERMS

All Caps Short for all capitals or all capitalized, refers to text in which all letters are capital letters. Example: ALL CAPS.

Cold Type Types generated by photographic or digital methods without involvement of heat.

Colour Copy Copy containing coloured images such as photographs, drawings, paintings, positive films, and digital information meant for printing.

Colour Separation The process of extraction of the component hues of a colour image in order that each of these hues can be recorded on photographic emulsion.

Copy Fitting The process of specifying types in a particular font and style intended to fit into the area estimated or specified for the final composition.

Crop Tool A tool in the shape of an icon available in computer applications which helps select and eliminate part of an image.

Cropping The process of eliminating part of a photograph or illustration by trimming its edges to make it fit into a given space or to remove its unnecessary parts.

Digitized Copy Copy created on computer by digital information and viewed by illumination of screen.

Digitized Typesetting Typesetting that uses digital technology in which arranged letter image are printed directly from the computer to paper or a printing plate.

Drop Letter An initial capital letter that is set larger than the text by 2 to 6 lines for emphasis.

Flat Assembled masking sheet with attached pieces of films.

Hot Metal Type Types that are cast by melting metal and injecting that into moulds of type, associated with the letterpress process of printing.

Interface Technology A boundary across which two systems communicate. An interface might be a hardware connector used to link to other devices, or a convention used to allow communication between two software systems.

Leading The vertical space between lines of type, measured in points.

Linotype A set of types in line or slug, cast mechanically by hot metal methods.

Manuscript Original text written by hand or typed (typescript) meant for editing or typesetting.

Movable Type An invention attributed to Johann Gutenberg in which each letter character is cast in metal that can be used multiple times for multiple printing simply by rearranging or moving them.

Optical Character Recognition (OCR) The process of converting an electronic image of text into a format that can be read by text-based applications such as word processors.

Photo Typesetting One of the cold typesetting methods in which letter images are obtained on photosensitive paper or film by passing light through negatives of font.

Reflective Copy Photographic prints, drawings, or paintings that can be viewed due to the light reflected when it strikes an object.

Scaling The process of determining the desired size for an image that will be reduced or enlarged to fit a particular area of the layout.

Sentence Case A style of typesetting the text in the way a sentence is usually written, that is, the first letter of the sentence is capitalized, all other letters are usually in lower case. Example: Sentence case.

Title Case A style of typesetting the text such that the first letter of each word is capitalized, and the remaining letters are in lower case. In some cases, the first letter of articles, prepositions, and conjunctions is not capitalized. Example: Title Case.

Transmission Copy Copy that can be viewed because of light projected through positive transparencies or films.

Verbal Copy Original copy with words for the purpose of printing, meant for rough layout, final paste-up, or final press-sheet.

Visual Copy Copy containing photographs, drawings, paintings, and other visual images that are scaled, cropped, and altered for the purpose of printing.

REFERENCES

Adler, Elizabeth W. 1991, *Print That Works*, Bull Publishing Company, California.

Adams, Michael J. 2002, *Printing Technology* 5E, Delmar Thomson Learning, USA.

Adobe 1995, *Print Publishing Guide*, Adobe System Incorporated, USA.

Agfa Prepress Education Resources 1992, *An Introduction to Digital Colour Prepress*, Agfa Prepress Education Resources, USA.

Bann, David 1985, *Production Handbook*, Macdonald & Co., London.

Barnhill, Suzanne 2004, 'Tips and Tricks for Copy Fitting', Microsoft Word MVP Site.

www.citationsoftware.com, accessed in October 2006.

Clair, Kate and Busic-Snyder, Cynthia 1995, *A Typographic Workbook*, Second Edition, John Wiley & Sons, Inc., New Jersey.

Conover, Theodore E. 1990, *Graphic Communication Today*, West Publishing Company, St. Paul.

http://www.bitstream.com/corporate/news press_2004/pf_041213_nexpress.html, accessed on 3 August 2007.

Kane, John 2003, *A Type Primer*, Prentice Hall Inc., New Jersey.

Padwik, Gordon 1994, *Guide to Colour Printing Techniques*, Random House, New York.

Schlemmer, Richard M. 1990, *Handbook of Advertising Art and Production*, Prentice Hall, New Jersey.

Stevenson, George A. 1968, *Graphic Arts Encyclopedia*, McGraw-Hill, New York.

Strans, Victor 1988, *The Printing Industry*, Printing Industries of America Inc., Washington DC.

Turnbull, Arthur T. and Baird, Russell N. 1980, *The Graphics of Communication*, Holt, Rinehart and Winston, USA.

REVIEW QUESTIONS

1. Identify and explain the three commonly used types of copy for printing.
2. Discuss the steps involved in preparation of verbal copy.
3. What do you understand by copy fitting? Mention the points to be taken care of while fitting text matter within the specified area on computer.
4. Calculate the number of words to be written for an area with dimensions of 4" × 7", when 11 point type with 2 point leading is used.
5. What is typesetting? Note the development of typesetting from hot metal type to digitized methods.
6. What are the points to be considered while reading proofs? Mark three proofreading symbols each for deletions, additions, and corrections.
7. What is a visual copy for printing?
8. Where is the purpose of sealing and cropping a visual image?
9. How are scaling and cropping handled on a computer?
10. Calculate the cropped proportionate size of a photograph which will be printed within the area of 9 cm × 17 cm. The original size of the photo is 10.5 cm × 17 cm.
11. Define reflective copy, transmission copy, and digitized copy in relation to colour printing.
12. What is the purpose of colour separation? Write the basic concept of spot colour and process colour separation.
13. What are the situations in which only spot colour or only process colour is used? Also, mention situations when both are used.

PROJECTS

1. Type 250 words in 12 point Courier type. Take a printout on an A4-size paper. Now, set the text in Arial 10 point with 24 pica line length and 2 point leading and find out the galley depth in picas. Prepare a layout with this text block using an appropriate heading.
2. Use the text you have typed for the first assignment. Determine the space for the following situations. Show your calculation against each text block.
   (a) New Times Roman 9/11, 20 pica line length
   (b) Helvetica Bold 10/13, 16 pica line length
   (c) Avant Garde 11/14, 15 pica line length
   (d) Book Antigua 11/13, 22 pica line length
   (e) Futura Bold 6/8, 14 pica line length
3. Prepare a working rough of two facing pages for a newsletter. The pages contain six stories with four photographs. Determine the space available for heading and text for each story. Calculate the number of words that should be written for each story, leaving 3 pica space vertically for headings. The text should be set in 9 point type with 2 point leading.
4. Take a printed page having mainly typographical content. Identify the type blocks of the page. Give them numbers. Write the instructions that must have been given to set the type on a sheet of paper as per the number of each block.
5. Scan a typographical text page with OCR system and save it in a word document. Take a printout and proofread it using proofreaders' marks. Carry out the necessary corrections on the computer and arrange the text in a different type style and format.
6. A given page layout contains space for three photographs and a text block. The photo areas are 9 cm × 11 cm, 8 cm × 15 cm, and 8 cm × 6 cm. Cut three halftone pictures from a magazine. Naturally, they will be of different sizes. Calculate the proportionate size of these pictures that will fit within the area of the layout. Use a separate sheet for the purpose of calculation but mark the crop area on the picture itself to judge your content selection.
7. Carry out the exercise in the previous question on your computer screen by scanning three

pictures. Use the crop tool or masking command of any one of the page layout programs. Note the sequence of actions you have taken to accomplish the job.

8. Choose a coloured advertisement in which all the elements are easily identifiable. Keep a transparent sheet on the advertisement and trace the outline along with various colour blocks. Identify and mark each of the blocks as spot, process, and tints. Mention the approximate percentage of colour where colours are mixed or blended.

9. Scan a coloured photograph and open it in Photoshop. Do the necessary retouching and colour correction for the purpose of printing. Use the channel command in Photoshop for CYMK separation. Write your observation on each separation and combination of two, three, and four colours.

CHAPTER

Printing Processes

Learning Objectives

After reading this chapter, you should be able to
- trace the history and development of printing processes and technology
- gain an overview of the various revolutions in printing technology that have come about over the years
- understand the three major categories of printing—on-demand, major, and specialized printing
- understand the various processes and techniques used in each of these methods
- gain an insight into the advantages and limitations of the various processes of printing

INTRODUCTION

Printing is the process of reproducing an image by pressing an inked surface to a substrate that receives the impression. The art of printing was fairly developed and in use in China by the second century AD. China was in a position to pioneer printing because it had already invented the three necessary elements of printing—paper, ink, and engraving. Engraving refers to the process of carving an image relief on a surface. The most common method of engraving was to cut blocks of wood in relief and ink them with a water-based ink. Paper was laid on the block and gently rubbed with a bamboo stick or dry brush to produce an impression. The art spread to other parts of East Asia. Today, books printed from woodblocks by the Japanese and the Koreans in the eighth century are still in existence.

Printing became mechanized after the invention of the movable type system by Johann Gutenberg in the fifteenth century. Although the Chinese are known to have used movable types in the eleventh century, mechanized printing is considered to be a European invention. Gutenberg's solution was to last more than four centuries. Due to the need for speed and the invention of photography and personal computers, newer printing processes have now overtaken this traditional printing method. Figure 8.1 shows an illustration of Gutenberg's printing press.

Along with wood carving, in which an *image relief* is carved on a surface, another method of printing—intaglio—was becoming popular. This process of printing originated with the work of creative artists of the Italian Renaissance in the 1300s. The word *intaglio* (in-tal-yo) means 'engraved' or 'cut in' in Italian. In intaglio printing,

Figure 8.1 Gutenberg's printing press

the impression is obtained from a *depressed area*. Since this method was not compatible with movable type, it was limited only to the printing of illustrations and was mainly used by artists for their creative work and for reproductions of such works. The intaglio process was refined by Karl Klic of Germany and an Englishman called Samuel Fawcett. The process continued to improve with electrochemical engravers being introduced in 1968 and digital control added in 1983.

In 1798, the planographic process arrived on the scene. It was based on the principle that water and oil do not mix. In planography, the image and non-image area of the printing surface are on the same *plain*. Lithography—a planographic process where a flat limestone surface is used as the image carrier—served as a medium for artists until the stone printing surface was replaced with the metal sheet of offset printing. Figure 8.2 illustrates how impressions are made in relief printing, planography, and intaglio. As shown in the figure, images are obtained from a raised surface in relief printing, plain surface in planography, and depressed surface in intaglio printing.

Printing techniques advanced further after the invention of photography in the early nineteenth century, enabling printers to duplicate images accurately without much manual skill. Offset lithography has since emerged as a pre-eminent printing process.

In India, the first printing press was installed in Goa by the Portuguese in 1556. Within a short period, some other coastal towns of the South added printing centres. Credit goes to the Roman Catholic mission for introducing printing on the west coast and in the South, and to the Protestants for introducing it on the east coast and in the North.

The early printing presses were used mainly for spreading Christianity. This did not lead to a general development of printing.

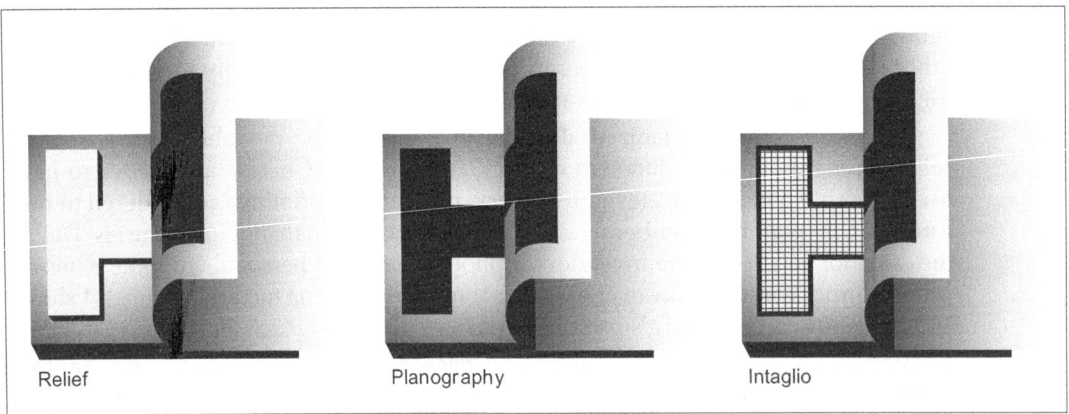

Figure 8.2 Impressions made from relief printing, planography, and intaglio

The advent of the printing press in Bengal may be traced to political considerations and the selfless and dedicated efforts of pioneers such as Charles Wilkins and William Carey in the late eighteenth and early nineteenth centuries. Nationalistic opposition to the established order led to the birth of journalism in India. *The Bengal Gazette*, published by James Augustus Hickey in 1780, added a new dimension to the development of printing in India.

We shall discuss the growth and development of printing technology in the following section.

TREND TOWARDS MODERNIZATION

The growth and development of printing techniques is a continuous process. The real revolution in printing technology came in the second half of the last century, when the computer was introduced in information processing. Printing is now no longer seen as a reproduction technology—it is viewed more as a communication technology. Communicators, who used to work in isolation only a few years ago, now find themselves in the role of designers-cum-composers-cum-writers. Not too long ago, a copy was written and edited at one end of an office and passed through as many as half a dozen stations before being printed. Today, automation has eliminated the need for most of these intermediary stations.

New technology has opened up a world of wide-ranging alternatives. These days, colour separation is done by a colour scanner. Complete page layouts can be made on a computer terminal with several flexible options. Digitized typesetting, image manipulations, on-demand printing, and automatic binding have contributed to substantial changes. In the newspaper field, facsimile transmission via co-axial cable or satellite has added a new dimension to modern printing technology. Thanks to this system, simultaneous publications can be brought out from different centres. For example, local editions of newspapers such as *The Hindu* and *The Times of India* can be brought out from different centres with the help of advanced technology.

Figure 8.3 illustrates the various steps involved in the old, relatively new, and recent techniques used for printing. Over the years, there have been considerable changes in printing technology. In the old printing process, hot metal composing was in use. This was followed by the use of the relatively new method of photocomposing. In the recent times, desktop publishing has gained popularity over all these printing techniques for many types of printing jobs. Let us now take a look at the various developments in printing technology over the years.

The *first* revolution in printing technology was Gutenberg's invention of the movable type system, discussed earlier.

The *second* revolution came at the end of the nineteenth century, when two methods of mechanical typesetting were invented, speeding up the process of setting type in hot and molten metal. The first one was the *monotype system*, which consisted of a keyboard to perforate a paper tape, and this perforated paper tape was then fed to a separate machine called a 'caster'. The second system of setting a line mechanically in hot and molten metal was the *linotype system*.

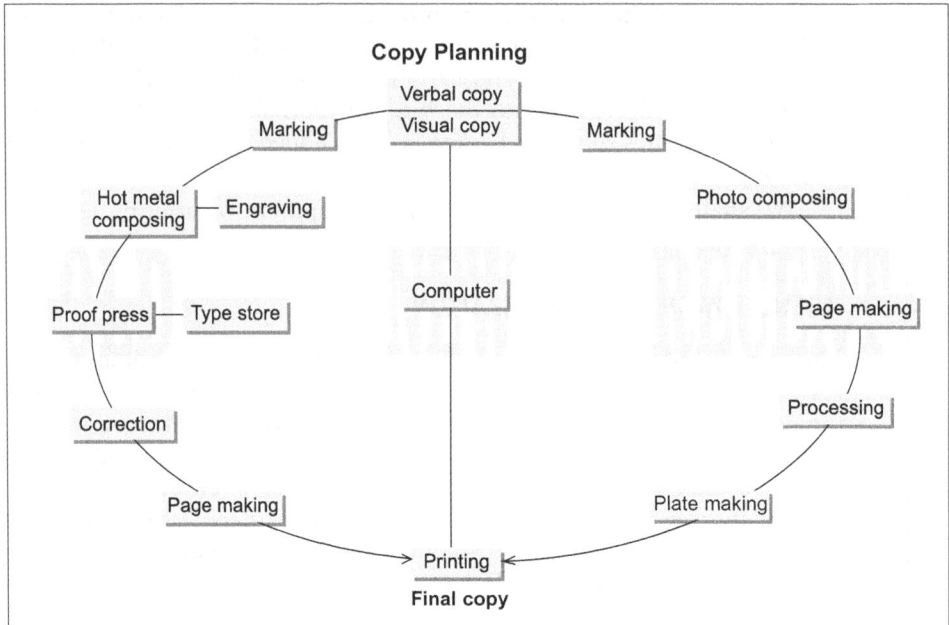

Figure 8.3 Steps in obtaining the final printed copy in the original old, recent, and latest methods

The *third* revolution in printing technology was phototypesetting, which is based on simple physics. In phototypesetting, high-intensity light flashes through the transparent type images, which move on a spinning disc. The images are projected through one of the lenses meant for creating different sizes of characters. The projected characters pass through a moving prism, which positions them on a photo-sensitive paper or film. The advent of this electronic process increased the use of *offset lithography*. The impact of this revolution on the other processes of printing is also clearly visible.

Desktop publishing (DTP) is considered to be the *fourth* revolution in printing. A DTP system is basically a computer that facilitates the designing of a page with graphics or any line or tone image, in any specific typeface and size, with a screen backdrop in any area of the page. The computer is connected to a laser printer. The manuscript is written and fed (through key punching) into the computer and decisions about type style and size, spacing and placement of elements, and graphics are all handled by the communicator directly on the computer.

With DTP, a designer can singly accomplish what earlier would have required a team. The laser printer provides almost typeset-quality printouts on ordinary paper as well as on film. The DTP system has reduced the composing cost substantially, at least in comparison to phototypesetting.

Developments in India

The Indian printing industry has three major segments—(i) newspapers and magazines, (ii) general commercial printing, and (iii) packaging. Newspapers and magazines have witnessed some of the most momentous and revolutionary changes since the mid-eighties. The impact of these changes is visible in computerized typesetting, word processing, image manipulation in a desktop environment, text and image integration, use of portable personal computers and laptops, and networks between computers and printing units. As a result, conventional technology such as hot metal composing and letterpress printing is rapidly being replaced with offset printing, which is capable of meeting the demands for high-speed printing by newspapers and magazines such as *India Today, Outlook,* and *Frontline.*

All the above-mentioned changes have wrought an incredible change in general commercial printing, telephone directories, posters, point of sales material, catalogues, etc. Most presses of metropolitan towns have adopted the new technology to meet the demands of advertisers for top quality printing. A few multinational printing presses like Quebecor and Donneley have already made inroads into the Indian printing scene. Colour now plays an increasingly greater role in printing because of the availability of digital proofing of four-colour separation and integration of text and continuous tone illustrations.

In order to enter the packaging horizon, high-speed presses (with sophisticated tension-control systems, web guiders, automatic register controls, controlled temp-drying facility, automatic control of ink viscosities, and web viewing devices) have made mass production of packages economical. Multi-colour printing on diversified substrates has thus made for uninterrupted consistency and quality and opened vast new vistas for the packaging industry.

PRINTING PROCESSES

Printing is a very high-pressure business. Technological advancements are taking place so fast that printers are forced to upgrade their equipment and improve the skills of their employees continuously to survive in the competitive market. Print buyers are also becoming more and more demanding in terms of price, quality, and speed.

With the increasing number of processes available in the market, we must be aware of the printing processes and their capabilities. Before deciding on a printer for a specific job, we must also understand our own requirements. Many a time, we find that the job does not require a very high-quality output but needs to be done very quickly. Sometimes, a quality job is obtained by compromising on the price. Both quality and quantity may be required for certain kinds of jobs. We may need a specialized effect be given an exclusive look on a printed page. To meet all these and other needs, there are various processes available in the market. These processes can be divided into three categories: (i) on-demand printing, (ii) major printing, and (iii) specialized printing. Figure 8.4 presents a flow chart showing the various printing processes that are based on the principles of on-demand, major, and stencil printing. We shall discuss each of these in detail in the following sections.

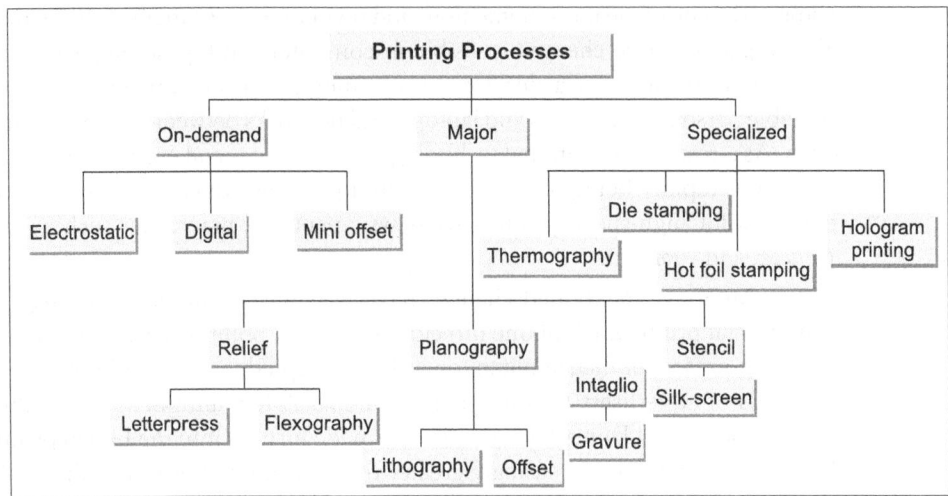

Figure 8.4 Flow chart showing various printing processes

ON-DEMAND PRINTING

On-demand printing can also be referred to as quick, digital, or custom printing. In the printing industry, it is also associated with shorter and usually more economical print runs.

Digital on-demand printing is revolutionizing the publishing industry in Western countries. New machines from Xerox and Kodak have eliminated the need for complex and difficult prepress work and to create, capture, store, and distribute documents digitally. In India also, its influence is felt in all sorts of print documents.

Traditional offset printing is a multi-step process—a document is created, made ready on a plate, printed, collated after folding, stored, and distributed. On-demand printing has, however, enabled publishing units to print the copies they actually require, when they require them. It is more cost effective than traditional printing for shorter runs of up to about 500 copies—which currently account for around 10 to 15 per cent of all print jobs in India.

Conventional printing has a minimum run of around 250 copies. This means that if the actual demand is for fewer copies, some will remain unsold. In many ways, digital printing takes the risk out of publishing and speeds up cash flow. In the language of the publishing industry, digital on-demand printing means 'no more dead horses in the warehouse'. New on-demand printing machines also highlight the move towards more cost-effective integrated multi-functional digital devices. For example, Xerox's Docu-Tech Production Publisher series of machines integrate scanning, network input, digital processing, printing, and on-line finishing capabilities into a single machine. Using dial-up modem lines, satellite up-links, Internet access, and advanced networking functionality, users can also distribute and print the right document in the right place at the right time and in required quantities.

Many a time, we mix and match various types of machines to get our job on-demand. Let us discuss some of them in terms of their characteristics, capabilities, and cost effectiveness.

Electrostatic Printing

Some printing machines available in the market can duplicate a job instantly. Electrostating devices or photocopiers may be the most commonly used devices in today's fast speed communication business. These machines utilize the principle of static electricity. They employ photosensitive materials that may be electrically charged in the form of a desired image and then caused to attract dry ink, which is known as 'toner'. The toner prints the image on paper or any other substrate.

There are various copiers available in the market with several features. They can be handled by a casual user. These copies can be used not only as printed outputs but also for instant imaging by a graphic artist. These machines can enlarge, reduce, and crop images to the desired size. Printers find these machines very handy for stapling, collating, and gluing the pages. Colour photocopiers, though a bit costly, can be used for various purposes when a few copies are required. They prove to be very cost effective if compared with coloured photography or scanned image outputs. Colour photocopies also aid presentations on overhead projectors (OHP) and act as useful teaching aids.

Some photocopiers can be connected with computers. In other words, images created and modified on the computer can be transferred to the copier and the output can be obtained instantly.

Digital Printing

Desktop digital printing has probably had the greatest impact in the modern printing industry. It has helped to evolve print production from a craft-based to a technology-based business. It is especially useful when printed copies are needed immediately. Since the copies are reproduced directly from computer memory, bypassing the steps of film- and plate-making, it reduces the lead time needed for printing and for changing the image on each revolution of the press. Desktop printing has therefore altered the publishing procedure from 'print and distribute' to 'distribute and print'. Two types of digital technology are involved in on-demand printing—inkjet and laser printing.

Inkjet printing In inkjet printing, digitized computer information directs the outputting device to force or spray tiny individual drops of charged liquid ink. The ink is sprayed to the printing surface from a small opening.

There are various types of inkjet printers available in the market. The most popular one is continuous flow inkjet, for its ability to print on a wide range of substrates. High resolution image technology is capable of providing acceptable proofs to customers. Low resolution images can be used for layout and dummy approval of a design solution. As the inkjet printing is a *non-impact* process, it can print on almost any surface regardless of surface texture and pressure resistance.

Laser printing In digital laser printing, laser light passes through a finely tuned optical system and lands on a light-sensitive negatively charged rotating drum. It scans the surface of the drum as it is activated by the computer. Wherever it strikes, it neutralizes the spot and dots are formed at the points on the drum. A series of dots create the image to be printed. A negatively charged roller containing powdered ink, known as toner, is used to form the image, when it rolls over the drum. The neutralized area of the drum adheres to the powder from the toner, whereas the negatively charged area repels the ink. This process is based on the principle that like charges attract, whereas unlike charges repel each other. The paper receives a positive charge as it enters the printer and the dots formed on the drum are transferred to the paper. The heated rollers fuse the dots on the paper, creating a permanent image.

Laser printing is used for typesetting, creating visuals on the computer, and even for very small runs for presentations, for group discussions, etc. The quality of production depends on the density of the dots. The more the dots, the more superior the quality. A printer that uses 300 dots per inch (dpi) is considered to be a low resolution printer. Laser technology is used for printing house journals, booklets, folders, etc. where high quality production is not the prime aim. A range of 300 to 600 dpi is considered good resolution suitable for fine quality printing. High resolution images, that is, images between 1200 and 1600 dots and above, are used for camera-ready copies or mechanicals. Low and good resolution printouts can be obtained from a desktop publishing system on various types of paper, and high resolution images can be obtained from an image setting system on bromide or directly on film.

Due to some disadvantages in laser printing, print buyers continue to use conventional printing processes and utilize digital printers as peripheral devices. The drawbacks include the high costs of consumables, especially toners, which are many more times higher than a set of process colours needed to print a job by offset process. Laser printing is also a slow process for a high run job. Most of the desktop digital printers can print only up to A3 size paper. Although the quality of colour print obtained from digital printing is impressive, in many cases; it is much inferior to similar prints obtained through offset printing.

Mini Offset Printing

The term *offset* refers to the transfer of image from the plate to a rubber cylinder which offsets it onto the paper. The process is based on the principle that water and oil do not mix. Offset printing is an elaborate process. For quick copy where quality can be compromised, however, it is a simple and cost effective process.

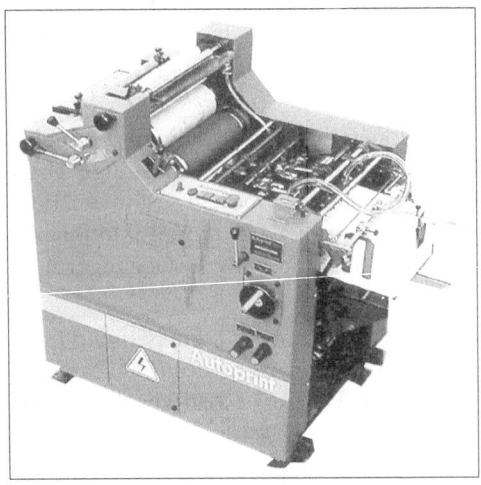

Figure 8.5 Mini offset machine

In offset printing, the image is exposed onto a flexible, chemically-coated paper plate or synthetic sheet by the electrostating or laser printing method. The freshly exposed plate is passed through a heating system so that the image gets fixed on the plate capable of holding ink. Since the rest of the plate can hold not only the image but also the non-image area, only the image area takes ink from the ink roller and transfers it to the rubber cylinder and then to paper. Figure 8.5 shows a mini offset machine.

Mini offset is mainly used for medium and small run jobs such as circulars, questionnaires for research, business forms, etc. In recent times, the mini offset machine has replaced the stencil duplicator. It can normally print on A4 and A3 size paper in single colour as well in multi-colour. The quality of halftone reproductions on this machine is mediocre.

Satisfactory results can be obtained from quick printing machines such as swift offset, autoprint, etc., if the design is simple and clean. The use of a large solid area with reverse image should be avoided. Hand drawn illustrations, vector graphics, and designs with typographic images from any output device can be duplicated by quick printing machines.

MAJOR PRINTING

Major printing processes include relief printing, planography, intaglio, and stencil printing. The various processes and methods that are based on these principles are discussed in this section.

Relief Printing

Printing technology as we know it today has, in some form or the other, developed from the letterpress process of printing, which is based on the principle of relief printing. New printing methods, particularly offset printing, have surpassed letterpress printing in terms of market share. These new developments, however, have not been able to eliminate letterpress printing from the market due to its use in finishing operations and some types of jobs where letterpress printing is particularly economical and handy in Indian conditions. Finishing operations include perforating, scoring, die cutting, and embossing. Today, most relief printing is done today with flexography—a process that prints from a raised rubber surface in the same way as impressions are made from rubber stamps. Although flexography is now more common, it is important to understand the letterpress process as much of the terminology that printers use even today comes from the traditional metal type and letterpress printing.

Letterpress printing

The term *letterpress* brings to mind images of raised letters pressing against a surface, onto which their shape is transferred in ink. Letterpress printing is also called *relief printing* because the mirror image of the letter to be printed is raised in relief above the surface that carries it and the non-printing area is depressed. Thus, while ink is applied on the image area by rollers, only the raised surface receives ink. This surface is then pressed against the paper to make the impression. The non-image area, which is depressed, does not come into contact with the inking roller or the paper. So, it leaves no impression on the paper.

Types Letterpress printing is meant for printing text comprising of not only letters but also other visuals such as borders, rules, and illustrations in black and white or colour. The term *letter* press, however, still persists as the early attempts were focused on printing *letters*. Since the letters are cast separately for letterpress printing, other visuals can also be made separately, and then arranged together on a page or pages. Then, a forme can be made for printing.

There are three types of processes involved in letterpress printing. In chronological order, these are—platen, flatbed cylinder, and rotary. The operations of inking, paper-feeding, printing and delivery are common to all these processes.

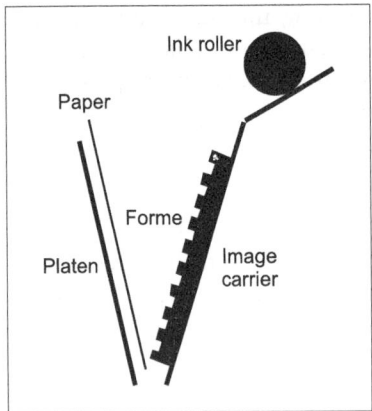

Figure 8.6 Printing process in a platen letterpress

Platen letterpress The platen press takes its name from the *platen*, which is one of the two plain surfaces on which paper is placed for printing. The other surface, on which the arranged images (formes) are locked firmly, is known as the *image carrier*. Inking is done by *ink rollers*, which pick up ink from a revolving disc fixed above the machine, and then pass it across the forme. Paper is fed by inserting it between the two flat surfaces. These surfaces are brought together to print the required image. Finally, the printed image is delivered. This output is taken out in the form of printed paper from the machine when the two surfaces are open or separated. The feeding and delivery system of the platen press may be automatic or hand operated. Naturally, the automatic system is faster than the hand-operated one. Figure 8.6 shows the printing process of a platen letterpress.

The platen press is slow, but it is well-suited for printing letterheads, cards, bill forms, small format booklets, and leaflets. It can also be used for embossing, die cutting, creasing, perforating, and hot-foil stamping, which are not possible on other presses.

In India, a platen press can be set up by small investors and can be run by just one or two persons. In our country, where many people are unemployed, the platen press is one of the major sources of self-employment. As labour is very cheap here in comparison to many developed countries, the unit cost of production is quite low.

Flatbed cylinder letterpress The first development of the flatbed cylinder press came as many as 350 years later than the invention of the platen press. The credit for it goes to Frederick Koening of Germany. This development had two features—(i) the press was operated by steam power, and (ii) one of the printing surfaces was cylindrical, that is, the surface of the type forme remained flat on a bed while the ink rollers rotated over it and a cylinder was used to roll over and press the paper against it. Figure 8.7 shows how a flatbed cylinder letterpress works.

Since there was a revolving impression cylinder and the machine was power-driven, the printing speed was quite high, bringing about a revolution in the industry. It was efficient enough to print considerably longer-run jobs and for much bigger paper sizes.

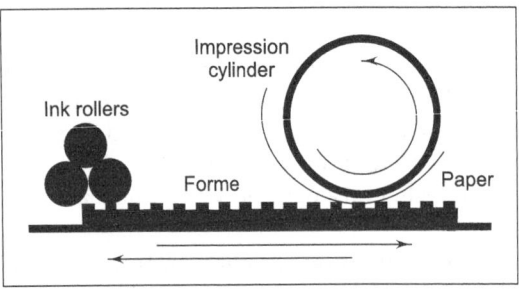

Figure 8.7 Printing process in a flatbed cylinder letterpress

Rotary letterpress Letterpress printing improved further when both the printing surfaces were made cylindrical. Therein lay the beginning of the rotary press and high-speed printing. The type forme in a rotary press is converted into a cylindrical plate and another cylinder is rolled against it. The paper passes between the two cylinders, as shown in Figure 8.8. The rotary press is faster than any flatbed press because of

Printing Processes   169

the continuous action of the cylindrical image carrier. The printing speed is enhanced further by using a paper web in the feeding system instead of sheets.

A rotary press requires elaborate make-ready procedures before printing can begin. The purpose is to convert the flat page forme into a half-cylinder for rotary printing. To achieve this, the copy is set on a hot metal composing system and blocks are made for illustrations, etc. and then arranged according to the layout plan on a metal frame called *chase*. The arranged page is locked up and images are transferred to it via flexible flongs made of *papier mâché* by applying high pressure against the metal types. Now, the paper flong with depressed images is fed into a casting box where it is converted into a lead version, called a *stereo*. This stereo is now in a half-cylindrical shape. The stereo plates are then fitted on to cylinders on the rotary machine. With a view to adopting the modern pagination system, flexible photo-polymer plates are sometimes used in place of a stereo.

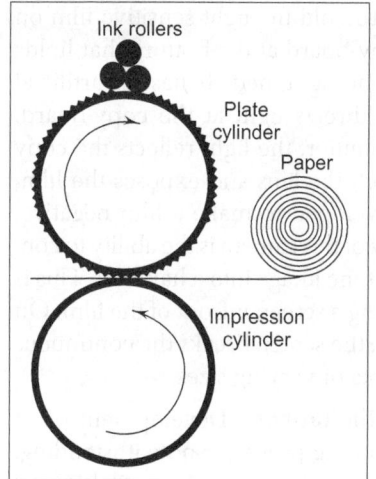

Figure 8.8   Printing process in rotary letterpress

The rotary letterpress had been a favourite of the newspaper industry till the early 1980s. It has now been almost completely replaced with web-offset presses, which, while adopting the rotary system, have discarded its cumbersome hot metal make ready procedure.

Process of engraving   In any type of letterpress printing, the make-ready is accomplished with a combination of cast types and photo-engraved illustrations, locked together in a forme. The process of arranging the metallic types in sequence is known as typesetting. Relief printing plates for illustrative materials are made by taking a film negative through a process camera and contact printing it backwards on to a sensitized metal plate, usually made of zinc (for longer print runs and better reproduction, copper is also used). Exposed light passes through the image area, which is transparent, strikes the sensitized emulsion of the plate, and makes only the image area hard.

The exposed plate is then dipped into etching acid, which eats away the non-image area. The image area, being hard, is acid-resistant and retains the printing image in relief on the surface of the metal sheet. The metal plate is then mounted on a wooden or straw-board platform. Etched metal sheets are also used to make flexographic plates. A sheet of the rubber is positioned over the plate and curved by heat and pressure. The photo engraving process is commonly known as block-making.

Process camera   Process camera is a large camera used for graphic art photography. Figure 8.9 shows a process camera. It is large because it must hold a large sheet of film needed for printing. It should be noted that, while printing, the outputting film should be of the same size as that of the image to be printed. A vertical non-portable camera

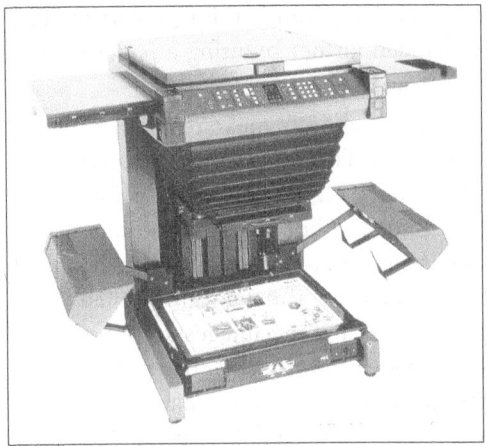

Figure 8.9 Process camera

has a film-board to hold the light sensitive film on the top and a copy-board at the bottom that holds the copy to be photographed. It has an artificial light source that directs light at the copy-board. On opening the shutter, the light reflects the copy that passes through the lens and exposes the film, which is then developed to make a film negative. Another speciality of this camera is the ability to convert a continuous tone image into a halftone. This is achieved by placing a screen infront of the film. On exposing the film, the screen breaks the continuous tone copy into dots of varying sizes.

Advantages and limitations Development of so many modern printing processes notwithstanding, letterpress technology is still easily available and accessible to all kinds of print buyers in India. In many cases, letterpress printing is a cost effective process. The direct impression on paper with dense ink makes a high quality typographic reproduction. Paper wastage is comparatively less in letterpress printing than in other processes.

Letterpress printing has some limitations as well, because of which print buyers are increasingly shifting to offset presses. Letterpress printing requires a large area for the composing unit. Its make-ready procedure is quite costly because of the high cost of metal type and engravings of illustrations. Reproduction of photographs is generally not of high quality, especially on coarse and uncalendered paper. Letterpress needs calendered or costly art paper to produce satisfactory results, thereby increasing the unit cost of production. Most letterpress machines are not capable of carrying out larger print orders due to their slow speed and because the image gets blurred after a few thousand impressions. Printing from a raised surface also leaves a blank raised impression on the back side of the paper if it is too thin. Sometimes, the right impression is not achieved even with proper make-ready procedures before the final run. Although the rotary letterpress has a high printing speed, it is not used these days. This is because of the cumbersome make-ready procedure required for rotary letterpress printing. Moreover, several other processes are available these days, which are compatible with computers and need less floor space for operation.

Flexography

The invention of plastic material and the need of printing on it gave birth to flexography printing in the early 1900s. At that time, flexographic printing was called *aniline printing* because the inks used were made from organic aniline dyes. It was termed as *flexographic printing* in 1952 so that the process could be made popular by removing the association with aniline dyes, which were mistakenly believed to be poisonous. It was believed that aniline dyes would contaminate food products packed in printed plastic.

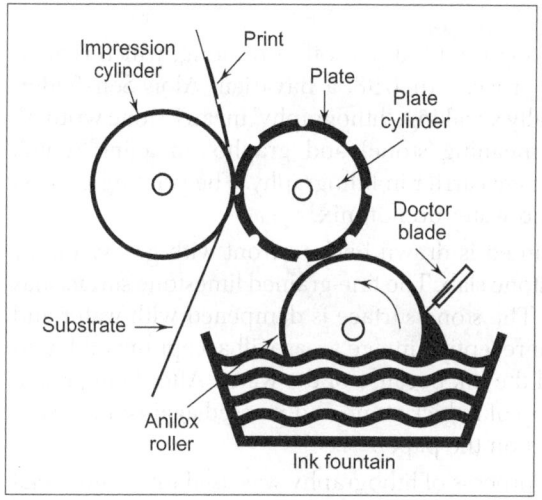

Figure 8.10 Printing process in flexography

Flexography is a rotary relief printing process. Here, the images are made in relief on a rubber plate moulded from an intervening matrix plate or photopolymer plate exposed to ultraviolet light. The plate is thin and mounted onto the plate cylinder as in a rotary letterpress. A thin and fast-drying ink is applied to the plate with a metal roller, known as *anilox roller*. This hard-surfaced roller is etched to create millions of tiny cells of equal size and depth. The ink is filled in these cells of the roller while revolving into the ink drum. The excess ink carried on the anilox roller is wiped off by a doctor blade. Hence, the function of the depressed surface is to distribute the ink to the plate uniformly. The inked plate then makes the impression onto the paper. Figure 8.10 shows how images are printed in a flexographic process.

The majority of flexographic printing is done on roll-fed material such as film, foil, and laminates. The substrate is then rewound into roll for processing it later. Sheet-fed flexography is mainly used for printing on corrugated board.

Advantages and limitations The flexography process can be used to print on a wide variety of materials such as paper, plastic, foil, and foil-laminated or corrugated materials used for modern packaging. Fast-drying ink and the rotary principle facilitate high-speed printing. Four-colour printing is possible in this process. The make-ready procedure is quite simple and inexpensive. There is less wastage of paper than in the offset process. Moreover, there is no show-through even when printing is done on a low-quality paper.

The limitations of flexography include the inability to reproduce fine details and a tendency towards colour variation. Also, the evaporating solvent of flexo-ink is known to pollute the environment.

In India, flexographic printing is mainly used in the packaging industry. In developed countries too, it is often used in the packaging industry alongside book and newspaper printing.

Planography

Planographic printing is the process of printing from a flat surface, as opposed to printing from a raised surface, as with relief printing, or an incised surface, as with intaglio printing. The planographic process is based on the principle that water does not mix with oil. This process is used to produce lithographs or offset lithographs by applying a greasy substance to a metallic plate or stone.

Lithography

The most common type of major printing used today is offset printing, which is actually a modification of the lithography process. In 1798, a Bavarian, Alois Senefelder, invented this process by accident. Literally speaking, 'lithography' means 'stone writing', derived from the Greek words 'litho', meaning 'stone', and 'grapho', meaning 'write'. A flat limestone surface is used as an image carrier in lithography. The printing process is based on the principle that grease and water do not mix.

In lithography, the image to be printed is drawn back to front with greasy ink or crayon on a flat, smooth surface of the stone slab. The fine-grained limestone surface has an excellent capacity to absorb water. The stone surface is dampened with water and then inked by an ink roller. The grease-receptive image areas will accept the oil-based ink, but the non-image areas will repel the ink because of the water. After being inked and watered, the paper is laid on the top of a thick stone and pressed against the inked stone and the readable image is printed on the paper.

In the early nineteenth century, the process of lithography was used for commercial reproduction. It could not, however, maintain its primacy in the mass production era that followed, as stones were in short supply and expensive, prone to damage, and difficult to store. Moreover, the flatbed system was slow. Despite these limitations, lithography became quite popular among master artists, who used it for limited circulation of art reproductions.

The lithography process was first improved in 1889, when limestone was replaced with grained metal plates of zinc. It was further improved by converting the flat surface into a cylindrical form. The image is printed on a cylinder covered with a rubber sheet which then becomes the printing plate. The offset press as we know it today was born in 1906. The credit for this development was given to Ira W. Rubel of USA, a printer.

Offset printing

For most printing jobs, publishers' and advertisers' first choice is offset printing. The factors that have determined this choice are—elimination of costly make-ready needed in other processes, easy plate-making, ability to print fine-screen halftones on less expensive paper, and a series of computer and photographic techniques in coordination.

In offset printing, the image area and non-printing area are on the same plane of the surface of a thin metal plate, the difference between them being maintained chemically. Printing is from a flat surface—one which is neither raised nor depressed—and three surfaces are used instead of two. Here, the additional surface receives the image from the image carrier surface and then sets it off to the paper. This is why this process is called *offset* printing. As photography is the key to the modern make-ready procedure, it is called *photo offset*. Where the lithography principle is used, it is called *litho offset*, and where printing is done from plain surface, it is called planography.

An offset press is generally rotary. It has an additional operation system besides feeding, inking, printing, and delivery. This system also has a dampening unit, which applies water to the plate. There are three cylinders—a plate carrier, a rubber blanket, and an impression cylinder. A thin metal sheet with a planographic image is wrapped around the plate cylinder, the dampening rollers coat the plate with water, the ink roller inks the image area of the plate, and the inked image is then transferred to the rubber blanketed cylinder. The image on the rubber blanket is in reverse. This is turned the right way round when it is transferred to paper. The paper comes between the rubber blanket and the impression cylinder. The rubber blanket is water repellent and protects the paper from distortion. The paper picks up the image as it passes between the blanket cylinder and the impression cylinder.

Prepress procedures Offset printing requires an elaborate make-ready procedure, which is known as prepress. It includes the steps involved before the material to be printed goes to the printing unit. Prepress procedures are handled through either the traditional or the digital method, or, in some cases, through a combination of both.

Digital prepress This prepress process has almost entirely changed the classical division of the areas of typesetting, film outputting, and plate-making. Since the introduction of desktop publishing at the end of the 80s, it has become a dominant alternative in prepress. The advent of the personal computer, computerized page planning, image processing software, PostScript page description language, and high-resolution imagesetters with raster image processors revolutionized the prepress work. These days, there is greater participation of designers and communicators in printing work, and some part of the prepress work is being handled by them.

We shall discuss digital prepress in greater detail in Chapter 9. In this chapter, we shall discuss the working of traditional prepress, which is still vogue in India. In combination with digital outputting devices, traditional prepress proves to be cost effective.

Traditional prepress There are three steps in traditional prepress—(i) typesetting of text matter, formatting the text pagination, and arranging the pictures and graphics; (ii) film outputting of formatted text and visual elements, particularly colour separation for multi-colour printing; and (iii) assembly of film- and plate-making.

Whatever text material is to be printed should be pasted on the paper. Alternatively, a black and white printout can be obtained from a laser printer. Thin outlined boxes should then be marked on the page for pictures and solid black graphic areas. This combined visual and text matter is commonly known as *artwork*.

Line visuals in the artwork are pasted in position exactly as they are to appear in the final printed job or supplied separately if they are not of the required size. Type and other solid coloured elements are considered line artwork, from which line negatives are made. Continuous tone illustrations like photographs are generally submitted separately so that the process camera can sort them out through a screen and make a second (halftone) negative, which is then stripped into position with the line negative.

The visual elements may not always be available in the required same size. They can be reduced or enlarged to the required size separately and placed in a pre-determined position as per the layout. Such placement is referred to as *stripping*. The compositions of stripped negatives or positives are called *flats*. In the case of coloured continuous tone visuals, the colours are separated and a computer-driven imagesetter obtains the film output. This is followed by multi-flat stripping for four-colour process printing. Flats are used to make the offset plates.

Various materials, such as zinc, paper, plastic, and foil, can be used for the offset plate, but the most common one is aluminium. The plates are mechanically grained to hold the necessary moisture at the time of printing. They can be coated with a wipe-on solution that will enable them to be imaged from either a negative or a positive film. A plate made from a negative is known as a surface plate or helio plate.

The plate is coated with a light-sensitive emulsion and then dried. The negative flat is positioned over the plate and exposed under a high-intensity arc lamp. Light is passed through the transparent (image) area of the negative, thus making the plate coating hard and water repellant. The coating on the non-image area remains soft or water soluble and is washed off in running water, thus retaining the image on the surface of the plate. When the image is developed, it becomes visible and greasy. Figure 8.11 shows the steps involved in traditional offset printing.

These types of plates are economical for short-run jobs without halftone illustrations. This is because the surface image starts breaking after a few thousand impressions due to continuous friction between the rubber blanket and the plate cylinder. The exposure time for the surface is very little. Printers do use recycled plates for short-run jobs.

Deep-etch plates Plates made from film positives are called deep-etch plates. Here, the non-printing area is exposed to light whereas the image area remains soft and is etched when the plate is developed chemically. The etched area is filled with greasy ink in order to give the ink a receptive quality. The light, hardened coating is cleaned off by another chemical. Since the image is in micro-recessed form, there is less possibility for it to wear away during the press run. Deep-etch plates are suitable for long run jobs and fine halftone and multi-colour work.

Pre-sensitized plates Another variety of readymade coated plates are now commonly used in offset printing. These are known as pre-sensitized (PS) plates. Pre-sensitized plates can be exposed by passing light through either negative or positive film and developed by an automatic processor. Accordingly, they are called negative working plates or positive working plates. The exposed emulsion of the positive working plate is removed by wiping it with a special developer. The unexposed or image area remains in place. In the case of negative working plates, the unexposed emulsion is removed with a developer and lacquer is rubbed on the plate to make the image area strong.

Pre-sensitized plates are popular in commercial printing because they have eliminated the hassle of making and coating the plates using several chemical and equipment. In addition, coating is standardized and processed with ease, and these plates have long shelf lives (up to 6 months). Pre-sensitized plates are available in a wide range of capabilities—from short to long run jobs, say, from 1,000 to 3,00,000 impressions. These qualities of PS plates enable the offset press to be more efficient and clean, and they also save time. Figure 8.12 (a) and (b) shows how the imagesetter is used for making film negatives or positives, which are then placed on a PS plate for exposure in the modern offset printing process.

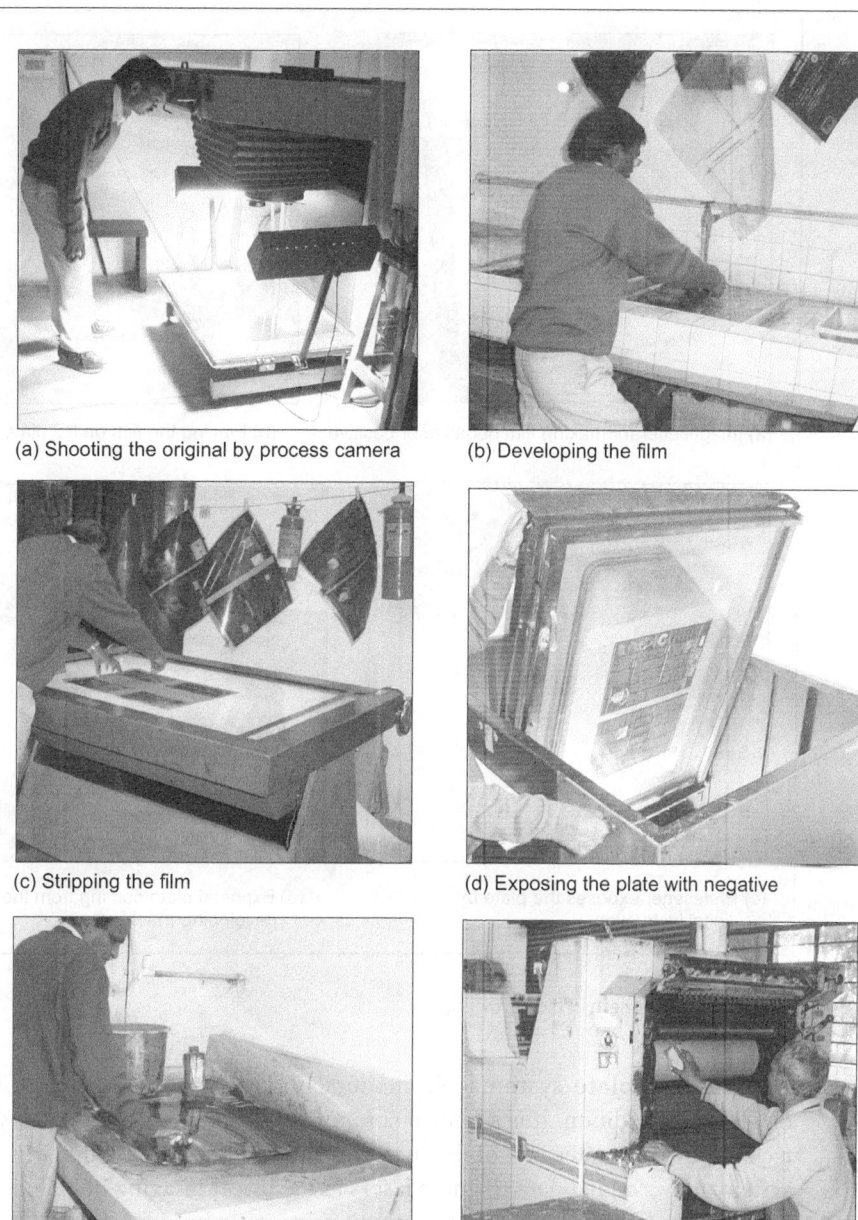

Figure 8.11 Conventional offset process

176 *Art and Print Production*

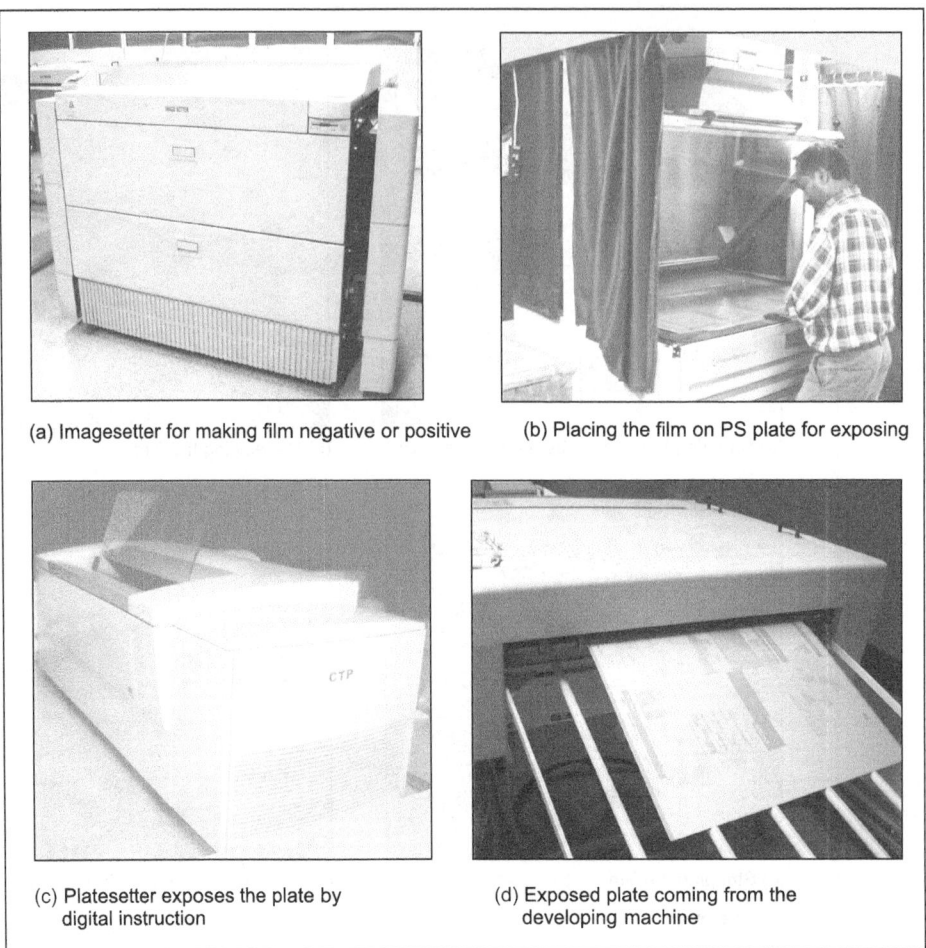

(a) Imagesetter for making film negative or positive

(b) Placing the film on PS plate for exposing

(c) Platesetter exposes the plate by digital instruction

(d) Exposed plate coming from the developing machine

Figure 8.12 Modern offset printing

Computer-to-plate systems In modern printing, computer-to-plate (CtP) technology is a new addition. It is a critical component of a completely digital work flow. This technology eliminates one of the most important steps of plate-making—the film. The system allows digital data to guide lasers in the direct imaging of a flexible plate that is loaded in a dedicated plate exposer unit commonly known as a platesetter. It greatly reduces mechanical concerns such as registration problems and dot gains, because there is no generation loss between media. This makes the plate a high-quality one and ensures extremely accurate dot placement. Figure 8.12 (c) and (d) shows how the platesetter exposes the plate and how the exposed plate emerges from the developing machine in a computer-to-plate system.

In India, CtP technology is slowly gaining popularity. However, it may not be possible for presses of all sizes to make use of its many benefits until the prices of plates and equipment, which are presently imported, drop. Moreover, CtP loses out to conventional film-based plate-making when duplicate plates or reprints are needed. In the CtP system, the imaging process has to be repeated, while a conventional plate-making system requires only re-exposure of the film. Film is a convenient storage medium that is cheaper than archiving rasterized data on magnetic media.

Types of offset presses An offset press can be set up to perform a great variety of printing combinations. It can be single colour to six colour press, sheet-fed to web-fed press, or a blanket-to-blanket printing press.

Sheet-fed presses can handle paper in a vast range of sizes and offer the most flexible printing method for everything from one colour, single-page leaflets to complete four colour illustrated books. The choice between single colour sheet-fed and multi-colour sheet-fed press depends on the format of the job. Here, format refers to number of colours, size of the page forme, type of paper, and print run. Figure 8.13 shows a single-colour and four-colour sheet-fed offset machine. Figure 8.14 shows the printing process in a sheet-fed offset machine.

A *web-fed offset press* prints on a continuous roll of paper and operates at a higher speed than sheet-fed presses. As the web of paper flies through

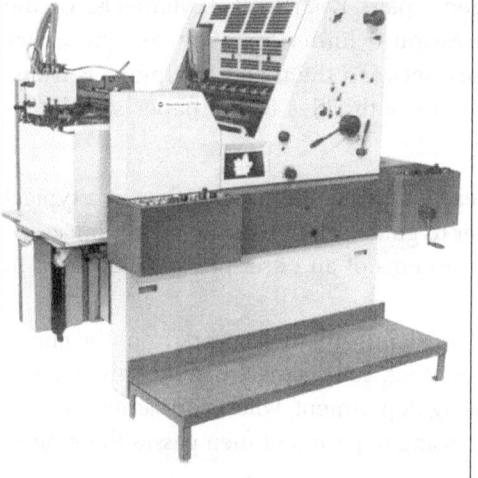

(a) Single-colour sheet-fed offset machine

(b) Four-colour machine with digital control

Figure 8.13 Sheet-fed offset machine

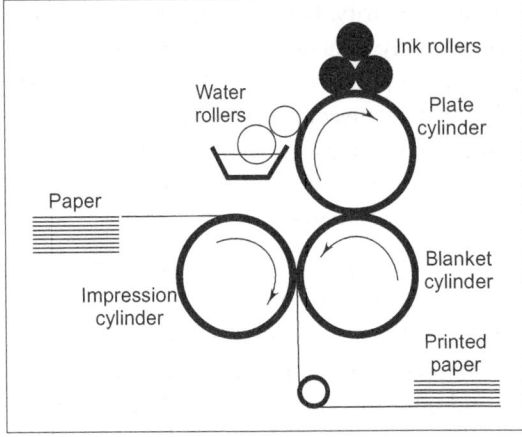

Figure 8.14 Sheet-fed offset process

the cylinders, both sides of paper are printed at the same time. High-speed multi-colour web-fed presses are controlled by computerized sensors and feedback devices that help in adjusting the ink flow, critical registration, and number of copies being printed. Figure 8.15 shows a web-fed offset machine used for newspaper printing.

Publications like newspapers are printed on *blanket-to-blanket web-fed presses*. Here, plate cylinders and their blanket cylinders are arranged in pairs. Each blanket cylinder acts as the impression cylinder for its mate. The paper passes between them and the image is transferred to both sides of the paper simultaneously.

Process flow in a typical offset printing press The general process flow in a typical offset printing press is described here in order to guide print buyers or communicators. This process flow between the various departments of an offset press is illustrated in Figure 8.16.

The office of the offset press receives orders along with the artwork from the client. Some presses handle both artwork and typesetting; some others handle only typesetting. The job is then passed on to the processing department, where the camera section prepares line and halftone images. The processing department then passes these on to

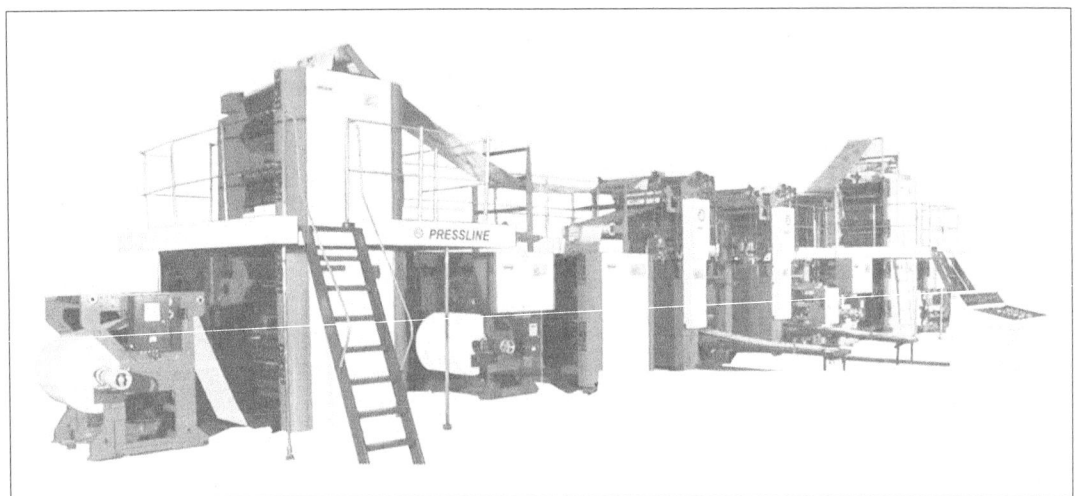

Figure 8.15 Web-fed offset machine for printing newspapers

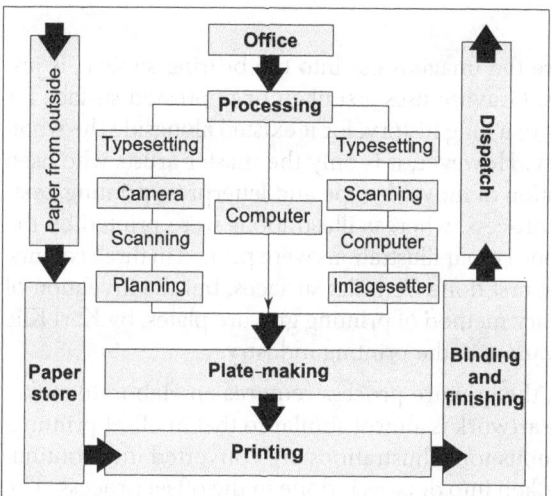

Figure 8.16 Process flow between various departments in a typical offset press

the planning section for stripping. Some printing houses have modern imagesetters which can convert composite text and illustrations directly into single-piece positives or negatives ready for exposition on the PS plate. The plate-making section keeps the coated plate ready and exposes it on receiving the flat or positive from the processing department. Modern printing establishments are equipped with the latest technology (CtP system) in which the image is processed on computer and directly exposed on to the plate. The exposed plates are fixed around the plate cylinder of the printing machine.

Meanwhile, paper comes from the paper store and is loaded on the machine. Paper should be properly stored and brought to the same temperature as in the press room before the printing starts. Printed sheets then go to the binding department for folding, stitching, cutting, packing, etc. The final department of an offset press is the dispatch department, which delivers the finished goods to the client.

Advantages and limitations Offset printing is the most popular modern method of printing because of its ability to print images of near-original quality by fine screen halftones. The use of the rubber blanket facilitates printing on less expensive paper. The printing plate for offset printing is inexpensive and can be easily curved to fit around the cylinder. It also occupies less storage space. Wipe-on plates are economical for short-run jobs without fine halftone illustrations. Deep-etch and pre-sensitized plates give a long print run and can be stored for some time for a second print run. Computer-to-plate systems with electronic imposition of complete flats eliminate the need for films entirely. This eliminates a major prepress production stage. The preparation copy of the offset process is mainly photographic or involves image-assembly, which goes well with modern reproduction methods.

The elaborate pre-printing make-ready procedure notwithstanding, the offset process is less time consuming, cleaner, and less cumbersome. It is generally rotary, which enhances the printing speed. It can also print on large-sized paper and on materials other than paper, such as tin, board, corrugated card, and plastic.

A major disadvantage of this process is the problem of controlling the balance between ink and water. If there is less dampening of the non-printing areas of the plate, the ink sticks, and if there is too much dampening, it can cause the paper to stretch, affecting printing registration. Line reproduction in dense ink is often difficult to achieve, especially in wide areas. A last-minute correction, which is sometimes inevitable, means that the pre-printing job has to be re-done in entirety. The routine maintenance of an offset press is comparatively expensive as, in order to get high-quality print, some of the departments need air-conditioning and humidity control.

Intaglio or Gravure

The gravure or intaglio process, where the image is cut into the bearing surface, is just the opposite of the letterpress process. Gravure uses a sunken or depressed surface for transferring the image. It too can boast of a long history, for it existed alongside the wood carving process in the fifteenth century. However, it is only the master artists who used it for art reproduction. After the invention of movable type and letterpress printing, text-matter was printed by the letterpress process, whereas illustrations were printed by the intaglio process. The first continuous-tone colour illustrations were printed in three colours. Printing by the gravure process was at first done from flat surfaces, but the invention of the rotogravure process, which is a rotary method of printing gravure plates, by Karl Klic in 1894, brought about significant advances in the printing industry.

The process Like the offset process, the gravure process requires an elaborate make-ready procedure. The handling of the artwork is almost similar to that in offset printing. The only difference is that the continuous-tone illustrations are converted into continuous-tone positives instead of being broken into dots, as is done in the offset process. The positive is then placed on a carbon tissue—a transfer paper coated with light-sensitive gelatin. The carbon tissue is pre-screened and appears as a graph where the lines are transparent and the spaces between them are opaque because of the gelatin. Here, the screen performs only a mechanical task—it creates walls between the cells of ink to be etched on the plate. On exposure, light hardens the gelatin. Unexposed and less exposed areas remain soft and water-soluble on the transfer paper. The carbon tissue is squeezed upside down into the cylinder (image-carrier). Then, the paper backing is soaked and peeled off like a sticker. Soft gelatin is also washed off in that action. Square-shaped gelatin of varying thickness is, however, retained by the plate surface. The plate is etched with acid. The acid eats the plate surface on the basis of the thickness of gelatin. Acid bites thinner gelatin faster than the thicker one. The space between gelatin screens is acid resistant. The result is the creation of cells or wells of different depths. The deeper cells or wells carry more ink while the shallower ones carry less ink. On giving an impression on paper, they create deeper and lighter images respectively.

Figure 8.17 illustrates a carbon tissue, a continuous-tone image, the image broken into cells, and cells of varying depths.

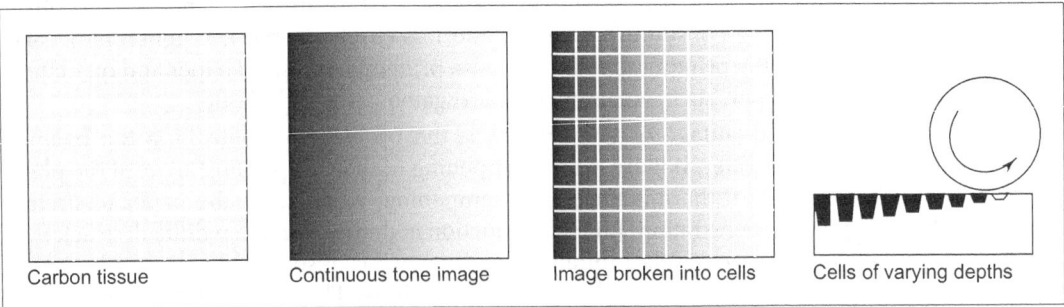

Figure 8.17 Carbon tissue, continuous tone image, image broken into cells, cells of varying depths

Printing Processes **181**

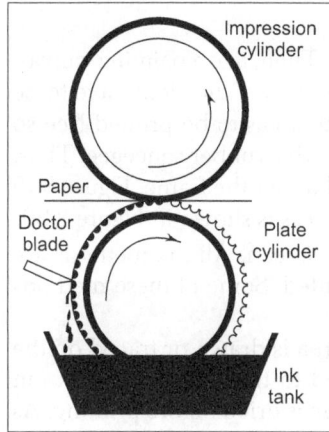

Figure 8.18 Gravure process

The etched cylindrical plate is fixed on the press. The inking of the cylinder is done by rotating it in a bath of ink. The ink is quick-dry and volatile. The pits of varying sizes and depths of the plate are filled with liquid ink. The excess ink on the plate surface is wiped clean by a thin and flexible steel blade known as 'doctor blade', leaving ink only in the depressed areas. A paper is fed between the impression and plate cylinders, which then picks up the ink from the depressed area that forms the image. Figure 8.18 shows how printing is done in the gravure process.

Advantages and limitations The gravure process allows a high-speed print run with consistent colour impression throughout the run. Quick-drying ink and images engraved into the hard surface help achieve this. Halftone reproduction in gravure is generally superior to reproduction in other processes, as the screens are not visible and look like the original continuous tone. Liquid ink spreads a bit, making a slightly blurred impression on paper. Halftone illustrations printed by gravure have a greater contrast between light and dark areas, as the darker areas are printed from deeper pits with more ink and the lighter areas are printed from shallow pits with less ink. The ability to print on inexpensive paper is probably the biggest advantage of this process. Though expensive, the gravure plates are extremely durable, saving costs for a long-run print order.

The expensive gravure plates are not suitable for short print runs. The job may not be cost effective unless the print order is more than 100,000. A distinctive feature that helps in recognizing gravure is that the entire image is screened type—line drawings as well as halftones. Line reproduction is not quite as sharp, because this area is also printed by screens (pits) and the edges of the image become soft and rugged due to the liquid ink of the pits. Correction is often done by hand on the cylinder, which is quite time consuming. The copper or steel cylindrical plates are very expensive and take more time and etchants before these can be used for printing. Proofing and last-minute alterations, which are also manual in nature, are expensive and time consuming. The introduction of modem photographic and computer systems is, however, mitigating these disadvantages. The exorbitant investments required for setting up a gravure press and the very selective print buyers have, however, impeded the growth of such presses in India.

Stencil or Silk-screen Printing

Commonly known as screen printing, this type of printing is obtained by spreading and forcing ink through a stencil, screen, or mesh of silk fabrics. Nowadays, silk is not the only fabric used. Nylon, Dacron, and wire screens are also being used with equal effect. The origin of this process has not been recorded like the other main processes of printing. The stencil, which is the main feature of the process, existed in Egypt, China, and Japan before woven silk. In Europe, it existed in the late nineteenth century. Like the other printing processes, early silk-screen or stencil printing was used by artists for their creative work. This process came into full-scale commercial use only in the early part of the twentieth century in Japan, and then in America.

The process

In screen painting, the woven fabric is first stretched tightly. Then, like a painting canvas, it is tacked or stapled on a wooden frame. The non-image parts of the cloth have to be blocked out by paper, adhesives, or chemicals, leaving the areas to be printed free so that ink or colour can be spread and forced through them with a rubber squeegee. Thus, the images are obtained by depositing ink on paper placed under the frame. Figure 8.19 shows how silk-screen printing is done, and a silk-screen press is shown in Figure 8.20.

There are various methods for blocking out the fabric screen. All the methods are in use today, depending on the type of material to be printed. Some of these methods are discussed here.

Block-out solution method In this method, the image area is drawn or traced on the screen and then a water-based fine-quality glue is applied to the screen to block out the non-image area. The glue is dried before printing. As the glue is water soluble, oil-based ink does not affect the non-image area. This method is suitable only where areas to be printed are large and flat and fine details are not required. Reverse printing of designs can be easily done by applying the block-out solution directly on the screen. Artists use the block-out solution method for creating a textural effect by scratching the screen when the solution is half-dry.

Tusche glue method This method is based on the non-mixability of oil and water. Tusche glue is an oil-based chemical. The image area is drawn directly on the screen with a thin and uniform solution of tusche glue. When the tusche is completely dry, water-based block-out solution is applied on the whole of the screen, including the tusche area. Tusche and block-out solutions have non-affinity, so the block-out solution does not stick to the areas drawn or filled by tusche. When the block-out solution is dry, tusche is removed with a piece of cloth dipped in turpentine or kerosene and the mesh of the cloth is opened for printing. This method is useful for preparing posters, greetings cards, and patterns on textiles.

Photographic stencil method This method requires that the stencil be produced with an emulsion that is sensitive to light. A photo stencil can be prepared either by transferring the image indirectly or by exposing the light-sensitive emulsion directly. Both the methods require a film positive.

The indirect method employs a pre-sensitized transfer sheet, commonly known as a five-star film, which is placed in contact with the film positive and exposed to light. The emulsion of the transfer sheet becomes hard

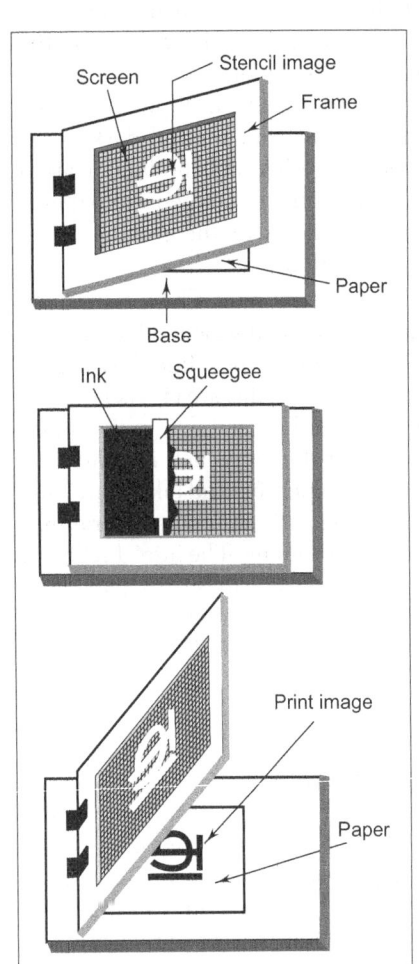

Figure 8.19 Process of silk-screen printing

Figure 8.20 Silk-screen press

in the exposed area while the unexposed area remains soft, so that it can be washed away by hot water with chemical-developing solutions. The transfer film stencil is then squeezed off the screen and the backing film is removed. This leaves the mesh blocked by hardened emulsion.

In the direct method, light-sensitive solution is applied directly to the screen and dried. A film positive is exposed to the coated screen. As a result, the non-image areas become hard and remain on the screen by blocking its mesh, whereas, on developing the film, the image area is washed away. It is possible to print delicate designs and small type by this method.

Hand-cut stencil method In this method, a lacquer film sheet made of transparent paper (backing sheet) and a transparent lacquer is used for making the stencil. The sheet is placed on the original drawing or areas to be printed, and cut with a stencil knife along the outline of the drawing instead of tracing it. These cuts are made in such a way that only the thin layer of lacquer is cut and pulled off, leaving all the non-image areas with the backing sheet. The sheet is then placed under the screen. When the film lacquer is properly melted by thinner and stuck, the backing sheet is pulled off. Now, the screen is ready for printing. This method is useful for printing bold letters and simple forms with sharp edges.

Printing

As discussed earlier, the manual printing process involves hinging the screen frame to the base board. The ink or colour is spread on the upper side of the screen and brought into contact with the paper placed below the screen in the correct position on the base board. The colour is forced through the pores of the screen with a rubber squeegee, thus creating an image on the surface placed under it. The screen is then raised and the printed piece is removed. The action is repeated till the copies required are printed.

These days, most commercial screen printing is done on automated presses. There are both web-fed and sheet-fed presses with hot air dryers which run at speeds up to 300 feet per minute or over 4000 impressions per hour. There are two types of power-operated presses. One type uses flat screens which require an intermittent motion as each screen is printed. A pair of hinges is the critical component to ensure close registration. The operator takes considerable care before running the press to maintain the desired speed. The latest type uses rotary screens with the squeegee mounted inside the cylinder and the ink pumped automatically. These processes are continuous and fast, and they print continuous multi-colour images with ease.

The printed piece should be allowed to dry for some time. Any number of colours can be printed by using this process. Each colour must, however, have a separate screen.

For accurate registration in a multi-colour job, it is better to have all the stencils made on screens of equal sizes and at the corresponding places on the screens.

Advantages and limitations

Screen printing is simple and, in many cases, it is a very cost effective method of printing. The image can be transferred to almost any surface, whether flat or odd-shaped. Any colour—opaque, transparent, glossy or matt enamel paints, plastic colour, fluorescent paint, or textile colours—may be used. The main charm of the printed image is that it looks like the original because of its high relief quality and brilliant colours. This is the only process where over-printing by light colours is possible. All the materials used are simple, inexpensive, and easy to handle. The silk-screen printing business can thus be taken up with very little capital.

The screen printing process has some limitations too. It cannot achieve fine details and mechanical characteristics like halftones and process colours. Use of photographic systems has brought about some degree of screen but not the quality achieved by other printing processes. The amount of ink applied is far greater than in letterpress, offset, or gravure, which accounts for some of the unusual effects in screen printing, since thick ink takes time to dry after the printing. Availability of many fast-drying inks nowadays has solved this problem considerably. Long-run jobs with fine details are, however, still expensive.

The versatility of the screen printing process has brought it into wide-spread use, necessitating automated production. Automation includes raising and lowering the screen frame, pulling the squeegee across the screen, and feeding and delivery of paper and drying equipment. Silk-screen is an ideal medium for printing small numbers and is very effective if used appropriately.

SPECIALIZED PRINTING

Thermography, die stamping, hot foil stamping, and hologram printing are some specialized printing techniques. We shall discuss each of these briefly in this section. Table 8.1 provides a brief description of the various methods of printing. This table would serve as an useful guideline before one gets his/her communication material printed.

Thermography

This process is called *thermography* because printing is accomplished with a relief image caused by heat or temperature. The image is first printed by letterpress, using adhesive ink. Before the ink dries up, the surface is dusted with resinous powder. The wet printed image holds the powder and the surplus powder is shaken off. The dusted sheets are placed on a moving belt made of wire net, where two to four electric heating rods are positioned under the belt. The heat created by electric rods melts the resinous powder. The mixture of melted powder and ink is hardened by means of cooling with a fan fixed on the other side of the moving belt. In most printing houses, this process is manual in nature.

Table 8.1 Factor-process selection

Category		Process	Type of job	Print order	Type of copy	Type of substrate	Make-ready	Availability
On-demand		Photostating	Letter, form, flyer, research questionnaire	Small/Medium	Typographic/line is good, colour halftone expensive	Ordinary paper for black and white smooth for colour	Cost and time involved negligible	Ubiquitous
		Digital	Simple brochure, presentation layout, report, proposal	Small/Medium	Any image which is digitized	Ordinary paper for b/w, smooth for colour, transparent sheet	Simple and low cost	Cities and small towns
		Mini Offset	Forms, newsletter, office stationery, research questionnaire	Small/Medium	Line job satisfactory, colour medicore	Ordinary paper for both black and white and colour	Simple and low cost and colour	Cities and small towns
Major	Relief	Letter Press	Book, magazine, gen. commercial, packaging	Small/Medium	Line job	Paper and card	Cumbersome but low cost	Ubiquitous
		Flexography	Package of various kinds	Medium and high print run	Line and half-tone	Paper, Plastic, foil, and corrugated materials	Simple and less expensive	Cities and towns
	Planography	Offset Planography	Newspaper, book, general commercial, metal decoration, packaging	Suitable for both big and small print order	Reasonably good line reproduction, quality half-tone is very good	Paper, thin card, thin metal sheet	High cost for quality job but low cost for ordinary job	Proliferating to cities and small towns
	Intaglio	Gravure	Packaging, magazine, catalogue, illustrated book, stamp, security printing	Suitable for only large print order	Line reproduction often not of good quality but gives good half-tone result	Paper, thin card, plastic film, and foil	High cost	Confined to big cities
	Stencil	Screen	Packaging, stationery, sticker, any job with unusual printing	Very effective for small print run	Line reproduction, coarse grain half-tone	Virtually any type of surface either flat or of any shape	Lower than other main processes	Can be set up anywhere
Specialized		Die Stamping	Letterhead, visiting card, certificate, security printing	Suitable for small run job	Only line work	Paper and card	Simple and less expensive	Cities and towns
		Thermography	Packaging, letterhead visiting card, greeting card	Suitable for small run job	Only line work	Paper and card	Simple and less expensive	Cities and towns
		Foil Stamping	Book cover, packaging, greeting card	Small and medium run job	Only line work	Paper, card, plastic, leather	Simple and less expensive	Cities and towns
		Hologram	Logos, brand name, and masterhead	Small/Medium	3D effect and flat	Foil and plastic	Complicated and costly	Cities and towns

In automatic thermographic machines, dusting, fusing, and cooling is done in an enclosed box containing a conveyor belt to carry the printed sheet, a vacuum-reclaimer system which sucks up the excess powder to re-circulate it for further use, and heating and cooling chambers. Printing is done by the letterpress process. The paper or card is fed from one side of the machine and delivered on the other side. The output is a glossy raised image.

Materials commonly printed by the thermographic process include visiting cards, letterheads, greetings cards, and packages. Thermographed products look like embossed ones; the printed images are raised in a relatively high relief on the printing stock.

Die Stamping

Die stamping is another printing process which gives a raised image. It is mainly manual but in big presses, die stamping is done on very powerful platen presses and automatic machines. Figures 8.21 and 8.22 show the manual stamping process and an automatic die stamping unit, respectively. Die stamping follows the principle of intaglio printing. It is different from thermography, for its printing images are sharper, more permanent, and highly glossy. Also, the raised image can be accomplished even without ink.

In die stamping, the design to be printed is transferred onto a piece of copper or steel plate, either manually or photographically. The design is then engraved on the plate manually. Such a plate is called a *die*. A simple die stamping machine is one in which two surfaces are prepared—one by putting the die on the bed of the machine, and the other by putting paper loading. The two surfaces are pressed hard with the paper or card lying between them. The paper falling in the impression surface is forced into the depressed area of the die along with the card to be printed. On releasing the pressure, a raised image is formed on the surface of the paper or the card. For automatic machines, two dies are used, referred to as the 'male' and 'female' die. The raised image can be obtained in colour if the depressed area is filled with ink and the excess is wiped clean. The technique can also be used for blind embossing when a raised image is produced but no ink is used.

Die stamping is a very good raised-image-making process for visiting cards, letterheads, packaging, greetings cards, certificates, and security printing material. It is used mainly for short jobs and in jobs where backside printing is

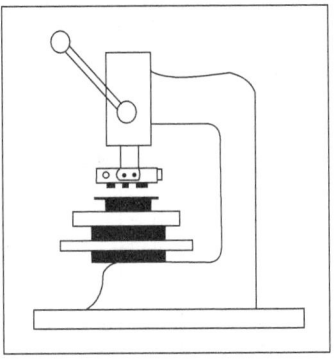

Figure 8.21 Manual die stamping process

Figure 8.22 Automatic die stamping unit

not required, the image being depressed on the backside of the printed sheet. Modern banknote presses do use this process of die stamping in certain areas of currency notes but these presses are rotaries. Their printing unit consists of a plate cylinder and impression cylinder and they use highly viscous inks.

Hot Foil Stamping

Hot foil stamping is a process in which a thin layer of foil is applied on a particular design or a pattern is applied onto a substrate. It is also called *gold leaf printing*. The three items needed to accomplish a job in this process are foil, die, and the machine for stamping.

Figure 8.23 Automatic hot foil stamping machine

A foil is a thin sheet composed either entirely of aluminium metal or a tissue-like material coated on one or both sides with metal or metal colouring. The die is the metal piece made of brass, copper, or steel. Brass and copper are especially useful for long-run jobs. In order to make the image area raised, the non-image area on the metal piece can be chemically etched, machine cut, or hand tooled. Dies are increasingly manufactured using laser, guided by computer software.

The machine can be automatic or manual. Automatic machines work like a platen press where the image carrier holds the die, which is connected with the heating system. The substrate, along with the foil sheet, is placed on the platen and then pressed by the heated die. As the heated die touches the foil, it melts and gets transferred to the substrate that is to be decorated. Figure 8.23 shows an automatic hot foil stamping machine. A manual press works almost like a die stamping process. The only difference is that the image to be printed is raised and heated before stamping.

Many paperback books, hard cover book jackets, and various types of packaging and greeting cards are foil stamped. Foil is available in different colours, patterns, finishes, textures, etc. Foil stamping that occurs in tandem with embossing is known as *foil embossing*.

Hologram Printing

A hologram image creates a floating three-dimensional look on a two-dimensional surface. It is produced by photographing an object with laser light from different angles and superimposing the image optically to create the original in a three-dimensional effect. Nearly anything that can be photographed can be made into a hologram image.

There are different types of holograms but, for printing purposes, the most commonly used is the embossed hologram. Here, embossing refers to the subtle variations in the surface structure of the metallized films, which are a few microns in thickness. This film image is then stamped on to the mirror-like surface of the hot foil, followed by a protective film layer or coating.

A hologram image is an unique expression of creativity. A communicator can select any one of the available effects from the following to make the communication material exclusive and attention-grabbing.

- Patterned foil that creates an image depth and a rainbow of shifting colours as it is viewed from different angles.
- Three-dimensional illusion in which the object seems to rotate in space as the angle of viewing changes.
- Multiple-plane hologram that creates a floating illusion at the depth of the planes.

Hologram images are ideal for security documents such as trademarks, logos, credit cards, and identity cards. They can also be used as anti-duplication devices. Holograms can also be used on book and magazine covers for creating a special effect. They lend an exclusive look to advertisement designs and promotional literature and packages. Holograms are a preferred method of brand protection because these images are difficult to photograph and tamper by any other means.

HANDLING A PRINT PROJECT

All the printing methods discussed in this chapter can help in some kind of job or the other. Each one has got some unique features to efficiently handle certain jobs. At the same time they also have some limitations. Some methods may not be available at the workplace or in the vicinity. Some methods may not be able to do all the work needed for the project. Therefore one needs to not only understand the printing processes but also understand the print shop. Before getting involved in a print project the following points need to be noted. These will make it easier to handle the job both as a print buyer and also as a service provider.

Identifying the job It may be a book, booklet, brochure, office stationery, flyer, or annual report of a company. The selection of the print shop will be determined by the approximate size, number of pages, number of colours, number of visuals, typesetting, binding, etc.

Identifying the printer It would be essential to know the machines available with the printer to handle the job from prepress processing to finishing. In order to reduce costs and have greater control over the work, it may be practical to choose a printer with only printing facility. Look for the services of a dedicated processing house that will provide films to make plates at printing press. If the job to be printed is from computer-to-plate, the facility should be available with the printing press.

Number of copies needed In most cases the required number of copies is an arbitrary decision often based on rough estimation of target readers. Sometimes the required number of copies is decided by economy of printing. For example, if only 600 copies of a coloured brochure are to be printed at a commercial print shop, it may cost ₹12,000 or ₹20 per copy. But if 1000 copies are printed, it may cost ₹13,000, or ₹13 per copy. Many will decide on printing 1000 copies as the rest could be utilized without any extra cost. The number of finished copies is called the print run.

Time needed to print the job Each print job requires a certain amount of time to print. The print buyer will fix the time or the deadline with the print shop. It can be a year, a month, a week, a weekend or immediately. Some jobs may be flexible. Setting a deadline is beneficial for both the print buyer and the printer. As a print buyer other parts of the project can be planned so that all processes will be ready on time. The printer on the other hand will be able to schedule the other jobs and the assigned job will be delivered on the due date.

Quality of the job Each printed piece needs certain quality or standard depending on its function. A promotion literature requires a much more superior look than a newsletter to be distributed among the employees of the organization. A circular in multicolour will be avoided as finances may be a constraint. When copies of class notes can be photocopied for distribution among students, colour laser printouts are obviously ruled out. Cost and number of copies required also determine the factor of quality. The latter is often compromised due to cost.

Number of colours to be printed The number of colours used in printing a page is not necessarily those many colours used while printing. In most cases they are printed by four colour ink (cyan, magenta, yellow, and black). These are mixed in different proportions at the time of printing and create various colour hues on the page. Some of the pages are printed solid or in pre-mix colours and their tints to get a desired effect. They are called processes and spot colour printing, respectively. In some situations both the techniques are used.

Kind of substrate to be used Substrate refers to all kinds of materials on which the job can be printed. Besides paper it may be cloth, plastic, foil, etc. Printing on T-shirt for an event management show, naturally printing will be on cloth, while materials of a folder for participants of a workshop may be plastic or rexin. In case of paper, there is a wide variety available. Some are versatile while some are suitable for printing a specific type of job.

Way the job will be handed over to the printer The printing lexicon describes the job for printing as copy for printing or artwork. Most of the artwork is done by the print buyer on the computer. If the job is to be photocopied, the artwork can be made on the computer and print taken on laser printer. Artwork is a bit tricky if it is meant for commercial printing. Read more about it in Chapter 9. If there is any doubt, consult the print service provider.

Budget for the project As always cost is one of the major factors for any commercial project. How much money is available for spending helps one know the budget for the project. One cannot take the services of Thomson Press (one of the top commercial presses of India) for printing office stationery. At the same time for the printing of a multicolour time bound annual report of a company, one cannot rely on local print shop. Budget low or high, one must know one's limitation and also the limitations of the service provider. There are various ways one can cut down costs, such as using thinner paper, reducing number of colours, or even reducing number of copies.

SUMMARY

Printing or duplication of images was practised in China as early as the second century. With the invention of movable type, the process was first mechanized by Johann Gutenberg in the mid-fifteenth century. Since then, printing techniques have grown in several ways.

Today, fast-paced technological development has made the printing business a high-pressure and competitive one. Several printing processes are now available with various features to meet the requirements of printers and print buyers. These processes can be grouped into three categories—on-demand, major, and specialized printing.

On-demand printing is useful for quick, economical, and short-run printing jobs. Digital, electrostatic, and mini offset printing are some of the printing techniques in this category. Various qualities of output can be obtained using these techniques, affecting the cost and quantity of output.

Most printing jobs are done by *major printing*. On the basis of the basic principle of printing, there are of four types of major printing processes—relief, planography, intaglio, and stencil. In relief printing, the image to be printed is raised in relief above the surface that carries it. The relief image is inked and makes the required impression on paper. Two methods that are based on the principles of relief printing are letterpress printing and flexography. Letterpress printing—the oldest among all printing processes—is now almost obsolete. Most printing using relief images are done by flexography, which is mainly used in printing plastic packages.

Offset printing is the dominant printing process in today's print business. It is based on the principle of planography, where the image and non-image areas are on the same plane. These are separated chemically. The printing process is based on the principle of non-mixability of oil and water. Offset printing is a modification of lithography, in which flattened limestone is used as an image carrier.

In *gravure* or *intaglio* printing, the image to be printed is cut into the bearing surface, which is filled by fast-drying liquid ink that transfers on to paper. The process allows high-speed printing for long-run jobs. The packaging industry mainly uses this process.

In stencil or screen printing, the image is printed by forcing ink through a stencil image made on cloth. It is considered one of the major processes of printing because of its ability to print on almost any surface with various effects of colour.

Specialized printing lends a special look to the printed image. It is used very selectively and can be an expensive process, especially when a large number of copies are required. Some special effects created by this process are raised images, shiny foil images, and floating three-dimensional images on a two-dimensional space. These effects may be obtained by thermography, die stamping, hot foil stamping, and hologram printing.

A brief overview of the various printing processes, as presented in Table 8.1, can be an useful aid for communicators wishing to get their material printed.

KEY TERMS

Aniline Dye An ingredient of liquid flexographic ink.

Anilox Roller A roller containing tiny cavities to carry liquid ink from the ink tank to the relief plate of flexographic printing.

Blanket-to-blanket Press In web-fed press in which plate cylinders and blanket cylinders are arranged in pairs. Each blanket cylinder acts as the impression cylinder for its mate. The image is transferred to both sides simultaneously as paper passes through the two cylinders.

Block Relief printing plates of illustrative materials, which are mounted on a wooden or strawboard platform for letterpress printing. The process of making a block is called engraving or block-making.

Carbon Tissue An image transfer sheet of gravure printing that is coated with light-sensitive gelatin tissue with paper backing.

Collation One of the finishing operations of printing in which individual printed sheets are assembled in the correct sequence.

Die Cutting A process of cutting printed sheets in irregular shapes using a die—a sharp-edged steel rule mounted on a wooden platform.

Doctor Blade A device used in the ink clean-up system of gravure and flexographic printing.

Embossing A process in which a raised image is created on a sheet of paper by pressing the paper against an engraved steel die.

Facsimile Transmission An electronic transmission system which can send written messages, photographs, and drawings over telephone lines.

Film for Printing A strip of plastic coated with light sensitive emulsion that is exposed by a process camera or imagesetter to make a positive or a negative. It is a requirement for many printing processes.

Flong A paper mache mould for a semi-circular metal plate for printing a newspaper page on a web-fed rotary letterpress machine.

Image Assembly Alternate term for stripping, cutting out, and placing in position, particularly with reference to arranging a photographic negative on a masking paper for a plate.

Imagesetter A high-resolution outputting device that produces images on photographic paper or film, used by the printer to make plates for printing.

Ink Fountain A tank or fountain that holds liquid ink that is passed to the inking system at the time of printing in gravure and flexographic printing.

Ink Viscosity Measure of a semi fluid ink's resistance to flow. High viscosity ensures that the printed image is as dense as possible.

Linotype Mechanical typesetting method in which a line of type or slug is cast by the machine's outputting device.

Molten Metal Metals that are melted by heat to cast a type.

Monotype Mechanical typesetting method in which single characters were cast by using two machines—a keyboard and a caster.

Perforating A finishing operation to tear away part of paper along the tiny narrow holes punched into a stock of paper.

Planography A printing principle in which the image and non-image area of the printing surface are on the same plain and the image is transferred on to paper. This procedure is based on the principle of non-mixability of oil and water.

Plate-setter The machine that gives the plate output for printing in a CtP system.

Pre-sensitized Plate Also known as PS plates, these are readymade coated plates that can be exposed by passing light through either negative or positive film. Accordingly, they are known as negatives or positives.

Process Camera A large camera used for graphic art photography, such as shooting negatives and positives as a prelude to plate-making, colour separation, or screening continuous-tone images into halftones.

Rasterization The process of converting graphic information into bitmap information that the output device understands.

Rubber Blanket One of the cylinders in an offset printing machine covered with a rubber sheet to transfer the image on to paper without water.

Rubber Squeegee A thick rubber blade with a handle of wood or metal, similar to a floor wiper, used in silk-screen printing to spread and force the ink through the stencil.

Screen Printing The process of obtaining an image by spreading and forcing ink through a stencil made on a screen or mesh of cloth.

Sheet-fed Press A press in which an individual sheet of paper goes in for printing.

Stripping Cutting out and placing in position, particularly with reference to arranging a photographic negative, in masking paper for a plate.

Synthetic Plate Light-sensitive coated direct image synthetic plates used in offset duplicator machines that are made directly from the copy. They eliminate the need for films.

Web-fed Press A press in which a continuous flow of paper goes in from a roll or web of paper for printing.

Woodblock Printing An early method of printing practised by the Chinese. In this process, a block of wood is cut to carve the image in relief, which is then inked to make an impression on paper.

REFERENCES

Adler, Elizabeth W. 1991, *Print That Works*, Bull Publishing Company, California.

Adams, Michael J. 2002, *Printing Technology 5E*, Delmar Thomson Learning, USA.

Adobe 1995, *Print Publishing Guide*, Adobe System Incorporated, USA.

Agfa Prepress Education Resources 1992, *An Introduction to Digital Colour Prepress*, USA.

All India Federation of Master Printers 1993, *Printing Times*, WPC5 Special Issue on Print Communication: A Global Vision, New Delhi.

Bann, David 1985, *Production Handbook*, Macdonald & Co., London.

Kipplan, Helmut 2001, Handbook of Print Media, Springer-Verllay Berlin Heidelberg, Germany.

National Institute of Industrial Research, *The Complete Book on Printing Technology*, Asia Pacific Business

Press Inc., Delhi.

Rogers, Geoffrey 1986, *Editing for Print*, Macdonald & Co., London.

Schlemmer, Richard M. 1990, *Handbook of Advertising Art and Production*, Prentice Hall, New Jersey.

Stevenson, George A. 1968, *Graphic Arts Encyclopedia*, McGraw-Hill, New York.

Strans, Victor 1988, *The Printing Industry*, Printing Industries of America Inc., Washington DC.

REVIEW QUESTIONS

1. Discuss the brief history of printing, starting from Chinese woodblock printing.
2. What were the major factors that revolutionized printing from time to time?
3. Discuss the trend towards modernization in printing in the Indian context.
4. Define on-demand printing. How does this category of printing meet the requirements of commercial printing?
5. List all the major printing processes that are being used today. Describe their basic principles and working process in brief.
6. Why is the offset process of printing the first choice of publishers and advertisers? Illustrate your answer in light of the costs, make-ready processes, availability, print orders, subtract, etc. involved in offset printing.
7. What are the types of plates used in offset printing? Discuss the advantages and disadvantages of each plate.
8. Both process cameras and imagesetters are used for film outputting. Compare the two.
9. Why is the silk-screen printing process considered one of the major printing processes despite its slow speed and manual operating processes? Describe one of the stencil making methods.
10. Why is specialized printing so called? Mention the various types of specialized printing and their applications.

PROJECTS

1. Prepare a project on printing processes. Do the following:
   (a) Collect printed samples of all the printing processes you are familiar with.
   (b) Paste them on the left pages of your project.
   (c) Label them and write a paragraph on the printing principle of each.
   (d) Write two or three paragraphs about the samples on the right-facing pages.
2. Visit a printing plant. Write a report on the working sequence of the plant.
3. Spend some time in the processing and plate-making departments of an offset press. Note your observations in relation to page planning, film output, film assembly, and plate-making.
4. Organize a silk-screen printing workshop in your institute with the help of a local silk-screen printing operator. Let the person bring all the materials needed for printing. Prepare an artwork for a greeting card or a small poster suitable for printing by this process. Take a printout on an OHP transparency, which will serve the purpose of a film positive. Transfer the image on to a framed cloth through 'five star film'. Print it on paper with the help of the operator.
5. Take a printout of the lab-journal you have prepared on the computer. Assume that 250 copies of it will be printed by the offset process. Go to a press with this copy and write the interaction you had with the printer to get the final printed copies.
6. Involve yourself in preparing a multi-colour placement brochure for your class, which will be distributed among prospective employers. You need one thousand copies of this publication, which will be printed on art paper. Prepare a print file and have a dialogue with a printer. While printing the job, be present there to supervise all the steps of operations. Get a printed copy in hand and write about your experience.

CHAPTER

Digital Prepress

Learning Objectives

After reading this chapter, you should be able to
- define the types of images that are used in digital prepress
- discuss image resolution, file formats, and their storage and transportation
- identify digital input devices and discuss how they work
- discuss digital image processing, including halftone and colour image processing
- understand digital image assembly and page planning
- list the various types of proofs to be checked at various stages of development of a publication

INTRODUCTION

Computers have revolutionized all walks of life, including printing technology. There has been considerable development in the printing industry since the introduction of the desktop computer in the mid-80s. These days, computers have enabled us to print hard copies of what we see on our desktops, transfer images through satellites, and customize size, colour, file formats, etc. to suit our requirements.

Not long ago, most of the prepress tasks were handled by skilled technicians through the use of expensive machines and complicated tools. Today, most of these tasks can be performed on a computer. Compared to the traditional prepress process, digital prepress offers much more flexibility by allowing the user to control and edit the matter with ease. The new technology has also changed the traditional role of designers and prepress professionals. Designers can now handle their own prepress work by acquiring knowledge of new technologies. With changing times, prepress professionals have changed their prepress environment with new equipment and services required for today's diverse printing needs.

The uniqueness of digital prepress lies in the integration of three areas of printing —image making, image processing, and outputting. Images can now be made as imagined, outputting has become economical and reliable, and the digital technology is so efficient and sophisticated that it has become an integral part of the industry. This chapter discusses the issues and processes involved in preparing print documents digitally. The set of tasks needed to accomplish this is referred to as *digital prepress*.

BASIC CONCEPTS

Before we discuss the digital prepress process, it is essential to develop a basic understanding of some basic concepts, terms, and tools related to related to digital prepress. We shall discuss some basic aspects of digital prepress in this section.

Image Types

We have already discussed two types of digital images—bitmap and vector—in the previous chapters. Let us now look at these images in greater detail.

Bitmap images

A bitmap image is a collection of pixels arranged on a rectangular grid. Pixels are the basic elements that make up a bitmap image. A pixel may be in black and white or in colour. The number of distinct colours that can be represented by a pixel depends on the number of bits per pixel (bpp). In the case of black and white, each pixel is formed by one bit, which means that the element is either black or white. A bit is a binary digit of a computer. In a greyscale image such as a black and white photograph, 8 bits are used for each pixel. This is because 8 bits form 256 levels of grey. An image composed of 256 shades of grey would appear photo-realistic or continuous tone on the computer screen.

In the case of colour images, there is a minimum need of 8 bits of each primary colour. A colour image with 8 bits would have 256 levels of red, 256 levels of green, and 256 levels of blue. With a combination of these three, we can get $256 \times 256 \times 256 = 16,777,216$ possible colours.

Eight bits or 256 levels of colour are adequate for most designs, but some situations may demand a more realistic presentation of colours. For instance, when colours are to be faded smoothly with another, then 16 bits or even 32 bits of colour are used. Here, one should note that bitmap images are resolution dependent. They lose details and look less sharp if enlarged.

All scanned images and images from digital cameras are bitmap images.

Vector images

These images are made up of mathematically defined lines and curves. Unlike bitmap images, vector images remain sharp even when enlarged. The vector format is ideal for typographical content, line art such as logos and drawings, and flat-coloured graphics. Vector objects may consist of lines, curves, and shapes with editable attributes such as colour fill and outline. Vector images need to be handled carefully in digital prepress because, in a computer, vector does not exist as an image but as a formula. Vector images are unsuitable for producing photorealistic visuals. Despite the fact that vector images are usually made up of solid areas of colour or gradients, they cannot depict the continuous subtle tones of a photograph.

These days, with advanced vector graphic tools, it is possible to achieve much more than was possible a few years ago. Modern vector tools allow the user to apply bitmapped textures to objects, giving them a photorealistic appearance. Moreover, soft blends, transparency, and shading can be applied using these tools.

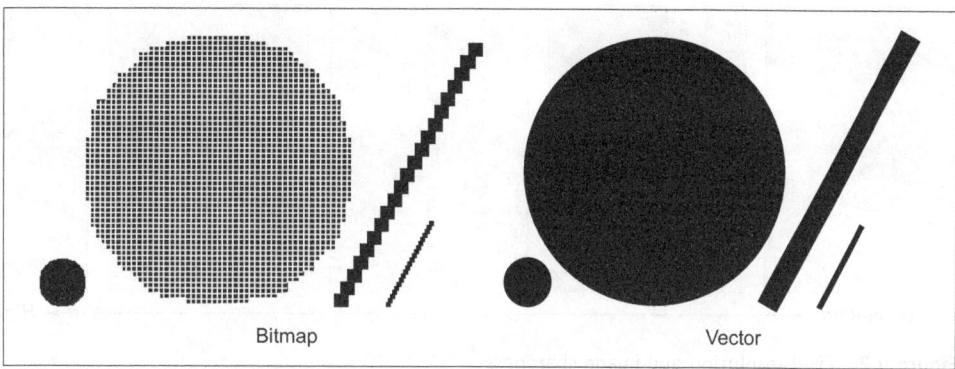

Figure 9.1 Characteristics of bitmapped and vector images

Prepress professionals should prepare vector images on the computer screen in the same way as they would appear on a printed page. There are two ways to achieve this—(i) by using the computer language of PostScript and (ii) by converting the vector image into a bitmap image through the process of rasterizing.

The characteristics of bitmap and vector images are illustrated in Figure 9.1 by showing an enlarged dot and a line in a bitmap form as well as a vector form.

Image Resolution

Resolution refers to number of dots or pixels available to represent graphic details in a given area. The resolution of an image on a computer screen can be expressed in terms of *pixels per inch* (ppi). It can be expressed in dots per inch (dpi) if the image output is produced on a laser printer or imagesetter.

The resolution of an image determines its quality or the degree of details and definition in the image. Figure 9.2 illustrates how the sharpness of an image is determined by its pixel resolution. The higher the ppi, the more space the file takes up, the slower it is to edit and work with, and, sometimes, the harder it is to print. Another factor that influences the image quality is screen frequency or lines per inch (lpi). There is a relationship between ppi, dpi, and lpi in commercial printing. The best resolution for an image can be obtained by multiplying its screen frequency by 2, that is, image resolution (in lpi) = 2 × screen frequency (in dpi). Therefore, if the screen frequency is 150 lpi, the best image resolution should be 300 ppi. Also, as mentioned earlier, 8 bits per pixel can create 256 levels of grey. Therefore, 150 lpi = 300 ppi × 8 = 2400 dpi. In other words, there will be 2400 dpi to create the 150 lpi.

The existing applications in the market can be divided into the following two categories.

Pixel-based applications These are the applications where bitmap files can be edited. Adobe Photoshop and Corel PHOTO-PAINT are examples of bitmap files.

Vector-based applications These are the applications where vector files can be edited. Adobe Illustrator and CorelDRAW are examples of such applications.

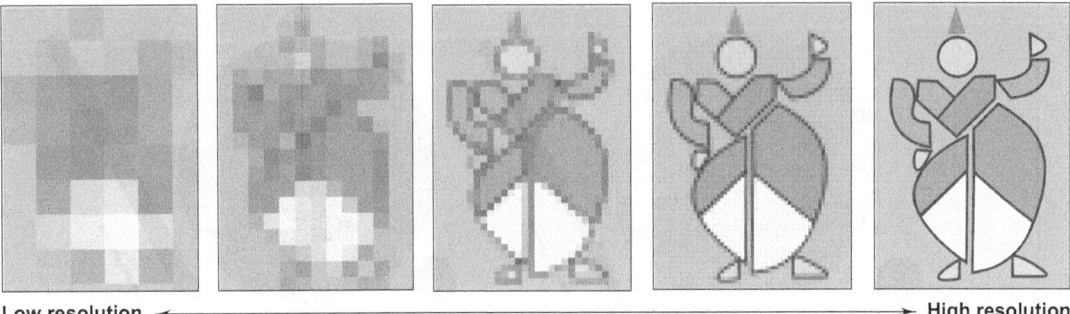

Figure 9.2 Pixel resolution and image sharpness

File Formats

Image files are saved, stored, opened, and transported in specific formats before the final printing. Knowledge of these formats would help us in choosing the right format for various kinds of images.

Native format

The native file format of an application is also known as its default file format or proprietary format. The native file formats of applications are proprietary and these types of files are not meant to be transferred to other applications. Usually, special software-specific image properties can only be retained when an image is saved in the software's native format.

PSD Adobe Photoshop's native format is PSD. It saves all its layers, channels, paths, and so on in the most flexible way. All that can be done in Photoshop is supported by the PSD format. Other formats do not have this capability.

CDR CDR is CorelDRAW's native format. The file takes up the smallest amount of disk space if it is saved in the native format. It opens and saves the fastest, and is always fully editable. After working in CorelDRAW, the user needs to save the artwork in the CDR format. The saved CDR file can be re-opened and edited.

AI Adobe Illustrator now has three native formats—AI, PDF, and EPS. In older versions of Illustrator, AI was the only native format. In the latest versions, when a PDF or EPS file from Illustrator is saved, one section saves the matter in native AI and the second section saves it in PDF. When the PDF file is opened in Acrobat, it appears in a normal PDF format, and when the same PDF is opened in Illustrator, the file can be edited.

When an image is being sent to another application, it should be converted or exported to a standard image format. This, however, does not need to be done when transferring an image between applications from the same publisher. For example, there should be no problem sending Adobe Illustrator files to Adobe Photoshop, or Corel PHOTO-PAINT files to CorelDRAW.

Standard image format

It is important to keep in mind that an earlier version of a program cannot be used to open files saved from a latter version of the same software. In most cases, image properties that are specific to the latter version will be lost if this is attempted.

The various types of standard images are described here.

TIFF A Tagged Image File (TIFF) format is a standard image file format which is used for saving material that is to be sent to the printer or for importing matter into a page layout application. Usually, a graphic designer works in a PSD format (as this format supports all attributes of the Photoshop application) but saves the file in a TIFF format to send the file to printer or to a page layout program.

PS PostScript (PS) is a page description language developed by Adobe Systems. The key feature of PostScript is device independence which allows many different outputs devices from different manufacturers to print the same file in more or less the same way. A PostScript file contains all relevant information needed to print the document. It embeds in itself the contents of the layout, its multiple pages, fonts, colours, and a variety of other information.

EPS Encapsulated PostScript (EPS) is a graphic file format which is widely recognized by computer applications and printers. A variety of applications generate and read EPS files. When saving a file in EPS format, a lot of information gets attached to it for later interpretation by other applications. Embedded images, paths, font information, clipping masks, and bounding boxes are some of them. The EPS format is excellent for use where vector graphics information is to be retained. The Encapsulated PostScript format scores over the PostScript format in that it can be placed in any graphic application.

PDF The Portable Document Format (PDF) is a widely used document format for a variety of purposes. These files can be viewed using Adobe Acrobat Reader or any other PDF viewer application. Images, graphics, fonts, etc. are embedded within the file and can be easily shared with computers across different platforms. The PDF format is gradually becoming the standard transport file format for the commercial prepress industry. Security features can be attached to PDF files for preventing unauthorized viewing, editing, and printing. It is a perfect document format for business, engineering, and creative professionals to create, distribute, and exchange secure and reliable information.

File Transportation and Storage

The image files that are created for prepress processing are usually large. It may sometimes be difficult to send such heavy folders to the printer or elsewhere. They may also be difficult to store or archive.

Image files can either be transported electronically—through e-mail—or sent in the form of pen drives, CDs, DVDs, etc. It may be difficult to transport very heavy files through e-mail. Moreover, when files are sent electronically, it may pose a problem if the person at the other end does not have the same software application to open it.

Besides e-mail, portable media disks can be used to transport files. Not long ago, there were limited options to store or transport required files to the prepress service provider for imaging. These days, a host of options are available for data transportation as data storage has become less expensive. Depending on the file size, an appropriate portable disk can be chosen.

Floppy disks can store only up to 1.44 MB data. They are very handy, but not quite reliable. Read only or re-writable CDs can store up to 700 MB data. They are highly efficient and can be opened in any computer. Magnetic Optical Devices (MOD or MO) can store up to 250 MB data. Most service bureaus have the drive for MODs, but an external drive is required for MODs on a personal computer. DVDs can transport large files of up to 9.4 GB data, and can also be used as backup devices. Auxiliary hard drives or tape backup systems can also be used for data storage purposes.

Compressed file format

For easy storage and transportation of information, heavy files may be saved in a *compressed format* and then e-mailed or stored in a CD or DVD. Compression is primarily used to shrink the information in a file. It may be of two types—*lossy* and *lossless*. The lossless type can be compressed without losing any data, and the image looks exactly the same when compressed. A lossy compression, however, leads to some data loss, thus, the image may lose some details after being compressed. Some compressed file formats are as follows:

LZW   Lemple, Ziff, and Welch developed the LZW lossless compressive format, which is named after them. Images in TIFF can be saved with LZW compression. Such a format is completely lossless, but it may be difficult to open such files in any other format.

ZIP   It is another lossless format. It works best with images containing large areas of a single colour.

JPEG   It is the standard lossy format for bitmap images. It was developed by the Joint Photographers' Expert Group. JPEG is a commonly used format on the Internet. It is, however, not suitable for high-quality printing.

Locating data

It is sometimes difficult to locate data stored on the computer. One should therefore store it systematically on the hard drive of the computer. Previews, customized thumbnails, and slide shows can be used for systematic storage of data. These are especially helpful when one is working on multiple files.

IMAGE INPUT

The first stage of digital prepress is that of image inputting. Several input devices are available for this. Once an image input has been obtained, it needs to be processed. In this section, we shall discuss the various devices used to obtain image inputs and their characteristics in a digital format.

Input Devices

Keyboard, mouse, electronic tablet, scanner, and digital camera are some computer input devices. Scanners and digital cameras are considered to be the major input devices for digital prepress.

Scanners

Scanning refers to the conversion of information in a reflective or transparent flat object into digital information that a computer can understand and process. Photographs, for instance, can be scanned to obtain a digital image on the computer.

Two types of scanners are normally used in prepress work—the flatbed scanner and the drum scanner.

Flatbed scanner A flatbed scanner uses charge-couple device (CCD) technology. It is characterized by the use of an array of light-sensitive elements which translate analogue signals into digital information. The image to be scanned remains flat and stationary on a glass surface on the scanner and, like a photocopy machine, the scanning head moves down the length of the image in 1-pixel increments. Scanning quality depends on three characters of a CCD scanner—*dynamic range, bit depth,* and *resolution.*

- The *dynamic range* of a scanner is the scanner's ability to capture a range of densities representing both highlight and shadow details in the original copy.
- The *bit depth* of a scanner is the number of colours or amount of information it can capture. The bit depth has an effect on the size of the file and smoothness of image gradation. For example, 8 bit colours capture 256 levels while 24 colours capture more than 16 million colours.
- *Resolution* refers to the number of pixels per liner inch captured by the scanner. To determine the best scanning resolution for a particular job, the quality requirement needs to be known. The scan resolution should be based on the enlargement, reduction, and screen ruling of the original. For images that need to be resized, the required scan resolution can be obtained by calculating the scaling factor and multiplying it by twice the screen ruling. For example, if an original of 4″ height is to be reproduced in 6″ height with 120 lpi, the required scan resolution would be $6/4 \times 120 \times 2 = 360$ ppi. Line art scanning needs three to four times higher resolution than a continuous tone art. The user should first ensure that his/her output device can support this resolution. Otherwise, the quality of the printed image may suffer.

For best results, decisions regarding scan resolution and scaling need to be taken at the time of the scanning. Editing images later in an application will not bring in much improve in the quality of the image. Figure 9.3 shows a high-end flatbed scanner.

Figure 9.3 High-end flatbed scanner

Drum scanner In drum scanning, the image to be printed—which is usually a transparency—is mounted on a drum using adhesive tape. During scanning, the drum spins rapidly, exposing each part of the image to the light source which moves in tiny increments across the original. The reflected or transmitted lights are then sent through a photo multiplier tube (PMT), which breaks the light into RGB components. Other circuitry converts the analogue light information to digital, CMYK separations.

Figure 9.4 Drum scanner

High-quality imaging needs drum scanning. Since the equipment is costly and requires expert operators, the facility is usually available with commercial printers only, and is a little expensive. Figure 9.4 shows a drum scanner for scanning images from colour transparencies.

Digital cameras

All cameras—be they digital or film cameras—capture images. The requirements for working on film cameras and digital cameras are, however, different. The output (bromide and transparency) of film cameras need to be scanned for prepress work. Digital images, however, do not require this step of scanning. A digital camera is basically a little scanner, and works almost on the same technology as that of a CCD scanner. All the concepts of pixels, file size, and resolution apply to digital cameras as well. Images are captured as RGB data, typically in the TIFF format, and then converted to various colour spaces and file formats as required. A digital device is required for storing, editing, and printing pictures captured with a digital camera.

Some of the advantages of digital photography are as follows:
- There is no time wastage between the stages of exposure and the final image.
- There is no generation loss from the original to the copies.
- There is no requirement for films that need to be processed.
- Images are sharper, clearer, and show more details than films.
- The images can be edited according to one's requirement, and bromide prints of the same can be taken.
- The storage capacity of digital cameras can be extended by updating memory cards.

IMAGE PROCESSING

Once the image inputting is over, these images need to be processed for printing. Continuous tone images need to be converted to halftones. Colour images also need to be processed and separated. In this section, we shall discuss the process of creating digital halftones and the processing of colour images.

Halftones

For the purpose of printing, continuous tone images should be converted into screens termed as halftones. A screen in the traditional method of printing consists of a fine grid of lines on film, which break the image up into dots and thus produce a halftone film. In the digitized method, these dots are created through computer programming.

Digital halftones are generated for outputs to imagesetters, computer to plate, and laser printers. The functions of digital halftones and traditional halftones are the same. In traditional halftones, screening dots are of variable sizes with fixed spacing. In digital

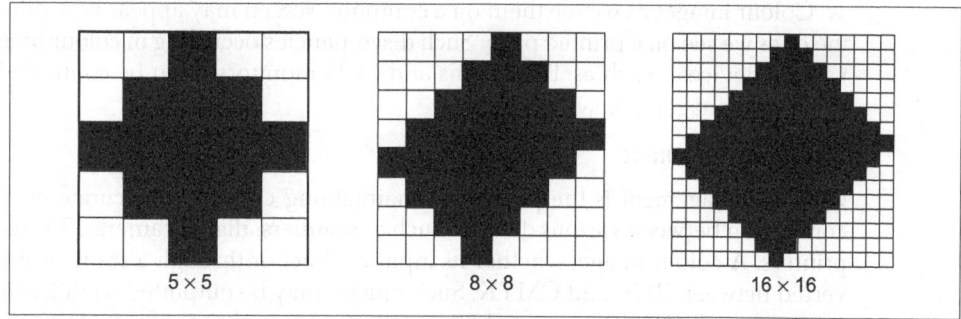

Figure 9.5 Halftone cell of varying spots and changing shapes

halftones, each halftone cell is made up of a number of spots, as shown in Figure 9.5. The sizes of dots are determined by the number of spots either off or on within the halftone cell. Each halftone cell can produce different levels of tonal value, as shown in Figure 9.6.

Halftone dots or screens can be fine or coarse, depending on the eventual printing method and paper being used. Most books and magazines use 133 to 150 lpi screens, whereas newspapers can be as coarse as 65 to 100 lpi screens. The figures used to describe screens relate to the number of lines per inch on the screen (lpi), often termed as *screen frequency*.

Screen angles are another important aspect of colour halftone printing. If the screen angles of all the colour plates for four colour printing are the same, the result will be almost black and white printing because the dots are overlapping. If the angles of the dots are too irregular, say, 80° for cyan, 20° for yellow, and 30° for other colours, a different colour is created. In order to enable the eye to perceive the colour, dots of each colour must be printed close to each other. This is achieved by changing the screen angle of each colour. The standard screen angles are 45°, 75°, 90°, and 105° for black, magenta, yellow, and cyan, as shown in Figure 9.10 in the section on process colour printing.

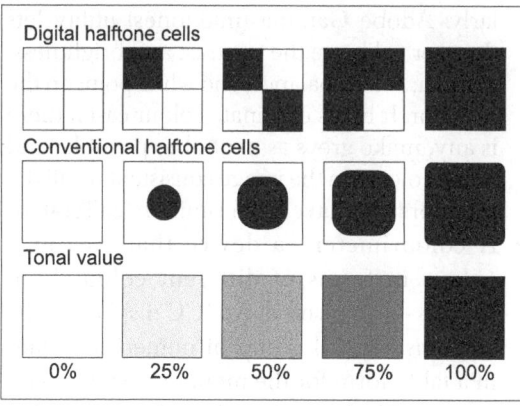

Figure 9.6 Halftone cells with different tonal values

Colour Images

Colour plays an important role in visual communication. In this section, we shall discuss how colour images are handled digitally. Some of the commonly used colour modes are RGB, CMYK, and greyscale. The RGB mode, which stands for red, green, and blue, is based on additive theory. The CMYK mode, which stands for cyan, magenta, yellow, and black, is based on subtractive theory. The CMYK mode is used for printing. Greyscale is a black and white colour space.

Colour images as we see them on a computer screen may appear very different from the ones we see on a printed page. Such discrepancies occurring in colour images across various devices—such as TV screens and LCD monitors—can be controlled by using a colour management system (CMS).

Colour management

Colour management is the process of maintaining consistent, accurate colour during conversion between various devices, such as scanners, digital cameras, TV screens, and printers. A colour image, whether its input is direct or through a scanner, may be converted between RGB and CMYK. Such images may be outputted on different software applications (in RGB) or printed from various output devices (in CMYK). The colour of the outputted image does not appear the same on all devices, be it an LCD monitor, a video frame, or a plasma TV screen. This can be attributed to several factors:

- Human eyes can see more colours than can be reproduced by digital devices such as scanners, cameras, monitors, and printers.
- The colour gamut of all devices is different. Monitors can display more colours than can be printed, and some printing colours cannot be seen on a monitor.
- Monitors and printers process colour in completely different ways. Monitors use the additive colour system while printers use the subtractive system.
- Colours printed on paper look different from those on the original. The smoothness of the page and its colour and ink absorbing qualities determine the look of the colour image on the printed page.

The problem of colour discrepancy can be solved in the following ways:

- The colour management system (CMS) can be uploaded on the computer as a software solution to the problems in all digital images. Apple ColorSync and Microsoft ICM2 are two standard colour management systems used in the industry. Figure 9.7 shows how a colour management system works.
- Computer monitors can be calibrated regularly. Adobe Gamma (mid-tones) utility lets the user calibrate the contrast and brightness, gamma, colour balance, and white point on the monitor. It helps eliminate colour cast if there is any, make greys as neutral as possible, and make colours in the image consistent on all the monitors that have been similarly calibrated.
- A colourimeter—a device that measures colour in terms of different colour light sources—can be used. An ICC display profile contains a small group of numerical values in a table-form for the monitor's white point, gamma, black point, and the balance of the RGB primaries.

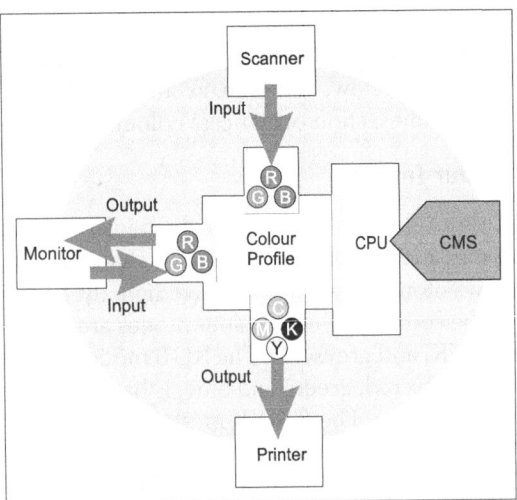

Figure 9.7 Colour management system

- Prepress work should always be reviewed throughout its development by checking the proofs. Proofs should always be taken on the paper on which the matter will finally be printed.

Colour separation

The most common way of printing colour artwork is by producing a positive or negative image of the artwork on paper or film and then transferring the image to a printing plate to be run on a press. *Colour separation* is required for preparing artwork for this process. This is done by first separating the composite art into its component colours used in the printing process—cyan, magenta, yellow, black, and any spot colours needed to print the artwork. To produce high-quality separations, it helps to be familiar with the basics of printing, including line screens, resolution, process colours, and spot colours. By working closely with the print shop that will produce the separations and consulting its experts before beginning each job and during the process, one can achieve high-quality colour images.

To reproduce colour and continuous-tone images, printers usually separate artwork into four plates—one plate for each of the cyan, magenta, yellow, and black portions of the image. When inked with the appropriate colour and printed in register with one another, these colours combine to reproduce the original artwork. The process of dividing the image into two or more colours is called *colour separating*, and the films from which the plates are created are called the *separations*.

Spot colour printing   *Spot colour printing* is the printing of line image in colour. Spot colour is also called an extra colour in printing. If an image is printed in cyan, magenta, yellow, black (CMYK) and an extra colour, this extra colour is a spot colour. Spot colours are usually used when we are not able to obtain a desired output in CMYK printing. Colours such as gold and silver, which cannot be obtained by mixing CMYK, are printed as spot colours. 'Specifying a spot colour' means that any page element assigned that colour will appear on the same colour separation. Each spot colour is reproduced using a single plate. Spot colour can also be used to add solid and screened blocks of colour to an image. By screening the spot colour, one can create the illusion of adding an extra, lighter colour to the printed piece.

Process colour printing   Printing of continuous tone colour images in cyan, magenta, yellow, and black (CMYK) is called *process colour printing*. It creates the illusion of full colour with a precise halftone pattern. The CMYK model is based on the light-absorbing quality of ink printed on paper. We have already discussed this aspect of colour in Chapter 6.

On the computer, colours are separated by the channel command of the image editing program in the CMYK mode. Figure 9.8 shows a screenshot of the channel command in Adobe Photoshop. The channels show the amount of each process colour that will be printed. They are viewed on films and plates in grey as default channel colours.

Figure 9.8 Computerized process colour separation

In theory, pure cyan (C), magenta (M), and yellow (Y) pigments should combine to absorb all colours and produce black. For this reason, these colours are called *subtractive colours*. However, as all printing inks contain some impurities, these three inks actually produce a muddy brown and must be combined with black (K) ink to produce a true black. The symbol 'K' is used instead of 'B' for black to avoid confusion with blue, which also starts with the letter 'B'. The process of combining these inks to produce colour is called *four-colour process* printing. Figure 9.9 (*see also Colour Plate 4*) shows how these colours combine to form the final image.

Font

Digital typography is still handled in the same manner as traditional typography in terms of kerning, tracking, formatting, and leading. Three basic types of fonts are in use

Figure 9.9 Combination of four colours (*see also Colour Plate 4*)

today—PostScript, TrueType, and OpenType. These fonts have already been discussed in Chapter 2. PostScript fonts have two components—screen fonts and printer fonts—whereas TrueType fonts include display and output information in a single file. Open Type fonts are platform-independent fonts. That is why the same OpenType font can be use for Windows and for Macintosh.

IMAGE ASSEMBLY

Image assembly is required to make all the components of a design suitable for printing. It is an art as well as a science. Issues such as page layout, preparing the artwork for printing, and characteristics of artwork are discussed here to enable successful digital workflow.

Page Layout

Page-layout software allows digital assembly of all page elements prior to being sent to the specified output device. Software such as Adobe PageMaker, Adobe InDesign, and QuarkXPress are used for this purpose.

Conventionally, page layout is done on design grids and involves the visual organization of the design and editorial parameters for a particular book, magazine, or promotional literature. Each grid is an actual size plan of a double page spread, showing the position and extent of the text and illustration areas, location of headings, page numbers, trim size of the page, and so on. In fact, all the positional information that everybody needs—right from the editor and designer to the typesetter and printer—is there on the design grid. Design grids are discussed in greater detail in Chapter 4.

These days, grids can be created easily on computer screens. The design process converts the empty grids into layouts that show the text and illustrations fit together within the grids. This process can be carried out much faster digitally than through the conventional method.

Artwork

Photographs, sketches, types, etc., are the raw materials for preparing artwork. These elements are turned into art when combined with creative vision. The first step for preparing the artwork or original for printing is the integration of words and pictures.

Artwork can be prepared by using one of the three main methods, depending on the requirement of the publication. These are line, halftone, and page planning.

Line art

In line art, the original artwork is a black and white solid image. Most typographic images are in the form of line art. Line art is made by laying out the typographic content and drawing outlines of the illustrative area or graphic shapes. In case the design contains tint areas or flat colours, the art should carry the outlines for these as well. The line art should carry trim marks at the four corner of the page. These marks indicate where the page will be trimmed after printing.

Art that is prepared on a DTP system can be checked by taking a proof print of the piece. It should be ensured that all types are in the right position. Special attention needs to be paid to areas where widow/orphan lines or words occur. Further, it should be ensured that page numbers, running heads, titles, and captions are accurate and placed correctly.

Despite careful checking, some spelling errors in the artwork may be overlooked. Errors at the proof stage are relatively inexpensive. Changes on the camera-ready art or the film output of a digital file, however, may prove to be costly. The proofs, therefore, need to be checked thoroughly, particularly if the typesetting work has been outsourced.

Halftone art

This is the process used to produce a halftone negative or positive from a continuous tone original such as a photograph or scanned bitmap image. A photograph, unlike a line original, does not consist only of areas that are either black or white. It is made up of infinite shades of grey. In other words, it is a continuous tone image. Continuous tone images cannot be printed as such by the offset process. The picture first needs to be broken up into very small dots that simulate the greys. These dots are larger in the dark areas and smaller in the pale areas, creating the effect of dark and light tones of grey, although printed in black ink. Colour continuous tone images are also converted into halftones by separating and screening four colours—cyan, magenta, yellow, and black. Here, dots of varying sizes from the four different colour separations overlap to accurately reproduce the colour original (Figure 9.10, *see also Colour Plate 4*).

The originals need to be sent to the printer so that continuous tone images can be converted into halftones. Before sending the originals to the printer, it should be ensured that these images are cropped proportionately so that they fit into the space indicated for them on the original art. Necessary instructions for size enlargement or reduction, the page number on which the will appear, etc., should be marked clearly. The back side of the original can be used for this purpose.

Page planning

The success of the finally produced design largely depends on careful planning of the prepress work. The tasks discussed in this section help to keep the project on schedule and save money. Proper planning ensures that the document is printed properly and reduces re-work required from the prepress service provider.

Image integration All pictures are scanned with the help of scanning software, which come along with the scanner. The scanned files are stored in a format such as TIFF, is easily understood by the digital prepress format.

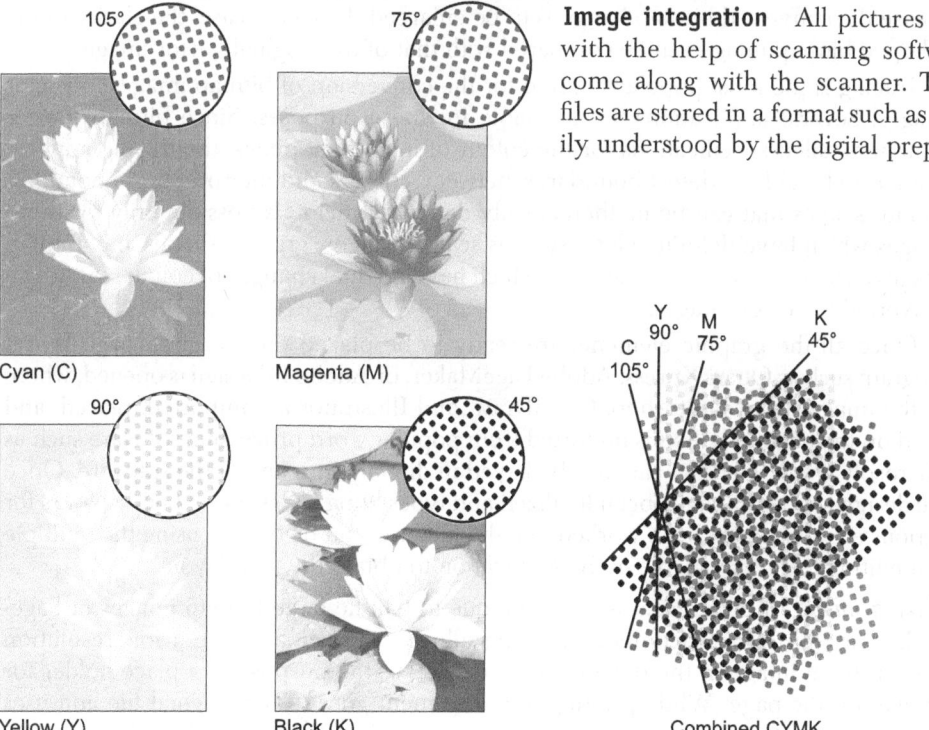

Figure 9.10 Film separation of four colours with enlarged dots in respective angles (*see also Colour Plate 4*)

Touch-up of images for dust and scratch removal, colour corrections, effects, etc., is done using software like Photoshop. These tasks should be carried out before the file is saved in the TIFF format. This is because Photoshop files (PSD) work on layers and can be edited easily layer by layer. The moment the file is saved in TIFF, the layers of the image are merged and no alteration is possible after that. Line art illustrations are created in programs such as Adobe Illustrator and CorelDRAW.

Conversion of images Two types of images are processed in digital page planning—vector and bitmap. These are easily handled if created in their respective applications. Problems are encountered when one type of image is to be converted to another, that is, from vector to bitmap or from bitmap to vector. The reasons for this will be apparent if we consider what such conversions involve.

We already know that vector images are resolution independent and retain their sharpness when enlarged. Another characteristic of vector images is that these images can be converted into bitmap images. On conversion, the quality of these images in display or in print is largely dependent on the number of pixels or dots making the image. Therefore, before converting the vector image, it is mandatory to specify the output resolution of the final bitmap as per the size in which the output is required. It is advisable to keep a copy of the original image in the native vector format before converting it to bitmap. Once it has been converted to bitmap, the image loses all the wonderful qualities it had to its vector state. The original vector image will be required in case the converted bitmap image is to be enlarged. In such a case, the clarity of the enlarged bitmap image can be compared with that of the original vector image.

Tracing is the most popular method for the conversion of bitmap images to vector images. Several applications are available for these purposes. Since bitmap images contain detailed specifications for the colour of individual pixels, the tracing application has to be able to detect boundaries between colours and interpret those boundaries into shapes that can be mathematically defined. Tracing is possible only for those images which have definite edges, such as scanned logos, graphic shapes, etc. Bitmap images such as scanned photographs, which have gradual changes of colour, cannot be converted to vector images.

Once all the graphic elements are ready to be placed on a page, a page layout program such as QuarkXpress, Adobe PageMaker, or Adobe InDesign is opened, where all the images from Photoshop, CorelDraw, and Illustrator are imported, placed, and sized on the page. The text is imported from popular word processing software such as Microsoft Word. The text can also be keyed in directly into any of the software. Once the design and layout have been finalized and typesetting styles for text and colours for various elements have been worked out, the material can be typeset using the multiple text editing feature available in the application to obtain the final layout.

Linking image Linking is a useful technique to handle large bitmap images in PageMaker or Illustrator documents. Linking allows the user to place a low-resolution version of an image in the document, which serves the purpose of a place-holder for display on the page. While printing, the document goes to the original file and uses the high-resolution information to print the image where it belongs. The file cannot be printed without that original bitmap image.

Digital Prepress **209**

Imposition For planning a multi-page publication, the pages need to be arranged in the sequence in which they will be printed and folded for binding. The process of arranging single pages is called *imposition*, and each set of pages is called a *signature*.

Imposition is done at the page planning stage. In the conventional method, a paste-up artist does the imposition after films are made. These days, the imposition is done digitally in the Adobe PressWise software, which arranges the digital document in the proper sequence. In the software, the pages are arranged so they appear in the correct order once the signature sheet has been printed, folded, and trimmed.

Trapping Trapping is the method of expanding or shrinking an adjacent colour area into another area minutely in order to compensate for misregistration and resultant gaps between colours. Traditionally, designers used to provide trapping on their artwork, and the prepress technicians incorporated this into the film stripping. In digital prepress software such as Adobe Illustrator and QuarkXpress, trapping can be handled efficiently. Hence, the printing or the prepress service provider may be asked to handle the trapping choices at the stage of colour separation and outputting the film. Adobe TrapWise is a trapping software that can trap complex artwork by choking the background or spreading the foreground. Figure 9.11 shows how trapping can solve the problems of knockout, overprint, and misregistration.

All designs do not require trapping. Such designs include those that contain isolated solid colours and process colours that share sufficient percentage of ink components. Overlapping may compensate misregistration but can change the colour value of the image. Text type with trapping distorts its character. A thin black outline can hide any misregistration. One should avoid resizing graphics which have already been trapped in another application.

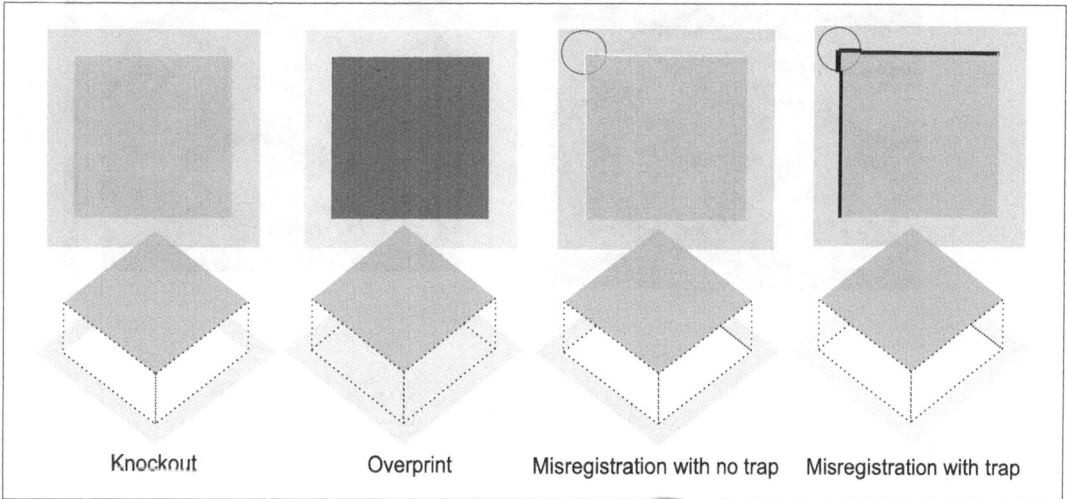

Figure 9.11 Trapping to solve knockout, overprinting, and misregistration

Crop marks It is imperative that before the mechanical is begun, the exact size of the printed piece should be determined. The exact size of the publication is called its *trim size*. Trim size is indicated with crop marks on the mechanical, often called trim marks or corner marks. These are thin ruled black lines placed at the edges of the boundary box of artwork that indicate the actual finished size, as illustrated in Figure 9.12. These marks are retained on the printing plate as well as the printed sheet and serve as guides for positioning it in a press form or for aligning the cutting knives when the printed piece is to be trimmed. The size of the marks should be short (approx. 2 cm) and placed slightly away from the corner of the bounding box so that they do not interfere with bleed lines. Many desktop publishing systems are capable of automatically printing crop marks for the camera-ready copy.

Bleed The content of an image in a design extend to the edge of a printed sheet. It should be ensured during page planning that, when the printed paper is trimmed during the finishing process, that part of the bleed that was printed beyond the trim mark is cut away, leaving only the content required in the design. Figure 9.13 shows how a bleed area that goes beyond the trim marks is cropped. While creating bleed, objects aligning exactly with the edge of the page should be avoided and it should be ensured that no important image content falls beyond the bleed area. The size of the bleed, that is, an image that bleeds off the edge of the printed sheet, should be at least 18 points. If the bleed is to ensure that an image fits a key line, it needs to be no more than 2 to 3 points. In case of doubt, the print shop can be consulted for advice on the size of bleed necessary for a particular job.

Figure 9.12 Crop marks **Figure 9.13** Cropping of bleed area on crop marks

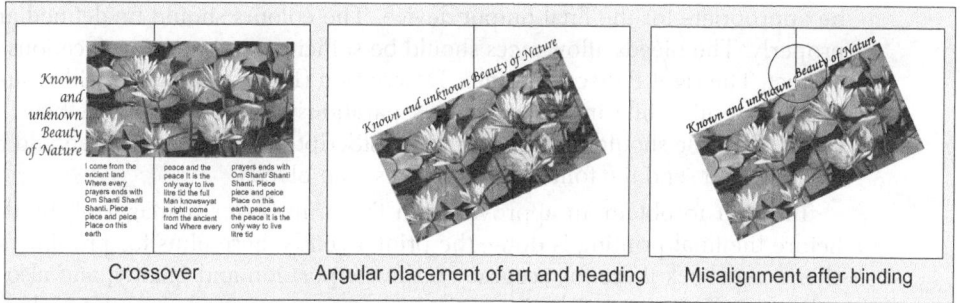

Figure 9.14 Crossovers on a centrespread

Crossover Some elements of the design layout may spread across two pages. Such elements are known as crossovers. There is no difficulty in printing crossovers when they appear on a centre spread, but problems may be encountered if they are printed on two separate sheets of paper. Figure 9.14 illustrates a crossover on a centre spread and one printed on two different sheets. As can be seen in the figure, the latter is not displayed properly once the pages have been bound.

The criteria for a good crossover is the alignment of elements in the two parts that have been printed on two pages. When pages are folded and gathered together for binding, some pages may be pushed out slightly, causing gaps or misalignment between the two parts of the crossover. Care must therefore be taken while creating a crossover. Visuals should never be placed at an angle across the gutter. As can be seen in Figure 9.14, headlines or text blocks become less legible as they cross the gutter. It should also be noted that it is very difficult to align thin rules in a crossover. If the colour of two facing pages is expected to be the same, the pages should be printed on the same side of a forme.

IMAGE OUTPUTTING

For the output, the final files of all artwork, scanned images, and page layouts, along with the relevant types used, bitmap images, and PostScript fonts, are stored and forwarded to the output station in a printing file format such as EPS. These files are opened, trapped, and imposed if required, and then made ready and passed on to the raster image processor (RIP). The raster image processor converts the PostScript data into rasterized data so that it is in a format that is readable for the imagesetter and can be outputted on to a film. For a single colour layout, the imagesetter exposes a single film. A four-colour layout will, therefore, have four separate films.

Handing Over

Once all the elements have been put together in a file, it should be handed over to the printer or prepress service provider for imaging. A systematic check of the files at this stage will ensure that the document will be printed without any problem. It should be ensured that there is no file missing from the document. The fonts that have been used on the pages should be provided separately. The print and document settings should be appropriate for the final output device. The colours should be defined and named properly. The bleeds allowances should be sufficient and trap specifications should be correct. The right Postscript Printer Description (PPD) format that will ensure the best possible result while imaging colour separations should be used. A black-and-white proof of the file should be taken on the PostScript laser printer. One should remember to check and send the fonts, linked images, and bleeds.

In order to obtain an approval from the print buyer/manager of the department before the final printing is done, the printer sends these films for proofing so that the client can check these for accuracy or image position and quality, and also assess the colours used. In case of discrepancies, corrections are made and the cycle is repeated again. The final approved films are then sent to the printer for final printing.

Proof Checking

The print buyer or designer is the person who knows what the printed product should look like. The proofs need to be checked throughout the development of the publication. They allow the designer/print buyer to check the layout, verify the accuracy of text and graphics, and anticipate and solve potential printing problems for which he/she is ultimately responsible. Preliminary proofs may give a good idea of the page layout and placement of graphic elements, etc., but they may not be accurate predictors of the colours that are expected from a finely produced page. When working on a four-colour process publication, the designer/print buyer needs to check the film separation and machine output on paper. This will give him/her an accurate idea about whether the colour will print on the correct separation.

It is always useful to preview one's publication at the early stage of workflow and identify problems that can be corrected easily. The same problems, when identified on film separations or at the final printing stage, are more time-consuming, expensive, and difficult to rectify.

Proofs can be obtained and checked at several stages. There are various proofing devices to meet the requirements and quality of different stages of proofs and correct them within the limitation of each stage.

Before stepping through at the any stage of proofs, the designer/print buyer should organize the prepress work, performing a digital preflight check. *Preflight* is the term used among prepress professionals for checking digital files before they go to press, in order to catch errors and to ensure smooth passage through to output.

Desktop proofs

Desktop proofs are checked before the final document is handed over for printing. During the process of designing, one can always preview the page on-screen and evaluate it from time to time. This on-screen proof is also called *soft proof.* While checking colour images on a soft proof, one should remember that a reliable colour display cannot be obtained on-screen if one's monitor is not calibrated with a correct colour management profile. One should thus check to see that appropriate colours have been assigned to each object of the design, and not just rely on the on-screen appearance of colours to proof the colours in the publication.

Desktop inkjet printouts as proofs are cost-effective means to identify problems with layout and design. They can be used to check the appearance of the text and to see the overall layout. The outputs of PostScript laser printers are good for proofing purposes if the design involves colour separations. Besides, they allow one to preview the overall page design, show colour relationships, and verify bitmap image resolution in large size. Many printers these days provide direct digital colour proofs—proofs that indicate the colours that are expected in the final multipage document. Figure 9.15 shows a large-format digital printer.

Once the layout is ready, the PostScript files need to be sent to the printer. The PostScript data is converted into a rasterized format through RIP and separated into four pigments—cyan, magenta, yellow, and black. These four separations are then printed on transparent sheets from the imagesetter.

Film separation proofs

Colour originals need to be separated by four basic colours of pigments—cyan, yellow, magenta, and black. A colour scanner is used for this purpose. The colour scanner produces four films for the respective colours. These are stripped on transparent sheets with registration marks on each sheet. Some tasks are necessary for checking film quality at this stage.

During film separation, one should look for streaking, scratches, or other damage to the film and work with the prepress service provider to determine the screen angle and ruling for each separation. One should also ensure that bleed objects extend beyond the boundary indicated by the crop marks and areas one expects to trap. A light box should be used to view films by placing them one on others. This is the best way to check the alignment of the separations. If even a single separation for a page is wrong, the printer should be asked to produce all the separations for that page to ensure that the separations do not misregister. Figure 9.16 shows professionals engaged in registering the film separation on a well-lit table.

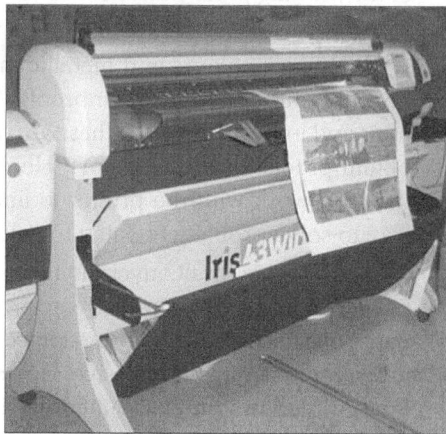 

Figure 9.15 Large-format digital proof printer   **Figure 9.16** Registering the film separation

Film separation proofs are also taken on photographic contact prints, known as *blue-line prints*. These proofs are of a single colour. If the document is in more than one colour, each colour will be shown as a different shade of blue on a blue-line. Blue-line proofs are in the same size as the press sheet, which can be folded and bound to check the bleed, crossover, page sequence, etc. Blue-lines are also used for checking the sharpness of type, missing fonts, cropping and positioning of photographs on the page, and alignment of page elements.

Machine proofs

To check the quality of colour printing, a *machine proof* of the same types of ink and paper that are used on the final job should be obtained from the film separations. This may be done by making an offset plate and printing from these on a proofing press. A proofing press is a slower hand-fed version of an offset printing machine. Machine proofs are a little expensive, but give the designer/print buyer a better idea of the actual print. Figure 9.17 shows a flatbed proofing machine.

Since the prints of individual colours are built up one at a time, it shows the progression to the eventual four-colour result. These prints are called *progressive proofs*. Progressive proofs show the result of four individual colours and also the combination of two, three, and four colours. The printer uses these as guide to set the ink on the printing machine to the correct strength. The ribbon of colours and their tints that can be seen at one side of progressive proofs denote the actual colour strength used at the time of taking proofs.

When checking the colour proofs, it is best to tell the printer *what* result one wants to achieve, rather than providing instructions on *how* it should be achieved. For example, if a darker green is required, it is better to say 'darker green' as an instruction rather than saying 'increase blue', because the best way to achieve a darker green may be to reduce yellow rather than increase blue. The technicians of the printing press can be consulted when one is in doubt about these matters.

Some spot colours and metallic inks cannot be represented by four colour proofs. Additional films and impressions from these are required to obtain proofs for these colours. Here also, one needs to work with the printer to find the best way to solve problems related to colour.

The designer/print buyer should insist that the printer should supply the machine proofs on the paper on which it will finally be printed. Proofs on art paper look quite impressive. However, if the final printed output is obtained on some other paper that soaks the ink, the result will be very different from those seen on the proofs.

Figure 9.17 Flatbed proofing machine

Press proofs

After the film separation/machine proofs are approved, plates are made from the output films and mounted on the cylinder of an offset press. The press is prepared with correct inks and paper and several trial runs are carried out to ensure correct ink coverage and register.

When an action is complete, a sheet is available for final checking. Such sheets are called *press proofs*. Single-colour printing machines can show only one colour proof at a time, which is often difficult to evaluate. It is better to wait for the full-colour printing proofs.

Press proofs should be checked at the printing press only. They should be checked according to the printer's schedule as the machine is stopped temporarily for this purpose. Press time is precious. If the designer/print buyer wants to check the printed piece, he/she needs to do so by visiting the press when called. Press proofs offer the final chance to see the piece before it is printed. At this point, one should concentrate on changes that can be made by adjusting the machine, paper, and ink. Other changes, such as changes in the text and replacement of photographs, should be avoided at this stage as they would require all the steps of printing to be repeated, right from the artwork to plate fixing. If, however, some error in page sequence, folding marks, etc., has been introduced by the printer, it should be rectified by the printer. The client should not be charged for such errors.

While going through press proofs, one should check whether changes marked on the earlier proofs have been carried out. It should be ensured that the publication is being printed on the paper supplied/suggested. Press proofs are exact representations of the final printed sheets. The neatness of these sheets should, therefore, be checked. They should also be compared to the machine proofs, as shown in Figure 9.18. The press operator should be asked to adjust the ink density in case the colours do not match.

Printing of wide solid areas with halftones is a little complicated. This is because the ink flow required for the solid area is more than that for the halftone area. If the proofs show the inconsistencies of the solid colour, the printer should be asked to give a separate impression for the solid area. These days, ink flow identifiers can be used to control the flow of ink in the printing machine. Figure 9.19 shows a modern high-speed web-offset machine configured with a scanner for colour registration, which is controlled by the computerized system of the machine.

Apart from the consistency of ink flow, the alignment of both sides of a sheet should be checked by folding the sheet. This also helps in checking the page sequence. Finally, the page should be glanced through to ensure that the colours and their registration is satisfactory. The designer/print buyer can sign on the checked proofs at this stage if they are satisfactory.

Figure 9.18 Checking of press proof

(a) Scanning of colour registration (b) Controlling of ink flow digitally

Figure 9.19 Modern web-offset machine with ink flow identifier

COMPUTER TO TECHNOLOGY

Once an established standard digital prepress was popularized, more and more pages were output to film with all elements in position. This increased the use of scanners and colour workstations and led the different segments of the printing industry adopt digital as a supplement to, or replacement for offset printing. In India small to medium sized quick print shops, which have been printing offset successfully for many years and have been slower to embrace digital due to investment on new technology in terms of equipment and trained manpower, are also discarding the system followed so far. Switching over to digital from analogue has proved successful for offset printers who have adopted it, especially those who were experienced in digital on-demand printing.

Historically, experiments with computer to plate started in the early 1980s, but it was named as *paper print master* because the base material was paper. The next development was polyester-based plate which was stronger than paper and also could give better quality print output. Both the paper and polyester print master used only a single colour for short print run jobs.

Technova, the company that makes all kinds of plates, created a polyester-based, zero-process, dry-to-dry, offset printing plate. The *computer-to-plate-to-print* (CPP) is a system of imaging the plate directly on a standard laser printer. After imaging, the plate goes direct-to-press without any further processing. It allows small to medium sized printers the ability to produce press-ready offset printing plates in their individual set-up.

Computer to Film

Computer to film (CTF) represents the conventional process for imaging printing plates. The film is silver halide coated plastic film, which is very similar to normal black and white photographic film. In CTF, data and text are transmitted from the data source to a film using laser technology. The laser exposes the film on exact predetermined positions. In an additional process step the exposed film information is transferred to the printing plate by the photo-chemical process. This data transfer needs to be carried out very precisely because the resulting printing quality depends on the position of the information on the film and printing plate. However, even now a large number of printing presses are making plates by exposing them through films.

Imagesetter In digital work flow, film output is obtained through imagesetter, which is a high resolution large format computer device. After ripping the image on computer, it exposes rolls or sheets of films to a laser light source.

Once imaged, the film must be developed in a separate unit called processor that involves chemical use. The film used with this technology is known for its extreme quality and accuracy. The offset lithography industry heavily utilized imagesetters to produce printing plate. A large majority of the printing industry has now migrated to computer to plate (CtP). As a result, the use of film is reduced and printers rely on digital imaging directly to the plate.

Computer to Plate

In this section, we shall discuss the CtP process of printing.

Printing sans plate The first non-press computer to plate exposure pioneered by Heidelberg and Presstek was created in 1992. In 1993, digital colour presses from Indigo and Xeikon allowed short runs of plain paper colour printing. New technologies are predicted to bypass plates and go directly to press cylinder. These innovations have been possible because of the laser and laser dot technology. Text and image are just agglomerations of dots. Thus, the printing industry has entered a new century with a totally digital orientation.

As we already know that when the sequence of prepress work is digital, it is the computer controlled direct imaging of printing plate that becomes an important component.

Computer to plate in general refers to making of offset printing plate. Now the technology has extended to making of flexography polymer plate, direct engraving of gravure cylinder, and also making of stencil for silk-screen printing. In this chapter we will deal only with CtP in relation to offset printing.

Technology in India According to Delhi Printer's Association, the first attempt at CtP in India was taken by *Deccan Herald* and *Malayalam Manorama* in the newspaper segment and their partial success made all the others to wait and watch. In 2001, Print Pack, which is an annual show of print trade, CtP got a real boost when Vamsi offset of Hyderabad suddenly decided to go for CtP instead of an imagesetter. In a true sense, it was the first commercial use of CtP in India.

Since then, doubts about CtP have vanished; the technology has matured; and the printers have embraced the new digital way of working.

In order to achieve direct image on plate, there are three components to accomplish the task: computer, platesetter, and plate for printing.

Computer

It is the heart of the entire prepress work flow. On receiving the digital artwork, all the adjustments of the page, such as colour, font, margin, and screen angle have to be done. In print trade it is called preflight checking. Imposition (if the print document is of multiple pages) another critical task, is also done here. This is the number of pages to be exposed on the plate and the sequence in which they will print paper. It is obvious that electronically imposed pages are far faster than manually arranged films on light table. Before exposing, the image is to be rasterized. Rasterization is accomplished by the raster image processing unit of the computer (RIP).

Rasterization It is the task that connects the digital information about font graphics, colour into dots or pixels. Rasterized image in computer is a translator between the computer file and printer. An image is created on the computer screen using various file formats in either vector or bitmap or combination of both. Each one has a language of its own. Rasterization converts the instructions into the language of the printer. Rasterization is needed for most of the output devices such as desktop printer, imagesetter, and platesetter.

Many desktop printers have some built-in RIP. But some are dedicated pieces of devices configured to process digital files for outputting through imagesetter or platesetter. This high-end RIP is capable of meeting the requirement of large design houses or print service providers. It can do the queuing print job, batch processing, imposition, trapping, colour separation, and halftone screening.

Platesetter

This is a computerized plate outputting device that carries images suitable for the offset process of printing. The plates are flat with necessary grains to hold moisture. These are coated with laser sensitive coating for imaging. The platesetter burns the coating on a plate with laser thus forming image that is not visible when it comes out from the imaging unit. The processor develops the plate with chemicals that dissolve the non-image area which is then washed and cleaned by water followed by gumming that makes the image strong on the plate. Figure 9.20 (a) shows the workflow of the CtP system and Figure 9.20 (b) shows the CtP system.

The platesetter has two different machines—exposing and processing work in sequence. Often they are connected with each other so that the plate first gets burnt and then automatically moves into the processor for developing.

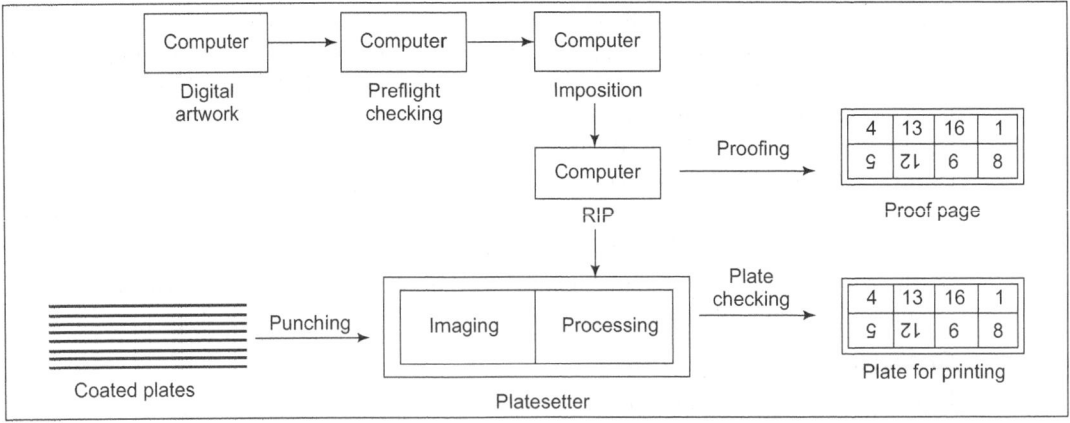

Figure 9.20 (a) Workflow of CtP system

There are three types of platesetter mostly used by the print houses—flatbed, external drum, and internal drum.

Flatbed platesetter During imaging the printing plate is held on a flat surface of the imaging unit, hence the name, 'flatbed'. The laser beam that is deflected by a rotating polygon mirror and then onto the printing plate, exposes the image line by line. In a flatbed setup the laser beam is not very accurate at the edges of the printing plate. The ease of plate handling makes this method suitable for smaller printing formats where quality can be compromised.

External drum platesetters They have a plate fixed on the outside of a rotating drum as is done with the plate cylinder of a printing machine. The imaging head moves

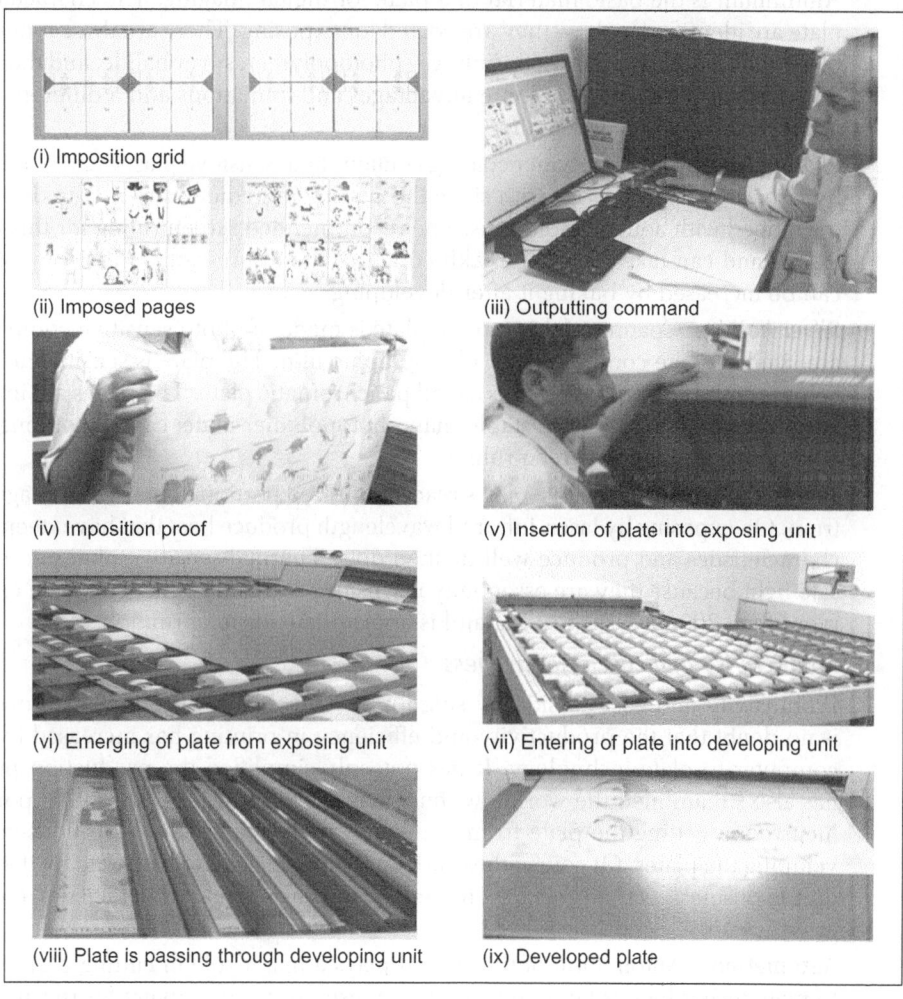

Figure 9.20 (b) CtP system

parallel along the length of the drum that burns the image on the plate while it rotates. The plates are punched with holes before loading on the drum that facilitates colour registration at the time of printing.

Internal drum platesetters They have plate set inside the drum which is designed as open concave like the letter 'C'. The plate is held in place with a vacuum pressure. The imaging unit is a spinning mirror that deflects the laser beam on to the plate. The mirror travels down the axis of the drum scan a line per revolution of the mirror and burnt on to the plate. The concave drum remains stationary. To ensure registration, the internal drum imagesetter is also punched with holes.

Plate

Aluminium is the basic material of a plate for digital imaging. The characteristics of a plate are identified by how they are coated for exposing. There are three types of coated plates which are used in offset printing—photopolymer, silver halide, and thermal sensitive. Each type of plate has some advantages and limitations and a different sensitivity in the visible light wavelength.

Photopolymer Photopolymer coating contains light sensitive plastic and is auto exposed by laser. It is safer to work with since the coating ingredients are non-toxic and can be developed with aqueous solutions. The recommended screen ruling for this plate is up to 200 and can take about one lakh copies of the impressions. Efficiency of the plate can be increased by baking it after developing.

Silver halide Coating of this type of plate is made of photo sensitive compounds that are similar to the compounds of photographic film. The plate is sensitive to all visible colours of the spectrum and thus called panchromatic plate. The plates are imaged with various lasers and are more stable than photopolymer plate, capable of long print run with higher resolution screen ruling.

Thermal Thermal-sensitive plates react to infrared portion of the electromagnetic spectrum. On exposing by laser, infrared wavelength produce heat that have steep threshold characteristics and produce well defined dots. Thermal-sensitive plates do not need a safe light because they are essentially insensitive to visible light. The plate can support more than 300 lpi screen ruling and is appropriate for long run job.

Productivity and cost effectiveness

Productivity and cost go side by side for any mechanical production process. There is no doubt that the productivity and efficiency in printing has increased by adapting computer to plate technology. It has not only simplified the production process but has also streamlined the workflow thus saving the cost. There are still important costs incurred in getting the plate from the plate suppliers and chemicals consumed in developing the plates. Of course these are unavoidable costs to be borne by the printer to do the business as the pressure on them to increase speed and efficiency continues to grow.

Automation Automation of the system plays a major role in cutting costs. Computer to plate technology is favoured by print houses and print buyers for this fundamental factor. Automation starts with saving make-ready time of prepress work. Digital imposition of CtP system is far more faster than assembly of the film for imaging the printing plate. Productivity refers to the number of printing plates produced per unit time. This is determined by the exposure and imaging time within the platesetter and also how quickly plates are loaded into the imagesetter that is developing the first plate in the processor and simultaneous imaging of the next plate in the imaging unit. Replacement of damaged CtP plate is faster in comparison to that of film plate.

Work in shifts Highly automated CtP system can work a number of shifts and also requires no operator. To increase productivity there are even systems which combine with CtP platesetter and plate imagesetter. These are controlled by a common computer, the raster image processor and the server, but can be imaged independent of each other.

Production time Imaging time depends on the size of the plate and the resolution of the image. As an example: if a plate size 70 cm x 100 cm with 1200 dpi takes two minuets imaging time then 100 cm x 140 cm size plate with same dpi or 70 cm x 100 cm size plate with 2400 dpi may take around three minutes. Due to this factor plates are produced slower for commercial printing jobs in comparison with book and newspaper printing. Quality requirements are different for both.

CtP vs Film Plate

Many printers use film plate or both despite many favouring CtP technology. Some points should be noted for the situations when the film plates or the CtP plates are efficient vis-à-vis cost effectiveness.

(a) CtP is better than film plate where dot quality is concerned, especially the size of dots which contribute a lot in the final output.
(b) Colour printing flexibility is more in film plate in comparison to CtP. Exposed CtP plate has to be changed if the colour output is not as per requirement. However, time and exposure adjustment can control the colour and also optimize certain parts of colour without affecting the rest.
(c) Mistakes identified at the proofing stage have to be re-worked for the whole signature on computer and the plate has to be exposed again. For a film, the correction can be done on a particular page without affecting the rest.
(d) CtP has a small advantage on cost for one time book printing. In case of reprinting, the whole set of CtP plates have to be outputted again because CtP cannot be reused after some days. On the other hand, a film can be reused as many times as required.
(e) CtP plates are in general exposed on in-house platesetter. Film processing and even making of plates can be outsourced. This may add some extra cost for plate-making but often proves less expensive as the print house is not carrying the additional cost of the platesetter.

In India this technology is slowly gaining its popularity. However, it may not get the necessary momentum and allow presses of all sizes to adopt its many benefits until the technology drops the price of plate and equipment which are at present imported. CtP loses out to conventional film-based plate-making when duplicate plates or reprints are needed. A CtP system has to repeat the imaging process, while a conventional plate-making system has only to re-expose the film. Film is a convenient storage medium that is cheaper than archiving rasterized data on magnetic media.

SUMMARY

Prepress is the set of steps for traditional copy preparation prior to the stage when the proofs reach the printing machine. Today, most of the prepress tasks can be carried out digitally. Digital prepress offers much more flexibility and ease of operation. The steps involved in a digital prepress procedure are—image input, image processing, image assembly, image output, and proof checking.

In order to understand the digital prepress process, it is imperative to first have a basic understanding of image types, resolution, file formats, and file storage and transfer. All these concepts have been described briefly at the beginning of the chapter.

Image input is the first step of digital prepress. Although, keyboard, mouse, and electronic tablet are some commonly used input devices, scanner is the main input device for digital prepress. Digital cameras are also used for this purpose.

Image processing is the next stage of digital prepress. An image needs to be processed before it can be printed. Continuous tone images need to be converted into halftones, and colour separation is required for processing colour images. Digital colour separation for both spot and process colour printing is fast. In order to ensure that the colour displayed on various types of monitors is consistent, a colour management system can be used. Colour management systems help to maintain colour consistency and accuracy.

All the elements of the design—photographs, sketches, types, etc.—are assembled in a page layout software such as PageMaker or InDesign. In doing the page planning, an artwork is helpful to organize the line and halftone art like traditional methods, the only difference is these are to be done on digital requirement. The success of the finally produced design depends largely on careful planning of the prepress work. Careful page planning helps save time and costs. Various aspects of page planning, such as image integration, conversion, and linking; imposition, trapping; bleed; etc. have been discussed in the chapter.

Assembled digital files are handed over to the printer in order to obtain the final output. Film output is obtained from an imagesetter in order to make plates. These may also be exposed directly on to the plate through the page setter. Digital prepress work is not complete unless different sets of proofs are checked during various stages of the workflow. Proof checking encompasses checking of desktop proofs for revision/approval, film separation proofs for imposition dummies, machine proofs to check the quality of colour printing and, finally, press proofs for checking the ink coverage and register. Careful proof checking ensures that there are minimal errors in the final printed piece.

Digital prepress is linked with computer to technologies. The technology is being used in many segments of printing industry as a supplement to or substitute to offset printing. The printing industry enters a new era with computer to plate technology when complete prepress work-flow is digital. Computer to plate refers to direct imaging of high quality offset plate bypassing any intermediate medium like a film. The technology is gaining popularity but not yet filly matured in India as all sizes of press cannot afford the costs to run the system.

KEY TERMS

Bitmap Image Images formed by rectangular grids of small squares known as pixels.

Charged Couple Device (CCD) A technology characterized by the use of an array of light sensitive elements which translate analogue signals into digital information.

Colour Management System (CMS) A technique used to obtain matching colours across devices, such that a scanned image, the image displayed on a computer screen, and the image printed on paper have consistent colours.

Developer A unit of the machine where chemical bath is used to make the image visible on a light sensitive emulsion.

Digital Halftone In traditional printing, greys are represented by black dots of various sizes. In digital halftones also, dots serve the same purpose but each dot is made up of a number of spots (bits).

Digital Imposition Proofs Low resolution light colour inkjet output to check all artwork and text in position as well as trim and binding edges.

Digital Typography The style, arrangement, and appearance of typeset matter that is stored as digital information. It also encompasses creation and manipulation of letterforms to use them in graphic communication.

Digital Video Disk (DVD) A transportable storage medium that can store and transport files of up to 9.4 GB. It is often used as a backup device.

Drum Scanner A high-end optical scanning device in which the original is mounted on a revolving drum. A light source is then moved in tiny increments across the original, so that the image is converted into digital information.

Electronic Tablet A flat-surface computer input device that allows one to hand-draw images and graphics with a stylus—a pen-like drawing apparatus—just as we draw images on paper with a pencil. These are also known as graphic tablets.

Encapsulated PostScript (EPS) Files containing PostScript data.

File Format A set of related data stored on a disk, which can be opened and transported in a specific application.

Flatbed Scanner A device that converts a printed image or flat object into digital information. It is so called because its shape is flat and it stays on the ground like a bed.

Gutter The adjoining inner margins of two facing printed pages.

Imagesetter A high resolution computerized outputting device that produces images on photographic paper or film used by the printer to make plate for printing.

Line Per Inch (lpi) The resolution of halftones is expressed in terms of lines per inch (lpi). The higher the number of lines per inch, the higher is the image resolution.

Magneto Optical Disk (MOD) A kind of optical disc drive capable of writing and rewriting data on a magneto-optical disc. Both 5.25" and 3.5" form factors exist.

Native Format The default file format used by a specific software application. The native file format of an application is proprietary and these types of files are not meant to be transferred to other applications.

Pixels Per Inch (ppi) A pixel is the smallest element on a computer screen, formed by a number of bits. The resolution of an image on a computer screen can be expressed in terms of pixels per inch (ppi). The higher the number of pixels per inch, the higher is the resolution of the image.

Platesetter A computerized high quality plate outputting device that creates image on plate directly by laser eliminating the need of film, suitable for offset process of printing.

Portable Document Format (PDF) A standard file format that preserves all the fonts, colours, and graphics of any source document regardless of the application used to create it.

PostScript A device-independent page description language use to transmit text and graphic information to a printer.

PostScript Font (PS) Font characterized by the vector-based program with page description language, which is required by a printer to print the font.

Preflight A procedure for checking digital file before they go to press in order to find errors that need to be fixed. The term is taken from aviation in which a pilot goes through a set of procedures to make sure the plane is in a position to fly.

Rasterization The process of converting digital file containing various formats of images into pixels or dots for output on film, plate, or other surfaces.

Resolution Clarity of the graphic image, which depends on several factors, such as the number of dots per inch, size and shape of dots, dot placement, type of paper on which the image is printed, and printer driver setting.

Screen Font A font that is designed for displaying characters on a monitor, and is not designed for printing.

Tagged Image File Format (TIFF) A standard file format for graphics files. Most graphic applications can read and write TIFF files.

TrueType Font (TT) A vector-based object-oriented scaleable font format which can be used to generate printer and screen fonts.

Vector Image Also called object-oriented graphics, these are images made up of mathematically defined curves and line segments called vectors.

REFERENCES

Adams, Michael J. 2002, *Printing Technology 5E*, Delmar Thomson Learning, USA.

Adobe 1995, *Print Publishing Guide*, Adobe System Incorporated, USA.

Adobe Illustrator 10 Users guide.

Agfa Prepress Education Resources 1992, *An Introduction to Digital Colour Prepress*, USA.

Chastain, Sue 2006, *Your Guide to Graphic Software*, http://graphocssoft.about.com, accessed in July 2006.

Cohen, Sandee and Robin Williams 1999, *The Non-Designer's Scan and Print Book*, Peachpit Press, USA.

Gorden, Bob and Maggie Gorden (consultant eds) 2002, *Digital Graphic Design*, Thames & Hudson Ltd, UK.

Johnson, Harald 2003, *Mastering Digital Printing*, Muska & Lipman, Cincinnati, Ohio.

Kipphan, Helmut 2001, *Handbook of Print Media*, Springer-Verllay Berlin Heidelberg, Germany.

Padwick, Gordon 1994, *Guide to Color Printing Techniques*, Random House Electronic Publishing, New York.

Sterling Publishers Printing Press, Noida UP, visited in May 2012.

The GATF Encyclopaedia of Graphic Communication, Prentice Hal PTR (NJ 07458).

www.allionprinting.com/wordpress, accessed in June 2012.

www.digitalprintingtips.com, accessed in May 2012.

www.wikipedia.org/wiki/Computer_to_plate, accessed in May 2012.

REVIEW QUESTIONS

1. Describe bitmap and vector images.
2. Discuss the various file formats used in prepress work.
3. What are the ways in which digital data can be stored and transported to the prepress service provider?
4. What are the main input devices in digital prepress? Explain how they work, mentioning the various advantages attached with each of them.
5. Compare traditional halftones and digital halftones with the help of a diagram.
6. What is digital colour? What are the problems that can be encountered while working with digital colour for printing? How can such problems be solved?
7. How is a layout developed on a computer? Discuss this in relation to artwork, line art, and halftone art.
8. Page planning in digital prepress involves image integration, file linking, and film output. Discuss the purpose of each.
9. Prepare a checklist that can be used for handing over files to the printer.
10. Define trapping and imposition. Discuss their function in page planning.
11. Why should one check the proofs of a publication at every stage of its development?
12. When would you use a desktop proof, machine proof, and press proof?
13. Explain computer to technology. Compare between imagesetter and platesetter in terms of quality and cost effectiveness.
14. Computer to plate system is now parts and parcel of modern printing. Describe its use in Indian context.
15. Write in brief the steps involved from artwork to plate outputting in CtP system.

PROJECTS

1. You have already prepared a layout in your design assignment. Prepare this layout in the form of a digital artwork and carry out the following activities:

(a) Describe the steps you have followed and the action you are expecting from your prepress service provider.

(b) You have done some of the prepress work, such as scanning, colour correction, trapping, trim marking, and file preparation, on your own. You are now looking for a commercial printer. Prepare a questionnaire on the lines of the information required to find out the capabilities of the press. Visit at least two presses with your questionnaire, have it filled up, and write a report on the same. Your questionnaire may include questions on the following:
- Name of the printer
- Experience of the printer
- Type of work done/sample work
- Facility available: prepress, printing, post-press
- Printing machine available: sheet-fed, web-fed, single colour, multi-colour
- Proofing facility

(c) In case the job is to be handled by a prepress service provider (PPSP), prepare a questionnaire based on the following lines to find out the organization's capability.
- Name of the organization
- Rate: System charges, film outputting
- File format acceptable
- Scanning quality
- Fonts available
- Trapping software facility
- Electronic imposition facility
- Type of imagesetter
- Availability of colour profile system
- Responsibility of film checking: Client/PPSP

(d) Prepare a written report on the information that the prepress service provider will need while processing your job. The report should contain the following information:
- Setting for imaging: Output resolution, PPD used, screen ruling, film setting (negative/positive), device profile
- Fonts used in the document
- Detailed page listing: Numbered, blank, and special pages
- Filenames and location of artwork
- Separation: Number of separation for each page including spot and varnish
- Special requirement, if any

2. You are involved in a job from origination to final printing. Prepare a checklist for each stage of proofing for this job. Answer each question you have posed in your checklist. Write the summary of the whole exercise in relation to the job you have handled.

CHAPTER

10 Desktop Publishing

Learning Objectives

After reading this chapter, you should be able to
- understand the desktop publishing (DTP) environment
- delve into the capabilities of a DTP system
- identify the users of DTP systems
- understand the hardware and software support required for DTP
- look at some specific features of commonly used software
- understand the dos and don'ts of desktop publishing

INTRODUCTION

'Publishing' traditionally conjures up visions of only composing and printing. However, it encompasses a whole range of tasks that go much beyond typesetting and printing. Publishing includes everything from origination of the message to generation of text and graphic design and assembly of text and graphics into a functional form. Copy-editing, proof-reading, and, finally, converting the assembled page into a camera-ready copy—all this is a long labour-intensive process, involving various specialists and expensive equipment. The traditional, labour-intensive process of publishing had a high incidence of errors and required more money and time. Computers are now being increasingly used in all significant aspects of publishing, not only removing most of the bottlenecks in publishing but also offering tools and techniques for carrying out all the tasks related to printing. Above all, all the phases of publishing can now be controlled by one person directly with the help of computer commands.

Desktop publishing (DTP) has provided entirely new means to create a print document in less time, with less cost and less bother. Desktop publishing is so called because, in a DTP system, most of the publishing tasks can be carried out on relatively small equipment that can be placed on a table. The advantages of DTP over the traditional methods of publishing include increased control over the end-product and savings in turnaround time as the product can be created and printed at the same place.

Desktop publishing can be said to have begun with the advent of early phototypesetters (second generation), which were a combination of typesetting and computing. Traditionally, typesetting is an expensive and labour-intensive process for producing high-quality print documents. It involves cutting and pasting jobs to combine type with headlines, charts, diagrams, and other graphic elements. The inevitable last-minute changes are difficult to incorporate in traditional typesetting when type must be reset, art redrawn, and headlines, type, and art shuffled around on a paste-up board. Desktop publishing goes beyond typesetting, as it produces typeset matter and graphics, and a combination of the two.

Pasting is done electronically in DTP. It is far easier to draw several geometrical shapes using DTP than to draw them by hand. Also, undoing a mistake electronically is far easier than using an eraser or white-out manually. Perhaps the most important advantage of DTP is that it makes it possible to re-arrange a page with a simple computer command.

CAPABILITIES

Almost anything that can be achieved on a dedicated publishing system can also be achieved on a DTP system. This includes handling of text, generation of graphics, editing of images, and outputting.

Handling of text DTP allows one to compose text in a manner that comes close to the requirement of typesetting. It is possible to compose text with well-designed, proportionately spaced characters along with justified lines, if desired, and automatic and customized hyphenation. Type composition in a DTP system allows the use of more than one type of font and size, and a character set more varied than that available on a typewriter or with hot metal composing methods.

An in-built dictionary helps in checking spellings. Desktop publishing also takes care of the setting of tabular matter, indents of all kinds, and aesthetic character kerning. The system accepts processed words from pen drives, disks, tapes, OCRs, or directly from the keyboard. It also alerts the user to grammatical mistakes in the text.

Desktop publishing also enables the user to create a particular style for the word processing document as per the look or image desired for the publication. The style may include elements such as font, font size, leading, space before and after paragraphs, alignment, and indention. The style created can easily be exported to the application of desktop publishing. Every detail of the style can be reproduced accurately through DTP.

Generation of graphics Artwork and design can be created with the commands of the operator in DTP. Business graphics can be generated by programs that use figures from the data and convert them into required charts or graphics.

Other than text, graphics may be either free-hand graphics or drawings made by using computer-aided design (CAD) programs. Graphics may also be scanned through a peripheral device such as a scanner or drawn with the help of a digitizer. The pictures used in the publication do not need to be derived from photographs and then screened to convert them into halftones for the purpose of reproduction. The system performs a variety of manipulative tasks, such as sizing, cropping, and image rotation. Images can also be enhanced using several visual effects—strokes, washes, and textures that simulate conventional art techniques.

Editing of images The visual documents created by the user can easily be viewed on the computer monitor/VDU. It is also convenient to edit and shift around composed matter in a DTP system. Illustration areas can also be edited by cutting, cropping, deleting, superimposing, and colouring. The image quality of the on-screen matter is as fine as the output quality.

Desktop publishing clearly demands an effective and experienced editor and an imaginative designer who can make good use of the various facilities available in a DTP system.

Outputting The DTP system must be able to produce output on at least one of the devices available. Today's publishing standards require the output of a DTP system to be at least 600 dpi or more for the master to be camera-ready, or for the film in positive form.

Laser printers can produce acceptable outputs for many users. For some, however, laser output is of too low a quality to be used for publishing. In such cases, the master copy for printing is created through imagesetters, which produce higher resolution output. Printouts of 300 dpi or less serve as proofing copies in these cases.

Since a DTP system requires a small area and less of running around, one person can easily take control of the entire process and keep track of both the creative and the production aspects.

USERS OF DESKTOP PUBLISHING SYSTEMS

DTP systems can be used by an individual or by small groups and organizations. The individual may be an author, a journalist, or an artist. *Authors* and *journalists* can prepare their manuscripts on their personal computers. A low-cost laser printout of the same can be obtained as per the publication's format, thus avoiding the need for costly and time-consuming typesetting. *Artists*, with their basic skills of drawing and layout designing, can use the DTP system to create graphics, illustrations, etc., and arrange them aesthetically on a page along with the text created by other individuals.

A simple typist or a traditional composer can also operate a DTP system. In most cases, the composer's task is limited to entering the text. He/she may also be trained to handle layout aspects gradually. Publishing houses seek the services of *typists/composers* for basic composing purposes and page layout formats before the editor and designer decide on the final pages and give them the final touch.

Magazine editors use DTP to test their ideas, producing near-typeset quality pages showing the layouts, graphics, etc. *Corporate* or *business houses* can produce brochures, direct mail or communication materials, and other promotional tools quickly and easily with data-base assisted publishing solutions, eliminating the involvement of any third party.

Public relations departments of organizations can use DTP to produce consumer newsletters, press material, etc., much more efficiently, which help to enhance the organization's image. *Advertising departments* and *advertising agencies* also use DTP to produce advertisements, test new ideas, and to make presentations for clients. Alterations and change of design elements are now a matter of pressing a keyboard button, eliminating the need for manual cutting and pasting that earlier used to take several hours or days. Some agencies are using DTP not only in their creative departments but

Table 10.1 The users of DTP and the application area of their work

Users ▶ ▼Applications	Job shop	Processing house	Advertising agency	Newspaper	Magazine	Publishing house
Word processing	Yes	Yes	Yes	Yes	Yes	Yes
Page layout/Artwork	Yes	No	Yes	Yes	Yes	Yes
High-resolution scanning	Yes	Yes	Yes	Yes	Yes	Optional
Image processing	Yes	Yes	Yes	No	Yes	Yes
Colour prepress	Optional	Yes	Yes	No	Yes	Yes
Painting and drawing	Yes	No	Yes	Yes	Yes	Yes
Business and infographics	Yes	No	Yes	Yes	Yes	Yes
3D modelling/rendering	Yes	Optional	Yes	No	No	No

☐ Yes ☐ No ☐ Optional

also in their media and administrative departments to take care of campaign scheduling, accounting, and other aspects of advertising.

These days, *newspapers* gets news, pictures, and advertisements from various sources, which are stored in a server and accessed by the various departments involved in the production process. These elements are manipulated in DTP systems to compose a page in much less time than required in traditional composing and page make-up systems. The ability to save time is vital for efficient production of a newspaper. Many big newspapers use the DTP system for handling not only text matter but also graphics. Photographs can be touched up using the special effects of the system.

Many users of DTP systems obtain camera-ready copies on ordinary paper through a laser printer. In order to reduce production costs, one can obtain laser prints directly on a transparent sheet, Gateway tracing paper, or butter paper, which can then be used as a positive for plate-making. For this purpose, prints must be taken as mirror images so that, at the time of exposing the film, there will be no gap between the film image and the plate. Desktop publishing thus enables the user to save on the use of costly photographic films.

Table 10.1 provides an overview of the users of various DTP applications.

EQUIPMENT REQUIRED FOR DESKTOP PUBLISHING

A typical DTP system needs two basic components—hardware and software. Hardware includes a computer, a printer, and an optional peripheral such as a scanner. Software includes the programs that interact with the hardware. The hardware performs various tasks under software instructions and manipulations.

Hardware

As discussed, hardware includes computers, printers, scanners, etc. A computer has various units, such as the monitor, keyboard, etc. Let us now look at various elements of computers.

Computer

A basic requirement of a DTP system is a micro-computer, which is a single work station unit. It is also called a personal computer (PC). The computer should have a screen to display exactly what is printed on a page. A DTP system displays an accurate presentation of the page layout, typeface, type size, graphics, etc., so that 'what you see is what you get' (WYSIWYG).

Computers are also equipped with an input unit. Keyboards are one of the most common input devices used for giving commands to the computer as well as for entering the text and graphics. Its operations resemble those of conventional typewriters. In multi-language cultures such as India, special keyboards have been designed. These keyboards provide characters set in different languages. Personal computers with a DTP system are attached with a hand-held device known as a 'mouse'. The mouse is used for pointing at and selecting a precise location on the screen.

Another critical requirement of a DTP computer system is a large random access memory (RAM). This memory contains the programs that the user works with and the information he/she manipulates with those programs.

Several types of computers are available in the market today, and these perform various functions. For the purpose of desktop publishing, however, two types of personal computers are commonly used—the Apple Macintosh and the IBM PC.

Macintosh vs IBM PC Macintosh (Mac) became the leader of desktop publishing after entering the market in 1984. Known for its 'user friendliness', an average user without a background in computers can easily operate a Macintosh effectively and in less time compared to an IBM PC and its compatibles.

Applications developed for the Macintosh in the absence of Macintosh clones have far more reliability in terms of software performance. Applications available for the Macintosh platform are more standardized than those for the IBM PC. In Macintosh, data files created using one application program and standard formats are fully usable in other application programs. The sequence of commands to perform a particular task or operation and the syntax of commands—such as cut, copy, paste, save, and quit—remain identical in different application software.

In IBM PCs, languages other than English require language-specific software such as Lingua, Lipi, Ankur, etc., whereas just the font of a particular language is enough to allow the user to use any language in any application in the case of Macintosh.

Constant development and refinement of operating systems has today wrought major changes in the concepts of file interchangeability and common commands. Documents created in Mac can be opened in an IBM PC or vice-versa.

Constant change and improvement of IBM PC's hardware operation over a period of time has rendered some software programs obsolete and redundant, whereas

Macintosh, even after improvement and enhancement of hardware and operating systems, still continues to honour the earliest developed application packages. Despite the advantages of Macintosh, IBM PCs are also highly popular these days. In recent years, the IBM PC has become so popular that it is the *de facto* industry standard in personal computing. Since hardware manufacturing of IBM PCs is not restricted to a single company as in the case of Macintosh, access to the equipment is easier. Thanks to the easy availability and large number of IBM PC users, compatible software is far more in number and diversity. The most popular these days are Microsoft Windows 2000, XP, and Vista operating systems. These programs have more flexibility and graphic manoeuvrability.

Although IBM PC and Macintosh systems differ in practice, optional software can let us enjoy the advantages of both. For example, a text file created in an IBM PC can be transferred to a Macintosh for final page layout, integration, or other manipulation.

Choosing the right system is becoming increasingly difficult. A few years ago, Macintosh was the primary choice for desktop publishing, but today, the IBM PC environment, with its amazing software programs, is quite elaborate and satisfactory.

Printer

A computer is connected with a printer which prints out the images—both text and graphics—created in it. There are two types of printers—impact printers and non-impact printers. *Impact printers* create an impression of the image on paper either by an image slug which is struck by a hammer or by depositing the image on the paper in the form of dots. Such printers are commonly known as *dot matrix printers*. The output of impact printers is not good enough for printing quality work. Since the output cost is quite low and printouts can be obtained fast, these printouts are considered as proofing prints. Unlike impact printers, non-impact printers do not use direct mechanical contact with the paper to create an image. Laser and inkjet printers are non-impact printers. Laser printers give letter quality impressions which are good enough for all kinds of publications.

The requirements for the finished printed piece depend on the type of job and length of final print run. A laser printer can produce text and graphics in more detail and in higher resolution. Three hundred dpi resolution laser printers are common and good enough for short-run in-house material which can be photocopied. For longer runs and reasonably good quality publications, however, high resolution laser imagesetters are used to create output on film or bromide paper.

The terms *dpi* and *lpi* should not be mixed up. Dpi refers to the number of distinct pixels that can be created on each linear inch of output, whether on a printer or on a computer screen. It is a measure of resolution. Lpi, on the other hand, is a measure of screen frequency. The normal range of a halftone screen is 55–200 lpi, and the higher the lpi is, the finer the screen looks.

Printers can also be classified as dumb printers and intelligent printers. A *dumb printer* does not possess a typeface library of its own. An *intelligent printer*, on the other hand, uses a built-in library of typefaces to produce true to the character types of the file sent to it for printing. A person working on an intelligent printer can either use fonts from the built-in library of the printer or download them from the computer.

Within the category of intelligent printers, there is a class of laser printers that uses PostScript printing language developed by Adobe Systems, Inc., which instructs the printer how to reproduce a page containing text and/or graphic images. As explained earlier, a laser printer cannot be used as a production device. The unit cost of output on laser printers is very high due to the limited life of the laser engine and high toner and operational cost. These printers may, however, be used for obtaining camera-ready copies for offset printing.

Colour laser printers use four different toners of cyan, magenta, yellow, and black to create colour images. Due to the cost of the toner and quality of paper needed to print colour images, the unit cost of production is a little higher, and this may deter one from obtaining multiple copies on a colour laser printer. However, there are some high-end multi-user applications, such as printers with fax, copy, and print facilities, which can justify the cost. Some printers can now print matter on both sides of a page and collate and staple them as well.

Commercial printers use a high-end computerized film outputting device known as imagesetter to obtain high-resolution cost-effective multiple-copy output on paper.

The output generated by a desktop laser printer is not considered to be as professional as that produced by an imagesetter. This is because the capability of creating a high-dpi output is much higher in the case of an imagesetter. Moreover, the output obtained on substrates such as film or photographic paper (bromide) is very sharp and clean. On the other hand, the dots transferred on plain paper by a laser printer often do not print evenly due to the texture of the paper or because the ink of the toner may be peeled or split off on paper.

Inkjet printers are one of the most successful printing technologies developed during the last few years. Inkjet printers can print not only black and white text but also coloured graphics, including photographs. The quality of photographic images printed on an inkjet printer is closer to the original. Since the output can be obtained on ordinary paper, the unit cost of printing becomes very low. Many people use inkjet printers for office work or for regular work at home. Professionals who are engaged in planning or designing and need impressive printouts, may take printouts on specially manufactured paper available in most computer consumable supply stores.

Scanner

A scanner is a peripheral electronic device of a DTP system which converts a graphic image into digital information in the computer. The image may be a photograph or a line art with text which has been drawn or created outside the computer. Through scanning, these images can be manipulated in several ways and stored in the computer memory. They can be reproduced in any desired size. They can also be inverted to obtain a negative, flipped to create a mirror image, or copied and cropped to focus attention on a particular detail. Images can be distorted to achieve an expressive effect. One of the most exciting aspects of a scanned image is the option of experimenting with several possibilities, which would have taken several hours to accomplish by traditional methods. Moreover, several images can be merged into one composite image through scanning to create a multi-dimensional image.

Most users avoid purchasing low-lpi scanners as the equipment cost is very high and the images reproduced through low-lpi scanners are not suitable for direct quality printing.

Most scanners produce satisfactory image outputs for line illustrations. Scanned images of line illustrations are formed by pixels where dots are square in shape and uniform in size. Such images are called *single-bit scanned images.* For the scanned image to be a continuous tone image, a *multi-bit scanner* is used. This device breaks down the image into round dots and, sometimes, lines of varying sizes. A multi-bit scanner records the original in many levels of grey shades. The laser output of a 300 dpi scanned halftone is not of reproducible quality. It can, however, be used for layout purposes and once the designer is happy with the laser proof of his/her layout, the same file can be output to either film or bromide paper through a high resolution imagesetter for the purpose of printing.

Multi-bit scanners capture colour information in red, green, and blue (RGB). These scanners are compatible with the default colour of computers, which is also RGB and, therefore, it is easy to handle images scanned in RGB. These days, some scanners are also equipped with the ability to process colour information in CMYK, but colours produced in CMYK are not as reliable as those produced in RGB. In case an image is required in CYMK, especially if the image is to be printed by a commercial printer, it is advisable to work on the file in RGB, convert it to CMYK, and then place it on a layout page and obtain colour separations for printing.

Scanners scan pictures as images and text as types. A special software called Optical Character Recognition (OCR) is inbuilt in scanners. This software recognizes the shapes of letters and creates an editable text file from the page on the scanner. There is great demand for this facility in desktop publishing, especially when a large amount of printed documents are to be retyped or keyed in.

Software

In DTP, there are many software programs to choose from, depending on the type of job in hand and the computer platform being used. The commonly used software in DTP are word processing software, graphics software, spreadsheet software, and layout software.

Word processing software

The raw copy is keyed into the computer using a keyboard and a word processing software is used to process the matter. It can be edited and corrected at the terminal/console as the system is sophisticated enough to allow the user to look at a composed page on the screen, identify a paragraph that needs rewriting, and make that change then and there, without having to refer to the proof prints. Most word processing programs can check spellings, justify columns of type, and adjust the space between lines. Once the copy has been keyed in and edited, it is time to make any required changes in the document before the copy is sent to the printer/layout artist for further modification.

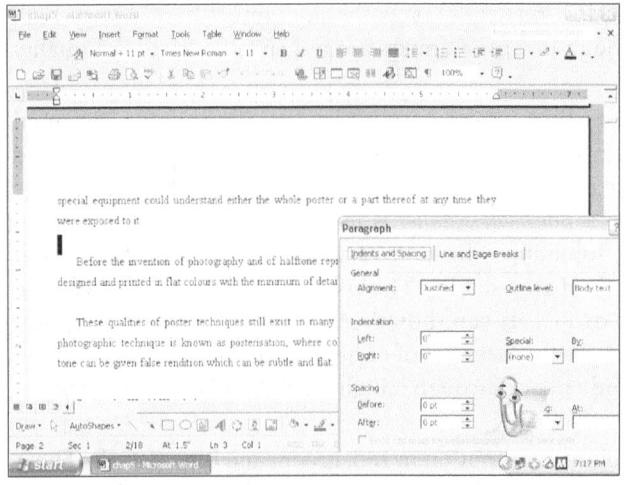

Figure 10.1 Microsoft Word window

Figure 10.1 shows a screen-shot where instructions for paragraph alignment, indentation, and spacing are being specified in a Microsoft Word document.

Although word processing applications are easy to use, they should not be used to create professional documents with graphics. One should also avoid formatting text, making column tabs, and using text effects, drop caps, etc., in this application as it does not have the right features for such changes. Word processing applications do provide a few graphic features, but these features may bring more trouble than ease when they are imported to another application. The graphic features available in these applications should be used only to create graphics that will be printed directly from a word processing program on a desktop printer. Documents processed on word processing software should never be sent to the prepress service bureau directly for film outputting.

MacWrite is the word processing software of Apple Macintosh, while WordStar, WordPerfect, Microsoft Word, etc. are the word processing software of IBM. All word processors have their respective advantages and limitations, so they should be investigated carefully before deciding on the appropriate software.

Spreadsheet applications

Spreadsheet applications are used to create complicated tables with easy-to-read columns, charts, graphs, and various other formats. Statistical information is converted into charts and graphs as per the samples inbuilt in the application. All such statistical data can be coloured, reformatted, and printed directly from a spreadsheet application through a desktop printer. Microsoft Excel is the most popular spreadsheet application and images created on Excel can easily be incorporated with Microsoft Word documents. Applications such as CorelCHART, Lotus 1-2-3, and Harvard Graphics can be used to create an even wider variety of graphs and charts. As with word processing documents, information in spreadsheet applications cannot be easily imported to another application. In order to give a professional touch to charts and graphs created on a spreadsheet application, the images should be created on the respective program. Another alternative is to save the spreadsheet file in the EPS file format.

Graphics software

Graphics software is used for creating and editing freehand drawings, charts, graphs, illustrations, diagrams, etc. Here, again, the capabilities of a program depend on its compatibility with the computer and the features the software contains.

Graphics software gives the designer access to hundreds of possible choices that he/she might never have thought of. Myriad tools of an artist are available in a few minute icons. The same pictures can instantly be 'tried' in different sizes and styles and moved to a new layout. The designer needs to make the aesthetic choice and is in control of the images that are produced by various manipulations on such software. Graphics software may be an object-oriented drawing program or a pixels form paint program.

Object-oriented drawing programs Object-oriented drawing programs are those which clearly define each element of a graphic formed by lines and curves. In computer language, these programs are referred to as vector programs. Figure 10.2 shows graphics drawn on CorelDRAW—an object-oriented program. Types and thickness of lines created on such programs can be manipulated at will. Figure 10.3 shows types created in different styles in an object-oriented program. Logos can be created with tint and shade on these programs. Graphics formed on object-oriented programs can be reproduced accurately on a high-resolution laser printer. These images, when stored on a computer, do not occupy much memory space.

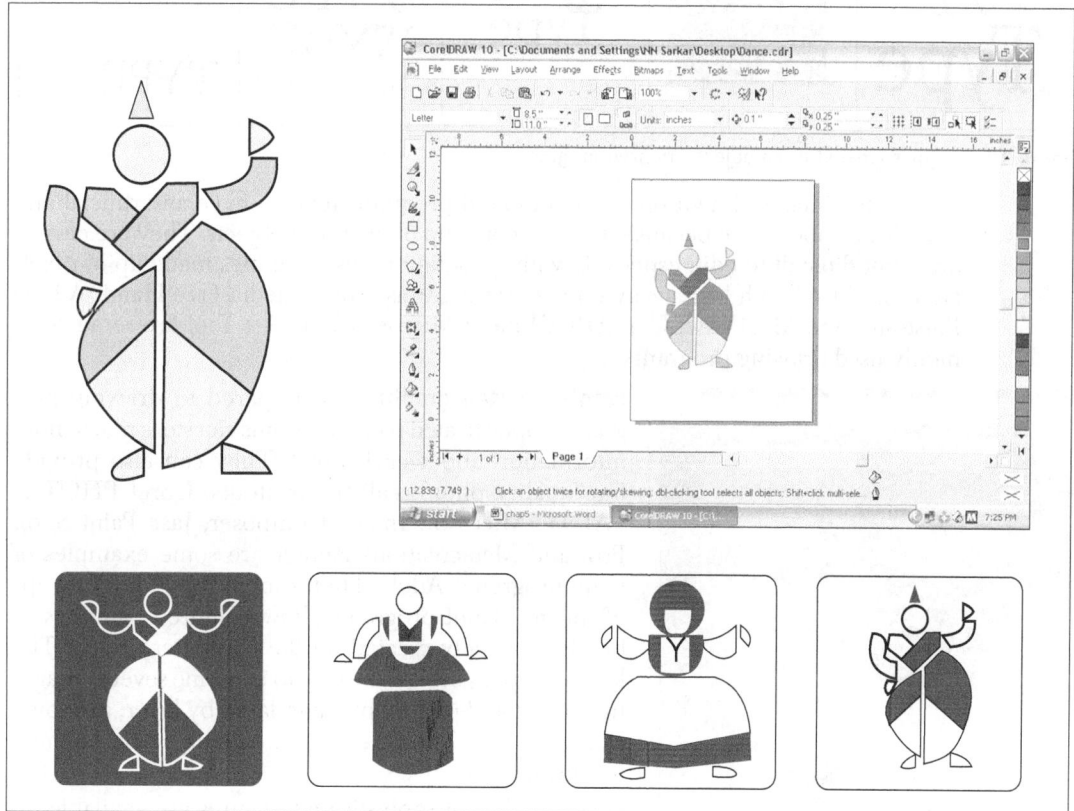

Figure 10.2 Graphics in CorelDRAW

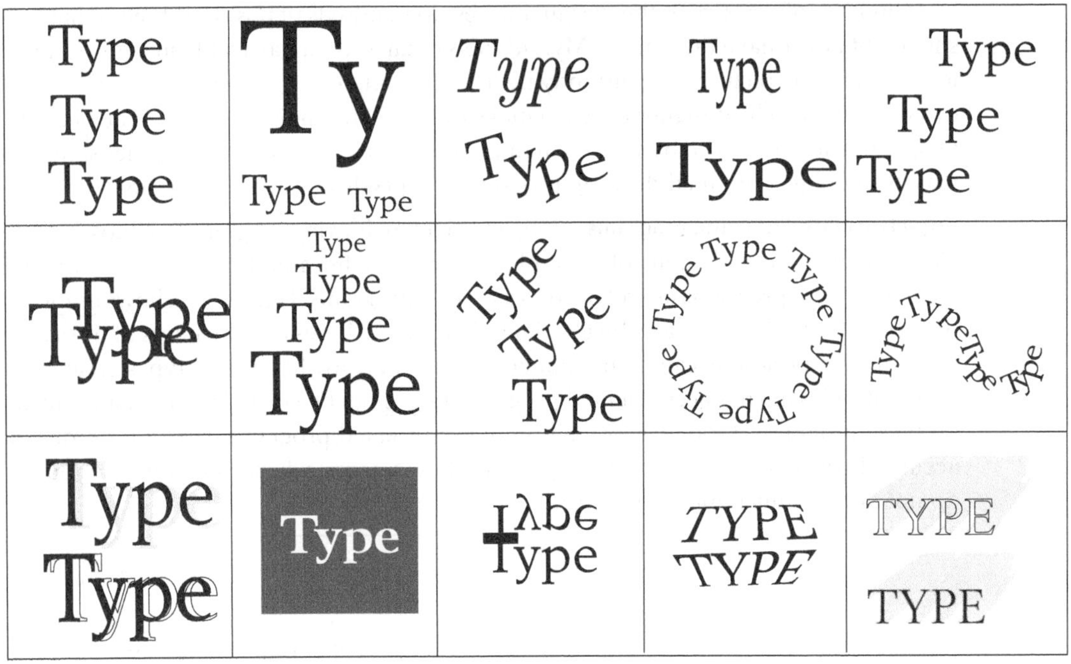

Figure 10.3 Types created in an object-oriented program

Usually, images drawn on object-oriented programs tend to have an artificial and unrealistic appearance because they are made up of lines and objects. They are easy to draw but difficult to edit, especially with gradation tones. Graphics made up of pixels are reproduced with less clarity on vector programs. Macromedia Free Hand; Adobe Illustrator and MacDraw; CorelDRAW; and Microsoft Line Art Tool are some commonly used drawing programs.

Figure 10.4 Layering options

Paint-oriented graphics Compared to drawing programs, sophisticated paint programs can store much more information about each pixel. They can also provide fine quality photo-realistic printouts. Corel PHOTO-PAINT, Microsoft Image Composer, Jasc Paint Shop Pro, and Metacreations Painter are some examples of paint programs. Adobe Photoshop is used for touch-ups of images. Paint programs allow coloured paintings to be electronically created on the computer screen. The layering options allow the user to combine several images that are edited part by part and layer by layer, as shown in Figure 10.4. The layers are then merged or flattened for further use.

A number of sophisticated features are available on paint programs. Paint software provides tools such as different brush shapes and sizes, pencils, and erasers.

It also has tools for spraying, shading, image rotation, scaling, and sizing, and the option of choosing from hundreds of colour shades. Several screen patterns are available on paint programs. An artist can change his/her painting in a few seconds with the help of cut and paste features available in paint programs. AutoCAD, PC Paint, Lotus, Photoshop, and Symphony are examples of software used in a Windows environment. Today, most software is being developed for cross-platform use, which enables the user to open a file created in Windows in Macintosh or vice versa.

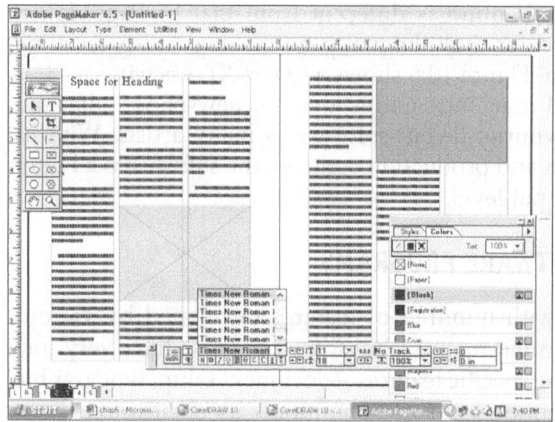
Figure 10.5 Magazine layout on Adobe PageMaker

Layout software

Layout software allows the user to create text-based pages in many styles and formats—they may be multi-column and multiple-font pages with special indents, drop letters, and ruling lines between columns. These programs normally feature style sheets. *Style sheets* are a type of pre-formatted page layout where all parameters like the number of columns; type style and size for body text, headings, subheadings, and headers and footers; alignment; and other controls are defined. All that one needs to do once the style sheet has been finalized is to import the word-processed text from another program and apply the style sheet, and the text is automatically laid out. Layout software accepts graphics created in other applications or scanned images with the help of import facility or data file transfer of the system. It can build a spread that runs across the gutter between two pages. Layout software can even be used to prepare the layout of a tabloid or broadsheet newspaper page, as shown in Figure 10.5. For such jobs, printouts are taken in more than one A4 size paper by tiling. Each sheet contains a little matter of other sheets. A big single-sheet page is prepared by overlapping and pasting the sheets together.

The first true layout software was a program called PageMaker, which was developed on the classic design studio environment of a drawing board and paste-up tools. The page is the basic unit on which the user operates. PageMaker was initially available only to IBM-compatible machines. Another popular layout software which is available only to IBM machines and compatibles is Corel Ventura. It works almost like PageMaker

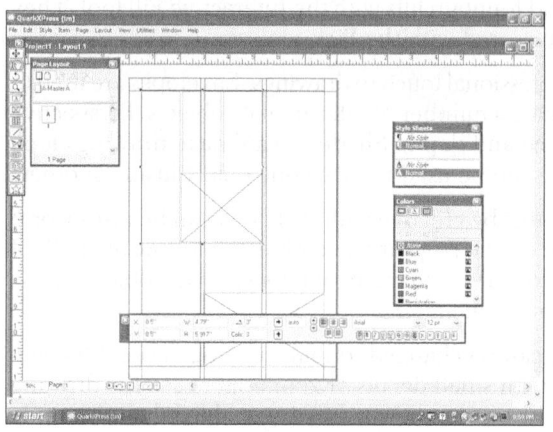
Figure 10.6 QuarkXPress window

although the basic way of operating Ventura is different from that of PageMaker. QuarkXPress is a software that is used for multi-lingual page making and typesetting and has proved quite effective in India. Figure 10.6 shows a QuarkXPress window. It is available to both Macintosh and IBM machines, and is ideal for newspaper edits and art rooms. Adobe InDesign is the favourite layout software of many artists. With its near-natural colour display and design and production controls, the software is a better choice for page layout at the professional level.

FEATURES OF SOME SPECIFIC SOFTWARE PROGRAMS

There are many software programs with hundred of features developed by various companies. Some of them work in a similar manner, but some programs have very specific features. We shall now look at some specific features—document setup, typographic controls, image manipulation, and printing—of some commonly used software.

CorelDRAW

Some basic features of CorelDRAW are discussed here. A basic knowledge of these features will help the user to draw images on this software with ease.

Create an object CorelDRAW documents are made up of separate elements called *objects*. An object's edge is called a *path*. Paths can be closed or open. An object with a closed path can be filled with colour, but this is not possible in the case of an object with an open path. The path of an object passes through nodes that shape the path. Some CorelDRAW tools automatically create closed path objects.

Modify an object In order to modify an object, it must first be selected. When an object is selected, handles appear in a rectangular formation around it. Objects can be modified using a variety of program features, such as menu commands, dialog boxes, and tools. For instance, an object's path can be shaped by moving its nodes and control points with the Shape tool.

Fill an object An object can be uniformly filled with a spot or process color. Objects can be filled with patterns, textures, and fountain fills with the Interactive Fill tool. They can be rotated, skewed, scaled, and mirrored with the Pick tool.

Special effect Special effects add a professional touch to drawings. Envelopes are used to distort the shape of objects, Blends create a number of intermediate objects, Perspective lets the user add the illusion of distance and depth, Shadows can make drawings look three dimensional, and the PowerClip can be used to place one object inside another.

Handling text CorelDRAW lets the user be creative with text. Text can be artistic or it can be in a paragraph. It can float free on the page as a text object or follow the path of an object. Text can also be converted to curves, changing it into a graphic object whose outline can be modified like any other outline.

Change view The view of a drawing can be changed to make editing easier. One can zoom in to get a close look and work with small details or zoom out to see the drawing as a whole. CorelDRAW also allows the user to view a drawing in the enhanced mode or as a full-screen preview.

Place objects One can use precision tools such as guidelines, grids, rulers, and the align and distribute dialog box to place objects exactly where he/she wants them.

Import and export Many types of files, such as clip art, text, and graphics, can be imported into a drawing. Drawings can also be exported in a format that enables them to be read by another program or be used on a Web page.

Print document When a drawing is completed, it can be printed or saved to file for a high resolution output. The Print Preview mode allows the user to see what the printed document will look like.

Photoshop

Photoshop is a powerful graphics program, primarily used for photo re-touching and image manipulation. It can also be used to create original art, either from scratch or from a base such as a photograph or painting.

Starting a new page The Photoshop New Page dialog box allows the user to indicate the image size, resolution, and colour mode. On opening the window, a large white area appears with the toolbox at the corner.

Toolbox The toolbox, like an artist's worktable or paint box, holds all the tools that are used to draw, paint, erase, and otherwise work on a picture. There are four types of tools in the box—Selection, Painting, Viewing, and Specialized.

Working on window One can start working with the menu displayed on the top of the screen. The File menu lets the user work with files—opening, closing, saving, exporting, and printing the same. The Edit menu is for actions such as cut, copy, paste, and undo. The Image menu is for choosing a colour mode, changing image size, rotation, etc. The Filter menu can bring dozens of physical changes to an image.

Working with layers The most powerful feature of Photoshop is the layering option. This tool allows the user to combine images and create collages by working on one part of an image at a time.

Merging layers One needs to merge the layers or flatten the image if the file is to be used for anything else. It should be kept in mind that no change or alteration is possible once the image is flattened.

Selection tools There are several ways to select a specific piece of a picture. Any of the selection tools—Marquee, Lasso, or Magic Wand—can be used for this purpose.

Cutting, copying, and cropping The Cut and Paste options enable the user to borrow from one picture to add to another. Cropping is an artist's term for trimming the unwanted parts of a picture.

Image scanning Usually, flatbed scanners are used for digital scanning. A flatbed scanner works by making a bit-by-bit image of a document, photo, or piece of artwork fed into it. Scanned documents can be imported into Photoshop, where they can be worked upon.

Digital painting Photoshop allows the user to choose and apply colour to the picture in different ways. The Colour Picker is a colour palette that contains all the colours that one can paint with. At the beginning, one can work with two available colours—foreground and background colour. One serves as the colour of a brush/pencil on the painting and the other serves as its canvas.

Image alteration Images in Photoshop can be turned into an imitation of an oil painting, water colour, or drawing by using the various filters and brushes available in this software. Filters are also used to improve an image, distort it, and to make it artistic and achieve other special effects.

Masking This option enables the user to apply changes to an image selectively, protecting parts of the image that he/she does not want to change.

Adding type In Photoshop, type images are in pixel form. They can be given special effects using all the attributes of Photoshop.

Saving files Photoshop can save documents in all the formats it can open. Besides PHD, its native format, JPEG, TIFF, and EPS are some examples of formats in which Photoshop can open and save files. Different formats have different purposes and file sizes. Some are specially intended for web users while others are more appropriate for printing.

Printing Obtaining printouts of Photoshop images involves quite a few variables and decisions—choosing a printer, setting the page up, deciding on paper quality, etc.

PageMaker

PageMaker is a layout software program that automates all the steps in developing a printed document.

Requisites for creating new document Before one begins to work on a document in PageMaker, it is important to feed in data about the paper size, margin, and page extent of the document.

Creating master pages For multi-page documents, it is important to create master pages. PageMaker displays a two-page spread, labeled L and R. Headers, footers, graphics, and column grids applied on the master pages appear on all the pages of the layout automatically.

Changing page size view On this software, it is possible to shrink an image to see the whole page or to see varying enlargements on the page up to 400 per cent of its actual size.

Using rulers PageMaker allows the user to draw horizontal and vertical rulers on the page. Measurement of ruler can be changed into millimeters, inches, and picas. Rulers provide accuracy in laying a page.

Using guidelines A fundamental aid to page layout is the grid, which helps one to visualize the basic format of a page and provides an accurate reference for positioning text and graphics.

Entering text Text can be typed directly or placed/pasted from word documents. Text is typed in text blocks in PageMaker. The blocks can be moved like any other graphic object. Text blocks have sizing handles that allow the user to resize their width.

Formatting type PageMaker offers highly accurate typographic contents of letters, words, lines, and paragraphs. With PageMaker, one is free to experiment with different formats.

Changing font families A font family consists of the basic typeface and (usually) the bold, normal, and italic forms of the typeface. The type can be changed by selecting a section of the text and applying the required type attributes to it.

Character specification This involves specifying the space between lines—known as *leading*—and between letters, which is adjusted by tracking.

Editing text One can add, change, or delete words in the document layout window in PageMaker. The view size of the window can be enlarged to make the text easier to read.

Adding graphics Graphics can be added anywhere in a document by drawing with PageMaker drawing tools or by importing images from other programs or scanned photographs.

Text wrap PageMaker normally considers graphics to be independent objects on the page. If the graphic is inserted on the text page, it can make room for itself by shifting the text around it with the help of the text wrap command.

Adding colour Colour can be added to text as well as graphics. Colours are displayed and activated with the colour palette which contains default colours and custom colours defined by the user.

Saving a document While working on a document, it should be saved every ten minutes. The first time one saves a particular document, he/she needs to use the Save dialog box to assign a file name and directory path.

Printing a document One should select the printer according to the quality requirement for the job. He/she should ensure that the printer can recognize the fonts used on the page. If the job is meant for commercial printing, one should discuss the page information with the service bureau.

QuarkXPress

QuarkXPress is a layout program like PageMaker. It is known for its box-based interface. It contains three types of boxes—text, picture, and fill.

Pages and spread The most basic concept in QuarkXPress is the page—all documents are made up of one or more pages, which can face each other to create a spread.

Pasteboard The work surface of QuarkXPress is the pasteboard, which is as big as a document.

Using the palettes QuarkXPress has several floating palettes such as tools, measurement, style, colour, etc.

Handling text and graphics Any object created on QuarkXPress can be moved, resized, reshaped, locked, and grouped with other objects.

Importing text One can create a text box in QuarkXPress and import the text from a Word document. Any overset text will flow into another box if both the boxes are linked.

Editing text QuarkXPress has tools that allow the user to replace text and check spelling. It also has the standard cut, copy, and paste commands.

Formatting text There are two ways to apply text formatting in QuarkXPress—locally and by using a style sheet.

Importing graphics QuarkXpress lets the user import scanned images and images created in other applications. They can be manipulated to some degree and integrated into the design in QuarkXPress.

Use of master page One must have a master page when all the pages need to look alike in terms of style and database information.

Use of colour Every QuarkXPress document starts with a set of default colours including the four basic colours. One can also combine colours one has defined to create multi-ink colours.

Trapping Trapping consists of making sure that different coloured elements overlap enough so that there will be no gaps between them. QuarkXpress has built-in trapping system.

Printing As with most modern software, printing is easy and works in the same way. The quality of prints sometimes depends on the output medium, such as film or paper. At other times, it depends on the purpose of the prints, such as obtaining proofs or final outputs.

SOME DOS AND DON'TS WHILE WORKING

Discussed here are some general guidelines to be followed while working on a software in a DTP environment.

Make a thumbnail sketch It is essential to have a plan in mind before one starts working on a software. One should know where one is going with the design. Even the roughest of sketches can be useful. Although this step can be skipped, one can notice the difference thumbnail sketches bring to the planning of a document.

Apply the design rules The layout should be fine-tuned by applying basic design rules. This will give a professional look of the design. One should develop a relationship between the elements in a design by using the design syntax of harmony, rhythm, balance, and unity.

Check the colours on screen One should never rely on the colour displayed on the screen. The look of a colour may differ in different areas of the screen and across various screens. To obtain the desired colour on the printed page, it is essential to understand the colour management system.

Send font file with print document One should never forget to send type files to the printer along with the document to be printed. This is especially necessary when the outputting device is in another place where the computer used may not have the fonts used in the document.

Print a draft and proofread it Although proofreading can be done on-screen, it is always good to do the same on a printout of the document. Proofs should be printed out not only to check for colours (colours on screen do not always print as expected) but also to spot typographical errors and errors in the placement of elements. If the document is to be folded or trimmed, one should ensure that it folds properly and that trim marks are printed correctly.

Print the document Once one is satisfied with the layout and it has been ensured that the proofs are printing properly, one can print the document on a desktop printer.

Software-specific Guidelines

Discussed here are some software-specific guidelines for working on a DTP system.

Choose an appropriate template Each software has several templates. One should make sure that the template chosen by him/her is suitable for the type of project he/she is working on. If required, one can modify the project slightly to fit the template.

Set up the document While using a template, one may need to modify some of the template settings. If starting from scratch, one should set the size and orientation of the document. The margins should also be set at this stage. Text columns should be set up if one wants to set the text in columns.

Place text in the document If the document mostly contains text, it should be placed in the layout by importing it from a file. Copying substantial amount of text from another program or typing it directly in the program is not the best choice.

Format the text One should set the text spacing by choosing an alignment format. The desired type style, size, and spacing should be used to format the text. Although one may later want to make some changes in the style, one needs to select appropriate fonts for the document before starting work. Embellishments such as plain or fancy drop caps can be used. One should never format text or use graphics in a word processing software if the document is to be used in some other software.

Place graphics in the document If the document is mostly graphics-based, one may want to place the images before adding bits of text. In this case, one can import the graphics from a file, copy them from another program, or create them directly on a page layout software.

Adjust the placement of graphics One can move the graphics around so that they line up the way one wants them. Graphics can be set up in a way that the *text wraps* around them. They may be *cropped* or *resized* in the graphics software if necessary. This can be done on a layout software as well if the document is meant for desktop printing.

Graphics in word documents Graphic features of word processing programs or graphics/photographs imported from another application should not be used as they do not print well and create problems if one wants to output a file using a professional process.

Copy paste One should not try to copy paste charts and graphs from a spreadsheet file into a page layout program. They may look fine onscreen, but they usually are difficult to print.

Special effect to text One can use a paint-oriented program to achieve special effects such as glow, shadow, texture, and embossing. Paint-oriented programs are formed by pixels and they create jagged edges. They are good for creating special effects, but unsuitable for creating plain text, which needs to be sharp.

Resize the artwork Graphics should be enlarged and reduced in their respective programs. They should not be enlarged after being placed on a page layout program. Doing so will make the image blurry.

Keep the file size small One should avoid unnecessary white space between the images in a paint-oriented program. It is advisable to make separate files for each image. This will reduce the file size and ensure that the image is printed faster.

Merge layers Layers should be merged carefully. One should not merge the layers of images developed in a paint-oriented program before keeping a copy of that file. This is because, once the layers of an image have been merged, it will be impossible to alter the image in case of need.

SUMMARY

Traditional publishing is a long, labour-intensive process that involves the creation of the intended message, assembly of text and graphics, and preparation of a camera-ready copy that is used for printing. Several specialists and a lot of expensive equipment are required for this process. Desktop publishing (DTP) has revolutionalized the publishing process by making it possible to create print documents in much less time and with less money and effort. Almost everything that a dedicated publishing system does can be done on DTP.

Desktop publishing has opened up several possibilities for creating print material. Documents can be typeset with well-designed, proportionately spaced characters in DTP. It offers flexible options of font size and formatting. Graphics can be created with simple computer commands. Images taken from elsewhere can be scanned and modified digitally for an enhanced effect. Typeset matter can be edited, shifted, changed, and corrected on a DTP system. Illustrations can also be cut, cropped, and coloured on DTP. A DTP system can create the output on paper or film/plate by one of the devices available.

A typical DTP system has two basic components—hardware and software. Hardware includes a computer, printer, and scanner. The basic hardware requirement of a DTP system is a microcomputer, which may be of two types—Apple Macintosh and IBM PC.

A scanner is required to convert a pictorial image into digitized information that can be read by a computer. The DTP scanner is a flatbed scanner. It is called a CCD scanner.

There are several types of printers available today, which can produce printouts for diversified requirements. The most inexpensive type of printer is a low-resolution dot-matrix printer, which serves the purpose of a typewriter. The inkjet printer produces moderate quality output of both text and graphics with colour, ideal for layout purposes. The output of the laser printer is comparable to a finally produced printed page. Its black and white printout is used as a master for printing. Commercial printers use imagesetters to obtain output on film. Some printers get the plate for printing exposed through a plate setter.

All hardware work under software instructions. There are three categories of software for desktop publishing—word processing software, graphics software, and layout software. Word processing software is used for entering text into the computer, normally by using a keyboard. Graphics software may be an object-oriented drawing program or a pixilated paint program. The images created in different programs are imported or assembled in layout software to make a page. Various types of software and specific features of some commonly used ones have been discussed in the chapter in order to enable students to work on a DTP system with ease. Finally, some dos and don'ts for working on a DTP system have also been discussed.

KEY TERMS

Apple Macintosh A personal computer based on Motorola microprocessor, employing graphical user interface (GUI)—an enhanced environment for computer users. It was introduced by US-based Apple Corporation in 1984.

Bromide Paper Photography paper coated with a light-sensitive emulsion of silver bromide in gelatin.

Camera-ready Copy The complete page or a publication assembled with text and graphics and ready to be photographed as part of the first step in the process of making plates for offset printing.

Central Processing Unit (CPU) The main operating part of a computer. It provides the fundamental commands and instructions environment for the computer. It contains a processor, resisters, control unit, and an arithmetic logic unit. Each one performs its respective function on a single chip called the microprocessor.

Character Kerning The practice of adjusting the space between two adjacent letters so that a part of the type body is positioned within another type body.

Column Grid The underlying structure of a layout program that includes the column width and height and gutter.

Drop Caps An initial capital letter that is set larger than the body text by 2 to 4/5 lines in height for emphasis at the beginning of a text composition.

Graphics Software An application used for painting and drawing on the computer screen and also for manipulating the scanned images in various ways with the help of various tools.

Gutter The space between two facing pages. The space between two columns is often referred to as gutter, but it is actually an alley.

Headers and Footers The information appearing on the top or bottom of every page of a multi-page publication, which includes the margin, title, chapter name, page number, folio, etc.

IBM PC A personal computer (PC) based on microprocessor developed by International Business Machines (IBM)—a large US-based multinational corporation. Originally, it was used to perform routine tasks by a user or a small group of users. Today, it is a powerful machine that has a large memory and can perform multifunctional tasks with incredible speed.

Impact Printer A printer that gives an impression of the image on paper either by hammering an image of slug or by the impact of different combinations of print pins. Typewriters and dot-matrix printers are impact printers.

In-built Dictionary A facility available in most word processors, which provides a thorough, but not infallible spellings check of text files.

Inkjet Printer A non-impact printer that shoots minute bubbles of ink on to the print surface to form the image.

Laser Printer A printer that uses laser technology to project an intense light beam with a very narrow band width to charge the printer drum that picks up the ink from the toner and transfers it to the paper.

Layout Software An application used for assembling and creating text base in many styles and formats in combination with imported graphics.

Master Page The particular page style of a layout program that appears on every page of a multi-page publication with automatic changing page number.

Mouse An electro-mechanical device used as a pointer to select items from the on-screen menu. It was originally designed with the idea of reducing the number of key strokes required for a particular task.

Multi-bit Scanner A scanner that captures 8 to 36 bit-depth information. An 8-bit scanner captures grayscale or 256 shades of a colour. A 24-bit scanner captures millions of colours. Most office desktop scanners are 30-bit, whereas higher quality graphics scanners are 36-bit scanners.

Non-impact Printer A printer that does not use direct mechanical contact with the paper to create an image. Laser printers and inkjet printers are non-impact printers.

Random Access Memory (RAM) The primary memory of a computer that stores information temporarily.

Resolution A measure of image quality of computer output on hard copy or soft copy. It is expressed in terms of dots per inch (dpi) on hard copy (paper) and pixel per inch (ppi) on the monitor.

Single-bit Scanner A scanner captures information from the original bit by bit. The amount of information captured by a scanner is measured by bit-depth. A scanner that captures 1-bit or line image is called a single-bit scanner.

Spreadsheet An application used for converting statistical data into graphic images such as charts, graphs, tables, etc.

Template A pre-formatted file that serves as a starting point for a new document. Users can either create their own templates or use the existing ones that come in-built with the program.

Video Display Unit (VDU) A display screen, also known as the monitor. It is used to check the status and progress of the computer.

Word Processing Software An application used for typing text, checking spellings, automating repetitive typing task, writing reports with footnotes, making data tables, etc.

REFERENCES

Adler, Elizabeth W. 1991, *Print That Works*, Bull Publishing Company, USA.

Adobe 1995, *Print Publishing Guide*, Adobe System Incorporated, USA.

Agfa Prepress 1992, *An Introduction to Digital Colour Prepress*, Agfa Prepress Education Resources, USA.

Burns, Diane, Sharyn Venit, and Rebecca Hansen 1988, *The Electronic Publisher*, Brandy, Simon & Schuster Inc., New York, USA.

Cohen, Sandee and Robin Williams 1999, *The Non-Designer's Scan and Print Book*, Peachpit Press, USA.

Collier, David and Bob Cotton 1989, *Basic Desktop Design and Layout*, Quarto Publishing Plc, USA.

Conover, Theodore E. 1990, *Graphic Communication Today*, West Publishing Company, USA.

Gorden, Bob and Maggie Gorden 2002, Consultant Editors, *Digital Graphic Design*, Thames & Hudson Ltd, UK.

Jones, Graham 1988, *Desktop Publishing Companion*, Galgotia Publications, India.

Paddock, Bruce T. 1993, *Graphics for the Desktop Publishers*, Management Information Source Inc., USA.

Padwick, Gordon 1994, *Guide to Color Printing Techniques*, Random House Electronic Publishing, USA.

Romano, Frank J. and M. Romano Richard 1998, *Encyclopedia of Graphic Communications*, Prentice Hall PTR, USA.

Simmons, Ian 1991, *Computer Dictionary* 1991, BPB Publications, India.

http://desktoppub.about.com, accessed in March 2007.

REVIEW QUESTIONS

1. Define publishing. Compare traditional publishing with desktop publishing.
2. What are the capabilities of desktop publishing? Describe them in brief.
3. What are the advantages of using a DTP system? Mention some of its limitations as well.
4. What equipment is required to run a DTP system? Discuss the function and working of each.
5. Discuss the software support required for desktop publishing.
6. List the software features of CorelDRAW, Photoshop, and PageMaker.
7. What are the important points to be kept in mind while working on DTP?

PROJECTS

1. If you are a beginner in desktop publishing, familiarize yourself with the fundamentals of computers and basic input devices such as keyboard and mouse. Open a Word window and locate the Word menu bar, standard tool bar, rule, insertion point, split bar, style box, formatting tool bar, and status area. Discuss the content and feature of each element. Start typing some text from a printed page of a magazine or a newspaper article. Note experiences of pressing a wrong key, such as the delete key, space bar, caps lock, etc. Make a folder in the chosen drive of your computer, save the typed material in a word document with a name, and save it in your folder.

2. Open the word document you had saved. Select the text and change the font to Book Antiqua medium, 11 pt size with 2 pt leading and 2 pica paragraph indentation. Set the text within 6 inches line length, format it to justify. If some of the words on the document appear with a red underline, run a spell check and make the necessary corrections. Type a headline on the top of the text matter, change the type font to 30 pt Helvetica bold, and place it on the centre of the page. Prepare a table on the weekly schedule of your class and insert it in the document. Now, take a printout of the page and write a review of the entire process.

3. Draw a picture of a butterfly sitting on a flower using one of the draw programs of desktop publishing. You may copy the image from a printed page if you find it difficult to create a free-hand drawing. Note the set of commands you have used to develop the image. Fill the image with appropriate colours and take a printout for assessment.

4. Open a picture from sample pictures or a scanned file in Photoshop. Cut the main content of the picture and paste it on a layer. Give it a background colour of your choice. Create another picture for a second cut-out picture. Do the necessary colour correction, moving from one layer to another layer. If your main content and background colour are sharply divided, use the feathering effect behind the main content to obtain a soft blending. Save the file in a .psd format alteration if required for future use. Merge the layers of the images and save in a tiff format for use in other programs.

5. Assume that you are one of the members of a production team and have been given the responsibility of publishing a four-page magazine for your college. Build your plan around the capabilities of QuarkXpress, in which you will have to display seven stories and six photographs. Divide the space into seven rectangles of text boxes excluding margins. Then, divide these rectangles further into a number of column grids. Bring in text from the word document and allow it to flow along with the column grids of respective text boxes. Give a heading to each story. Insert picture boxes as per your plan and place pictures in it from image-editing software. Give a fine tone to your text pictures in terms of formatting text and resizing pictures. Judge your arrangement by taking a black and white desktop proof.

6. Prepare a dummy of a 32-page prospectus of your institute using the PageMaker software. Given that you have the text content in a soft copy, plan the pages with some space-holder photographs. After getting the dummy approved, replace the space holder by actual photographs and prepare a print file.

7. Your new communication consultancy firm needs a desktop publishing system. Make a list of your requirements, keeping in mind the expected expansion of your company in the next 2–3 years. Go to the market and meet at least three vendors. Note their suggestions in terms of hardware configuration and software capabilities. Do not forget to note down the price of each item. Discuss the available products with a group of friends or colleagues. Decide on which products you should purchase immediately and which can be bought later. Prepare a report on all the action you have taken.

CHAPTER 11
Paper and Finishing

Learning Objectives
After reading this chapter, you should be able to
- gain an overview of the basic paper-making processes
- understand the physical and surface characteristics of printing paper
- identify the different varieties of paper available in the market
- look at various sizes of paper used in print production
- understand paper weight and calculate the required quantity of paper for a particular job
- discuss various criteria for paper selection
- outline the methods of paper folding, assembling, cutting and trimming, binding, and finishing

INTRODUCTION

Paper is one of the major cost factors in the production of printed material today. It is important for us to familiarize ourselves with the processes of manufacturing paper, its aesthetic and physical characteristics, and the types of paper available in the market—their standard sizes, weight, and quantity.

The word *paper* is derived from the word papyrus, which is the name of a plant whose dried stem was first used by the Egyptians before 2000 BC as writing material. The next credit for the development of paper goes to the Chinese, who used wood and cotton fibres to make paper around 100 AD. During this period, palm leaves were used as writing material in India. The knowledge of papermaking came to the other parts of the world during the middle of the eighth century. The first paper mill in India was set up at Serampore (West Bengal) in 1832.

Till about two hundred years ago, practically all paper was made by hand. Today, the process of making paper by hand is so expensive that only certain types of paper are manufactured in this way. The basic material used in this process is the pulp of cellulose fibres. The fibres of wood, hemp, linen, or cotton rags are reduced to pulp and mixed in water to make slurry in a wooden tub. The mixed slurry (95 per cent water and five per cent fibres) is then placed in moulds made of fine wires stretched across wooden frames. As the water drains off through the mesh of the wire net, the mould is gently withdrawn, leaving the fibre mat, which is then flattened by passing it through rollers or by pressing it with a squeegee. The sheet is then hung to dry.

Now, of course, sophisticated machines are used to manufacture paper. However, the basic principle of papermaking remains the same. These days, the slurry is prepared in a large vat and undergoes various types of mechanical and chemical treatments. The water of compound slurry is drained through a fine-mesh moving screen. A steel frame known as deckle holds the pulp in place and determines the width of the paper. The screen movement shakes the fibres that float along the direction of belt's movement. The direction of fibres defines the paper grain. Paper grain runs with the long dimension of the parent-size sheet. The paper is pressed and dried at the end of the process. While it is still wet, it is passed through a variety of rollers to impart different characteristics. The rollers may be used for polishing the paper or for creating a special texture, design, or watermark. The watermark in paper is produced by bending the wires of the mould or by wires bent into the shape of the required letter or device, and sewed to the surface of the mould. It has the effect of making the paper thinner in places.

Finally, the paper is wound onto a large roll. Some rolls are cut into rectangular sheets by slicing the roll vertically and horizontally according to the desired size.

PAPER CHARACTERISTICS

Paper is available in an unlimited array of characteristics for the print industry's use. The several terms used to describe these characteristics are often confusing and misleading. Durability, for example, is often confused with permanence. Similarly, formation is confused with grain, and finish is confused with surface. Understanding the appropriate terms will greatly improve one's chances of getting the desired specifications when deciding on the paper to be used for printing.

The physical and surface characteristics provide the basis for choosing the paper for a particular printing job. These are discussed here. The physical characteristics may be the natural consequences of the physical properties of paper while the surface characteristics may be controlled according to the requirements of optical properties or quality.

Physical Characteristics

This section discusses the physical characteristics of paper, such as strength, thickness, opacity, and stretch.

Strength The strength of paper depends on the quality and length of the fibres and on how firmly they are intertwined. The fibres of the paper laid horizontally are referred to as short grain fibres and fibres that are laid vertically are termed as long grain fibres. The direction of the fibre or grain is related to the strength of the paper. It is thus an important consideration for the binding department of a printing press.

Paper folds, bends, or tears easily in the machine along the grain direction and has a great strength across the grain. This characteristic of paper can be easily identified by folding a sheet in two right-angle directions (horizontally and vertically). The paper folded in the long grain direction gives a smooth fold, whereas the other gives a rough or ragged edge due to the breakage of grain. In order to get the smooth folding of short-grain direction paper, binders often score the paper along the line of folding. A score is a crease in a sheet of paper that establishes position for a fold. This is especially necessary when the paper is thick.

Thickness Thickness is often referred to as bulk. Weight and finish determine the thickness of paper. It is possible to have two sheets that weigh the same, but they may have different thickness. The thickness of paper can be increased by boiling the fibres for a longer time during the process of papermaking. These fibres contain air and make the paper light and voluminous. Sheet bulk or thickness is related to many other sheet properties. Decrease in bulk makes the sheet smoother, glossier, less opaque, and lower in strength. Coated and antique finish papers are generally heavier than other papers of similar substance. Calendered or super-calendered paper is thinner, as its fibres are compressed by calendering rollers.

Opacity The quality of a paper is often judged by its opacity. If a paper is held against light, it can be observed whether it is opaque or transparent. Printing paper, particularly thin paper, where two-side impressions are needed, should be opaque enough to avoid the ink showing through.

Stretch It refers to the shrinkage and expansion characteristics of paper. Since the main ingredient of paper slurry is water, freshly manufactured paper contains some moisture and has a tendency to expand or shrink during the process of evaporation of moisture. It also changes its size after coming in contact with the moisture on an offset printing machine. These changes are more visible along the long-grain direction than along the short-grain direction. All these affect printing, especially coloured registration. Printers take care of atmospheric conditions, grain, and stretch while feeding paper into a printing machine.

Surface Characteristics

Different surface characteristics of paper are referred to as paper finish. Machine-made paper broadly comes in the following types of finishings—antique, English, calendered, coated, textured, and coloured.

Antique finish This finish imitates the appearance of handmade paper. The fresh paper roll coming off the papermaking machine displays various surface characteristics on both sides. This surface is generally rough in character due to minimum pressure. There are several sub-categories of antique finish paper, including eggshell finish and vellum finish. The roughness of eggshell finish resembles an eggshell. Vellum finish, which resembles a calf skin, is smoother than the eggshell finish.

English finish When the surface of paper is made smoother by machine, it is called English finish paper. To obtain a smooth surface, the paper material should have high clay content and short fibres.

Calendered finish It is the process of smoothing the surface of paper by rolling it between heavy iron calendering rollers. When this operation is done only once, the quality of surface obtained is known as calendered paper. For obtaining super-calendered paper, this operation is done more than once and the paper is dampened by steam. The finish of super-calendered paper is smoother than calendered paper. Both calendered and super-calendered paper may be of either matt or glossy finish. A glossy finish is obtained by the friction of steel rollers at the time of calendering.

Coated finish   In this finish, the surface of the paper becomes very smooth, because the cellulose fibres are covered by a coating substance. The coating substance is China clay, which is enhanced with whitening and adhesive agents. It is applied to the surface of the paper by immersing it in the coating solution or is distributed by a suitable arrangement of rollers. The operation is completed by drying the paper with hot air. Like calendered paper, coated paper may have glossy or matt finish. Since the coated stock is finished by an additional operation with additional coating material, the paper becomes costly vis-à-vis other varieties of paper.

Textured finish   This surface quality is obtained by the embossing process. Such finishes are commonly used for cover papers when a decorative or fancy surface is required, as an uneven surface is often unsuitable for printing.

Coloured finish   Most varieties of printing paper are bleached to make the paper white and ideal for four colour printing. Unbleached paper is slightly brownish and is mainly used for single colour printing. For aesthetic considerations, some varieties of paper are coloured using special bleaches, dyes, or pigments.

PAPER VARIETIES

Paper manufacturers produce a wide variety of paper. Different types of paper are used for different purposes. The choice of paper is of critical importance. For a particular job, various kinds of paper may be manufactured by various paper mills. It is, therefore, essential for us to study the physical characteristics of paper and their suitability. We may classify paper into five basic categories.

Book paper

This is a very important group with a wide variety of finishes. As its very name suggests, its quality makes it suitable for books, magazines, booklets, annual reports, and various promotional literature. Its quality ensures the lasting value of the publication. The paper is not discoloured or torn-off along the folding during its shelf life. Due to its opacity, images on the two sides of a page do no clash with each other. Most book paper is made of wood pulp, cotton pulp, or a combination of the two. Chemical processes are used to change the pulp into cellulose fibres, thereby removing the impurities of the pulp. These treatments ensure that the paper is tough and long lasting.

Due to the burgeoning demand of consumers, various cheaper varieties of paper made of mechanical wood pulp have been introduced in the market. This variety of paper is less smooth than others and is slightly coloured. White Printing Paper is an example of this kind of cheap paper.

Book paper stocks are produced under different brand names by various paper mills. Some of the brand names indicate the qualities possessed by the paper. For example, Maplitho Paper is meant for offset printing, where the quality prevents the paper from curling due to moisture. In the case of Sunshine or Super Sunshine Paper, opacity and whiteness are the distinguishing features. The names of White Printing Paper and Coloured Printing Paper speak for themselves. A comparatively superior quality paper in different light colours, including white, is available under the brand name Lucky Parchment. This is an imitation parchment made of high-grade fibre. Real parchment is extremely expensive, as it is made of goat/sheep skin.

Newsprint

This variety of paper is mostly made of mechanical wood or bamboo pulp and is a low-grade economical stock, used mainly for daily newspapers. It is also available in sheets for handbills and other low-quality items. It discolours quickly due to the impurities contained in and around the fibre. Due to the huge demand and scarcity of indigenous newsprint, distribution of this type of paper in India is greatly controlled by the Government of India. In order to make better quality newsprint, some chemical pulp is used to increase its strength. The newsprint is bleached to make it white. Many magazines and Sunday editions of newspapers use a superior variety of newsprint so as to be able to print coloured halftones with fine screen. This superior variety of paper is known as calendered or super-calendered newsprint.

Art paper

Art paper refers to coated finish paper available in varying thickness and finish. It may come with a high gloss or matt surface. It is called art paper because photographs and paintings can be printed on this kind of paper. It can carry a good reproduction of halftone. Indian art paper has not yet come up to the mark of imported art paper, for it cannot carry the number of line screens for halftone or coloured reproduction. Therefore, for much superior quality reproduction, we still have to depend on imported art paper.

One-side coated paper is called chromo art paper. It is cheaper and used where only one-side printing is required, as in the case of labels and posters. The cheaper variety of art paper tends to get discoloured soon.

Writing and stationery paper

This variety of paper is used for letterheads, envelopes, ledger sheets, exercise books, etc. Since it is meant for writing, its surface is made to prevent absorption and soakage. Bank paper and bond paper are examples of this variety of paper.

Better grades of bond paper are called 'executive bond' and are made from rags. Wood pulp is commonly used for cheaper varieties of writing paper, such as that used in concessional exercise books. However, care is taken to make its surface reasonably smooth for writing. Ledger sheets are strong, because they have to withstand repeated handling. Since the surface of ledger sheets should not strain the eye, they are often light green or light blue in colour.

For laser printing and photocopying purposes, the paper has a surface that is smooth enough to carry the dense image of the toner. Computer paper is a variety of low-grade paper available in continuous sheets with perforations and is suitable for dot matrix printers. There is a large variety of inkjet paper available in various thicknesses and finish. Some are termed as Photoglossy paper. A near bromide print output can be obtained on this quality of paper.

Plastic-coated variety of paper is smooth and shiny. The surface of this kind of paper is washable. Ivory card is a high-rag content stiff cardboard used for greater durability and ease of handling. This hot pressed card is ideal for delicate line work and precise mechanical art. It is commonly used for visiting cards, invitation cards, etc. Although this paper is of good quality, halftone reproduction is often avoided on its surface.

Cover paper

Cover paper refers to a very thick variety of paper. This variety of paper is available in a wide range of thickness, colours, and textures. Most of the paper under this category is strong enough to withstand rough handling and has long fibres for easy folding. Paper with a weight of 160 gsm or upwards is called card or board.

Pulpboard is a commonly used type of cover paper. Generally, both sides have a smooth finish suitable for the processes of printing. Pulpboard coated with China clay is called art board. If only one side is coated, then it is called chromo board. Paper with a metallic surface of silver, gold, copper, etc. is called metallic board.

Strawboards are made from straw pulp. They are used for book-binding, and not for printing. Mount board is a better variety than strawboard. It may be smooth-surfaced on one or both sides. It is used for the artists' rough layouts, mounting of photographs, and dummy boxes. Handmade paper—a comparatively thick paper—is available in a variety of textures and thicknesses. It is suitable for covers, certificates, invitation cards, and water-colour paintings.

Besides the above-mentioned varieties of boards and paper, there are many types of highly specialized paper. These include the kind of paper used for wrapping, tracing, currency notes, photography, cheques, postage stamps, etc.

PAPER SIZES

Paper is supplied to printers in reels for web-fed printing and in sheets for sheet-fed printing. All varieties of paper, with the exception of handmade paper, are first manufactured in the reel or web form and then cut into sheets of different sizes.

In India we are still in a period of transition from the Imperial size to the metric size system. Both the systems are used in this country, even though the sizes officially standardized by the International Standards Organization (ISO) are in metric measurement. Metric measurement is scientific and reduces wastage.

Despite the adoption of metric sizes by the Bureau of Indian Standards (BIS), Indian paper mills are still supplying paper in traditional British sizes. This is due to two factors—(i) the fixity of deckle size, a stainless steel board used in the papermaking machine for supporting the pulp stock, and (ii) the natural resistance to change.

Traditional British Sizes

Paper is available in many sizes. However, the common sizes used for the production of books and other publications are known by the brand names of Crown, Demy, Medium, Royal, Imperial, etc. There is no proportional relationship between them. Multiples and sub-divisions of all these sizes also exist.

The dimensions of British size paper are still expressed in inches. The particular size of a paper refers to the whole sheet of paper, which is called a *broadsheet*. Twice of a broadsheet is called a *double* of that particular size and four times of a broadsheet is called a *quad*.

Sub-divisions

When a piece of paper is folded once lengthwise, we get two leaves or four pages. Each leaf is called a *folio*. When the sheet is folded first length-wise and then breadth-wise, we get one quarter of a sheet, which is called a *quarto*. One-eighth part of a sheet is called an *octavo*, that is, the long side of the sheet is divided by four and the short side by two. If both the sides are divided by four, we get a sixteenth part of a sheet or *sextodecimo*. To get one-sixth part of a sheet, the long dimension is divided by three and the short one by two and it is called a *sexto*. Figure 11.1 illustrates the sub-divisions of British paper sizes.

Traditionally, the kind of paper used for books and other publications are Crown, Royal, Demy, and Medium sizes. Foolscap, Demy, and Medium sizes are used mainly for writing material, such as letterheads, writing pads, exercise and ledger books, etc. Card and board sizes come in Imperial, Largepost, and other sizes, and can be used to make packages, invitation and greeting cards, and covers for paperback and casebound books. Standard names and their sub-divisions are given in Exhibit 11.1.

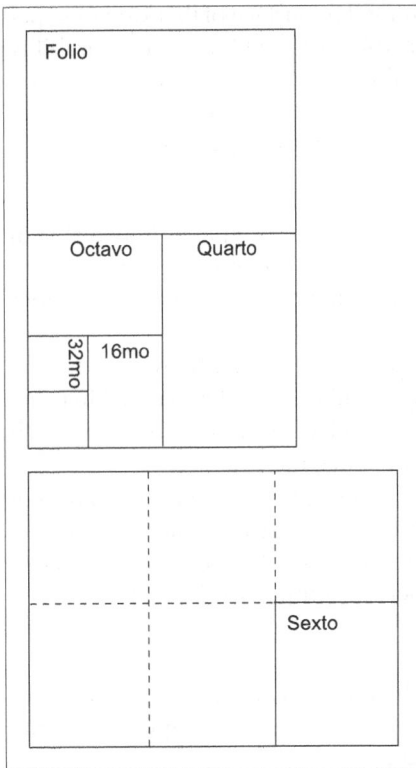

Figure 11.1 Sub-divisions of British paper sizes

Exhibit 11.1 Traditional paper sizes and their sub-divisions

(Size in inches)

Size name	Double	Broadsheet	Folio	Quarto	Octavo	Sexto
Crown	20×30	15×20	10 × 15	7.50 × 10	5 × 7.50	6.66 × 7.50
Demy	22.50×35	17.50×22.50	11.25 × 17.50	8.75 × 11.25	5.62 × 8.75	7.50 × 8.75
Medium	23×36	18×23	11.50 × 18	9 × 11.50	5.75 × 9	7.66 × 9
Royal	26×40	20×26	13 × 20	10 × 13	6.50 × 10	8.66 × 10
Imperial	30×44	22×30	15 × 22	11 × 15	7.50 × 11	10 × 11
Foolscap	17×27	13.50 × 17	8.50 × 13.50	6.75 × 8.50	4.25 × 6.75	5.66 × 6.75

Exhibit 11.2 Comparative sizes of ISO paper

(Size in millimetres)

	A	B	C
Basic sheet 0	841 × 1189	1000 × 1414	917 × 1296
Subdivision 1	594 × 841	707 × 1000	648 × 917
Subdivision 2	420 × 594	500 × 707	458 × 648
Subdivision 3	297 × 420	353 × 500	324 × 458
Subdivision 4	210 × 297	250 × 353	229 × 324
Subdivision 5	148 × 210	176 × 250	162 × 229
Subdivision 6	105 × 148	125 × 176	114 × 162
Subdivision 7	74 × 105	88 × 125	81 × 114
Subdivision 8	52 × 74	62 × 88	57 × 81

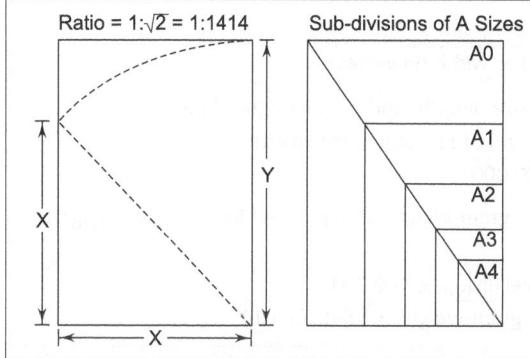

Figure 11.2 Sub-divisions of A sizes of ISO paper

International Sizes (ISO)

Unlike traditional British sizes, international sizes have alphabetical designations such as 'A', 'B', and 'C'. All the sizes are interrelated, that is, proportionate to one another, and a wide range of sizes and folds can be obtained. Most printing work such as books, magazines, and stationery is accomplished with 'A' size paper. The 'B' series is intended for posters, charts, maps, etc. The 'C' size is for envelopes in which 'A' size products are enclosed. The basic size in each series is A0, B0, and C0. Here, half of A0 is A1 or folio; one-fourth is A2; one-eighth is A3; and one-sixteenth is A4, as shown in Figure 11.2. Further, Exhibit 11.2 lists the comparative sizes and sub-divisons of ISO sizes of paper.

WEIGHT AND QUANTITY

Paper is first manufactured in reels and then cut into sheets of the required size for printing and processing on the sheet-fed machine. The price of paper is based on its weight, size, and finish. Most paper is sold in lots of a given number of sheets as well as weight. The standard quantity of paper, termed as a *ream*, has 500 sheets. The next smaller quantity is *gross*, which contains 144 sheets. Boards and cards are available in 100- or 150-sheet packets. Paper reels for web-fed machines come in large quantities and sell in tonnes. Substance is often identified by the grammage and width of the reel in metres or inches.

It is difficult to identify the weight of a single sheet of paper. Therefore, it is expressed in terms of the number of kilograms (kg) for a ream of sheets of a basic size. Moreover, the

> ### Exhibit 11.3 Calculations for paper in sheets/reels
>
> 1. To find the weight (in kg) of a ream containing 500 sheets of a given size in inches and gram-weight:
>
> $$\frac{\text{Length (in inches)} \times \text{width (in inches)} \times \text{gram-weight}}{3{,}100}$$
>
> 2. To find the weight (in kg) of a ream containing 500 sheets of a given size in centimetres and gram-weight
>
> $$\frac{\text{Length (in cm)} \times \text{width (in cm)} \times \text{gram-weight}}{20{,}000}$$
>
> 3. To find the gram-weight of a ream containing 500 sheets of a given size in centimetres and weight (in kg) per ream:
>
> $$\frac{\text{Weight (in kg) per ream} \times 20{,}000}{\text{Length (in cm)} \times \text{width (in cm)}}$$
>
> 4. To find the gram-weight (in kg) of a ream containing 500 sheets of a given size in inches and weight (in kg) per ream:
>
> $$\frac{\text{Weight (in kg) per ream} \times 3{,}100}{\text{Length (in inches)} \times \text{width (in inches)}}$$
>
> 5. To find the total weight (in kg) of a reel of a given size, length, and gram-weight of paper:
>
> $$\frac{\text{Gram-weight} \times \text{width (in cm) of reel} \times \text{length in metre}}{100{,}000}$$
>
> 6. To find the length in metres of a reel of a given size, gram-weight of paper, and total weight (in kg) of the reel:
>
> $$\frac{\text{Weight of reel (in kg)} \times 100{,}000}{\text{Substance of paper in gram-weight} \times \text{width (in cm)}}$$

basic sizes of all kinds of paper are not the same. For example, a booklet in Crown Octavo printed on 20 kg paper will be thicker than a booklet in Demy Octavo, printed on paper of the same weight. The international method of expressing paper weight in grammage has solved much of this problem. Grammage is measured in grams per square metre (gsm)—this refers to the weight in grams of a single sheet that has an area equal to one square metre. Weight is thus independent of the size and number of sheets in a packet.

At times, it is necessary to convert the weight of paper in kg to gsm or vice versa to meet the requirements of a particular printing job. The formulae for such conversions are given in Exhibit 11.3.

Calculation of Paper Requirement

As mentioned earlier, paper is sold by weight, that is, at a price per kg and, if the quantity involved is large, at a price per tonne. It is necessary to calculate the number of sheets required for a particular job. The formulae provided in Exhibit 11.4 will help in estimating the requirement of paper.

> **Exhibit 11.4   Formulae for estimating paper requirement**
>
> 1. To calculate the number of sheets of paper required to print a folder:
>
> $$\frac{\text{No. of pp. in the folder} \times \text{No. of copies to be printed}}{\text{No. of pp. to be printed on both sides of a sheet}}$$
>
> 2. To calculate the number of reams of paper required to print a book:
>
> $$\frac{\text{No. of pp. in the book} \times \text{No. of copies to be printed}}{\text{No. of pp. to be printed on both sides of a sheet} \times 500}$$
>
> 3. To calculate the number of copies obtainable from a given quantity of paper:
>
> $$\frac{\text{No. of sheets} \times \text{No. of pp. to be printed on both sides of a sheet}}{\text{No. of pp. in the book}}$$

A few extra sheets to account for wastage need to be added to the total quantity of paper to get the exact number of printed copies required. This is especially necessary when the publication is highly priced or is of high quality. The provision for wastage is based on the number of press runs and the total number of printed copies required. For example, let us assume that 10,000 copies of a Crown Sexto folder are to be printed in three colours. The size can be obtained from Crown size paper (allowing for gripper space). One sheet of this size yields two units, therefore, 5,000 sheets are required. Wastage may be calculated at three per cent, that is, 150 sheets for three press runs. Thus, 5,150 sheets of paper need to be purchased. If 150 loose sheets are not available, a packet of 250 sheets may be available. There is no fixed formula for determining the percentage of wastage. Most often, it is based on an understanding between the printer and the print buyer.

PAPER SELECTION

In print communication, paper is the only material that can be seen and felt in the finished product. The quality of a printed publication is thus dependent on paper selection. Several factors need to be considered while selecting paper. The cost, as always, is a pre-eminent factor. These costs can be kept under control by selecting the right type of paper for the right job. Some of the considerations for selecting paper are as follows:

Printing process   Paper should be selected on the basis of the printing process being used. Some varieties of paper are suitable for only one printing process, while others can be used for several processes. Good quality coated paper is required to reproduce fine screen engravings on dry or wet offset processes of printing. Maplitho or mechanical newsprint reproduces fine details in offset lithography or gravure processes.

Space requirements   To avoid wastage, paper should be selected from the available sizes. While selecting a paper size, we also need to take into consideration the space requirements for grippers (a row of metal tabs or clips located on an impression cylinder or transfer cylinder that grab a sheet of paper and feed it through a printing press), bleeds, trimming, etc.

Requirements of colour and smoothness These should be judged according to their aesthetic contribution. From the reader's viewpoint, this may indeed be the vital role of paper. Straight matter printed on a coloured or glossy surface is tiring for the eyes. Continuous tone illustrations printed on a glossy surface reduce the shine. For any printing job, white is the safest choice. The right choice of coloured stock often enhances the publication's aesthetic value and reduces monotony.

Weight and opacity These are some other important considerations while selecting paper. Text or images printed on both sides of a thin paper often show through. A thin paper with good opacity should be used to prevent this problem. Generally, heavy paper has more opacity, but it increases the publication's bulk and distribution costs.

Strength and resistance Printing paper must have resistance. Paper resistance depends on the chemical and physical properties of paper and methodology of manufacturing. Sometimes, the printing ink spreads out when an impression is made on paper if the paper is not absorbent enough. This is due to the porosity and strength of the paper. Weak paper often releases undesirable paper particles during the press run, which wastes precious press time in frequent cleanup and results in production loss.

FOLDING, BINDING, AND FINISHING

Most paper sheets must undergo folding, assembling, cutting and trimming, binding, and finishing operations after printing. These may be classified as the final touches of the printing operation.

Folding

The sheets must be folded after printing. The folding may be done either manually or mechanically. Manual folding refers to the process of folding a sheet simply by hand, aligning the edges of the sheet. The stiff or thicker sheets are folded using a solid strip of hardened steel sheets to crush the grain of the paper to create a straight line on folding. This process is called *creasing* or *scoring*. High-speed mechanical folding, called *buckle* folding, is achieved by pulling the paper through rollers, as shown in Figure 11.3. The arrangement of these pages is done in a certain order so that, after folding, they appear in consecutive numerical order. This arrangement of a page forme is known as an *imposition*, and each printed and folded sheet is called a *signature*. Imposition is the responsibility of the printer. Designers generally do not prepare the pages in the manner required for a page forme to go into the machine.

Signatures come in multiples of four pages. They may be eight, sixteen, thirty two, and so on, depending on the size of the press and the paper stock. Planning a printing job is easier if

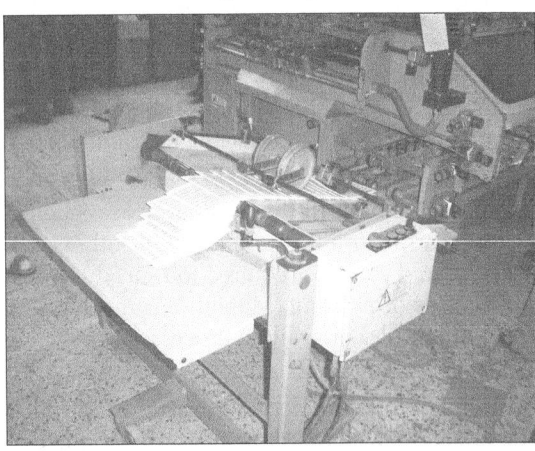

Figure 11.3 Mechanical folding

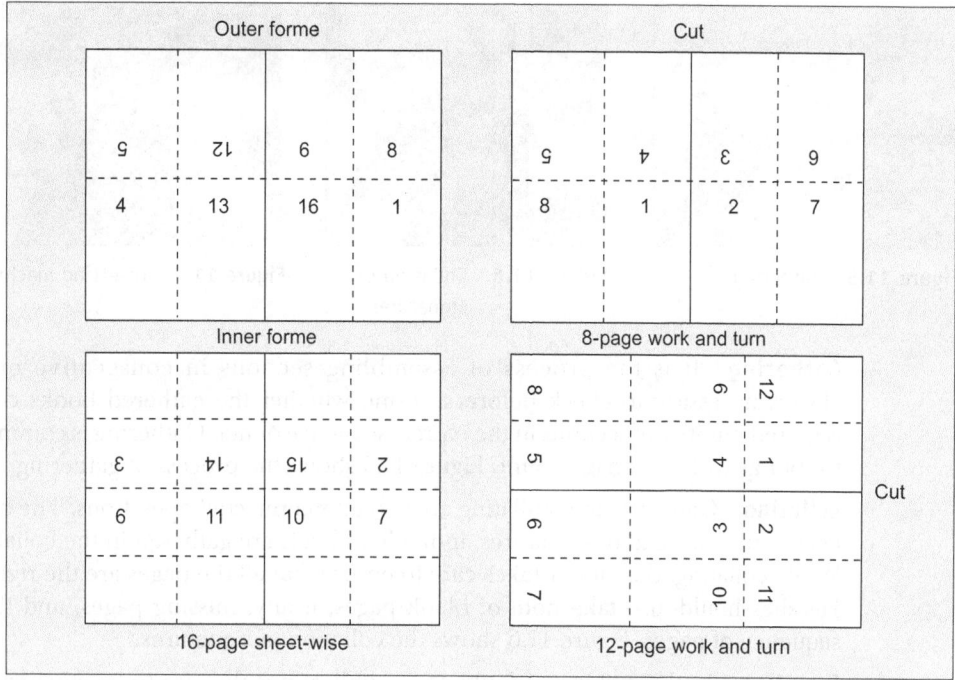

Figure 11.4 Folding of a forme

these factors are taken into account. For example, let us assume that we want to use some other colour besides black on some pages. The cost factor should also be within the budget. One impression takes care of one side of the sheet. The pages on the sheet are not in numerical order (see the diagram of a 16-page signature in Figure 11.4). If we plan page 4 and 14 in colour, an additional printing impression will be needed, which translates into an extra cost for the job.

There are two basic kinds of imposition: *sheet-wise* and *work and turn*. In sheet-wise imposition, half of the pages are imposed on one side of the sheet and the other half on the back of the sheet. In the second process, all the pages of a forme are imposed on one side of the sheet for half the press run and the sheet is then turned over for the same pages to be printed on the opposite side. The sheet is then cut into two pieces to form two signatures. Figure 11.4 shows the sheet-wise and work and turn imposition of a forme.

Assembling

It includes all the simple binding operations which are performed without using any material such as adhesives, thread, or wire. In assembling, the separate pages are brought together into a single unit. This involves gathering, collating, and insetting irrespective of the size of the unit. The process may be manual; semi-automatic, that is, partly manual and partly by machine; or automatic.

  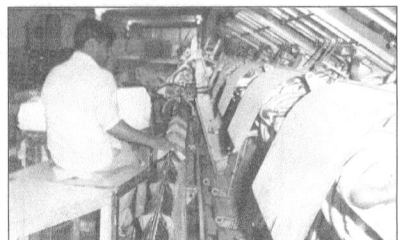

Figure 11.5 Gathering   **Figure 11.6** Collation of signatures   **Figure 11.7** Insetting machine

Gathering It is the process of assembling sections in consecutive order. It is always necessary to check before securing whether the gathered books contain the required number of sections in the correct sequence or not. Gathering is commonly used for books with high page count. Figure 11.5 shows the process of gathering.

Collating Gathering and collating are two interconnected operations. The only difference is that, instead of signatures, individual sheets are gathered in the collation stage. While collating, the binder takes care to ensure that all the pages are the right way up. He/she should also take note of blank pages, if any, missing pages, and the correct sequence of pages. Figure 11.6 shows the collation of signatures.

Insetting In the making of multi-page publications that are to be stitched centrally, sections have to be inserted in between each other, and finally into a cover. This is called insetting. It can also be done manually or on a machine often with a stitcher and a three-knife trimmer for mass production. The output of insetting depends upon the total number of sections to be inset and, to a little extent, on the format of the publication. Figure 11.7 shows a person working on an insetting machine.

Cutting and trimming

Reams of paper are cut or trimmed before being put on the printing machine and after the printed signatures are stitched or bound. The main difference between cutting and trimming is that in cutting a pile of paper is converted into the required number of pieces of the desired size. During the process of trimming, 1/8 inch or 3-4 mm of paper is removed from the edge of a ream or a printed product in order to make the pages rectangular in shape and flushed at the edges. Figure 11.8 shows a cutting and trimming machine.

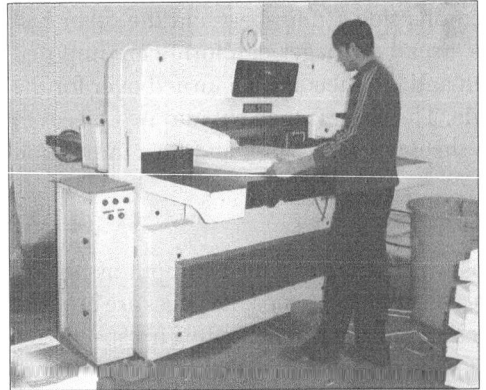

Figure 11.8 Cutting and trimming machine

Binding

The folded signatures then go through the processes of binding and trimming. Binding may be very simple or very complicated, depending on the type of the job in hand.

Wire stitching There are two methods of wire stitching—saddle and side stitching. These methods are the simplest and most widely used binding methods. In the first method, signatures are inserted one into the other and wire staples are driven into the fold through the centre of the publication. This binding method is called saddle stitching because stitching is accomplished by positioning the signatures on a metal 'saddle'. Figure 11.9 shows a sewing machine.

Thick publications with more than one signature should preferably be side-stitched. Here signatures are stacked one upon the other and the staples are forced through the side. Since the side stitch takes up about one-fourth of an inch for binding, the publication does not open flat. The designer must, therefore, plan a wide inside margin (gutter) to compensate for this.

Perfect binding Folded sections are gathered in the right order and roughened along the back fold by trimming and grinding. The pages are then glued at the spine on which a lining cloth is pasted. The cloth piece holds the pages together, and then the paper cover is glued on. Now, with the availability of better quality rubber-based glue, there is no need for a cloth lining to hold the pages together. Figure 11.10 shows a perfect binding machine.

Sewn binding In this method, the signatures or sections are gathered and sewn together to form the book block. These sections are then joined by further sewing. The cover is then glued to the spine. Both perfect binding and sewn binding are commonly used in paperback publications.

Case binding This traditional method of binding is often called 'hard binding'. It is mainly used for books that need to last long. After the signatures or sections have been assembled, end-papers are pasted on the spine edge of the first and the last signature. These are then sewn together with a strong thread. A strip of cloth is glued on to the spine. The end-papers are glued down to the case. The case is created by covering the cardboard covers with paper, cloth, or even leather. Case binding is the most expensive

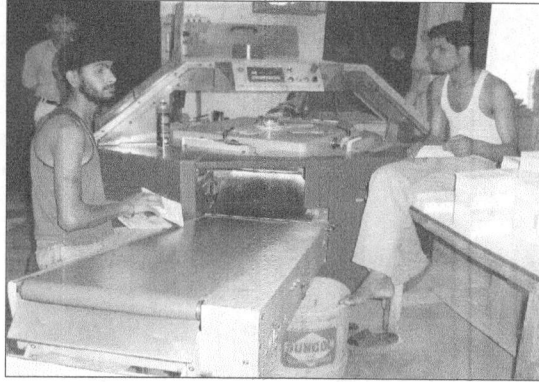

Figure 11.9 Sewing machine **Figure 11.10** Perfect binding machine

Figure 11.11 Case binding machine

binding method. In the USA and Europe, some publishers insert perfect bound, rather than sewn, signatures into cases to cut down costs. Figure 11.11 shows the process of case binding.

Spiral/spico binding This is a modern mechanical method of binding, used mainly for various types of reports, background papers, catalogues, etc. Here paper folding and imposition are not required, as the pages are independent sheets which can be printed using small size machines or photocopied. In spiral or spico binding, sheets are punched with holes along the binding edge. Plastic or metal rings, coils, or combs are inserted through them to hold the pages together.

Finishing

This is the final stage of a printing operation. Some of the finishing techniques are very simple. Some are very complicated. Their application calls for specialized skills. For example, to obtain a printed piece in a non-rectangular form, die cutting is required. Three-side trimming machines are used to obtain perfect rectangle trimmings.

Varnishing A glossy finish can be achieved by applying lacquer or varnish after printing. This is called varnishing. Varnish is essentially ink without pigment. It requires its own printing unit on press. From an artistic standpoint, one can place a dull-varnished portion of the sheet against a portion without varnish or with a gloss varnish. This contrast can give emphasis to certain areas and/or give the impression of depth.

Ultraviolet coating To coat a paper with ultraviolet coating, a clear liquid is spread over paper like ink and then cured instantly with ultraviolet light. It can be a glossy or dull coating, and can be used as a spot covering to give accent to an image created on a raised surface by embossing. Alternately, a metallic glitter effect can be created on the sheet or as an overall (flood) coating. Ultraviolet coating gives more protection and brightness than varnish coating. Since it is cured with light and not heat, no solvents enter the atmosphere. However, it is more difficult to recycle as compared to other coatings.

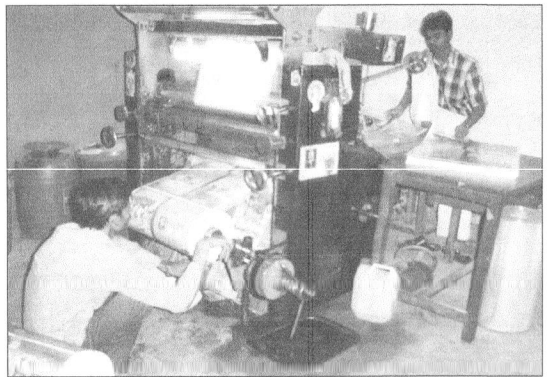

Figure 11.12 Lamination machine

Ultraviolet coating is applied as a separate finishing operation of one of the printing units of a flexo or offset machine as a flood coating. Screen printing is ideal for spot coating. It should be kept in mind that this thick coating may crack when scored or folded.

Lamination This highly glossy or matt finish and waterproof surface is achieved by applying a thin clear plastic sheet or spreading liquid on the printed matter. A laminate is a material constructed by uniting two or more layers of material. The process of creating a laminate by sandwiching the paper between layers of plastic and sealing them with heat and/or pressure, as shown in Figure 11.12, is known as lamination. Laminates are available in two types: film and liquid. As their name suggests, in one case a clear plastic film is laid down over the sheet of paper, and in the other case a clear liquid is spread over the sheet and dried (or cured) like a varnish. Laminates protect the sheet from water (including perspiration from the hands) and are, therefore, good for coating items such as restaurant menus and book covers. Laminates are slow to apply and costly but provide a strong, washable surface. They are the superior choice for protecting loose books in transit.

Other finishings The simplest finishing method is cutting the printed sheets on the sides. Die stamping, thermography printing, and leaf printing are some of the other specialized finishing techniques.

Finishing operations also include *perforating* for clean and straight tearing of pages; *numbering* for loose printed sheets, application forms, etc. *Eyelet punching* is ideal for card making and general art and craft projects.

SUMMARY

In print communication, paper is the only material that can be seen and felt in its finished product in terms of aesthetic quality and cost. Therefore, anyone concerned with printing should be aware of how paper is made, its physical characteristics, types of paper available, standard sizes, etc.

The basic materials of papermaking are the cellulose fibres of wood, hemp, linen, or cotton. These are mixed with water to make paper. Paper was earlier made manually, but now sophisticated machines manufacture most of the paper. However, the basic principle of making paper remains the same. The aesthetic quality of machine-made paper comes from various surface characteristics such as antique finish, English finish, calendered, coated finish, etc. The paper to be used for printing depends on four other characteristics: strength, thickness, opacity, and stretch.

There are wide varieties of paper used for different purposes. We may classify them into five basic categories. Book paper is long lasting. It maintains whiteness during its shelf life and is opaque enough to be printed on both sides of a page. It does not crack along its folding. Newsprint is a low-grade economical stock, meant for printing short-lived publications such as newspapers.

Better quality newsprint is known as calendered finish. It is mainly used for special editions of newspapers and magazines. Art paper is a costly paper with a coated finish. It can carry a good reproduction of halftone. One-side coated paper is known as chromo art paper. It is useful for label and poster printing. A wide variety of paper comes within stationary paper. This includes paper used for writing, photocopying, wrapping, etc.

Paperweight is determined by gram per square metre (gsm). Thick paper is called cover paper or card, and generally has a thickness above 150 gsm.

Paper is available in many standard sizes. In India we have two varieties—(i) traditional, such as Crown. Demy, Royal, etc., and (ii) international sizes having alphabetical designations such as 'A', 'B', and 'C'.

Most paper is sold in a bundles containing 500, 144, and 100 sheets. These are called ream, gross, and packet of hundred respectively.

In printing business, paper calculation is must to calculate the number of sheets required to print a particular job or the number of publications that can be obtained from the available quantity of paper.

Most paper sheets must undergo folding, binding, and finishing operations after printing.

KEY TERMS

Antique Finish Paper Printing paper that has a coarse and uneven finish. The term 'antique' refers to the similarity between this finish and the paper of the early print days.

Art Paper Coated finish paper generally used to print photographs, paintings, and graphics in order to get sharp and bright images.

Book Paper A type of paper generally used for offset printing. It is known for its durability and resistance to water.

Broadsheet The traditional basic size of paper is called broadsheet.

Buckle Folding This high-speed mechanical folding is achieved by pulling the paper through rollers.

Bulk A term used to indicate volume or thickness of paper in relation to its weight.

Calendered Paper Degree of smoothness imparted to paper during the papermaking process by pressing it between rollers.

Case Binding Traditional method of binding, often called hard binding, used mainly for long-lasting books.

Coated Finish Paper Paper with clay or other coating applied to one or both sides.

Cover Paper Thick variety of paper having enough strength to withstand rough handling and facilitate easy folding.

Die Cutting A printed piece cut into a special shape by dies made by shaping steel blades into the desired form.

End Papers Paper that is used at the ends of a book. There are two leaves of paper at the end and front that hold the case bound cover to the body of the book.

English Finish Paper A smooth finish on uncoated paper that is smoother than a machine finish, but not as smooth as calendered finish.

Folio, Quarto, and Octavo Broadsheet paper folded once, twice, and thrice to get two, four, and eight sheets or four, eight, and sixteen pages respectively.

Gripper Space Non-printing area of a sheet meant for pulling by the mechanical fingers of a printing machine.

Gross Quantity of paper in a packet containing 144 sheets.

Handmade Paper Non-standard rough or semirough surface paper made without the use of any machine.

Imposition Arrangement of pages for printing in such a way that, when folded, the pages fall in a proper sequence.

International Size ISO standard sizes of paper have alphabetical dimension such as 'A', 'B', and 'C'. These are proportionate to each other and wide range of sizes and folds are obtainable.

Lamination Paper developed by gluing or fusing layers of metal or plastic together to a desired thickness and quality.

Newsprint A cheap variety of paper used primarily for publications with a short life span; for example, newspapers.

Opacity The measure of how opaque or see-through a piece of paper is.

Papyrus An early form of paper made from the pith of papyrus plant that used to grow in the wetlands of the Nile Delta in ancient Egypt.

Perfect Binding This process involves putting all the pages or signatures together, roughening, and flattening the edge. A flexible adhesive is used to attach the paper cover to the spine.

Print Run Total number of copies of a publication to be printed in one impression.

Pulp Fibrous material prepared from wood or recovered waste paper for the use of manufacturing paper.

Ream Quantity of paper in a packet containing 500 sheets.

Reel of Paper A web of paper wrapped around a core or shaft used for printing on a web-based press.

Saddle Stitch Mechanical binding method for a booklet/magazine that opens to the centre spread and is wire-stapled.

Sewn Binding Sewing of the gathered signatures to form a book block.

Signature A sheet of paper printed on both sides and folded to make a part of a publication. It is also called a section.

Spiral Binding Binding method that uses wires inserted through specially punched holes along the margin.

Stationery Paper Paper that is used as stationery, such as paper that is used for computers, photocopiers, ledgers, crafts, etc.

Strength of Paper Quality and length of the fibres used in making paper. Strength of paper also depends on how firmly the fibres are intertwined with each other.

Traditional Size Paper This kind of paper is available in the market by size names such as Crown, Demy, Royal, Foolscap, etc. The dimension of the size is expressed in inches.

Trimming Cutting the edges of a folded sheet to page size.

Varnishing Applying fixative to printed matter to increase its durability and improve its appearance.

Water Mark A translucent design impressed on paper during the manufacturing process and visible when the paper is held to light.

Weight in Gsm The basic weight of paper is the weight per unit area. This is expressed as the weight in gram per square metre (gsm or g/m^2).

Weight in Kg Weight in kilogram of one ream or 500 sheets of the basic size of a particular paper type.

Writing Paper The surface of this paper is so made as to prevent absorption, soakage, perforation, and depression.

REFERENCES

Adams, Michael J. 2002, *Printing Technology*, 5e, Delmar Thomson Learning, USA.

Kipplan, Helmut 2001, *Handbook of Print Media*, Springer-Verlag Berlin Heidelberg, Germany.

Kumar, Sunil 2006, *Paper for Book Production*, Seminar presentation during the 19th condensed course organized by IBP, New Delhi.

Martin, A.G. 1988, *Finishing Process of Printing*, Focal Press, London and USA.

Mendiratta, B.D. 1999, *Printer's Costing and Estimating*, Print Trade India Publications Pvt. Ltd, New Delhi.

National Institute of Industrial Research, *The Complete Book on Printing Technology*, Asia Pacific Business Press Inc., Delhi.

Rogers, Geofferey 1986, *Editing for Print*, Macdonald, London.

Schlemmer, Richard M. 1990, *Handbook of Advertising Art Production*, Pretice Hall, New Jersey, USA.

Waxman, Steve 2003, *Printing and Design Tips*, print-industry.com, vol. 18.

REVIEW QUESTIONS

1. What is the need to know the basics of papermaking? Compare the traditional and modern methods of papermaking.
2. Describe the various surface qualities of paper and the aesthetic and functional considerations regarding the same in printing a job.
3. Why should the print buyer be aware of the paper's strength, thickness, opacity, and stretch?
4. What are the common varieties of paper available in the market? Discuss their characteristics and suitability for different kinds of printing jobs.
5. Crown, Demy, Medium, Royal, and Imperial are the brand names of traditional paper. Mention the dimensions of each in inches and the subdivision terms of any one of these.
6. How are international size papers identified? Mention the dimension of basic sizes and subdivision terms.
7. What information is needed to calculate the quantity of paper to print a job? Provide the paper calculation formula.
8. How are paper weight and paper quantity determined?
9. What criteria determine the selection of paper for printing?
10. What are the steps involved in the finishing process of printed paper? Discuss the commonly used binding methods of multi-page publications.
11. Define imposition. Discuss 'work and turn' and 'sheet-wise' imposition.

PROJECTS

1. Collect at least 15 samples of various kinds of paper by visiting a paper market or a printing press near your locality. Cut them into 8.25 × 11.50 (A4) size and pile them up by cutting each one half inch shorter then the next one. Make the sequence of piling paper thick to thin. Spiral bind them by aligning all at the short side. Note the kind of paper (or brand name) and weight in gsm of each type paper on the respective sheet.

2. Pick up some of the samples you have collected with different weight and texture. Identify the wire side of the sheet by shading a portion of both sides of paper with a soft pencil. You may use a magnifying glass in case you experience difficulty in identifying it with naked eyes. Make a folder of 8 pages (use coloured card), paste the samples (two pieces of each kind) on each panel and label them as wire side and smooth side.

3. Take some of the samples again and identify their grain direction. Try the following two methods and note your observation.
   (a) Fold the sheet in two right-angle directions and move your index finger on the fold gently.
   (b) Gently tear the paper horizontally and vertically.

4. Take a paperback printed book. Write the specification of the book in terms of size, number of text pages, and cover pages. Calculate the quantity of text and cover paper used to print 2100 copies of this book. Also, mention the type of paper/card and the weight used for printing this book.

5. A multi-coloured folder of size 4.0″ × 9.5″ containing six pages of 130 gsm art paper is to be used for printing 5000 copies. Calculate the quantity of paper in reams to be supplied to the printer. Explain the details of your calculation.

6. There are 230 sheets Demy, 200 sheets Royal, and 150 sheets of Crown paper lying idle in a store room. The papers are to be utilized by developing a self-cover booklet of 24 pages. Calculate the number of booklets that can be printed with the available sheets. Prepare a detailed proposal to get an approval from your superior.

7. Select the most suitable binding method for the following publications. Consider size, weight, quality of paper/card for each publication. Special finishing, if needed, should be mentioned. Explain the reasons.
   (a) A magazine on journalism education containing mainly typographical matter.
   (b) A book on a bird sanctuary containing lot of coloured photographs and graphics but less of text matter.
   (c) A brochure promoting a mobile phone among the rural audience. One of the pages of the brochure contains a pocket to carry a cut-out printed card of a mobile phone.

CHAPTER 12
Costing and Estimating

Learning Objectives

After reading this chapter, you should be able to
- define costing and estimating
- understand the difference and relationship between costing and estimating
- handle estimates for design and artwork
- understand the graphic design business
- analyse the cost factor of various printing operations
- handle estimates for the print production stage
- oversee the costing of a printed publication

INTRODUCTION

'In the modern world of business, it is useless to be a creative original thinker unless you can also sell what you create. Management cannot be expected to recognize a good idea unless it is presented to them by a good salesman.' Professionals pursuing a career in the field of graphic art can benefit from these words of advertising guru David Ogilvy. Graphic art is undeniably an exciting profession. It gives a professional the satisfaction of creating new ideas. These ideas, however, are considered successful only when they are financially rewarding. Accurate costing and estimating techniques help an organization to ensure that its business is profitable. This chapter addresses some of the basic financial issues in the field of art and print production.

Printing technology gives physical form to the creative ideas of a graphic designer and enables these ideas to reach millions of people. In an industry that caters to such a large audience, organizations need to work with a multitude of other organizations and people, work hard, and take risks at many fronts. All this effort is aimed at one main motive—that of earning profit. *Profit* can be defined as a financial reward for the risk borne by an entrepreneur in establishing and operating a business. An entrepreneur will establish and operate a business only when there is a reasonable return after meeting all the costs incurred to run the business. The amount of profit earned is largely dependent on the price—a remuneration against which a firm is prepared to sell a product and/or service to a customer. The profit in the field of graphic art is dependent on the price of the product, and is determined by costing and estimating techniques.

Estimating and costing a design work is a relatively difficult job. A correct and scientific estimation of costs is almost impossible, because each material for printing has its own distinctive features. Moreover, the professions of printing and publishing are growing fast. Many individuals and organizations have started producing and selling printed material. Many new advertising agencies are coming up, and the existing ones are expanding fast. In such a competitive scenario, some organizations are fading away and some have achieved success. One of the main reasons for their decline in success is the costing and estimating techniques adopted by them. Lack of proper costing and estimation techniques can negatively affect the growth of an organization.

Both over- and under-estimation cause damage to advertising agencies, printers, and customers. Over-estimation leads to high prices, which negatively affect customer satisfaction. Under-estimation, on the other hand, leads to low prices, which affect the organization's bottom line negatively. Accurate estimation results in reasonable prices and profit, which is satisfying for both the buyer and the seller.

In a business transaction, the buyer looks forward to a quality product at a reasonable price and the seller seeks a profit. Both buyers and sellers participate in developing a design and involve themselves in the selection of printing processes, materials, and finishing processes. Clients can gain a lot of relevant knowledge during the process of art and print production and can demand a complete break-up of costs from the seller or service provider. This helps the agency to deliver a product that matches the client's expectations and helps the clients to plan a future project judiciously.

COSTING

Costing is the process of deriving the cost of production. In order to manage and operate a business successfully, a reasonable profit over and above the actual cost must be recovered. It is, therefore, essential to know the actual cost of a job. Hence, the role of costing is crucial in art and print production.

Costing also involves the process of analysing the costs and benefits of different options. It helps to determine the various approaches that can be adopted for a particular job and the solution that should be chosen once the various options have been considered. Costing, thus, is carried out early on in the process, when parties decide whether and how they should respond to a task in hand.

The following are the main advantages of costing:
- It helps to determine the cost of each and every production operation carried out by a firm.
- It makes it possible for the firm to submit estimates of various jobs based on the actual production costs.
- It provides data for the comparison of the actual cost of a particular job with its originally estimated cost.
- It helps the management to ascertain the profit or loss to be made by a firm on a particular job.
- It provides information necessary for eliminating waste and inefficiency, if any, prevailing in the firm.

ESTIMATING

Estimating is the technique of assessing the sale price of a job or a service. In other words, it is a forecast of the sale price before the execution of a job. Like costing, estimating is also primarily concerned with the processes involving a large number of items of expenditure. Sale price in these circumstances cannot be ascertained without the use of accounting methods.

Estimating is also termed as *advance costing* or *standard costing*. Advance costing refers to the method where costing is done before the job has been undertaken. In standard costing, a standard or an average cost is assessed on the basis of certain norms. Estimating can also help the agency to forecast the time needed for the completion of a job.

The following guidelines need to be kept in mind while estimating an art and production job:
- The directly chargeable operations that are to be carried out in the execution of the job need to be ascertained.
- The time likely to be consumed in carrying out each and every operation needs to be estimated.
- The hours likely to be used in each and every operation should be multiplied with the hourly rates of the respective operations.
- The labour cost needs to be furnished on the basis of hourly rates.
- The costs of directly chargeable materials and outwork, such as paper, binding, covering materials, etc., need to be added to the labour cost of the job.
- Service charges (in percentage) should be added to the directly chargeable materials and outwork.
- The profit should be added as per the policy laid down by the management.

Relationship between Costing and Estimating

Costing and estimating are inter-related. This section will throw light into how these processes are related to each other:
- The unit of costing as well as estimating is common, that is, 'hourly rate', which is a rate for one chargeable hour of work. This unit is applied to the actual hours of work done in costing and to the anticipated hours of work in estimating.
- Estimating is essentially done on the basis of hourly rates, output records, and other data as furnished by costing. In this way, costing provides the basis for estimating and both are related to each other.
- Accuracy in estimating depends entirely upon accuracy in costing. In case the data provided by the costing is incorrect, it is impossible to prepare a correct estimate.
- A sound, coordinated costing and estimating system creates the much-needed goodwill and understanding between the client and the printing/design firm. Transparency in costing and estimating procedures satisfy the customer with respect to the genuineness of the rates charged.

Stages of Estimation

Estimation is done for two broad stages—(i) design and creative work, and (ii) production.

Design and creative work

Some agencies and organizations deal with only the design and creative work for the client. In such cases, the print production is taken care of by the client. Some other agencies and firms take up the complete job. Besides these organizations and agencies, many freelance consultants are active in this field. Clients often find freelancers cost-effective for small jobs. Working with freelancers also gives them more control over the work. However, for assignments such as a sustained advertising campaign in newspapers and magazines, where the services of a team are necessary, an in-house department or outside advertising agency is more cost-effective than a freelancer.

We shall now look at the various bodies that may take care of the design and creative work for printed material.

Design studio/freelancer An important decision a client needs to take is whether to delegate the work to an agency or a freelancer.

Freelance artists may work individually or in groups. All freelance artists are not specialized in all sorts of work; nor do they have all the equipment required to accomplish a job. Therefore, they may, in turn, outsource some specialized jobs to specialized artists. Instead of outsourcing the work to freelancers, the client may also choose to assign the complete design work to one agency. In this case, too, the agency may outsource assignments related to photography, scanning, illustrations, typesetting, bromides, image processing, paste-up jobs, etc. to specialized suppliers. These suppliers work from their own offices and charge the agency according to their specialization and brand name in the market. While estimating the charges for the complete design work, the agency or the freelancer who hires the specialized supplier/artist must take into account the money spent for specialized jobs. In addition to the overall costs, the effort and resources spent on coordination should also be considered in order to yield good profits.

Sometimes, a group of artists who are specialized in a particular area of design operates from one place. This helps individual artists to seek work from the market easily. The place of work of such a group of artists is called an art studio. The studio may be a sole proprietorship, a partnership, or a company.

Advertising agency Many organizations get their artwork done by an advertising agency instead of relying on their in-house studio or on a freelancer. Artists of the agency work in close coordination with a team of specialists from the client's side. This makes for a successful design output, which ultimately gives clients value for their money.

In most cases, an advertising agency handles jobs on a turnkey basis, that is, from design and production to ultimate release in different media. The agency charges for the artwork under the head of 'design and creative charges'. It calculates this fee on the basis of how much time its staff devotes to each problem of the client—the time spent by executives, number of days utilized by the creative team, number of outside service hours involved, and so forth.

Most advertising agencies maintain a catalogue for standard creative and design charges. A sample catalogue for these charges is displayed in Exhibit 12.1. The design

Exhibit 12.1 Art charges rate card

Creative charges

DESIGN FEES

	Amount (₹)
Corporate Identity	
Package deal	50000
Brand name/logo (each)	15000
Stationery (each)	6000
Corporate Identity Manual	50000
Packaging—Pack/Label	
Original	10000
Adaptation	20000
Mock-up	5000
Flash on pack	2000
Press Advt.	
Original—B & W	
Up to 500 sq.cm.	3000
501 sq.cm.–1000 sq.cm.	5000
1001 sq.cm.–1200 sq.cm.	8000
Adaptation in different sizes or per language	50% extra of master design
Colour	50% extra of above
POP Material	
Category A (poster, dangler, streamer, backing-paper, dispenser)	
Original	7000
Adaptation	5000
Category B (sticker, shelf strip, head card, tent-card, C slide, greeting card, certificate, T-shirt)	
Original	3000
Adaptation	2000
Category C (outdoor hoarding, display board, wall painting, bus shelter, kiosk, glowsigns, banners)	
Original	5000
Category D	
Display window	8000
Bus/van design	8000
Trophy	10000
Print Literature	
Brochure: 8 pages	20000
Additional: per 4 pages	8000
Single sheet leaflet	5000
Folder	15000
Dummy paste-up per page	500
Charts, graphs	2000
Docket folder	5000
Calendar	
Master page	20000
Fly leaf	3000
Per sheet	12000
Table calendar master	6000
Per sheet	5000
Diary	5000
Per page	1500
Specialized Demonstration/Interactive Devices	5000–15000
(design conceptualization cost dependent upon complexity of specific job in question)	
Phototype cost extra	

Contd

Exhibit 12.1 *Contd*

Artwork charges

Photography Rates

(a) Photography assignment fees	½ day	8000
	Full day	12000
	Out station	100% extra
(b) TP of negative rolls (120 mm/35 mm)		750
(c) Photography by freelance photographer		at actual + 17.65

Translation Cost

Original per 50 words	750
Additional per 50 words	350
Checking A/W	300
Translation into foreign languages	
Minimum 50 words	2000
Additional 50 words per unit	1500

Charges for Miscellaneous Artwork Input

(a) B/W halftone finishing per sq. cm (Minimum ₹ 750 area 100 sq. cm)	8
(b) Colour halftone finishing per sq. cm (Minimum ₹ 1500 area 100 sq. cm)	10
(c) Vignette (spray finishing) per sq. cm (Minimum ₹ 300 area 100 sq. cm)	3

Q/T

(a) Minimum area 300 sq. cm ₹ 4 per sq. cm	1200
(b) Sharpline Q/T 300 sq. cm ₹ 15 per sq. cm	6000

Handlettering
(a) Ordinary minimum charges: ₹ 750 upto 5 words and ₹ 75 for each additional word.
(b) Special type minimum charges: ₹ 750 upto 5 words and ₹ 75 for each additional letter.
(c) Special type with outline minimum charges: ₹ 950 upto 5 words and ₹ 95 for each additional letter. 50% extra for circular and curve types.
(d) Logo type-banner lettering: ₹ 2000 per language.

Slides

Slide A.V. Simple	₹ 325
Tabular	₹ 450
Bar charts	₹ 650
Charts	₹ 1300
Slide from printed material	₹ 300 each

Calligraphy
Urdu, Sindhi, Persian/Arabic calligraphy charges as per labour involved. Minimum charges ₹ 2000 (50 words/above ₹ 1500 per unit of 50 words.)

Contd

Exhibit 12.1 *Contd*

Digital charges

	Amount (₹)
Page Make-up	
Minimum 300 sq. cm	5000
Additional unit 100 sq. cm	1250
Below 300 sq. cm	2500
Adaptation: (English or Language)	50% of the master page make-up
CD Transfer	3000
Colour Printout	
(a) A4	100
(b) A3	200
Master Artworks Illustration	
Illustration (B/W)	5000
Line (simple)	3000
Line (complex)	7000
Halftone (simple)	4500
Halftone (complex)	8500
Colour illustration	50% extra
Outsourced illustrations	Actual + 17.65

Processing charges

- Processing charges for all colour and B/W jobs @ ₹ 15/- per sq. cm. It includes system time, planning, tinting, superimposition, outputting, and proofing.
- Processing charges for all colour and B/W jobs without four colour positive and proof @ ₹ 9.25/- per sq. cm. It includes system time, planning, tinting, and superimposition.
- Scanning upto 300 sq. cm is ₹ 510/-; above 300 sq. cm @ ₹ 1.70/- per sq. cm. Scanning above the used size will be charged again.
- Duplicate set of positive @ ₹ 2.50 per sq. cm.
- Duplicate set of proofing @ ₹ 1.50 per sq. cm.
- CD @ ₹ 3000 per file.

	Amount (₹)
Colour Prints/Negatives/Enlargements	
Copy negative 120 mm size	325
Print 4″ × 5″ (post card size)	50
Print 5″ × 7″	100
Print 8″ × 10″	225
Print 10″ × 12″	425
Print 12″ × 15″	600
Print 16″ × 20″	1100
Print 20″ × 24″	1560
Print 30″ × 40″	4550

Note: Rates given in this table are fictitious.

Notes
1. All estimates raised to be returned approved within 15 days of receipt, failing which it will be deemed approved and bills raised thereof.
2. Any revisions in final artworks prepared on the basis of approved layouts/copy will be charged extra at 25% of the total cost of artwork.

Contd

Exhibit 12.1 *Contd*

3. Urgency charges of 50% over and above the rate quoted will be charged, if the job is wanted in less than the normal time.
4. Materials not specified in the rate card will be charged as per suppliers' rates + agency commission (eg. Props, location, hire-charges, model fee, TP hire charges, etc.)
5. Out-of-pocket expenses incurred on your behalf on account of travel and hotel stay will be billed at actual.
6. The rate card is subject to annual revision.

charges vary widely from agency to agency. In many cases, these are quite high in comparison to those of a freelancer or a design studio. The designing cost when seen in isolation may seem high, but when calculated per unit of the print order of a particular job, appears to be more economical. Clients in most cases understand the creative process and the need for involvement of a number of people and time in such jobs. Hence, they do not mind paying for quality work.

Traditionally, the main source of an advertising agency's income was the 15 per cent commission from the media, which was good enough to generate revenues to meet the expenses and earn some profit. These days, however, independent media buying agencies have virtually taken away one of the most important jobs from these agencies. Today, it is not uncommon to find media buying agencies settling for a fee of 2.5 to 5 per cent. Thus, clients have started to question the traditional 15 per cent commission quoted by advertising agencies for such jobs. Clients, especially large ones, now retain agencies only for creative work on a pre-determined fee.

In-house department Many organizations find it quite convenient and cost effective to set up their own creative section. This section may exist within the department of communication or as a small group which works under the guidance of the subject expert of the organization. The decision to set up an in-house department rather than getting the work done from an advertising agency may have several pros and cons. In-house designers understand the requirement of the company very well. Explaining the same to an outside designer is often a difficult and time-consuming process. Moreover, an in-house person would also be available for odd design work—posters for conferences, sales literature, office stationery, and even calligraphic work on award certificates. Working with in-house designers, however, may also have some limitations. It is not uncommon to find employees getting bored with the same job over a period of time, especially when working on the same brand. Advertising agencies thus employ various kinds of people to work on a number of brands.

As design and artwork these days are largely computer-based, many printers provide this service to the client either free of cost or at a reasonable cost. Small companies who do not have advertising agencies on their panel prefer this service.

Business process outsourcing The IT revolution has brought new trends in various fields. Business process outsourcing (BPO) services have gained prominence during the last decade. Many companies are now delegating their non-core activities that require man power, investment in fixed assets, etc. to external service providers. Companies are concentrating more on understanding and servicing their customers.

Besides saving time, the cost reductions in capital investment such as fixed assets are the major benefits of the BPO revolution.

The outsourcing trend has been seen in the field of print publishing too. The main drivers remain the same—high quality at low cost. The cost saving process starts at the lowest entry level; a trainee copywriter is available in India at one-fourth of the cost of one in the USA. The same is the case with other developed countries as well. Overall, the costs are about 60–70 per cent lower in India. If a computer designer earns a salary of £30,000 in the UK she receives about £10,000 in India and if the cost of an illustration is £200 in the UK, a comparable Indian job costs about £80. The huge cost difference is, needless to say, the main reason for the surge in outsourcing. However, the availability of an excellent, educated, cheap English-speaking workforce is also an important criteria for outsourcing. Indians possess excellent skills in copy writing, editing, and proof reading. India also has a mature publishing and advertising industry, which makes a ready pool of talent available to international companies.

Production

Like artwork, printing jobs are also bought on a made-to-order basis. Capabilities and limitations of the printing plant, operations involved in producing a job, time taken for different operations, hourly or piece wage rates of each operation, materials used for the job—all affect the costing and estimating of a printing job. While securing a job, a printer prepares an estimate in such a way that it gives the client a feeling of quality at an economical price and gets him/her a reasonable profit after recovering the expenses. Exhibit 12.2 presents one such sample estimate form.

Cost estimates of printing jobs vary widely from one press to another. However, all presses should be aware of costing standards in the market because of the competitive market conditions. The print buyer strives to purchase the best quality at a reasonable price. He/she judges a press on the basis of its schedule rates for price and past performance for quality. All presses may not have all the facilities. Most of them have an arrangement with other presses and while preparing an estimate, they include the cost of getting work done at another press as well as their profit. Regular print buyers are aware of the prevailing market rates of each operation and do not hesitate to pay a little extra to get a turnkey job at one place. Some print buyers, of course, prefer to handle some operations separately to bring down the total printing cost.

Estimation is done by various methods, based on different types of cost information. Such information is available within the press and, in some cases, the tariff rates of trade associations are also referred to. For discussing estimation, it is imperative that certain other terms such as 'casting off' and 'costing' are defined.

The process by which the number of printed pages of a publication is estimated before they are sent for printing is known as *casting off*. As explained earlier, costing is the calculation of the exact cost of production after a job has been printed and delivered. Post-print costing is required to evaluate the profitability of the job and to make

Exhibit 12.2 Estimate form

Date ....

Name of the customer ....

Job details .... Special instructions ....

Job	Operation	No. of Hours	Rate	Amount
Design/Artwork	(a) Layout preparation (b) Final design and artwork		Total:	
Printing and Machining	(a) Preparation for job (b) Actual running		Total:	
Processing/Planning	(a) Negative/positive making (b) Linework processing (c) Scanning/col. seperation (d) Planning (e) Contact printing		Total:	
Typesetting	(a) Keyboarding (b) Proof printout (c) Page make-up (d) Imposing		Total:	
Binding and Finishing	(a) Cutting and folding, trimming (b) Perforating/purchasing (c) Centre/side stitch binding (d) Section-sewn binding (e) Paperback/adhesive binding (f) Pad making (g) Specialized work (h) Others		Total:	
Surface Preparation	(a) Wipe-on plate (b) PS/Deep-etch plate (c) CTP		Total:	
Materials and Outwork	(a) Paper (b) Binding (c) Outwork		Total:	
Summary	(a) Design/artwork (b) Typesetting (c) Processing/planning/scanning (d) Surface preparation (e) Printing/machining (f) Binding and finishing (g) Materials and outwork		Total:	

Add: Profit....%, therefore estimated price...

Prepared by.. Checked by..................

necessary amendments in the estimation of such jobs in future. Similarly, estimating is the process of calculating the total cost of production of a job before it is actually printed. It is essential for quoting the price for a printing job or for fixing the price of a publication.

As discussed earlier, the costing and estimating functions are interrelated and yet different from one another. The estimator should know the sequence of operations involved in doing each job. He/she should also know the work performed in each operation and the time taken to perform each operation. He/she should be able to recognize conditions that might necessitate an alteration in the normal sequence of operations of doing a job. This is sometimes necessary to enforce cost control in the press.

Principal Printing Operations

This section deals with the estimation of principal printing operations such as typesetting and layout, processing, plate-making, printing, and binding and finishing.

A sample costing sheet has been presented in Exhibit 12.3. Students are advised to prepare a costing sheet as per the sample. This will help them to calculate the total cost of production and unit cost of publication, which, in turn, will help them in fixing the price of a publication.

Typesetting and layout Casting off, which is the estimation of the number of printed pages, is also related to the cost of typesetting. These days, most of the typesetting is done using word processing software. Layout software is used to develop the layout of the typeset matter. For the purpose of estimating, the task may be of three categories, namely:

(i) Job work—mainly for short copy for advertising design, booklets, labels, cover design, etc. The charges will be on 'per job' basis.
(ii) Book work—since only textual matter is used with limited headlines and uniform layout, charges are normally on 'per page' or 'per square inch' basis.
(iii) Magazines and periodicals—display type and body copy are set mechanically by word processing software or DTP. For word processing and designing, 'per page' rates are employed and the rates vary according to page size, type size, tabular matter, and complexity of the page with graphics and visuals.

Typesetting in Indian languages or foreign languages other than English always costs more for all categories and methods of typesetting.

Typesetting involves proofing and making of a print file. It also involves setting the structure and layout (composition) as well as the text of the piece to be produced. The best way to determine the job cost for a typesetting project is to estimate the time involved in this process. This is largely dependent on the complexity of the job, the timely response to proofs supplied to the customer, and the number of required revisions. Although often underestimated, the importance of proper proofing cannot be overstated. Once approval is given on a proof, any errors become the responsibility of the signatory, and subsequent returns are charged accordingly.

Typeset matter that is ready to be printed is converted to PDF file format at no extra charge. 'Ready-to-print' refers to pages of the same size as the publication's final trim

Exhibit 12.3 Costing sheet

1. **Details of Specifications:**
   (a) Name of the book and author _____
   (b) Size of the book _____ Finished Size _____
   (c) Number of pages: (i) Text _____ (ii) Prelims pages _____ (iii) Back pages _____
   (iv) Illustrations _____ (v) Total _____ Pages
   (d) No. of colours: Text _____ Illustrations _____ Cover/jacket _____
   (e) Print run _____
   (f) Specifications for paper:
   Text _____ Illustrations _____ Cover/jacket _____
   End paper _____ Any other paper _____
   (g) Style of binding _____
2. **Cost Estimates:**
   (i) Editorial expenses @ ₹ _____ per page × _____ pps = _____
   (ii) Preparation of Ilustrations @ ₹ _____ × _____ illustrations = _____
   (iii) Composing @ ₹ _____ pp × _____ pps = _____
   (iv) Proofreading @ ₹ _____ pp × _____ pps = _____
   (v) System charges (in case any designing is involved) = _____
   (vi) Processing (outputting) @ ₹ _____ per sq. inch × _____ inches = _____
   (vii) Plate-making @ ₹ _____ per plate × _____ plates = _____
   @ ₹ _____ per plate × _____ plates = _____
   @ ₹ _____ per plate × _____ plates = _____
   (viii) Printing
   Text: 16 pp forme @ ₹ _____ per forme/1000 × _____ formes = _____
   8 pp forme @ ₹ _____ per forme/1000 × _____ formes = _____
   4 pp forme @ ₹ _____ per forme/1000 × _____ formes = _____
   Illustrations: 16 pp forme @ ₹ _____ per forme/1000 × _____ formes = _____
   8 pp forme @ ₹ _____ per forme/1000 × _____ formes = _____
   4 pp forme @ ₹ _____ per forme/1000 × _____ formes = _____
   Cover/jacket: @ ₹ _____ per col × _____ Col. per 1000 = _____
   (ix) Binding: Hard binding (section sewing/centre stitching/perfect binding)
   @ ₹ _____ per copy × copies = _____
   (x) Lamination (matt/gloss) @ ₹ _____ per copy × _____ copies = _____
   (xi) Packing and forwarding = _____
   (xi) Paper
   Text _____ reams _____ sheets @ ₹ _____ per ream = _____
   Illustrations _____ reams _____ sheets @ ₹ _____ per ream = _____
   End paper _____ reams _____ sheets @ ₹ _____ per ream = _____
   Cover/jacket _____ reams _____ sheets @ ₹ _____ per ream = _____

Total Cost of Production
Unit cost = ₹ _____ Price = ₹ _____   --------------

size, with proper margins. It includes all graphics, page numbers, and design elements as specified by the client, as with the conventional 'camera-ready' artwork. In the case of any design work that involves typesetting, the typesetting costs should be added to the print-ready printing price.

Processing Film making and stripping are done by the processing unit of the offset press. The need for stripping is eliminated in computerized processing units. In many presses, both the systems are used in order to obtain the most cost-effective output. Processing of halftone jobs and stripping them with line work is costlier than simple line work. The chargeable area of an output film is one cm more on each of the four sides of the printing area. Schedule rates are generally in per sq. cm. The minimum area is 300 sq. cm. Continuous tone colour processing is done by a colour scanner. A four-colour halftone job is usually done nowadays using a scanner. Processing charges also include the planning of colour work. Many printers offer computer facilities to their client in order to make their artwork suitable for printing requirements. These services are charged by the printers under the head, 'system charges' on a per hour basis.

For a satisfactory result of printed work, especially of a colour job, print buyers demand proofs of the processed work. These proofs are known as progressive proofs. The processor charges extra for this service.

Low-cost film outputs are in demand for most of the printing processes today. Through desktop publishing, it is possible to produce images through a laser printer directly on a transparent film or on a special quality cellophane sheet or butter paper, which can be directly used as a positive for plate-making. This provides a lot of savings on the use of costly photographic film.

Plate-making Charges of offset plate-making depend on the plate's grain quality, size, and emulsion. Albumin or wipe-on plates, which are used for line and short-run jobs, are the cheapest. Pre-sensitized (PS) plates and deep-etch plates are the costliest. They are mainly used for colour and quality jobs. Computer to plate (CtP), the new entrant in India's print industry, is a bit costly in the present market condition, but is gaining popularity because of its quality and elimination of the need for films for plate-making. Wipe-on plates are cheaper than PS plates but are hardly suitable for colour jobs. Plate-making charges are always on a per plate basis. In one plate, a number of pages can be accommodated, depending on the plate size and size of the page to be printed.

The cost of plate-making may be reduced by using pre-sensitized plates only for such parts of the job where it is absolutely necessary and, for the remaining part, one may use either wipe-on or deep-etch plates keeping in view the length of the run. Due to considerations of quality and speed, CtP is suitable for digital workflow and goes well with the new changes in the field of art and print production.

Printing Except for some specialized jobs, printing is generally charged per thousand of each impression. Half-sheet and sheet-work impositions also affect printing charges. Take, for example, a sheet-work imposition where 2,000 impressions are needed to print 1,000 copies. In half-sheet imposition, the printer gets both sides of a given number of copies. This is accomplished by imposing all pages on a single sheet, and then turning to print the other side from the same plate. Two copies can be extracted from one sheet by cutting the sheet into two parts.

Jobs of less than a thousand impressions are also charged at the rate of a thousand. For long-run jobs, most printers offer reduced rates for subsequent thousand or a part thereof. Printing charges are higher if a colour other than black is used, or if some area is solid. In such cases, the estimator adds the additional ink cost to the total cost estimate. For the same reason, metallic colour printing is also expensive. Often, printers charge per colour, per forme, or as otherwise agreed upon.

The cost effectiveness of a printing job is largely dependent on the selection of a right type and size of printing machine within the same process of printing. It is more economical to print textbooks on a web-offset machine provided the print order is very large, running into a few lakh copies. The overall cost of printing is also reduced by printing text pages on a bigger size machine, but it should be kept in mind that sometimes it becomes essential to print high-quality jobs on smaller format machines too.

Paper costs As paper constitutes a major cost factor in today's printed communication, the paper cost should be estimated very carefully. The cost of paper fluctuates a lot—sometimes unpredictably. So, even a slight miscalculation might result in substantial losses for the printer or the print buyer who takes the responsibility to supply paper. The estimator first calculates the quantity of paper required for the job, including wastage, which depends on the number of ups or pages to be accommodated in a sheet, whether worked half sheet or full sheet. We have already dealt with the paper calculation formula in the case of formes where a number of them are combined, given the print order or the number of impressions, in Chapter 11.

The consumer of paper is supposed to pay sales tax to either the retailer or the manufacturer. When print buyers purchase paper from the printer, the printer usually charges 10 per cent extra on the price paid to the manufacturer or retailer. Thus, it is costlier to buy paper from printers. The printed items become taxable if the paper is supplied by the printer. Otherwise, printing, being a service and a process of conversion of raw material (paper) into its final shape, is not taxable.

There are varieties of paper under different brand names available in the market. While selecting paper, the characteristics of paper in terms of weight, strength, opacity, surface texture, folding qualities, grain direction, printability, moisture resistance, etc. should be considered. The correct choice of paper often leads to cost effectiveness.

Binding and finishing For a binding estimate, full specifications of the work along with a sample copy or dummy should be obtained. The charges are different for different kinds of binding and finishing. Centre stitched and side stitched binding are cheaper than section sewn and perfect binding. For book work, case binding is still costlier due to the labour involved and materials required. Specialized binding such as spiral and spico is charged mainly on the basis of the size and the thickness of the publication, material of the spiral, protective covers, etc. Printers add creasing and folding costs to the binding charges.

Different kinds of printed jobs need different kinds of finishing. Lamination and varnishing are charged on a per page and size basis. Some printers charge at a per square inch rate for lamination. Automatic numbering, perforation, die cutting, etc. may be charged at per hundred or per thousand. The die cutting rate varies widely from simple to complicated cutting. Wrapping, packing, and delivery costs are also included in binding and finishing costs.

GRAPHIC DESIGN BUSINESS

To handle costing and estimating efficiently, a design firm needs a clear understanding of the graphic design business. This includes knowledge of the types of businesses and the process of developing a plan, taking a design brief, and selling the design by presenting it to the client.

Type of business Like any other business, the size of the firm and the product and/or service it is selling are the primary concerns of the business. The firm may be a sole proprietorship in which an individual handles all the aspects of the business, a partnership with more than one person, or an agency employing diversified professionals.

Design firms, whether big or small, undertake various kinds of work. Some offer specialized services such as exhibition design, web design, multimedia design, and design for print media. There are specializations within print media graphics as well. These specializations are newspaper graphics, corporate identity graphics, advertising graphics, publishing graphics, etc. Organizations which do not focus on graphic design hire individual graphic designers or design firms to carry out their work.

Developing a plan This stage starts with setting the goals and objectives for the business. The plan goes on to discuss the area of specialization, product, or service the firm can provide and the potential clients to be served. It also includes in detail the profitability and growth opportunities of the firm. It lists the names of suppliers, professionals, and agencies who will be working with the agency.

A marketing plan is set by studying the obstacles and opportunities of the business and through competition analysis. Identification of potential clients, their characteristics, and requirements is another important area of a plan. A client base is developed gradually as the agency grows. Pricing strategy also contributes to a marketing plan by using costing and estimating techniques.

Taking a brief from the client Graphic design is a communication process by means of creative design. Its creative aspect may be very subjective, but not the process. The process starts with taking a brief from the client.

What is a design brief? According to Peter L. Phillips, the author of *Creating the Perfect Design Brief*, 'A design brief is a written document outlining, in complete detail, the business objectives and corresponding design strategies for a design project. Some prefer the term *creative brief*. Among a number of other things, the most critical elements of a design brief are: a complete description of the project—what is it that is to be done; why is this needed now; what business outcomes are expected; who is this being done for (the target audience); and who are the key stakeholders in this project. The design brief must also address current industry trends, the competition, scope, time-line, budget and measurement of success metrics.'

Self-employed designers and those who work for small firms take the brief themselves. A big firm or advertising agency is represented by a person often referred to as the account executive or client servicing person. The knowledge of art and production and the costs involved in executing the job are critical to the success of any design firm.

The popular belief, 'the client is the boss', should be ignored while taking a brief from the client. One should make the client a friend by demonstrating a positive attitude and giving him/her the assurance of quality and a long-term professional relationship. It is important to listen to the client patiently and to understand the client's expectations. For this, one needs to identify the problem areas and ask questions for clarification. One should be analytical and should view things from the end users' perspective. Many a times, clients may overlook the users' perspective in the proposed solution. Although one needs to remind the client about aspects that have been overlooked, it is important to keep a balance between one's own view and that of the client, so as to let the client know that their needs have been understood.

To facilitate brief-taking from the client, a sample brief form is presented in Exhibit 12.4. Students are advised to copy this form and fill in as many details as possible. The items mentioned in the form may be altered on the basis of one's requirements.

Selling a design A design is also a product. It should be sold to the client like any other product or service. Some designers believe that 'a design speaks for itself'. In most cases, building a relation with the client may be the first step in selling a design. The design should be very professional in terms of its visual quality and its concept. If a firm has any hesitation in developing all the parts of the design, it can hire some professionals or collaborate with others—such as a research bureau, copywriter, photographer, printer, etc. Another method of developing the design is to involve the client in the design development process. Many of them find it exciting to work with designers. The design knowledge of clients and the credentials of their representatives in their own organization need to be respected.

Presenting a solution Many a time, a well-executed design may fail to convince the client due to improper presentation. The computer and the Internet can help the designer present his/her work effectively. In today's environment, it is not enough to get a computer printout. Shortcomings in one agency's presentation will work in favour of its rival.

The mode of presentation should be decided beforehand. It is always a good idea to carry two sets of the work; one in traditional form, that is, on paper or card, and the other on a computer file. It is easier to assess the work on paper because the finally produced work will be on paper.

The design should be well-mounted on a stiff board. A tracing flap should be used to protect it from dust or scratching. A coloured pastel paper cover always gives the layout a professional look and protects it from handling hazards. A portfolio should consist of relevant papers/handouts.

Exhibit 12.4 Client/design brief

Design Firm _____
Description of Customer _____
_____ Date _____
Project: _____

Project Objectives: _____

Target Audience: 1. _____ 2. _____ 3. _____

Product Description: ☐ Publication   ☐ Report   ☐ Direct mail   ☐ Advertising
                      ☐ Brochure   ☐ Website   ☐ (Specify)

Customer (User) Benefits: _____

Support for Benefit Claims: _____

Competition: _____

Distribution: _____

Relative Consideration: _____

Key Message: _____

Current/Desired Perception: 1. _____ 2. _____ 3. _____

Strategic Focus: _____

Tone and Manner: _____
_____

Project Mandates: Project lifespan _____
                  1. _____ 2. _____ 3. _____

Budget: _____ Quote required? _____
        | Creative required | Date: |
        | Art approval | Date: |
        | Film/digital output | Date: |
        | Client sign-off | Date: |
        | Deliver project | Date: |

Delivery Instructions: _____

A PowerPoint presentation is ideal for a larger group. The slides should list only relevant points of the agency's proposal. The presentation should be prepared in advance. It helps the agency to explain the various aspects of their work and prepares it for the client's queries. This may include a copy of the original design brief, originals or copy of all previous design work prepared for the same project, and estimated amount to be charged. It is a good idea to show an executive summary, which should be brief and precise, at the presentation. The process of negotiations will start after this stage. A list of settlement options is usually developed and the parties then need to assess the relative benefits and costs of each of the options, comparing their 'best alternative negotiated agreement'.

Cost of services A design firm's financial viability is largely dependent on this particular aspect of design business. Graphic art is an exciting profession. It involves creativity, skill, devotion, and service that bring satisfaction along with financial rewards. The financial part is more critical as it is difficult to determine the value of a service.

Cost estimates of an agency's service may not be simply based on amount of money spent in developing the design, that is, materials used and number of hours spent by the designer along with other members of the organization. More practical costing should be determined by generating the rate structure annually and considering both fixed costs and variable costs.

Fixed costs have no direct relationship with the number of hours spent in developing a design and remain constant throughout the year. Fixed cost is incurred even if no business is generated by an agency. These costs include rent of office premises, maintenance of computers, utility and telephone bills, etc.

Variable costs vary in direct proportion to output. They generally increase or decrease in the same proportion in which the output increases or decreases. For example, in order to accomplish a job, an agency needs a senior designer, a junior designer, DTP operator, and the outside services of a photographer. This will cost more than a job done by a junior designer and a photographer.

A satisfactory gross profit can be achieved by maintaining a docket sheet or requisition form that leads to scientific billing to the client. Exhibit 12.5 presents a sample of a press/non-press requisition form.

Rejection or cancellation fee At times, for reasons known or unknown, the client may cancel the whole project. Hence, a provision for cancellation in the form of a cancellation fee should be incorporated at the beginning of the proposal. There is no set norm to fix the cancellation fee. In most cases, it comprises of mutually acceptable charges. At other times, a fee is quoted on the basis of actual costs incurred to develop the project till the cancellation time. Some suggest that the cancellation fee should be 50 per cent of the estimated fee. It is always better to have an in-house policy that is also made known to the client before signing a business contract.

Exhibit 12.5 Press/non-press requisitions

Date _____ Product _____ Art No. _____
To _____ Job No. _____ Headline _____
Client _____ Art Director _____
Creative Group Head _____ Copywriter _____

PLEASE SUPPLY : ☐ ARTWORK   ☐ TRANSLATION   ☐ POSITIVE   ☐ PROOFING

Sl no.	Job description	Size language	B&W/colour	Orig/flap	No. of positive B&W/colour	Screen ruling

DIGITAL BILLING

	English	Language	Size	Rate	Amount
Creative Charges					
Colour Printout					
B&W Printout					
Translations					
No. of Words					
Checking					
Photography					
Half Day					
Full Day					
No. of Rolls					
35 mm					
120 mm					
Master Colour A/W					
Master B&W A/W					
Q/Tone					
Handlettering					
Calligraphy					
Colour Prints					
B&W Prints					

Total

ATTACHMENTS : ☐ Original layout   ☐ Language translations   ☐ English copy   ☐ B&W drawing
☐ Photography   ☐ Master A/W B&W colour   ☐ Positive
☐ No. of colour TP 35 mm   ☐ No. of colour TP 120 mm

Account Representative

SUMMARY

Before any job goes into production, it is essential to prepare a quotation or a binding agreement between the client and the service provider. Post-production costing is also called for to evaluate the profitability of the job. Estimating and costing help in evaluating the profitability of a job. In definition, they are different from each other, but in function they are interrelated.

Estimating is the process of calculating the total cost of production of a job *before* it is actually printed. Costing is the calculation of the exact cost of production *after* a job has been printed.

Estimation is done in two broad stages: (i) design and creative work, and (ii) production. There are agencies and organizations involved in producing creative artwork. The charges vary from firm to firm, depending on their size in terms of creative staff and other in-house facilities. Freelancers or a group of creative people can also do the artwork. In many cases, their work is cost effective. The agency has the option to choose specialized people and has more control over the work.

Advertising agencies handle turnkey jobs including printing. The agency maintains a catalogue of standard creative and design charges for creative work. However, in many cases, the charges are negotiable. The agency may also get its printing work done from an outside printing press and bill it to the client. Commission from printing jobs is also one of the sources of revenue for an advertising agency.

Cost estimation of printing is done by various methods, based on information about costs under different heads, which are available within the plant, or on the tariff rates of different service providers.

There are five principle operations in a printing job. These are typesetting, processing, plate-making, printing, and binding and finishing. Charges are calculated for each head with further break-ups.

Paper is the major cost factor in any print job. It should be calculated on the basis of current market rates, which fluctuate constantly.

To handle costing and estimating, a design firm needs a clear understanding of the graphic design business. This may include the type of business, planning, taking a design brief, and selling the design by presenting it to the client. All these aspects have been discussed in the chapter.

KEY TERMS

Advertising Agency A service business dedicated to creating, planning, and handling advertising and other forms of promotion for its clients.

Casting Off The process by which the number of printed pages of a publication are estimated before they are sent for printing.

Cost The total money calculated for the time used and resources associated with a purchase or activity.

Design Studio Organization specializing in designing. It offers professional graphical solutions for various kinds of businesses.

Docket Sheet Document or label listing the job done, goods delivered, contents of package, etc. in order to enable the user to find new references with ease.

Freelancer A person who pursues a profession without a long-term commitment to any one employer.

Price Remuneration in terms of money against which a business is prepared to sell a product or a service to a customer.

Profit Reward for the risk borne by an entrepreneur in operating a business.

Quotation An estimate of how much money a particular work will cost.

Tariff Rates Table of fixed charges for particular goods or services.

Trade Association It is generally a public relations organization founded and funded by corporations that operate in a specific industry. Its purpose is generally to promote the industry through public relations activities such as advertising, education, business deals, legal help, etc.

Turnkey Job Various kinds of jobs undertaken and managed together.

REFERENCES

Ashwoth, Hilary (ed) 2004, *The Business in Graphic Design: A Professional's Handbook*, The Association of Registered Graphic Designers of Ontario, Ontario, Canada.

Jethwaney, Jaishri and Shruti Jain 2006, *Advertising Management*, Oxford University Press, New Delhi, pp. 370–372.

Kulkarni, Sarika 2006, *Business Process Outsourcing*, Jaico Publishing House, India, p.175.

Mendiratta, B.D. 1999, *Printer's Costing and Estimating*, Printrade India Publications Pvt. Ltd, New Delhi, pp. 6–15.

Sarkar, N.N. 2001, *Art and Production*, Sagar Publications, New Delhi.

www.graphics.com/modules.php, accessed in January 2007.

www.southwestern.edu/utsw/cda, Printing Service Users' Guide.

REVIEW QUESTIONS

1. Define cost, price, and profit. How do these affect the business?
2. What is estimating? Discuss its role in the art and production business.
3. What do you mean by costing? What are the objects of costing in print publication?
4. How is a creative work charged by an advertising agency and a freelancer?
5. How is an advertising agency different from a design studio in terms of cost effectiveness?
6. Explain the graphic design business in terms of scope and marketing plan.
7. What do you understand by fixed cost and variable cost?
8. What are the principal printing operations? Discuss the methods of estimating for typesetting, processing, and printing.
9. Why is paper a major factor in a print job? What precautions should be taken by the estimator while deciding on the paper to be used for printing?
10. Identify the different binding and finishing methods. Give the estimating methods of each.

PROJECTS

1. A monthly magazine of 104 pages plus 4 cover pages, all in colour with lot of photographs, is being published by the in-house facility. The publishers want to use the services of a freelance artist for the cover design.

   Prepare a project on cost effectiveness of cover design despite the fact that the firm has three full-time designers. The firm is also equipped with computer and photography facilities.

2. Prepare an estimate for a coloured dummy and artwork for the prospectus of an educational institution. The size of the publication is 7.25″ × 9.50″ and it contains 32 pages including the cover. The work involves photographs of student activities and infrastructure of the institute, re-structuring of copy based on the information provided, layout of pages including the cover, and preparation of a complete dummy for approval. Artwork should be prepared after necessary changes or alteration and a PDF file is to be provided for printing. You will also have to supervise the printing at the press selected by the institute to monitor the quality.

3. Pick up an advertisement (service or product) published in a magazine. Debrief it and fill all the points in the client/design brief form.

4. Take a catalogue of a manufacturing company. Go to a design firm and show the design to them. Take their rates on a design estimate form. Then take the printing estimate on a printing estimate

form from a printer. Find out the paper cost from a paper dealer. Prepare a summary of the whole exercise and find out the cost of production of 5000 copies of that catalogue.

5. A paperback book has to be printed with the following specifications:

 (a) Book size   Demy octavo (text in black and white, cover in 4 colours)
 (b) Print area   24 × 42 pica
 (c) Manuscript   3,25,0000 words
 (d) Print order   2,500 copies
 (e) Text paper   90 gsm superprint
 (f) Cover paper   250 gsm chromo art card

Costing rate

 (a) Typesetting   ₹ 25 per page
 (b) Processing   ₹ 0.18/1.70 per sq. cm (4 col)
 (c) Plate-making (Helio)   ₹ 100 per forme of 8 pages (text)
 (d) Plate-making (PS)   ₹ 200 per forme of 8 pages (cover)
 (e) Printing   ₹ 100 per forme per 1000 (text)
 (f) Printing   ₹ 150 per forme per 1000 (cover)
 (g) Binding   ₹ 25 per copy
 (h) Paper   ₹ 350 per ream (text), ₹ 800 (cover)

Calculate the total cost of production of the book.

6. To start a business in art and print production, prepare a 'data bank' on the following and keep on updating it quarterly.

 (a) List the names of six design firms/agencies and their area of specialization including in-house facilities.

 (b) List the names of three processing houses and their schedule tariff rate.

 (c) List the names of three paper dealers and collect the samples of papers you would normally use. Weight and rates should be duly written on each sample.

 (d) List the names of six printers including their in-house facilities.

CHAPTER

13 Newspaper Make-up

Learning Objectives

After reading this chapter, you should be able to
- understand the purpose of a newspaper design
- examine the constraints in designing newspaper pages
- discuss the effect of television and new media on newspaper design
- discuss the form and format of a newspaper design
- identify the elements of design and their impact on newspaper pages
- describe and analyse different parts of a newspaper in relation to design
- discuss the role and functions of colour in a newspaper

INTRODUCTION

A newspaper is an ephemeral publication. It has a shelf-life of just a few hours, and most information published in the morning newspaper becomes stale by the afternoon. In spite of its short life, the morning daily is the most eagerly awaited material for the information-hungry masses, be it in the metropolises, towns, or villages. The morning daily attracts the average reader with not only its news coverage but also the elaborate design of the pages.

As in the case of all other printed matter, it is the design that attracts the reader's initial attention to a newspaper. Before we even begin to read a newspaper, the pictorial depiction of news and specific subjects—be it news on the day's events, business, economy, or sports—grasps our attention. The design then guides us through the contents of the pages. It indicates the relative importance of the news or article and, above all, lends a visual 'personality' to the newspaper. By doing so, the design contributes to the reader's emotional bond with the newspaper. It is this emotional bond that prevents the reader from shifting his/her loyalties to another newspaper.

The reader is accustomed to the style of the newspaper that he/she reads. It helps him/her to find the required information. For example, the reader is aware of the fact that the editorial page has a bigger column width, and the business page has occasional graphics. These style characteristics help him/her locate information in the newspaper pages. Readers usually flip through the pages to find graphics that are of interest, such as human interest photographs or political cartoons. Very few readers can think of *The Times of India* without R.K. Laxman's pocket cartoon on the front page.

NEWSPAPER DESIGNING

The emotional bond created by a newspaper is unlikely to last if, despite its consistent style and 'personality', it fails to offer variety in its design. Thus, each day, there should be something fresh about the look of the paper—this creates the need for layout and make-up planning in newspaper production.

A newspaper make-up can attract negative feedback if it is bizarre. Newspaper designers must, therefore, know how much designing is required and where designing should take a back seat. The key to a successful newspaper design lies in helping the reader locate and pursue the day's news and other vital information with ease.

Newspaper designing is done under inexorable time constraint. Designers and other professionals working in the area of newspaper production need to abide by the deadlines at all times. This requirement had kept designers out of the newspaper world for decades. Until recently, newspaper make-up was designed by chief sub-editors, sub-editors, and printers, whose focus, naturally, was on aspects other than the design. Today, newspaper publishers can no longer afford to overlook the importance of design and layout. This is because of the cut-throat competition from commercial TV channels, the Internet, and other dailies. The higher literacy rate has also affected newspaper readership, and today's readers are much more demanding that those of the yesteryears. In order to meet these challenges and fill the void left by other newspapers, many new newspapers are now coming up, with new ideas to catch the attention of different sections of the society. The design of the newspaper is a key to achieving this end.

In order to face the challenge of competition successfully, and to add colour and zest to the pages of newspapers, more and more newspaper publishers are engaging professional designers these days. We may also refer to professional newspaper designers as graphic journalists. Graphic journalists may work as part of a team in a newspaper publishing house or agency, or as freelancers. They are responsible for depicting news in a pictorial, lucid, and easy-to-understand format.

Graphic journalists may have a design background with formal or informal training in journalism or a journalism background with training in the graphic arts. Thanks to new technology, which has reduced the gap between the designer and the journalist, pages that took hours to design can now be designed in minutes through computer commands.

Apart from time constraints, graphic journalists work with the difficulty of accommodating advertisement space in the overall layout. The rigid requirements of size, tone, and placement of an advertisement on a page often restrict the creative process of a designer. However, these need to be handled carefully as advertisements bring revenue to the newspaper, which is essential for its survival. Although newspapers are not primarily an instrument of profit, they must yield enough returns to sustain the viability and independence of the newspaper.

We know that the credibility of the news published in a newspaper and the views therein are essential elements in creating an identity for a newspaper. Where, then, do design techniques come in? The answer to this is that a newspaper is a product for marketing. Like any other product, it needs attractive packaging so that it can be marketed well and its existence can be established. Newspaper marketing is much more difficult than the marketing of a non-media product. This is because, a newspaper is primarily a product that stimulates the intellect. Over a period of time, newspaper reading becomes a habit, and, frequently, an addiction. In order for a reader to change his/her loyalties from one newspaper to another, considerable time and a strong reason is required. Quality in terms of content and packaging plays a critical role in sustaining and developing readership.

In order to produce an attractive and functional paper, graphic journalists should keep in mind that—(a) the design should be attractive enough to compete with media such as television and the Internet and sustain the reader's attention; (b) a good design alone is not sufficient to satisfy the readers, unless the publication is strong on content. We shall discuss these issues in the following section.

Effect of Television and New Media

The eighties and the early nineties of the last century were a trying period for Indian newspapers. This was the time when television came to India in a big way, first with colour and then with the satellite link and cable network. These had a direct effect on newspapers, as they lost valuable advertisement revenue. Many advertisers shifted a part of their advertisement budget to buy more TV time. Also, more people started watching TV due to the impact of sight, sound, and motion.

Television programmes have enabled people to derive information and entertainment without a fraction of the effort they earlier exerted in reading newspapers and books. Television has much more reach than newspapers because of its sensory appeal. Moreover, there is no literacy barrier and problem of clutter on TV. As a result of constantly moving images on the TV screen, many people have lost the ability to concentrate on a page for long. Youngsters these days often have a shorter attention span and are passive watchers. Newspaper editors and proprietors, therefore, need to take effective steps to make newspapers more attractive than ever before. They need to devise ways to grab the attention of people, sustain their interest, and develop the reading habit.

In order to lure the readers back to the newspaper page and reduce their TV viewing time, it is essential to be aware of the weaknesses and limitations of this powerful audio-visual medium. For delivering a message that has an impact on the audience, the audio-visual system requires them to concentrate well. One of the limitations is that transmission disturbance or shrill music affects the understanding of the message negatively. Second, newspapers can go into greater depths while presenting spot news, news analysis, and items on specific subjects such as health care, stock markets, local events, sports, and music. Television is less capable of doing so. Third, newspapers have the advantage of repetitive effect and archival value. Television programmes cannot be aired according to the convenience of the audience. Newspapers, on the other hand, can be picked up and read according to the readers' convenience. These advantages of a newspaper over TV should be leveraged by newspaper professionals, including designers, to increase its popularity and sales.

Another noticeable development in newspaper publishing was the emergence of a new medium—web journalism—in the early nineties of the last century. Web journalism made it possible for readers to have instant access to the latest news. Fortunately for newspaper publishers, though, it emerged as a support medium rather than a threat to newspapers. Most mainstream newspapers have used its strengths, such as global networking and instant interactivity, to enhance their readership. Newspaper publishing is geared more towards garnering profits, while web journalism is aimed more at communication and dissemination of ideas and concepts. Design, thus, remains an important concern in newspaper publishing. An attractive design enhances the sales of newspapers.

DESIGN APPROACH

Traditionally, work on the design of a newspaper page starts after the dummy sheet with clearly marked areas for advertisements has been received. A *dummy sheet* is a simple page sheet, normally 35 cm × 55.6 cm in dimension, for the average broadsheet with nine vertical lines making up eight columns. It may have two scales in centimetres on either side, with 0–52 marked on one side and 52–0 marked on the other side. These scales facilitate calculations on either side of the dummy sheet. Figure 13.1 shows a sample dummy sheet.

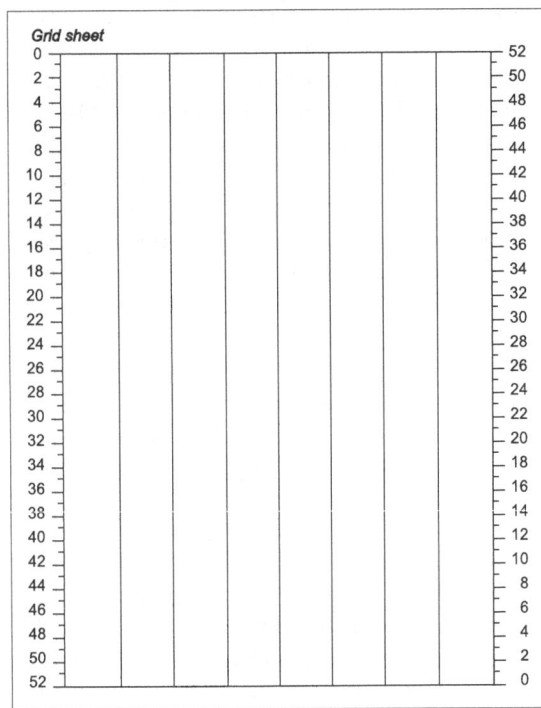

Figure 13.1 Dummy sheet

These days, most newspapers are composed on the computer in a desktop environment, using programs such as QuarkXPress or Adobe InDesign. However, an understanding of the traditional method of designing pages it is still helpful. There are two reasons for this—(i) it is easy to visualize the pages in the actual physical form; and (ii) even now, many newspapers find it convenient to combination the digital and traditional methods of newspaper publishing.

Students may find it exciting to design the pages on the computer. However, with inadequate knowledge of computers, it may take hours to make a page. Moreover, it is difficult to view the complete page on the computer screen in an adequate size. When one wishes to view a headline in relation to a picture or text, he/she can focus on a part of the page by enlarging the area. Enlargement of that area will, however, show only a small part of the page.

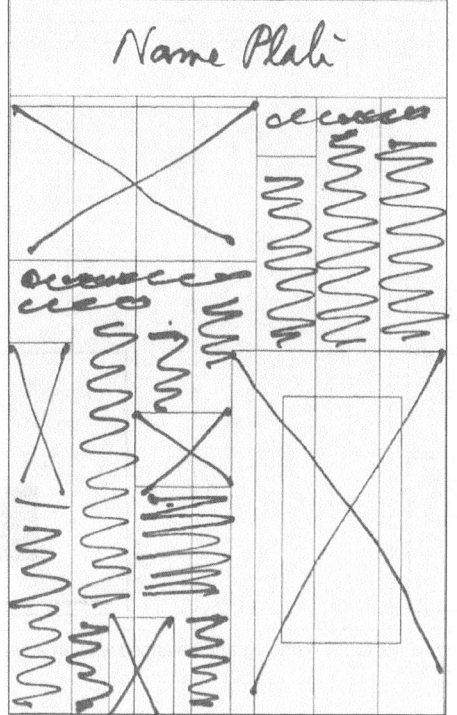 

Figure 13.2 Thumbnail sketch and its layout on a computer screen

Students are advised to familiarize themselves with the designing of newspaper pages by placing design elements on dummy pages. The first dummy may be proportionately smaller in size (which we call a thumbnail sketch) for easy handling and fast working. This initial dummy may later be developed in the actual size, indicating all the details roughly. This will enable the computer operator to make the pages up according to the given instructions. Figure 13.2 shows the initial sketch, that is, thumbnail sketch, and the layout of a newspaper page on a computer screen with non-printable lines and column grids.

Design Principles

As in the case of other graphic designs, newspapers must follow some basic design principles. Some of these are discussed here.

Rhythm The first design principle is rhythm. The newspaper columns should have a rhythmic pattern in order to help the reader move his/her eyes on the page.

Balance On a newspaper page, 'balance' refers to the distribution of headlines, pictures, and other display elements along with advertisements that dominate the page visually, according to their size, tone, shape, and edges. Balance gives the page an equilibrium that makes the reader perceive all the elements of the page as settled at their respective places.

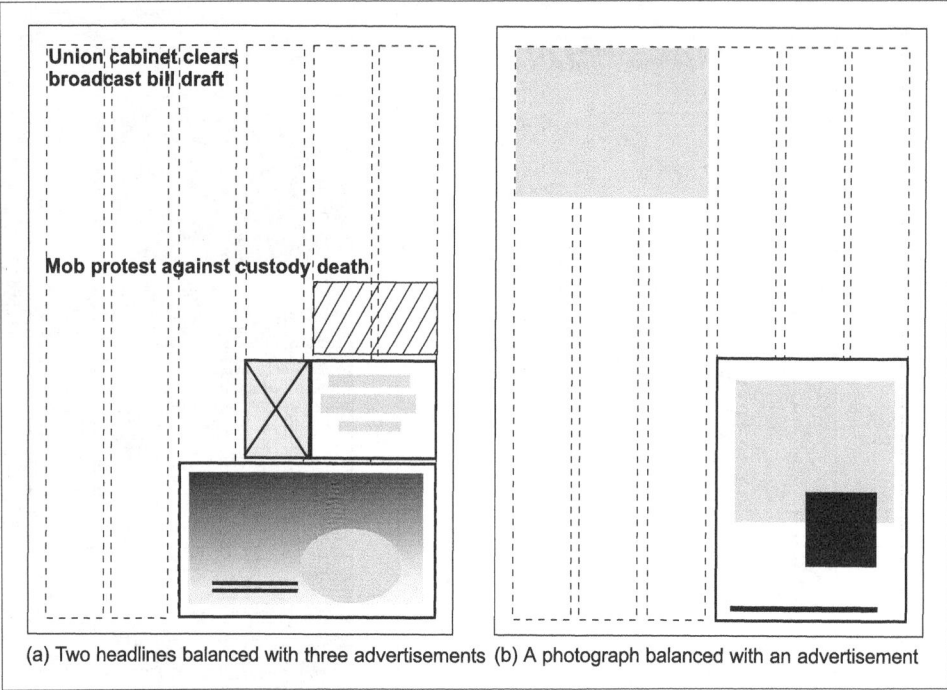

(a) Two headlines balanced with three advertisements (b) A photograph balanced with an advertisement

Figure 13.3 Asymmetrical balance

These days, most papers follow an *asymmetrical* pattern of balance. In such a design, a big picture on the left corner counterbalances an advertisement at the bottom right corner. In case there is a group of advertisements in a pyramid shape, they are balanced with two top headlines. Figure 13.3 shows samples of asymmetrical designs. Readers can observe the page of *Business Sphere* presented in Figure 13.4 and judge it in terms of the balance of the page.

Symmetrical balance is easier to achieve than the asymmetrical one. In a symmetrical design, uniform design elements are placed on both sides of a page in such a way that they are equidistant from an imaginary centre line that divides the page. In a newspaper, an asymmetrical design is uninteresting, stiff, and often unworkable because two news stories cannot be made completely equal both in content and typographic format to fit them in a pre-determined pattern.

Contrast Another key design syntax is contrast—it imparts graphic emphasis to design elements in proper proportion and sequence. Otherwise, all the elements in a design compete for attention, frustrating the reader and negating one another in effect. Contrast can be achieved by using big and bold headlines. A dark-toned photograph stands out within a light-toned text. Graphics in unusual shapes have more contrast value than regular shaped photographs. These facts can be used to create contrast in a design.

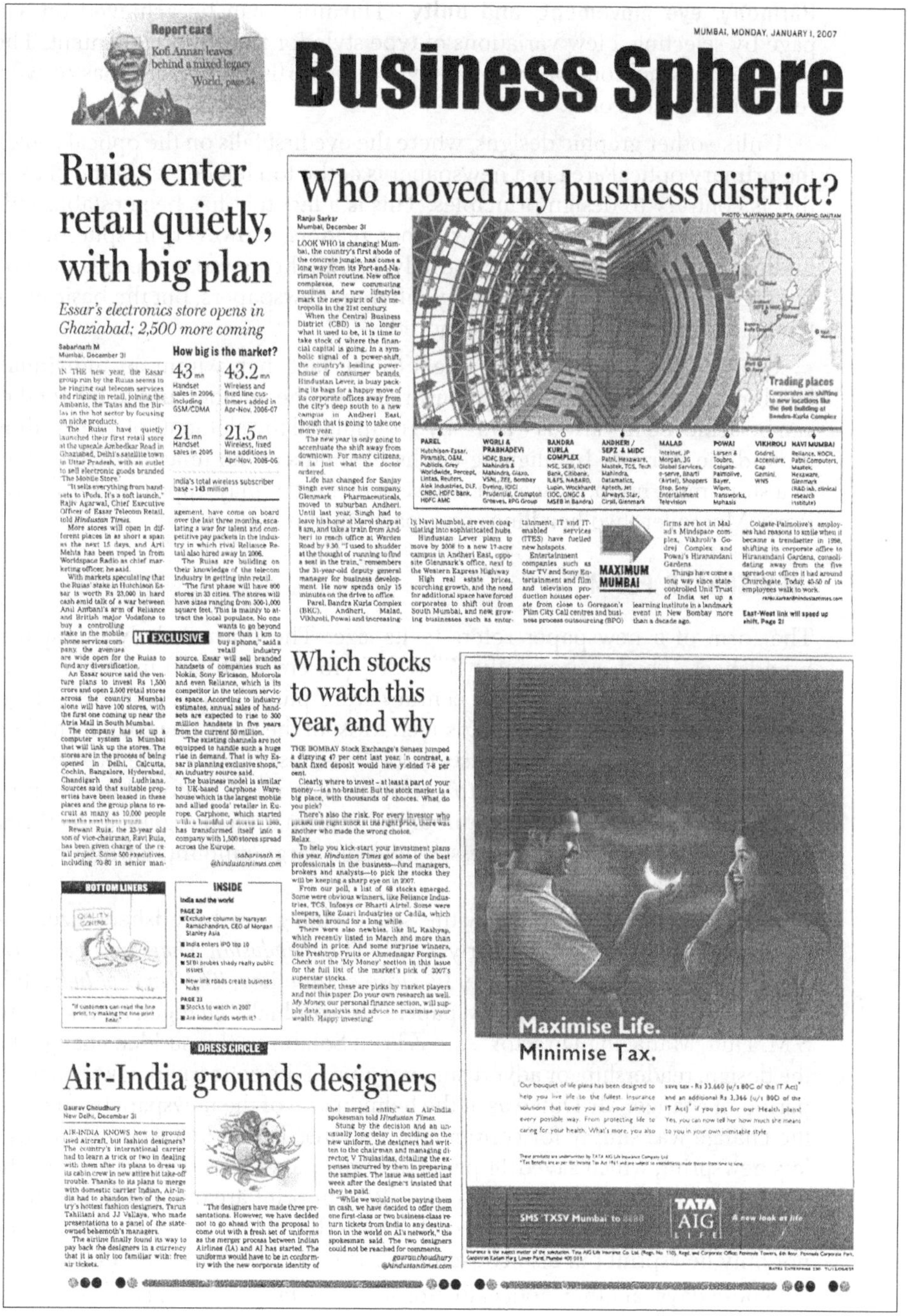

Figure 13.4 A page from *Business Sphere*

Harmony, eye movement, and unity Harmony can be achieved on a newspaper page by selecting a few variations of type style for the editorial content. The designer, however, has no control over the style of advertisements, and has to work with the remaining content only.

Unlike other graphic designs, where the eye first falls on the optical centre of a page, the primary optical area in a newspaper is at the top left corner of the page—a position that is contrary to design principles. This is a fact that has been established by studies on the reading habits of the newspaper readers. However, in spite of such research findings, this rule is not followed strictly, lest all the newspaper pages should look alike. Different principles are followed by different newspapers, but the basic eye movement tendency of the reader is never ignored.

Unity in newspaper design refers to the fact that, within an individual story, the headlines, text, and illustrations must relate to one another and to the total page. Unity can be achieved in various ways—by grouping all the elements of a story, drawing a rule around the story, or by aligning all the elements on an imaginary line. A photograph in a story must not be placed in a position where it may appear to be a part of another story. Moreover, two headlines on a page must not clash with each other.

NEWSPAPER FORM

The form of a newspaper refers to its size. The normal daily newspaper size is a broadsheet, which is normally 17″ × 22″ (43 cm × 56 cm) in dimension. The early newspapers of the seventeenth century were published in a slightly bigger size, but they existed along with the broadsheet. Most of the early newspapers had been started by printers rather than journalists or big business houses. The broadsheet became a standard by accident, perhaps to accommodate more editorial items on one page so that a reader can view a large amount of information at a glance. As this size gained acceptance, many printing presses invested large amounts of money to be able to print a newspaper in this size.

In recent times, we have witnessed a change in broadsheet size, and this was conspicuously noticeable in early 2002. The *Hindustan Times* first came out with the 35 cm × 57.8 cm broadsheet size. Its close competitor, *The Times of India*, followed suit. With this, other mainstream newspapers also gradually changed their size. According to S.M. Dutt, Managing Director, A to Z Print Solutions, this sudden change did not affect the design, readership, or advertising revenue of the concerned newspapers. During that period of change, Mr Dutt was at the helm in one of the newspapers. According to him, the change was simply for commercial reasons. The reduced size naturally consumed less newsprint, which saved 14 per cent of the paper cost. The size was further reduced to 35 cm × 54.6 cm (with a 33.2 cm × 52.5 cm print area) in 2005, which saved an additional 3 per cent in newsprint cost. The reduced size resulted in savings in terms of not only newsprint but also consumables such as plate, ink, and film.

These days, another noticeable format—the tabloid—has emerged. Since a tabloid is almost half the size of a broadsheet paper, it is easier to print even on big-sized machines. The desktop phenomenon has given this size a boost and multiplied the number of tabloid publications. Companies publish tabloid journals to build their corporate image, and small publishing houses publish them to purvey social gossip, labour problems, or human interest journalism. R.K. Karanjia, founder and editor of *Blitz*, is the pioneer of tabloid journalism in India.

Tabloids are usually identified with sensational news and, therefore, the broadsheet size remains popular among both conservative and radical people.

NEWSPAPER FORMAT

A newspaper format is like a stage play. In theatre, artists have to work within the given stage dimensions, lighting, sound effects, and stage background. Within these limitations, actors and directors have to display their creative talent and lure us to watch and appreciate the play. Similarly, newspaper professionals work within the limitations of form and the format, which are fixed by practical, technical, and economic considerations. Editors, designers, and the make-up persons work within the limitations given to them.

Practical considerations Space is a practical limitation for editors. They have to constantly estimate how many news items or comments can be accommodated on a page, and with what emphasis. This is especially the case when they need to fill the columns within their overall dimensions, either vertically or horizontally. Traditionally, the newspaper format has had a narrow column width. With new digital technology, however, the column width can be manipulated in a minute.

Before the advent of TV and the design revolution in newspapers, newspapers were set in the old system, with a masthead flanked by ear pieces, the cut-off rules separating news stories, photographs, and even columns, and many headlines set in capital and small letters. Pages set in this style used to be overcrowded, with little white space. The front page of a newspaper published in 1940 in Figure 13.5 illustrates a page set in the old style.

These days, newspaper production journalists have brought in many innovations. Formats are becoming more visual-oriented now, with a wide use of graphics, pictures, and shapes. In fact, the look of some news-

Figure 13.5 Front page of a newspaper in 1940

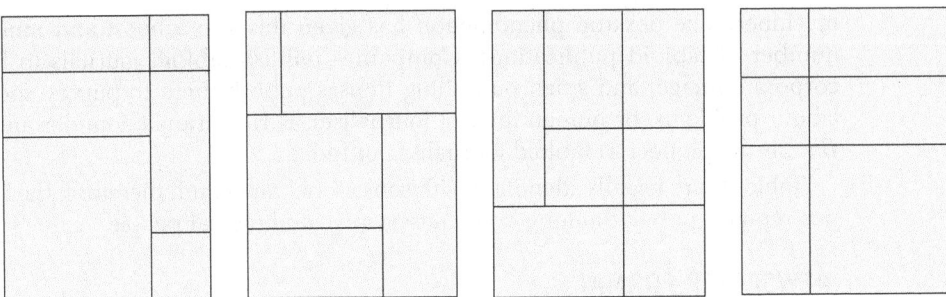

Figure 13.6 Some common modular grids

papers is getting closer to that of magazines. Some experimental formats have become the model for some newspaper layouts.

In order to decide on the arrangement of matter on a page, the editor/designer makes use of a design grid. The design grid is the basic guideline for a newspaper page, made up of squares and rectangles in subtle proportions. The headlines and the pictures are arranged within these rectangular portions to form a total page in a pleasing pattern. These flexible grids are also referred to as a *modular pattern*. The inspiration for a modular grid came from the French architect and planner of Chandigarh, Le Corbusier, and a Dutch painter, Piet Mondrian. Figure 13.6 shows some common modular grids used in newspapers.

Technical considerations Other than the spacing and arrangement of matter on a page, decisions on technical aspects such as the handling of type, pictures, and the final production have to be taken. Types are the basic elements in a newspaper format. The text matter forms a solid squared-off mass in small types, which is combined with bold and big-sized headlines or pictures. This requires knowledge of the physical structures of types and typefaces and their suitability for a newspaper format. It is the type format which imparts a distinct identity to a newspaper.

Typesetting techniques also influence the development of newspaper formats. The advent of phototypesetting and desktop publishing systems are significant developments in the world of printing. During the mid-1980s, which was a period of transition, most national dailies changed from linotypesetting to phototypesetting. Linotypesetting was compatible with letterpress printing, where printing was done from a raised surface. In phototypesetting, however, the printing image is flat on paper. In order to use this typeset image and to avoid discarding the expensive letterpress printing machines which were not compatible with phototypesetting, the typeset image was transferred from the phototypeset copy to the photopolymer plate in a raised image form. This process was far less cumbersome than fitting the hard metal plate around the cylinder of a rotary letterpress. Moreover, it is easier to make a polymer plate.

These days, most newspapers are printed by the offset process, which is highly compatible with the modern typesetting system.

Economic considerations A newspaper is one of the few items in the world which sell below the cost of production. Unlike any other product, a publisher who sells more copies of a newspaper does not necessarily make more money. In fact, in the short term, the publisher loses revenue by selling more copies, for there is a time lag before the higher circulation figures get translated into higher advertisement revenue.

The production of a newspaper becomes very expensive when the circulation crosses the break-even point. Thereafter, the production cost is so high that it becomes uneconomical to print more copies, unless, of course, it is supported by massive advertising.

The newspaper page layout starts from the advertisement department, where all the advertisements are placed on the dummy sheet. This gives the page a certain shape before the editor or the make-up person begins to think about what to do with editorial content. In order to avoid cluttered layouts due to rigid placement of advertisements, certain formats are developed, keeping certain pages light, heavy, or clear of ads. Even the advertisement department may follow a guideline and stipulate the available shapes and sizes and the policy of the newspaper in regard to the sale and placing of advertisements in a pattern that broadly meets the editorial equirements.

DESIGN ELEMENTS

The format is mainly filled up by four design elements—advertisements, text matter, headlines, and pictures.

Advertisements

As discussed earlier, the designer has no control over the placement of advertisements on a page; neither can he/she tamper with the content of any advertisement. Since advertisements are placed along with other elements on a page, the placement of these elements should be decided keeping the size, shape, tone, and edges of the advertisements in mind.

A copy-heavy advertisement will be inappropriate in a space that is surrounded by editorial text matter with the same or similar type style. A photograph of a news story will lose its identity when placed alongside an advertisement which has a photograph of the same tone and shape. Even two advertisements on a page may clash with each other if they are not separated by a border rule or some other distinguishing device.

There are two kinds of advertisements in newspapers—classified and display. Display advertisements are measured and the advertisement space is sold in square centimetres, while classified advertisements are measured in terms of the number of words or lines per centimetre.

The classified advertisement page is a group of rectangular solid masses (normally in 5.5 point type size). It is the most neglected page in terms of design, as the reader is more interested in the contents of this page than in the graphics, if any. There are occasional reverse type faces, a few thumbnail sketches of the product being advertised, logos of companies for tender notices, and stylized sketches of men and women in matrimonial advertisements. These design elements are, however, exceptions to the rule.

Some standard patterns are used for advertisement placement in newspapers. Some commonly used patterns for placing advertisements are displayed in Figure 13.7. A *group display advertisement* is a standard advertising unit that may be placed on the right or bottom right position, leaving the rest of the page for the editorial content. This gives the reader an easy flow of reading material. The white space shown in these samples is used for editorial content. Another standard advertising unit is a *full-page advertisement.* It frees other pages for more editorial matter.

Whatever pattern is chosen, unless there is coordination between the editorial and advertisement departments, no successful make-up is possible. It is essential for the advertisement department to provide the dummy that shows not only the size and positioning of advertisements on a page but also all necessary details about whether the matter is in line or half-tone, typographic or illustrative, fixed or flexible position. Such a close coordination is a prerequisite for optimum results. A proof or pull of the advertisement will yield positive results.

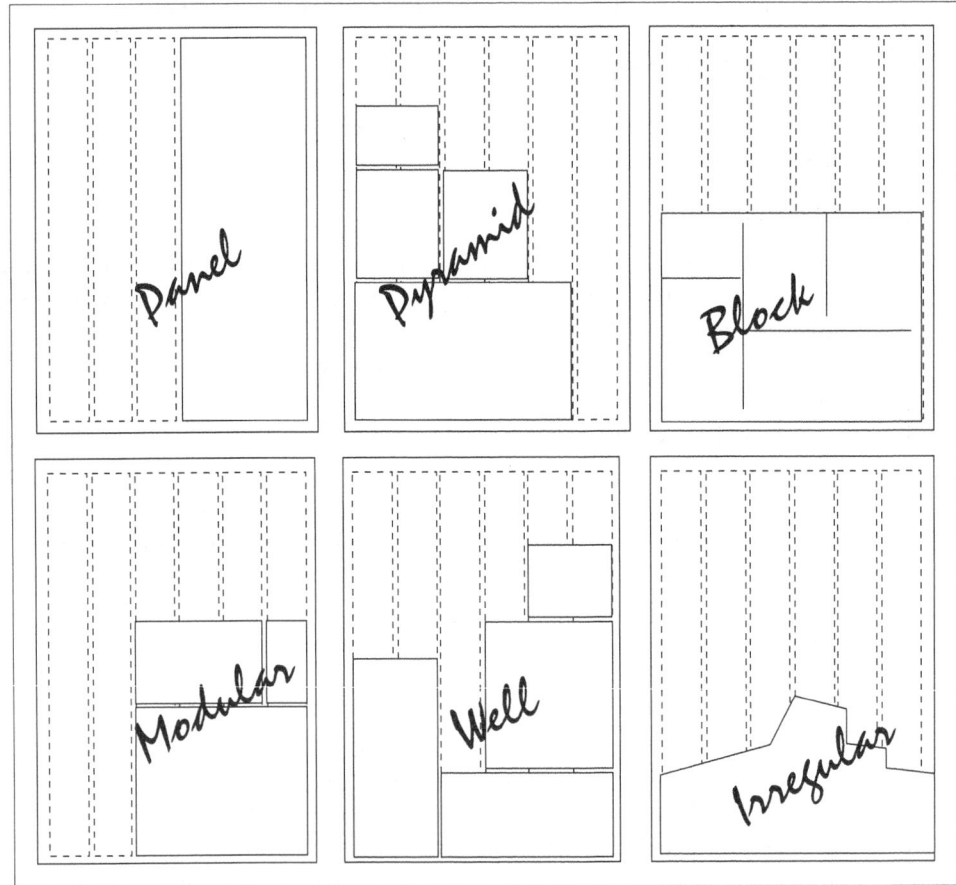

Figure 13.7 Some common patterns for placing advertisements

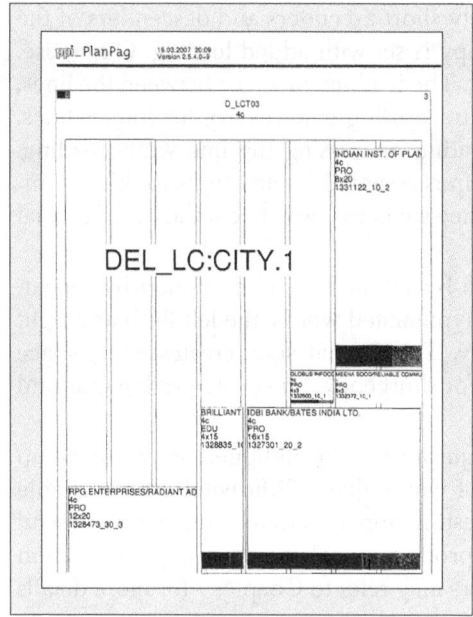

Figure 13.8 A page plan on PlanPag

In the case of advertisements that are developed digitally, the advertisements are placed on the grid templates of the specific application. These are then circulated among various departments through LAN, so that each department can add its inputs to the page. All the information is stored in a server in the respective file format, and all the professionals working on the advertisement have access to it. PlanPag, a ppi software program is an example of a popular software used by mainstream newspapers for advertisement booking and advertisement page planning, respectively. PlanPag supports parallel activities with Q. Link (Quark Link), such as dropping the advertisements into the hot folder where the actual advertisements are stored and allowing the incursion of editorial content and auto generation of PS files. This helps the art room to give a final shape to the pages on QuarkXPress. Figure 13.8 shows a page plan on PlanPag.

Text Matter

The primary objective of a newspaper is to involve the customer in reading. So the next step in creating a design should be to locate the text matter that is to go into the day's paper. The matter is then set in appropriate typefaces and sizes. Certain typefaces are more suitable for newspapers because of their distinct characteristics. The text matter is set in a particular format. The column width of a paper determines its basic format. The typeset format (justified, left-aligned, etc.) is identified by the grey mass of small type.

The text matter of a newspaper is generally set in a standard size (8 points), which is legible even on inferior-grade paper like newsprint. Newspaper text types are specially designed. The most commonly used text face for newspapers is the classical Roman face, whose design structure has thick and thin strokes within a letter, with a short crossline attached to the main stroke of the letter, known as a serif. Type experts feel that the thick and thin strokes create rhythm and the serif accelerates horizontal movement. Sans serif Lineal typefaces, which have a monotonal design character, are generally avoided in newspaper text matter.

The x-height of the face style is another criterion for type selection. The faces used for newspapers are a bit condensed. They are also relatively bold, and have a larger x-height, so that the words formed by these typefaces are more noticeable. Condensed faces can accommodate more words in a short line length and slightly bold letters in small size are legible on even an inexpensive paper like newsprint.

Due to the large x-height and the relatively short ascenders and descenders of the type faces chosen for text matter, the text copy is set with added leading. Otherwise, the text may look tight which impede reading. The leading, or space between the lines, is taken in one or half-point increments. Extra leading is necessary for longer lines. Otherwise, the reader runs the risk of repeating or missing the line while reading. Maintaining a steady, constant reading rhythm is essential for any typographical composition. It is more so for a newspaper, as a newspaper is largely composed of textual matter.

Most newspapers achieve reading rhythm by setting type composition by repeating the columns. For variation and to avoid hyphenated words, the left flush and right ragged format is also used, though sparingly. This format style creates white space between columns, which looks quite jarring. For short copy, however, it is dynamic and more contemporary in style.

Copy estimation is a very important requisite for the designer or the make-up person. It involves calculating the number of words that will fit within the available space. There are different formulae for copy estimation, but none of them are as useful as the experience of working in newspaper production. These days, copy estimation can also be carried out on a computer. Readers may refer to Chapter 7 for more details on copy estimation.

Headlines

Newspaper headlines demonstrate two aspects—content of the headline and physical form of the headline type. By providing an overview of the news content and summarizing the news, they create curiosity and attract the reader on to the pages. Through the physical form of the type, they indicate the relative importance of the stories. Headlines are conspicuous elements in newspaper design and exist on the page in harmony and balance with other elements such as pictures and text. They lend a distinct identity to a newspaper.

In order ensure that the headlines of a paper convey the right information about its content, and, at the same time, are of an appropriate form, editors and designers work on them together. A sub-editor who possesses basic knowledge of typography can play a dual role, deciding on the form as well as the content of headlines.

There is no set type style rule for headlines. The harmony rule may not always work, as the page may look very passive and monotonous even when it is harmonious. Lineal and classical faces are widely accepted for headline style in most newspapers. A slightly fancy style is not inappropriate in some places such as features.

Headlines in an irregular line length are preferable, but they should not be in a justified format. They may be centered and left or right flush in accordance with the style adopted by a newspaper.

Using big, bold headlines for the main or lead story of a newspaper is a very common practice. The alternative to this may be a number of lines stacked on top of one another.

Some of the old-style headlines such as decks and inverted pyramids have now been replaced by headlines with subheads and those followed by credit lines supported by rules.

A *kicker* or a shoulder headline is small and is usually placed above the main headline, as shown in Figure 13.12. It is frequently underlined for some extra optical weight. As the eye should move from the kicker to the main headline, left placement of the kicker is preferable to a central one. Reverse lettering with border and flat tones, thumbnail graphics, and photographs of newspaper columnists are used commonly. The effectiveness of these depends on how creatively they are treated.

Headlines are expected to be in regular sizes, widths, weights, and positions. Headline type sizes are generally big and bold, ranging from 16 to 40 points, with the exception perhaps of the lead story, which should reflect the mood of the story through a bigger type size. Normal width and the Roman posture are the simplest forms, but expanded, bold, medium, or italics may be used for variation. It is better, however, to stick to one style to give the newspaper a particular visual character.

Headlines with wide white spaces are more legible than those surrounded by other types and visual elements. As white space in a newspaper design is a scarce element, deciding on how much white space to leave around the headline is another creative task for the designer. Figure 13.9 shows some headline styles that are commonly used in newspapers.

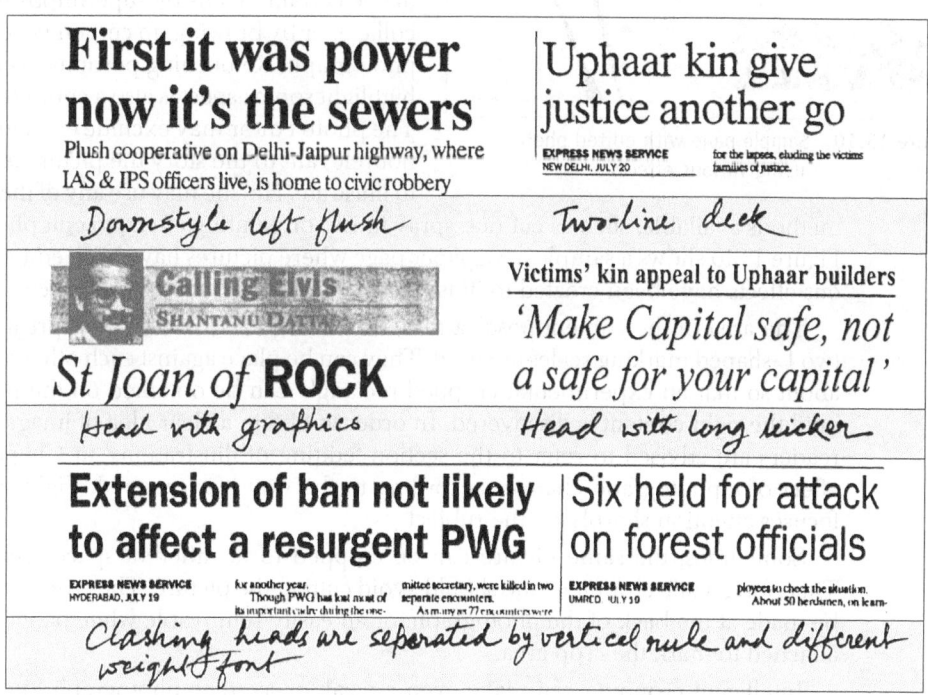

Figure 13.9 Some common heading styles

304 *Art and Print Production*

Figure 13.10 Sample page with edited photos using various effects

Pictures

Pictures on a newspaper page are noticed at first glance. Pictures that are weak, ugly, meaningless, and without credibility can do more harm than good to the page and the newspaper as a whole. Unlike other printed literature, newspaper pictures are generally not commissioned. They come from various sources, such as staff photographers, paparazzi, stock photographers, picture libraries, television channels, and handouts. Pictures obtained from these sources are not always suitable for use in a newspaper unless they are edited and/or cropped to suit the content. The size of the picture has an indelible effect on the importance of a news story.

Selecting the right picture content is the job of a photo editor. Aesthetic quality and functional role are the two parameters of editing. To get the best possible image combined with line drawing and special screening, the editor may enhance certain details by superimposing, using a collage, or by blowing up certain portions of the photograph. Retouching portions to enhance or highlight some aspect is also a common practice. The photo editor may exclude elements that are not relevant to the story the picture is supposed to illustrate. He/she may use any of the dozens of methods available, such as cut-out, spray finish, or painting effect, to edit photographs. Figure 13.10 shows a sample newspaper page where pictures have been edited and various effects have been created to illustrate different aspects of a news piece.

The area of the content poses a rather difficult job. It is, however, greatly eased if two L-shaped marking scales are used. They can be place against each other and moved about so that an experimental cropped rectangle can be obtained on the photograph until the right content is discovered. In order to obtain a clear idea of image cropping, readers are advised to refer to the section 'editing of illustrations' in Chapter 3. The effect of a photograph changes according to the way it is cropped. Tighter cropping focuses attention sharply on the subject.

Sometimes, the same picture can be cropped to fit different space requirements. Therefore, while cropping, one should avoid cutting the picture. The crop marks should be made at the back of the photograph, or an easily-removable white paper should be attached to mark the crop area.

Intelligent cropping can make even a weak or average photograph look great. In the case of a picture created by combining the portraits of several people, the picture will look better if the area covered by each portrait is consistent, and if all of them are shot from the same angle. When a portrait has a strong directional line, it will look best facing inwards on the page or inwards to the story with which it is attached. It will be a cause of annoyance to the reader if an individual's ears, chin, forehead, etc. are cut in the process of cropping. Moreover, one should be careful while using a border around a photograph. It will help when the edges of the photograph are very light, but may be unnecessary when the photo content has enough tonal contrast with the background. Readers may refer to Chapter 3 for details on cropping and scaling.

Photographs are the primary choice for illustrating a graphic design. This is more so for newspapers, because photographs represent real life. People tend to believe photographs more than any other form of illustration.

Hand-drawn graphics such as charts, maps, cartoons, and comic strips have maintained an important place in newspapers. They can inform, instruct, guide, entertain, and set the mood for a story. Most readers enjoy a light cartoon before settling down to read the serious matter in a newspaper. A graphic improves readability by explaining complicated parts in the text. It also adds realism to writing. It may also present the data in an easy-to-understand way and guides the reader to a place of travel or helps him/her locate a particular place.

Hand-drawn illustrations can be made more effective by graphically manipulating them to enhance their content. Such images are referred to as graphics. Graphics may be typographic images, photographic images, hand art, or even computer manipulated

Figure 13.11 Digitally created graphic image

images. Charts can be made more interesting by adding some pictures to them. A photo background may be eliminated form an image to make room for text or another visual element. A tonal effect may be added to a line illustration by applying tone and shade to it. There are a lot of possibilities of manipulation of photographs or hand art through computers. Figure 13.11 shows one such digitally created graphic image. Copyright-free illustrations and graphic symbols are available in printed books as well as computer software programs. These images, when used creatively, can be effective graphics without the help of a skilled artist.

PAGE MAKE-UP

Page make-up is the final editorial job. It is usually finished in a hurry. The traditional method of page make-up, which was practised till a decade back, was a time-consuming process. It has now been replaced with electronic page designing, which offers immense freedom to the editor and the graphic artist.

These days, a number of software programs are available for page make-up. They are quite convenient to use, and, as discussed earlier, offer a lot of flexibility. In order to design the page make-up of a newspaper, designers and editors need to rely on their knowledge of the available technology. Many new technologies keep coming up, and they need to familiarize themselves with the same in order to update their knowledge of various software programs. They should not let the lack of knowledge about new technology limit their creativity.

Another development highlighting the widespread use of computerized typesetting and electronic pagination is the emergence of the photo-offset system as the pre-eminent printing process in newspaper production.

Let us now discuss the page make-up of various important sections of a newspaper, such as the front page, editorial page, section pages, and pages in colour.

Front Page

The front page is usually the first page to be designed. This page calls for the most creative use of typography. This page helps the editor give the audience the feeling that all the news of the world has been covered. The front-page style helps in developing a recognizable identity for the paper. The daily task of page designing is done within the parameters dictated by the paper's accepted style. This style pertains to type style, column number, and column width. The front page serves the purpose of a shop window. After reading the day's hot news and other main stories, the reader obtains information about the features of other pages from the front page.

The front page is visualized on the basis of the number of stories appearing on it and their relative importance in terms of the length and value of the news items. The common elements of the front page design are—nameplate with or without ear pieces; one or two news photos or advertisements, normally in the solus position; or graphics such as map charts, cartoons, and indexes. Figure 13.12 shows some common elements on the front page of a newspaper.

Newspaper Make-up 307

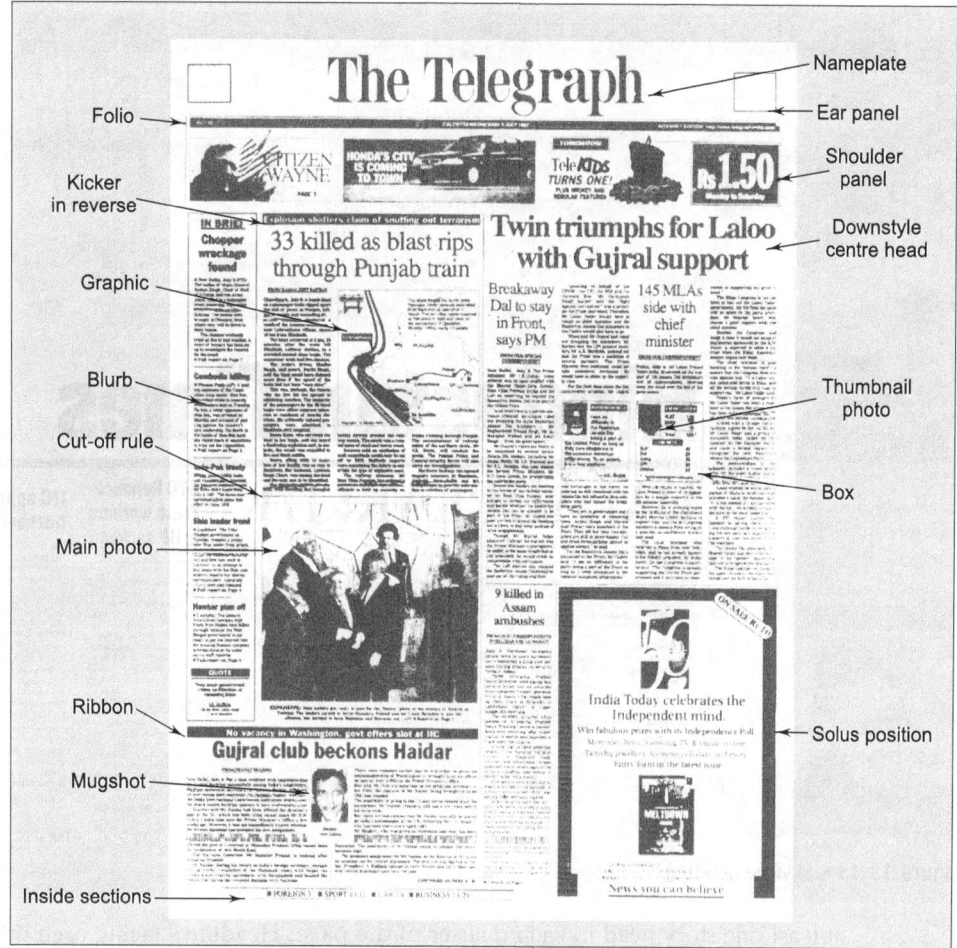

Figure 13.12 Design elements on a front page

The *nameplate* always runs at the top of the page. Sometimes, *skyline matter* in the form of a headline alone or in combination with body type and art may run above the nameplate. Figure 13.13 illustrates an example of skyline matter used by *Hindustan Times* when India won the T20 World Cup in September 2007.

A *bannerhead* that runs across the page with bold letters is common for spectacular news items such as the assassination or death of the head of a state, the toppling of a government, or a world cup victory. Usually, a bannerhead is set in somewhat larger type than the rest of the text and is printed in boldface. In normal circumstances, such pieces are broken into multiple columns to give the page a dynamic look if few words are given graphic treatment. The rest of the head's size and weight may be decided in proportion to the lead story. An almost equally important story may be placed above the lead story with a smaller sized headline to avoid confusion in the page. Effort should be made to get

308 *Art and Print Production*

Figure 13.13   Skyline heading

at least one story head in each quarter of the page. Headlines facing each other create confusion for the reader, and may be avoided by providing significant variations. In case there are more than one news photographs on the front page, the top one should look much heavier. The headline should be wide enough to cover the entire story.

Grouping of pictures on the front page is not very common. However, grouped pictures may be used in order to cover events such as cabinet reshuffles, where new ministers suddenly come to the centre-stage. In such cases, pictures that run across the fold should be planned very cautiously. It should be ensured that one of the folds gets most of the content related to the picture.

Boxes, reverse letters, and thick lines may be used to separate the stories or to highlight a particular portion. They should, however, be used sparingly, and not used as substitutes for pictures. Indian dailies usually avoid the use of dominant graphics on the front page, but these graphics can create a lot of impact if used creatively. In the case of train accidents, deaths, etc., photographs of the actual incident may be difficult to obtain. Such events may be illustrated with appropriate graphics.

Since several stories need to be accommodated on the front page, jumps of the page are unavoidable. These jumps, however, should be minimized as much as possible, as they hamper the reader's interest in the story.

The *index* is the content of a newspaper. The index should be a simple listing of the stories with their page numbers. Many newspapers not only give it elaborate graphic treatment but also place it in a key position such as the top of the nameplate or the first or the last column. The index carries a short write-up on the stories, often with a small illustration. There are some disadvantages in using an elaborate index. Such indexes occupy a lot of space and the reader may skip the actual story as he has already got an overview of the news through the index.

Editorial Page

The editorial page is actually the opinion page of the newspaper, and hence it is designed differently from the other pages. Figure 13.14 shows the editorial page of a popular Indian daily. The style adopted for the editorial page reflects the seriousness of the views expressed for or against certain ideas, which is in contrast to the style of the news pages; this creates a feeling of immediacy and excitement. The function of the editorial page can be substantiated by using various graphic devices such as a bigger column width, larger text type size, and different type styles. Graphics may be added to make the page subtle and interesting. A topical political cartoon is usually an acceptable graphic for an editorial page. Many papers, however, keep the editorial page free of graphics to maintain seriousness. The editorial expresses the opinions of the newspaper and its logo and nameplate show that the newspaper is responsible for the opinions expressed on this page.

Section Pages

The section pages of a newspaper are designed in such a manner that each page is unique enough to reflect the mood of the section, and yet it is consistent with the overall style of the paper. For example, all the section pages may start with a thick toned line across the page with stylized type at the end of the line and some highlighting lines on or above the toned line, but the lettering style for each page may differ to reflect the mood of the section. The sports page may be composed in square serif type and the business page may have sans serif type. In order to make the sections more distinct, each section panel may carry a photo or graphic related to the section.

Typographic treatment of text matter for section pages will, of course, be the same as that of the front page. Since most of the pages are dominated by

Figure 13.14   Editorial page

advertisements, care should be taken while placing the headline and the text on section pages. News headlines should not be aligned with the content of an advertisement or clash with its headline. If a story runs to the next page, a feeling of continuity should be developed. In case the starting point of a story is not distinct, drop letters may be used. In addition to indicating the opening of a story, drop letters add beauty to the page unobtrusively. One-column mug shots also break the monotony of the page, especially where excessive ribbon-type text copy has been used.

Two types of pictures are used in section pages—(a) those pertaining to news items, and (b) those related to feature articles. As discussed earlier, news pictures need to be related to the news stories. Pictures that illustrate feature articles, however, can have much freer treatment in terms of shape, size, and placement. Graphics or pictures combined with headlines make a composite block that gives the page a contemporary look. In some newspaper pages, portions of the text matter are wrapped around a cut-out photo to give the page an interesting arrangement. An example of a cut-out photo can be seen in the photograph used in the article titled 'Going, Going…?' in Figure 13.10.

Sections with feature articles ought to be more dynamic. They are designed to hold the reader through the whole of the run. As shown in Figure 13.15, generous white space, occasional blurbs, subtle column width, non-justified formats, and reverse or tinted head blocks enliven a section page with features and make it look like a page out of a magazine. Symmetrical balance can also be achieved on a section page when covering a story like that of two equally strong sports teams clashing in finals.

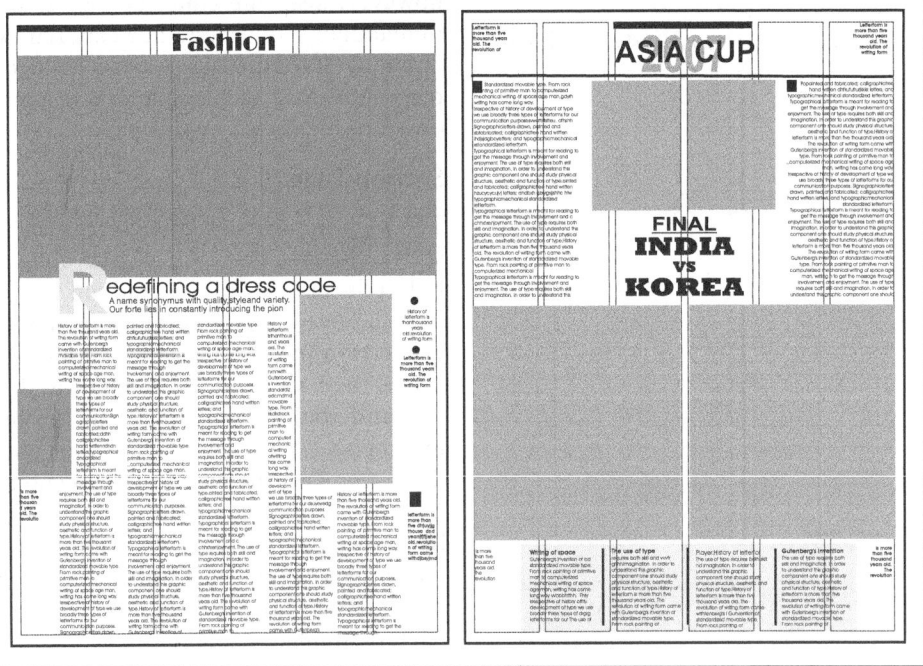

Figure 13.15 Page make-up of section pages

Colour Pages

Despite the fact that most publishers and advertisers use colour in their printed material and television, the closest competitor of newspapers, also presents programmes in colour, newspapers are lagging behind in this aspect. The reason for this is not the unavailability of the required technology but the inferior quality of newsprint. The rough surface of newsprint can just not take the fine dots of half-tone, making fine results impossible.

The inescapable blotting factor makes the printed image immeasurably dull. Time and cost are two other constraints. Despite the fact that colour scanning and electronic page make-up give the graphic journalists the greatest opportunities, manual page planning continues to be practised in newspaper art rooms and processing units in many newspaper publishing houses in India. This is because colour page planning requires more time. Four-colour processing, plate-making, and printing cost not only additional time but also money. Because of these constraints, many newspapers refrain from using colour. Some use it sparingly and some use it only in special supplements or Sunday editions, which are almost free from the constraints mentioned here.

Colour is most effective when used functionally. This is as applicable to a newspaper as to any other product. Colours are more functional in features than news pages, as they create a mood and atmosphere that make the reader stay on the page. Besides colour, half-tone features, logos or motifs, tint blocks, and headlines are very effective.

Until we overcome the problem of inferior quality newsprint, news photos in black and white will continue to be most appropriate. News photos in colour can do more harm than good if they are not printed properly. Photographs taken in colour may be printed in black and white, but it should be remembered that doing so will make them lose a part of their intrinsic quality. Photographs from other sources such as printed material or the Internet should be avoided as these may result in poor image reproduction. Halftone dots applied on a pre-printed image not only reduce the quality but also create flowery patches (moiré effect) that distort the image. Colour photos can be reproduced best from colour transparencies and high resolution digital photographs. A news picture from the camera lens can be transmitted straight to the make-up screen by using digital method. This method offers a designer the scope of colour correction along with image manipulation.

It is important to note that, for newspaper pages, flat colour or spot colour printing is comparatively safer than colour photo (process colour) printing. Line illustrations may be used for both editorial and advertising material. It should, however, be ensured that the area of the solid colour is not too big; otherwise, the colour impression will be seen through the back of the page. Tinting of spot colours should be avoided, especially for text matter. The heads and subheads should be bold enough, in a colour that is deep and dark. Reverse letters do well in many situations.

In recent times, some newspapers have started the use of colour newsprint and, through that, have created an identity for their group and their field of work. The use of pink pages for economic journalism and yellow pages for classified advertisements are some examples of the use of a specific colour for a specific field.

SUMMARY

A newspaper has a very short life. Its look is different from that of other forms of literature, but it is no less important to readers. The overall look or design of the paper, which is developed by a designer, gets the reader's initial attention and then guides him/her through the pages. It lends a distinct identity to the paper and contributes to the reader's emotional relationship with it.

Professionals who are involved in designing newspapers are called graphic journalists. Low reading habits, growing popularity of television, inferior quality content, and time constraints are some of the challenged faced by graphic journalists. Advanced technology and professionalism in design approach help them overcome these constraints to a great extent.

Designers work within the limitations of form and format. The form of a newspaper refers to its size. The two commonly used forms are the broadsheet and the tabloid. The main considerations in designing a newspaper format are the column width, type style, standard graphics, and design grid.

The main design elements of a newspaper are advertisements, headlines, text matter, and pictures. These are the rigid elements of a design. In no way can their size, tone, and edges be tampered; sometimes even their position on a page is fixed. The commonly used text type for a newspaper is classical Roman, which has thick and thin strokes with serifs. The design style of type creates rhythm and horizontal movement. The headlines summarize the news, attract attention, and indicate the relative importance of stories. News pictures come from various sources such as staff photographers, freelancers, stock photographs, picture libraries, television, and handouts. No matter what the source of a picture is, it should be strong, appropriate, professionally done, and credible.

The design of a newspaper page starts soon after the dummy sheet, marking the areas for advertisements, is received. Here again, designers follow the basic principles of design in arranging the elements. Most of the pages are balanced asymmetrically, and contrast is achieved by using bold and big headlines and, sometimes, by using pictures and graphics. Harmony and eye movement are the other requirements of a newspaper design.

For the purpose of designing, a newspaper may be divided into four part—the front page, the editorial page, and section pages, and colour pages. Front page designs are dictated by the newspaper style, which includes the chosen style of headings, format, picture arrangement, and index. The appearance of the front page is also dependent on the number of stories on the page and their relative importance.

The editorial page reflects the seriousness of the opinions expressed therein by means of bigger column width, different type style, and various graphic devices including occasional cartoons. The editorial page is free of advertisements.

Section pages develop the mood for the concerned topic/area by using appropriate type faces and visuals. They are also designed in a way that an overall harmony is maintained with the other pages. Section pages with feature articles look dynamic with generous white space, occasional blurbs, subtle column widths, reverse head blocks, etc.

The use of colour on newspaper pages are limited by the inferior quality of paper used for printing and the time constraint. Some newspapers use good quality paper sparingly and some use it only for their special supplements. Colour planning should be done on the basis of the need of a page and the role and function of colour in page make-up.

KEY TERMS

Broadsheet The format used by mainstream newspapers such as *The Times of India*, *Hindustan Times*, and *The Hindu*. It also refers to the size of a standard newspaper, which is approximately 35 cm × 55.6 cm.

Deck One or more lines of text found between the headline and the body of the article. The deck elaborates or expands on the headline and the accompanying text.

Dummy A prototype of a newspaper on which the placement of advertisements and allocation of stories are decided.

Ear Piece An advertisement that is placed next to the nameplate.

Graphic Journalists Graphic designers who specialize in the process of art and production, fulfilling the journalistic requirements of being able to create quick, newsworthy, and informative material.

Grid Subtle division of space to position columns and other elements that may occur repeatedly on various pages or screens.

Gutter The blank margin between two printed pages or two columns.

Jump The part of a story from where it is continued on another page.

Kicker A short phrase above the headline usually set in a smaller type. It serves as an introduction to a headline.

Lead The first and most important paragraph of any news story. It attracts the reader and states the important facts first.

Make-up The art of arranging elements on a newspaper page for the purpose of printing.

Nameplate The title of a newspaper, which is set in a distinctive typestyle. The nameplate is also called the flag or the masthead.

News Editor Professionals responsible for the news pages in a newspaper. They work in co-ordination with reporters and decide which stories to use for a particular edition.

Paparazzi Freelance news photographers.

Shoulder Panel Brief inside stories graphically presented under the nameplate and above the stories.

Solus Position The bottom right corner of a front page used for publishing a single advertisement.

Tabloid A newspaper size that is smaller than broadsheet, often identified with sensational journalism.

REFERENCES

Arnold, Edmund C. 1981, *Designing the Total Newspaper*, Harper & Row Publishers, New York.

Bowles, Dorothy and Diane L Borden 1999, *Creative Editing*, Third Edition, Wadsworth Thomson Learning Company, St. Paul.

Conover, Theodore E. 1990, *Graphic Communication Today*, West Publishing.

Dehadrai, Anant P. 1989, *Newspaper Production*, paper presented at printing technology seminar organized by DAVP, New Delhi.

Frost, Chris 2005, *Designing for Newspaper and Magazine*, Routledge, Taylor & Francis Group, London and New York.

Hodgson, F.W. and Giles, Vic 1990, *Creative Newspaper Design*, Heinemann Professional http: shop.net.e2bn/glossary, accessed in March 2007.

Hutt, Allen 1960, *Newspaper Design*, Oxford University Press, London.

Khurana, S.K. (ed), *All About Newspapers*, July–Sept 06, Quarterly publication of Newspaper Industry in India, New Delhi.

Quinn, Stephen 2001, *Digital Sub-editing & Design*, Focal Press Publishing, London.

REVIEW QUESTIONS

1. What are the characteristics of a newspaper? How do these affect the development of its design?
2. 'Newspaper design is as important as any other printed publication.' Elaborate this statement.
3. Why is the term 'make-up' used for the layout of a newspaper?
4. What are the effects of television and the Internet on modern newspaper designing? Elaborate these in light of the strengths and weaknesses of these media.
5. What are the sections that a newspaper can be divided into for the purpose of page make-up? Describe the characteristics and functions of each section.
6. Define grids and modular patterns. Why is the modular pattern popular in newspaper design? Support your answer by comparing the digital era of newspaper production with the pre-digital era.
7. Panels, pyramids, blocks, and modular designs are some of the advertisement styles used in a

newspaper. Describe the look and importance of each for presenting the editorial content of a page.

8. What are the roles of a sub-editor and designer in handling text matter, headlines, and pictures in newspaper make-up?

9. Compare broadsheet forms with tabloid newspapers in terms of their size, format content, and visual look.

10. How is the design of a front page different from that of an editorial page? Discuss the differences in the format, text, visual style, and use of colour in each.

PROJECTS

1. Go to a nearby news-stand and purchase five newspapers of the same day (two national dailies and three regional newspapers, irrespective of their language). Prepare a comparative list of the front page on the following lines:
   (a) Typographical details for both text and headlines
   (b) Number of visuals and their physical characteristics
   (c) Number of advertisements and their placement
   (d) Lead story or entry point
   (e) Layout style and production quality
   (f) Appropriateness of type style in relation to the content of the story and intended target audience

2. Take a broadsheet newspaper. Identify the design elements on it and label them on the page as per the sample given in the book. Mention their placement on the page and discuss how these elements illustrate the application of basic design principles.

3. Copy a page of newspaper but as per the style of newspaper make-up within the time limit of one hour. Pass it to your fellow student without the original. Ask him/her to write the details of the placement of the elements including typographical details. You do the same exercise for his or her layout as well and make sure that both the layouts are prepared as per the computer operator's requirement.

4. Trace the grids on a newspaper page. Copy the same on a page layout software (preferably QuarkXPress). Make two alternative grid pages. Arrange the same stories in your own style. Type the headlines and sub headlines and fill the text block with any text available in your word document. Use graphics and pictures or tint blocks as space holders.

5. Organize a mock newsroom involving all the students of your class. Divide the class and designate an editor, a chief sub-editor, and four sub-editors. Let some of your classmates who have good visual sense play the role of graphic artists, and let the remaining students play the role of reporters. Organize a brainstorming session comprising all the members of the team. Make a plan for an 'ideal newspaper'. Write the main story from the day's teleprinter copy or television news. Write other stories by interviewing people or base them on research and survey. Allocate the articles and visuals, if any, on a dummy according to your plan. Go through the details on a grid sheet. Develop the layout on computer. Take a proof of the pages and carry out the necessary corrections. Take a laser printout on paper and make a PDF file for film output. Now, print your paper on a sheet-fed offset printing machine and distribute it.

CHAPTER 14

Advertising Design

Learning Objectives

After reading this chapter, you should be able to
- understand advertising in relation to designing
- appreciate graphic design in advertising
- look at the process of deciding on the strategy and appeal for an advertisement, based on advertisers' objectives and the design brief
- understand the use of creativity in advertising art
- discuss the design approaches used to appeal to the target audience and develop a desire for the product/service in their minds
- discuss visualization and its importance in developing an advertisement
- understand some important considerations for executing a graphic design successfully

INTRODUCTION

In today's world, thousands of messages reach us in the form of advertisements. Newspapers and magazines are heavily loaded with classifieds and other advertisements. All kinds of products and services, such as personal care products, consumer goods, automobiles, telecom, insurance, etc., are being launched and advertised daily.

It is difficult to escape advertisements. Advertisements reach our homes through the print media (newspapers and magazines) and the electronic media (radio, television, and the Internet). The graphics on posters, billboards, bus panels, etc. vie for our attention outside our homes. At the workplace too, there is no escape from advertisements. Many flyers and mailers are received daily in offices. Most of the junk mail downloaded in the inbox consists of advertisements.

With so many advertisements surrounding the consumer today, it has become difficult to catch his/her attention in the first place. This is more so because an advertisement competes with not only other advertisements in the same medium but also advertisements in other media.

ADVERTISING COMMUNICATION

Advertising is a non-personal, paid form of communication that depends on mediated channels of mass communication such as television, radio, or newspapers and magazines.

Advertisements in the print media consist of written copy and graphic design. The creative task of an advertisement is not the responsibility of a single individual. In most cases, it is a team effort. Although the success or failure of an advertisement is attributed primarily to the creative team comprising the copywriter and the designer, teams from other areas such as media planning and production too have a big role to play. The creative team always works within a medium's limitations and bottlenecks. To generate a creative advertisement in an atmosphere of conflict and compromise is a big achievement for the creative team.

Designers do not always work on advertisements for a single medium at a time. They may work on an entire advertising campaign. An *advertising campaign* comprises a series of advertisements that reach the largest target audience with one basic message through different media. An advertising campaign, in general, does not urge immediate action but creates a mood that simultaneously induces attention, interest, and desire. Most advertising campaigns are based on a careful analysis of the situation and intensive research data. The success of the campaign is always determined by a well-defined action plan that includes major selling points, media selection, and advertising objectives.

The creative team's role in planning the advertising campaign lies in creating a common message in all the advertisements across different media. This may take various forms, such as slogans or headlines, particular styles of illustrations, layout, colour, tone, shapes, logos, and brand names. Figure 14.1 presents an image-building campaign using various success stories of an organization. The common element across these advertisements is the use of drawn visuals of various concepts, such as a flying kite for 'growth', waves for 'change', etc.

An advertising campaign uses more than one advertisement and one medium to target the potential customer. This helps to capture and retain the target audience's attention. This reinforces the message in the mind of the target audience. Advertisements that are part of a campaign should have a common flavour. Yet, care should be taken to avoid repetition of the same design as it may cause monotony, thus leading to a passive impact.

Graphic Design

As discussed earlier, advertisements in the print media consist of—(i) written copy and (ii) graphic design. We shall focus on the graphic design aspect for our purposes.

Graphic design plays a big role in making an advertisement stand out in this competitive environment. In selling a product or service, the design must reflect its uniqueness based on tangible elements such as illustration, type, and colour and intangible elements such as human values and emotions.

Advertising communication is usually aimed at making people buy something or accept an idea. Therefore, for achieving this purpose, it must use all the attributes of the communication process—transmitting, receiving, and comprehending the message. For maximum effect, the advertisement must be creative. These creative techniques must persuade the prospective buyers or consumers to accept the viewpoint of the advertiser. People generally interpret messages in accordance with their surroundings, sociological patterns, and ethnic complexities. A good-looking photograph or an attractive

Figure 14.1 An image-building campaign

caption is not enough to persuade the prospective customer. The advertisement should be bold, dramatic, interesting, and convincing.

Design brief

An effective design cannot be created without understanding the objective of the advertisement and the message the design must convey.

In order to ensure the success of an advertising design, the creative team (comprising the copywriter and the designer) goes through the client's marketing objectives. The client's brief provides the agency with a clear understanding of the product and its marketing objectives. The brief is a written statement supported by research findings. In the absence of a formal client brief, the designer can benefit from an oral briefing. Whatever the method of briefing, the creative team should be clear about the following issues:

- What do the advertisers want to achieve?
- What is the marketing goal—to increase sales volume or to create a new market?
- What is the advertising goal—to establish awareness, create interest, or ask readers to take action?
- Is it a one-off advertisement or part of a campaign series?
- What is the chosen print medium—newspapers, magazines, or any other?
- What is the budget for creative work including the rejection fee?
- What are the characteristics of the advertisement's target audience?

Strategy development

The design brief helps the creative team to develop a strategy of execution. The costs involved in getting an advertisement designed and placed are so exorbitant that no advertiser can afford to experiment with advertising without a proper media plan, that is, planning about which and how much of advertising to be allocated to which media. Using the design brief, the creative team develops the key communication message for the required media so that a physical and/or an emotional rapport is established with the target audience. The physical benefit is demonstrated as the possession of the product, and the emotional message brings excitement to the target audience in the form of happiness, entertainment, fear, humour, etc.

The creative team may decide on the use of various strategies to appeal to the audience's emotions, sense of fear, humour, etc. The various strategies used by advertisers are discussed here.

Direct sale appeal In this approach, the design is developed by showing the product or demonstrating its use. Demonstration is another technique used in direct sale. The designer can demonstrate the product's superiority by presenting it in comparison with a competitor's product. Figure 14.2 illustrates an advertisement for flooring material wherein the client's product has been compared with other similar products. Direct appeal is usually used for advertising products such as instant tea, shoes, detergents, etc. Such advertisements try to appeal to the target audience by demonstrating the product in use.

The use of celebrities to sell a product or idea may also be considered as an instance of direct appeal. Such celebrities generally give an assurance about the product or testify to its quality by mentioning their personal experience. The designer's role is to present it in such a way that the visual in relation to the product gives a feeling of credibility. A real-life photograph is much more believable than a hand-drawn or manipulated picture.

Emotional appeal The most creative advertising demonstrates the emotional appeal, or the mood and feeling created by the visual and the copy. It tends to achieve an impact on the mind of the target audience for a longer period than direct appeal. It also registers a high recall rate. Creativity works in a very subtle way. The advertisement seeks to creatively target different groups of people irrespective of their ethnic, regional, or cultural association.

Figure 14.2 Direct sale appeal advertisement

Figure 14.3 shows the creative use of a picture of two animals to depict the concept of 'harmony'. In the first advertisement, a cat and a dog are shown to be sleeping cozily, although cats and dogs are not harmonious by nature. Similarly, the second advertisement depicts a deer and a lion co-existing peacefully. The word *harmony* has also been printed using two fonts that are not coherent in style. The creativity of these advertisements is very subtle, and they appeal to the emotions of the target audience.

Advertisements also appeal to the humorous side in each of us. Amul Butter's advertisements hardly escape anybody's attention due to their humorous appeal. The selection of a current subject in the advertisements accentuates the viewers' interest.

Fear appeal Many products/services such as insurance covers and social causes such as awareness against drugs, alcoholism, HIV/AIDS, etc. use fear appeal. Social awareness messages reinforce the individual's anxiety when he/she has to decide whether to continue with or discontinue a potentially harmful habit.

Entertainment appeal Hotels, travel agents, and tourism promoters colourfully emphasize the delights, comforts, and entertainment appeal of their services. They may do so either directly or indirectly.

Sex appeal Advertisements often use sex appeal to attract attention. This approach has a strong attraction value in terms of sales and recall, but its impact is hard to judge. As the use of sex appeal may lead to controversies, it is advisable to use sex appeal if it synergizes with the product and/or services, and the advertisement's copy and layout. In all cases, the basic code of ethics of advertising must be followed. Figure 14.4 presents an advertisement that uses sex appeal to make the prospective buyers notice the advertisement. Like many other advertisements in this genre, this advertisement too

Figure 14.3 Advertisements using emotional appeal

was a subject of controversy when complaints were made to the Advertising Council regarding the use of sex appeal in the advertisement. The Council endorsed the advertiser's viewpoint that it was not used as a sex appeal advertisement. It agreed with the advertiser's view that the advertisement reflects the values of the manufacturers in terms of natural leather, the softness of leather, and the artistic nature of the designing.

Creativity in advertising art

Creativity employs a well-thought-out strategy to influence the target audience. Strategy includes the *uniqueness of presentation* in the form of words, pictures, and layout and the *plan of execution* to achieve the desired goal. The advertisement's basic purpose is to grab attention, provoke interest, build an image, and, finally, sell the product or idea.

Figure 14.4 A sex appeal advertisement

The word 'create' means to bring into existence or to give rise to something that is original in nature. Creativity is the primary impulse of all forms of art. Advertising creativity is no exception. However, an advertisement cannot afford to be abstract. Abstract art pieces are generally conceived by the imaginative instincts of the artist's mind solely for the purpose of self-expression. An advertisement, however creative, needs to be directed at one or more specific goals, such as promoting sales, spreading awareness, etc. Yet, we see scores of advertisements that are so unique that they deserve appreciation, but fail to achieve the objectives for which they had been designed in the first place.

Advertising art should be aesthetically appealing and functional, but this is not enough. It must link the mind of the artist with the mind of the reader/viewer. If the message is misunderstood, the advertisement will fail to strike a cord with the target audience, even if the artwork is creative in purely aesthetic or functional terms. Thus, the true measurement of creativity in advertising art is its effectiveness.

The needs of the client too sometimes restrict the creative team's artistic approach. Since clients invest money and are most affected by the advertisement's success or failure, they are usually demanding.

Handling advertisements for the print media is a big challenge for designers. Competition from television, formidable as it is, forces the creative team to use more eye-catching images in big sizes and, wherever possible, in varied colours. These days, designers are coming up with print advertisements that have a strong impact. Dramatic image manipulation and persuasive headlines used in print advertisements are emerging as a challenge to the sight, sound, and motion impact of advertisements in visual media.

Economic liberalization and globalization have led to open markets. As a result, such markets are flooded with hundreds of brands of the same product. All these brands perform almost the same basic functions. Yet, each brand must stand on its own individual strength. Listing the benefits of using the product with the help of eye-catching visuals is not enough. The creative team must try to position the brand in such a way that the consumer identifies with the product.

The use of technology in designing has led to some challenges in the field of creative designing. Creative designers should constantly update themselves with new developments in technology.

Creative artists will do well to use technology, but they should not become slaves to it. The ethnic and cultural ethos of the region in which the product/service is being advertised should be kept in mind while creating advertisements.

The creative team works out the approach that will be adopted to achieve the objectives, visualizes the advertising campaign, and, finally, works toward the execution of the design. We shall discuss these stages in the following sections.

DESIGN APPROACH

Design approach is the action that needs to be taken about the task or the problem of an advertising concept. In fact, it is an effect of the thought process and strategy discussed earlier. The major aims of an advertising design are—attracting the target audience, holding the target audience's interest, creating a desire, and facilitating action. In this section, we shall discuss the design approaches used by advertisers to achieve these objectives.

Attracting the Target Audience

The target audience can be attracted with the use of visuals, contrast, type-style, colours, and layout. Advertisers use many devices to attract the target audience to the advertisement page. The visual impact of an advertisement is the first thing that catches the eye of the reader. The size of an advertisement plays an important role here. A bigger advertisement will score over a smaller one. *Size* works well since it helps the advertisement to come within the focus of the reader's eye. *Contrast*, another attention-getting device, is often the source of decision-making. It is the designer's most potent tool for bringing an advertisement's meaning into sharp focus.

Contrast can be achieved by manipulating the design elements with respect to their size, shape, tone, texture, and direction. A big-size picture may stand out prominently among many small ones. Lighter tones always give accent to darker tones. An

Figure 14.5 Contrast by placing visual in unusual direction

unusual shape stands out against usual shapes. Contrast in direction helps eye movement on the page. Rough-edged elements outdo smooth-edged ones in contrast. Figure 14.5 presents an advertisement that creates contrast by placing the visual in an unusual direction, which is well-matched with the appeal of the advertisement.

An effective *type style* is another interesting device to attract the target audience. Most of the text in an advertisement is dressed in type. Type dressing refers to design style with various formats of letterforms. Each design style has subtle qualities that influence the reader. The size, tone, and composition of these qualities make all the difference.

Any *picture* that is used in an advertisement will be noticed before the reader moves on to the accompanying copy. Well-illustrated visuals not only catch the eye but also hold the attention of the target audience. Good visuals are determined by the technique, style, professional quality, and appropriateness of the advertisement's message.

Colours in an advertisement provide an enormous attraction value. They sustain a viewer's attention by creating a visual impact. Despite the additional cost involved in colour printing and the mechanical constraints (in some cases), most advertisers prefer to use colours in advertisements. These advertisers realize that the cost can be recovered by gaining the target audience's attention and creating the desired impact.

Figure 14.6 Use of creative layout to attract the audience

Well-planned *layouts* do not go unnoticed by the reader. A layout which is unusual, stylish, balanced, and brilliantly executed is so distinctive that it becomes the single-most eye-catching feature of an advertisement. This, in turn, creates a strong desire to go through the advertisement or to know more about the product. Figure 14.6 depicts an advertisement used for the inauguration of an FM channel. The layout of the advertisement is such that, at first glance, it appears to be a newspaper page. A closer look, however, shows that it is, in fact, an advertisement to launch the channel. Such creative use of layout captures the reader's attention and his/her desire to take a closer look at the advertisement.

Non-information-bearing visual elements such as unusual shapes, tones, borders, and patterns may be used to attract attention. However, if not used creatively, these may fail to sustain the target audience's interest.

Holding the Audience's Interest

Immediately after attracting the reader's attention, an effort should be made to stimulate interest; otherwise, it is difficult to sustain attention. Some advertisements are able to hold on to a reader's attention long enough to stimulate interest. However, if the message is not well-structured in the form of an interesting copy, attractive visuals, and an imaginative layout, the target audience may not understand the full context of the advertisement. The message then fails to register in the mind of the viewer/reader.

The creative team of an agency tries to awaken interest by appealing to the readers' material needs. For instance, the advertisement for a service may stress its intangible attributes such as security, prestige, and reliability.

The acceptability of all these appeals depends largely on the advertisement's copy and on visuals that are sincere, believable, stylish, and approachable. The potential customer may relate to some physical characteristics of the brand, such as a logo. Most advertisements focus on the benefits of the product and/or service. In general, it has been observed that people take more interest in the advertisement's content if it is sober in approach and does not overstate product benefits. In case an advertisement requires an authoritative approach, creative artists must first think of the possible consequences before implementing the design. An authoritative approach is usually useful in the case of consumers who have already set their minds about the advertised product/service.

In order to sustain the audience's interest, headlines, copy, and familiar visuals can be used. The copy should be simple and coherent with the other elements of the advertisement. The advertisement should be in a language that the audience is familiar with.

Developing a Desire

Interest is turned into desire when the target audience is satisfied with the advertisement's message. If this happens, a desire is developed in the audience to acquire the product, to know more about it, or to endorse the idea. Desire may be established by emphasizing features such as the size or volume of the product, special or exclusive features, manufacturing processes, easy-to-handle packaging, or low prices.

A desire cannot be created by conveying the message abruptly. Prospective customers must be exposed to advertisements through several media.

In order to create a desire for a product/service, a number of product features are taken into consideration, depending on the characteristics of the target audience. The desire of a group of people may be satisfied by the physical proportions of the product such as size, weight, strength, and shape. Others may be more interested in the performance of the product, comfort in handling, efficiency, durability, storability, etc. Many consumers are also stimulated by a product's aesthetic qualities such as a well-planned surface design, elegant shape, appropriate colour scheme, or distinctive texture. Figure 14.7 shows an advertisement where the texture of the product is emphasized by using a visual that displays the product benefits.

The intangible qualities of a product also contribute towards developing a desire. The product may be a fashionable designer product or ethnic khadi cloth. Amongst the scores of toilet soap brands that are advertised, Lifebuoy and Cinthol are identified as masculine, whereas Lux, Evita, and Liril are considered feminine. Advertisers develop a desire for a product/service by appealing to the tastes and lifestyle of the target

Figure 14.7 Advertisement emphasizing the texture of the product

audience. As shown in Figure 14.8, a telecom service provider appeals to the new generation's lifestyle to create a desire for its services.

Advertisements of services try to make the target audience accept the advertiser's viewpoint by clearly depicting the purpose of the advertisement. If the advertisement is for a tour and travel package, the information relating to booking for a journey, hotel accommodation, places to visit, tariffs, etc. can develop a desire in the mind of the potential customer. Some advertisements in the services sector can develop a desire much more easily than others because a class of readers is actively seeking these services. This includes advertisements of financial services, recreation and entertainment, health, and education. Advertisements of services promoting cleanliness, environmental norms, traffic rule compliance, donations, de-addiction, etc. need a hard-hitting appeal to develop a change in attitude. Some of the advertisements promoting cleanliness and a green environment may appeal to audiences by using images of comfort, a better life, health, etc., while images of safety and punishment may be used for messages promoting de-addiction and traffic rule compliance. Fund-raising advertisements may be developed by stressing sentiments of duty, tax benefits, social respectability, etc. Large organizations develop a positive image among their customers, employees, shareholders, etc. by informing them about the company's productivity, efficiency, authority, and dependability. This is achieved through advertisements, internal newsletters, and the company's website.

Figure 14.8 Advertisement that appeals to the new generation's lifestyle

Facilitating Action

After the advertising message has been conveyed, there can be two different customer reactions. The potential customer may either change his/her attitude or preference towards the product/service, or decide to acquire/accept the product/service. Potential customers in the second category will be interested in knowing the product availability or further details such as addresses of retailers or dealers, phone/fax numbers, service warranties, etc.

Most advertisements have a specific objective. Many of these advertisements are linked to promotional offers designed to induce the purchase of the product or to some other desired end-result. It may be achieved by creating a favourable image or mood by constant campaigning or by urging an immediate response. It may also be done by offering a product at a nominal price within a limited time-period. Some companies provide incentives such as coupons to their buyers. These days, companies promote special deals such as free hotel accommodation for a package tour and five years' subscription at four years' price. Perhaps, advertisements that offer 'sale until stocks last' gain the maximum attention. Many companies offer free products with some items. Figure 14.9 shows an advertisement where the customer is urged to buy a product by offering freebies. Despite the fact that most people think that the sale price is first escalated and then reduced, more and more people respond to 'sale' advertisements than to awareness advertisements of the same product range. Sometimes, service providers advertise tax benefits to encourage taxpayers to choose their services.

Encouraging the target audience to participate in competitions and games is another time-tested method to promote a product. Similarly, comparative advertisements create a lot of interest because they compare their rivals' attributes with their own.

Figure 14.9 Advertisement promoting sales by offering free products

Some advertisers attach a sample of their product with the advertisement. For example, free shampoo and face cream sachets are often enclosed with magazines with a large base of female readers.

Creative designers at times pave the way for action by providing necessary information on when and how the product can be purchased, or by providing a map to locate the particular sales point. A sample of the gift offered, in visual or written form, at an appropriate place in the advertisement also helps.

VISUALIZATION

The creative process begins with visualization. It provides a mental picture of the advertisement. The art director and the copywriter discuss the visualization process. During this stage, different ideas are collected before translating them into visuals. The idea may be put forward by any member of the team that is handling the advertisement—artist, copywriter, or the accounts executive.

Even though an artist is adept at drawing and painting, he/she may not possess problem-solving skills. Artists with creative imagination and problem-solving skills have an advantage during visualization and often rise to the position of art directors.

In retail advertising, the advertiser or client himself/herself visualizes the advertisement and takes the help of artists and other professionals to execute the job.

The visualization process starts by noting the different issues on a big-size flip sheet or whiteboard. The problems are then shortlisted. Next, appropriate suggestions for headlines are invited. This is usually followed by the visual. The visual may come first and the copy may be finalized later. There is no particular visualization approach that is considered the best. The copy chief suggests the headline and the art director suggests the visual. All these ideas are noted on the flip sheet or board. These ideas are then thrown open for discussion. Each member of the team is free to appreciate or criticize and react to the ideas until the team comes closer to the desired goal.

Visualization may be a group effort or an individual work. In the group situation, it is termed as a brain-storming session, in which each individual throws up ideas that stimulate the minds of the others. Ideas beget ideas. This encourages the members to come out with better and more effective ideas. The various ideas are then shared by the group. The group finalizes a composite idea to solve the problem. Some advertisers rely on an individual's talent. Some creative people also feel comfortable working alone or only with professionals who will translate their ideas into an advertisement. In an advertising agency, such individuals are called visualizers.

A visualizer, either as an individual or as a member of a group, must be creative. In advertising, a truly creative person is one who has the habit of reading, a knack of observation, patience to listen, and eagerness for research.

DESIGN EXECUTION

An advertising design must be visually appealing. This helps in achieving the advertisement's goal of making the potential customer buy the product or accept the advertiser's viewpoint. Since an advertisement is usually limited to a single page or less, the design syntax must be effectively used to convey the intended message to the target audience. Thumbnail sketches are the best starting point for a design. The best thumbnail sketch should be selected to develop a rough layout. The degree of finish of the rough is dependent on the client's demand and the designer's skills. The accepted layout must be converted into camera-ready artwork or digital image.

Technicalities apart, while handling the design elements for an advertisement, some points should be borne in mind. The designer should identify the design elements, select effective illustrations, making the headlines and copy harmonious, develop a presentable layout, and fit the layout within the limitations of production.

Identifying Design Elements

Headlines, illustrations, copy blocks, logos, colours, and white spaces are some design elements used in an advertisement. Visuals, headlines, logos, and trade names are considered to be the major elements while the others are called sub-elements. Figure 14.10 displays some elements used in a typical advertisement. Copy block refers to the portion of grey mass formed by the text type in an advertisement. Each design element serves a different function in design. These elements are also visually different from one another in their size, tone, texture, and edges. They may be very distinctive, separated clearly by background space, or subtle and vague, with various tones merging with one another.

328 *Art and Print Production*

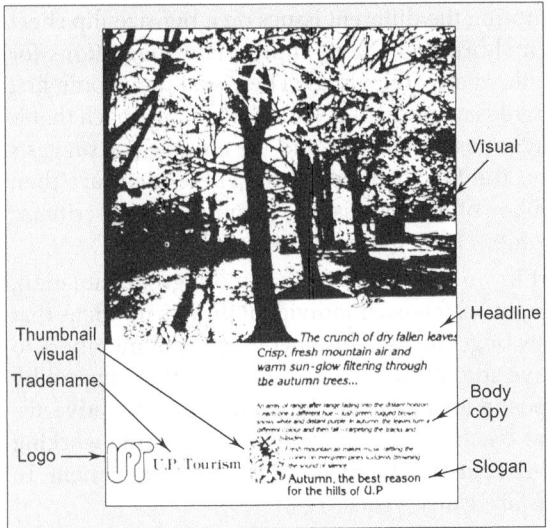

Figure 14.10 Elements of a typical advertisement

The design elements should be selected according to their proportions in terms of size, shape, and tone. The proportion of elements is manipulated by placing two or more elements together in relation to the total size of an advertisement or by placing an individual element in different proportions of length and breadth. This develops a relationship of size and strength between one element and the other or the design as a whole. On the basis of proportion, the reader decides which element of the advertisement to read first, which one to read next, and which one to skip.

Selecting Effective Illustrations

An illustration is a predominant display element and the single most memorable feature in most advertisements. Besides attracting attention, it creates the desired mood. There is always a great deal of discussion in the advertising industry about the relative merits of illustrations such as hand-drawn pictures, photographs, and computer-generated images. However, no consensus regarding this issue has emerged so far. The selection of the style of visual is based on the designer's personal taste and the objective of the advertising message.

Hand-drawn illustrations offer the maximum variety of styles and provide the greatest freedom to experiment. However, they need an illustrator's diversified skills and talents. Simple line drawings with pen or brush with tone and colour can be enhanced using an artist's imagination. Line drawings are well suited for designs that are to be printed on coarse grain paper or for certain printing processes such as silk-screen printing.

Most advertisements are printed using the offset process. It can print fine-screen halftones even on ordinary paper like newsprint, thus creating near-original reproductions. It also helps the designer show minute details and authentic realism in form and colour. The content can also be dramatized by using various physical alteration techniques such as cut-out, vignette, superimposition, and special screen.

Illustrations can be generated on the computer by using suitable graphic programs. Alternatively, an illustration can be drawn or photographed and transferred to a computer using a scanner. The scanner, with the help of the available software, can be used to retouch or manipulate the illustration in accordance with the designer's imagination.

Whatever may be the technique adopted to develop an illustration, the advertisement's appeal lies in the integration of the content with the illustration. This can be achieved by engaging the target audience in different moods of nostalgia, emotion, humour, incongruousness, etc.

Creating Harmony in Headlines and Copy

The headline identifies the target audience and tries to involve them further. It serves its function not only with forceful language but also with an appropriate type style and an imaginative arrangement.

A big-size and bold typeface is used for advertisements hard-selling a product. A dominant type style is especially appropriate when the advertising content asks the prospects to take action by offering a benefit or a piece of advice, or by providing news and information.

A type style that is harmonious with the other elements of the design should be selected. An ornamentally illustrated advertisement calls for a fancy headline, whereas an advertisement for computer hardware requires a lineal modern face. The headline for cosmetic products may look as delicate as the product itself. Many advertisements provide a personal touch by using script or cursive type style. Copy-heavy advertisements need division of text block and appropriate headings that can enable the advertisement to stand out within the limited available space. Figure 14.11 shows how text blocks and reverse types can make a copy-heavy advertisement stand out.

Playful and gimmicky headlines with a manipulated type style provoke curiosity and induce the reader to read the text for further information. Headlines covering an event or incident, on the other hand, are usually straightforward and follow the style of news stories.

Some advertisements may be designed without headlines, in case the product's packaging serves the purpose. This kind of advertisement gives the feeling that the message on the label is too obvious to be stated in a headline. There may be exceptions in cases where the advertisement functions as a reminder.

Figure 14.11 Simple text blocks and reverse types

In case of an appeal headline, the approach should be sober and subtle both in terms of content and physical form. A small-size type surrounded by empty space, all letters in lower case, tint or thin letters, and a common face style like classical Roman or lineal can create the desired image.

There is always an argument on whether to choose short headlines or long headlines. A short headline, if it can say enough, is ideal. The short headline can be placed strategically in the advertisement so that it stands out. Long headlines should be broken into the main headline and sub-headlines.

Setting the format and placing the headline in the advertisement are dependent on two elements—(i) elements of the design, and (ii) the nature of the advertisement. Centre settings are very formal and are used with a formal design and a justified copy. Flush left is a common setting and is used with an informal design. Ragged left setting is comparatively dull. It should be used in balance with other elements. If used imaginatively, a free setting can lead to dynamic advertising effects.

The physical appearance of the headline composition is quite often a function of the arrangement of lines and the division of phrases. To accentuate and enhance the meaning of an advertisement's message, the headline words should be grouped logically.

The copy follows the headline and elaborates the message which has been communicated in the headline in brief or shown in the visual. Like the headline, the copy can also be informative, narrative, gimmicky, emotional, appealing, or factual. The copy may be very short or very long. The style selected should be in harmony with the headline and other elements of the design. The legibility of the composition should be an important consideration. It should be kept in mind that, 'When we see a headline, we see letters; when we see the copy, we see words.' The text copy should be separated from the headline. The text should be broken down into units, with the initial word(s) in bigger type, bold face, or tint/colour.

Developing a Layout Style

All the material that is to be displayed, whether it is in the form of visuals, written text, or just scribbled text, should be collected. A style that helps to place the elements logically should be developed. The most commonly used style is the *advertising space grid*. The space is divided into subtle forms of rectangles. This helps one to allocate the graphic elements in unity.

Another style is the *grouping of elements*. Here, all the white space with the elements is thrown on the border, thus giving the elements a composite shape or a silhouette.

A good *silhouette style* provides an identity to each element despite its grouping and overlapping.

A white or coloured border around the elements makes a *frame* and becomes a style. The style makes the elements stand out. It also separates the advertisement from the other advertisements when printed in a newspaper.

Aligning headlines or any verbal copy with an interesting or precise part of the visual or copy is another layout style. Here the visual and the headline complement each other. The reader is first directed to the starting-point of the advertisement and then to the other elements. This helps him/her to read and understand the advertisement's message.

A *rhythmic style* can be obtained by repeating some elements that have homogeneous characteristics in terms of shape, tone, and colour. It is ideal when the number of elements to be handled carries a uniform weight. Rhythm allows the eye to move to other elements after the initial fixation on one element.

If different products of the same manufacturer are displayed in a single advertisement, it may look cluttered. Yet, this serves the purpose of a shop window. This style of layout may be made distinctive by occasional graphics, colour tint, etc. An effort should be made to list the products in a sequence. For the purpose of contrast, one of the products may be allowed to stand out prominently.

The space bought for the advertisement may not be filled with all the elements. A simple style using generous white space, a few type styles, and regular shapes makes the advertisement easier to read.

Ornamental styles are used in certain types of advertisements. Hotels, restaurants, fast food giants, jewellery brands, toys and handicraft shops, etc. often use fancy type styles, ornamental elements, and a complementary colour scheme.

A style can even be developed by typography. This layout style consists of only copy with a subdued headline, accompanied by a small picture for the message. It also consists of a headline with minimum copy. A big-size headline serves the purpose of a picture. Hence, this type of layout is often termed as the poster layout.

Design elements, when arranged in sequence with each one explaining something to provide a story, is called a *storyboard style*. This style sometimes looks like a comic strip with dialogue balloons or a brief text in each frame.

A *bleed* advertising style refers to a photograph or advertisement content running across the page. This style of advertisement helps in attracting extra attention. Since the border is absent, it often provides a feel of a visual's continuity.

Many hard-sell advertisements use the gimmicky style with manipulated types, reverse blocks, and sunbursts. All these are capable of arresting the viewer's attention. If not used in proper proportions, they will divert the viewers' attention to something else.

Figure 14.12 shows some layout styles for advertisements.

Making the Layout Presentable

Whatever may be the idea or style adopted to develop a layout, it must be acceptable to the client. Therefore, the only real criterion regarding the standard of presentation is effective communication of the advertisement. For many clients, a photograph, an illustration, a roughly drawn headline, or copy block separated by parallel or simulated lines is sufficient. Some clients or senior executives may expect the layout to be finished to the extent that it can be easily evaluated and discussed in the context of the proposed idea in the form of a visual. Some clients, especially those who invest a good deal of money in developing a campaign, demand layouts that are as polished as printed advertisements.

Not long ago, illustrations were drawn and photographs were copied by a fine artist. A finishing artist used to draw the headline and other elements. For a very finished or comprehensive layout, the duly finished actual photograph was pasted on the layout. The headline and copy were pasted after typesetting. Bromide prints for the logo and the elements were taken and a lot of cutting and pasting was involved in making a

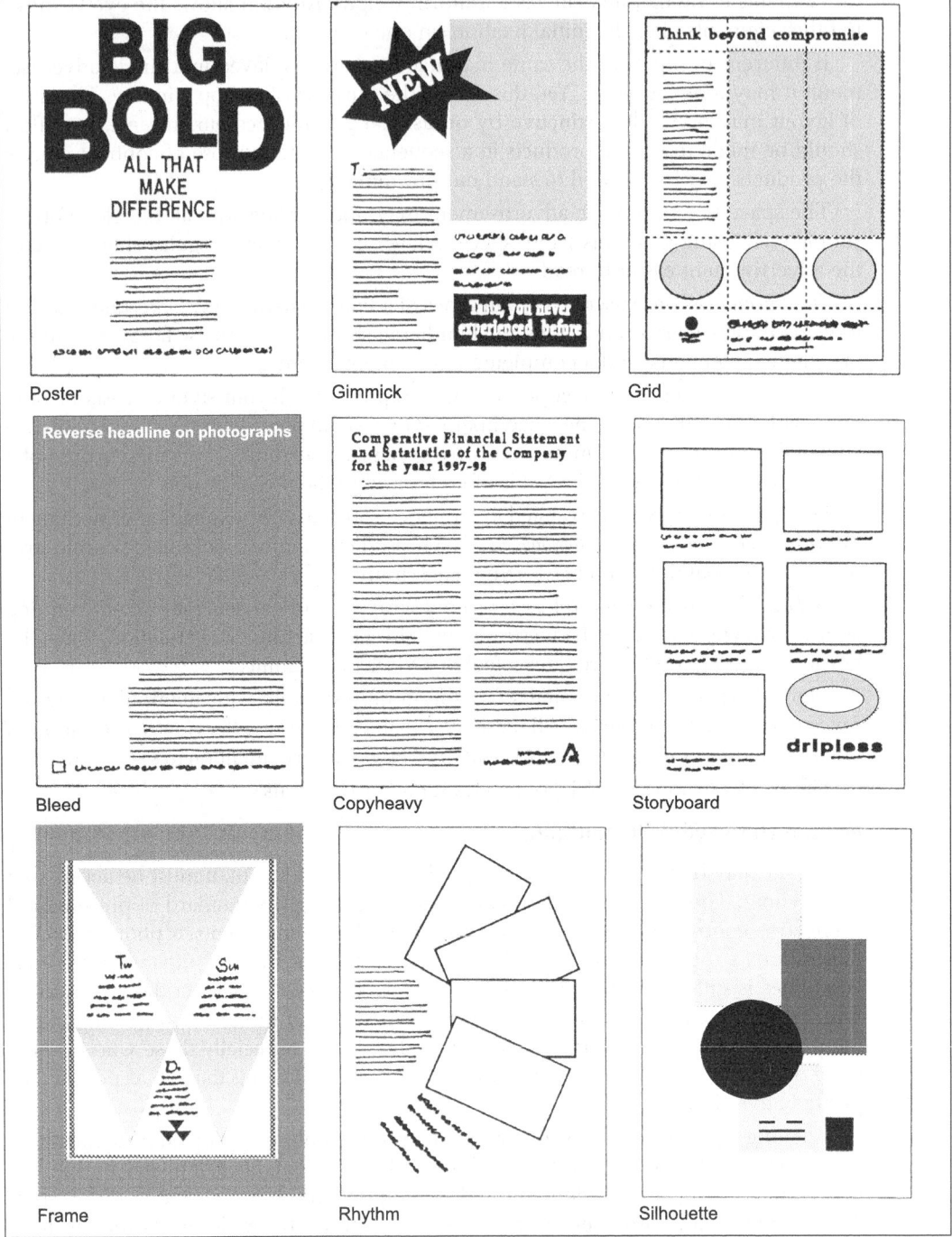

Figure 14.12 Some layout styles

layout. Today, the presentation of the layout has become a sophisticated process. The whole layout is done in a digitized form. The client receives the layout in a CD or through e-mail. This leads to shorter lead times as an addition or alteration suggested by the client can be carried out without wasting time.

The traditional form of presentation has not been eliminated. Thanks to modern technology, even a very rough layout now comes close to a comprehensive one. The layout can be pasted on a chromoboard or ivory card. A tracing flap helps in protecting it from dust or scratches. A colour pastel paper cover always gives the layout a professional look and protects it from handling hazards.

In case the advertisements are part of a campaign, they should be presented using PowerPoint. Digital images can create a greater impact in case a compatible PC terminal is available at the place of presentation. A portable image-magnifying system can be used when the presentation is meant for a larger audience.

Fitting the Layout within the Production Limitations

A creative idea may be well executed and may look excellent, but unless it fits into the mechanical limitations of the printing process, it will lack effectiveness. Mechanical limitations refer to the adaptability of the content to the machine and the process camera, electronic scanner, printing process, paper type, etc.

Therefore, the layout for this purpose must be handled by a trained artist with considerable knowledge of printing and its limitations. Conventionally known as artwork, it is drawn on a white paper by black ink lines for the area that is to be filled with colour. The area for the illustration is demarcated. The illustration may be supplied separately after due cropping and scaling. It is important to supply the rough layout or comprehensive with the artwork.

Electronic page planning is a recent development in layout for printers. Here, both the line and the halftone elements can be scanned and stored in digital form. This information can be used to create a complete advertisement. All these machines have a colour monitor. This helps the operator or layout person to assess the layout and colour before converting it into a film positive.

Computers can generate graphics or manipulate scanned images, which are integrated with types brought from the source of the system. It is important for designers to know about various software programs for designing and to have a working knowledge of computers.

An effective design and layout is an integral part of an advertisement. If it can arrest the attention of the viewer, half the battle is won!

SUMMARY

Advertising design is one of the most challenging tasks faced by graphic designers. There is stiff competition in the field of advertising, and media buying costs are very high. Designers thus need to create advertisements that can effectively convey the desired message and stand out in the clutter.

Some advertisements do not urge the viewers to make an immediate purchase but create a mood that involves attention, interest, and desire. The mood is created by a series of advertisements in print, often supported by other media. This is known as an advertising campaign. A campaign makes a viewer see more than one unit of a series and helps him/her to remember the earlier unit that was similar to the present one. The designs of all the advertisements in a campaign should be similar in character or style, but they should have a distinctive identity when viewed in isolation.

For success in designing advertisements, the creative team should understand the advertiser's objectives and also get a clear briefing based on research findings. All this information facilitates the creative team to develop a strategy to attract the target audience to the advertisement. This strategy may consist of an offer of benefits, an emotional appeal, or a psychological feeling. No advertising strategy can succeed without a creative touch that is unique and original in terms of art and ideas. In the case of advertising, no art or the idea is considered creative, unless it sells a product or an idea.

The creative task of an advertisement is not the idea of a single individual. A creative team consisting of a copywriter and a design artist work on the task. Despite being separate entities and working under two units, their work is highly interrelated and interdependent.

The creative process begins with visualization, which is basically a mental picture of the advertisement's message. It may be developed by a group or through individual effort. Any individual with creative ideas can visualize an advertisement.

While developing content, an effort should be made to attract the target audience by creating a visual appeal with imaginative images and effective headlines. The advertisement may strive to hold the attention of the target audience by appealing to the readers' needs. Developing a design is the third step. A design aims at motivating the customers to acquire a product, know more about it, or endorse an idea. With a view to facilitate action, the design may create a favourable mood or image by offering product coupons, discounts, free gifts, etc.

Some important points should be borne in mind while handling a design. The first step is to identify design elements such as headlines, illustrations, and copy block by sizing, shaping, and toning in subtle proportions. Next, the design elements are placed on a given area based on design syntax. A particular illustration or image can be used as a predominant display element. The headlines should convey the message of an advertisement in a powerful language backed by type styles and imaginative arrangement styles. The style may be grid, grouping, bleed, shop window, rhythm, simple, luxurious, typographical, etc. Style not only facilitates the logical placement of elements but also identifies the mood of the advertisement. An advertisement in the finished form should be used to sell the design to the client. For production purposes, the approved layout needs to be converted into artwork.

KEY TERMS

Advertising Campaign A series of advertisements having homogeneous characteristics. It strives to reach the largest target audience through different media.

Advertising Strategy A well-defined strategy that uses creative thought and unique presentation to influence the target audience.

Appeal An approach adopted by the creative team to communicate a message that establishes a physical or emotional rapport with the target audience.

Art Director An advertising executive responsible for visual presentation of an advertisement. He/she works with the copywriter and visualizer at the concept level.

Brainstorming A technique in which people work together on a problem, collect ideas from everybody, and finally narrow down to one 'big idea'.

Campaign Planning An organized and careful planning for advertising that targets the potential customer through different channels of communication (media).

Copy Block The portion of grey mass formed by the text type in an advertisement.

Design Brief A document that expresses the scope of work and desired objectives as required by the client. It helps an advertising agency or design firm to understand the client's project needs.

Display Element Picture, type, or any other graphic shape that is clearly visible in a design.

Media Planning It encompasses all decisions related to the timing and placement of advertising. This includes the selection of media and the frequency of the advertisement or the campaign.

Retail Advertising Advertising which promotes the goods/services of local merchandisers. Also referred to as local advertising, these advertisements are not part of a campaign.

Sunburst A design element representing the sun and its rays.

Visualization The process of forming a mental picture. It can be a picture, design, or representation of an object or idea.

REFERENCES

Baker, Stephen 1979, *Systematic Approach of Advertising Creativity*, McGraw-Hill, London, UK.

Banerjee, Subrata 1996, *Advertising as a Career*, National Book Trust, India.

Chunawalla, S.A. 2003, *Advertising—An Introductory Text*, Himalaya Publishing House, Mumbai.

Conover, Theodore E. 1990, *Graphic Communication Today*, West Publishing Company, St. Paul, USA.

Evans, Robin B. 1992, *Production and Creativity in Advertising*, Wheeler Publishing, India.

Jewler, A. Jerome and Bonnie L. Drewniny 2001, *Creative Strategy in Advertising*, Wadsworth/Thomson Learning, USA.

Mathur, U.C. 2002, *Advertising Management*, New Age International (P) Ltd, New Delhi.

Nelson, Roy Paul 1989, *The Design of Advertising*, William C. Brown Publishers, USA.

Ray, Murray 1977, FSIAD, *Designers and Art Directors' Manual of Technique*, Business Books, London, UK.

Rege, C.M. 1984, *Advertising Art and Ideas*, Ashutosh Prakashan, Mumbai.

Schlemmer, Richard M. 1990, *Handbook of Advertising Art and Production*, Prentice Hall, New Jersey, USA.

REVIEW QUESTIONS

1. What role do graphics play in communicating the advertising message?
2. Advertising graphics is considered more challenging in comparison to other media graphics. Why?
3. Explain the terms—design brief and advertising appeal. What is the relationship between the two? Support your answer with appropriate visuals.
4. What does advertising creativity mean?
5. How is advertising strategy linked to creative thinking?
6. What do you understand by an advertising campaign? Explain the role of the creative team in developing a campaign.
7. The idea is the key in the visualization process. Explain.
8. Design an advertisement for a premium suiting brand based on the idea 'he stood like a rock'. Design this advertisement in comparison with a similar product.
9. Headline, illustration, copy block, colour, and white space are the design elements of an advertisement. How are these handled while executing a design?
10. An advertisement's layout style is used to attract readers. Mention some of the commonly used styles and the design effects created by using them.
11. Why should the creative team take the production aspect of advertisements seriously? Explain the technicalities involved in producing an advertisement.

PROJECTS

1. Buy a spiral bound sketch book containing 32 pages (approximately 16" × 11" in size). Collect a recently published press advertisement of your choice. Paste it on the left page of the sketch book. Write a few lines about the advertisement under the sub-heads—source, target audience, communication objective, advertising objective, and creative idea. Appreciate or criticize the design in relation to these factors. Do this exercise every week by collecting a new advertisement. Prepare a comparative report at the end of the month and judge the improvement in your ability to appreciate design.

2. Collect three to four print advertisements of an advertising campaign. Analyse the visuals, headline, copy block, and colour in each advertisement. Mention the similarities of the advertisements in terms of content and design style. According to you, what effect will the advertisement have among the prospective target audience?

3. Find an advertisement, which, according to you, is poorly executed. Note down the areas that have scope of improvement. Make an alternative rough and compare it with the original. Write your views against each point noted earlier.

4. Make a series of three advertisements for a mobile phone company that wants to expand its market among the rural audience. Involve some of your classmates in this exercise. Conduct research on product features, objectives of the advertising message, and characteristics of the target audience. Organize a brainstorming session and get ideas from everybody. Once you have agreed on a solution, translate the idea into a visual form and prepare a note.

5. Take a day out of class and collect advertisements from various sources. Prepare the list of advertisements (social, lifestyle, image building, product, etc.). See the list after a week and note why some advertisements are still vivid in your mind and others are not. Write a brief note on their positive qualities.

CHAPTER

15 Identity Design

Learning Objectives

After reading this chapter, you should be able to
- understand the significance of identity marks
- describe various types of identity marks
- look at symbolism in India and study its influence in modern identity mark designing
- discuss the effect of colour symbolism and language and culture on identity mark designing
- look at some basic symbols that are commonly used in identity marks
- describe the rules and procedures for creating an identity mark
- understand how effective identity marks can be created

INTRODUCTION

Human beings have devised various names, signs, and symbols to identify the multitude of objects in the world. The world would be a chaotic place if we did not have ways to create a distinct identity for various people, species, concepts, ideas, etc. For example, it would be difficult for us to call everyone at our workplace by gestures if we didn't know their names. Similarly, it would be impossible for us to convey to a motorist that there is a school ahead and hence he/she should drive carefully, if there were no traffic signals to indicate the same.

Names are one of the most commonly used ways of identifying a person or object. Every human being has a name for identification. In early childhood, the name is used primarily to differentiate one child from the other. The same name becomes a part of one's consciousness when he/she realizes his/her separate identity. One soon starts feeling attached to his/her name, and feels proud of it, protecting if from distortion and attempting to make it distinctive and identifiable.

Names are used not only for human beings but also other things in the world, such as animals, birds, trees, groups, and organizations. Any thing or idea, however abstract, has a name. These names have been coined by human beings for ease of identification and communication. Thus, names can be thought of as codes of communication.

The practice of identifying codes through visual form has been in existence for centuries. In fact, psychologists and scholars feel that the roots of identity codes in non-verbal communication are embedded in primitive thinking, when human beings in early society became aware of themselves and their relations with others. Human beings' quest for communication brought into being verbal identity codes such as linguistic signs. Today, a mark of any kind, verbal or visual, has a far deeper significance than ever before. By itself, it takes on a special meaning with the power of communication.

A wide variety of signs, visual concepts, and codes exist in all walks of life in the form of letters, names, logos, trademarks, etc. This wealth of signs and visual concepts and their forms and content is being abundantly used in the field of design and communication. New ways of symbolic expression of old ideas are also being devised by contemporary identity designers. These symbols strike people at a deep, sub-conscious level. They help us not only in identifying objects but also in understanding them.

IDENTITY MARKS

A discussion on identity codes and symbols brings to the fore several terms. For a layperson, they may not differ much from one another, but the differences need to be understood clearly by those who are involved in creating and using such identity marks.

Sign

A sign is a conventional or arbitrary mark, seen and felt mostly by its surface character. Musical notations, road signs, mathematical signs, and motions or gestures to convey an idea are some common examples of signs used in our day-to-day lives. Indications of a change of weather or change in health conditions are some examples of signs that are felt. These are means of expressing what we *feel*, and no logical and conditional statements can be made about them.

The concept of a sign can be understood by considering the letters of an alphabet. Each letter is a sign and its name and meaning are accepted by people on the basis of an agreement between the type designer and the type user. Since letters in a group convey a meaning and impose a logical order, they are termed as verbal signs. Besides these, non-verbal signs can also exist for a group or groups of words and convey a complete message. Figure 15.1 shows a few non-verbal signs.

Letters arranged in a sequence provide a linear progression of ideas. Ideograms in the Chinese and Japanese languages are an exception to this. Accepted signs can cross the barriers of language and literacy.

Symbol

A symbol is a two- or three-dimensional object that represents an idea, concept, or abstraction. Symbols may have roots in the past, and they always have some meaning. For instance, a lamp is a symbol of life, glass symbolizes fragility, and a flower symbolizes happiness. Hands joined to form a *namastey*, elephants, peacocks, and the Swastika represent the

Figure 15.1 Non-verbal signs

Identity Design   339

unique cultural ethos of India. A dove is the universal symbol of peace, and a red cross symbolizes care of the sick. Figure 15.2 shows some commonly accepted symbols.

Figure 15.2   Commonly used symbols

Trademark

A trademark is a symbol, figure, word, or mark adopted and used by a manufacturer or merchant in order to designate his/her goods and to distinguish them from other such goods. It is usually registered with a government agency to ensure its exclusive use by the owner.

A trademark indicates the origin of a product, provides a constant guarantee, and also serves as an advertisement in miniature form. It tells the prospective buyer that the product is the same as an earlier unit bought and presumably enjoyed. Sometimes, the logo and the trademark work together for an identity mark, representing both the product and the company. As shown in Figure 15.3, Bata, Godrej, and Escorts are some such examples.

Figure 15.3   Trademarks

Trade Name

A trade name is a word or a phrase used in a trade to designate a business or a particular class of goods. In other words, it is the name or style under which a firm does its business. Hindustan Unilever Ltd, Colgate-Palmolive, and Steel Authority of India Ltd are trade names. The company ED Parry manufactures different products but does business on the product line of sanitaryware under the trade name of Parryware. Some examples of trade names are shown in Figure 15.4.

Logo

The word *logo* is derived from the Greek word *logos*, meaning a word or speech. If we stick to the dictionary meaning, the word *logotype* will be much more appropriate to describe a group of letters that is cast in one piece, stands for an organization, and is used in advertisements, publicity material, etc.

punjab national bank

Life Insurance Corporation of India

Hindustan Unilever Limited

Figure 15.4   Trade names

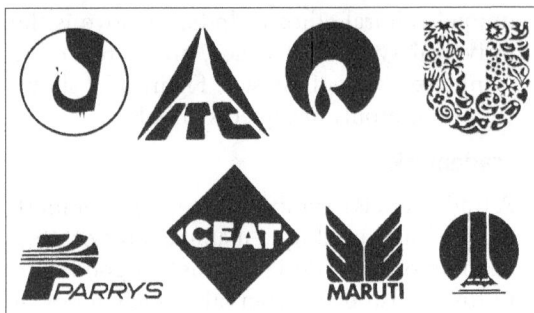

Figure 15.5 Logos

Figure 15.6 Brand names

Semantics apart, the word 'logo' today is no longer esoteric, nor is it restricted to the jargon of marketing and advertising parlance. Logos have been adopted as a means for creating brand recognition and corporate image. Figure 15.5 shows the logos of some well-known organizations.

Brand Name

A brand comprises all the symbols and information connected to a specific product or service, and creates expectations and associations around the same. A brand name is made up of the linguistic elements of a brand. It is meant to distinguish a product or service from a competitor's product or service. Some common examples are Lifebuoy, Liril, Pepsodent, Lakmé, and Sunsilk—brand names sold by Hindustan Unilever Ltd (formerly Hindustan Lever Ltd); and Power, North Star, and Ambassador—brand names sold by Bata India Ltd. Occasionally, a brand name and trade name become the same, that is, the company or the manufacturer and its products are identified by the same name. One such example is Godrej, whose products carry the same brand name as the trade name despite the fact that Godrej manufactures goods in different product lines. Figure 15.6 shows some examples of brand names.

For a company or a product, the trademark and the brand may not differ much as identification and communication devices. The major difference lies in the legal connotations. The Consumer Protection Act 1986 of the Government of India protects logos, brands, trademarks, and colour schemes against infringement. An unprotected brand name may be protected by the registered trademark or the logo of a company.

Other Identity Marks

Some other identity marks used to identify distinct objects, concepts, and ideas are service marks, collective marks, certification marks, emblems, insignia, crests, mascots, etc. We shall now discuss these marks briefly.

Organizations such as educational institutions, insurance companies, hospitals, and hotels offer services to the people. Therefore, the marks used by them are technically *service marks*. The marks used by organizations such as the Public Relations Society of India, the Association of Advertising Professionals, or the All India Federation of Master Printers are called *collective marks*, because members of these organizations work together to promote and develop the aims and objectives of their

Figure 15.7 Collective marks

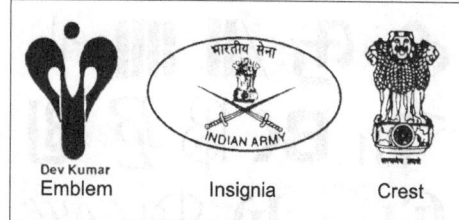

Figure 15.8 Emblem, insignia, and crest

respective organizations instead of selling a particular product. Figure 15.7 shows a few collective marks. Some marks, such as the Bureau of Indian Standards' 'ISI mark', FPO, Hallmark, Agmark, etc. give the guarantee of a standard product. They are termed *certification marks*.

An *emblem* is pictorial image, abstract or representational, that epitomizes a concept, deity, tribe, nation, virtue, or vice. The emblem designed by Sudarshan Dhir for Dev Kumar, (shown in Figure 15.8) shows the personal identity of a painter who believes in the Tantric way of life. *Insignia* is a distinguishing mark of honour and belonging. The badge of the army is an insignia; it not only identifies the troops but also becomes a representation of loyalty, pride, courage, and honour.

A *crest* means a tuft or some other natural growth on top of the head of an animal. An identity mark developed in this form is called a crest. An ideal example of a crest is the national emblem of India, in which three lions are seated back to back on an abacus in the centre. An emblem, an insignia, and a crest are shown in Figure 15.8.

A *mascot* is also known as a trade character. It may be an illustration of either a real or an imaginary figure of a person, animal, event, or object. Believed to bring good luck to business, mascots are designed as the symbol of sports events, trade fairs, etc. The Maharaja mascot of Air India, the mascot Appu for the 1982 Asian Games, and the tiger mascot for the Commonwealth Games in Delhi are some examples of popular mascots. Figure 15.9 shows some of these mascots.

Identity marks can be seen in newspapers, magazines, and personal belongings of people. The identity mark of a newspaper is the nameplate or flag. In the case of a magazine, it is the masthead. People often use monograms on their stationery and

Figure 15.9 Mascots

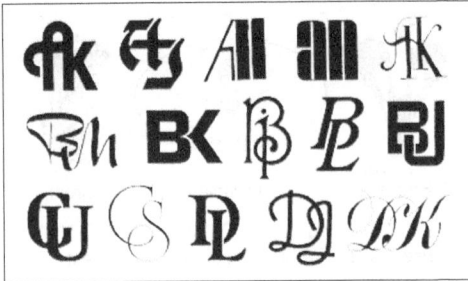

Figure 15.10 Monograms

other articles. A monogram is a mark consisting of two or more letters—generally one's initials—combined or interlaced and printed on stationery or embroidered on clothing. Figure 15.10 illustrates a few monograms.

SYMBOLISM IN INDIA

India has a rich tradition of art and cuture, which is largely based on symbolism. This is reflected in our traditional forms of dance, music, handicrafts, folk arts, and religious rituals. All these demonstrate the cultural ethos of India. An understanding of cultural elements will help us appreciate and design meaningful symbols for various purposes.

Clay craft is probably man's earliest creation and marks his coming of age. In fact, our ancient writings in moulded bricks can be traced back to the Vedic times. Symbols on earthenware found during excavations in Harappa and Mohenjodaro show the skills of people in those ancient days. Over a period of time, Indian traditions have witnessed several changes, but the art of making clay objects and their symbolism remain an integral part of our socio-cultural life. A water pot filled with water is considered a symbol of good omen and is, for that reason, indispensable in any ritual. For ceremonies and rituals, a *mangal kalash*, the sacred vessel, is a common religious symbol.

The folk art of various parts of the country help us identify the various communities they belong to. Rock paintings in caves are the earliest specimens of folk art in India. Folk art is present in all parts of India, especially in the rural regions, and is visible on various objects on the floors, walls, and objects of everyday use. Various symbols used in our daily lives today have originated from the Vedic and Tantric traditions. These symbols are usually based on the knowledge of the world around us, which were expressed in an abstract form by wise persons. Many of these symbols represent objects in the natural world, and are used to express abstract philosophical concepts. Figure 15.11 shows some common symbols used in our country.

The three shapes predominant in Indian folk art are the square, circle, and the triangle. The square represents the earth. According to scholars, it is the most stable shape. The circle is the cosmos and beyond. This symbol was derived from the circular movement of the planet. The triangle of the three worlds—the positive, negative, and the balance of apex—represents the male, whereas the inverted triangle represents the female. Combinations of these shapes are extensively used in *Tantric* art and provide different meanings. For example, one square within another symbolizes the qualities (*gunas*) of human life.

Figure 15.11 Indian symbols

Mohenjodaro seal   Mangal kalash   Folk art

Figure 15.12 Symbols of tantric faith and Islamic faith

India was invaded by several foreign rulers and some of them ruled the country for centuries. They brought their own art and culture, which got assimilated into the Indian culture over the years. Islamic rulers brought architectural designs with arches, *minars*, and domes from Persia and Central Asia. Geometric shapes became a symbol of Islamic faith, when combined with calligraphic images and arabesque figures. A few religious symbols of *Tantric* and Islamic faiths are shown in Figure 15.12.

Several religions and faiths originated in India. Their philosophy and rituals have found expression in various graphic forms. Indians have been firm believers in co-existence, be it with animals or other forms of nature. In India, a symbolic representation of the animal and nature has continued since the dawn of history. Interpretations of animals in sculpture and paintings in consonance with Buddhist philosophy have given a new dimension to art. In Buddhist symbolism, the *elephant* represents the conception of the Buddha. The *lion* is the Buddha himself. Its majestic appearance in front of temples, *mahals*, and on auspicious occasions is associated with strength and purity. King Ashoka erected his pillar with the lion at Sarnath to mark the spot where the spread of Buddhism began. The *horse* is energetic and symbolizes the solar animal, depicted as the mount of the Sun god who rides on his seven radiant horses. The *bull* shows great physical strength in astrological symbolism of the zodiac. In Hindu mythology, the bull is taken to represent justice or virtue. The *peacock*, one of the most beautiful creatures on earth, is India's national bird. It is the symbol of victory over falsehood and malice. It is also related to the performing arts for its ability to dance.

The *lotus* is our national flower. It symbolically represents life itself in ancient Indian thought. Lotus petals represent purity and spirituality. The circumference of a blooming lotus forms the shape of a wheel, which symbolizes the moving force of life. A *banyan tree* symbolizes several things to people in India. It is a symbol of shelter because people rest under it. It is also a symbol of knowledge. It is big and grows over a long period of time, symbolizing experience and wisdom. Ancient *munis* and *rishis* gave lessons to their pupils under banyan trees. The banyan tree is also a symbol of festivals. People assemble under it during various festivals. It is also worshipped in a number of religious rituals.

Agni or fire is by far the most important element of many Indian rituals. It symbolizes energy, transformation, and purification, which are vital factors in human progress.

The *swastika*, the most distinctive graphic symbol claimed to be of Indian origin, means many things to many people: the supreme deity, infinity, the sun's power, well being, the succession of generations, etc. However, its association with the Nazi holocaust has, of late, given it a sinister meaning. Figure 15.13 depicts some commonly used symbols in the Hindu faith.

The *wheel*, which stands for the cycle of birth, life, death, and rebirth, is an important Buddhist symbol. The Buddha's eight guidelines for living are represented by eight

Figure 15.13 Symbols used in Hindu faith

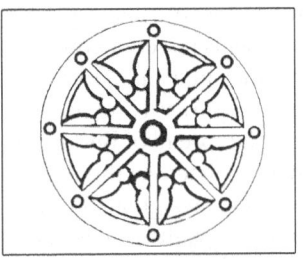

Figure 15.14 The wheel—a Budhist symbol

spokes of the wheel, as shown in Figure 15.14. These spokes radiate from the centre of a small circle. This centre represents the goal of one's thinking, feelings, and behaviour.

The *sun* is a self-luminous heavenly body. Its use in symbolic form is universal. Numerous shapes and characters based on the sun have been developed to convey various kinds of messages. Some of these are shown in Figure 15.15.

Colour Symbolism

Our response to most visual imagery is emotional and often subjective, based on human experience. Common experience confirms that colour can affect our subjective assessment of ideas and information. Selection of colours which evoke particular responses in the thoughts and feelings of various groups of people is an important element of design. Since there is no specific law of colour preferences, designers use colour in terms of its symbolism.

Despite the fact that each family of colours has negative and positive associations, the emphasis in identity mark design is almost always on the positive nature of the product or company. Before choosing a suitable colour or colour combination, the designer must have a look at the colour symbolism chart to find out if it is being used to convey the right information or feelings.

Most banks use blue for their identity programs as it symbolizes efficiency, loyalty, and security. The green of the New Delhi Municipal Council (NDMC) logo shows the organization's effort to keep the city green and pollution free. The two wings in the logo of Maruti Udyog Limited are in dark blue, which is associated with the company's engineering activities. The red logo of Ray Ban sunglasses symbolizes the passionate and active mindset of the young. Yellow is the happy colour used in combination with red for identity marks designed for children's products such as Leo toys. Many products gain added value when their identity mark is in gold or silver colour.

Figure 15.15 Symbolic form of the sun in graphic shapes

Exhibit 15.1   Colour symbolism

Red	:	vitality, excitement, courage, and enterprise
Yellow	:	sunshine, cheerfulness, radiance, and optimism
Green	:	peace, balance, prosperity, freshness, and nature
Dark green	:	tradition, reliability, and reassurance
Blue	:	coolness, vastness, truth, intellect, loyalty, security, and contemplation
Dark blue	:	industriousness, efficiency, and authority
White	:	purity, truth, peace, and virtue
Deep red	:	aristocracy
Pink	:	femininity and cosmetics
Orange	:	knowledge, civilization, luxury, and flame
Bright green	:	spring and fertility
Black	:	beauty, sophistication, and exclusiveness
Gold	:	wealth, majesticness, honour, and wisdom
Grey	:	maturity, patience, and retrospection
Brown	:	richness and fertility

There are some identity marks which use colour for its negative connotation. Red, for instance, is the symbol of danger. The red of the family planning symbol alerts the audience to the possible disadvantages of having more than two children. The skull and cross bones in red is another example of a danger symbol colouring red. Yellow suggests poison, and hence is used as an identity mark for pesticides. Exhibit 15.1 provides a comprehensive list of various colours and what they symbolize.

Effect of Language and Culture

The rich treasure of the symbols of the Indian culture notwithstanding, graphic designers have to work hard to develop the right visual concepts. As India is a multilingual society, a letterform symbol or identity mark developed in a particular language will not be understood by the other linguistic groups. In other words, the mark will have a limited audience. Roman letterform is the most acceptable language in logo designs. However, since the Devanagari letterform relates to Hindi, the official language of India, it is almost imperative to design bilingual identity marks in Roman and Devanagari letterforms for Government-controlled organizations. It is a difficult task to design bilingual logos, especially when the designer has to create harmony between the two languages along with the image, if possible.

The logo of Bharat Heavy Electricals Limited (BHEL) is an example of a bilingual logo. As shown in Figure 15.16, its Roman letters are well-structured. The graphic form of the electric spark on one of the letters is highly suggestive, throwing light on the activities of BHEL. The Devanagari letters, however, do not appear to be a part of the logo, despite the fact that an effort has been made to hold the Devanagari elements with other elements by enclosing everything within a border. In comparison, the Devanagari

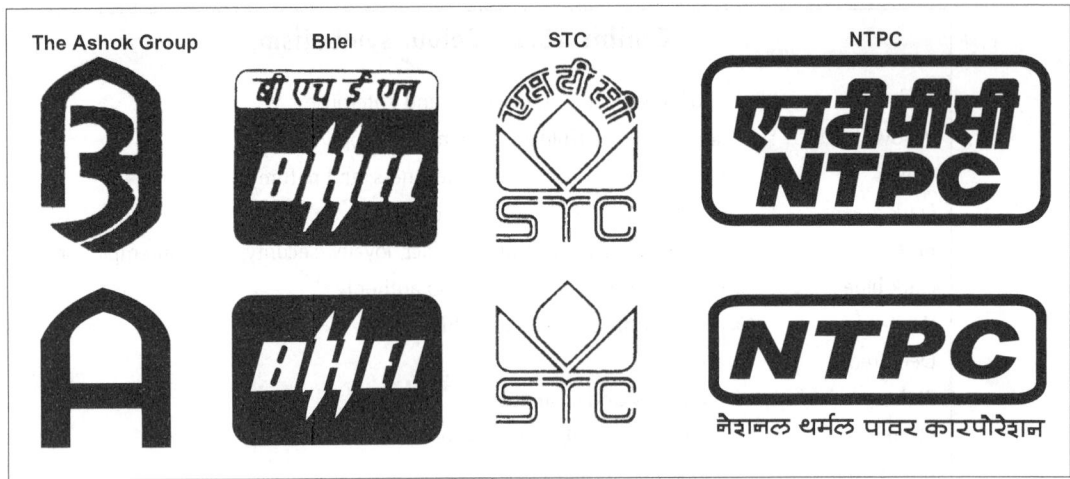

Figure 15.16 Bilingual logos

letters of the NTPC logo are harmonious with the Roman letters in terms of style and boldness.

Despite the difficulties in designing harmonious bilingual logos, some bilingual logos have been quite successful. Four such examples are shown in Figure 15.16. The Ashok group logo, designed by Shekhar Kamath, has an arch that resembles the physical appearance of the hotel building, which is full of arches. The concept of the bilingual logo for the group came in the early 1970s. The initial logo was an 'A' in the shape of an arch. The logo was redesigned by adding the first letter of the word 'Ashok' in Devanagari in a very imaginative style, maintaining the flavour of the old logo.

The logo of the State Trading Corporation (STC) is another good example. As shown in the figure, three petals of the lotus, our national flower, have been used in an interesting graphic shape accompanied by a Eurostyle double-line letterform harmonized with the Devanagari letters placed on the logo in a semi-circular shape.

Indian culture, like its language, is heterogeneous. The differences between the various streams are based largely on the diversified topography and religious faiths of the people. One should be careful while using symbols and colours in a design as ours is a country of many faiths, and a symbol or colour that may appear to be otherwise neutral may offend some religious groups if it occupies a significant place in their faith. A designer should therefore be aware of the religious connotations of various symbols and colours and use symbols that may have even a remote association with some religion with extreme care. As discussed in Chapter 6, green holds a special significance in Islamic cultures, while saffron-yellow is considered holy in Buddhist cultures. Shapes such as the swastika and the conch are associated with Hindu cultures.

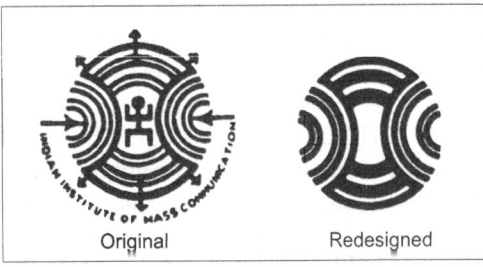

Figure 15.17 Redesigned logo of IIMC

Identity Design   347

A designer should use colours and shapes such as the ones discussed above with extreme care in corporate logo designs. Let us take up an example of a logo that had to be changed because of its symbolic significance to a religious group. The original logo of the Indian Institute of Mass Communication (IIMC), as shown in Figure 15.17, had a human figure in folk style at the centre of the design and there were two arrows pointing towards the figure, while some were going away from it. This figure had to be removed in the re-designed logo on the ground that it resembled a Hindu religious symbol.

Some symbols that may have special cultural meaning may be used in logo design after a lot of deliberation. In our country, there are many prominent logo designs that depict cultural symbols. The lion is the symbol of royalty and power. It has been adopted by the Government of India as our national emblem from the Sarnath lion capital of Emperor Ashoka. The folded hands of the Welcom-group logo depicts hands folded in a 'namastey', a typical Indian gesture denoting hospitality. Several organizations, such as the Haryana Tourism Development Corporation, the Directorate of Film Festivals, and the Vilaza Hotel, use the symbol of the peacock, the national bird of India, in their logos. The Tourism Development Corporation uses a motif style logo of an elephant adapted from the Ajanta paintings. Figure 15.8 presents the logos discussed here.

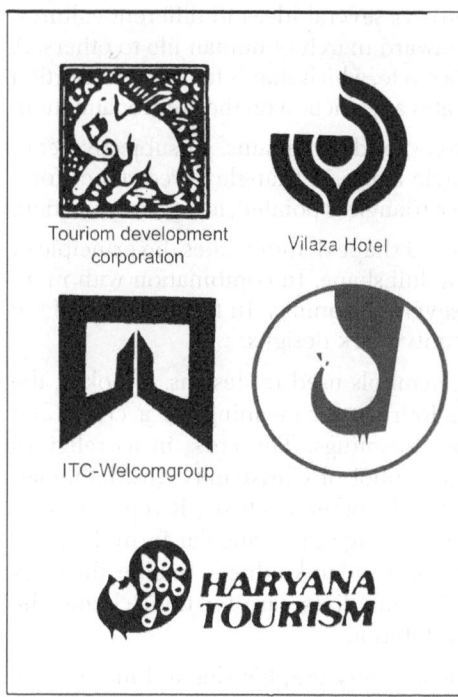

Figure 15.18   Logos based on Indian culture

BASIC SYMBOLS USED IN IDENTITY MARKS

Certain graphic symbols become basic to coded communication and represent or express certain qualities, attributes, or characteristics. Their appearance in our day-to-day life is so common that their meaning is understood and followed universally. They figure in our interpretation of complex directions and are fundamental to the understanding of any symbolic system.

Symbols may be in the form of shapes, letterforms, or images. Some symbols such as letterforms are well-defined and well-documented and become a language of communication. Some, however, are arbitrary, and lead to either ambiguous meanings.

Shapes

Shapes may be divided into three categories on the basis of their characteristics. These may be used as symbols that may convey different meanings in different contexts.

Circle   The circle is a universal sign. In our country, it is believed to be based on the ancient Indian philosophy of cyclic movement. It is patterned on the shape of the earth, the moon, the sun, and the wheel. A circle conveys several ideas in different cultures. It symbolizes life and death to some; and the onward march of human life to others. A wrong answer on an answer sheet is marked by a circle, which stands for 'zero'. A portion of visual or verbal copy marked by a circle indicates a restriction on the area for attention.

Triangle This sign represents the pyramid, trees, and mountains. In subjective connotation, a triangle shows three aspects of a single figure. A triangle in red stands for a warning, danger, and caution. When the apex of a triangle is pointed, it suggests direction.

Square The square, rectangle, or any other closed shape demonstrates the principle of inclusion or exclusion. The square by itself is a dull shape. In combination with more squares or other shapes, however, it conveys several meanings. In fact, it is one of the most widely used basic shapes for modern identity mark designs.

Cross Although the cross is one of the basic symbols used in designs, a look at the dictionary would reveal as many as three to four dozen meanings of a cross; and in combination with other words, many more meanings. The cross in its religious connotation means durability and is used as a symbol of Christianity. In Mathematics, it means addition (+) and multiplication (×). In other contexts, it represents an intersection. It is used in cancellation or as a 'wrong' sign in an angular form. It is also used negatively to contradict and to denote ill nature and unkindness. In blue, the cross symbolizes nature and agreeableness; in red it symbolizes care for the sick and the wounded. An angular red cross symbolizes prohibition.

Lines These are the most fundamental element of any graphic shape. Lines can be straight or curved, bold or light, continuous or broken. For a detailed discussion on the various effects created by using lines, students are advised to refer to the section titled 'line' in Chapter 5.

Letterforms

The letter characters chosen for an identity mark act as subtle identifiers and provide a subliminal message, conveying something that is classical or modern, industrial or pastoral, delicate or bold, and so on. *Calligraphic letterforms* are hand-written letters. In symbolic expression, calligraphy is associated with casualness, personal art and aesthetics, and a free style. Signographic letterforms are flexible and ideal for most identity mark designs. Since signographic letterforms are mainly developed in painted letters, the logo or mark may be creatively manipulated to express a specific mood or meaning. *Signographic letterforms* may be structured in various applications to form 3D logos, illuminated signs, and so on. *Typographic letterforms* are the most fundamental and well-defined verbal codes. They are available in thousands of design styles and characters. Some of them are versatile enough for all sorts of designs for communication purposes, and may be used to reflect various human emotions and moods. Exhibit 15.2 presents various attributions associated with some standard typefaces.

Modern technology has triggered off a revolution in most fields of human activity. This is true of letterform and identity mark designing too. Technology has enabled a transformation of writing from the ancient 'pictographic' form to the modern-day digital, 'compugraphic' form. Today, letters can be created in a very imaginative way. A rich variety of graphic treatments is also possible.

Identity Design **349**

Exhibit 15.2 Typefaces and their attribution

Helvetica	:	modern, straightforward, and versatile
Eurostile	:	industrial, European, and monotonal
Optima	:	elegant, soothing, corporate, and novel
Palatino	:	modern flavour with 16th century influence
Futura	:	geometric, authority and attention with bold face
Hobo	:	novel, friendly, and comical
Tiffany	:	nostalgic, delicate in light and elegant in boldface
Souvenir	:	warm, friendly, and combination of casualness with tradition
Garamond	:	classical, contemporary, with large x-height
Bodoni	:	modern and poster in boldface
Goudy	:	old style and versatile face
Avant garde	:	geometric and contemporary
Rockwell	:	industrial, corporate, and architectural
Times Roman	:	classical, familiar, and all-purpose

Images

The requirement of visual images for identity mark designs is somewhat different from that for graphic communication material. A mark or symbol condenses or compresses meaning and represents that meaning in a simple graphic image. The visual image gets integrated within a mark to imply a much larger message or to connote a particular style or association. Sometimes, commissioning the illustrative part of the identity mark design to an illustrator or a photographer may not yield the desired result. In case an illustration is commissioned to a specialist, the designer should be allowed to alter it to suit his or her requirements. Most designers depend on their reference manual or scrapbook as well as their own skills.

A wide range of books and catalogues with graphic symbols, borders, and motifs are available in the market. These can be traced, photocopied, or scanned for use in

Figure 15.19 Graphic symbols: clip art and motifs

Figure 15.20 Use of images to reflect a thought

logo designs. There is no copyright protection against the use of such symbols. Clip art is another source of copyright-free image available in software programs and on the Web. There are thousands of such designs and motifs that can become strong identity marks, and some of these are presented in Figure 15.19. However, if these motifs and designs are not used creatively, the logos may be deficient in quality and originality.

Some images are widely used in our communication material as well as in identity mark designs. These images have some obvious reference to a specific object, activity, or thought. Their use has become so common that they are termed as symbols. A list of such image symbols is presented in Exhibit 15.3. These images enable a viewer to recognize something at a glance. Any verbal explanation is then just superfluous. For instance, the crown on the logo type Elpar, as shown in Figure 15.20, clearly conveys the fact that the product has a royal or majestic touch. Similarly, a silhouette glass peg on a package indicates that the product inside the pack is breakable and should, therefore, be handled with care.

Exhibit 15.3 Image symbols

Pigeon	:	messenger and peace
Anchor	:	stability, security, and hope
Rose	:	beauty, romance, fragrance, promising, and optimistic
Glass	:	fragile, breakable, and transparent
Umbrella	:	shelter, protection, and upright
Vulture	:	rapacious and famine
Dog	:	faithful, vigilant, and neglect
Eagle	:	sharp eyesight and strength
Garland	:	respect and wedlock
Horse	:	energy, speed, and obedience
Tortoise	:	slow speed and long-lasting life
Feather	:	light weight, grace, and glory
Fist	:	show of strength and fighting
Heart	:	love, affection, friendly, pleasing, and gratifying
Diamond	:	precious and rhomboid figure
Flower	:	happiness, blossom, and ornamentation
Fruit	:	productive, enjoyment, and hope
Fox	:	cunning and perplexity
Skull & cross bones	:	danger, death, and poison

CREATING AN IDENTITY MARK

As discussed earlier, identity marks may be in the form of signs, symbols, trademarks, logos, brand names, etc. As the design approach for most of these marks is similar, we shall discuss the designing of one of these marks, logos, in detail in this section.

The simplicity of a logo may make one feel that designing a logo would be a simple job for a skilled designer. On the contrary, it requires much more than just graphic skills. The logo should look aesthetically pleasing and, at the same time, express a lot with the limited graphic elements. It is more difficult to design an identity mark than to create a full-fledged advertisement or promotional literature. Moreover, the mark or logo should not irritate the viewer with repeated exposure over a long period. All this notwithstanding, the logo is considered an advertisement of the company or product in miniature. Therefore, in creating a logo, one should follow all the rules and procedures of an advertisement or ad campaign. These rules and procedures are: (i) conducting intensive research, (ii) developing a design brief, (iii) designing a creative concept, (iv) presenting the solution and justifying it, (v) implementing the chosen solution, and (vi) changing the logo and redesigning, if required.

Research

The research work may start with a study of the company and its business information—how it operates, what products/services it offers, etc. The research should also include information on competitors, the company's areas of activity, and a description of its target market and consumer profile so that the designer knows how to create an identity that appeals to them. The company's publications, both present and past, may be of great help to the designer in his/her research. Information regarding the company is provided by the client, either in response to the designer's questions or at their own initiative.

Design Brief

The client is the source of information for the designer. In order to develop a design brief, the designer needs to question the client about relevant issues. The design brief acts as the basis for the creative work for the logo design. The brief can yield several creative design options, but these need to be narrowed down by asking the following simple questions:
- What form of visual image would identify with the organization or its product/service?
- Can it be developed with minimal graphic elements?
- What style and ideas can be tried to make the mark or logo distinctive?
- Can it be enlarged or reduced without loss of its basic characteristics?
- Is it contemporary enough and could it become outdated in the near future?
- Is it flexible enough to be adapted to other than a two-dimensional surface?
- Can it be legally protected?

Creative Concept

This initial approach of a designer is to try out several thumbnail alternatives on a tracing pad or on ordinary paper with a sketch pen or 4B pencil. The best design will, however, emerge only on getting satisfactory answers to the questions posed earlier.

Thumbnails The initial sketches of the logo may be in the form of thumbnails, which may contain types and colour, besides the chosen symbol(s). We shall discuss these elements here. The first few sketches of the designer may be based on the various activities of the company. These may be narrowed down to a handful as the designer progresses. For creating the logo sketches, the designer may combine symbols of more than one activity if he/she feels that it is difficult to isolate a single activity of the organization. The design can be tried out in both letterform and image. These can also be combined to see the result. The images should be drawn in bold lines or solid blocks unless thin and delicate lines are required to imply specific connotations. The images may be bound with a basic shape or developed as a subtle silhouette. If the design is to be in colour, different colours should be experimented with only after the designer is satisfied with the shape of the developed images. Figure 15.21 illustrates a designer's experimentation while developing a logo for an organization.

Figure 15.21 Designer's experimentation while designing a logo

Types In case the logo contains any type content or tagline, an appropriate type style needs to be chosen for the same. In doing so, one should be aware of the fact that each type style may have some specific meaning or connotation. Several type styles can be tried out on a computer. Moreover, it is possible to create one's own style, including calligraphic letters, digitally. Commonly used graphic software programs such as CorelDRAW and Adobe Illustrator not only allow us to draw images but also help us fill the area with several tints, textures, and colours. These programs can be used to try out images in several angles with perspective. Repetition of an image, reversing, flipping, rotating, and several other options are available through simple computer commands. Programs such as Photoshop can be used to alter or retouch photographs and drawings, creating a spectacular identity mark or logo design. The image can also be animated in 2D or 3D with sound in a multi-media environment.

The *dhrupadam* logo shown in Figure 15.22 is computer generated. The concept of Indian classical music is depicted by an image of a *tabla*. The calligraphic letterform in

Devanagari style has been developed in CorelDRAW with the calligraphic pen option, which simulates the effect created by a conventional flat-nib pen. This option can be selected from the artistic media tools and the curve and the nib angle can be selected as per the requirement. The pen can then be dragged on the screen to obtain the desired curve, which can be smoothened by using the shape tool.

Colour Apart from symbols and types, the creative concept may also include colour. The use of colour for an identity mark is different from that of other two-dimensional designs such as book covers, folders, or advertisements. In logo designs, the aesthetic aspect of colour is often sacrificed for functional considerations. This is because most logos are reproduced as line art on various kinds of surfaces and surroundings, and hence they need to be in colours that are functional. Although black and its tones are the most safe colours for a logo design, primary and vivid colours are often good choices when colours other than black are to be used. Bata's bright red, Unilever's blue, and Kodak's yellow, red, and black combinations are examples of attractive logos designed in such colours.

Subtle gradation of tones and shades of colours are not uncommon in a logo design. Figure 15.23 shows some logos where a gradation of tones has been used. The effectiveness of the colours in a logo will depend on the combinations that have been used and their appropriateness for the product and activities of the company. While working on logo designing, designers should ensure that the colours in the printed design match their colour specifications as there is a strong possibility that the colours of the results that come back from the printer or some duplication device will be different from the original. Logos and marks developed in colour should work well if converted into black and white, because many application areas of the company can take only black and white images. For instance, if a press advertisement carrying a logo is to be released in a newspaper the company would have to bear a lot of additional costs if the logo is in colour and does not look good when converted into black and white.

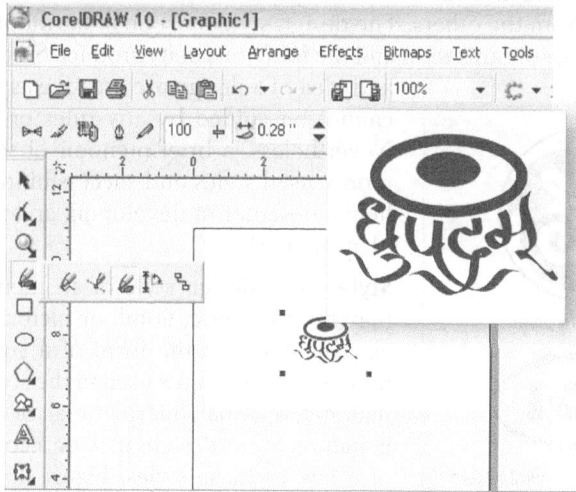

Figure 15.22 Computer-generated logo

Figure 15.23 Logos with gradation of tones

Characteristics of effective identity marks

An identity mark is considered to be effective if it is aesthetically pleasing and functional. Its shape, form, and colour, developed skilfully, must be unique, making it stand out from others. It must create a positive image. The mark should be created with minimal graphic elements. This will facilitate its easy recognition. The design should not allow the viewer to think or respond differently from what it is intended to do. It should spare the viewer from too much effort to understand it. At the same time, the mark should not be a literal translation of the company or organization name, which makes the viewer passive towards the mark or mix it up with other marks or visual elements. In case the mark is a corporate logo, it should be ensured that it will be visible on any item in any size. It should be small enough to go on a visiting card, big enough to be at the entrance of the company, and flexible enough for use in a digital signboard or television commercial. Figure 15.24 shows identity marks, simple as well as intricate, in various sizes.

Figure 15.24 Simple and intricate identity marks in various sizes

Reproducibility is a must for an effective identity mark. Any printing process or copying device should be able to duplicate the identity mark with ease. Colour, tone, shade, and shape must not be distorted during reproduction. Identity marks are distinct from any other graphic design because of their timeless value. A good mark must represent not only the current period but also a period many years from now.

As in any other communication device, style and idea play an important role in the development of an effective identity mark. Style brings distinctiveness that separates one identity mark from the others. The design style must be in harmony with the activities of the company or organization and the functions of its product. Since the style and idea of a design are creative aspects, they cannot be guided by any rules or formulae. Nevertheless, a brief mention of some commonly used styles and successful ideas might help a designer in developing an appropriate identity mark.

Figure 15.25 Identity marks in different styles

Style The design style of an identity mark may be geometric, floral, or pictorial. It may also be styled in the form of a signature or initials. The elements used in the style may be national, regional, international, or traditional in nature. Some designs may be a combination of a few of these styles. Figure 15.25 shows some examples of geometric and pictorial styles and styles with initial letters.

Some of the styles have been in use for years. The signature style evolved from the times of early craftsmen and entrepreneurs, who put their signatures on the products created or manufactured by the company. These signatures became a distinctive style once their businesses expanded. The identity marks of Bata, Johnson & Johnson, Godrej, etc. fall in this category. Some of these marks maintain the style of a hand-written signature. The signature-style mark may be even more distinctive if designed in various shapes and lines. It may have a better chance of longevity if it is stylized. General electric's (GE) identity mark, shown in Figure 15.25, is an example of a stylized signature-style mark.

Some of the identity mark styles, as discussed earlier, are based on the initial letters of a name. An identity mark style is simple and straight-forward, occasionally accompanied by simple graphics or bound by a basic shape. A mark in this style can be quite successful if it becomes popular. The identity marks of NTPC, BHEL, and ACC are examples of logos with initial letters. The marks, however, may appear quite confusing, unless accompanied by a descriptive name, such as a signature or a logotype. A look at the distinctive IDI mark with thick and thin lines in oval shape, as shown in Figure 15.25, will illustrate this point. Such a mark may leave the audience wondering what it stand for—Industrial Design Institute, Indian Diamond Industry, or something else. Moreover, the initial letters of the names of many organizations are sometimes the same, and hence it is difficult to get a registration for exclusive right to use the mark unless it is accompanied by a descriptive name.

Idea Ideas for identity marks may range from the obvious, that is, literal, to the abstract. Although an obvious idea can help us link an identity mark directly to the product/brand/organization concerned, the mark will be remembered only if it is distinct enough to stay on in our memories. Thus, an identity mark should not be over-simplistic—this will help it stand out from the scores of marks designed for similar products. It should also be developed in a distinctive style which, together with the idea, makes the identity mark distinguishable from that of competitors' marks.

An idea for an identity can be successful if it evokes any of the following associations with the company or product—direct, indirect, abstract, or arbitrary.

Direct association A distinctive visual symbol, when linked with a name, can lead to an identifying mark that evokes strong association with the company or its products. For instance, a simple drawing of three leaves for a company dealing in pesticides would suggest directly and meaningfully that the company has something to do with plants and crops. Some marks that evoke direct association are presented in Figure 15.26. The hexagonal nut and spanner locked in forming the letter 'E' is representative not only of the first letter of 'Escorts' but also of technology and the company's engineering commitment to the people. Another interesting mark is the L'affaire logo. The designer, Satish Sood, perceived the logo as a woman's love affair with herself. L'affaire is a sari boutique offering a line of up-market

Figure 15.26 Direct association marks

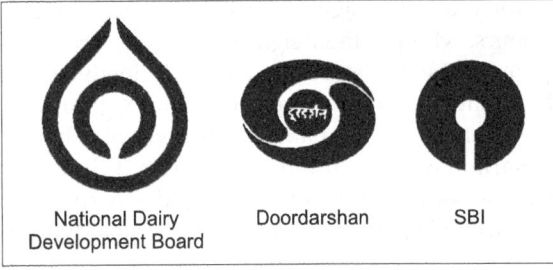

Figure 15.27 Indirect association marks

saris. Considering the idea that every woman is beautiful, the logo with the name L'affaire in relaxed flourishes reflects the basic theme of the boutique beautifully.

Indirect association A mark which encapsulates the essence of a company's name, product, or philosophy is usually very interesting. Such a mark may not contain the representational element of the product, but it does have allusions to the organization's activities. It expresses common thoughts in uncommon ways. The symbolic idea and simplified style give the viewer an easy understanding, helping the mark to register in one's memory. Figure 15.27 presents some marks that evoke indirect associations. An example of such a mark is that of the National Dairy Development Board. This mark is an inverted form of a liquid drop held within a large drop, intended to suggest the collection and processing of milk and milk products. As can be seen in the figure, the skilfully developed graphic device represents the product and the company in a simple and subtle way. Doordarshan's logo is another example of a mark that evokes indirect associations. One can easily perceive an eye in the Doordarshan symbol, which represents the visual medium. The two curved shapes give the feeling of space through which all TV signals are communicated. In another case, a keyhole represented graphically in a large solid circle conveys the idea that the State Bank of India provides safety and security.

Abstract association Some identity marks are completely in an abstract form. Sometimes, a very remote allusion or meaning is made to suggest the connotation of the mark. The symbol of the Indian Institute of Mass Communication (IIMC), shown in Figure 15.28, is a typical abstract mark. IIMC is an institute of communication. Its mark suggests the information flow which comes from, or goes out to, all the four sides of the world. The semi-circular lines of different thicknesses create that feeling. The circular shape of the mark suggests the world.

The three elements—flame, protective circle, and the letter 'R'—of the Reliance Industries Ltd logo denote the reliability of the company. This logo is also shown in Figure 15.28. The flame is the symbolic presentation of Reliance's ongoing activities, which are protected by the surrounding circle. The circle has been depicted by inverting a circular graphic shape. Besides, the letter 'R', which is Reliance's initial letter, is formed by the protective circle.

Protection of life has been symbolized in the service mark of the Life Insurance Corporation (LIC), as shown in the figure. The earthen lamp is traditionally a very popular Indian symbol of life. The end of life may come any moment, bringing unforeseen misery to the dependents. The LIC symbol suggests that a person will remain alive to his/her family if

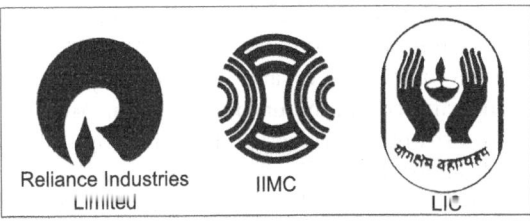

Figure 15.28 Abstract association marks

Identity Design 357

he/she is protected by life insurance. The two hands of the logo protect the flame (life) from being blown off.

Astrological signs are good examples of abstract symbols. The realistic presentation of figures can be replaced by simple lines and shapes that convey the same meaning, as shown in Figure 15.29.

Arbitrary association Much of the ancient imagery and symbolism used the world over is based on arbitrary associations. Some of these associations have entered so deep into our psyches that they are in use even today. These symbols may signify issues of life and death, eternity and infinity, modern science and technology, human values, or issues of global concern.

The symbol of yin and yang, as shown in Figure 15.30, is made of two semi-circular shapes, one's narrowed tail facing the other's broad head and thus making a complete circle. This well-established symbol is based on Chinese philosophy and religion. The two shapes in the symbol—one dark and the other bright—correspond to the principles of the negative and the positive. They symbolize the unity of opposites, such as heaven and earth, night and day, or male and female.

The male and female biological signs are frequently used in identity marks and visual communication. The male sign has a circle and a 45-degree-angle arrow from the circle. In biology, it also represents a steminate flower or plant. In the female sign, the circle with a plus sign attached at the bottom not only symbolizes the female organism but also represents a pistillate flower or plant or the seed-bearing parent of a hybrid. The logo for the International Women's Year, as shown in Figure 15.30, is a classic example of adaptation of this arbitrary symbol.

The solid red triangle for family planning became so popular that it was able to penetrate the vast illiterate section of the Indian population. The triangle is simply a mark; it is no inherent idea, intellectual thought, or even an intricate shape. This makes it possible to reproduce it on any surface ranging from smooth paper to rough surface trees or the mud walls of a village. A remote association may be found only in the red colour, which symbolizes danger. The logic may be that it is dangerous to have more than two children. A few years ago, it was re-designed, maintaining the basic shape and colour but inserting a silhouette illustration of a family. The red triangle has continued to date to be the code for family planning.

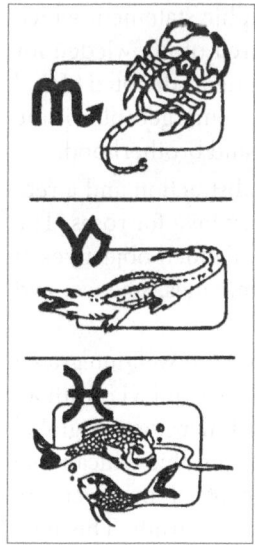

Figure 15.29 Simplified symbols

Yin and yang

Symbolic representation of the male and female

Figure 15.30 Symbols for opposites

Presenting a Solution

The presentation of the designed logo is not simply an event where clients pick one from the alternative designs which have been prepared. This event is as important as the presentation of an advertisement campaign. The designer should prepare a summary of the whole process for the presentation and show it to the client with the aid of slides.

For the presentation, the designer should prepare the prototype of the application area in a 2D or 3D format and place the logo at the appropriate position of each format. In case the house style needs to be adhered to, the designer should plan the position of the logo well with the other elements of the design, such as the typestyle, colour, and shape. This works towards helping the client develop a positive opinion about the design. For the convenience of the designer as well as the client, it is advisable to store the designs and present them on a computer.

Identity mark designing is a field where the designer and the client need to understand each other's needs and perspectives. The designer should be mentally prepared to change the design, if so desired by the client, because the client invests a lot of money and has the right to ask for a satisfactory design. Clients too need to appreciate the fact that designing is a creative process, and any unnecessary change or demand for further alternatives may result in poor designs, as designing is basically an emotional activity.

Designers usually present a few alternative designs to the client, and the client selects the one that is most appropriate. The client may, of course, ask for more alternatives. Let us discuss a real-life example, which will further illustrate this process. The logo design of the Jawaharlal Nehru University (JNU) was outsourced to Ulka Advertising Private Ltd. Ulka presented a few alternative logos designed by R.K. Joshi. These alternatives are illustrated in Figure 15.31. One alternative was a graphic statement which stood for international academic exchange and the onward search of knowledge for the betterment of the human being. The overlapping circular segments denoted global interaction, creating a flame emitting enlightenment. This flame emerged out of the traditional Indian *diya* (lamp)—a source of light, understanding, and brotherhood.

Among the other two alternatives, one was a highly stylized abstraction and a representative drawing of a rose bud, suggestive of Nehru's legendary love for roses. The petals were chiseled out in a geometric pattern to reflect the well-defined objectives of JNU, with its multifold educational activities in the field of humanities, science, and technology.

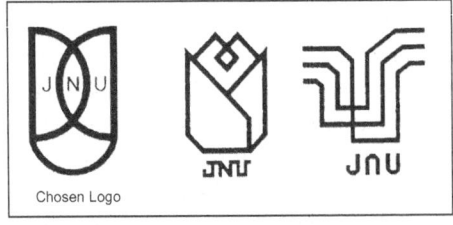

Figure 15.31 Alternative ideas for JNU logo

The third alternative depicted the well-integrated courses at various schools and levels of JNU, with an emerging form, exploring new dimensions in global understanding and exchange within this educational environment, reflecting the concepts of the adventure of ideas and the on-going search for truth. This logo sought to highlight ever-higher objectives for the betterment of the human race.

Out of these three alternatives, the client chose the first alternative, that is, the one signifying international academic exchange and the onward search of knowledge.

In case the client requires a design for a complete identity program, the presentation should be made more elaborate. The designer should also use an audio-visual system for the presentation. There should be a specific house style for matter other than the logo, such as the typography, logotype, slogan, colour, etc.

Implementing the Chosen Solution

Once a design has been selected, it is implemented by the client. For this, the designer should compile the chosen solution and prepare it in the form of an identity manual. This should be used as a guide-book by the implementer of the company, who will consistently and correctly adhere to the rules laid down in the manual. The implementer(s) may be public relations (PR) personnel who supervise the printing of stationery and publicity material, personnel of the purchasing and marketing departments, and/or the top management of the company. Ideally, all of them should work in cooperation, checking for any distortions or wrongful applications. Figure 15.32 shows the 'look book' developed for 7UP, a soft-drink brand. The 'look book' is an identity manual that lays down specific guidelines for the implementation of the identity marks created for the brand.

In cases where a new identity is sought to be established, the company's PR department should launch an elaborate publicity program for its internal and external customers, including staff and employees. This may include an advertisement campaign focusing on the logo and a booklet or special issue of the newsletter of the company for the internal customers.

It is a very common practice to design posters with the logo as the main visual element. The Delhi Administration came out with an interesting poster depicting its multifarious activities through simple graphics attached to the main logo. Each graphic, as shown in Figure 15.33, tells its own independent story, but the one which represents all its activities is a fully bloomed flower symbolizing happiness—the ultimate result of all the activities. After the Reliance Industries split occurred in 2006, the blue logo of Reliance Communications became a common sight on the walls of city streets. This is another example of the implementation of identity mark designs on posters for creating a brand identity.

A novel way was adopted to popularize the logo of the New Delhi Municipal Council (NDMC). All the design elements of the logo were arranged in a subtle form. These were then used in a six-division calendar, which would be on the desk for the whole year. This calendar is shown in Figure 15.34. Had the designer used only one shape for each of these divisions, the calendar would have been awfully monotonous.

Change and Redesign

Some marks are used year after year as originally designed, while some are gradually revised with minor modifications. There are still others, which undergo a total change. There may be several reasons for these changes or modifications. The company's

Figure 15.32 Identity manual: 7UP look book

Identity Design **361**

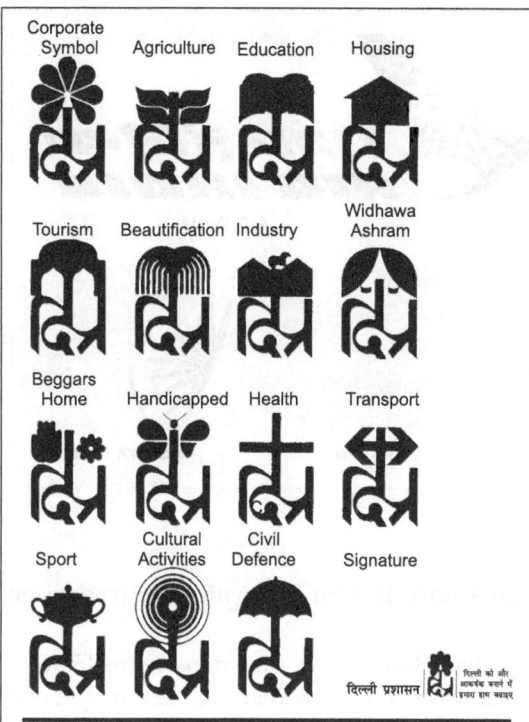

Figure 15.33 Poster depicting activities of the Delhi Administration

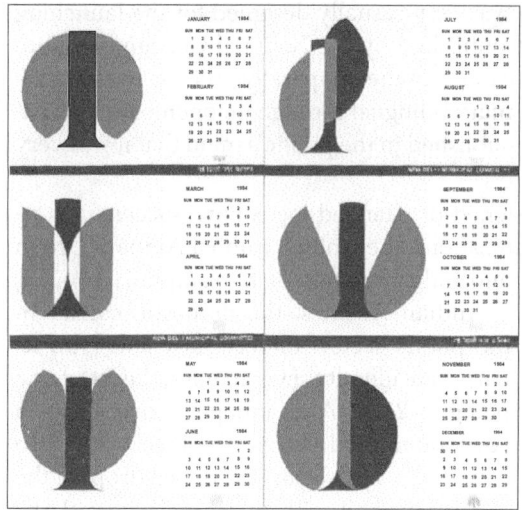

Figure 15.34 Calendar using NDMC logo

philosophy may have changed over the years, or the company may have entered a different business, for which the logo is no longer appropriate. The rapid change in values is another reason for change. During the past two decades, the world has witnessed drastic technological and economic developments which have affected our socio-cultural life powerfully. These changes need to be borne in mind while redesigning a logo. The old logo should be redesigned to suit new trends, or a new one should be developed to suit the needs of the present day as well as the future. Many old marks had been developed casually, symbolizing the appropriate concept, but lacking in visual appeal. Such designs now look outdated and amateurish, and are often difficult to adopt for other media such as television or the Internet, which require a 3D display.

Changing an identity mark design is not as simple as it appears to be on the surface. It takes a lot of time and effort to establish an identity mark in the public mind. Let us discuss some instances where efforts at redesigning an established logo were not successful.

At the end of the last century, when Air India decided that it needed a change in image, it hired an international design firm, who changed the logo from the Centaur to the red sun—a change that turned out to be a disaster for the company as people failed to associate the new logo with Air India. Realizing this, Air India came out with a new logo in July 2007. This logo was formed by merging the former logos of Air India and Indian Airlines, as shown in Figure 15.35. The red and orange colours signify 'vigour and advancement'. The symbol of the 'flying swan' is partly from the Air India Centaur logo (Figure 15.36), with the Konark Chakra from the Indian Airlines logo embedded inside it. The company decided to

362 *Art and Print Production*

Figure 15.35 Changed and redesigned logos

go ahead with the 'Air India' brand name since it is an internationally recognized one.

The steam engine in the logo of the Indian Railways, as shown in Figure 15.36, is also quite outdated. Realizing this, an effort was made a few years ago to redesign and update it by announcing an open competition. The Selection Committee, however, failed to choose one from the hundreds of entries. The impact of the old design is perhaps so great that, despite the change of values, the public may be less inclined to accept a new design.

The 'Coop' mark shown in the figure was very casually designed for the launching issue of the journal, *Consumer Cooperator*, published by the National Consumer Cooperative Federation. It became the identity mark of the cooperative sector. In the early 1970s, an attempt was made to make the mark bilingual through an open competition, but the 'Coop' mark had been so firmly established in the public's mind that it was very difficult to change.

There are also instances where redesigned or changed logos have successfully established the changed identity of an organization. The Anil Dhirubhai Ambani Group and Indian are two such examples.

Indian Airlines, the domestic carrier in the public sector, underwent changes in its corporate identity several times, the latest one being in 2006. After independence, it was a corporation and carried the logo of the two wings of a bird against the backdrop of the sun, combined with the three letters 'IAC' directly related with flight. In the early 1980s,

Figure 15.36 Marks that resisted the change effort

it changed its trade name from 'Indian Airlines Corporation' to 'Indian Airlines', and so the logo with 'IA', two stylized lineal letters graphically shaped in the runway of an airport, came into being.

Now, Indian Airlines is simply 'Indian'. The new logo is a graphical image of a partial wheel inspired by the wheel of the Konark Sun Temple. It abstractly creates the feeling of openness and vastness, and symbolizes timeless motion. The new identity, accompanied by the word 'Indian' in Devanagari and Roman type, emanates from its core value of being the epitome of Indian hospitality. The current design retains the type font and colour of the previous mark to maintain a sense of continuity.

In 2006, the Anil Dhirubhai Ambani Group came out with a new group logo without any visual association with the original Reliance logo. The new logo consisted of the word 'Reliance' in capital letters in an entirely new font along with the lineage—the Anil Dhirubhai Ambani Group. A combination of blue and red colours was used, which conveyed solidity, and the letter 'A' in 'Reliance' was converted into two arrows arching upwards. The new logo was designed to reflect the group's business interests from telecommunications to entertainment, urban infrastructure to financial services, and from energy to areas such as healthcare. The need, therefore, was to evolve a logo that did not reflect any specific product category. This logo is presented in Figure 15.35.

A good and established logo may be continued though it can be redesigned, when necessary, retaining the key visual elements of the old design so that a feeling of continuity of the old mark lingers and the loyalty and values evoked by the old design are not dissipated. The logos of STC, Ashoka Hotel, and IIMC are some examples of redesigned logos.

In the case of a complete overhaul, the design may be commissioned to professional designers who have already established their credibility in the field. When it comes to large scale changes in a corporate identity design, a designer or design firm well known for their visual designs may be engaged.

SUMMARY

The most fundamental element of an identity mark is the name. A name helps us identify objects in the world around us and communicate about them. It is the basis for coded communication. Besides names, identity marks can be in various other forms—signs, symbols, trademarks, trade names, logos, and brand names. These are used in the day-to-day activities of most companies and organizations and adopted for ease in recognition and for building a corporate image.

For designing identity marks, designers need to possess knowledge about symbols used in the local culture. India has a rich symbolic culture. Our varied dance forms, music, handicraft, folk art, and religious rituals demonstrate our cultural ethos. In our country, these cultural elements have a tremendous influence on identity mark designing. The lotus logo of the State Trading Corporation and the Welcomgroup logo with hands folded in a *namastey* are examples of cultural elements used in identity mark designing.

Some graphic symbols become basic to coded communication and represent or express certain qualities, attributes, or characteristics. The basic symbols in identity mark designs are shapes, letterforms, and/or images. Marks within different shapes provide different meanings. Letterforms may have classical, modern, industrial, delicate, and bold connotations. Visual images used in identity marks have some obvious reference to some object, activity, or thought related to the subject. They enable a viewer to recognize something at a glance.

A logo should not only look good but also communicate the intended message with the minimum of graphic elements. The logo should therefore be treated as an integral part of an advertisement campaign. The procedures involved in logo designing are: conducting intensive research, developing a design brief, developing the creative concept, presenting the designed solution, and implementing the desired solution.

The design process starts with the collection of information, which leads to a design brief. Based on the design brief, a creative concept is developed. The creative concept may be developed in the form of thumbnail sketches of the types, symbols, and colours to be used in the design. In order to create an effective identity mark, the designer should develop a distinctive style and idea. An idea can be successful if it evokes a direct, indirect, abstract, or arbitrary association with the product or organization concerned. An identity mark should be aesthetically pleasing. It must create a positive image. An effective mark spares the viewer from straining himself/herself to understand it. A corporate mark should relate to the identity of the business or organization. It should also be visible on any item in any size. Reproducibility and timelessness are the hallmarks of a good logo.

For presenting the design to the client, a summary of the entire design-solving process should be prepared. The designer should also prepare a prototype of the areas of application in a 2D or 3D format for complete identity programs. This should be accompanied by a logic note on the chosen colours and shapes. A guide book or manual of the chosen solutions should be developed for ease in implementation.

There may be times when a change or modification of a logo design is inevitable. Changing trends and change in the organization's corporate identity or line of business are instances where a redesigned logo may be desirable. Nevertheless, effort should be taken to avoid changing one's identity mark frequently as a mark, once established in the peoples' minds, may be difficult to change. There are many instances when a complete change in identity mark has failed. Even when such changes are necessary, it is advisable to maintain a sense of visual continuity with the old design or to assign the job to a professional designer or designing firm.

KEY TERMS

Arabesque Figure A style of ornamentation, painted, inlaid, or carved in low relief. It consists of a pattern in which plants, fruits, foliage, etc. as well as figures of men and animals are fantastically interlaced or put together.

Brand Name A product, service, or concept that is publicly distinguished from other products, services, or concepts so that it can be easily communicated and marketed.

Corporate Identity The 'persona' of a corporation, designed to facilitate the attainment of the business objectives of a company or organization. It is usually visibly manifested by way of branding and the use of trademarks.

Crest An ornamental tuft, ridge, or similar projection on the head of a bird or other animal.

Emblem A pictorial image, abstract or representational, that epitomizes a concept, deity, tribe, nation, virtue, or vice.

House Style A company or organization's preferred style of presentation and layout of written material and graphics.

Identity Manual The collection of conventions set out in the internal style guide of a company focusing on elements of graphic shapes, typography, colour, etc.

Insignia A distinguishing sign to show official position, rank, membership, or nationality.

Mascot A person, animal, or object believed to bring good luck, especially one kept as the symbol of an organization or event such as a sports event, trade fair, etc.

Logo Distinctive graphic design element, often including a name, symbol, or trademark, representing an organization, product, service, or persons either independently or collectively.

Motif A feature in a design or decoration that consists of recurring ideas, shapes, or colours.

Non-verbal Communication Communication through wordless messages, such as gestures, tone, body posture, etc.

Sign A non-verbal code by which something is made known or represented.

Swastika In India, a symbol for good luck, protection, and auspiciousness. It is derived from the word 'su-vasti', and means 'the essence of all goodness'.

Symbol A two- or three-dimensional object that represents an idea, concept, or abstraction.

Tantra Art A special representation of Indian art and religion, especially *tantric* imagery, in which deities are often in geometric shapes.

Trade Name A word or a phrase used in a trade to designate a business or a particular class of goods. It is the name or style under which a firm does its business.

Trademark A symbol, figure, word, or mark adopted and used by a manufacturer or merchant in order to designate his/her goods and to distinguish them from other such goods.

Vedic Tradition Philosophy, culture, and civilization based on Vedic scriptures, believed to contain all knowledge, both material and transcendental.

Verbal Code Typographical letterforms are the most fundamental and well-defined verbal code. Each letter of typography is an arbitrary sign, seen and felt by its surface character.

Zodiac The band of sky through which the sun, moon, and planets apparently move during the course of the year.

REFERENCES

'Logos Not Mere Symbols', *The Economic Times*, New Delhi, 25 January 1992.

Dhir, Sudarshan 1987, 'Symbol Designs for Corporate Use', *Indian Symbology*, Proceedings of the Seminar on Indian Symbology, Industrial Design Centre, IIT, Bombay 1987.

Dreyfuss, Henry 1972, *Symbol Sourcebook*, McGraw-Hill Book Company, New York.

Ganguly, Dibyendu 1996, *Designing the Corporate Gift*, Indian Express, Ahmedabad.

Indian Symbology, Proceedings of the Seminar on Indian Symbology, Industrial Design Centre, IIT, Bombay 1987.

Joseph, Denis 1992, 'Paradise Regained', *The Economic Times*, New Delhi, 25 January.

Joshi, R.K., 'Calligraphy—The Art of Writing', *CALTIS-84 Souvenir*, Institute of Typographical Research, Pune.

Nasar, Sayyed Hossin 1987, *Islamic Art and Spirituality* Golgonooza Press, Ipswich, Suffolk.

Romano, Frank J. and Richard M. Romano 1998, *Encyclopedia of Graphic Communication*, Prentice Hall PTR, USA.

Sud, Satish 1992, 'Logic of Logo: Corporate Identity', *The Economic Times*, New Delhi, 25 January.

REVIEW QUESTIONS

1. Define sign, symbol, trademark, trade name, brand name, and logo with examples.
2. Identify some service marks and certification marks. Explain their functions in communication.
3. Emblems, mascots, crests, insignia, and monograms are all identity marks for something or other. Describe their characteristics and application areas.
4. 'India has a rich tradition of symbolic culture.' Elaborate this statement in relation to identity marks designed in the past and in the modern day.
5. What is the significance of colour symbolism in identity mark design? Explain it with the support of some commonly used logos.
6. What are the constraints in developing an identity mark keeping the language and culture of

a place in mind? How can these be overcome? Explain with cases.

7. What are the basic visual elements of an identity mark design? Describe their characteristics and role in shaping a mark.

8. Compare a logo design with an advertisement design and establish that logo design requires much more than just graphic skills.

9. What criteria determine the selection of effective identity marks?

10. 'Style and idea bring distinctiveness that separates one identity mark from others.' Elaborate the statement with the help of some commonly used identity marks.

11. What are the reasons for changing and redesigning a logo? Identify and explain some identity marks that have been changed successfully.

12. How can a design solution be created for a complete identity program? Describe the ways in which the solution should be presented and the chosen solution should be implemented.

PROJECTS

1. Prepare a portfolio collecting several identity marks. Segregate them as per their style (for example, ethnic, modern, national, and international).

2. Pick up five commonly used identity marks. Discuss the style and idea used in their design, which have some association with the organization's activities and philosophy. Display all these in a presentation folder.

3. Create a name for an imaginary company. Describe the profile of the company in terms of its aims, objectives, and present activities. Mention the future expansion plans of the company. List the probable application areas. Suggest three alternative identity marks supported by rough sketches in colour. Explain the concept behind your designs.

4. Select the best logo from the rough sketch you have prepared for the previous assignment. Develop it on a computer, using an appropriate software program. Take printouts of various sizes on a sheet or two. Cut and paste them on some of the application areas you have already identified. Judge them on the basis of the criteria for the selection of an effective logo.

5. From any print advertisement, select a logo that you feel is not up to the mark. Discuss the areas of improvement. Redesign the logo, retaining some of its basic elements, or overhaul it completely. Prepare a questionnaire on the criteria by which an effective mark can be identified. Test your design, showing it to some people who had seen the existing identity mark earlier.

CHAPTER

16 Periodicals

Learning Objectives

After reading this chapter, you should be able to
- understand the types and characteristics of printed literature that are issued periodically
- discuss the functions and characteristics of magazines and categorize them on the basis of their content
- understand the editorial, design, and production planning of a magazine
- analyse the parts of a magazine for the purpose of designing
- discuss the roles, formats, and production aspects of newsletters

INTRODUCTION

Periodicals are publications that are issued at regular intervals. Newspapers, tabloids, journals, magazines, newsletters, bulletins, etc. fall in this category of publications. These publications may be issued daily, weekly, bi-weekly, fortnightly, monthly, quarterly, or at other intervals. Periodicals are different from books because, unlike books, they are short-lived in nature. They are also different from advertising and packaging because of their diversified aims and objectives. Despite their distinct identity, however, periodicals are strongly influenced by advertisements, books, and television—a fact that is reflected in the editorial content and design of periodicals.

Periodicals such as newspapers, tabloids, journals, magazines, newsletters, and bulletins have substantial differences from each other in terms of the content and format of presentation. Each individual periodical has a character of its own. For ease of understanding, however, periodicals can be divided into three categories—ephemeral, leisure reading, and specialized/official.

Modern consumers buy information like any other daily necessity. They store and consume it according to their requirements and the freshness of the commodity/content. Ephemeral periodicals become stale at the end of the day, whereas leisure reading material can be stored for some time and used according to the convenience and need of the consumer. Official periodicals are usually offered at highly subsidized rates.

Newspapers and tabloids are ephemeral periodicals. Their demand is so high and their design and production requirements are so different that we have dealt with them separately, in Chapter 13. In this chapter, we shall discuss leisure reading periodicals such as journals and magazines and official periodicals such as newsletters and bulletins.

MAGAZINES AND JOURNALS

The basic approach of design for leisure reading material, be it a magazine or a journal, is the same. In this chapter, we have referred to all leisure material as 'magazines' for our convenience.

Functions

The functions of a magazine fall between those of a newspaper and a book. The role of a magazine is similar to that of a newspaper in that it carries news of events or happenings which have relatively less lasting value. However, a magazine also carries information that has a longer life, in the form of features and articles for entertainment and knowledge. This brings a magazine close to a book.

Physical Characteristics

Each magazine has its own aims and objectives. Each has developed a distinct character of its own. Physical appearance is the primary factor that helps create a distinct character for a magazine. Every day, we see hundreds of magazines at news-stands, and each magazine is distinct from the ones that surround it.

The physical appearance of a magazine depends, among other things, on the nature of the magazine. Technical magazines have covers and pages that look so formal that they give them a book-like appearance. Magazines that cover news of events or topical features have design elements such as headlines, photographs, and graphics arranged in such a way that they resemble a newspaper. Magazines aimed at a select target audience may follow the style of promotional literature and, sometimes, of a formal book design. In order to create an effective design for a magazine, it is helpful if the designer knows who the target audience is. This may, however, not be possible in all cases as some magazines serve a large geographical area with people having varied interests while others have a very precise audience.

Magazines can be classified in several ways. For our purpose, we have categorized them into news magazines, glamour magazines, special interest magazines, and aesthetics and culture magazines.

News magazines These magazines are aimed at the general reading public. In order to satisfy the interests of varied kinds of consumers, most magazines cover different types of topics. It becomes necessary to break the whole magazine into sections. In most general news magazines, the first section is the political section. This may be followed by sections such as business, states, sports, film/television, etc. A news magazine that serves a particular business or profession focuses on news in that area instead of general politics. Whatever be the area covered by a magazine, its physical characteristics include photographs of current events, packed with type, narrow column grids, occasional blurbs, cartoons, etc. Charts and graphs facilitate easy understanding of financial and business topics. The page layout of news magazines is always influenced

Figure 16.1 Political, way of life, and business features in news magazines

by newspapers and advertisements. *India Today, Sunday, The Week*, and *Business India* are some of the examples of news magazines. Some of these are displayed in Figure 16.1.

Glamour magazines With their glossy pages, stylish graphics, and fancy designs, glamour magazines are meant more for viewing and less for reading. Movie, design, and lifestyle magazines are a feast for cinema lovers, television viewers, and fashion-conscious people. These magazines show the target groups' favourite stars in action or carry visuals of human interest or utility, with types and copy block mainly used to support the visuals. Sometimes, types are also made to serve the purpose of a visual. Designers of glamour magazines strive to create designs that will not only stand out at the news-stand but also be able to compete with the strong visual appeal of television.

Big photographs, subtle graphics, collages, fancy headings, reverse copy blocks, and different page style are some ingredients of magazine design. Most magazines are big enough to accommodate big visuals. Some of them use glossy paper which not only reproduces the continuous tone visuals well but also adds additional glamour to the magazine. *Cosmopolitan, Sports*, and *Fashion N Life* are some examples of popular glamour magazines. Some of these are shown in Figure 16.2.

Figure 16.2 Glamour magazines

Special interest magazines These magazines cover a wide range of interest groups, ranging from homemakers to astronauts and school-going children to research scholars. They also cover a variety of topics, from neighbourhood gossip, religious preaching, and palmistry to computer science, travel destinations, photography, and automobiles. Figure 16.3 presents some special interest magazines.

The design style for special interest magazines cannot be generalized. Magazines with good financial support either from advertising revenue or from a rich publisher allow the creative team to experiment and present a visually effective magazine. Sometimes, they even attract readers beyond the targeted group. For example, a beautifully illustrated magazine on food items would attract a person who is otherwise interested in computer science magazines only.

Low-budget magazines do not have the advantage of a large circulation. They are meant for reading rather than viewing. *Mainstream* is an example of a low-budget magazine. Most low-budget magazines are published with commercial advertisements as revenue support. These magazines also depend on donations from patrons and subscriptions of very loyal readers. Such a magazine may also benefit from funds from another organization or body if it takes care of the interests of the concerned body. Low-budget special interest magazines are bound to be modest in physical appearance, as can be seen in Figure 16.4.

Figure 16.3 Magazines for special interest groups

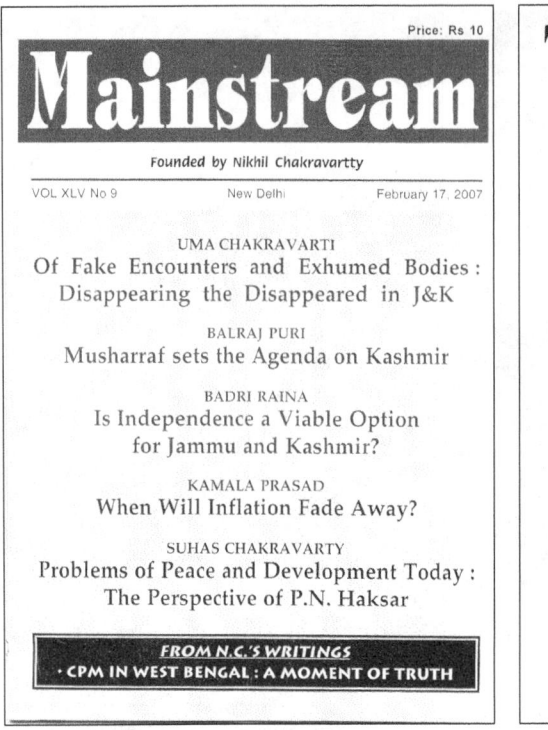

Figure 16.4 Low-budget magazines

Aesthetic and culture magazines These magazines may be visual-oriented or simply typographic in nature. They are aimed at the intellectual sections of society, which have a special interest in art with literary material. Although these magazines are appreciated for their individuality, intellectual influence, and artistic quality, their commercial success is usually very poor. Most of these magazines, as can be seen in Figure 16.5, are serious-looking even with visuals. Some magazines on culture and aesthetics are available in colour, with beautiful visuals of pictures, paintings, picturesque destinations, etc. on glossy paper and well-designed pages and covers, but their prices are so high that very few people can afford them. Lack of competition and commercial appeal often restrict the options of designers in this field. To deal with this problem, they can strive to build an image with a sober and serious-looking style that can then be followed issue after issue.

The style for aesthetic and culture magazines may be varied. Magazines such as *Communication Arts* and *Inside Outside* are developed in a style that is between news and glamour magazines, but the content of the visuals separate them instantly from the other groups. Figure 16.6 shows the covers of these two magazines. Magazines such as *India Perspective* and *Swagat* look similar to promotional literature with their liberal white spaces and subtle column grids. In fact, these magazines are published to promote Indian art and culture by the Government of India and Indian Airlines, respectively. The magazine *Marg* may be considered a pure art magazine. Among literary

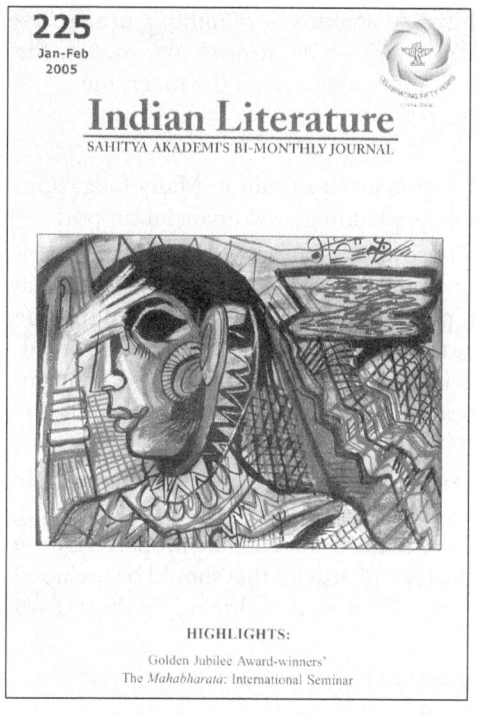

Figure 16.5 Literary magazines with a serious look

Figure 16.6 Aesthetic magazines with a style between glamour and news magazines

magazines, *Seminar* and *Indian Literature*, Sahitya Akademi's bi-monthly journals, are packed with thought-provoking articles without any visuals. In such magazines, the advertisements are usually selected to match with the aesthetics of the magazine.

Editorial Planning

A magazine can be started by anyone, but it is difficult to sustain it. Many magazines die prematurely due to the lack of editorial policy, planning, and financial support.

No editor likes to work under financial constraints. The magazine management should, therefore, take care that the editor is an equal partner in the business. Editorial planning, which affects the design, includes (i) planning several issues ahead of the due date; (ii) developing a broad idea about the articles received or likely to be received; (iii) making provisions for advertisement space (both flexible and fixed); (iv) allocating space for departments, if any; and (v) working out the target date for sending the manuscript/artwork to the press.

A magazine editor who plans in advance can identify the right people to contribute to the publication or assign various jobs relating to writing, photography, and designing to freelancers. All the contributors need to adhere to the time schedule prepared by the editor. Further, the editor needs to decide on the type of articles that should be included in a particular issue. This is an important decision for him/her. Briefing in this regard is mandatory for developing a design.

Most magazines survive on advertisement revenue. Some organizations pay extra money for getting their advertisements printed on a particular space or section or along with a particular article. Some magazines carry a policy in terms of the percentage of space for advertisements in comparison with the editorial content. Sometimes, second and back covers too carry advertisements, and, in rare cases, some magazines may allow advertisements on their front cover if they are in need of financial support. The editor should enquire about such policies before deciding on the layout of the pages.

Allocation of space for articles or sections is primarily the job of the editor. If the planning is done with the inputs of a designer, the pages of the magazine can be designed in a very cost-effective manner. For example, if magazine pages are printed four or eight pages to a sheet, the designer and the editor can work together to decide on the positioning of the colour images on the basis of the folding of the sheets, which forms a sequence of pages. If some images are in colour, these can be assigned to pages that fall on the same side of a sheet. This results in substantial cost savings as it eliminates the need for an additional press run for printing colour separately on each page. Planning for long headlines and large photographs that run across two facing pages should also be done at this stage. The designer can plan the layout on four-page or eight-page units by placing photographs and headlines in such a way that, after folding, they fall on facing pages and the headline and the photograph appear to be running across the page. This gives the page a strong visual appeal.

In order to build the image and credibility of a magazine, it is essential that it reaches its readers on time. The editor plans and allocates work to his/her colleagues and freelancers, supervises their work giving sufficient freedom to creative professionals, and adheres firmly to the deadline to endure timely production.

Design Planning

The editorial plan goes into action with design planning. It may start with a decision on the appropriate size for the magazine. Although this decision is primarily a part of editorial planning, the designer too has an important role to play in it.

Size

While deciding the appropriate size for the magazine, the editor and the designer should keep in mind the functional as well as aesthetic aspects of this communication medium. The functional aspect includes production feasibility and ease in handling, mailing, distribution, and accommodation of the content. The aesthetic aspect is concerned with the type style and size, number of columns, size of visuals and graphics, affordability of white space, etc.

The size of a magazine is partly determined by the size of the paper available in the market. The most common size for magazines is demy quarto (8.5″ × 11″), which can be obtained from 17.5″ × 22.5″ size paper by folding it twice. An odd-sized magazine results in wastage of paper, which ultimately increases the cost burden on the magazine owner. Magazines with large circulation are not constrained by the available paper sizes as they are printed in web-fed machines, which can produce paper in any desirable size. Despite the flexibility of web-fed machines, most magazines printed on such a system are closer to the demy quarto size, which is perhaps easy to hold, fold, open, and store.

Adaptability of the content is another consideration while deciding on the size of the magazine. A magazine with big photographs would require a larger page size. Text-dominated magazines may be published in smaller sizes. This is because formal two-column or single-column text matter is easy to read if the page is in a smaller size. Some magazines also come in pocketbook sizes so that they are convenient to carry.

Format

Once the size has been decided, an appropriate format has to be worked out for the magazine. The 'format' of a magazine refers to the arrangement of column grids, margins, space between columns, type size, style of text matter, and graphic style in which the magazine is expected to appear, issue after issue. If the format is standardized, it facilitates easy recognition on the part of the customer and provides the designer with the much-desired convenience to work within a pre-decided framework. This simplifies the production process.

Grid sheet Whatever may be the size and format of a magazine, no layout should be started without a grid sheet. The *grid sheet* is the dummy page of a magazine. In order to prepare a grid sheet, the decided number of columns is drawn as per the format size, preferably indicating the scale vertically on the outer column of each page. In case it has been decided that the magazine will carry some articles in two columns and some in three, one group of columns should be drawn in dotted lines and the other should be drawn in plain lines so that, while filling the two-column content of an article, the three-column grid can be ignored. The grid sheet may contain a line above or under the column grids for the folio. The grid for two facing pages should be prepared

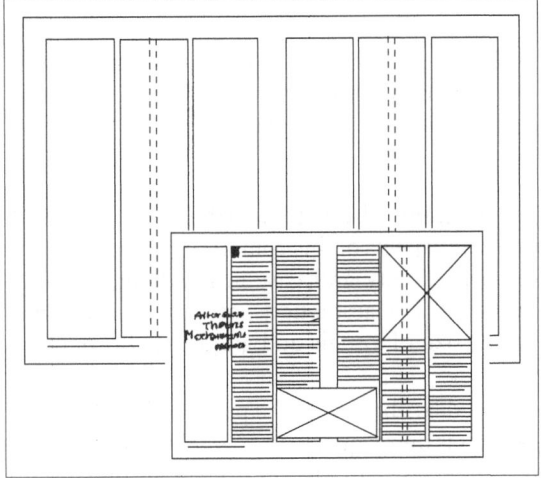

Figure 16.7 Grid sheet for two facing pages

together, for this establishes a relationship between the pages in terms of look, balance, and unity, which contributes to an easy flow of reading. Figure 16.7 shows a sample grid sheet for two facing pages. A grid sheet can easily be designed on the computer. Any page layout program can be used to create a grid with appropriate computer commands.

White space The white space on a page is often considered to be an unutilized area and a waste of paper, but imaginative designers utilize this white space positively in relation to the other design elements. White space in proper proportions improves readability and adds beauty and a feeling of spaciousness to it. It unites the copy block and other visual elements. Depending on the content of the pages and the type of magazine being designed, a standard design decision may be taken on white space, which may range from 25 to 60 per cent.

Margins All magazines need a margin for both functional and aesthetic purposes. In fact, the margin is also white space. The proportion of space to be devoted to the margin may be decided before making the grid sheet. Equal margins on all sides of a page may make the page look too rigid and mechanical. A page with equal top and outer margins, wider bottom margins, and narrow inner margins is considered to have the most pleasing margin spacing. On such a page, the inner margins are kept small so that, when two facing pages are opened, the two combined inner margins or gutter space will look as big as the outer margin.

Column width and space between columns Column width and the space between columns are essential aspects of the page format. These should be selected in such a way that they enhance reading comfort. For this, one may experiment with various arrangements and create a few samples before taking a decision. We know that a wider column can accommodate more words even in bigger type sizes. A narrow column width accommodates smaller type sizes. In both the cases, legibility can be hampered if the column width is not proportionate to the type size. Most designers follow a thumb rule for deciding on the column width—the width of the line or column (in picas) should be double the type size being used. For example, text set in 10 pt type size should have a 20 pica line length.

The space between the columns should be sufficient to separate the columns. It should not be so wide that it seems to separate the columns, and neither should it be so narrow that it hampers the readability of the text.

Masthead The masthead is a permanent element of a magazine. It is the magazine's name in a visual or typographic form. The masthead of a magazine or newspaper is referred to as its logo, banner, or flag. Once decided upon, the masthead continues to

(a) Magazines on news-stand showing mastheads   (b) Some masthead styles

Figure 16.8 Mastheads

be used for many years. It functions as a logo or symbol meant for identifying the magazine. The masthead, therefore, must be designed with utmost care and thought, making sure that it identifies with the aims and objectives of the magazine and that its style will not be outdated in the near future. Further, the masthead should be distinctive enough to make the magazine stand out at the news-stand or elsewhere.

While designing the masthead, the designer can use type with fancy elements such as borders, colours, and tints. Different manipulations of normal typefaces such as bold, expanded, or condensed faces; shading; reversing; and outlines may make the masthead stand out. The masthead may even be drawn by hand. It is, however, advisable to avoid using a type style that is very fancy, such as Script or Old English. The masthead should be planned along with the date of issue, volume number, etc. If the magazine is to carry an identity mark and a tag line, these elements should be made a part of the composite masthead. Figure 16.8 shows some mastheads on magazines displayed at a news-stand and a few styles for mastheads.

Design approach

What should be the sequence of steps in designing a magazine? Some designers first lay out the pages on the basis of the hard copy or the typeset proofs supplied to them. Some prefer to start with the cover design, because the cover is the attention-grabber in the news-stands. Some may concentrate first on the centrespread, because they feel that it is the most interesting part in a magazine. For the purpose of our discussion on layout planning, we shall divide the whole magazine into six parts on the basis of the sequence of pages and production planning. These parts are—(i) cover page, (ii) contents page, (iii) editorial page, (iv) running pages, (v) centrespread, and (vi) colour pages.

Cover page   The cover is the first thing to be noticed in a magazine. It must, therefore, not only attract but also create a curiosity about the inside content in the mind of the reader. It may be rather easy to attract attention through interesting photographs, well-structured graphics, and a catchy type display. These elements, however, need to be used in such a manner that they lend a distinctive identity to the magazine, which suits the content as well. Only then can the readers' interest be sustained. A reader should be able to identify a magazine with a glance at its cover, and yet, the style across various issues should not become monotonous.

Covers may range from the simple, with only typographical display, to the elaborate, with multicolour graphics, photographs, and type combinations. In all types of covers, the design starts with the placing of the masthead on the page. Generally, the position of the masthead is fixed. As the term 'masthead' implies, its conventional placement is at the top of the cover page. In this position, the magazine can be easily located by its masthead at the news-stand or in a pile of magazines. Modern-day designers may not like to be restricted by this conventional style. They may prefer to place it on one side or in the middle of the page. Vertical or angular placement is also being experimented with. Caution should be exercised while experimenting with the positioning of a masthead. An unusual placement sometimes proves dangerous. Such a style may confuse the reader if the letters in the typographic display are not adequately separated. Moreover, the placement of the masthead often breaks up the pages into two parts.

Most magazines rely on photographs for the cover design. Usually, big photographs are preferable to small ones. Techniques such as bleeding (making the photo run beyond the page) can be used in photographs to catch the readers' attention. On a cover page with multiple photographs, one photograph can be allowed to stand out to create a contrast effect. Hand-drawn illustrations, cartoons, computer generated graphics, etc. can be used either independently or in combination with photographs and type displays to create an effective cover with an element of surprise.

The cover illustrations, whether they are in the form of photographs, hand-drawn illustrations, or computer-generated graphics, must be related to one of the stories covered in the issue. These illustrations may represent the story symbolically. In order to involve the reader at the cover stage itself, some of the features of the issue are displayed on the cover by way of type messages alongside the main illustration. The designer should make good use of the various available type styles to make the cover page look unique and inviting.

Reproduction of covers calls for special attention. Even for a low-budget magazine, professional help must be sought to make the mechanical process of cover printing come alive. The paper quality of the cover page should be superior to that used for the inside pages in terms of thickness, smoothness, and strength. Textured and coloured paper can create a particular mood, but these may not be suitable for halftone reproduction. The printing process should be selected on the basis of the complexities involved. To print the cover page, a process that is different from the one used for printing the inside pages may be used.

Contents page   The cover page initially attracts the reader to the magazine, and the contents page attempts to sustain his/her interest by providing an idea about the issues

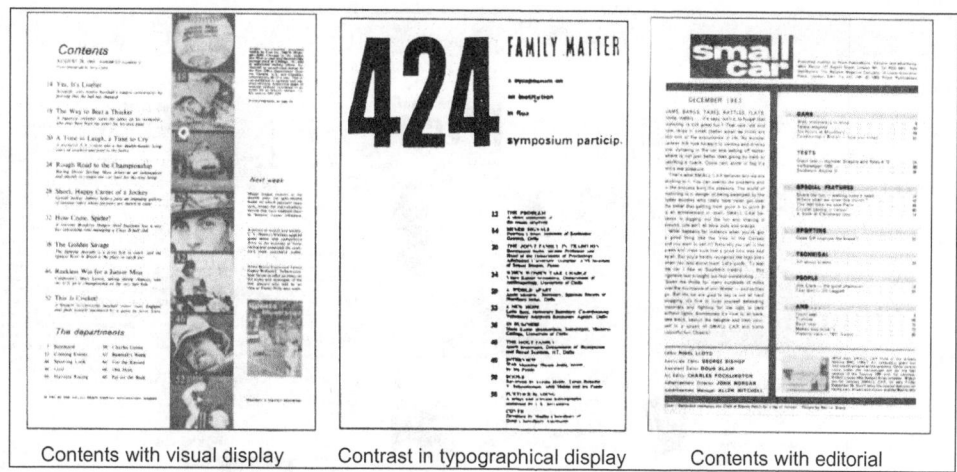

Figure 16.9 Variations in style for contents page

and topics that are covered in the inside pages. As the reader opens the magazine, the first page that is encountered is the contents page. This page provides an answer to his/her foremost question—what is there inside the magazine? It also kindles the reader's interest to go through the magazine from cover to cover.

The contents page is made up of four basic pieces of information—(i) the masthead with the date of issue and number; (ii) list of articles with their respective writers; (iii) page numbers of respective articles; and (iv) the name of the editor and the publisher's address.

For some magazines, 50 per cent of the page area is sufficient for this information and the remaining 50 per cent may be occupied by blurbs, cover description, credits, print line, and any other information that is considered vital during editorial planning. An advertisement on the contents page is also not uncommon. Some magazines prefer to provide minimal information on this page, with liberal white space, occasional bold types, rules, etc. which together make the page stand out and look sober. Some variations of content page style are shown in Figure 16.9.

The format of the contents page may be standardized or changed with every issue. A new design for every issue is expensive, besides being time-consuming. Heavily funded magazines not only change the style of the contents page for each issue but also experiment with several treatments. For instance, they may include a brief summary of some articles accompanied by a small photograph that is used in a bigger size in the inside pages. Tint block, colour, etc. add exclusiveness and dynamism to the contents page. Figure 16.10 shows one such elaborately designed content and editorial page. The idea behind a contents page is to involve the reader and to allow him/her to select reading material of his/her interest.

Editorial page The editorial page of a magazine, also referred to as the editorial, carries a letter or write-up from the editor, in which he/she may talk about the way the magazine wants to achieve some objective or provide suggestions and express his/her views about a particular topic discussed in the issue. Often, the editorial is subtle and

380 Art and Print Production

Figure 16.10 Elaborate content and editorial page

abstract, and is not based on any standard format or pattern. A fearless editor can bring about change and influence public opinion through the views and facts expressed in his/her editorials.

The editorial page should be made distinct from the other pages. It can be made more interesting and different by using a format with a wider column grid, slightly bigger typeface than that used for running pages, and a right-ragged setting for the text. Graphics, cartoons, charts, and graphs can be used with the text, depending on the category of the magazine and the contents of the issue. The editor's photograph may be published on the top of the editorial, and his/her signature can be placed at the bottom of the editorial, as shown in Figure 16.10.

Although the design of the editorial page should look different from that of the other pages, it should be harmonious with the other pages. Harmony can be achieved by using a standard border, uniform type family, repeated pattern of ruled lines, etc. in the editorial page as well as the inside pages.

The right-hand side page shown in Figure 16.10 presents the editorial page of a popular advertising, marketing, and media review magazine.

Running pages The main body of a magazine, containing a series of articles, is known as the running pages. These pages are distinct from the introductory pages such as the contents, editorial, etc.

Figure 16.11 Two-page spread running page

Each running page is designed individually, but not as a series of isolated pages. Although this group of pages consists of different sections or series of individual features, the objective of these pages is to take the reader from page to page smoothly. Since the eyes of the reader run through these pages, they are termed as running pages.

A two-page grid sheet is mandatory in laying out the design elements for running pages. As the reader opens a magazine, he/she sees the facing pages together as one unit of design. The grid sheet is the replica of these pages. It establishes a regular rhythm so that one page flows easily to the next, and makes the text easy to read. Figure 16.11 shows a two-page spread of running pages.

Before using the grid sheet, one should make a rough estimate of the text copy to be used. The headlines, illustrations, and other visual inputs should be selected on the basis of their sizes, tones, and shapes. The sizes of these elements should be kept flexible as far as possible because one has more control over these compared to the running text. It is always more convenient to work on a thumbnail sketch than to work on the actual image straightaway.

The most important elements, which may be either an illustration or a headline, should be placed on the actual page. The other visual devices should be allocated, leaving the column grid empty for a while. The page should then be judged on the basis of design principles. Is the headline of the left side page counterbalancing the photograph placed on the right side page? Are the shapes of the photographs/graphics harmonious? Is there enough contrast on the page? These are some issues that need to be considered at this stage.

Once the designer/editor is satisfied with his/her layout, the column grids can be filled with the text copy either from the galley proofs received from the press or by drawing parallel lines resembling lines of text. This should be arranged in such a way that the reader can go from one end of the article to the other in a flow. One should make sure that the elements placed earlier are not an obstruction to this flow. If necessary, the position of those elements can be shifted, or they can be resized. One or two can go as bleeds. In other words, the edges of photographs or illustrations can run across the page and may even occupy the gutter space. The running text, however, should always be within the print area or the column grids.

Pages filled with only text type with a heading at the top look sober and are just what is needed for a serious magazine. Most magazine pages designed in this manner, however, become monotonous and dull-looking unless a little thought is given to the selection of types and the layout of the pages. In such situations, one can use a larger-size type or a couple of blurbs to create contrast. Blurbs not only break the monotony of the page but also help the reader decide whether he/she should read the whole article.

Drop-letters, oversized punctuation marks, rules, etc. may also be used for the purpose of contrast. Drop-letters are also helpful when the reader is trying to find the starting point of a piece on a crowded page.

These days, computer page layout programs such as Adobe PageMaker, InDesign, and QuarkXPress are available, and are of great help to designers and editors. Layout software programs allow one to create text-base pages in many styles and formats. They may be multi-column and multiple formatted pages with special indents, drop-letters, and rule lines between columns. These programs normally feature style sheets. Style sheets are a type of pre-formatted page layout where all parameters such as the number of columns, type style and size of body text, headings, subheadings, headers and footers, alignment, and other controls are defined. All that one has to do is to import the word-processed text from another programme and apply the style sheet, and the text is automatically laid out. Layout software embraces graphics or scanned images with the help of import facility or data file transfer of the system. It can build a spread that runs across the gutter between the two pages.

Centrespread The two pages opposite each other in the middle of a magazine are referred to as the centrespread. This spread is like any other two-page unit but is considered special. Most magazines are centre-stitched or centre-stapled, and the two pages that actually constitute a spread are a single sheet, unlike other spreads, which are made up of two separate sheets.

Designers enjoy a lot of creative freedom in the planning of the centrespread. They can run art and type across the gutter and experiment with various styles for this spread. Headlines can be placed across the page so that they create a horizontal movement and form a graphic bridge between the pages. Photo features can be effectively planned on the centrespread, with a few photographs on the fold. Grouping and aligning of visuals are far easier in a centrespread as compared to other pages in a magazine.

In the case of magazines that are not centre-stapled, such as section sewn magazines, visuals and headlines that are printed in two parts—one each on facing pages—may not be aligned properly unless a sophisticated binding system is used. The designer should be aware that, in such magazines, a headline on a centrespread may not come in a straight line once the magazine has been bound. This may make the page look uninviting.

Glamour and special interest magazines make good use of the centrespread by printing big-sized photographs of celebrities, beautiful locations, etc. Celebrity pictures printed on centrespreads are much sought-after objects as fans use them as posters on the walls of their rooms.

The centrespread is also used for printing calendars or year planners by most magazines in their year-end issues. This creates a lot of interest among the readers. They can conveniently take out the page from the magazine and display it in their homes or work places, so that the centrespread acts not only as a poster but also as an advertisement of the magazine itself.

The centrespread is of great importance to advertisers as well. This space is often sold to advertisers at a premium. While printing a visual-dominated advertisement on a two-page spread, care should be taken to ensure that the alignment of the pages is right, so that the printed pages have the look and finish desired by the advertisers.

Colour pages As we stop by a news-stand, the attractive covers of many different magazines vie for our attention. Colour plays a dominant role in attracting our attention to a cover. The importance of colour hardly needs to be stressed, as editors and designers are well aware of the fact that, besides attracting attention, colour can also be used to create the right mood or atmosphere and to provide accent and contrast to specific areas as desired. It can also guide the reader through the messages.

Colour has a strong effect on the readers' minds. Hence, colour should not be used just to give the page a bright and colourful look, without putting much thought behind the choice of colours. Sometimes, misuse of colour can do more harm than good to the magazine. Poorly used colour combinations can be quite distracting, and can create a sense of revulsion in the minds of the readers despite the fact that a lot of additional money may have been spent on colour printing. Colour planning should thus be done with a lot of care and understanding.

Reproduction of colour photographs involves four-colour printing. This results in extra costs for colour separation, planning, and printing. The decision to use colour visuals should be taken after considering the costs involved. If, for instance, there are about ten photographs in black and white and one in colour for a specific issue of a magazine, the colour photograph can be avoided to cut down costs. Optimum utilization of colour is always appreciated. Most magazines are printed in four or eight-page formes. The positioning of colour visuals and text can be decided in such a manner that they fall in one or more selected formes. This helps to ensure that colour elements are not scattered across several formes, and thus cuts down the cost of printing several pages in four colour. In the selected formes, colour can be spread across the pages, using colour tones in boxes, borders, headlines, etc., besides visuals images. This can lend variety and colour to the magazine pages at little or no extra cost. Here, again, colour should be used in an effective way.

Since the legibility of typographical matter is of utmost importance, colour should preferably be used for display types only, as these types are bold enough. The colour should also be in contrast to the background. Text matter should never be printed in a colour other than black or a very dark colour. Long copy of reverse on any colour, flat or halftone, should be avoided. Colour tone areas can attract attention to provide power to the various elements of a page. Such areas can be used as a background panel for a copy block, an underlay of a headline or a blurb, a frame of an illustration, or even as an extension of a phototone. The colour pages should be designed in accordance with the production plan, so that, on folding the printed sheet, all the pages are in harmony and fall in the right sequence.

Magazines with shoestring budgets should plan only the cover page in colour. If designed imaginatively, a two-colour cover page or a single-colour image printed on colour paper can look attractive. A few formes may be printed in colour in case the funds available are limited. In such cases, the designer should ensure that these colour pages are in harmony and coherence with the pages in other formes. Halftone illustrations require a smooth-surface paper like art paper or calendered paper. If such paper is used for printing only a few formes, they may look separated from the rest of the magazine. The cover page, however, can be printed on better quality paper, and this is a common practice in most magazines. Colour pages are also planned on the basis of the colour scheme used in some advertisements printed in the magazine.

Production Planning

Editorial planning, design planning, and production planning are highly interrelated processes. For a magazine to be successful, all three processes need to be planned with care. Lack of proper planning in any one of these processes can ruin the work done in the other two processes.

High-quality content, well-designed pages, and liberally invested money may yield a shabby-looking magazine if the production planning is poor. Care should, therefore, be taken to plan the production process properly, so that the magazine is able to face the stiff competition in today's world, and the money invested is used wisely.

Production planning starts with the selection of a printing process. The most commonly used printing process for magazines is offset printing. Offset printing is usually preferred for printing magazines because of its easy make-ready facility and the possibilities of printing fine-screen halftones and using less expensive paper. Moreover, offset printing is compatible with modern typesetting methods and computer imagery systems. Anything that can be photographed can serve as a copy for offset printing.

The offset process is suitable for both low- and high-budget magazines. Selection of the right printing plant is important. A multicolour web-offset plant is most suitable for magazines such as *India Today*, which need to be printed in higher quantities and better quality, but a sheet-fed single-colour small-sized (19″ × 25″) machine is good enough for magazines such as *Mainstream*, which do not need to be of very high quality, and are printed in smaller quantities. Such a machine is also capable of printing multicolour pages.

Another important decision of production planning concerns the paper stock. A substantial part of the magazine budget goes into buying paper. The quality, weight, and surface texture of the paper should be chosen with care, keeping in mind the cost of the paper. Moreover, the content should be adaptable to the quality of paper chosen. It would not be judicious to use costly art paper for a magazine that has no coloured halftone illustrations, or in a magazine where the illustrations and the editorial matter are not likely to improve in quality even if superior-quality paper is used. On the other hand, inferior-quality paper like newsprint may make a magazine look cheap, unattractive, or unreliable. In order to keep the magazine light for easy handling and distribution, calendered newsprint is the safest choice. Fine-screen halftones can also be printed on calendered paper. Other varieties of paper such as maplitho, superprint, and lucky parchment can also be experimented with, depending on the printing process selected and the type of copy.

The cover paper of a magazine needs special attention. To protect and hold the inside pages, it should be thicker and stiffer. It should be superior in surface quality, so that any type of printing is possible on it. The cover paper should also be slightly bigger in size so that any bleed illustration or ground colour can be accommodated within the size.

The camera-ready copy of the artwork is another important part of production planning. It is a positional guide for the printer, in which all the typographical matter is pasted on to a master set of layout grids, leaving spaces for pictorial elements. Alternatively, it can be created by outlining the areas for pictures. These days, desktop publishing has made it possible to generate accurate artwork and obtain a laser printout as a master copy for the printer.

Electronic page planning is used for commercial magazines, which not only separates the colours but also stores the separation information on a disk in a digital form. This information can be used to create a complete page, even if the page consists of several photographs and extensive typographic matter. These facilities give the editor and the designer tremendous flexibility.

NEWSLETTERS

A newsletter is a report, open letter, or bulletin that periodically provides informal or confidential news to the members of a particular group. It is very similar to a magazine, but its aims and objectives are limited to communicating specific messages to a particular group of people.

The two words, 'news' and 'letter', indicate that a newsletter carries information or news, and is in the format of a letter. These days, with the increasing emphasis on design and style, the format of newsletters has shifted from the established letter format to a format that stands somewhere between a newspaper, magazine, and promotional literature. Thus, a modern-day newsletter may have style elements from all these forms of printed literature. For example, the masthead may be in a letterhead style, the column grid may be similar to that of a magazine, the headlines may be in a newspaper style, and the pictorial placement may be similar to that of promotional literature. Figure 16.12 shows the front page of a newsletter, which contains design elements from all the forms of printed literature mentioned here.

Newsletters are important tools for maintaining public relations. They serve as catalysts between the management and the employees of an organization, or between a company as a whole and its external stakeholders. The management uses the newsletter to inform the staff about the progress made by the company and some developments within the organization, thus boosting employee

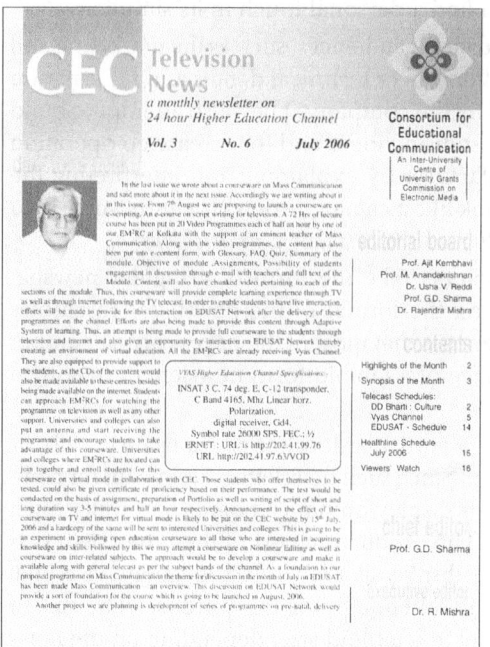

Figure 16.12 Front page of a newsletter

morale. Employees may also contribute articles and news items to their newsletters. The newsletter is thus a two-way communication tool. It is a forum through which the thoughts and visions of the management, its employees, and others who are interested in the organization's fortunes can be expressed and shared. It serves as a vehicle for fostering unity in an organization and for binding the readers together so that they strive for a common goal.

Newsletter Formats

Big companies or organizations dealing with specialized markets often publish more than one newsletter in order to satisfy the specific and distinct interests of varied target groups. Some newsletters, however, cater exclusively to select target audiences. Depending on the target audience at which it is aimed, the design and format of a newsletter also may vary.

If a newsletter is meant for the in-house staff of a magazine, and the resources are limited, it may be designed in the style of a conventional letter, with a masthead on top, as in a regular letterhead, followed by the text in simple typewritten copy. This style may sound very simple, but readers often find a personal touch in its simplicity.

Figure 16.13 Tabloid size newsletter displaying diversified topics

Some newsletters are aimed at specialized target audiences, such as the marketing and sales personnel of a company. Such newsletters cover technical details and information about the products that are being marketed by the company. They also attempt to build brand awareness by publishing their merchandising ideas and to increase co-operation between the merchandisers and the manufacturer by explaining and interpreting the company policies. Such a newsletter may look like a catalogue or a brochure, and is also referred to as a *company bulletin, trade bulletin, sales bulletin,* or a *dealers' journal.*

Newsletters that primarily cover news items take the form of a regular newspaper, mainly in a tabloid form. In such cases, the format of the newsletter resembles that of popular tabloids, and the only difference is that most of the pages carry a number of stories. Figure 16.13 presents the front page of a tabloid-form newsletter covering a variety of topics.

Newsletters meant for target audiences at a particular location like a factory, club, or health centre usually take an interesting shape. Since such newsletters are meant for community reading, their sizes are big enough for display on notice boards and walls. Such newsletters are often called *wall newspapers.* The production cost of these newsletters is very low as very few copies are required for display at a few select locations. A typed, photocopied, or handwritten copy may be good enough for this purpose. The size of such newsletters may vary from a broadsheet to a tabloid size, depending on the news and information to be conveyed.

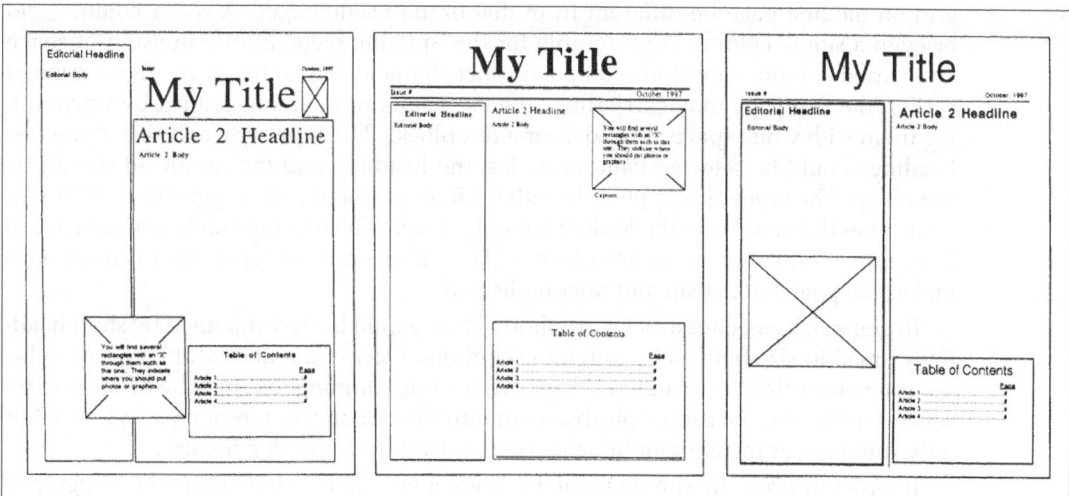

Figure 16.14 Some newsletter formats available in computer software

The publishers of newsletters usually consider its design a peripheral matter. Designers, too, may become complacent about newsletter designing as it seems to be a rather uncomplicated printed communication. Since each newsletter has a captive audience and no other newsletter competes with it, designers sometimes do not take the task of designing seriously. As a result, we come across many ugly, amateurish newsletters in our everyday lives. It is a fact that, many a time, a newsletter designer, who may perhaps be the editor him/herself or a hired professional, works under the multiple limitations of typesetting methods, printing processes, and paper quality, besides the limited amount of money allotted for these purposes. Successful designers, however, strive to make the newsletter design attractive, easy to read, memorable, and effective in spite of all these constraints, even if they have to work with plain printed text. This can be achieved through the creative use of typography, box items, headings, subheadings, blurbs, graphics, etc. In the absence of adequate design knowledge or funds to engage a professional designer, a publisher may rely on the computer template, which is a tool specially developed for designing newsletters. Figure 16.14 shows some newsletter formats available in software programs.

Newsletter Designing

Magazine designing and newsletter designing are closely related. The size, format, masthead, and grid sheet of a newsletter follow the magazine design. Newsletters can, however, be made distinct and separate from magazines and other publications by choosing appropriate type style, graphics, and photographs and by placing them at the right place on a page.

The masthead of a newsletter should always be placed on top, and it should be ensured that it does not occupy more than one-sixth of the page. In most newsletters, the editorial content is started on the front page itself. Designers should let the column grid on the first page be different from that of the inside pages. A wider column grid or even a single column is preferable for the opening page. Subtle division of space and varied column widths also lend a distinct characteristic to the page. As mentioned earlier, the first page may carry the contents. They can be made distinct by surrounding them with white space, a border, or a tint block. The type style and size of the first heading should be selected cautiously, lest the headline and the masthead should be mixed up. The typewriter type style with a left-aligned and right-ragged format for text copy gives the newsletter the look of a regular letter. The text type style may be chosen from Lineal sans serif or modern Roman faces if mechanical typesetting is used. This makes the page look clean and uncomplicated.

In general, newsletter articles are short. They should be accompanied by short headlines, small in size but bold enough to stand out. Occasional lines and boxes can also separate one article from another. Pages with a long running text may be broken up by several subheads, occasional blurbs, or an introduction in a different type style that not only summarizes the content but also creates a vigorous graphic texture.

In order to stress the simplicity of the newsletter, graphic elements and photographs should be used sparingly. In case these are to be used, their size and placement should be such that they do not look too much like a magazine's illustrations.

The back page of the newsletter can be given special treatment. A regular feature, which is particularly fun to look at, may be printed on this page. It may be a cartoon, a special service provided by the company, an interesting off-beat photograph, or a quiz or activity. The back page should also include the mailing address space if it is to be circulated by post. Many organizations mail their newsletters to people's homes by wrapping and stapling the newsletter. The back page should be designed after consulting the postal authorities about their requirements.

Newsletter Production

An electronic typewriter and a duplicating machine are sufficient for producing some newsletters, but wide use of computers and modern offset printing is required for some. Among the duplicating processes, photocopiers are suitable for short-run jobs. Photocopiers can instantly produce an output from a master copy, and this makes the newsletter inexpensive.

In-house printing with a tabletop or small offset machine provides fast and inexpensive printouts. This process does not require an elaborate make-ready system. The text can be typed on a low-cost paper master, which can be heated up to make the image firm and a bit raised, and wrapped around the cylinder of the machine for printing. This master can receive images from artwork as well. In such cases, the image is transferred on to it by photocopying. The image can also be obtained directly on the master from the laser printer.

Since most parts of the newsletter that come from the quick print shop are in black and white, the masthead can be printed in colour in bulk at one time, using one of the major printing machines. This masthead-printed paper can then be supplied to the printer for every issue. The rest of the matter can be printed in black and white as and when required. This will give the newsletter a touch of colour and also save a great deal of money.

Newsletters are generally very thin. The pages of a newsletter can thus be held together by stapling them at the top corner or at the side. Centre stitching or one or two folds to a sheet can also be used to bind a newsletter.

Desktop publishing has become very popular for newsletter production these days. Desktop systems can be used to carry out all the processes required for printing a newsletter. It allows the text to be arranged in a manner that makes it appear similar to typeset text. The time-consuming paste-up process is completely eliminated in page formatting. The system also provides a printout on inexpensive paper by laser. This printout can be used as a master copy or artwork, and the newsletter can be printed using any of the processes discussed earlier.

SUMMARY

Periodicals are publications that are issued at regular intervals. They are usually short-lived in nature. Periodicals may be divided into three categories—ephemeral periodicals such as newspapers and tabloids, leisure reading periodicals such as magazines and journals, and official periodicals such as newsletters and bulletins. Newspapers and tabloids have already been discussed in Chapter 13. In this chapter, we have focused on magazines and newsletters. The designing of other leisure reading and official periodicals is similar to that of magazines and newsletters, respectively.

The format of a periodical depends on the adaptability of its contents to a particular form. In other words, the nature of the magazine influences its format to a great extent. For example, technical magazines have a formal and book-like appearance, news and current affairs magazines resemble the newspaper format, and glamour magazines have stylish and fancy pages. Depending on their role, magazine formats are influenced by books, newspapers, and television.

These days, hundreds of magazines are issued at regular intervals. Each of them has developed a character of its own. Based on their physical characteristics and contents, they may be classified as news magazines, glamour magazines, special interest magazines, and magazines on aesthetics and culture.

A news magazine covers different kinds of topics with vivid photographs of events. It is packed with type, narrow column grids, blurbs, cartoons, etc. Glamour magazines, with their big-sized photographs, subtle graphics, and fancy headings, are meant more for viewing than for reading. Special interest magazines cater to a wide range of interest groups, from homemakers to children to astronauts. The physical appearance of such magazines depends on their aims and objectives and the availability of funds. The content of aesthetic and cultural magazines may be visual-oriented or simply typographic. They are aimed at specific sections of society, such as those who have a special interest in art.

Work on a magazine starts with editorial planning, which includes a concrete plan for publishing the issue by the due date, selection of appropriate articles for the issue, planning for advertisement space, and sending the manuscript/artwork to the press as per the schedule. Editorial planning goes into action with design planning. Most of the decisions relating to the size of the magazine, format of column grid, margin, space between columns, type size, style of text matter, etc. are taken at this stage.

Production planning starts with the selection of the printing process. Offset printing is the most commonly used process for magazine printing. Paper stock, typesetting methods, nature of artwork, etc. are the crucial decisions of production planning.

Editorial, design, and production plans influence the planning and designing of the various pages of a magazine. For our convenience, we may discuss magazine designing by dividing a magazine into the following parts—cover, contents, editorial, running pages, centrespread, and colour pages. Covers may range from the simple, with only typographical display, to the elaborate, with multicolour graphics with photographs and type combinations to attract attention and to create the desired mood. The contents page is designed to involve the reader and to arouse his/her interest so that he/she is inclined towards going through the magazine. The editorial page should look different from the other pages without losing the basic harmony of all the pages. Running pages are designed to take the reader from page to page smoothly. The centrespread of a magazine is a special page. The elements running across the page or gutter space of a centrespread should be placed with care, as improper binding may disturb the alignment of such matter. The designing of colour pages should be based on aesthetics, legibility, and appropriateness. Since colour reproduction is expensive, this aspect needs to be planned professionally.

Newsletters are official periodicals that carry information or news that is sent to the readers generally in the format of a letter. The format of newsletters may vary from that of a letter to a newspaper, magazine, or promotional literature. As an important public relations tool, they serve as a catalyst in promoting cordial relations between the management and the employees.

Newsletter designing is similar to magazine designing, but they can be given a distinct look by choosing appropriate type styles and graphics and by placing them at appropriate locations. The production methods for newsletters may range from duplication of a typed copy to elaborate offset printing.

KEY TERMS

Blurb A brief paragraph of verbal copy written as promotional text for a book jacket or in order to highlight the essence of an article or some parts of it in a magazine or book.

Centrespread Two facing pages in the middle of a publication that are center stitched.

Column Grid Non-printable structured lines on paper or on a computer screen, determined by the designer, and used to indicate column width, height, number of columns, and space between them.

Credit Line The place where the name of artist, photographer, or writer appears, usually close to his/her contribution in a publication.

Galley Proof A term derived from the hot metal days' hand proofs from galley trays. Today, the term refers to non-formatted typeset proof from the service bureau.

Header The information at the top portion of a page margin. It may be title, chapter name, and/or page number or folio.

Introduction Brief introductory lines of an article or story normally set in a slightly bigger type size than the text. Also referred to as the 'intro'.

Magazine A term derived from the Arabic word 'mahazin' or the French word 'magasin', both meaning 'warehouse' or 'store'.

Newsletter A report, open letter, or bulletin that periodically provides informal or confidential news to the members of a particular group.

News-stand A stall for small business that sells newspapers, magazines, stationery, postcards, and clothing emblazoned with sports team mascots.

Pocketbook Pocket-sized small book, usually paperbound (paperback). Also called a 'pocket edition'.

Press Run The number of copies of a forthcoming publication that is aimed at the commercial market that will be printed. The press run is also referred to as the 'print run'.

Print Line The place where the name and address of the printing press appear on the publication.

REFERENCES

Conover, Theodore E. 1990, *Graphic Communication Today*, West Publishing Company, St. Paul.

Frost, Chris 2005, *Designing for Newspaper and Magazine*, Routledge Taylor & Francis Group, London and New York.

Nelson, Roy Paul 1991, *Publication Design*, Wm. C. Brown Publishers, USA.

Sarkar, N.N. 1998, *Designing Print Communication*, Sagar Publications, New Delhi.

Turnbull, Arthur T. and Baird, Russell N. 1980, *The Graphics of Communication*, Holt, Rinehart and Winston, USA.

White, Jan V. 1976, *Designing for Magazine*, R.R. Bowker Company, New York.

www.printusa.com/glos, accessed in June 2007.

Yadin, Daniel L. 1994, *Creative Marketing Communication*, Kogan Page Ltd, London.

REVIEW QUESTIONS

1. Define periodicals. Mention the categories of publications that can be classified as periodicals. Why are the design and contents of periodicals influenced by books, advertising, and television?
2. Periodicals can be categorized into ephemeral, leisure reading, and official publications. Describe the characteristics of each category with the help of appropriate examples.
3. What are the functions of a magazine? How is the physical form of a magazine developed? Categorize magazines on the basis of their physical characteristics.
4. What are the roles of an editor in publishing a magazine? Describe the working of an editor in financially sound as well as constrained situations.
5. How can a designer show creativity in designing a magazine within the framework of editorial planning? What do you understand by design planning?
6. What are the parts a magazine can be divided into for the purpose of design planning? Describe the design approach for each part in relation to its content.
7. Why is the centrespread of a magazine considered to be a special page? How can designers make the best use of this page?
8. The use of colour in magazine pages is as important as in any other field of media communication. This involves aesthetics, legibility of information-bearing elements, cost, and time, and hence requires a lot of planning. Support this statement by suggesting ways for the optimum use of colour.
9. How are the editorial, design, and production planning of a magazine interrelated? Elaborate the steps involved in the production of a magazine.
10. How is a newsletter different from a magazine? Describe the physical appearance of some common style of newsletter in relation to its contents.
11. 'Newsletters are a tool to maintain public relations, and design plays a peripheral role in most new sletters.' Write a note on the statement.
12. Compare a newsletter with a magazine, based on its design and production planning.

PROJECTS

1. Plan a magazine for a young urban target audience. The aims and objectives of the magazine are to educate and entertain through stories based on music. Design an appropriate masthead accompanied by a slogan for the magazine.
2. Prepare a grid sheet on a demy quarto size paper as per the sample given in Figure 16.7. Make a prototype page paste-up for an article spread over two facing pages. Cut text copy, heading, photographs, and other elements from an old magazine and paste them on the grid sheet in your own style. There may not be any relation between all the elements you have cut out in terms of their content. Judge your arrangement on the basis of its visual look and use of design principles and typographical rules.
3. Pick up some magazines from a news-stand. Redesign one of them, retaining only the masthead. Make sure that the design created by you has a harmonious look with its regular editions, so that it gives the readers a feeling of continuity and oneness with the magazine he/she has been reading.
4. Prepare a centrespread photo feature on the computer, using a layout software. Give it an appropriate heading and add captions for the photographs. Photographs chosen should be harmonious in terms of content and style. You may use graphic effects on the computer to create a style that enhances the content of the photographs.
5. Take a poorly designed newsletter that has only typographical content. Redesign it on your computer within the same limitations. Take a printout of the same and evaluate the improvement made by you.

CHAPTER

17 Poster Design

Learning Objectives

After reading this chapter, you should be able to
- trace the developments in the field of poster designing and the role of posters as a communication medium
- look at the designing and reach of posters in the Indian context
- discuss the advantages and limitations of posters as a communication medium
- understand some basic rules for poster designing
- discuss the steps involved in creating a poster and look at various methods of poster production

INTRODUCTION

In the era of information technology, when messages constantly come to us through visuals in a moving form, the poster, a static visual medium, could be expected to take a back seat in the field of mass communication. However, this has not happened. New developments in technology have given the poster medium a boost not known in the 200 years of its existence since the invention of the lithographic process. Posters have their own place in the field of communication and continue to be used widely. Modern technology has not only helped produce posters accurately on a large scale in less time but also allowed poster designers to try out several options in terms of style, colour, etc. This has given a new dimension to poster design.

The poster is one of the oldest forms of communication. It existed even before the invention of Gutenberg's movable type. Most of the posters before Gutenberg's invention were produced in limited numbers and were mainly painted by hand, or produced by stencil or wood-cut blocks. In those days, posters were in single colour and usually carried government or religious propaganda.

With the invention of the lithography process in 1798, posters got a new look with dominating visuals in dynamic colours. Many famous artists of that period made the poster form a piece of art with the help of lithography. At the end of the nineteenth century, the offset process, which is an improved form of lithography, facilitated mass production of posters.

Before the invention of photography and halftone reproduction, posters were designed and printed in flat colours with the minimum of details. These qualities of poster techniques still exist in many poster designs. Posterization is a photographic technique that converts colour or monochrome photographs into images consisting of subtle, but flat areas of tones or colours.

During World War I, the poster was an important medium of communication, as the radio and other electronic means of public communication had not yet come into prominence. During this war, governments turned to the poster as a major means of propaganda and visual persuasion. Posters were used to recruit troops and boost public morale.

In many situations, posters, with their powerful use of graphics and messages, have helped bring about incredible change in the social, political, cultural, and economic aspects of the human condition. Figure 17.1 shows an anti-war poster that seeks to have an impact on human society by urging people to say 'NO' to war. Here, the letter 'N' in the word 'NO' has been creatively written in the form of a missile.

The role of the poster has also been substantial in the independence struggle of many countries, during demands for peace and public demonstrations. Posters are used extensively in elections and advertising campaigns. Events such as exhibitions, conferences, and seminars use posters for publicity.

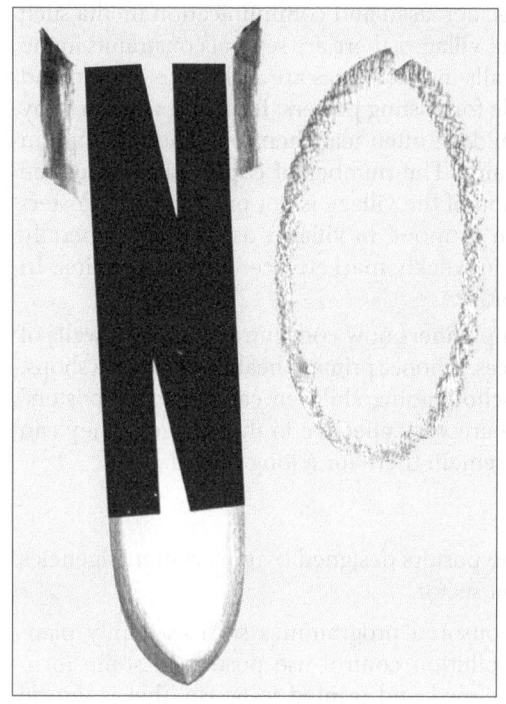

Figure 17.1 Say 'NO' to war: an anti-war poster

INDIAN CONTEXT

In this section, we shall look at the designing, reach, and advantages and limitations of posters as a medium of communication in our country.

Reach of Posters

The use of posters in Indian mass communication is not a novelty. Posters have been extensively used in our country to disseminate information. The poster message is generally presented in a written form supported by strong visuals; hence, a minimum level of literacy is a must to understand the message.

For many years, posters in India had largely been confined to cities and towns. With the development of trade and industry and with governments more actively promoting development programmes such as literacy campaigns, a large number of rural people are now exposed to posters, and are able to understand the communicated message.

The reach of communication into rural areas has been multiplied with the growing penetration of television. Posters and television can together serve as an effective medium of communication. Television is a strong audio-visual medium, to which the poster can serve as a reminder medium. In other cases, the poster may serve as the primary medium and television may remind people of the message.

Despite the fact that the literacy rate has increased and communication media such as television and posters have entered Indian villages, there are several constraints in the use of posters in rural areas. Most of the walls in rural areas are still made of mud and dried tree parts. These walls are not suitable for pasting posters. Rain and wind destroy the pasted posters very fast. Moreover, children often tear them off. The distribution system of posters presents another constraint. The number of copies printed for the village audience in relation to the population of the village is not proportional. Posters often fail to create the desired atmosphere or mood in villages as they are generally pasted far away from one another, except in weekly marketplaces and *melas* (fairs). In these places too, their impact is just temporary.

In view of the above constraints, media planners now concentrate on brick walls of community centres, block development offices, schools, primary health centres, tea shops, and marketplaces. Literate villagers and school-going children can carry the posters' message home. Posters printed on tinplate are very effective in the villages. They can be nailed to trees and wooden pillars and remain there for a long period.

Quality of Posters

In India, vast differences can be seen in the posters designed by government agencies and those designed by the non-government sector.

Government sector Most government-sponsored programmes such as family planning, health care, adult education, and pollution control use posters in some form or the other. These posters are largely designed and printed in-house, that is, in the departments of the central and state governments. There is a specialized department of the central government, namely, the Directorate of Advertising and Visual Publicity (DAVP), which produces and distributes a large number of posters. The quality of these posters in terms of design and production has often been criticized. Lack of competition is perhaps the main reason for the poor quality of these posters. Also, the designers' exposure to modern technology is usually negligible. The officers responsible for briefing the artist and selecting the final design are not well-versed in the subject and are usually unaware of the target audience. Lack of visual literacy may also lead to the selection of wrong designs. A major handicap of the process is the lowest tender system. Under it, the agency quoting the lowest price for a government job is awarded the tender. Quality is often compromised since the agency quoting the lowest price is more likely to do a shoddy job.

These days, however, the quality of posters designed by government organizations is showing improvement, as discussed in the section titled 'current scenario'.

Private sector The situation is different in the private sector. City streets always wear a festive look with a variety of posters, which are bold with striking graphic forms and brilliant colours. Every now and then, these posters surprise the viewers, hold their attention, and bring a significant fact, idea, or message to their minds.

Current Scenario

Economic liberalization has now forced trade and industry into hard competition to lure the target audience, who are now much more mature and selective. Specialized agencies are engaged in developing the required poster for its inclusion in the organizations' media planning, which involves decisions on when, how, and in what frequency the posters will be exposed to the viewers.

These changes are now slowly visible in government and government-controlled organizations too. Posters are being developed along with other publicity material by organizing workshops, seminars, and open competitions. Figure 17.2 shows an award-winning poster developed during an open competition organized by the National Literacy Mission.

In a workshop, the participants may be a homogeneous group of designers who come out with a functional and aesthetically good design after a series of lectures by experts in the field. This is followed by group discussions among themselves. Heterogeneous groups also work well when ideas are developed and get authenticated by the experts and implementers of the message. For example, in a health care poster workshop, a group can consist of a designer, a photographer, a copywriter/editor, a doctor, and a block-level health worker. Workshops and seminars are provided with background papers based on research and study of the subject, with perhaps a sample of work done earlier. Developed posters may also be taken to the intended target audience for pre-testing during these workshops. Figure 17.3 shows a poster on the dangers of deforestation developed during a workshop titled 'save your environment' at IIMC. All the entries were pre-tested, and the poster displayed in Figure 17.3 got a high rating. This poster was developed by participants from Kerala, and the Kerala Government used this poster extensively for promoting a green enviroment.

Figure 17.2 Literacy—a burning social issue

Figure 17.3 Dangers of deforestation

As we all know, there is no dearth of talented designers in our country. An open competition can be held to encourage such designers to contribute their work for posters. Such competitions can help the cause of poster-making in many ways—(i) by involving of a great number of people in the process; (ii) by facilitating the selection of the best works from a large number of entries, which can be duplicated and distributed; and (iii) by enabling people to appreciate the created designs by organizing exhibitions of selected entries on the subject. Press coverage of such exhibitions would give additional publicity to the whole exercise.

These days, various organizations and institutions have realized that, poster-making, like sports and music, is a stimulating activity. Many voluntary organizations, local bodies, and communities have begun to organize poster-making competitions for different levels of participants. In schools too, poster-making has become a major co-curricular activity. Thus, posters have become a part of our everyday lives.

STRENGTHS OF THE POSTER MEDIUM

The various strengths of the poster medium have been elaborated in this section.

Effort for communicating the intended message Posters requires minimum effort on the part of the viewer to understand the message conveyed. Since most posters are simple and convey only a brief message with striking visuals and the minimum number of words, potential consumers can take in the message at a glance and, in most cases, understand whether it is meant for them or not. It does not take a viewer too much time and effort to study a poster in detail.

Figure 17.4 Poster displayed at a point of purchase

Unit cost Since posters are generally reproduced on a mass scale, they have a relatively low unit cost. They are printed on one side and left blank on the other to facilitate pasting. Printing can be done on low-grade paper or on chromo paper for better halftone jobs. Since paper is the biggest cost factor in poster printing, it can reduce the unit cost of printing.

Versatility Posters are a versatile medium of communication. Poster sizes can range from $5'' \times 9''$ flyers to $12' \times 24'$ billboards. They may be printed in thousands or even lakhs for outdoor display for a mass audience. They may also be used for selective audiences, as in seminars and exhibitions, where a limited number of copies may be printed or drawn.

Posters can be displayed at the point of purchase, which permits the customers to have a close look at their contents. Figure 17.4 shows a poster of Maggi noodles displayed at a fast-food outlet. Use of posters as a teaching aid is an age-old practice. Posters printed on tinplate can be used for a longer duration. The poster's message may not only be restricted to a slogan

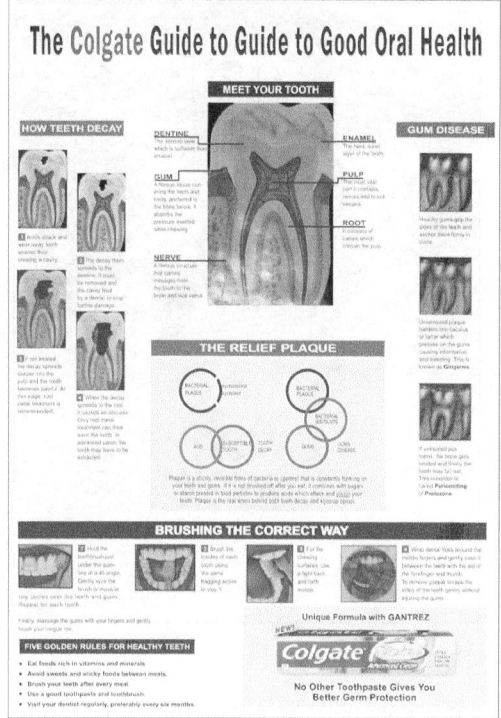 

Figure 17.5 Poster aimed at the captive audience in a dental clinic

Figure 17.6 Poster that can be used as a wall display

and a visual. On a number of occasions, particularly where the audience is captive, as in trains, buses, and health centres, there is an excellent opportunity for advertisers to convey more detailed messages. Figure 17.5 shows a poster of a toothpaste brand aimed at the captive audience at a dental clinic.

Scope for creativity Posters provide unlimited scope for creativity. A poster creates a good deal of excitement, surprise, and curiosity with the creative use of graphic shapes, visuals, colours, etc. A creative poster not only sells the product or idea effectively but also serves the purpose of a wall display. Figure 17.6 shows a poster for a folk art museum, which can also be used as a wall display.

Creating the right ambience Posters can create a suitable ambience or environment during local events such as a crafts *mela* or national events such as general elections. Reliance and Vodafone created an environment of awareness by displaying their posters on city streets to popularize their new image in 2006 and 2007, respectively. The ambience created by posters can cross the barriers of literacy and language as it can be easily comprehended. A positive ambience created by posters improves the ability of the viewers to appreciate the aesthetics of the posters and involves the viewers with the message. Figure 17.7 shows a poster that engages the viewer by posing a question and providing the answer to the same.

Figure 17.7 Poster that engages the viewer by posing a question

Reach   Posters have a strong reach, affecting even people who are on the move. Communication through posters is unique. A poster delivers its message while people travel, shop, or visit friends.

Exposure   Posters have a twenty-four-hour exposure as they are usually displayed in public places. Therefore, their message has the chance to reach a wide portion of the total population constantly. An individual may be exposed to a poster several times during the course of a single day.

'Real-life feeling'   Posters are usually seen from a distance. The visuals used in posters are usually printed in such a manner that the viewer perceives the object in its actual size. These visuals strive for appropriateness in subject-matter, which is vital to fulfil the purpose of a poster.

Market coverage   Posters enable controlled market coverage. Advertisers can localise their campaign to a street, town, area, or region. They can, in fact, choose sites where their products will be most visible to the target audience. This provides an opportunity to the advertiser to capture the attention of the population within a specific area.

LIMITATIONS OF THE POSTER MEDIUM

Even though the poster as a medium has many advantages, it has certain drawbacks as well. This section lists the drawbacks of posters.

Non-selectivity   The poster is a non-selective medium. As it is a mass medium, it cannot provide selective demographic coverage. When displayed, it is seen by all classes and groups of the society, some of whom may not be the target audience of the message. For example, a poster of a new car battery may not create any interest among those who generally travel by bicycle or scooter. Such a poster will not create any impact on the daily-wage earners whose number is so high in any city. Deciding just how many sites/areas to use to achieve an optimum coverage is another problem for the advertiser.

Limitations on message content Posters can allow only limited message content. A poster is seen at a glance, so it can carry only a brief and simple message. It needs the help of other media for detailed information. Posters are used as supplements to advertisements; they cannot attain the prestige of the major advertising tools. A short message that must be read is not as effective as one that needs to be seen. The opportunity-to-see (OTS) is very high but it is hard to gauge the impact per opportunity.

Limited visibility and life The visibility and life of posters depend on nature. The poster is an outdoor medium and is mainly visible in daylight. After sunset, it is only seen in limited places with the help of artificial light. Rain and winds cause great damage to posters. They are quickly discoloured by bright sunlight. Moreover, a poster can fade away without creating an impact if another poster is stuck over it.

High absolute cost In order to reach a large target audience, posters have to be printed on a large scale. The total cost of printing including paper becomes very high despite the low unit cost per poster. Each poster has to be pasted manually. The distribution system and monitoring of the pasting work at appropriate places also cost a lot of money. Paid sites such as kiosks and hoardings are quite expensive. Posters with a low print run and those printed on tinplate are also very expensive.

Effect on the natural environment Posters often pollute our natural environment. For those who care for environment, the poster is a nuisance that creates visual pollution. Posters pasted haphazardly not only deface streets, buildings, or flyovers but also destroy the natural beauty of parks and monuments. They can also cause a lot of inconvenience when pasted on signboards of local guide maps and road names. There are usually no set laws to prevent this. Even those who create and implement laws have been the subject of criticism on this account during times such as election campaigns.

RULES FOR POSTER DESIGNING

The poster is a visual form of expression. It is seen, read, and understood within a few seconds. In a poster, multi-dimensional design elements such as information-bearing, decoration, and background elements turn into composite two-dimensional graphic shapes. Like any other language, poster designing also follows some rules. One can mould an idea or an event based on these rules.

Visual comprehension is largely dependent on viewers' occupation, interests, experience, and frame of mind. The rules of poster are mainly framed to overcome the viewers' constraints. These broad rules are as follows.

Select as Few Design Elements as Possible

For effective communication, only a few design elements should be selected. For example, a poster of a soft drink may contain only the brand name of the product.

Two elements, such as a visual accompanied by a caption, work well together. Three elements may be considered in situations where they really help enhance the poster's visual quality and make it easier to recognize the idea. Multiple elements should be considered only when the poster is meant for a captive audience.

Restrict the Number of Words

The typographical element, that is, the number of words, should be restricted to three to five. The words should preferably be in a bold legible typeface. It is worthwhile to remember that a poster is exposed to the viewer only for an average of five seconds. If more words have to be used to create the message, the total number of words should not go beyond ten. The emphasis should be only on one, two, or three words. The remaining words may be used only in a subordinate role.

Try to Create the Maximum Impact through Visuals

The visual used in a poster may be a photograph, drawing, or simply a shape in colour or tone. Only the necessary portion of the visual should be used in the poster, covering as much area of the poster as possible. In order to facilitate recognition from a distance, unnecessary details need to be eliminated.

Different photo techniques such as cut-out, silhouette, posterization, and quartertone can be used for designing a poster. Hand-drawn illustrations such as line drawing, line and tone drawing, and dry-brush drawing offer greater freedom of expression than photographs. Bold lines make a poster attractive.

Exaggeration, distortion, and computer manipulation are some other techniques which help in attracting the attention of the target audience. These techniques are vital for this medium of communication.

Abstract and symbolic forms of visuals also have an important role to play in poster design. Although difficult, if an abstract form of expression is converted into a tangible form, it has a greater possibility of making an impact. However, it is better to avoid experimenting with abstract forms when the audience is rural and limited.

The size of the visual also influences the effectiveness of a poster. For example, in a poster advertising a pesticide, a large image of insects spoiling crops may not be identified by the majority of the farmers.

A poster should be able to communicate its message to both the illiterate and the literate section of the target audience. The visual must compensate for the inability of illiterate people to read the slogan. If the visual is able to generate sufficient interest, words will not stand in the way of comprehension of the message, as illiterate viewers will be motivated to seek an explanation from those who understand the message.

Never Think of the Visual and the Caption Separately

The visual and the caption should together create the desired effect. These two elements become the major force for attracting the target audience's attention in terms of idea generation and graphic presentation.

Posters are designed for display among an undifferentiated audience that may be loosely divided into the educated, semi-educated, and uneducated. Some of them may see the posters and completely ignore them. Through repeated exposure others may create some impression. Some potential consumers both see and read the poster. This helps in clarifying the concepts and creating a realization, which enables them to believe what they see. Therefore, visuals used in the poster must reinforce what the caption says and vice versa.

In case the photograph of a human face is selected for a poster, it is important to make sure that the target audience can associate themselves with the person.

Like any other visual form, posters require a centre of interest. In a poster, the centre of interest should be particularly strong and commanding. The message of a product shown in a poster is more effective if the visual is in actual size with a clearly visible label or brand name. The feeling of actual size can be created if, in the poster, the product is accompanied by a living being, especially a human figure. For example, in a poster advertising a refrigerator, a potential consumer can get an idea of the size of the refrigerator if it is accompanied by a human model.

Flat-tone pictures, charts, and maps have graphical characteristics and are used widely in poster designs to fulfil certain unique requirements. For instance, they are used to provide statistical information and locational guidelines. These images may be handled skilfully by toning, shaping, and sizing. To break the monotony, some illustrations may be added to the poster.

Treat All the Elements of Design as One Unit

To fulfil the poster's objective, all the elements of a design should be treated as one unit. When all the elements of a design are grouped together, it creates a sense of unity.

A proper visual sequence can be maintained by removing the non-essential elements of a design. Elements which emphasize the poster's message should be included in the design. Overlapping of elements is another well-tried method to create unity among the elements. As discussed in Chapter 5, this can be checked by placing a sheet of tracing paper on the poster and drawing an outline around the main design elements or making a silhouette of them.

Develop a Distinctive Style

A style can be created by a combination of five variables—forms, types, colours, images, and paper. The target audiences identify themselves with poster styles that are aimed at them. The effectiveness of a style is limited only by the characteristics of the target audience and their probable interest in the message. For example, a poster advertising products for women needs to be styled in such a manner that it appeals to the target group of women. Figure 17.8 shows a poster for Milk & Roses soap.

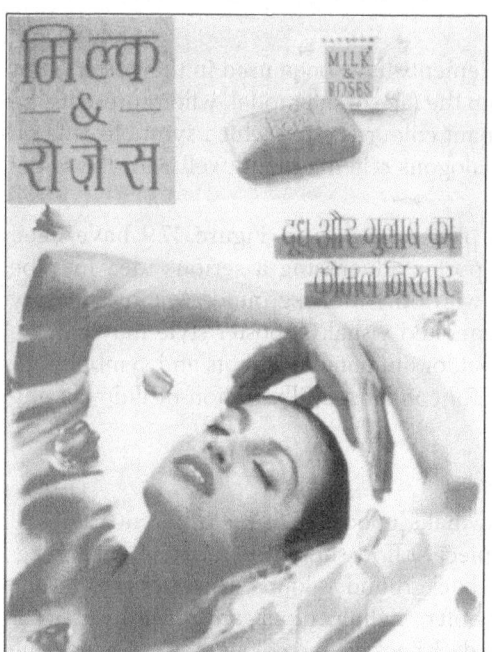

Figure 17.8 Poster specifically aimed at women

Youthful style

Animated style

Figure 17.9 Posters aimed at the youth

The proportion in which different design elements have been used in the poster helps in moving the potential consumer's eye from the face of the model, who represents the target audience, to the type. The predominant colour is pink, which symbolizes femininity. The novelty of the type and the analogous scheme blend well with the target audience's desire to look beautiful.

Similarly, the Hero Honda and 7Up posters shown in Figure 17.9 have been designed keeping the youth in mind. A poster advertising a serious idea may be developed by typographical arrangement with only a background. A contemporary style may be developed by a computer-generated visual. A poster style may contain rural, regional, Indian, classic, floral, abstract, or animated elements and symbols. For instance, the 7Up poster shown in Figure 17.9 contains an illustration of Fido, an animated character.

Make Use of the Full Value of Colour

While designing a poster, designers should make good use of the different values of colours to create a pleasing and effective piece. Effort should be made to ensure legibility and appropriateness. In general, the background colour is used to highlight the information-bearing elements of the poster. Soft or lighter colours are generally used for the background. However, in certain cases, a dark background colour may accentuate the lighter colours of the information-bearing elements by providing a striking contrast.

Audience preference and psychology cannot be ignored while selecting the colours for a poster, as each poster is designed for a particular group of target audience. Individual prejudices of the designer should not be allowed to influence the choice of colours. If and when required, the designer may have to break the rules of colour to achieve the basic objective, that is, to attract attention. At times, even symbolic and emotional appeal may have to be sacrificed for greater visibility.

A designer should not be disappointed if he/she has only one or two colours to work with. Sometimes, a multi-coloured poster may not be as effective as a well-designed single- or two-colour poster. Even if a poster is designed in bright, attractive colours, its basic purpose will be lost if its illustration is very small and the borders are too thin. The contents of such a poster will not be visible from a distance. In case only a limited number of colours is to be used, thick lines or solid colour bands that occupy a large area of the poster, reverse, or bleed may be used. The term *reverse* refers to an area fully covered with colour (solid or toned) and some elements like type and illustration appear in light colour or the colour of the paper. A *bleed* is where the colour goes right to the edges of the poster. Such effects give a more colourful look to posters and help them stand out in a cluttered environment.

In multi-coloured compositions, one of the colours should be allowed to dominate for the purpose of contrast. Other colours may be used in different proportions. This is especially necessary in a vivid colour scheme. Otherwise, the colours may create a flickering effect that kills the very purpose of the poster.

Grey and muted colours are not preferred in posters as much as pure colours as they tend to be depressing. They are best used as background colours or in situations where they are likely to have positive physiological or psychological effects on the target audience. For instance, if the poster is meant to be displayed indoors, it is preferable to use a simple colour scheme. Bright colours bring the image nearer to the eye. This may tire the eyes after some time. This is the physiological effect of colour. People feel cool in a blue-coloured or pre-eminently bluish design and warm in a red-coloured or pre-eminently reddish design. Designers may utilize these findings on the psychological impact of colour while creating posters.

Colours for a poster should be selected on the basis of their association with the product, environment, lifestyle, or with the specific theme that it desires to communicate. A poster of Fanta in a colour scheme consisting of red, orange, yellow, and bright green is immediately associated with the orange-coloured drink. The posters of Rajasthan Tourism generally carry a warm colour scheme. Posters on immunization meant for tribes in remote areas should not carry visuals of people from metros.

The visibility, readability, attraction, and recognition qualities of colour should be differentiated. Some combinations of colours are visible and appealing to the eye but not necessarily readable. A scheme of muted colours of blue, pink, and yellow may be very pleasing but none of the colours has the readable quality of typographic elements of the scheme. Certain colours are immediately associated by us with objects in the natural environment. Such familiar colours have more recognition value than unfamiliar ones, and can thus be used effectively in a poster to attract our attention. Another way to attract attention is to use elements that are in contrast. Black on white or yellow provides the maximum visibility. A complementary colour scheme enhances contrast and creates excitement; this is just what is required to attract attention.

STEPS IN POSTER DESIGNING

While developing a poster, it is important to gather information on the—(i) demography (age, sex, geographical spread, and occupation) and psychography (attitude, values, and tastes) of the target audience; (ii) communication objectives of the product or service (inform, educate, action, opinion-gathering, sale, etc.); and (iii) mechanical limitations such as size, language, printing process, and the number of colours.

Once the basic information has been gathered, a designer may then proceed with the following steps.

List some probable captions The designer should concentrate on reaching the target audience and achieving the poster's communication objectives. He/she can start this process by listing some probable captions. The captions need to be descriptive and flexible at this stage so that they easily blend with the visuals. The captions are short-listed keeping the following questions in mind—Is the caption simple and easy to read? Is the idea interesting and accurate? Does it have recall value?

Translate ideas into visual form The designer should think of a visual that blends well with the caption and vice versa. A number of thumbnail sketches should be prepared and the various alternatives should be laid out. The most appropriate thumbnail should then be selected. Usually, the most visually pleasing and functional thumbnail is selected.

Prepare a working rough from the selected thumbnail Next, a working rough should be prepared from the selected thumbnail for the purpose of client approval. A working poster rough may be one-fourth the size of the actual poster or even smaller. It is convenient to work in the small area without spending a lot of time and material. It is also easier to work by taking a printout of the working rough. Any correction or alteration can be carried out easily on this rough copy. Since the poster is a medium that is seen from a distance, the small-sized working rough may be evaluated by keeping the rough at a distance of 15 to 17 times of the width of the layout away from the viewer, just to judge the visual clarity and type legibility. We perceive the size of an object in relation to its distance from our eyes. Thus, it is difficult to determine the appropriate size for a poster and its elements independent of distance.

Make the actual size finished The poster's actual size layout may vary from the finished to the comprehensive. A mount board may be used for this purpose of layout, if a standard size poster ($18'' \times 23''$ or $20'' \times 30''$) needs to be prepared. It remains stiff, whether one paints, draws, or pastes photographs on coloured paper or any other material to get the desired effect. The selected thumbnail or working rough may serve the purpose of a guide. Photocopying and computer scanning are quite helpful in enlarging the drawing. A person relatively unskilled in drawing can comfortably depend on these techniques if someone else has drawn the illustration in a small size or if the illustration is taken from instant graphics, catalogues, or computer clip-art.

If the poster is planned with a photograph, it is advisable to draw a simulated image and paste the bromide print for comprehensiveness. This is all the more necessary when the poster illustration is to be printed from a colour transparency. All the elements of a comprehensive layout should be finished neatly to give the look of an actually printed poster.

Handle the artwork based on the selected printing process The final step or the artwork of the poster layout is almost the same as in other printed literature. It is important not to paste any portion meant for scanning on the mount board. The electronic scanner takes the artwork in a flexible form that can be wrapped around the cylinder of the scanner. A comprehensive layout that is finished in all respects is suitable for processing, if a colour transparency is taken from it.

POSTER PRODUCTION

There are various methods for the production of posters. Effective posters can be created by selecting appropriate methods of production and by utilizing digital technologies.

Production Methods

In this section, we shall discuss various methods of poster production, such as the manual method, conventional methods, and the common duplication method.

Manual production

The method of duplicating a poster may vary from hand-painting to high-tech digital printing. Naturally, the number of copies needed and the functions expected are the major factors influencing the method selected for poster production. A poster chart for display in the office room may be painted manually, and flat colours may be created from poster paper. Original photographs may be pasted on the poster, and typographical matter can be inserted by stencil lettering or by instant lettering. Announcement posters, commonly known as placards, are usually drawn with thick coloured markers.

Conventional methods

In situations where only a limited number of copies are needed, some of the conventional methods are still in use. One such example is the *stencil cut method*, where an image area is cut in stencil on paper or on a plastic sheet and ink is stamped on the stencil, thereby obtaining an image on the poster. *Silk-screen printing* is another conventional method that is widely used for commercial purposes. In the *photographic stencil method*, it is possible to print delicate designs such as halftones with sharp types in brilliant colours. Block-out solution and tusche-glue methods are processes of making stencils for silk-screen printing. These methods are mainly used when details are not required. These methods can be used for creating texture, reverse designs, and large areas in flat colours directly on the cloth.

Posters printed by the *lithographic process* may sound rather unusual, but in reality, some posters are still printed by the lithographic process. Although produced in limited numbers, these posters have some unique characteristics. The *letterpress* is also used in poster production, where normally typographic matter is used. For big size type, of course, some wooden letters are used. Due to the high cost of block-making, letterpress methods are not used for picture reproduction. Since the poster is basically a visual-dominated medium, the use of letterpress printing is very limited.

Common duplication method

The most commonly used method of poster replication is offset printing. Its ability to print fine-screen halftones on less expensive paper in large size is a major factor in its wide use. Since the offset process mostly works in coordination with digital and photographic techniques, poster production has kept pace with advances in technology. Offset printing can serve the needs of small-sized posters as well as big-sized panel posters such as billboards and film banners.

Single-sheet posters of normal size are printed like any other printed literature, whereas panel posters are printed on several sheets, providing space for overlapping on each sheet. The number of sheets needed to fill the panel is dependent on the size of the panel and the size of each printing machine is chosen so that a few sheets can be pasted to cover the panel.

Processing Techniques and New Technology

Posters can look brilliant when developed by the designer in coordination with computer and printing technologists. During the visualization process, a rough layout with different tints and colour patterns can be prepared. Overlapping of two or more colours or tints on solid colours to form a multicolour design can be used to great advantage. The appeal of a photograph or transparency selected for the poster may be enhanced in quality by using different effects such as posterization, superimposing, and blending of one picture content with another. Tone-lines can be obtained by selective or arbitrary manipulation with a colour scanner. Sharper picture details can be created by amplifying the shadow areas of the original.

Computer graphics are being increasingly used in poster design. Windows and Macintosh systems are compatible with a wide variety of software, which are specially developed to meet the designers' needs. Modern-day operating systems provide high-end technology, and memory capacity is not a constraint anymore.

Paint programs allow the user to paint on the screen with a digitizer or a mouse. Different brush strokes, brush widths, and colours are used to make the drawing look more realistic. Object-oriented programs such as CorelDRAW and Illustrator are meant for advanced users, who can draw complex geometrical shapes and manipulate different attributes (tint, colour, brightness, contrast) of the figure in these programs.

Software such as MS-Excel, Corel Chart, and Harvard Graphics are loaded with useful tools to draw charts and graphs. Using these tools saves time. Hand-drawn images can be scanned with a flatbed scanner. Any modification can be later done on the soft copy. Laser printouts of the created designs are suitable for reproduction. The output can be obtained either on film or bromide paper. The growth of large-format digital printing in recent times has revolutionized the poster medium, especially displays in all sizes on various surfaces.

Figure 17.10 Large poster around a public convenience

Advanced technology has changed the environment of our cities considerably. For instance, thanks to the digital outdoor makeover around public conveniences built all around Delhi, they are no longer an eye sore to people. Figure 17.10 shows one such public convenience after its makeover.

Figure 17.11 Large-format digital printer

According to the exhibitors participating in the exhibition PrintPack India 2005 held in Delhi, the cost of printing is dropping considerably due to the reducing prices of printers that are available in various sizes, operating costs, and input costs.

New-age printers with inkjet technology provide quality output at desired sizes for up to six colours (CMYK + two additional colours). The two extra colours increase the colour gamut and provide more finesse in mid-tone areas. Although the printing speed of these printers is nowhere near the conventional printing processes, they are suitable for printing limited copies of both high and low resolution printouts. The clarity of an image with a resolution of 30 to 70 dpi, though sufficient for many applications, depends on the distance from which it is viewed. Inkjet printers have the ability to print on various surfaces such as paper, canvas, vinyl, and cloth. Output can also be obtained on back-lit and front-lit materials. Figure 17.11 shows a large-format inkjet printer.

There are materials available that enable mounting of the print on different base materials. Various types of coating and lamination on the prints make ideal display for both indoor and outdoor posters. All these have created lot of interest among advertising agencies and signage companies.

SUMMARY

Posters are one of the oldest forms of communication. With the invention of the lithographic process in 1798, they got a new look with dominating visuals in dynamic colours. Many more people were exposed to posters due to fine quality printing through the offset process.

In many situations, a poster helps alter various aspects of the human condition, that is, the social, political, cultural, and financial aspects. A poster communicates its message using words and visuals. A minimum level of literacy is a must for understanding the message. Since many Indians are illiterate and live in rural areas, posters have largely been confined to cities and towns. With the development of trade and industry and various development programmes, efforts are being made to expose an ever increasing number of people to posters.

In order to make poster communication more effective, the communicator must understand the points of strength and basic characteristics of this medium. A poster's message is generally brief with a striking visual. Posters are produced on a mass scale, so their unit cost is low. It is a versatile medium that offers a designer scope for unlimited creativity.

The medium has some weaknesses too. The poster is a mass medium, but it cannot provide a selective demographic coverage. It normally contains a limited message. Posters destroy the natural environment. Considering these weaknesses, certain rules or guidelines should be followed to develop a poster design. A poster carries a few design elements for ease in comprehension. The typographical elements may be restricted to three to five. The maximum impact is created through visuals with only relevant content and minimum details. The visual and the caption should be handled together. All the elements of a design should be developed as a single unit by creating unity. A distinctive style identifies the target audience easily. It can be created by forms, colour, type, paper, and images. The full value of colour for a design is always preferable in a poster. Colour should be selected as per its association with the product, the environment, the life-style, or any other specific idea that needs to be communicated.

The creative strategy of a poster is always based on the information of demography and psychology of the intended target audience, communication objectives, and mechanical limitations. The creative process usually starts by listing some probable captions. Next, the caption chosen is translated into a visual form. The final layout might be a small-sized working rough that can be enlarged to actual size and finish as a comprehensive layout. The poster layout is then converted into artwork for printing.

Poster replication methods vary from hand-painted to conventional printing to hi-tech digital printing. These methods are dependent on the number of copies needed, functions to be performed, and how and when a poster is to be viewed.

KEY TERMS

Absolute Cost Impact of cost in relation to profit.

Captive Audience Viewers restrained by surroundings that prevent free choices.

Demography The numerical strength of the population in relation to age, sex, geographical spread, and occupation.

Economic Liberalization A broad term that usually refers to fewer government regulations and restrictions in the economy in exchange for greater participation of private entities.

Hoarding A large outdoor advertisement structure found in heavy traffic areas and highways. Also called a billboard, it shows distinctive visuals to promote an idea or product.

Kiosk Information booth for dispensing free information. It is normally displayed at street corners or other strategic points.

Large-format Printer Printing device that can handle sheets or reel of substrate 24 inches and wider. It is useful for printing small-run display jobs.

Market Coverage The territories within which the business activities are designed to achieve desired goals.

Mela A glittering public event in India with or without theme, combined with fun, shopping, eating, information exchange, and business activities.

Opportunity-to-see (OTS) Placement of an advertisement at a place where the target audience can conveniently see and read the message. It is intended to prompt action.

Point of Purchase (POP) Display materials, such as danglers, show cards, posters, etc., used by advertisers at the point sale of their goods.

Poster Eye-catching printed paper carrying an announcement or advertisement that is exhibited to promote a product, event, or idea.

Pre-testing Testing the rough design and its message on a cross section of people before investing money in production. It is used to ascertain whether the intended message is understood and comprehended.

Psychographics A form of market research that emphasizes understanding of the target audience's activities, attitude, values, and interests.

REFERENCES

Meggs, Philip B. 1992, A *History of Graphic Design*, Van Nostrand Reinhold.

Rahman, Saulat 1971, *Response to Visual in Poster*, TIMC Study of Visual Communication, New Delhi.

Sarkar, N.N. 1998, *Designing Print Communication*, Sagar Publications, New Delhi.

www.answer.com: Britannica concise encyclopaedia, accessed in June 2007.

REVIEW QUESTIONS

1. Define a poster. Mention the various forms of posters. Discuss the poster from its historical perspective.
2. In this era of information technology, the poster is still one of the important media in mass communication. Support this statement in the Indian context.
3. What are the constraints in disseminating messages using posters? Discuss ways to overcome these constraints.
4. Why should the poster be considered as a part of media planning? Answer the question using the various strengths of the poster medium. Mention the rules of poster design.
5. What are the weaknesses of the poster as a medium?
6. Although anyone can design a poster, it attains professional quality by following design rules. Elaborate.
7. Creativity in poster design is very important. Describe the steps involved in creating a poster.
8. Why are the rules of design often not followed in the use of colours in posters? Elaborate your answer citing a few examples.
9. Categorize posters in terms of copy. Write in detail their production methods.
10. What do you understand by large format digital printing? How has it revolutionized all kinds of outdoor displays?

PROJECTS

1. Visit some government departments and NGOs such as the Directorate of Advertising and Visual Publicity (DAVP), National Literacy Mission, National Aids Control Organization, Helpage India, etc. Collect some posters recently published by them. Take photocopies (colour, or black and white) on A4 size paper. Note your appreciation or criticism at the bottom margin of each print in terms of intended target audience, communication objective, and creative approach and send for evaluation.
2. Visit some private sector organizations and advertising agencies. Collect some posters they have designed and published to promote a product or idea. Take photocopies of the posters and write your comments. Spiral bind the pages of this assignment and use it for reference material.
3. Identify an issue that may be of interest to the youth of today. Write five slogans to motivate the target group. Make a poster using a slogan and/or visuals. The mechanical limitations are—size (18″ × 23″), colour limit (three), and printing process (offset). Take a printout of your layout on A4 size paper in case you are using a computer.
4. Form a group of five or six students of your class to develop a poster on 'caring for the aged'. Find out the problems of the people in question by visiting some old-age home or by collecting information from NGOs/websites. Organize a brainstorming session and develop a big idea. Convert the idea into a poster form. Show it to some social activist groups. Incorporate their suggestions to improve the design. Find a sponsor to print it.
5. You will find a lot of health-related information on various forms of posters on visiting some clinics. Improve one of them by the use of graphics. Prepare a comprehensive layout of that poster retaining all the information. Pin-up your poster next to the previous one. Collect comparative opinions from the audience in the clinic's waiting room.

CHAPTER

18 Packaging Design

Learning Objectives

After reading this chapter, you should be able to
- discuss the functions and characteristics of different types of packaging
- look at the Indian packaging scenario
- discuss the various materials that are used in making packages
- understand helpful tips in the design-solving process
- gain awareness of the emerging technology involved in package-making
- guard against the infringement of a design or tampering with goods

INTRODUCTION

The term 'package' can mean different things in different situations. Normally, a package is a bundle of related goods packed and wrapped for easy handling and carrying. When a set of objects, natural or man-made, is conceived as a compact unit having particular characteristics, it is called a 'package'.

Whatever may be the description of the term 'package', its outer layer is the first thing that comes to our notice. When we look around and observe carefully, everything that mother nature has to offer comes wrapped-up in a package. The conch shell which decorates our drawing room was once protecting the body of a gastropod. The round or oval-shaped egg shells of birds, snakes, and animals that protect their babies are among the most wonderful examples of packaging in nature. We can cite innumerable examples of natural packaging. Nature has inspired us to cover up the objects in our immediate surroundings to guard them from harmful elements as well as to add beauty to them. This is why we decorate our houses when it is sufficient to have four walls made of any material. Similarly, manufacturers use colourful packaging to attract the attention of potential customers. The colourful packages carefully displayed on the racks of a department store, as shown in Figure 18.1, never fail to catch our attention. The extra care and expenses are mainly meant to attract the shoppers and influence them to purchase the articles.

Packaging design combines art, beauty, and aesthetics in it. Art alone is not enough to produce a package design that serves the intended purpose. The basic purpose of the design is to attract attention, stand out from the competition, and develop a desire to uncover the package. A good packaging design quickly communicates what the product is about by reflecting an image of the product; moreover, it creates an impulse to buy.

Figure 18.1 Packages on display

Therefore, in package designing, the critical issue is what the package does. Packaging has a heterogeneous character and each package has a different function to perform.

Packaging can be divided into two broad categories—shipping packaging and retail packaging. Shipping packaging is mainly meant for storage, identification, and transportation. For this kind of packaging, the surface design is perfunctory.

Retail packaging is consumer-oriented. Consumer convenience is the main consideration for this category of packaging. It has two subcategories, viz. primary and secondary. *Primary packaging* is meant for products which need immediate containers; while *secondary packaging* is done to protect the primary packaging from external damage. Secondary packaging is discarded when the product is used. Figure 18.2 shows a product with its primary and secondary packaging.

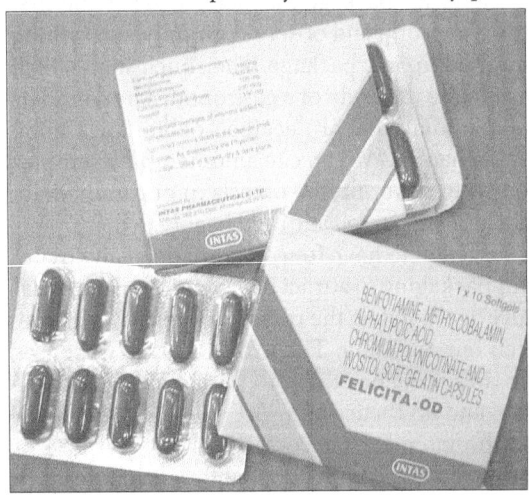

Figure 18.2 Primary and secondary packaging

Packaging must protect the product from environmental elements during transportation as well as during its period of use under anticipated conditions. Packaging preserves the product during its expected shelf life and contributes to the effective and convenient use of the contents.

Apart from protecting and preserving the contents, packaging also contributes towards advertising a product by providing not only its visual image, but also the necessary information about it, such as quality, quantity, price, date of packaging, and brand name. The package adds to the selling efficiency by motivating the customer, which ultimately brings profit to the manufacturer.

In short, a package must protect what it sells, and it must sell what it protects.

INDIAN PACKAGING INDUSTRY

For many years, India had been dominated by marketers who offered shoddily packaged products which were less useful than they actually could be. The Indian market gradually matured due to the development of trade and industry and ultimately emerged as a consumer-oriented economy. An era of competition has now arrived. These days, Indian manufacturers are, perhaps, for the first time, forced to face the harsh realities of a fiercely competitive global market. There is greater awareness among consumers about their right to obtain the right quality and correct quantity of a product at a reasonable price in an aesthetic, durable, and hygienic package.

A package is a vital link between the manufacturers of a product and its ultimate users, so the packaging industry must play an important role in Indian trade and industry. Many industries are now gaining prominence on account of their key role in both product promotion and product presentation. As it happens, the quality of the package of a product is a major determinant of its commercial success.

The packaging industry, in the post-independence era, started with a low profile. The Government of India, however, recognized the significant role of the industry, and a specialized institution, called the Indian Institute of Packaging (IIP), was established in 1966. The IIP endeavours to offer better service to the industry by evolving appropriate packaging systems, developing packaging technologists, and providing overall packaging information.

There is no dearth of artistic talent in our country. However, artistic talent alone is not enough to design a package. Often, a design cannot be executed by an individual artist or a design firm, however good their designing capabilities may be. Such situations call for creative professionals and industrial designers with specialized training in the field of designing. These professionals can come from engineering, architecture, or graphic arts backgrounds. A designing person may also gather the ability to design through training or because of innate talent. There are several art institutes in our country that help develop the creative talent of people. In the 1960s, two additional national institutes were started in India to cater to the packaging industry. These are the National Institute of Design (NID), Ahmedabad; and the Industrial Design Centre, IIT, Bombay. The number of printpack exhibitions organized in India from time to time have provided a platform to showcase Indian trade and industry. This has helped considerably in the modernization and growth of the Indian packaging industry, and enhanced the scope for introducing new concepts.

PACKAGING MEDIA

A wide variety of materials are used as packaging media. No design can be visualized without a clear understanding of materials. Some materials such as jute, glass, paper, metal, and wood have been used in packaging ever since the importance of packaging was realized. These are considered traditional packaging materials. They create a particular impression for a particular product. Some traditional packaging media are shown in Figure 18.3.

Figure 18.3 Traditional packaging media

Wine is always considered appropriately packaged when in a traditional glass bottle. A packet of tea in a wooden box looks much richer than it would if packed in a plastic bag. There is a tendency these days to replace traditional packaging materials with new and innovative plastic products, directly or in combination with other materials in accordance with the need of the product. Irrespective of the changing trend, the traditional packaging materials have maintained their constant lead over plastic. From the viewpoint of the material used, a package design can be divided into three categories—flexible packaging, folding cartons, and containers.

Flexible Packaging

The ever-widening range of flexible materials is a challenge to the package designers seeking to attain maximum protection for their products at a minimum cost. Flexible materials consist of paper, plastic films, and foils. These days, however, most materials are available as flexible laminates for packaging. These materials are bound together by heat, adhesive, or a composite substrate of molten polymer. Figure 18.4 shows some striking graphics on flexible packaging.

Paper is the simplest and the oldest form of packaging. It is useful in making designs for simple wrappers, boxes, or bags. There is a wide variety of paper products available in the market in terms of thickness, surface quality, and raw material used. The types of paper commonly used for flexible packs are poster paper, kraft paper, and chromo paper. The food industry is perhaps the biggest user of paper packaging. Among other industries which use paper are the cigarette, medical, electrical, agricultural, and publishing industry. Paper gets extra strength and flexibility by layers of plastics or superimposed foil made to stick by heat or by adhesives that create a formidable barrier to light, gas, liquid, and odour.

Figure 18.4 Striking graphics on flexible packaging

Foil and *foil laminates* are another variety of material used in flexible packaging. They are used successfully to package delicate products such as dehydrated or hygroscopic foods, drugs, and chemicals. They are non-magnetic, stress and crack resistant, and widely used in strip packaging of pharmaceutical products. Foils are mainly composed of aluminium, which makes them inexpensive. Foil is a thin and easily torn material. It can be easily moulded into any desired shape or texture. With suitable multi-layer laminates of films and foil, various types of collapsible tubes are made to package products such as toothpaste, cosmetics, medical ointments, adhesives, and paint tubes.

Plastic films and *cellophane* have dominated the modern packaging industry. They meet all the requirements relating to resistance to oil, fats, and even low temperature. Pouches and pre-formed bags have been developed in laminates, so that they can be heated or boiled. They can be recycled for repeated use, or can be made in such a way that they can be torn open along a straight line without perforation. The wide range of applications of plastic films has influenced not only the physical dimensions of the packages but also the designers' imagination. The transparent and shiny, glass-like surface of cellophane makes it an excellent wrapping material that adds value to the product.

Folding Cartons

A folding carton is basically a three-dimensional solid container made by cutting, folding, and gluing or locking a two-dimensional paperboard into its final shape, such as a cardboard box. The usages of folding cartons are virtually endless. They may be used for packing soaps, cereals, cosmetics, ice-cream, butter, biscuits, toys, cigarettes, and other such products. The scope of packaging expands further, when paperboards laminated with foil

Figure 18.5 Corrugated board lining

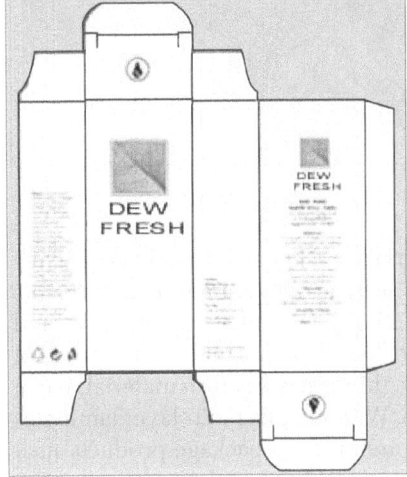

Figure 18.6 Packaging carton in collapsed state

or polyethylene are used. This kind of packaging suits beverages, tea, coffee, cocoa, etc. Corrugated board lining is used as a shock absorber for the product that is packaged inside it. Figure 18.5 shows a reel of corrugated board lining, with the structure of corrugated board.

Folding cartons provide various advantages to the designer. First of all, they can be easily manufactured using various machines. Intricate folding of decorated folding cartons can gain more value if we add some extra features to it, like hot-foil stamping, embossing, and surface film lamination.

Since a folding carton provides a flat surface, it can be used for innovative display of elements that can be effectively reproduced like any other high-quality promotional literature. The manufacturer can have the advantage of economy of space in storage. A package consumes less space in a collapsed state, as shown in Figure 18.6, and the consumer finds it to be of great use, thanks to the ease with which it is dispensed with.

Containers

The basic materials used for making containers are glass, tin, and plastics. The purpose of a container is to hold the product directly in the package. Some of the packages, especially multilayer ones that hold the product and can stand on their own, can also be termed as containers.

Glass containers Glass has some peculiar characteristics. It is very flexible in its liquid form, so it can be easily moulded into different shapes. At the same time, glass is very strong in its solid form, which is why it can carry dead weight. It can bear high temperature, and tolerate pressure when filled and sealed with caps. A glass container can be made transparent, opaque, coloured, or glazed. All these qualities make glass a very versatile material for packaging. Glass can perform a range of functions. Glass jars and bottles can be stacked by retailers without getting crushed. There are many good reasons why a product should be packaged in glass containers. It is a high-barrier material which does not leak or stain, and it is ideal for packaging food, drugs, wine, and cosmetics. The designer also has an opportunity to experiment with various innovative forms of colour as well as surface finishing. Glass, being a recyclable material, does not pose any risk towards environmental pollution. The surface design of a glass container is basically a label. The label design is best planned before moulding a glass container to maintain harmony between the label design and the shape and size of the container.

The brittleness of glass and its weight make most manufacturers shift their interest to new packaging materials like plastics, particularly PET and PVC. However, due to health-conscious consumers' distaste towards polyethene and pressure from environmentalists, glass is still a popular packaging material.

Metal containers The main metals used in packaging are mild steel sheets, tinplates, and aluminium alloys. Unlike glass, metal containers are strong and unbreakable. They can resist heat, cold, moisture, and rough handling during transportation and storage. Almost every food product one can name has, at some time or the other, been packed in a metal can. Tinplate is a steel sheet coated on both sides with a layer of pure tin, which has a shiny look and provides resistance to corrosion. Mild steel plate is the principal metal for making drums. It has been used for long to store oil. However, without any coating, it is prone to corrosion. Aluminium and its alloys have long been used for the manufacturing of rigid containers. The demand for cheaper and lighter containers with easy opening has made aluminium popular. Such containers are used to store products like beer and beverages. Tinplate also plays a significant role in the manufacture of caps for wide-mouthed glass jars.

Since metal sheets are generally printed in a flat condition, that is, before making a container, we may take the opportunity to decorate the cans. Offset lithography and silkscreen printing are the two methods used for the external decoration of cans. Unlike paper, metal sheets are non-absorbent. A special ink is used which dries instantly on the surface. Freshly printed sheets are passed through an oven to make the coloured pigment hard and scratch-proof. Thereafter, the printed sheet can be stacked, bent, and cut to make the container. However, majority of metal containers still carry paper labels. Printing on paper is easier and cheaper than printing on metal.

A design can be printed by the silkscreen process, either on the flat surface of the metal sheet or on a pre-constructed can. This process is economically acceptable where a good standard of decoration is essential and the quantity is limited.

The new scanning techniques provide a wide area of plain metal. This permits to decorate the entire body of the can.

Plastic containers Plastics have become the most common material in packaging in recent times. Plastic containers are extremely light and can be moulded into intricate shapes. A number of finishes, such as coloured, smooth, texture, opaque, and transparent, can be obtained. Plastic containers can also be made soft and rubber-like, which enables the product to be forced out from the container on squeezing. The development of PET (polyethylene terephthalate) and its availability in various forms is just what is required by the consumer today.

Plastic containers have already been successfully used to package soft drinks, mineral water, and beverages. Value-added packaging is being designed for a wide range of cosmetic items. Multi-layer plastic containers have been developed for oxygen-sensitive foods, giving them a longer shelf life. Several medical items are also packed in plastic containers. These are mainly developed from acrylic polymers, using the aseptic packaging system. The demand for plastic containers is steady. They are slowly replacing tin and glass containers, which have been hit by rising costs.

Figure 18.7 Plastic containers with labels

Labelling is the most common technique for the surface design of plastic containers. Figure 18.7 presents various plastic containers with labels. For direct printing on plastics (flat state), flexography and offset processes are used. Silk-screen printing and hot foil stamping are used in value-added packaging.

DESIGN BRIEF

Like graphic design and product design, package design is also a challenging task. The package is finalized on the basis of the design brief. A clear understanding of the product, marketing plan, consumer attitude, and competing brands leads to a comprehensive creative strategy for the package. Gathering all the details about the physical characteristics and the chemical composition of the product is vital. What is the function expected from the package in relation to the product? Will the product be identified by the brand image, or is it part of the corporate image of the company? The ultimate aim is to get the most effective pack.

The marketing plan refers to the targeted market to which the package must appeal. This will include the wholesale as well as the retail market. The wholesaler's need of the package design is different from the retailer's. The wholesaler may want a steady package to carry the bulk easily, whereas the retailer is primarily concerned with shelf-filling with eye-catching packages.

One needs to determine whether men, women, or children will be the decision-makers for a particular purchase, and design the product package accordingly. What are the purchasers' habits? Do they prefer to buy large or small quantities? What are their motivations, pleasures, necessities, or utilities? These are some important questions that need to be answered at this stage.

Figure 18.8 Competition in the shape of packages

The product must sell in the competitive market. What advantages does the product have over the competitors'? These should be emphasized in the design brief. A number of items and their brands get an edge over competing products, not because of superior features and quality, but due to innovative packaging. Figure 18.8 illustrates an example of competitive packaging for two similar products—Harpic and Sanifresh.

What also matters is the consumers' inclination towards a particular type of packaging for specific types of products. For example, consumers may prefer Bournvita when it is packed in a glass bottle instead of a tin container. In such cases, the manufacturers have to be sensitive to consumers' tastes and distastes.

The promotion plan of the product needs to be carefully evaluated. It should be coordinated with the package design.

The design brief may come from the client in a written format, which he/she has developed through sustained research and study. Whatever may be the compactness of the brief, many points may go over the head. The brief may contain some marketing jargon and technical terms of packaged material that would go beyond the designer's comprehension. Therefore, much of the briefing may best be accomplished verbally. The dialogue may spread over several days or even weeks. If possible, visiting the production plant may prove very fruitful.

PROBLEM-SOLVING STEPS

In the design-solving process, the AIDA principle, which stands for Attention–Interest–Desire–Action, is used in most of the cases. In case of packaging design, however, the 4C process (Walsh et al. 1988) is most suitable. The 4Cs are: concept, complexity, compromise, and choice. While working on a package design, the designer first develops a design concept. He/she then solves the complexities of the design by working on the appearance of the three-dimensional package, method of production, and so on. The third step is compromise. At this stage, the designer has to reach a compromise between the design concept, the materials used, and the package manufacturing process, which may be in conflict with each other. The final step is that of choosing the most appropriate option among many possible solutions. We shall discuss each of these steps in this section.

Concept

The design concept plays a crucial role in influencing people's purchase decision. People buy products not only for what they can do but also for what they mean. The design concept of the packaging must provide the elusive psychological bridge between the people and the product, and reflect what they would like the product to be. Concepts thus help in developing tangible characteristics with the help of various graphic elements such as shape, form, type, and colour. The concept includes functional aspects of packaging, such as holding the product, providing a closing and opening device, and a way to stack and handle the product. Concepts also bring intangible value to the package by arousing curiosity about the product, providing customer benefits, incorporating natural elements, acting as an active salesperson, and fulfilling the emotional needs of customers.

Excite curiosity The boundary of a concept is unlimited. The package may look dynamic when graphic elements of the package form additional patterns as the packages are arranged on the rack, side by side and one over the other. One should allow the package to surprise the customer. If striking features are not enough to excite curiosity, then the designers have to come out with other innovative ways to impress the consumers. For example, an interesting way of opening the package or a window to see the product may create the surprise element. One may create a design to hold, shake, and open the package. There is always a thrill in discovering the contents hidden under the outer layer of the package.

Provide customer benefits The design concept may emphasize the benefits being offered to the customer. Customers should get enough information to evaluate the worth of the product right at the time of purchase rather than at the time of use.

Incorporate natural elements Our eyes prefer concepts that are similar to elements, patterns, and shapes found in nature. The design elements should be free of unnecessary complexity in the form of abstract graphics, slogans, etc. Verbal explanations should be avoided.

Act as an active salesperson The product package is rightly considered to be the silent salesperson. It can be made active as well. A coffee pack may look active when the visual on the pack shows steam coming out of a hot cup of coffee. Products packed for children may be made as active as they themselves are.

Fulfil emotional needs Human beings are emotionally attached to certain forms and colours. A good package design seeks to appeal to various human emotions to sell the product. For instance, children are usually fond of multi-colour objects that are designed in attractive shapes. There are several examples of companies that have designed packages that fulfil the emotional needs of children. Milton, a manufacturer of a range of thermoware goods, designed a water bottle in a robot pack decorated with multi-colour graphics to entice children. The carton can be converted into a robot on fixing the easy-to-form organs, which can be purchased from the same shop and are supplied together. The pack has added value after use, meeting the emotional needs and creative instincts of children. The packaging for the Heinz Hummel range of children's shoes is at once a box and a carry-bag, with the handle reminding the child of his/her parents' briefcase. It uses primary colours, with a funny drawn turtle as an identity motif, which is an all-time favourite of children. Figure 18.9 shows the attractive packaging of Heinz Hummel shoes.

Complexity

The design concept gets a concrete shape when the design problems are solved. These design problems involve decisions regarding the materials to be used for the package, the appearance of the three-dimensional package, and the methods required to manufacture the pack. This is the complex part of the design process. The graphic designer should work as an active coordinator with the product designer, engineer, technician, and the manufacturer. The nature of the product may suggest the use of certain materials for the package. For example, for a food package, it is advisable to use packaging material that gives the package a neat and hygienic look and creates a feeling of security. Window packs of some flexible packaging materials like plastic jars or glass bottles may allow the customer to see the food inside it and judge its freshness. Zip Seal, an easy opening and closing device attached to a pouch, may add attraction and convenience to a package. Sometimes, materials may place restrictions on the design concept. The ideal design from the production point of view may be limited by constraints imposed by availability of machines and their operation system.

Figure 18.9 Packaging to meet the emotional needs of children

If the concept fits well with the available material, then the design is engineered keeping in mind the ease with which it can be manufactured. A production prototype is prepared with detailed working drawings and specifications. Modern manufacturing units are provided with computerized instructions.

Compromise

Design concepts, materials, and the package manufacturing processes may be conflicting with the requirements. A package may be perfectly satisfactory for all purposes, but it may add to the cost of the product to such an extent that the customer is deterred from buying it. A product with an excellent container and an eye-catching surface design may not succeed if ease of use is not considered. Sometimes, the materials selected are perfect for the design, but the container may not be durable enough to protect the product or make it stand upright without support. In all such cases, a compromise has to be reached, weighing the costs and benefits of the situation.

Choices

Design requires making choices among many possible solutions to a problem at all levels, from basic concepts to the smallest details of design elements—shape, form, colour, and typography. The choice of the design is dictated by the materials on which it is printed and whether they are economical and commercially viable.

DESIGN APPROACH

A package, like a sculpture, is a piece of art in a three-dimensional form. Consumers scrutinize the package from all sides before picking it up. It is also displayed on the rack at different angles to facilitate customer inspection. Therefore, all the sides of a package should be taken as one unit of design. The graphic elements should be arranged in such a way that the customer gets a feeling of movement on turning the package around. The basic principles of design—proportion, balance, contrast, harmony, etc.—should be kept in mind while designing the package for a product.

Shape and Proportion

The first thing the customer notices is the overall shape of the pack. The design of the various shapes of visual elements on the pack is dictated by proportion, which refers to the size of the label in relation to the overall pack size, the tone and size of illustrations in relation to the brand name, the background colour in comparison to the colour of the information-bearing elements, and so on. The decision on proportion is very subjective; it depends widely on the requirements of the product and the customer's attitude towards the product.

It is easier to achieve proportion in rectangular-shaped packages in comparison to odd-shaped ones. A rectangular shape offers a flat face to convey the main message and provides sufficient space to avoid mixing up with the messages of other products. The area for the brand name is another important decision of proportion. Though most packages are identified by the brand name, the brand name should not necessarily be big. Its proportion will depend on the total mood of the package and other accompanying elements like the illustration, product denomination, name of the manufacturer, and logo/trade mark, if any.

Figure 18.10 Innovative use of types to create brand identity

Types

The shape of a brand name is determined by the types that are used to create it. Since the brand name is the main identification element of a product, it should be developed with the use of the minimum possible number of letters. Six to eight letters are ideal for the purpose of facilitating recall. Letters may be as simple as possible, or may be stylized to harmonize them with the overall look of the product. If necessary, the lettering may be accompanied by some graphic elements. The idea is to give a distinct character to the package. The type style used for the Studds helmet is an example of a design that lends character to the product. The six letters of the word in thick type symbolize the strength of the product. The rounded edges of the letters, as shown in Figure 18.10, represent the physical characteristics of the product.

The bold, round-cornered letters of 'Frooti', as illustrated in the figure, combined with two mangoes in yellow, give the brand name a distinct look. One of the letters is developed in the shape of a mango. The brand name and its styling reflect the true characteristics of the product. Similarly, a leaf is added to the letter 'f' in Safal, a fruit and agricultural products brand, to suggest that it is a natural product.

The novelty letters NIVEA, as seen in the figure, tell us that the cream is a novelty item. Thin letters for a health-related product are inappropriate. Decorative letters for pharmaceutical and industrial products are best avoided. Since type legibility is an important factor for brand identification, handwritten types are uncommon. Handwritten types and calligraphic forms are, however, used for some products for which it is important to create a personal touch.

Logos

Sometimes, logos serve the purpose of brand identity. In cases where logos are used on the package, the product denomination or generic name may be written in an appropriate size, as in the case of Cadbury's chocolates and McDowell's whisky. Many people buy products after checking the name of the manufacturer. The logo or the trademark on the package takes responsibility for the genuineness of the product. It provides a sense of security to the customer, telling him/her unambiguously that this is the same product that he/she has earlier used and presumably enjoyed. The logo should be given as much importance as the brand name, especially in cases where the logo has already been positioned in the customers' minds. A logo with a distinctive shape and colour acts as a representative of the manufacturer.

Illustrations

Like any other graphic design, an illustration on a pack attracts attention and conveys a general impression about the product. The illustration can be a photograph or a hand-drawn art. Most products are covered by the package, and it is not possible to tell what the product looks or feels like until the package is opened or the seal is broken. Customers, especially those who have never used a particular product, would be interested in seeing the product and knowing of its benefits before making a purchase decision. A photographic illustration on the package is the best choice to satisfy such customers.

Take the example of any food product. A photographic illustration may stimulate the appetite and convey more than the brand and generic name. In our multilingual society, illustrations break the language barrier. Even the illiterate can identify the product through an illustration. However, one needs to be careful even while using an illustration that has a direct and obvious association with the product inside. For instance, a too-obvious photograph on a package of noodles, such as a photograph of noodles on a background of cooked food on a table, may make the viewer passive towards the package. Action photographs bring life to the package surface and often lead to impulse buying. Ideally, the photograph should occupy a wide area of the package. In case the photograph is proportionally smaller in comparison to other visual elements, it should be ensured that it is surrounded by empty spaces or less prominent elements. Human figures on the package should be carefully selected. The target audience should be able to identify themselves with the picture on the cover.

A hand-drawn illustration can be very effective at times, impressing the viewer much more than a photograph. It can present the hidden promise on the pack. For example, let us assume that we are preparing a new package for a low-cholesterol vegetable oil. Will it not be interesting if an incongruous illustration is thought of—like a hand-drawn heart with two wings attached on each side, symbolizing a light, cholestrol free, and active heart?

A hand-drawn illustration can bring the desired mood to a pack. It will look modern with smooth and easy-to-flow lines, which may be filled with flat colours rather than a photo finish. A few decades ago, hand-drawn illustrations on packages with a three-dimensional effect were a popular trend. Pop-art-like drawings with odd shapes, which was considered modern a few years ago, has become unacceptable for package illustrations these days. They may, however, still be used in some situations, such as junk food packaging, if the lines and shapes are made soft to suit the modern trend.

Most *aggarbatti* (incense stick) packages have a character of Indianness. Since the product is claimed to be of Indian origin, the illustrations on the packages are adapted from Indian motifs and figures. 'Nimantran' *aggarbatti*, as shown in Figure 18.11, is an example of a brand that uses modern packaging design, combined with figures from Indian mythology, applied to a typical Indian product.

Hand-drawn illustrations that remind the customers of their country or region's past glory may be effective in some situations. People can imagine the past more clearly than the future and feel proud to identify themselves with the values of the past. Thus, a hand-drawn illustration of a sage *(rishi)* on the cover of an ayurvedic medicine or tea pack, for instance, will effectively convey the message that the product has been created using a formula that was followed by our ancient sages. A butter packet with an illustration of Lord Krishna stealing butter *(makhan)* from Yashoda's kitchen is another example of an Indian value being put to work.

An illustration enhances the message of a product when it is juxtaposed with the graphic shapes on the package. Graphic shapes are active aids in promoting brand recall. This, of course, is achieved

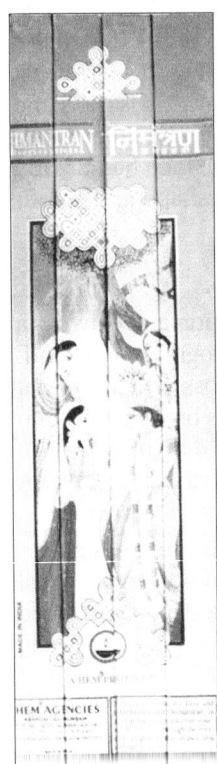

Figure 18.11 Indian motifs

Figure 18.12 Creative use of graphics

by following the basic rules of a graphic design, i.e., balance, harmony, proportion, etc. Hundreds of graphic shapes can be created on a package, either by using flat colours or vignettes; but simple shapes are preferred to complicated ones. Anything that is complicated tends to bother the eye and to create a mental block so that the impact of the package is lost.

The creative use of graphic shapes in the perfume pack with the brand name 'Limara' (morning sunrise) has been illustrated in Figure 18.12. The graphic shapes with different lines create a feeling of waves around the pack; a graphic sunflower is juxtaposed within the waves, giving an impression of the rising sun. The graphic shapes used in the package reflect the product characteristics, and convey the message that the perfume is fresh like the morning sun, clean like water, and active like sea waves. The package also gives the product a 'premium' look through its stylized graphic shapes in metallic colours.

Colour

Many successful designs have been created in print communication using monotones, that is, black and white and shades of grey. In product packaging, however, the use of monotone schemes is rare. Colour is the most prominent eye-catching feature of packages in display. Greater visibility is offered by a combination of vivid contrasting colours. Colourful packages of fast food, toys, sportswear, etc. are quite attractive and also successful in fulfilling the marketing strategy.

Colour should be used by designers with care. When many packages in vivid colours are stacked on the shelf, they create a flickering effect, causing rapid visual fatigue. The shopper cannot find at a glance what he/she is looking for, and often seeks another product. In order to satisfy the need of the customer, designers should strive to develop immediate visual interest, and consider carefully which colour combinations are most suitable. To this effect, colour elements may be divided into three broad categories—*information-bearing elements, background elements,* and *decorative elements*. Brand names, logos, illustrations, and types are the information-bearing elements of a package design, whereas the colour of the container, foil, or surface of the package printed in flat or continuous tone colour with or without a graphic shape may be the background elements. Borders, white space, and decorative shapes may carry no message. The designer may use them to enhance the visual quality. Normal visual preparation involves emphasizing the information-bearing elements by making their colour strong, while the background is kept soft by maintaining basic harmony.

The colour of the decorative elements in a package should be chosen very carefully. For instance, thin lines in colour may change the identity of the information-bearing elements and create optical confusion. However, there is no hard and fast rule about this. Even a thick line in soft colour on a hard background may serve the purpose.

Irrespective of the colour combination used, the designer will fail to catch and hold the attention of the customer unless he/she succeeds in creating an emotional relationship between the package and the customer. This, of course, depends largely on the characteristics of the target audience, their age, and cultural background. Most of the packages for the mass market are acceptable in vivid colours, but cosmetic products and premium products and those aimed at a specialized market may be a combination of muted tints or an analogous scheme. Most cosmetic and high-fashion products are packed with muted graphics, ideally agreeable for the target group of consumers.

Special attention is paid while selecting the colour scheme for food products. Since customers often need to judge the contents of a packed food item without opening the package, they make up their minds by looking at the colour of the package. That is why special attention is paid to make the colour and graphics look fresh, nutritious, and appetizing. Red, yellow, or orange and their combinations may have the desired effect for bakery products while green and blue are commonly used for vegetable products. Milk products such as ice cream and baby food look clean, soft, and even cool, if packed in a muted blue colour or in combination with pale yellow-green with pink. Most of the food package colours are selected on the basis of the colour associations the product has. Coffee packages are mostly packaged in dark brown. Tomato ketchup is usually packaged in red, but tea has no particular colour association.

PACKAGING TECHNOLOGY

Packaging technology involves surface designing, producing a package prototype, and printing and die cutting. Traditionally, the first rough idea is developed as a drawing with a sketch pen. Sometimes, a mock-up or model is developed by cutting and shaping plastic foam or cardboard. The mock-up is the first requirement of the client; it gives a better picture about what the final product will look like. Designers are usually more aware of the aesthetics of a design. They may not have much knowledge about production processes and materials used for packaging. Ideally, clients should provide information about these aspects to the concerned package designer. Designers should also be aware of the latest developments in these areas.

With the growing emphasis on packaging in the recent years and the availability of digital technology, designers are increasingly involving themselves in all aspects of package-making. Even an amateur designer can develop his/her ideas into realistic form and try out variants in a fast and cost-effective way. As the design can be viewed on the monitor with different options, the designer can get immediate feedback. The immense flexibility offered by some graphic design programs gives the liberty to adjust colours, reflections, and shadows at will. Some computer-aided design programs such as AutoCAD and

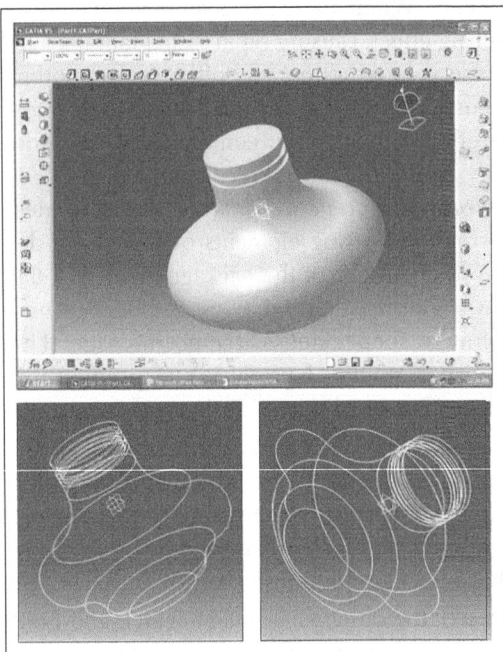

Figure 18.13 Design using CAD graphics

3D Graphics can accurately represent the package, including packaging strength and capacity. Figure 18.13 shows the design of a prototype container using CAD graphics. The physical shape of a package can be precisely cut by using computerized machines such as Kongsberg XE 10, which is basically a plotter used to make sample packages. Figure 18.14 shows a Kongsberg XE 10 plotter.

Offset printing is the best printing process for packaging such as paper, tin, and board; and flexo and rotogravure for bags and plastic packs. Dry offset is commonly used for cans and round containers, and screen printing is used for glass and bottles. In response to the market demand, packaging printers today are increasingly adopting high-speed processes with sophisticated tension control systems, web guiders, controlled temperature-drying facilities, automatic register controls, automatic control of ink viscosities, and web-viewing devices. Computer-based systems accurately measure crease-to-crease and crease-to-cut dimensions. Colour printing plays a greater role than ever before due to the availability of digital proofing of four-colour separation and various manipulation techniques for images.

Computers have made label designing very flexible. In the conventional process, labels are printed and then taken for lamination and gumming. They are then attached to the backing sheet. These days, after planning the number of ups to be printed on a sheet, the labels can be printed on a standalone unit. These standalone printers have all the facilities required to make a label, such as gumming, perforating, rewinding, etc. The new standalone label printer operates with its own LCD screen, so that one can customize labels directly through the label printer itself. Figure 18.15 shows a standalone label-making unit.

Die cutting is one of the major activities of packaging production. It is the method of using sharpened, thin, steel blades called dies to cut out a variety of shapes from all kinds of material. Figure 18.16 shows the making of dies. As shown in the left-hand-side

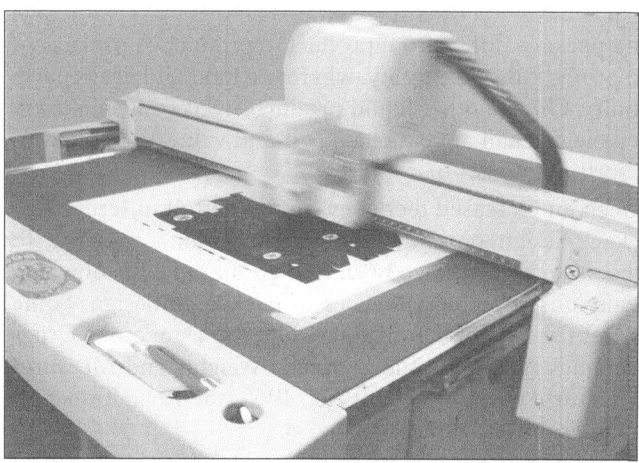

Figure 18.14 Kongsberg XE 10 plotter

Figure 18.15 Standalone label-making unit

Figure 18.16 Creating holes (left) and inserting blades into them (right) to make a die

figure, holes are created on a plywood surface and blades are inserted into the holes (right-hand figure) to make dies. There are several types of die cutting, viz. rotary, steel rule, ultrasonic, and laser. In rotary die cutting, the material is crush-cut between the angled blades on a cylindrical die. Typically, the material is cut in a continuous roll form, though sheets of metal can be fed through the rotary die. Steel-rule die cutting involves crush-cutting the material by placing it against a cutter tool (slightly raised blade fixed into high-density plywood) and pressing the two with several tons of force between two parallel plates. Ultrasonic die cutting is ideal for cutting thin plastic material that tends to fray easily. Laser die cutting is very useful for cutting materials that are impossible for conventional steel rule dies to cut, such as steel thicker than 0.5″.

LEGAL ISSUES

A consumer's requirement for a package differs from product to product. A package of electronic goods is expected to provide absolute safety, whereas a food and drugs package should lay stress on credibility. Oil and other liquid products need convenience in handling. Cosmetic goods need elegance in appearance. Cost and value are, however, ubiquitously important for all sorts of goods.

In recent years, there has been an increased tendency on the part of unscrupulous individuals to infringe the package design, or tamper with goods within a package. To protect the interests of consumers, some laws have been framed on the basis of which legal action can be taken against unscrupulous practices in packaging design. Some of the laws worth mentioning are: the Sale of Goods Act, 1930; the Dangerous Drugs Act, 1930; the Drugs and Cosmetics Act, 1940; the Standard Weights and Measures Act, 1976; the Export (Quality Control and Inspection) Act, 1963; the Road Transport Corporation Act, 1980; and the Poison Act, 1919.

The Consumer Protection Act, 1986, provides protection to the consumer against unfair trade practices adopted by traders, such as supplying defective goods or charging in excess of the fixed price. The Law on Patents is a government grant to an inventor of machines, products, and processes in any sector of industry for a stated period of time, conferring the exclusive right to use and vend an invention. In India, the Patent Act, 1970 provides these safeguards.

From the designer's point of view, the Copyright Act is the most important requirement for package design. India has a very strong and comprehensive Copyright Law based on the Indian Copyright Act, 1957, which was amended in 1983, 1992, 1994, and 1999. The amendments in 1994 were a response to technological changes in the means of communications like broadcasting and telecasting, and the emergence of new technology like computer software. The 1999 amendments have made the 'Copyright Act fully compatible with Trade Related Aspects of Intellectual Property Rights (TRIPS) agreements'. With these amendments, the Indian Copyright Law has become one of the most modern copyright laws in the world.

Copyright law protects and also promotes various artistic literary creations which include both two- and three-dimensional work. To be protected by copyright, the work does not necessarily have to be new and innovative; the work may not have any aesthetic value either. The only requirement is that the work has to be the result of independent intellectual effort. Being the sole proprietor of the work, the copyright-owner reserves all the rights to control the ways in which the work is exploited, including copying, adapting, etc.

Many design consultants are generally ignorant of the existing laws relating to package design. They sometimes get into trouble by copying a design suggested by the client. In case of any suspicion about the likelihood of copyright infringement or misguided information on the package, it is advisable to consult a legal agent or a lawyer before final production of the design. Small booklets on each Act mentioned above have been published by the Government of India. Besides, private publishers have brought out some law books as well. These books are low-priced and easily affordable; so it is worthwhile to refer to these books and be informed about the copyright acts.

SUMMARY

A package is basically a bundle of related goods packed or wrapped for easy handling and carrying. Since it is the outer layer of a package that first comes to consumers' notice, an aesthetic design is a must. The design of a package not only attracts attention, but also creates impulse buying and arouses a desire to unwrap the package.

Retail packages are of two categories, viz. primary and secondary. Primary packages are meant for products which need an immediate container. Secondary packages are packaging material that protect the primary package.

Trade and industry in India are now gaining prominence on account of the key role of packaging in both product promotion and product presentation.

A wide variety of materials are used as packaging media. Packaging may be divided into three broad groups, viz. flexible packaging, folding cartons, and containers. Flexible materials consist of paper, plastics, films, and foils. These materials provide the product with maximum protection at the minimum cost. A folding carton is basically a three-dimensional solid container made by cutting, gluing, or locking a two-dimensional paperboard into a final shape. Since it provides a flat surface, the designer can play with innovative display elements on it. The basic materials of containers are glass, tin, and plastics. Glass is a high-barrier material, but the weight and fragile nature of glass make it somewhat unpopular among manufacturers. Metal containers can resist heat, cold, and rough handling. Plastic containers are extremely light and can be moulded into various intricate shapes.

The design process of a package starts after a design brief is received from the client. The comprehensive creative strategy is prepared after analysing the marketing plan, consumer attitude, competing brands, and nature of the product. The package design-solving process should be based on the 4Cs principle. The 4Cs are concept, complexity, compromise, and choice.

The 'concept' is the basis on which the customer is attracted to the package. 'Complexity' refers to aspects such design and material. 'Compromise' is the stage where a balance has to be achieved between the costs and the benefits of the design solution. 'Choice' involves selecting a design amongst the various alternatives that are available.

A package is taken as a single unit, and it is viewed from all sides. The shape of the package and surface design are equally important for customer's inspection. Regular, appropriate, and convenient package shapes with proportionate balance and harmonious surface design are acceptable to most of the customers. In packaging, colour is often the single-most eye-catching display, so colour combination should be considered carefully to satisfy the needs of the customer.

All aspects of package-making, these days, are influenced by technology. Advanced computer technologies have enhanced the packaging process and redefined the way designers, manufacturers, and printers work.

The cut-throat competition among emerging brands sometimes influences manufacturers to infringe package designs of successful brands. This is considered illegal and the party guilty of infringement may face grave consequences according to the Copyright Act of India. Therefore, it is prudent to consult legal agents or refer to the rules/acts related to package designing before the final production of the design.

KEY TERMS

3D Graphics Three-dimensional representation of geometric data stored in the computer for the purpose of performing calculations and rendering 2D images. Such images may be used for later display or for real-time viewing.

AIDA A persuasive sequence used in advertisements: attention, interest, desire, and action.

Aseptic Packaging Packages free from microorganisms, through which a manufacturer ensures that a sterilized device remains in a sterile state until used in the manner intended.

AutoCAD A vector graphics drawing program. It uses primitive entities—such as lines, poly-lines, circles, arcs, and text—as the foundation for more complex objects.

Containers Packages made of glass, plastic, or tin used to pack solid or liquid products.

Corrugated Board Board consisting of one or more wave-shaped sheets between two flat layers. Corrugated board lining is used as a shock absorber for products.

Die Sharp, thin steel blades fitted into high-density plywood, used for cutting out a variety of shapes on cardboard, paper, etc.

Film A non-fibrous, non-metallic, flexible material available in a range of thickness.

Folding Carton A three-dimensional solid container used for packing soaps, cereals, cosmetics, ice-cream, butter, biscuit, toys, cigarettes, and other such products.

Generic Brand A brand that indicates only the product category and does not include the company name or other identifying terms.

Hygroscopic Food Food items having a tendency to absorb moisture from the atmosphere, which destroys the natural value of product. Hygroscopic foods have limited shelf life.

Ink Viscosities Semi-fluid state of ink that does not flow freely. It is critical in the press room as it determines the sharpness of the halftone dots and uniformity of flat colours.

Packaging Media Any material used in the fabrication or sealing of a packaging system or primary package to communicate information about the content inside it.

Packaging The science, art, and technology of enclosing or protecting products for distribution, storage, sale, and use. Packaging also refers to the process of design, evaluation, and production of packages.

PET (Polyethylene Terephthalate) Tough, temperature-resistant polymer. Biaxial oriented PET film is used in laminates for packaging because it provides strength, stiffness, and temperature resistance. It is usually combined with other films for heat stability and improved barrier properties.

Plotter A vector graphics printing and cutting device that connects to a computer. Plotters print or cut their output by moving a pen/knife across the surface of a piece of paper.

PVC (Polyvinyl Chloride) A tough, stiff, clear film. The oriented version is mainly used in shrink film applications.

Retailer An individual or a business group that purchases products from the wholesaler for the purpose of re-selling those to ultimate consumers—the general public.

Strip Pack A package used to protect solid dose pharmaceutical products, and to provide relatively inexpensive protection for individual dosages.

Ups The number of labels printed on a sheet with approximate crop marks.

Wholesaler An individual or a business group engaged in facilitating and expediting exchanges that are primarily wholesale transactions.

Zip Seal A re-closeable or re-sealable pouch produced with a plastic track in which two plastic components interlock to provide a mechanism that allows for re-closeablility in a flexible package.

REFERENCES

'Role of Packaging in 90s: New Horizon', Paper presented at PAMEX '91, India.

Danger, E.P. 1987, *Selecting Colour for Packaging*, Gower Technical Press, England.

Dighe, Srinivas 1991, 'Surface Design in Food Packaging', *Packaging India*, January.

Hancock, Marion 1992, *How to Buy Design*, Design Council, London.

Malhotra, D.N. and S.K. Ghai (eds) 2006, *Understanding Copyright Law*, The Federation of Indian Publishers, New Delhi.

Martin, A.G. 1988, *Finishing Process of Printing*, Focal Press, London and USA.

Murthy, C.N. 1993, 'Trends in Packaging and Package Printing', *Print Forum*, Madras, February–March.

Narayanan, R. 1977, *ABC Packaging Techniques*, Nanas Print Pack Service, Madras.

Paine, F.A. 1977, *The Packaging Media*, Blacke & Son Ltd, London.

Sonsino, Steven 1990, *Packaging Design*, Thames and Hudson.

Walsh, Vivien, Roy, Robin, Bruce, Margaret, and Potter, Stephen 1988, *Winning by Design*, Blackwell Publishers, UK.

REVIEW QUESTIONS

1. 'Package means different things in different situations.' Justify the statement.
2. Differentiate between shipping and retail packaging, and mention their basic functions.
3. Discuss the packaging scenario in India since independence.
4. What are the groups of materials used as packaging media? Mention the characteristics of each group.
5. Define flexible packaging, folding carton, and container. Discuss the suitability of these packages to carry various contents.

6. What are the points to be considered while taking briefs of a package design?
7. What is the difference between AIDA and the 4Cs formula in the design solving process?
8. What should be the design approach in developing a package?
9. What are the main components of surface design for a package? What is the criterion that determines the handling of these components? Discuss with the help of suitable examples.
10. How does modern technology boost the packaging explosion of recent years in terms of surface design, package manufacturing, and printing?
11. What is the need of understanding the legal aspects of packaging design? Mention some of the laws applicable to packaging.

PROJECTS

1. Collect various kinds of packages. Segregate them according to their type—flexible packaging, folding carton, and container. Pick up one from each group, and write a report on their design quality in relation to the function of the package.
2. Identify a printing press that specializes in printing packages. List the types of machines it has and the functions of each machine in developing a package.
3. Prepare a surface design for a carry bag meant for carrying designer shoes, common for both men and women. Make a prototype bag with the design on it.
4. Take a folding carton from your kitchen. Make it flat by unfolding it. Prepare a diagrammatic scheme on a standard sheet of card. Find out the number of packs that can be printed on each sheet without wasting much space. Indicate the area to be creased and die-cut for folding, pasting, and locking.
5. Develop a premium perfume bottle on a computer console using a 3D graphics software. Design the label of the perfume bottle using any 2D software. Import and paste the label on the model you have designed. See it from different angles by rotating the image. Take print-outs of the image from each angle, and evaluate the images from a consumer's point of view.

CHAPTER

19 Direct Communication

Learning Objectives

After reading this chapter, you should be able to
- discuss the characteristics and functions of direct communication material
- look at the role and design process of business correspondence material
- examine the importance and design of direct promotional material
- look at various souvenir items and discuss the designing of calendars and diaries
- discuss the various methods of distribution of direct communication material

INTRODUCTION

In our everyday lives, we use business correspondence material such as letterheads, business cards, and envelopes, and souvenir items such as calendars and diaries for business purposes as well as for personal use. Whether we are at work or at home, we are exposed to promotional literature in the form of leaflets, brochures, and booklets which may be mailed to us, distributed individually, or collected personally in case we are seeking information about something. These categories of printed communication, namely, business correspondence, souvenir items, and promotional material, are *direct* means of communication because, unlike indirect means, they are not dependent on other media such as radio and TV.

Usually, there is no competition in the designing of direct communication material. Moreover, these categories of printed material are free from constraints related to the medium, such as size, colour, paper quality, and date of issue. In most cases, items with a simple design serve the desired purpose. Because of these factors, the design aspect of these items is usually ignored. Little attention is paid to the aesthetic aspect of most stationery and promotional literature that we come across every day. Such unprofessional work usually ends up in the wastepaper basket without achieving the desired objective.

Whether the printed material has elaborate, imaginative copy with colour illustrations or it is a simple piece with a few words in a typographical arrangement with a plain background, it can serve the desired purpose if it is designed with some thought and attention to design principles. In this chapter, we shall discuss the designing of such printed material under three broad categories: (i) business correspondence items, comprising materials such as letterheads, business cards, and envelopes; (ii) promotional material such as brochures, leaflets, and booklets; and (iii) souvenir items such as calendars and diaries.

BUSINESS CORRESPONDENCE MATERIAL

Attractive business correspondence stationery is a means through which an organization can create a link with its clients, internal staff members, and the general public. Letterheads and business cards are the primary requirements for starting a business, as these help create an identity for the organization and promote its products and/or services. As the business progresses, specially designed envelopes that match the letterhead and other stationery items of the organization, invoices for goods and services bought and sold, and forms for various purposes become important requirements to run the business smoothly. Some of these forms may be specially designed for purchase purposes, with evaluation sheets with boxes and lines that make them easy to fill. Well-designed forms facilitate systematic documentation.

Memo sheets and notepads are some other commonly used stationery items in offices and businesses. A memo sheet is a simplified form of the organization's letterhead, where only one or two elements like the logo and company name may be displayed. Memo sheets are used when informal messages are exchanged, especially between two or more employees of the company. Unlike letterheads, memo sheets may not display the detailed address and telephone numbers of the company. The design style, however, may be the same as that of the company letterhead.

Well-designed memo sheets may serve the purpose of a cover for the company's proposals, reports, agenda of meetings, etc. Notepads are similar to memo sheets, but they are small in size, which makes them very handy. They too are used for internal or personal communication, besides jotting notes and points on which action is required.

Letterheads

A letterhead can be thought of as a form of package that contains information about the company or organization. Thus, the aesthetic and functional considerations for designing a letterhead are comparable to package designing. Since the message of a letter may be very personal and self-contained in nature, the design of the letterhead is often a secondary consideration for many communicators. Despite the fact that there is no competition in letterhead design, care should be taken while designing letterheads as a cluttered arrangement of elements may fail to guide the reader through the sequence of information, and this may ultimately lead to a negative effect on the recipient.

The design process may start with the identification of the design elements, viz. the name of the company/organization or person; the logo, if any; and the address with telephone and fax numbers, email i.d.s, etc. In case the logo design is part of the letterhead design, it should be handled separately, because the logo will be used not only on the letterhead but also on other materials of the company.

A distinctive type style should be selected for the company name from the type catalogue or computer software. Hand-drawn letters also look good. Often, a company name is accompanied by a stylized communicative name. For instance, SAIL and Blue Max are the communicative names of the Steel Authority of India Ltd and Blue Max Sportswear, respectively. The selection of type style should be governed by the organization's activities and the mood and impression they want to create among the audience. Most organizations dealing with tours and travel services use slanted bold letters in their company names, as such letters create a feeling of movement. Cursive letters would be inappropriate for the letterhead of a nursing home. To reflect the mood of neatness, health, and care associated with the activities of a nursing home, a simple Helvetica bold face may be most appropriate. In case the impression to be created is less authoritative, the letter's tone may be reduced to grey or some other pale colour up to the extent of optimum legibility. Addresses and other matter should be in smaller type, preferably in 10 or 8 pt. medium. To make the arrangement a bit fancier, a slightly bigger but light face type may be considered. Some organizations list their activities on the letterhead. In such letterheads, it should be ensured that such lists are not too long, and do not appear obtrusive to the reader.

While arranging the elements on the letterhead, one should experiment with various designs on a paper of the actual letterhead size. Three kinds of sizes are used in letterheads—official, demi-official (DO), and personal. The letterhead elements should be arranged in such a way that the design is appropriate for all the sizes. The white or blank space should be treated as a major element of design. Since white space is used for correspondence, the letterhead should have as much space as possible. The recommended ratio between white space and other elements is 6:1. All the elements will look mixed up if this ratio is not maintained. The best way to experiment with various letterhead designs is to type a letter on a blank page; crop one-third of it from top or bottom, or some portion on each of these two sides; and place this sample letter on every trial design. This gives the designer a fair idea of how the letterhead will look in a working situation.

The elements on a letterhead may be arranged either formally or informally. In a formal arrangement, all the elements are grouped together in one unit and placed on the top centre of the sheet. They are usually arranged in a rectangular or pyramid shape.

A formal arrangement provides a sober and traditional look. It also projects the company as conservative and well-established. Such a design has special significance if the company is in a business in which traditional values are of critical importance. In such situations, the design for the letterhead must fall within the existing designs on the company's correspondence material. The chosen logo, type style, colour, etc. should help create a visual identity for the company. The sequence of eye movement should be from the logo on top to the organization's name, address and phone number, etc. Inverted pyramids take the eye to the letter content. Placing all the elements in a centre format on the top right of the page is also common practice. In such cases, the composite element is balanced in an informal arrangement, with the address and the letter content left aligned. The main elements should not be placed on the left side of the letterhead because, when these are filed, a portion of the letter may remain hidden and inaccessible.

Informal arrangements, considered to be a contemporary approach, require more skill and ideas. The name of the organization, address, etc., when placed on the top right, can counterbalance the logo on the top left. All the elements can be grouped and aligned with imaginary left or right vertical or axis lines. Tone or colour lines, both

Figure 19.1 Alternatives letterhead designs

vertical and horizontal, can bring about unity and provide weight to the design. The address and other information-bearing elements can be placed at the bottom to allow the logo and the organization's name to stand out. Several alternative letterhead designs are presented in Figure 19.1. Each of these has a different typographical treatment and arrangement of elements.

The designer should try to create contrast either through the logo or through the company name. People always tend to read from the contrast to the normal, even if the contrast elements are placed in an unconventional place. Many a time, use of multiple visual devices brings dynamism to a modern letterhead design. In situations where such elements are used as a background, they should be light. Otherwise, the letter contents in these portions will be illegible.

Letterheads can also be fancy, with floral elements or graphic shapes as embellishments, as shown in the samples in Figure 19.2. Such elements should be designed with care, so that the design does not negate the use of die stamping, thermography, hot-foil printing, or very decorative styles. Figure 19.2 shows the use of floral graphic shapes on the letterhead, certificate, and envelope of a company. The use of such harmonious elements in various items of correspondence helps to attract consumers.

Paper is an important element in letterhead designing. Its surface quality, texture, colour, thickness, and other individual characteristics lend distinction to a letterhead. Some types of paper, such as bank and bond paper, are specially made for letterheads. The surface of such paper prevents absorption and soakage and also withstands the hammering of the type slug of a typewriter and the needles of a dot matrix printer.

Letterheads, like other printed material, look attractive when they are in colour. If the logo is in colour, it always dictates the colour scheme of the design. Line art logos allow one or two elements in colour. The address and related details, which are set in small type size, must be printed in black or in reasonable contrast colours to maintain legibility. Illustrative letterheads may carry continuous tone images. Usually, a simple illustration works better than an elaborate one in a letterhead design. A flat-tone or vignette background may also be used on letterheads.

It is advisable to plan the letterhead design with other stationery items for the organization, especially the business card and envelope. A uniform design style on all items helps in creating a consistent corporate image and also reduces the design cost as the same typefaces and art pieces can be arranged within the format with minor additions, alterations, or deletions.

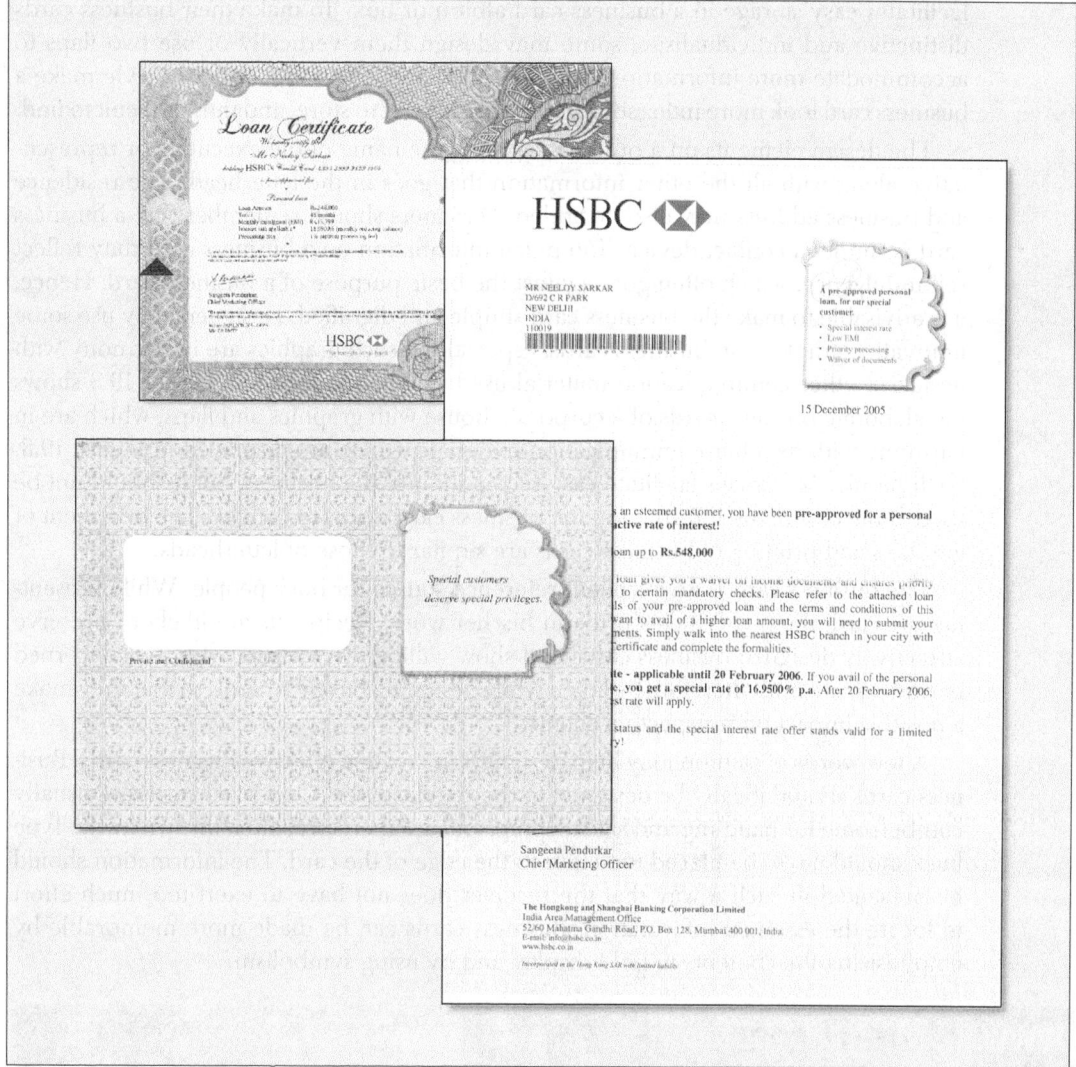

Figure 19.2 Visual harmony in the design of a corporate letterhead, certificate, and envelope

Business Cards

Business cards are small but powerful communication devices. Often, a business card is the only direct contact between an organization and its prospective clients. Since business cards are carried on one's person, the size and material of business cards should be decided in such a manner that they easily fit in one's pocket or wallet. The standard size for business cards is 2¼″ × 3½″, and the card thickness may range from 160 to 300 gsm. Business cards are usually printed horizontally on one side, which facilitates easy storage in a business card album or box. To make their business cards distinctive and individualistic, some may design them vertically or use two flaps to accommodate more information. Although variations from the standard style make a business card look more interesting, it may be difficult to store, and thus, difficult to find.

The design elements on a business card are the name of the executive or representative along with all the other information that goes in the letterhead. The residence and business address may also be added. Designers should remember that a business card is simply a contact device. Too much information on a business card may reflect self-indulgence, which often goes against the basic purpose of a business card. Hence, it is advisable to make the business card simple and dignified. Designers may use some innovative graphics on business cards, especially if such graphics are in harmony with design of other communication material used by the organization. Figure 19.3 shows the elaborate business cards of a corporate house with graphics and flaps, which are in harmony with its other communication materials, which are displayed in Figure 19.8. Such harmonized styles facilitate easy recognition of the business, but it should not be used at the cost of the information the business card needs to convey. The treatment of graphics and printing of business cards are similar to those of letterheads.

The business card is an excellent reference source for busy people. While presenting the card, the owner takes pride in his/her work. Recipients are likely to preserve attractively designed business cards and show willingness to work with the concerned business. Care must therefore be taken while designing business cards, so that they make a positive impact on prospective clients.

A few words of caution may help designers in creating effective business cards. Business cards should ideally be designed in the standard size. Odd-sized cards are usually cumbersome for handling and safekeeping, and are therefore, often thrown away. Type lines should never be placed too close to the edge of the card. The information should be presented in such a way that the receiver does not have to exert too much effort to locate the essential information. Business cards can be made more memorable by emphasizing the contents in bold display and by using symbolism.

Figure 19.3 Elaborate business card with graphics and flap

Envelopes

Often considered a subordinate device for main communication pieces, the envelope is paid little attention in design. It should, however, be kept in mind that the envelope makes the initial contact with the target audience for most direct mailers and printed pieces. It urges the recipient to open it not only because it is addressed to him/her, but also because it has an innovative shape, size, and graphics. The envelope also provides an idea about the nature of its contents. It creates curiosity in the mind of the recipient, who would like to find out what the actual contents of the envelope are. The envelope, therefore, does have an important role to play in printed communication.

Types of envelopes

There are several different kinds of envelopes that serve different purposes. They can be categorized on the basis of size, style of flaps and seams, closing devices, etc.

Figure 19.4 illustrates the various types of envelopes that will be discussed in this section.

Commercial envelopes These are the most commonly used envelopes for business correspondence. The standard size of commercial envelopes is 4″ × 9″ approximately. They are produced in several kinds of paper. Commercial envelopes with a window are used most often for bills and statements. Such envelopes save a lot of time because the name and address, once typed on the letter, do not need to be typed again on the envelope, as the address on the letter is visible through the window.

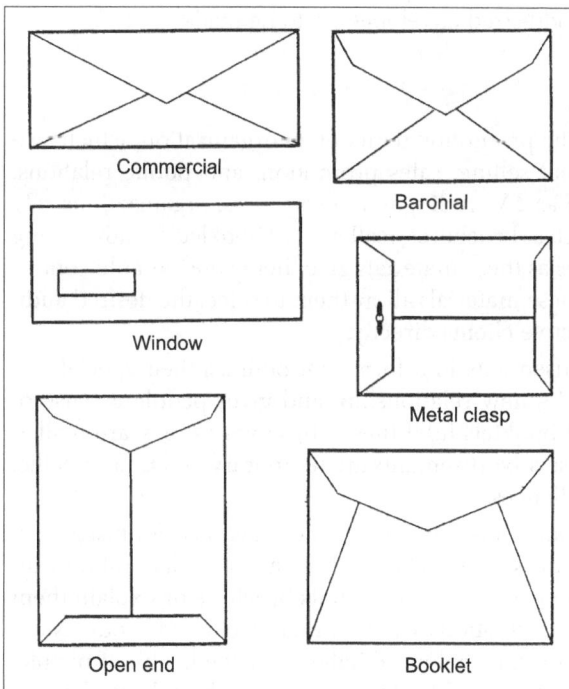

Figure 19.4 Some common envelope formats

Baronial envelopes The term 'baronial' is derived from the word 'baron', which signifies high social standing. These envelopes are traditionally used for announcements, invitations, and greetings cards. Baronial envelopes have a large pointed seal flap, and their shape is close to a square. They may range from the very simple white paper ones to those made of coloured and textured paper. The standard sizes for such envelopes is approximately 4½″ × 5½″.

Open-ended envelopes These envelopes have a seal flap and an opening on the short dimension. They are generally made of kraft paper, which is a relatively stronger variety of paper, so that they can withstand the weight of heavy publications.

Metal clasp envelopes These are another category of heavy-duty envelopes. Made of heavier-weight paper, these envelopes are specially used for publications that are meant to be taken out of the envelope and kept back in it more than once. The flap with the metal clasp serves as the button and string.

Booklet envelopes   As the name suggests, 'booklet' envelopes are envelopes that carry a booklet-sort of publication. Such envelopes are open on the long side. Occasionally, promotional matter of publications is also printed on booklet envelopes. They are, therefore, always designed to be attractive.

Design approach

Once the desired kind and size of an envelope are finalized, the arrangements of elements should be decided. Naturally, the graphic information to be placed on the envelope is dictated by the content it is to carry and the company's established house style. For envelopes that are meant only for carrying letters, the design of the letterhead is usually reproduced on the envelope, deleting some details of the information contained therein. Envelopes for cards, brochures, etc. may carry a part of the graphics used in the card/brochure to maintain a sense of harmony. Another alternative is to simply use an adapted style of the logo, the firm's name, and the address on its envelopes.

Graphics used on envelopes that carry publications should be treated as advertisements of the content. Design elements such as types, colours, shapes, etc. must create a composite design that is in harmony with the material the envelope is carrying. Odd-sized materials may be difficult to distribute by mail. The postal authorities should be consulted in situations where odd-shaped and odd-sized envelopes are to be made.

PROMOTIONAL LITERATURE

Advertising is an important part of the promotional mix of an organization, which also includes other tools such as personal selling, sales promotion, and public relations. Besides the use of mass media such as TV, radio, and newspapers, organizations rely heavily on promotional literature such as brochures, leaflets, and booklets for advertising various products, services, and issues as these materials give them considerable control in terms of production. Moreover, these materials allow them to select the desired audience and send copies to the prospective clients directly.

Organizations often need advertisements in a form that outlines their special services, demonstrates the benefit of the new relationship, and gives people a sense of immediacy. Brochures, leaflets, and booklets fulfil these objectives as they are mailed or delivered directly to people. These advertisements are temporary and time-specific, and are targeted only at specific audiences.

Direct promotional literature is extremely helpful in some situations. For instance, if a business group wants to inform its prospective clients about a new collaboration with a foreign investor, it may include the necessary details in its brochure or explain them in the form of a leaflet or booklet. In situations where a manufacturer's products are questioned because of their impact on the ecological balance or the health of people, they may provide the required explanations and quality assurance to their clients through direct literature. In such situations, organizations may also provide answers to frequently asked questions (FAQs) or include additional information in a booklet form to satisfy customers and to convey the desired message at the minimum cost. Organizations may also use direct literature to list their range of products and services with their respective special features and prices.

In all the situations mentioned above, a well-funded publicity campaign may not be as effective as a direct piece of communication. Publicity campaigns may include advertisements in specific magazines, regional newspapers, or even in some odd publication which the organization feels is read by the intended target audience. Many a time, however, these advertisements do not reach the intended target audience, and even when they do, they are diluted in the cluttered up or distorted situation by the time they are absorbed by the bulk of the audience. Direct literature plays an effective role in such situations. Brochures and flyers retain their individuality and distinctiveness while presenting the intended message. A brochure can range from a single or two-fold sheet to an elaborate publication printed on glossy paper with lots of information. A flyer, on the other hand, is a single sheet printed on one side with fewer details. It is usually easier and viable to promote a product/service through direct printed literature. Such materials should, however, be designed in such a way that they are convenient for the client to use. For keeping small messages afloat at regular intervals, the postcard is the best medium.

The advantages of direct promotional literature over other media are listed here.

They are selective An advertiser can use the method of personal communication by developing a mailing list of that target audience which will be specifically interested in its services or products. In this way, one can take full advantage of the directness and intimacy the medium offers.

They are personal These days, a personalized approach to marketing is becoming popular due to increasing media time and space buying costs. A piece of direct printed literature may look like a letter aimed at a specific individual, but can be run off in bulk, with the name and address 'matched in' at the head of each letter to give it the appearance of being individually typed. The sender's signature can be realistically reproduced to give it the effect of a personal letter.

They are flexible Since the format possibilities of direct literature are unlimited, the designer can tailor the piece according to the need and convenience of the target audience or simply to meet his/her own creative urge. Production techniques can vary from the very simple to the elaborate. The distribution method and the life expectancy of the piece are completely under the control of the advertiser.

They are stimulating A direct promotional piece can stimulate replies when a reply-paid postcard or no-postage-necessary envelope is included with it. An order form may also serve the purpose. The prospective customer can simply put in his/her name and address on the envelope and post it.

They are self-contained Direct promotional pieces are self-contained and exhaustive in the sense that they can include samples of the advertised product, detailed lists of dealers in various locations, etc., which can convince the target audience to take a decision in favour of buying the product and service advertised. Such communication may also provide suggestions, discussions related to the product/service, and details on how to buy, where to order, what to do, whom to pass it on, and so on.

Let us now discuss the designing of brochures, leaflets, and booklets in detail.

Brochures

Like all other forms of advertising and promotional literature, designers seek answers to the following questions while designing a brochure:
- Who is the piece going to and what are their characteristics?
- What is the piece trying to accomplish?
- What are the essential pieces of information to be included?
- Why should the recipient be interested?
- When will it be executed?
- When and how will it be distributed?

The designer's primary task is to ensure that the brochure gets picked up, opened, and read. He/she must then make decisions involving form, format, and paper stock.

Form

The form the brochure takes is limited only by the designer's creativity. Brochures may range from a single-fold paper to a three-dimensional object. Most advertisers consider folders to be the best form of a brochure. Some may also use brochures in the form of a pamphlet where a few loose sheets are used to cover a particular subject.

Format

The 'format' of a brochure refers to the (i) overall size of the piece; (ii) style in terms of the size, shape, and tone of the design elements; (iii) headline and copy block pattern and their placement; (iv) illustrations and techniques and their use; (v) use of other non-information-bearing elements like border, colour, and other graphic devices; and (vi) folding, opening, and closing style.

The design process can be started by cutting and folding the paper, preferably in the actual size. To avoid wasting time, complicated folding should be tried out in a miniature form. There are unlimited ways of folding paper for a brochure. We shall discuss a few standard folding styles in this section. Designers should remember that an unusually folded brochure may display his/her creative talent, but it may be difficult to fit such a brochure into a standard size envelope for distribution and mailing.

To make a folder, paper is folded to form distinct sections called panels. The elements or information contained in each panel may be complete in itself, or the panels may be combined to make one big panel. When such panels are opened out, they make a large spread. Some paper folding techniques for brochure-making are discussed here. Each of these folds has been illustrated in Figure 19.5.

Regular fold The paper may be folded along the centre line, either horizontally or vertically, to obtain a regular four page fold. Regular folds may be used to form the accordion style, in which each succeeding fold is parallel, but it turns the paper in the opposite direction. It may also form a standard parallel where each fold is in the same direction.

A sheet folded once forms a four-page signature. The signature, then folded further at a right angle, forms an eight-page signature. This is called the *French fold*. Since the paper is folded at right angles, it is also called the *right angle fold*. The French fold, when used for a forme, makes an eight-page signature.

Short fold A brochure can be given an interesting look if one or more sheets are intentionally made short by folding the page at a place slightly away from the centre. A display element can be placed on the larger inside page, which can be a common element for the front panel as well.

Gate fold This fold makes six pages. As shown in the figure, the front two pages, which are separated at the centre, become the doors of the folder. These two pages are designed to invite the reader and kindle a desire to open it. The wider inside panel is meant for the main display element.

Irrespective of the folding style that is chosen, a designer should always consider one question—what is the sequence of the panels, and what is the sequence of page

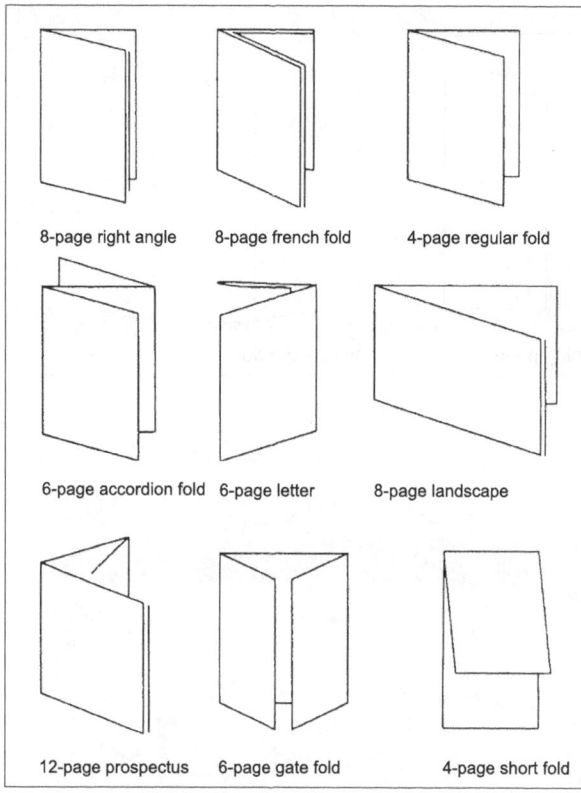

Figure 19.5 Common folding styles for brochures

numbers? It is important to note that these two sequences may not be the same. Although the sequence of pages remains the same, the sequence of the panels keeps changing, depending on the folding and opening style of the brochure. Take, for instance, a regular six-page folder, as shown in Figure 19.6. The cover of the folder is on the right outside page (O_3). As we open the folder, we get the left inside page (I_1) and the left outside page (O_1). They become one unit. For the purpose of sequence of information, these pages (I_1 and O_1) may be treated as Panel 1 and Panel 2. The elements of design can be displayed on this spread as well, following the design principle that the heading on the left panel may counterbalance the illustration on the right panel or the subheadings and graphs on the left panel are in harmony and unity with the copy block and illustration of the right panel.

On opening the last fold, we get the spread of all the three inside pages (I_1, I_2, and I_3). Now, the panel sequence becomes Panel 1, 2, and 3 for the pages I_1, I_2, and I_3, respectively. So, the information sequence and design unit is complete in itself. The left panel (I_1) is common for both the two-page and the three-page units. Care should be taken in providing information on the left outside page (O_1) as, on opening the fold, it is separated from the panels of the inside spread. It is preferable to allow the reader to read this page in isolation.

444 *Art and Print Production*

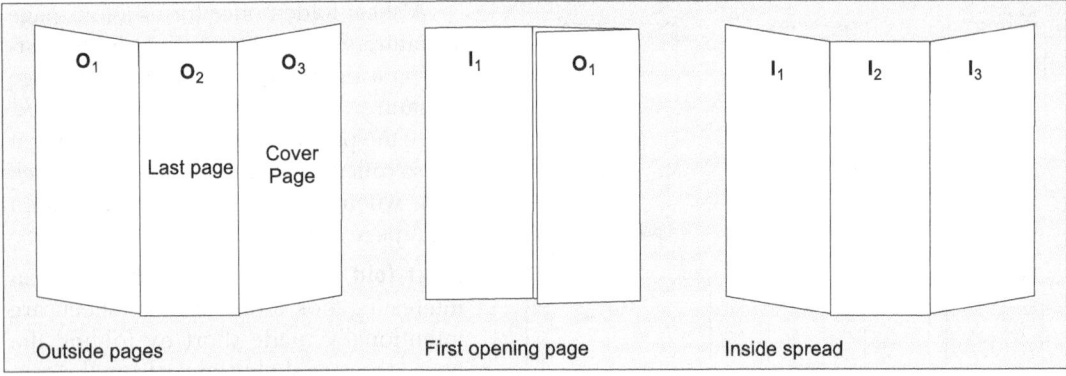

Figure 19.6 Folding of a regular 6-page folder

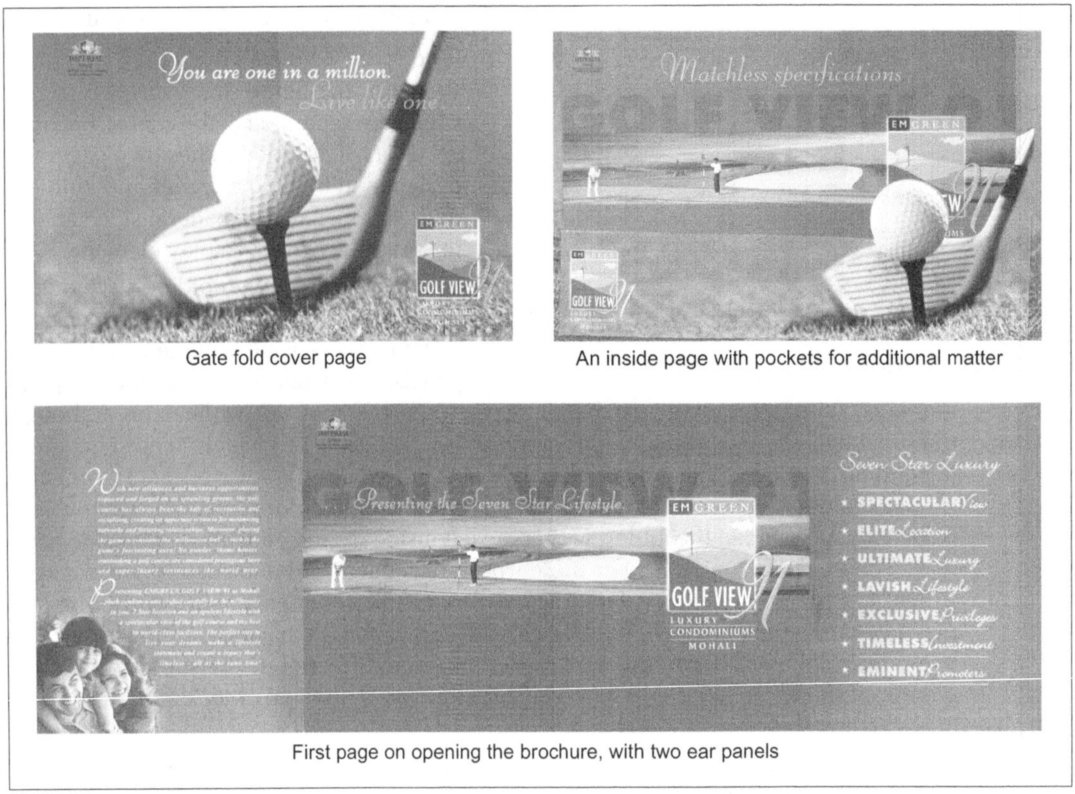

Figure 19.7 Fancy brochure aimed at a specific audience

The last page to be seen in the folder is the middle panel of the outside spread (O_2). This panel is read only when the recipient wants to take action on the information provided in the brochure. It is usually used for providing the address of the advertiser or some additional information that is not directly related to the issue being promoted in the brochure. For example, a publisher may list some of its publications on this page for promoting a particular book. If the brochure is used as a self-mailer, this page can be used for providing space for the postage stamp and lines for the recipient's address.

Organizing the sequence in which information will be presented is more complicated in the case of multifold brochures as compared to regular-fold brochures. The best way to present information is to capture the reader's attention with a strong or individualistic cover that guides him/her to open the fold or to let it open. The message content can be divided into groups which are independent in themselves but are related to the other pages and the overall mood of the brochure. The group(s) can be displayed on each opening unit of the brochure. Figure 19.7 shows a multi-fold, fancy brochure aimed at a specific target audience.

Design approach

Cutting and folding of paper is the initial step in designing a brochure. To proceed further, the designer requires adequate briefing. There are two approaches for proceeding with the brochure design. First, the designer may create the brochure on the basis of a written statement on the subject, details of its organization, and a visual as well as verbal copy. Second, the designer may have to proceed with a simple written statement alone.

In the first situation, the design may be restricted by the given length of the copy, its sequence, and also the visuals and their content. However, such situations are often convenient as the designer does not need to run around to find the appropriate copy and visuals for the design.

The cover should be designed first. A short description or line from the copy may used on the cover. Such a line can also be developed from the brief. It can then be displayed on the cover in an appropriate type style. In case a cover illustration is desired, the existing illustrations may be checked to select one that reflects the complete mood of the subject. Colour, graphics, slogans, etc., if used creatively, add aesthetic value to the cover of the brochure. Figure 19.8 presents a sample cover page of a corporate brochure in which graphic shapes, visuals, and type have been used creatively.

For the inside pages, a headline should be selected for each unit of the topic, so that it summarizes the whole theme of the unit. Distinctive shapes can be created for the headlines and their surroundings.

Copy block formatting is another creative task. An appropriate style of column width, line alignment, spacing, etc. for the copy block can, if combined with the heading, present a subject very effectively. These elements can also create a sense of rhythm and, when repeated on pages, add unity. Harmony and rhythm are essential in a brochure. Designers need to guard against styles that create monotony. Blurbs, boxes, graphics, and pictures of suitable sizes can be used to ward off monotony.

Designers should try to keep some pages free of literature, ideally the last page(s) or the one which is read last. These pages are the action pages. Application forms, reply coupons, box panels with suggestions or instructions for further inquiries, etc. may be provided on these pages.

While developing a brochure design on the basis of a brief provided only in the form of a written statement, the complete brochure needs to be visualized. Once this has been done, the designer may lay out the design elements, including the possible copy area, in the form of a rough layout. He/she may then fill the visual areas with roughly drawn illustrations. Another alternative is to simply paste simulated pictures in these areas. The copy area is usually indicated by parallel lines or simulated type.

The content filled in the rough layout does not necessarily need to be related to the subject of the brochure. The final copy written by the copywriter and the actual drawn or photographed illustrations are used to replace the simulated pictures and copy. The typesetting is carried out after the layout has been approved.

Leaflets

A leaflet is a form of advertisement on a loose sheet. This direct promotional piece is normally used for local issues and events—for announcing a cleanliness or water-saving drive, urging students to join study centre, advertising free gifts with the purchase of a new product, etc.

Figure 19.8 Cover page of a corporate brochure

The designing of leaflets is also a challenging task as most leaflets are usually thrown into the wastepaper basket without even a glance at their contents. In the huge mass of leaflets that we are flooded with every day, professionally designed leaflets tend to stand out.

In order to give a leaflet a professional look, it should be written and designed as a promotion in its own right. It should be printed in a handy size. The space should be divided into suitable grids, leaving adequate margins on all sides. The headline or the pictures should be big enough to attract the attention of as many people as possible. There should be a promise or benefit highlighted in the headlines or pictures. Sub-headlines should be used for readers who have no time to read copy in small letters. They can, however, be tempted to read further to find things of their interest. Generating enough interest to read all the important bits is the key to tempting a potential customer to take action.

Visual devices should be used creatively. In case it is difficult to find an appropriate photograph or it is too expensive to procure one, designers may rely on a striking arrangement of letters, graphic shapes, charts, graphs, tinted panels, sunbursts, white spaces, etc. to make the leaflet more attractive. Desktop publishing systems offer a lot of possibilities that are more accurate, faster, and less expensive than the conventional ones.

As always, the techniques used in the design should be tailored to convey the message to the target audience. Leaflets for general awareness issues such as health programmes or the dangers of pollution should be simple enough for everyone to understand the message. One should never try to accommodate more than one idea in one leaflet. The leaflet should have the visual look of a press advertisement that stands out in the cluttered atmosphere.

Leaflets which are to carry complete messages, such as the benefits of filing income-tax returns or opposition to the remarks of a political leader on a local issue, should provide a framework for action or at least persuade the reader to take the idea with him/her to discuss it with others at home. This type of leaflet often serves as a supplement of an advertisement published in the mass media or a meeting or workshop held on the subject. The designer should allow typography to play a major role in the design of such leaflets. The selling of new products is also matter for a supplementary leaflet. Such leaflets are usually aimed at a local or specific target group. The necessary facts and specific benefits are highlighted on the design. Sunbursts and oversized type work well in such designs.

A message for a new public school, an evening branch of a bank, or the weekly *pravachan* of a religious organization may be compared to institutional advertisements. Therefore, leaflets for these issues should talk more about the organization and its credibility. A sober, formal layout should be appropriate for the purpose. Besides headings, a tint panel or a few box items may be used for variation.

The ultimate goal of a leaflet is to obtain a direct response, so it should clearly indicate all the contact details, instructions, and sources for further information. Throughout the design, the readers' attention should be called to the reply elements at strategic places.

For the distribution of leaflets, people usually rely on inexpensive methods of distribution instead of a ready mailing list. They are used more as handouts at busy market places, crossroads, gatherings for events, etc.

Booklets

A booklet is basically a thin book, also referred to as a pamphlet. It is usually in the form of eight or more folded pages bound together. Three sides of a booklet are trimmed. Booklets have no format style of their own. Their visual look falls between that of a brochure and a book, so they are sometimes also taken as a brochure.

The booklet format is usually used for the promotion of a subject that requires detailed information or discussions that have a longer life. Once the complete manuscript or copy for the booklet has been received, the design process starts with a decision on the size of the booklet after calculating the number of pages that it will occupy after it is typeset. The most common size for booklets is demy octavo, which offers a 16-page signature. In the case of an eight-page booklet, two booklets can be obtained from one sheet. Odd-sized booklets usually cost more due to wastage of paper from each sheet, so these should be chosen after a lot of thought. Constructing a dummy booklet would be quite helpful at this stage.

While making the dummy, one should not overlook the quality of paper for both the cover and inside pages. A self-cover booklet is relatively cheaper and used when the booklet does not have too many pages. Booklets with elaborate design and multiple pages need extra protection. In such cases, a cover can be printed on one side of a four-page forme of heavier paper. The signatures of the inside pages can be inserted into the cover signature and then stitched together.

The pages of a booklet can be divided into the following design units: (i) front page or cover; (ii) preliminaries including the title page, introduction, preface, and contents; (iii) text pages; and (iv) the last pages including the back cover. As always, one first needs to design a cover that is strong enough to compete with other publications in capturing the interest of the readers.

The main consideration of the design should be the positioning, that is, creating an appropriate image of the inside copy on the reader's mind. This can be achieved by including a theme or a format on the cover that is maintained on the inside pages or vice versa. Since booklets carry promotional literature, their covers should have several typographical or visual elements. Both formal and informal ways of placements of elements are acceptable in a booklet design. A formal design looks sober, but is often less exciting. Informal designs, on the other hand, look challenging and contemporary. Oversized type, large icons, and other attention-getters make the cover stand out.

The preliminary pages of the booklet should be kept to the bare minimum—with or without a title and contents page. An elaborate leaflet may have a preface or a half-title and introduction. While designing these pages, it should be borne in mind that they too should serve promotional interests.

The text matter should be divided into groups with appropriate headings and sub-headings. It should then be arranged in a logical sequence on the pages of the dummy, which have been marked with grids. In case the booklet is designed on DTP, grids can be obtained on the screen in a PageMaker file. The two facing pages of a booklet should be treated as one unit of design. The placement of elements on the grid can be judged on the basis of the design principles. Serious and informative booklets that cover detailed discussions follow traditional book design techniques. On the other hand, when the information purports to be objective and precise, the page design should be closer to that of a magazine, with suitable placement of headers, footers, and text. Occasional bold lines, bullets, drop letters, tint blocks, etc. make the reader focus on the main points of the message and create a sense of continuity throughout the pages. Adequate white space and interesting folio-blocks can add a touch of professionalism to the booklet design.

Like any other printed literature, the last page should be treated as the action page. It should provide information to help the prospects respond to the theme of the booklet. The booklet cover should also carry some additional information or a brief write-up on the sponsor. The back page should be designed along with the cover so that the two are in harmony with each other. People just glance at the cover and then turn immediately to the back page. This is especially true for flat and thin publications.

Sometimes, it is difficult to differentiate between a brochure and a booklet. Some brochures are designed with elaborate graphic shapes and pictures. They are designed in the form of multi-page publications that are centre-stitched or perfect bound, and, hence, may be thought of as booklets. Designers may not follow the criteria for booklet

Figure 19.9 Two-page spread of a booklet promoting a winter-wear brand

designing for such material. Each page of booklet, thus, may look like an advertisement or a page out of a glossy magazine page, as shown in Figure 19.9.

SOUVENIR ITEMS

Everyone likes to receive gifts, be it a small token or an expensive present. Corporate houses, wholesalers, and retailers give away novelty useful items free of cost to the target audience in an effort to touch them emotionally. Although gift items are distributed free of cost, they are not thrown away like free distributed literature. They are distributed to select recipients, who may be patrons, prospective buyers, or clients of the organization. These items carry the organization's name, trademark, logo, slogan and, in some cases, information about the company and its products. By distributing these items, organizations earn a lot in the form of goodwill, good sales (indirect), and positive image.

There are several types of gift items that are given away as souvenirs. Some of the most common ones are calendars, diaries, key chains, caps, hats, T-shirts, pen sets, clocks, tea/coffee mugs, etc. In this chapter, we shall discuss printed souvenir items—calendars and diaries. For advertisers, there are many advantages of promoting the company's image through such items. Souvenirs are a selective medium. The selection of the target audience is completely controlled by the advertiser. Intimacy and directness are the major advantages of this medium despite the fact that it can reach only a selected few and the cost per contact is very high. In order to overcome these limitations, some of the items are produced on a large scale to reach wider audiences.

Like any other printed literature, printed souvenir pieces need specific write-ups and a good design. All the pieces can be tailor-made to suit the likes of the target audience.

Calendars

Any firm, big or small, is interested in pleasing its customers. Calendars are one of the most preferred gift items as they are acceptable to most people. Although the main function of a calendar is to provide information related to time and date, most people use them as decoration pieces. Thus, aesthetics and design play a big role in the design of calendars. Corporate and business houses spend enormous sums of money and take the help of professional design firms or advertising agencies to design their calendars.

The form and format of a calendar are always dependent on the available budget. With a good plan and idea, however, one can produce an aesthetically sound calendar even with a meagre budget. Most low-budget calendars are readymade ones, where pictures and date sheets are purchased separately and stapled together after printing the name of the company on the picture sheet. These types of calendars lack originality and aesthetic beauty. They are often distributed by local grocers and *paan* shops. A calendar with a beautiful illustration, say, a landscape, folk art, or human interest photograph, will evoke a lot of interest and may remain in the room even after the year is over. Paintings of gods and goddesses are also very popular among some people. A wide variety of inexpensive paintings are available in the market. The selection of the right one is a matter of one's aesthetic sense.

A good picture loses its aesthetic value when accompanied by the company name printed in an inappropriate type, along with a lot of information. People often hide such portions and retain the picture and date sheet for display. The basic objective of the company in distributing the calendar is thus lost if type and text is not chosen with care.

The selection of date sheet is also a critical job. Some people prefer date sheets with a lot of information, including the dates and timings of rituals, festivals, and holidays, while others consider calendars with too many details to be ugly. The date sheet should therefore be selected keeping the target audience in mind.

Big firms and organizations usually engage a design firm or an advertising agency to design and print calendars for them. Sometimes, the picture part is commissioned to an established painter/photographer or any other creative person by the company or by the design firm/agency. In this situation, the agency develops the layout, keeping in view the picture received or likely to be received. The comprehensive layout includes the picture(s)—actual or similar—with necessary display elements along with other display elements submitted to the client for approval. The picture content may have a direct or subtle association with the company's activities or may be a piece of art, design, or photograph that people can use to decorate their rooms. Beautiful calendars are often framed for longer use. Figure 19.10 shows a Caribbean woman on the March–April sheet of the 2007 calendar of KLM. The image is associated with the Cricket World Cup 2007 held in the West Indies.

There can be various different formats for calendars. The most common format is the hanging or wall calendar. Wall calendars may be in any size that can be hanged horizontally or vertically. Multi-sheet calendars have more impact than single-sheet ones, as they provide optical pleasure at regular intervals. However, the unit cost of production of such calendars is very high. Even a single-sheet calendar can create the desired impact if designed imaginatively.

Table or desk calendars are the choicest items for executives. The quality of the picture selected and the structural design of the calendar must match the tastes of the target audience. The structural design refers to the way in which the design elements are fitted within the selected size and shape of the calendar.

Figure 19.11 displays a novelty calendar with a unique structural design, aimed at medical professionals. Novelty calendars may perform different types of functions. They may, for instance, be designed in the form of stickers. Some of them may be sent as greeting cards, and some may be designed to fit into one's wallet or be placed under a glass table-top. Some calendars may be designed like a folding carton, as shown in Figure 19.12, so that they can stand up on their own. These calendars can be made by cutting, creasing, folding, and locking paperboard or card into the desired shape, as shown in the figure.

Calendar designers are increasingly using new technology for designing and producing different forms of calendars. Image assembly and manipulation by systems help develop images with improved quality vis à-vis the original. Besides such modern methods, there are some age-old techniques of securing loose printed sheets, such as spiral, wire-o, tin rimming, and perforating, which are still in use. These techniques are now being used in an innovative way. Modern machines not only provide superior quality printing and quick binding facilities but also enable newer designs and

Figure 19.10 Illustration on a calender that is directly associated with the Cricket World Cup 2007 held in the West Indies

Figure 19.11 Novelty calendar with stand

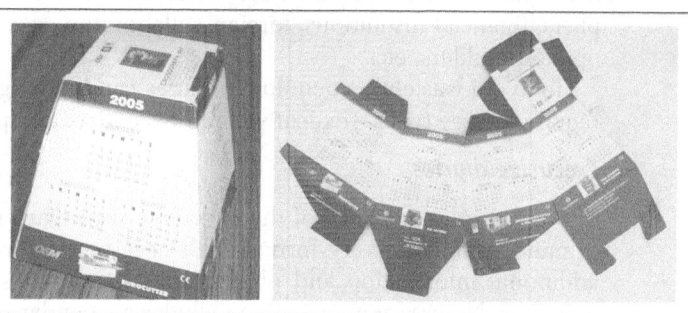

Figure 19.12 Novelty calendar as folding carton

innovative format possibilities. For example, tin rimming, which is a process in which the edge or border of a sheet is covered or held by a tin sheet, can be used innovatively by using a wider tin rim and printing the company or organization's name on it. By die cutting a part of the calendar, one can obtain an odd-shaped calendar or a three-dimensional one that can stand upright on its own.

Calendar images printed using the silk-screen process often resemble the original painted picture closely. Gradation of tone without using halftone dots, combination of glossy and matt ink, and metallic colour printing are some effects that can be obtained through the silk-screen printing process. Since silk-screen printing can be used to print images on any surface; it can be used to print calendars on cloth, plastic, or any other unconventional substrate. Such calendars are, however, viable only for a limited print run. Most calendars for mass distribution are printed by the offset process.

Diaries

Production and distribution of diaries within the selected target audience of a corporation or a company is part of its public relations activities. Diaries may also be considered a selective advertising medium, as a small logo and the company name can serve as a constant reminder to the user. Advertisers and publishers can find a number of opportunities to promote their cause and activities in a very subtle form by gifting diaries to their clients and customers.

Diary designers work in active coordination with the production people. Like calendars, diaries are available in a ready-made form in the market. It is sufficient for many companies to just print their name and logo on such ready-made dairies. Some companies may choose to have only the preliminary pages printed at their end and bind them with the ready-made inside pages to create an exclusive look. This strategy is also cost-effective.

As the organization expands, more and more diaries and other souvenirs need to be distributed among the internal and external stakeholders. Diaries are not meant for mass distribution. Even within the internal stakeholders of an organization, the top executives and some select supervisory members have a greater need for the various features provided in a diary for ease in noting down important engagements and other information. It is difficult to gauge the utility aspect of diaries for external stakeholders. Some stakeholders who are likely to find them useful are shareholders, dealers, suppliers, financial institutions, foreign collaborators, government agencies, legal bodies, opinion-builders, etc.

To avoid wasteful expenditure, diaries can be designed and produced in two or, if required, three types—executive, non-executive, and pocket diaries.

Executive diaries

The physical appearance of the executive type diary must be designed with the user in mind. It may be very formal, with necessary information only, or elaborate, with additional information and photographs or graphics accompanied by promotional write-ups. Necessary information includes a calendar of the present, previous, and following years; personal information and reminders; a year planner; company profile; holidays; important STD codes; etc. Additional information may be details about the temperature and rainfall of the country and area; its population; a weight and measure conversion table; maps of common interest; charts displaying some basic information; etc.

A little effort can make the pages inviting as well as stimulating. Designers should select a harmonious type style for the diary pages and make the main heading distinctive by making it bold or reverse. Also, the type used for sub-headings should be different from that used for the items under them by using bold type or any other style. Colour and tinted blocks can make the pages very interesting. Small icons or light background illustrations may add beauty to the page.

Running pages can also be designed in various interesting grids. Each page may contain one to three date-sheets with rules. A portion of the page, preferably the bottom few lines, may be provided for special notes. To provide more space for work days, the space for Sundays may be left at a minimum. It is desirable to accommodate a complete month's calendar on each page if possible. Rules should be very thin or in light colour to allow the notes written to stand out.

Illustrative diaries are handled like magazines or brochures. Art paper is appropriate for pages in which colour halftone images are to be printed. It is, however, inappropriate for pages meant for writing, in which only line images such as tables, tints, and types are used. The pages in an illustrative diary should therefore be planned in such a way that the colour halftone images can be printed separately on formes of art paper, and other pages can be printed on paper suitable for writing, such as superprint, bond, and lucky parchment paper. Smooth-surface paper such as executive bond paper can be used to print halftone as well as line images. Such paper, however, makes the unit cost quite high.

Different binding and finishing techniques impart a different look to a diary. An image printed on art paper using multicolour offset printing and pasted on a hard-bound cover makes the diary look costly, especially when a bordered box in metallic colour is used and the year and the name of the organization are printed in a gold leaf. Further value can be added by using raised images. Diaries look quite rich when the hardboard is covered with leather or leather-finished plastic with foam padding. To create an ethnic look, the hardboard may be covered with jute, khadi cloth, or handmade paper. Any folk design, motif, or line art can be successfully printed on such surfaces by the silk-screen process. A printed image on thick paper or a card with plastic lamination or protection plastic sheets can be bound with the inside pages by spico or spiral binding. Such diaries have a distinctive look and are convenient to use as the pages can be kept open if desired, without getting the pages mixed up.

Other novelty finishes for diaries are specially designed page marks, die-cut pages for instant access to specific months, detachable pages for addresses and telephone numbers, etc.

The executive diary must be packed in a carton for distribution, which too should be designed so that it is in harmony with the content. To create a personal touch, individual names may also be printed on each diary by the silk-screen or gold printing process.

Non-executive diaries

The non-executive diary needs the same design treatment as the executive diary. For keeping the cost of production low, some of the novelty binding and finishing techniques may be avoided. Inexpensive paper can be selected for such diaries. The paper should, however, be strong enough for writing with ink or roller ball pens.

Pocket diaries

The pocket diary should be thin enough to be fitted into one's pocket or wallet. The sequence of information to be provided in the pages, in order of importance, is space for telephone numbers, addresses, important engagements, and the year's date sheet. Bigger and more elaborate pocket diaries are also useful for most people. Such diaries can be conveniently carried in a briefcase or purse or used at home.

DISTRIBUTION

As the term 'direct communication material' suggests, these printed pieces reach the target audience directly. There may be several ways to distribute such material directly to the members of the audience. It is the management's task to select the right method for distribution.

Creative people play an important role in distribution, although their role may not be direct and obvious. This is because the distribution method affects the design and vice versa. In fact, the management personnel responsible for distribution should work in active coordination with the creative people involved in designing the product. It is in their interest that the designer be briefed about the distribution process and method well before he/she develops a format for the product.

The most common distribution method is to mail the copies to the intended recipient. When a printed piece arrives by mail, it gets the recipient's undivided attention for a moment. Designers can utilize this moment by holding the recipient's attention with interesting visuals, headings, or other graphic devices.

Postal regulations are another important aspect of distribution. The designer must be aware of the guidelines provided by the postal authorities and the ways of handling packages. Also, the permissible size for cards for business reply, envelopes, etc. should be known. All these details have a direct bearing on the design format.

The recipient's convenience is one of the major concerns of the designer and persons responsible for distribution. Whether a printed piece should be stuffed into an envelope/package or sent as a self-mailer depends on the nature of the piece and the characteristics of the recipient. For some, the envelope is a barrier, barring the opportunity to open it immediately. A self-mailer can generate immediate interest and save the cost of the envelope. An envelope, however, offers some protection against the contents being torn, bent, or dirtied. It also offers privacy and allows one to send additional enclosures.

The success of distribution through mail largely depends on the recipients on one's mailing list. The target audience can be selected carefully and the pieces can me tailored to suit the specific audience. The distributors can plan for the pieces to reach the audience at a convenient time. It should be ensured that the mailing list is up-to-date, otherwise the purpose of the entire exercise will be lost.

Some direct pieces are distributed at the point of sale or distribution of the organization. People come and collect the pieces in bulk or one each. This kind of distribution requires some publicity through other media. Many people collect the direct piece not for its own sake but for additional information of some product or service they are interested in. There is a possibility that some pieces will not reach the desired audience.

Another distribution method is hand-to-hand distribution at the place where the target audience is located. The distribution manager should be well aware of the movements of the target audience. For example, if the target audience is a group of students, the distributors should be aware that they go to school five days a week. If they want to target homemakers, they should know when they go for shopping, and so on.

Some direct pieces may be sent along with some other printed material. For example, a flyer may be sandwiched between newspaper pages, a brochure may be sent with a letter, a leaflet may be sent with a bill, a reply card may be placed inside a magazine, and so on.

A direct printed piece can be highly expensive when the cost per contact is considered. A well-planned distribution system often lowers the cost per inquiry or cost per sale.

SUMMARY

Printed pieces that are sent directly to the prospects either by mail or through individual distribution are termed as direct communication pieces. Each type of direct piece has a different function to perform. Some of them, such as letterheads and business cards, are meant for business correspondence; some, such as brochures, booklets, and leaflets, are used as promotional literature; and some others, such as calendars and diaries, are just given away as souvenirs.

Any type of business would require at least an official letterhead, a set of business cards, and envelopes. These should be designed professionally in order to have a positive impact on the clients or the consumers, so that the business can be expanded. Design elements such as logos, company name and addresses, etc., should be arranged keeping the organization's activities and the functions of the particular piece in mind. A simple design is considered dignified by most people. Some printed pieces look modern and sophisticated with special treatment, hot-foil and die stamping, thermography, and silk-screen printing.

Promotional literature as direct pieces in the form of leaflets, brochures, and booklets play an important role in the promotional mix of an organization. There are several advantages of advertising through direct promotional literature over using other media. Messages sent through direct promotional literature can be purely personal and targeted at specific audiences. Any format can be developed to suit the readers' convenience and the advertiser's budget and needs. Such promotional material can stimulate replies as they contain everything needed to take a decision in favour of the product or service.

The design process starts with decisions on the form, format, and paper stock. Brochures, leaflets, and booklets are some common forms of direct promotional material. The format refers to the overall size and the style of typographic and visual elements. The format also includes the way in which the piece can be folded, opened, and closed. The criteria for paper selection are aesthetic beauty, functional quality, and the standard size in which the paper is available.

A brochure format ranges from a single-fold paper to a three-dimensional object. In the case of a folded brochure, the sequence of panels is very important. The elements displayed on the panels must create an overall impression of harmony and unity. The leaflet is a form of advertisement normally meant for local issues. The booklet is basically a thin book and the format style falls between that of a brochure and a book. Multi-page promotional material such as booklets should have a distinctive cover, easy flow of inside pages, and the last page with the information that helps the prospects respond to the subject.

Souvenirs or give-away items such as calendars and diaries promote goodwill and sales, and also help build a positive image. Though they are distributed free of cost, they are not thrown away like other freely distributed printed material. They should therefore be designed with care. All the pieces can be tailor-made to suit the taste of the target audience. Calendars and diaries can be designed in several different formats.

Direct printed material should reach the target audience. Though distribution is primarily the task of the management, designers must be briefed about the methods of distribution well before they develop a format, for ease in distribution and the convenience of the recipients are the major concerns of a designer.

KEY TERMS

Brochure Promotional literature that is often used for promotional purposes. The physical form of brochures may range from folders to pamphlets. They may also be in the form of multi-page centre-stitched booklets.

Bullet A symbol in the form of a small, solid circle that is used to introduce listed items or categories.

Business Cards Cards bearing business information about a company or individual. They are shared during formal introductions for convenience and as a memory aid.

Catalogue An organized, detailed, descriptive list of items arranged systematically.

Demi-official (DO) Letter Letters written by officers while addressing equal-cadre or higher-rank officers, particularly in important/urgent matters. In such letters, the concerned officer is addressed by name (with an appropriate prefix consistent with the status of the addressee) to bring the matter to his/her personal/immediate attention, for an early reply, action, etc.

Direct Mailer Direct printed pieces that are sent directly to the prospective audience by mail or courier.

Flyer A single-page loose sheet advertisement for a product, service, event, or activity printed on one side of the page.

Leaflet Single-sheet advertisement printed on both sides.

Letterhead The standing information at the top of a sheet of letter paper, usually consisting of a name, address, and logo of the organization, individual, etc. It can also refer to a piece of letter paper imprinted with the standing information.

Memo Sheet Sheets of paper used for writing informal messages for future use, especially in business. The term 'memo' is the abbreviation of the term 'memorandum'.

Notepad Small paper pad for making brief notes as an aid to memory or internal communication.

Pamphlet An unbound booklet or leaflet often stuffed in the pocket of a folder.

Self-mailer A direct communication piece that is folded in such a way that the outside panels display the mailing indicia, return address, and promotional copy, so that no envelope or wrapper is required to mail the piece.

Signature Typically, a four-, eight-, or sixteen-page forme.

Tin Rimming The edge or border of paper sheets covered or held by strips of tin sheet.

REFERENCES

Adler, Elizabeth W. 1991, *Print That Works*, Bull Publishing Company, California.

Conover, Theodore E. 1990, *Graphic Communication Today*, West Publishing Company, St. Paul.

Ganguly, Dibyendu 1996, 'Designing the Corporate Gift', *Indian Express*, Ahmedabad.

Nelson, Roy Paul 1991, *Publication Design*, Wm. C. Brown Publishers, USA.

Sarkar, N.N. 1998, *Designing Print Communication*, Sagar Publications, New Delhi.

Yadin, Daniel L. 1994, *Creative Marketing Communication*, Kogan Page Ltd, London.

REVIEW QUESTIONS

1. What are the roles and scope of direct communication pieces in the promotional mix? Why do these pieces need attention at the time of writing and designing?
2. What are the basic functions of direct communication pieces? Discuss the categories under which all direct pieces can be grouped.
3. What are the forms of printed pieces required to start a business? Describe the designing of letterheads, business cards, and envelopes.
4. How is promotional literature different from other media advertisements? Identify some of the forms of promotional literature and discuss their characteristics.
5. A brochure is a form of promotional literature. Its physical forms are unlimited. Describe the various ways of folding a brochure in the folder format, with the characteristics of each.
6. What information would you need to develop brochures? Elaborate the design approach for brochures.
7. What kinds of issues are usually promoted through leaflets? How can you give a professional look to this uncomplicated direct promotional piece?
8. 'A booklet is neither a book nor a pamphlet.' Explain. When and why should this form of promotional literature be chosen? Describe the design process of a booklet, starting from the manuscript stage to the finished layout.
9. Write a note on souvenir items as tools for maintaining public relations. Identify some commonly used souvenir items and their use as promotional pieces.
10. 'Distribution of calendars among the general public is a wasteful expenditure for an organization.' Write an argument in favour or against the statement in light of the various characteristics and functions of a calendar.
11. What are the common categories of diaries? Why are they not distributed as freely as calendars? Descibe the design, printing, and finishing process for any one of these categories.
12. How do direct communication pieces reach the target audience? Discuss the role of the concerned organization's management and the designer in the distribution of direct pieces.

PROJECTS

1. Make a harmonious set of business correspondence material for a company. Use the company's logo on each piece of the set, along with other elements. Display your work on a two-fold (three panels) folder made of pastel sheet. Display the name of the assignment and your name and class details on the cover page.
2. Collect 3–4 admission forms of various mass communication institutes. Redesign any one form that, according to you, needs improvement. Use a single-colour design. You are free to use boxes, tints, and lines to enhance the aesthetics of the form and to make it more functional.

3. Design a multi-page brochure on a topic you are familiar with. Start your work by cutting and folding a sheet of standard size paper. Allocate simulated design elements (headings, text blocks, pictures, and graphics) on each panel of the folded sheet. Design an appropriate cover and back page. You may prepare all the pages on the computer and take printouts of each page. Cut and paste them on the folded sheet and make a dummy.

4. Create an exclusive T-shirt design for your institute/class. It may also be based on the theme of an event organized by your institute. Prepare a suitable design and print it yourself or by using the silk-screen printing method.

5. Choose an appropriate calendar format for your company/institute. Design a date sheet for three months, with the company name and a simulated visual on the page. Make a dummy calendar by spiral binding the page with three more blank sheets of the same size. Hang the calendar on the wall or make it stand on the table.

CHAPTER

20 Book Design

Learning Objectives

After reading this chapter, you should be able to
- understand how book design has gained prominence in the recent history of book making and publishing
- discuss the anatomy of a book for the purpose of designing
- look at the prerequisites for book designing: a well-organized manuscript, background information, and guidelines for page make-up
- examine the design approach for the integration of text and pictorial matter on a page
- gain an overview of the designing of various parts of a cover
- understand the role of paper quality and binding in book designing

INTRODUCTION

In the ancient days, before the development of written forms of language, knowledge and information were passed on from generation to generation through spoken language and non-verbal communication such as gestures, facial expressions, and sign language. Human beings, however, realized that these forms of communication had several limitations. Spoken transmission of language is dependent on human memory and, thus, is likely to be distorted and forgotten over time. Non-verbal language is rendered ineffective where large distances are involved. These limitations paved the way for newer ways of communication, in the form of symbols, followed by forms of writing based on pictographic elements. The evolution of writing systems has been discussed in Chapter 2.

With the coming of the letterform, knowledge began to be recorded on surfaces such as stone, clay, etc., and, with the passage of time, it was recorded in the form of books. The intricacies of book designing actually began with the invention of wood-block printing in the second century. It entered a new stage in the mid-fifteenth century after Gutenberg's invention of movable type and the printing press.

The earliest printed books were very similar to the calligraphic manuscript in ornate lettering illustrated in Figure 20.1. The illustrations had a symbolic narration. With the growth of typography and printing, book pages began to look less decorative and more functional.

Until recently, the designing of books was not considered a highly professional job. Publishers used to treat it perfunctorily and leave the aspects of layout and aesthetics

Figure 20.1 Fifteenth-century book with ornate design

to the printer. In the current age of information overload, however, publishers cannot afford to take the design aspect lightly as a poorly designed book, no matter how good the content is, may get lost among the numerous other printed materials in the market.

A book is not merely a functional object but also an aesthetic one. It is not only meant to be read; it is also to be looked at. The book must attract the buyer and generate in him/her a desire to possess it. The effort should be to make the book available to the purchaser with the best possible quality for the price that he/she is able and willing to pay.

Books are generally different from other forms of printed material in that they are long lasting in nature and contain literary, scientific, or other materials that can be preserved and read or consulted at any period of time. The physical structure of a book also differs from that of any other printed literature. A book usually has a higher number of pages, and is protected by a cover. The pages of most books are sewn into sections. Also, most book formats fall within some standard sizes that are easy to store in libraries and individual bookshelves.

The designing of books is also different from the handling of designs for other printed materials. Traditionally, book designers are freelancers who are not exclusive book designers. They design other materials as well. A big publishing house may have its own design team but, many a time, it too is largely dependent on freelancers, especially when a particular style of design or illustrations is needed for a book. Book publishers usually do not assign the designing of the whole book to the designer, unless the book needs special visual treatment. They normally follow the format suggested in their house style. In many cases, the cover page or the jacket of the book is the only item that is sent to the designer. In case the illustrations, diagrams, etc. required for a book are not supplied with the manuscript, an arrangement is made by the publisher, in consultation with the designer and the author, to procure the necessary material. Lack of coordination among designers, authors, and publishers is evident in most published products. This issue needs to be addressed as it may affect the final product negatively.

In traditional book publishing, various aspects such as writing, editing, designing, and production may be carried out independently by the author, editor, illustrator, designer, and the printer. These aspects are, however, handled in consultation with each other, so that the final product matches the author and the publisher's vision.

With the invention of electronic publishing systems, book publishing has become much more simple and convenient. The manuscript developed by the author can be edited online by the author himself/herself or by the editor, which brings down the scope of errors in printing. Several options are available on electronic systems vis-à-vis type style, column grids, setting formats, and page make-up. In cases where a short print run is required, the author himself/herself can write the book, edit it, work on the page make-up, and print the required number of copies on a desktop printing system. Various aspects of book publishing have thus become much more integrated with electronic publishing. It has also facilitated quicker, easier, and better quality work as attention can be paid to the finer details on such systems.

Whatever may be the method of publishing a book, the anatomy of the book and the design approach, which is the link between the manuscript and the final product, remains the same. The electronic method has only provided tools that help book publishing professionals carry out their tasks much faster and with less costs and effort.

BOOK ANATOMY

A book can be divided into: (i) the protective *cover* and *jacket*; (ii) the *spine*, or the portion of the covers used as the backbone of the book; (iii) *end-papers* that hold the text pages with the cover boards or cards; and (iv) reading matter. The entire reading matter can be further divided into a distinct sequence of parts: (i) the preliminaries or the front matter; (ii) running text; and (iii) the back matter.

Preliminaries The preliminary pages of a book refer to all the matter in a book that precedes the main text. Generally, these pages consist of the *half title*, that is, the first typographical page of the book, on which only the title of the book is displayed; the *title page*, or the second printed page, on which, along with the title, the names of the authors and the publishers also appear. Most books also carry *copyright*, *preface*, *acknowledgements*, and *contents* pages. Some books provide additional pages for the *dedication*, *foreword* (written by someone other than the author), *publisher's note*, and the *frontispiece*, an illustrated leaf facing the title page.

It is a common practice to have all the matter or at least the starting matter on the right-hand pages, except the copyright page and the frontispiece. However, the dedication and acknowledgements pages may sometimes appear on the left-hand page to suit the convenience of the publisher.

Running text The running text starts on a right-hand page, with an adequate sink, that is, wider white space from the top edge of the book. For books with chapters, the opening page of each chapter may start with the chapter title and number. The folios, that is, two facing pages of the book, are marked with page numbers. The left-hand (verso) pages display even page numbers and the title of the book whereas the right-hand (recto) pages display odd page numbers and the chapter title. The actual numbering of the book starts from the first running text page with Arabic numerals. Preliminary pages starting from the half-title page have Roman numerals in lower case. But the half-title, the title and the copyright pages do not display numbers. That is why they are known as blind folios.

Back matter The back matter includes the *appendices*, or the supplementary material for the book; the *glossary*, or the list of terms with accompanying definitions; the *bibliography*, or the list of resources for sourced materials that have been used or consulted in the preparation of the book; and the *index*, or the alphabetical listing of selected words along with the number of the pages on which they appear.

PREREQUISITES FOR BOOK DESIGNING

In order to proceed with the book design, a designer or the person responsible for the book design first of all requires a well-organized manuscript on which instructions can be clearly marked for the typesetter. He/she also requires information about the contents of the book, its target audience, the allotted budget, and so on. Further, the designer needs some guidelines regarding the size and format of the book, the type style and size, etc. Each of these requirements has been discussed in this section.

Well-organized Manuscript

The manuscript is the base for any design, and determines the final shape of the book to a great extent. The designer may receive a manuscript in various forms. In cases where the complete book design is assigned to the designer, he/she must obtain the edited manuscript with all the relevant materials and information. Some materials for the book may be camera-ready while some may be in the form of rough illustrations and matter for tables, graphs, charts, etc. Information about the book includes all the matter for the preliminaries and the back pages except the index, which can be made only after the pages have been finalized in print. The manuscript should preferably be typed out, or a computer printout should be provided with adequate white margins and space between the lines.

The margin enables the designer/editor to mark necessary instructions for the printer. The space between the lines should preferably be double the size of the line height, so that if there are any corrections, these can be made above the line without disturbing the readability of the script. This eliminates the need for retyping the entire matter, which is a time-consuming process. A clean manuscript should thus be provided to the typesetter. The typesetter or the operator is likely to introduce fresh errors or repeat the lines in the manuscript in the case of closely spaced typed matter or a shabbily corrected/edited manuscript.

When the publishers directly handle the designing of the main text in consultation with the author and the printer, the designer is assigned with only the preliminary pages, back matter, and the pictorial pages. In such cases, he/she must be fully briefed on the background and general planning of the book, besides being provided with the matter and information needed to develop those pages. Here, the editor or the publisher is responsible for organizing or shaping the manuscript. Although the designer's role is very limited in such projects, he/she should cooperate with the copy editor and the publisher, as a poorly organized manuscript not only hampers or slows down the design work but also introduces undesirable elements such as spelling errors, improper punctuation, and faulty language. Such errors remain on the printed pages until the book is re-printed with corrections, which lowers the quality of the book.

The manuscript, whether it comes directly from an author or through the publisher, must be thoroughly copy-edited. The copy editor helps the author present his/her ideas in a lucid and presentable manner. In order to ensure that the book has minimal errors, the copy editor may participate in proofreading as well. Designers need to cooperate actively with the copy editor and understand the need for changes, if any, to parts of the manuscript to enhance the quality of the book at the designing stage.

Information about the Project

Besides the manuscript of the book, the designer needs some additional information before going ahead with the design process. Like any other publication, a book too is targeted at a particular audience. Designers must keep the taste and needs of the target audience in mind. Most readers are concerned about the price of the book and judge its value on the basis of its physical appearance, so designers must have information about the price range in which the book will sell.

The designer must also have information regarding the budget for the book. This enables him/her to control the costs while taking decisions regarding the paper, type, illustrations, and the printing process, and while planning the pages.

In case the design assignment is separated from the production stage, the designer must be aware of the typesetting method, capability of printing process, binding requirement, permissible colours, number of pages estimated, etc.

If the book has illustrations, and these were not supplied to the designer with the manuscript, he/she should be informed about when and in what form they will be available. Accordingly, the designer can leave space in the layout or paste simulated illustrations. The actual illustrations, once received, can be cropped and scaled to fit the allotted space and then processed.

In case the publisher or the author has a special style in mind, or the designer needs to adhere to the publisher's house style, a sample book should be provided to the designer for reference. Moreover, the designer should either be provided all the physical details for the book or participate in the decision-making process for selecting the size of the book, paper quality and size, and covers (casebound or paperback). A sample binding case or dummy book helps the designer in developing a book design.

The designer must be aware of the points at which his/her services may be required. For instance, the designer may have to help the editor and the author in arranging the illustrations or making the artwork at the copy editing stage. He/she may also need to monitor the page make-up and supervise the printing operations. This knowledge helps freelance designers to quote their fees, and allows in-house designers to organize and delegate work.

Guidelines for Page Make-up

The author's ideas and the publisher's vision are converted into an aesthetic and functional physical object in the form of a book. While working on a book design and selecting types for the book, the designer needs to consider the author's ideas and the publisher's requirements and guidelines.

Most of the guidelines that designers need to consider while designing a book are applicable to a wide range of books; but some are meant for specific categories such as heavily illustrated books, technical books, and school text books.

Book size Size is the first consideration while working on a book design. Book sizes are usually identified on the basis of folded British-size paper. For example, a book in the size $5'' \times 7½''$ is identified as a crown octavo, as this size is obtained from crown-size paper ($15'' \times 20''$) that is folded thrice. If a book is obtained from international-size paper, its size will be identified as A4, A5, etc. Designers should be well-versed with the paper sizes available in the market.

The size of a book usually depends on the adaptability of its contents. Normally, a book with illustrative contents needs to be designed in a bigger size, whereas a single-column text base book can be designed in a smaller size. Some books are so small that they are referred to as pocket books. While designing the pages of a book, the designer needs to be aware of the trimmed size of the text pages and the size of the jacket. Otherwise, there is a danger that a part of the content of the text pages, especially the illustrative elements, may be chopped off at the time of finishing. In the case of a jacket design, the elements on the spine may not fall at a proper position or the contents of the cover may have an undesirable margin or be at a hanging position. Thus, designers need to exercise care while working on these elements.

Format Once the final size is decided, one needs to define the format that will be used throughout the book. Generally, it is an arbitrary decision based on some set practice or convenience in adapting the contents. A standardized format facilitates the production work and makes it economic.

The format refers to the general shape and appearance of a printed page, including its trim size, page margins, the size of the copy area, guides and positions of headers and footers, standard graphics, etc. Traditionally, all these are indicated on a grid sheet. These days, however, a design grid can be created in the form of a template on a page layout program. It can be duplicated to create a series of pages that follow the same design specifications, which saves repeated set-up steps, embodies the design, enforces consistency, and simplifies the page layout process. A sample page with layout specifications is illustrated in Figure 20.2.

Type style and size Choosing the type styles and determining their sizes is another important aspect of the design process. The type styles selected should be legible. In book design, typefaces for textual matter should be given special attention as the reader's involvement with the text is maximal. The selected typefaces should be not only aesthetically pleasing but also appropriate for the subject the book deals with. They should suit the overall mood created by the book. For instance, Souvenir may be an appropriate font for a novel, but it will be inappropriate for a science book.

Determining the length of the copy before typesetting is always helpful for designing. Different formulae are available for this purpose. For book designing, it may be sufficient to generate a rough estimate through the word counting system. Readers are advised to refer to Chapter 19 for details on such estimation. Among other standard decisions at this stage are—style of paragraph, text indentation, space between the lines, style of headings, sub-headings, tabular matter, etc.

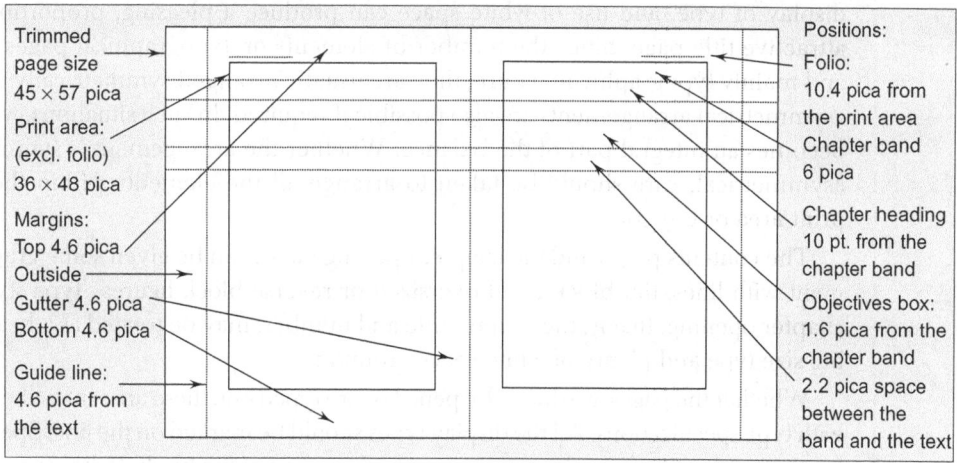

Figure 20.2 Page layout specification

STAGES IN BOOK DESIGN

In this section, we have divided the stages in book designing into (i) designing of typographical or text matter, (ii) designing of pictorial matter, (iii) integration of the typographical and pictorial matter during page layout, (iv) cover design, (v) deciding on the paper quality to be used, and (vi) deciding on the appropriate binding for a book. In actual practice, all these stages may not always be in sequence, and the designer may not be responsible for all of them. For instance, decisions on paper quality and binding techniques may be taken by the production persons of the publisher. Nonetheless, designers will benefit if they are aware of all these aspects and decisions as they will then be able to make well-informed choices.

Typographical Matter

The design of a book actually starts with the marking of the text matter for the typesetter. Most book designers are not even consulted for this purpose. Usually, the publisher or the person responsible for production looks at this aspect, keeping in mind the standard ways of page making discussed in the previous section. Since each book is unique, one needs to create a style guide to help the typesetter in laying out the matter as per the style. A *style guide* outlines the standards for designing a particular book, including specifications for the style of graphics, typographical matter, and white space to be used in the book. The need for a design guide is all the more when dealing with complex books. Let us now look at the specifications required for various parts of a book.

Pencil sketches may be prepared for the preliminary pages and the beginning page of the running text in actual size. Display types may be drawn roughly, but these should be close to the style desired. The display types may be the same as those used on the cover page, but this should not be taken as a rule. Judicious selection of typefaces, display of type, and use of white space can produce a pleasing, proportionate, and attractive title page. Since the number of elements on typographical pages is limited and mainly typographic in nature, they are usually arranged symmetrically. However, asymmetrical arrangements are also possible if required. In such situations, white space becomes an integral part of the balance. Whether the arrangement is symmetrical or asymmetrical, care should be taken to arrange all the elements within the decided print area or the grid.

The contents pages and the chapter opening pages can be given some graphic treatment with lines, tint blocks, and oversized or reverse block figures. Type style for the chapter opening, that is, the chapter title and number, may be treated as a heading with big size type and plenty of white space around it.

Whether the pages are drawn by pencil or are typed out, these are sent to the typesetter with type specifications. All the display types should be marked on the line. Specifications for the running text may be marked on the first page of the book. If, however, the book is more complicated, marking may be necessary on some more pages. If the manuscript handed to the typesetter is in a soft-copy format, it should be accompanied by printouts (hard copies) of the manuscript with necessary instructions for the typesetter.

In the style guide for a book, one is expected to mark the type size in points, with the name of the typeface and its weight, width, and posture. The text type should also be marked with leading (space between the lines) in points, and the length of the lines in which the text is to be set should also be clearly specified. For instance, the text copy for the book shown in Figure 20.3 has been set in 10.5 pt Baskerville BE Regular, 2 pt leading, 32 pica line length, and justified format. The marking on the margin for the main text would hence be: 10.5/12.5 pt Baskerville BE Regular, justified × 32 pica. The figure illustrates sample pages from the book that were created on the basis of the type specifications marked for the typesetter.

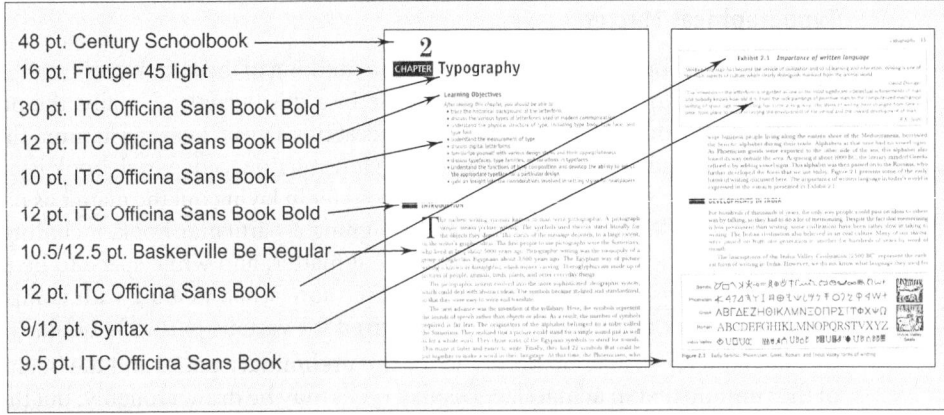

Figure 20.3 Pages made on the basis of type specifications

The manuscript is first sent to the typesetter along with the style guide. The typesetter then returns the material in the form of proofs. These proofs need to be checked carefully against the original instructions marked in the style guide in order to ensure that the instructions have been followed properly. Errors, if any, have to be marked clearly, using proofreading marks. Any adjustment in formatting may also be done at this stage. This may include providing space for headings, illustrations, tables (if set separately), sidebars, etc. Line adjustment is also to be taken care of at the proof stage. For instance, widow and orphan lines can be adjusted on the proofs. A page should not begin with a very short end-line of the paragraph continued from the preceding page. Such a line is referred to as a *widow*. Widow lines stand out from the remaining paragraphs and make the page look awkward. This is undesirable both aesthetically and pragmatically as it interrupts the reader's flow and thought process. One should make sure that the last line on a page is not too short, that is, it is not an *orphan*. An orphan at the end of a page may make two facing pages appear unequal. Indentation, bullet sizes, paragraph spacing, etc. can be adjusted on the proofs to make the page look more pleasing and legible.

On finalizing the page make-up, the running titles—small lines at the top or bottom of the inside pages along with the page numbers—should be decided. Running titles are in fact the elements of the folios. As discussed earlier, the book title normally goes on the left-hand pages and the chapter title goes on the right-hand pages. The volume and issue number may also be included in the folio, if necessary. In some technical and reference books, the chapter title comes on the left pages and the specific topic comes on the right pages. A little graphic treatment makes the pages positively different. Folios are useful for readers because they let them know which part/section/chapter of the book they are reading. Electronic publishing systems have automatic page number generators, which enable the designer or page maker to set the style and position for the folio on a master page.

Pictorial Matter

The illustrations for a book are usually provided by the author; the designer is only supposed to decide how these are to be presented in the book. This is especially true for books on technical or specialized subjects. Some books, however, demand greater inputs from the designer. Books with fast-moving stories, for instance, may require the designer to create visual images that illustrate the content and keep pace with the story or theme. Books on humour and fantasy are examples of books for which the designer needs to create realistic illustrations with, perhaps, some suggestions from the author and the publisher.

Pictorial pages are handled on the basis of the number and style of illustrations being used in the book. Heavily illustrated books such as comic books use mainly hand-drawn illustrations. Sometimes, books may be designed in non-standard shapes and formats to accommodate the illustrations, as shown in Figure 20.4. In most cases, the pictorial pages are designed by the illustrator in collaboration with the author. Sometimes, the author himself/herself may act as the illustrator (at least the originator of ideas), especially in children's books. In the absence of adequate skill, a professional illustrator's help may be sought to develop the final images.

468   *Art and Print Production*

Figure 20.4   Book designed in non-standard shape

In most cases, conversion of statistical information into visual form is the designer's responsibility. These days, visual forms such as charts, graphs, and maps can be generated on the computer. Graphic software programs such as Microsoft Excel and Harvard Graphics can easily covert statistical information into a chart. Various style options are available on these programs. Such illustrations can even be created while making the pages on the computer. The advantage of creating these illustrations online is that they can be tinted in various patterns, coloured, and shaped according to one's requirements. Moreover, the images can be scaled to fit into the page onscreen, so that they are integrated with the other elements of the page.

Photographic illustrations for books are mainly provided by the author or the publisher. Most photographs are collected from different sources. Rarely is a highly professional photographer asked to shoot fresh photographs. This is understandable, because, unlike a newspaper, a publishing house cannot afford to have a staff photographer. As a result, the quality of the photographs that come to the designer may not meet the desired standards. Some commonly noticed shortcomings in photographs are: clipping marks on photographs when they are sent in a bunch, scratches and undesirable spots, captions or instructions on the backside of the photographs that show through the content, too much contrast or low contrast, colour photographs for black and white printing jobs, already printed photographs with half-tone dots, and unbleached colour of bromides or transparencies.

It is necessary to use different tools and techniques to improve the quality of the photographs. One should not hesitate to reject photographs that cannot be reproduced well. Retouching is the most fundamental technique used to enhance the quality of photographs. Through retouching, one can not only remove several photographic imperfections but also make the photographic content sharp, emphasize highlights, change the background to create an appropriate mood, restore lost edges, remove undesirable contents, and maintain photo-quality images. All these can be accomplished with manual tools such as paint brushes, airbrushes, pens, pencils, and photographic chemicals such as dyes and bleaches. Tools available on software programs such as Photoshop can also be used to enhance the image quality.

Symbolic expressions or presentation of abstract idea in visual forms are quite common in book design, especially on the cover and title pages. Hand-drawn or computer-generated illustrations are ideal for most situations. Designers can exhibit their creative skills by designing covers and title pages that aptly represent abstract ideas and themes addressed in the book. Figure 20.5 displays book covers where symbols have been used to express the abstract subject of the books.

Photo conversion techniques such as cut-outs, vignettes, duotones, and special screens, though used sparingly in book design, can create the desired mood on a page. For example, a cutout image may be used to emphasize the main content and to allow the text to run into parts of the image area. Vignettes can create a feeling of age or beauty. Special screens may be used to create various effects. For instance, mezzotint may be used to make an image look as if it has been created with pen and ink dots, circle screen may be used to create a feeling of movement, and so on. Duotones create an effect of colour and can be used in harmony with other colour pictures used in the book. These tehniques have already been described in Chapter 3.

Figure 20.5 Use of symbols to express the subject of the book

Graphic images often need to be cropped and scaled to fit into the desired area. Care needs to be taken during the processes of cropping and scaling. These issues have also been covered in detail in Chapter 3.

Page Layout

During the page layout stage, the arrangement of the textual and pictorial matter is decided, and both these elements are integrated on each page of the book. Traditionally, the page layout of a book was done once the galleys were obtained from the typesetter. In the hot-metal days, two sets of galleys were required—one for pasting on a book-sized paper for page composition, and the other for reading the proofs. Both were returned to the press for correction and page make-up.

These days, page layout of books is done mostly in a desktop environment. The work that was earlier done manually can now be done electronically. Once the decisions on typographic matter and illustrations (in or outside the computer) have been taken, the page layout can be carried out on a software program, such as Adobe PageMaker, InDesign, or QuarkXPress. Some recently developed word-processing programs can also prepare page layouts, but layout programs are the most appropriate software for the same.

Layout packages, like most other software programs, enable the layout person to view portions of the pages up close and look at the finer details on a page. They also allow him/her to assess how the page looks after the layout and type specifications have been implemented. The Document Setup command allows the user to create the layout pages as per the required size with margins, etc., and also to create the master page with headers, footers, and automatic page numbering. When the text is imported from a word software and applied to this page, it not only automatically fills the grid but also goes on filling the following page with repeated elements indicated on the master page. Figure 20.6 displays the Document Setup command of Adobe PageMaker, a commonly used page layout program.

Layout programs offer a lot of flexibility. The text can be shifted to make room for a heading or an illustration. An illustration which has been scanned or created digitally can be pasted on the page on-screen. It is easy to scale illustrations, shuffle the text around, and set it in the desired format on a layout program. Despite all these advantages of layout programs, one should be careful in cases where camera-ready copies are handed to the printer on ordinary paper. In such cases, continuous tone illustrations should be sent separately in order to ensure that the print quality is good. Options for graphic effects such as line images, tints, and boxes help to make the pages look more interesting.

Books with numerous colour illustrations and occasional graphics require electronic page planning. Such books should be planned with a sufficient budget and time in hand. Specifications should be given for the layout of each page of the book, with precise instructions for colour and other elements. The colour images should be scanned with four-colour separations that are stored on a disk. This information can then be used to create a complete page. The output of these pages can be transferred onto film. The type and picture integration facility of some imagesetters has offered tremendous flexibility to publishers and designers.

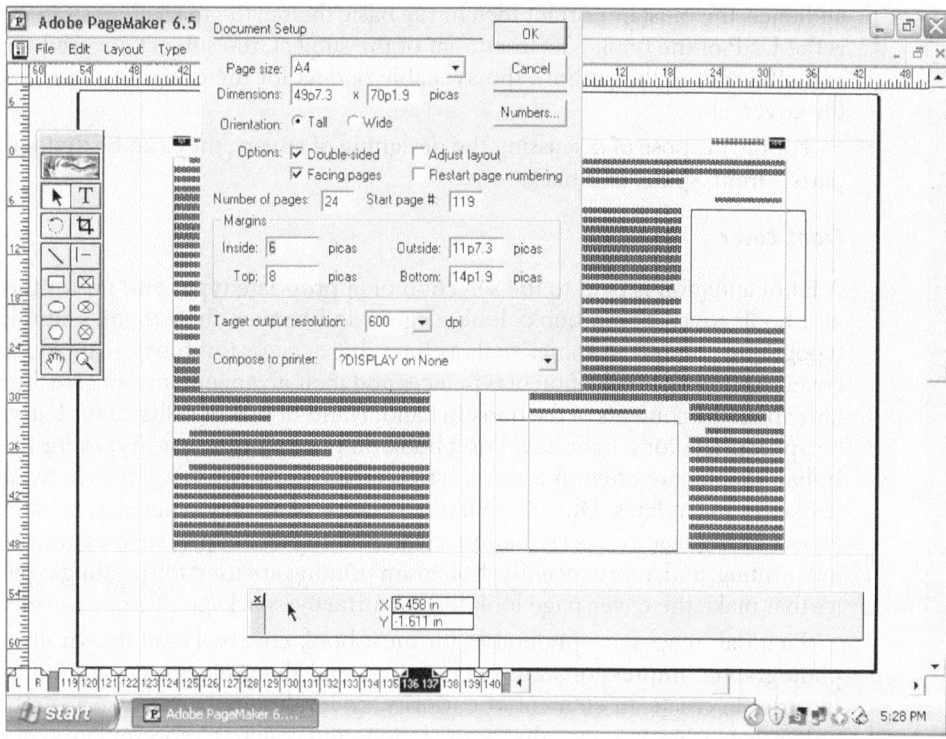

Figure 20.6 Adobe PageMaker—a page layout program

Cover Design

Many publishers do not consider cover design to be a part of the design activities for a book. They deal with this aspect separately once the manuscript has been finalized or the complete pages have been made. Sometimes, a highly specialized designer or an advertising agency may be engaged to design the cover.

The cover is not only a wrapper and protective layer for the book, it is also a poster or an advertisement to create a favourable impression that leads to a purchase decision. Therefore, cover art is of critical importance in the successful marketing of a book. A well-designed cover satisfies booksellers and publishers by promoting sales and provides aesthetic pleasure to designers, authors, and all other people involved in the book design.

It is essential for us to understand what makes a good cover. A good cover design should (a) be attractive and tasteful in the form of art, typography, colour, and graphics; (b) reflect the flavour/mood of the book directly or thematically; (c) stand out when displayed; and (d) look professional in terms of the arrangement of elements and the production of the cover.

The cover design of a book should be handled like an advertising design. The designer must be provided with a design brief, which may contain details about the target audience, the most important idea or the basic theme, the marketing strategy (i.e., what is the USP of the book—its treatment of the subject, the subject covered, or the name and affiliation of the author), the available budget for the designing and production of the cover, etc.

For the purpose of discussing the designing of covers, they can be divided into three parts—front, spine, and back.

Front cover

A lot of attention is paid to the selection of appropriate types and art for the front part of a book cover. Some books look elegant and convey their themes simply by using typography. Simple graphics such as lines, borders, or tint-blocks can add beauty to a cover. Appropriate selection of typefaces and their arrangement can give the readers an idea about the contents of the book in hand. Hand-drawn or calligraphic letterforms may be appropriate for a light novel or a book on poetry or theatre. Types for the covers of Indian classics are often in Roman script, created in a Devanagari style by adding serif strokes or mean lines. Due to the limited choice of display typefaces, most of the cover types for language books are hand-drawn. Printing techniques such as die stamping, hot foil printing, and, more recently, hologram printing are used for printing types or graphics that make the cover page look like an attractive package of some novelty item.

Pictorial images are preferable for most book covers. Hand-drawn illustrations or photographic impressions are expected to lend themselves to visual interpretations. In order to create an element of curiosity, cover designers may use a symbolic image rather than using an image that is an obvious and concrete representation of the subject addressed in the book. Some books carry the author's name and photograph on the front cover. The name of a celebrity author boosts the sale of a book.

Figure 20.7 shows the use of attractive typography and pictorial images on the front covers of some books. The cover for the book on Indo-Anglican poetry has been composed in Roman script in a Devanagari style, as discussed earlier. The illustration of an architectural structure directly depicts the theme of the period for the book on medieval India. The cover for the book on Mathura—considered to be the birthplace of Lord Krishna—has been designed using a delicate line drawing from *Mathura shaily*. The cover for a book in Bengali has been designed using a powerful single-line colour illustration.

Spine

Usually, books are not displayed like magazines on a news-stand. Most books stand on racks or shelves where only their spines are visible to the buyer. The designer must, therefore, pay as much attention to the spine design as to the front cover. The elements on the spine must provide the basic information about the book and display all the elements on the front cover in a subtle form.

A thicker spine offers more possibilities for the designer. It may include a small display of the cover art or a part thereof in a miniature form, an extension of graphics from the front sub-title for additional information, the title of the book, and the name of the

Book Design 473

A powerful single-colour line illustration for a cover page

Architectural form directly depicting the theme of the period

A cover with a delicate line drawing adopted from Mathura Shaily

A self-explanatory Indo-Anglican type form cover design

Figure 20.7 Attractive use of typography and images on book covers

474 *Art and Print Production*

Figure 20.8 Book spines

author(s) and the publisher. The title of the book is usually placed in a horizontal format on the spine, as shown in Figure 20.8. To sum up, a book cover must be conceived as an integral whole, visualizing both the front part and the spine together.

Back cover

The back cover of a book is generally used as promotional material by the publisher. The back cover may include a blurb covering the important subjects discussed in the book, its special features, and details about the authors. In some books, the back cover gives details about books published by the same publisher or the same author. In some books, and especially for children's books and centre-stitched books, an illustration may spread across the front cover, spine, and the back cover. A book is viewed and inspected like a package when picked up. Therefore, a sense of continuity between the three parts of the cover is a must. Books look elegant and neat without too much typographic elements on the back cover. Simple repetition of the cover graphics or a flat colour is often sufficient for the back cover.

Besides the three distinct parts of a book cover, there are two other parts that need to be discussed, especially in the case of book jackets. Jackets have two elongated flaps on each side. The front flap usually carries a description of the contents of the book, set in normal text type. The back flap may carry a short description of the author or a list of books written by the same author or related books published by the same publisher. Figure 20.9 shows the jacket of a book with its front and back flaps.

The jacket of a book may be treated as a promotional folder. The length of the copy, blank space around the copy, and the size of the illustrations (if any) should be handled with care. Many publishers print additional copies of the book jacket and send them to the prospective buyers as part of the promotional activities for the book.

Figure 20.9 Five parts of a book jacket

Paper for Book

Much of the physical appearance of a book depends on the quality of the paper selected for printing the book. Therefore, from the designer's point of view, paper selection is as crucial as the selection of types and illustrations. There are several factors that need to be considered for selecting the paper for a book. The cost, as always, is a pre-eminent factor. Although there is a tendency to select cheaper grade paper to keep the production costs low, some practical considerations cannot be ignored. A book should have longevity. The pulp and chemical process used for making paper should be of good quality, so that the book pages may not fall apart at the fold or get discoloured before the expiry of its life span.

The colour and smoothness of paper should be judged from their aesthetic contribution. One should be careful about the shades selected, for a dark-shade paper can impair readability. White is the safest colour for text pages for any book. Low-grade rough-surface paper looks cheap. Moreover, it cannot be used to print illustrations as it soaks too much ink. Long text on a glossy surface tires the eyes. However, a glossy and smooth surface is required for printing continuous tone images in illustrated books.

Weight and opacity are the other important considerations in selecting paper. These have been discussed in detail in Chapter 11. Most books are printed on both the sides of a sheet. Images may show through the pages in case they are printed on them. A thin paper with good opacity should be used to prevent this. Generally, heavy paper has more fibres and is thus more opaque, but it often affects the finishing because of the over-absorption of ink. Heavy paper also makes the book bulky and uncomfortable to handle. It also increases the transportation cost.

The thickness of paper is measured in grams per square metre (gsm). The commonly used paper weight for text pages is 80 to 135 gsm and that for jackets is 100 to 150 gsm. In case of a paperback, thicker stock is necessary for the cover to protect and hold the pages firmly. This is also true for books for school children. The weight of such stock may range from 160 gsm to 250 gsm, which is referred to as cards or boards. Thinner cover paper for jackets and paperbacks requires lamination, which makes the cover dust-proof, shiny, and stiff.

The strength and stretch of the paper are important concerns for the printer. Strength and stretch depend on the chemical and physical properties of paper. Weak paper often releases undesirable paper particles or tears off during the press run, which further extends the precious press time. Unseasoned paper has a tendency to expand or shrink, which affects printing, especially where colour registration is involved.

As the book publishing industry is one of the biggest consumers of paper, paper manufacturers produce a kind of paper specifically for book printing. This paper is referred to as book variety paper, although it may also be used for other publications. Book paper stocks are produced under different brand names by various paper mills, as already discussed in Chapter 11. Some of the commonly used brand names for text pages are: Maplitho, Sunshine, Super Sunshine, White Printing, Lucky Parchment, etc.

Book Binding

Although this step of book design is purely production-oriented and is done only after the complete text is printed, it is taken into consideration at the very planning of the book.

The binding process starts with the folding of the printed sheets and the making of signatures. The binding of a book may be very simple or very complicated, depending on the type of job in hand. The simplest, fastest, and least expensive binding method is saddle stitching. This method is generally used for thin publications such as comic books, school text books, and promotional booklets. Although the life of a book becomes short if saddle stitching is used, it has several advantages too. For instance, a saddle-stitched book can lie open and flat and is thus easier to handle and read.

A large number of books are bound without stitching or sewing. This method, known as perfect binding, is specially used for paperback editions. It keeps the cost of the book quite low. In this method, folded signatures are gathered in the right order and roughened along the back fold by trimming and grinding. The pages are then glued at the spine on which a lining cloth is pasted. The cloth-piece holds the pages together, and the cover is glued thereon.

Casebound books, also referred to as 'hardbound' books, are bound using the traditional method of book binding. When one looks at a casebound book from the top of the spine, it can be seen to consist of a number of *signatures* bound together. This kind of binding is used mainly for long lasting books. After the signatures or sections have been gathered, end papers are pasted on the first and the last signatures. These are then sewn together with a strong thread. A strip of cloth is glued on to the spine. The end papers are glued down to the case. The case is created by covering the cardboard covers with paper, cloth, or even leather. In art books, illustrated books, and other special categories, end papers are also used for displaying artwork or illustrations to make the book aesthetically pleasing. Figure 20.10 displays books with different kinds of binding.

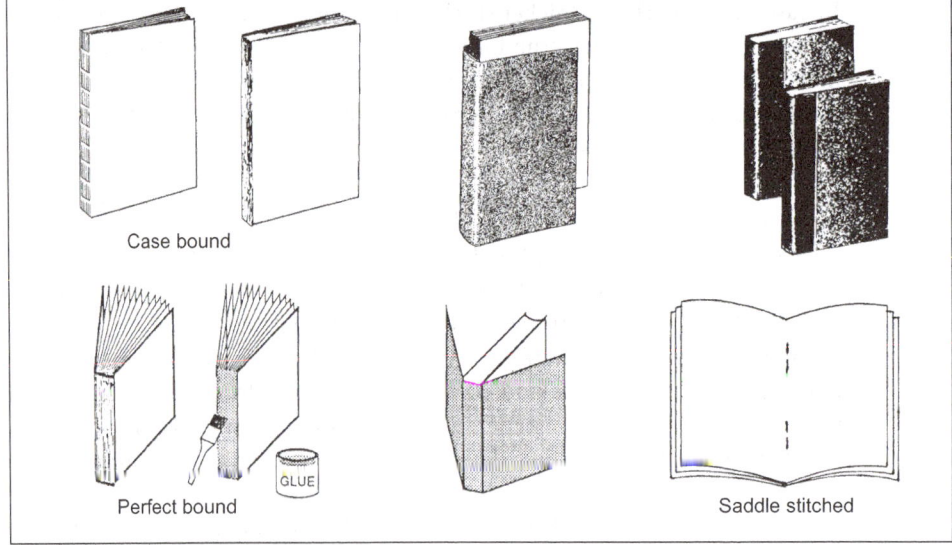

Figure 20.10 Types of book binding

SUMMARY

Books were in existence much before the invention of printing. Wood-block printing was the first faltering step in the designing of books. Book designing entered a new stage with the invention of movable types and the mechanical printing press in the mid-fifteenth century. The characteristics of the books that were printed earlier were very similar to a calligraphic manuscript in ornate lettering, and the illustrations were not realistic.

Until recently, the designing of books was not considered a highly professional job. Publishers used to treat it perfunctorily and leave the aspects of layout and aesthetics to the printer. In traditional book publishing, various aspects such as writing, editing, designing, and production may be carried out independently by the author, editor, illustrator, designer, and the printer, in consultation with each other. Today, the electronic publishing system has made the process of book publishing much more integrated. In cases where a short print run is required, the author himself/herself can write the book, edit it, work on the page make-up, and print the required number of copies on a desktop printing system. Electronic publishing has also facilitated quicker, easier, and better quality work as attention can be paid to the finer details on such systems.

No design can be handled without full knowledge of a book's anatomy. The various elements of this anatomy are: protective cover/jacket, spine, endpapers, and reading matter. The reading matter consists of preliminaries (front matter), text matter, and back matter. Preliminaries also include display pages like the half title page and the title page, which call for special attention on the part of the designer.

A well-organized manuscript is one of the most important prerequisites for the book designer. An organized manuscript helps the author present his/her ideas to the designer in a clearer and more accurate way. This involves editing, typing or word processing, copy editing, and the arranging of illustrations.

Besides the manuscript, book designers need a lot of information to develop a design. They must be told about the characteristics of the target audience, the budget of the publication, and the price range in which the book will be sold. They must also know all the technical details of the book, such as the typesetting method to be used, the capability of the printing process chosen, the binding requirements, permissible columns, and the number of pages estimated.

For page make-up, guidelines regarding the size of book, the format or general shape and appearance of the printed page, and type style are essential. These aspects are usually decided by the publisher, although some of them, such as type style and size, may be decided by the designer in consultation with the publisher. Before the book is typeset, it is helpful to estimate the length of copy.

The design of a book actually starts with marking the text matter for the typesetter and making a rough sketch for preliminaries. The facing pages are treated as one unit of design. The content and chapter opening pages are usually given some graphic treatment. Checking the proofs is also an integral part of handling the typographical matter.

The pictorial pages need to be handled on the basis of the number and style of illustrations being used in the book. Illustrations may be hand-drawn, computer-generated, or photographic. They usually need scaling and cropping for the purpose of printing.

Page layout is the stage where the text matter and the illustrations, if any, on a page are integrated and laid out. In the traditional method, the page layout of a book was done after the galleys were received from the typesetters. Nowadays, most of the page layout is done electronically or in a desktop environment.

Cover designing is another important aspect of book designing, although many publishers treat it as a step that is distinct from the designing of the book itself. The cover design may be assigned to a designer or even an advertising agency. In order to attract the maximum attention, the cover page of a book can be designed with art and type, as in the case of an advertising design. A book cover can be divided into three parts: the front cover, spine, and back cover. In the case of a jacket, two more parts need to be taken into consideration by the designer—the front flap and the back flap.

Much of the physical appearance of a book depends on the quality of paper selected and the binding and finishing methods adopted. Here, the designer needs to work in coordination with the publisher and the printer so that the cost of production is reasonable, and the final product offers the customers good value for money.

KEY TERMS

Bibliography A list of reference work detailing known published titles on a given subject or by a given author, or a list of resources for sourced materials that have been used or consulted in the preparation of the book.

Book As per UNESCO's definition a book, it is a non-periodical literary publication of 49 or more pages, excluding the cover.

Camera-ready Copy The complete page or a publication assembled with the text and the graphics, ready to be photographed as the first step in the process of making plates for offset printing.

Casebound Book A book that has rigid covers and is stitched in the spine.

Copy Editing The process of correcting the matter in a manuscript, presenting it in a precise and easy-to-understand form, and preparing the matter for typesetting, and printing.

End-papers Units of two or more leaves added to the front and back of a book by the binder so that one is pasted on the cover and the other becomes a free leaf inside the book. End-papers are used to secure the book with the cover. The end-paper at the front of the book is called front end-paper, and the one at the back is called the back end-paper.

Frontispiece An illustration that faces the title page or section of a book.

Half Title The title of a book printed at the top of the first page of the text preceding the main title page. It is also referred to as the bastard title.

Hologram A three-dimensional image that appears to float magically in space. It is made with laser technology.

Paperback A book bound with flexible paper covers; usually a term reserved for mass-market publications.

Preface A brief introduction to the book, stating its scope, purpose, etc., usually by the author.

Preliminaries The material that appears before the main text in a book, comprising the half-title, title, preface, acknowledgements, contents, etc.

Sidebar Short text block that appears on the side of the main text of a book page, used as supporting matter that highlights an important point.

Signature Four (or multiples of four) printed pages folded from a single sheet of paper for sewing or gluing into the binding to form a publication. It is also called a section.

Sink Distance from the top edge of a page at which the chapter title and similar material is set.

Spine The backbone, or back, of the book where the title is displayed when the book is placed upright on a shelf.

Title Page The page in front of a book indicating the title, subtitle, author, publisher, and its address.

Trimmed Size The finished size of the publication after three edges of a folded sheet have been cut.

Widow A very short end-line of a paragraph continued from the preceding page/column at the beginning of a page.

REFERENCES

Anthony, Garolyn 1988, 'The Cover Artists', *Publishers Weekly*, 24 January.

Malhotra, D.M. (ed) 2006, *60 Years of Book Publishing in India*, Federation of Indian Publishers, New Delhi.

Nelson, Roy Paul 1991, *Publication Design*, Wm. C. Brown Publishers, USA.

Rice, Stanley 1978, *Book Design: Systematic Approach*, R.R. Brown Company, New York and London.

Sarkar, N.N. 1998, *Designing Print Communication*, Sagar Publications, New Delhi.

Sherman, Steve 1984, 'Retailers Speak from Experience about Book Covers That Sell', *Publishers Weekly*, 26 October.

REVIEW QUESTIONS

1. What does a book mean to you? Write a historical perspective of books in relation to book designing.
2. Why, in your view, has book design gained prominence in recent times?

3. How is the handling of design for books different from the handling of design for other publications?
4. Describe the aspects of book designing within the electronic publishing environment.
5. What do you understand by the 'anatomy of book'? Identify the main parts of a book and mention the contents thereof and the normal practice of their placement.
6. Why is a well-organized manuscript important for book design? Describe how the printed book gets its physical shape from the manuscript.
7. What are the requirements for a book designer if he/she has to handle all the parts of the book design?
8. What are the guidelines within which the designer makes the pages?
9. Why is the cover design so important for the author, the designer, and the publisher of the book? Describe the role and scope of each part of a cover design.
10. Why is the quality of paper on which a book is printed given as much attention as the selection of types and illustrations in a book? Mention the criteria for the selection of paper for a book.
11. What role does the designer play in the binding of a book? Describe the aesthetic and functional aspects of some commonly used book binding methods.

PROJECTS

1. Pick up a casebound book. Analyse its anatomy and write a detailed report on the same.
2. Design the preliminary pages and a chapter heading of this book in your own style. You may make the designs on your computer or on paper by using a soft pencil, marking the necessary typographical instructions for the typesetter.
3. Identify some book title with an abstract theme. Design a suitable cover for the title with the help of graphic shapes to be printed on the jacket of the book in royal octavo size, with a ¾" spine.
4. Plan the design and production of a text book for higher education within a shoe-string budget. Assume that the book has the potential of a mass market and is also under the piracy threat through photocopying.
5. Develop a style for a page layout that will be repeated on all the pages of a modern poetry book. Format the typographical content in an appropriate type style. Each poem may be accompanied by some graphic image or typographical arrangement. Design a harmonious cover page. Compile the pages with the cover design to prepare a dummy.

CHAPTER

21 Outdoor Design

Learning Objectives

After reading this chapter, you should be able to
- trace the outdoor design that was practised a few decades ago
- gain an overview of the advantages and disadvantages of outdoor media
- understand the design and production process
- identify the outputting devices and how they work
- know the various substrates and their suitability for different formats of outdoor designs

INTRODUCTION

Travelling has always been considered as an enriching activity that enlightens and broadens one's knowledge. People travel for assignment, for leisure, for finding livelihood, and sometimes just for the sake of travelling. But travelling without reliable information may leave one directionless. According to available sources, outdoor information was conceived in ancient Egypt to meet the needs of the travelling people. It is believed to have begun with the *billboard*—bill or notice pasted on a board. Today, it comes in different formats and is also one of the major forms of outdoor design.

Getting noticed on a busy street or crowded marketplace is not easy and advertisers are consumed by the thought of how to reach out to the millions of prospective viewers. Outdoor designs adorn the city streets, walls, high-rise buildings, and even cinema houses. Earlier most of the outdoor designs were hand-painted. A few were printed by offset lithography process in pieces as tiles. Those pieces were then pasted manually on a hard surface, a bit overlapping each other, to get a big-sized banner. The original banners were also the handiwork of skilled artists.

Hand-painted *banners* were used in events such as election campaign, *mela*, and religious functions. Acclaimed artists would make banners for events using their expert brush strokes and painting techniques. Most of the banners were drawn on wall, plywood, or canvas drawing graphs which were identical to the original but proportionately bigger. Plywood surface was better for cut-out images, whereas canvases were frames used for display at select places.

In India, banner art was largely a family or community profession, such as clay artisans or folk artists. Some of the artists' works were so unique that they would be used as wall hangings in events. Some were hung in homes or in commercial establishments, such as office, restaurant, and music shop. To ensure longevity of a painting, a special blend of oil paints were used, which lent them a vintage look, distinct from commercial paintings.

Maqbool Fida Husain, the name associated with India's modern art movement, started his career as a banner artist and painted a number of film hoardings for popular Hindi cinema. His experience as a banner artist along with his early discipline of copying the Koran in fluid calligraphy helped him develop as a painter.

The nineties of the last century was the transitional period of India's outdoor design when digital imaging was introduced. Some banner artists quickly adopted the new technology, while others had to change their profession for survival. It became worse for them when the Supreme Court in its ruling of November 1997 ordered the removal of roadside hoardings in the wake of increasing instances of road accidents due to these hoardings. Despite the constraints, outdoor advertising has certainly evolved through the ages. Advertisers have to constantly think out of the box to come up with advertisements that capture the imagination of the target viewer.

OUTDOOR MEDIA

Outdoor design is a part of graphic design. It is synonymous with outdoor media, which has extensive forms and, therefore, no set of rules or practices govern its design process. Each piece of outdoor display has its own requirements. Before starting a design for outdoor coverage, the following forms of outdoor media may be considered.

Forms of Outdoor Media

Billboards are the most commonly used outdoor media. They are also known as hoardings of out-of-home (OOH) advertisements. Location is a major component for billboards as it helps in providing appropriate exposure. Therefore, every billboard is strategically located. In addition, billboards use presentations and material which are unconventional but effective in promoting the product. Advertisers prefer billboards for their high impact visuals.

The various forms include (a) *signs* and *banners—graphic shapes* with or without signographic letterforms on various surfaces are outdoor forms meant for providing information, direction, identification, etc. to a target audience; (b) *mobile graphics* for festivals, sports events, and *mobile billboards* fixed on trucks, vans, and other vehicles, even animals are other forms for conveying information; (c) *point of purchases* (POPs) that help consumers take purchasing decision at stores or malls; (d) *kiosks* that display structured information; (e) *bus shelters* for two-sided LED display, *bulletin boards* at distribution centre; and (f) *posters, striking 2D visual displays*, which are normally seen from a distance, as discussed in Chapter 17.

We shall now discuss some of the outdoor media forms.

Banner

Traditionally it is a long strip of cloth bearing a slogan or typographical design hung in a public place or carried in a demonstration or procession. The new technology facilitates creation of images on various materials like PVC and canvas, which are perfect for indoor and outdoor applications, respectively. The banner materials can be welded and eyeleted for easy hanging. Cloth banners can be hung either with the help of sticks to wrap the two cloth ends to keep the cloth straight or with a rope.

Banners can be used for advertising business to seminar or conferences, birthday functions to religious festivals, sports events to marriage functions. One can gauge the extensive use of the banner while watching a sports event like the IPL cricket matches.

Signage

Signage is any kind of visual graphics created to display information to a particular audience, as shown in Figure 21.1. This is typically manifested in the form of direction finding information displayed on the streets or inside/outside of buildings.

The main purpose of signage is communication. It aims to convey information so that its receiver can make cognitive decisions based on the information provided. In general, signage can be classified into the following functions:

Information Signs giving information about services and facilities, for example, maps, directories, instructions for use, etc.

Direction Signs leading to services, facilities, functional spaces and key areas, for example, sign posts, directional arrows, etc.

Identification Signs indicating services and facilities, for example, room names and numbers, toilet signs, number of floors, etc.

Safety and regulatory Signs giving warning or safety instructions, for example, warning signs, traffic signs, exit signs, rules and regulations, etc.

Figure 21.1 Various forms of signage

Vinyl signs Vinyl is a low cost, easy to cut but very effective signage material, suitable, for most of the functions mentioned above.

Neon signs Hollow glass tubes used to make neon lamps are available in various lengths. Skilled artisans shape the tubes by lit gas heating. Neon gas is then pumped into it that glows when it reaches a particular temperature using electric current. Although the basic colour of neon is red, it can produce up to 150 colours. One can also create moving images using a neon sign. All these are exploited by the designer to make the signs attractive.

Outdoor Design **483**

Figure 21.2 LED sign display

Figure 21.3 Kiosks

LED signs The fundamental elements of *light emitting diode* (LED) are anode and cathode. When switched on, it releases energy in the form of photon, which is a tiny packet of light emit to visible spectrum. The technology is used in various applications such as television, general lighting, and of course signage system. LEDs have helped create text, video display, and sensors. Their high switching rates are also useful in advance communication technology. Figure 21.2 shows a collection of LED sign displays.

Kiosk

This is a small two- or three-dimensional physical structure used to convey information for people, as shown in Figure 21.3. It has multifarious uses such as at the entrance of a shopping mall to guide the shoppers to different locations of various department or product display; stand-alone booth for marketing purposes; at trade shows that provide a festive look; or at professional conferences for creating theme. Kiosks at street poles or metro pillars provide repeated viewing opportunity. Some are illuminated at night by neon back light or solar light. Each kiosk is provided with a solar panel on top of the structure that illuminates automatically after sunset, thereby facilitating an effective use of renewable energy.

More sophisticated kiosks are now available at public places such as airports, banks, metro stations, and malls. Interactive facility of these kiosks, called *multimedia kiosks*, let the users operate the system by touch screen to choose the various options of text information illustrated by graphics, sound, video, and animation. Even simple kiosks can be created using HTML pages and graphics, setting the type size large enough to attract attention from a short distance. Display screen can be backed to 'kiosk mode' by removing the web browser tool bar. The presentation can be designed to simply loop through a series of pages or to allow user interaction and exploration. Many organizations are reaping the benefit of multimedia kiosks as apart from providing the necessary information it is also a lot of fun.

Advantages of Outdoor Media

Like any other media, outdoor media offers various advantages, as discussed here.

High coverage Outdoor designs displayed at appropriate places offer a broad base exposure that yields high level of opportunity to see (OTS).

Real-life image When seen from a distance, the visuals used on billboards appear close to real life. The impact is similar to the experience of watching a movie at the cinema, which is entirely different from watching it on a TV screen.

Display flexibility Communicators choose the site location and period of display considering where and when their product/message will be most visible to the prospective audience. It can be local, regional, or national displays, in front of a store, in city streets, on top of a building, or at the highways.

Creative flexibility New technology and production alternatives are the major sources of experimentation to make the outdoor designs stand out. *Large format digital printing* technology is a boost for the graphic designer. The designs created on computer can be reproduced on the desired surface instantly. It not only reduces the production cost (for limited copies) but also saves the turnaround time considerably.

Surface versatility Besides conventional flat surfaces, there are 3D forms, inflatable objects, computer-driven neon signs, LED signboards, etc., which are also used to meet the requirements of the communicator.

Disadvantages of Outdoor Media

Despite the widespread popularity of outdoor media, there are also some limitations.

Brief message Most outdoor displays carry only a few words to convey a message, which often fails to register in the mind of the viewer. It is because most people walk or quickly drive past the display.

Waste coverage Due to the high frequency of exposure, many outdoor designs become uninteresting and tiring for the eyes. As a result, the message quickly loses its effectiveness.

High absolute cost Despite its limited unit requirement, the cost associated with the fabrication of each display including lighting and technical support is considerably high.

Visual pollution Scattered outdoor designs do not look aesthetic. They also hinder public movement and distract drivers.

CREATIVE FACTORS

Designing outdoor displays requires a crisp and creative approach because of the limited time of exposure it gets. People look at the outdoor designs for merely seconds before moving on, but the frequent exposure ensures that the information is delivered and absorbed by the target audience.

Exhibit 21.1 Why outdoor designs?

'If designed well, it makes the country beautiful.'
—R. Balki, Creative Chief, Lowe Lintas

'Outdoor medium helps enhance the feel of the environment. Message has to be planted in such a way that it wouldn't create any clutter and add to the visual pollution. If you use the outdoor medium carefully, it's guaranteed to get people's attention and add value to the process of building brand.'
—Ravi Deshpande, Creative Chief, Contract Advertising

'Outdoor allows you to communicate your message in a tight telegraphic manner.'
—Rahul daCunha, daCunha Communication

'Outdoor is the only medium that has life as the backdrop. You see most other mediums are interspersed with entertainment created for that medium. Outdoor is interspersed with real life. Hence very specific kind of ideas and execution are required for this medium which in turn makes this a very interesting and challenging form of advertising.'
—Prasoon Joshi, CEO, McCann

Scope and Challenge

Outdoor images in general are stationary and large enough to attract attention of the moving audience from a distance. These aspects influence the way they are designed. From the advertising point of view, it is challenging for creative people. The message of an outdoor design should communicate within seconds, without clogging the mind with graphic elements, such as headlines, illustrations, and graphic shapes. Exhibit 21.1 gives a few important definitions of outdoor media.

Basic Design Rules

In this section we shall dwell upon the basic points to be kept in mind by a designer while constructing an outdoor display.

Minimum number of words The element used as the headline should be as brief as three to five words. If necessary, one or two sub-heads can be inserted to explain the concept. At first exposure, people merely look at the headline and develop an interest. In subsequent exposures, they try to understand the message from the sub-headlines and create a relation between the headline and the visual. Concepts or ideas cannot be copied in outdoor billboards.

Font style and size Like any other media, letters used in outdoor media are given due importance for legibility. Although the most visible type of design is poster type (above 72 points), the design for outdoor displays on computer screen is proportionately smaller in size. The designer must apply all the legibility rules of display type composition. When enlarged and viewed from a distance, it should be legible. Here also, the font types used should attract attention, give hints of the concept, and help in making an impression.

Work of graphics Pictorial content in any form plays a dominant role in outdoor media. It can be considered as the most important element for easy comprehension of the topic. Initially, the audience hardly looks for a message from a large outdoor format. However, pictures along with a headline and other typographical contents provide the message at a glance. Therefore, if you are thinking of a picture for your design, think

Figure 21.4 An image-manipulated billboard (*see also Colour Plate 3*)

of a picture and a headline together. Dramatize the picture using visual alteration techniques available in your computer program.

Image manipulation A billboard by the soft drink maker Pepsi created a lot of interest because of its visual manipulation. It showed three prominent players of the Indian Premier League (IPL) 4 dressed up with the flame of fire signifying the players' burning desire to fight and change the game, as shown in Figure 21.4 (*see also Colour Plate 3*). It demonstrated that the heat of the burning fire does not exhaust the players as Pepsi douses the fire and refreshes them during non-action period. The concept was used imaginatively by painting it in green colour, which signifies cool, along with orange flame on the body of the players.

Style of art Style separates one image from the others and helps identify the target audience. It may be realistic, high-tech, abstract, or folk. Figure 21.5 shows a billboard—part of a Vodafone campaign—depicting the concept of flying to Ambaji by helicopter using relief images in Gujarat folk art style. The style successfully created interest among its targeted audience.

Need of simplicity Elimination of details and perfect cropping are other considerations for outdoor art. Who can identify the details from 100′ to 300′ distance? Can the person on the move grasp the concept of eye make-up by looking at the full-length image of the model displaying the product? Outdoor designs need to be simple and united, which can be scanned at a glance. Viewers have no time to see each element separately and then join them together to get the message. Often graphic shapes, border colour block, etc. play an important role in helping the audience see the outdoor display as a whole.

Figure 21.5 A folk art style billboard

Figure 21.6 Relief structure coming out of a billboard

Backdrop of display It is essential to note and take care of the surroundings against which the outdoor design will be displayed. Surroundings may include the sky with changing colour and light as the day progresses, green patch created by trees and plants, concrete houses and buildings, or a countryside landscape. From the designer's point of view, these are merely textures of different colours and shapes. Whatever may be the surroundings, a simple layout will stand out more than an abstract. The reader can try a layout—that is 7" by 11"—placing slightly bigger sized pictures than that of the layout comprising the aforementioned content.

Viewing distance The area that will provide optimum viewing of a display is called the viewing distance. It may be calculated from the front or at an angle from the sides. When calculating viewing distance from the front, the greater the distance, the smaller the appearance of the message and vice versa. If the viewing position is angular, the image will be vague and distorted. The angle is determined by the horizontal and vertical points at which the measured light intensity is 50 per cent of that measured directly in front of the display. In other words, the maximum viewing angle is defined by the vertical and horizontal points where the information displayed can no longer be interpreted by the viewer.

Now the reader can try the layout in terms of visibility in relation to distance. Paste the layout on a wall; see it from about 12′ distance, 90° angle from front, 45° angle from the sides. Are the elements arranged on the layout clearly visible? If not, he/she will have to rethink the whole approach.

Structure of display An unusual structure inevitably attracts more attention than usual. The developer Supernova highlighted their area of work by using a cut-out image that was superimposed on the billboard keeping it a bit raised, as shown in Figure 21.6. Part of the image was deliberately kept out of the frame to make it more visible. Such 3D structures can be viewed from all the sides and thus get extra attention. Two or more sides of a display can be illuminated by a single light box which is economical in terms of fabrication of the structure and lighting support.

Role of colour Getting attention is the primary concern of an outdoor display and therefore colour is the most important component of design. Complementary colour schemes work best for this purpose. Colour association plays a big role. Interestingly, in most media designs, white is not considered as a colour. It normally serves as a base or background. White works well for outdoor designs as it separates texture from surroundings. Types and pictures displayed on a white surface are more visible

Figure 21.7 White background contributes to the elegant look

Figure 21.8 A lifestyle billboard

due to maximization of contrast. Soft and monotone scheme could be used to depict a situation.

As shown in Figure 21.7, dress materials have been elegantly depicted on the white background. Figure 21.8 shows how soothing colours on a white base creates an atmosphere of lifestyle.

Scope of Innovation

Outdoor advertising cannot be restricted within a standard format. Its versatility gives creative people an opportunity to experiment its structure with innovative materials. See, for example, the eco-friendly Woodland billboard in Figure 21.9. It has not only extended one of the elements beyond the conventional rectangular frame but has also

Outdoor Design **489**

Figure 21.9 An eco-friendly billboard

Figure 21.10 A cut-out billboard shaped like a bus with real people on it

Figure 21.11 A billboard with a big sofa against the backdrop of IPL players

executed the concept with innovative materials, such as real plants, plaster of Paris, and flex. To give it a 3D effect, the display included a cut-out with an extension at the top—a replica of the human brain on the head, and the environment around—all of which collectively compel one to think to save the planet. All these make the billboard interesting and attractive. The creative process of Woodland is inspired by the beauty of nature. They have positioned their products as the product of nature with the message 'Think Proplanet, Think Woodland'.

Cricket fever in India has reached a new level with its varied formats. Several sports channels use this opportunity to woo viewers by conceptualizing and executing an outdoor campaign targeted at the cricket crazy audience.

Figure 21.10 shows a billboard that is in the form of a huge cut-out bus displayed at a prominent place in Mumbai before the IPL 5. The bus is full of people—both inside and on its roof—heading to get the IPL entry ticket, with festive gestures and noise. There were real people sitting on the bus during peak hours. They were also inviting others to join them, assuring them that their seats were also reserved. A cloth banner was hung on the bus showing the number of days left before the start of the great cricketing event. It aimed at creating excitement among the viewers, not only for getting the ticket but also for enjoying the match on the media. The number of days left for the event was also changed daily. During periods of action the banner content was changed as per the match schedule of the day.

In Delhi, a real sofa was created in a bus shelter, with a big-framed group photo of cricketers, as shown in Figure 21.11. The display featuring the cricketers showed

490   Art and Print Production

Figure 21.12   Billboard with a model helicopter and relief figures

Figure 21.13   A cut-out tree highlighted by a frame

a perfect family picture set-up, aiming to highlight that the entire family can sit together and watch the IPL. A cut-out of a photographer with flashlights was also placed at the shelter.

The 'Fly to Ambaji in a helicopter' campaign by Vodafone launched in Gujarat on the eve of Navaratri is another creative example of innovation, as shown in Figure 21.12. The campaign's aim was to encourage people to download Navaratri caller tunes to participate in a *Garba* dance contest. Adding zing to the entire campaign were two larger-than-life sized figures on the billboard depicting Garba dance and a model lookalike of a helicopter installed on the top of the outdoor designs. The helicopter would rotate 360°, whilst the wings would rotate clock-wise and anti-clockwise, giving an impression that the helicopter is ready to take off to Ambaji.

'Save trees, save the earth' is the mantra against deforestation. 'Save paper, save trees' is the awareness mantra for over consumed natural resources. 'Use mobile, save paper' is the new campaign of the cellular brand Idea. The company introduced a unique idea to engage people to participate and spread the message of conserving the environment. The brand is promoting the idea of using mobile value-added services for a vast number of day-to-day activities, such as read newspapers, generate e-bills, make payment and transactions, and issue e-tickets, thereby saving paper. The subject of saving the environment is not new, but what is new is showcasing the ideas of how one can take a step towards saving the environment.

Another innovative and creative idea used by Idea was the 'Go green' concept. As shown in Figure 21.13, the billboard used a huge cut-out of a tree with the face of Abhishek Bachchan, the brand ambassador of Idea, embedded on the tree trunk. The tree had mobile phones hanging from its branches that illuminated the night. The outdoor display conveyed the message that this is our chance to do something for our environment.

The Idea campaign also used a bus shelter in Mumbai, as shown in Figure 21.14. To communicate the 'Go green' message, the bus shelter was judiciously covered

Outdoor Design **491**

Figure 21.14 A bus shelter within natural environment

Figure 21.15 Celebration of Pongal with Maaza
(*see also Colour Plate 3*)

with real plants. The stand thus provided shade and also gave the comfort of a natural environment. Passersby were seen stopping to appreciate the greenery.

Spreading the festive spirit and conveying best wishes, Maaza made sure that it was a fun time during the festival of *Pongal*. Maaza used OOH as a medium to spread the message and take festivities to a completely new level. The campaign was handled by Lodestar (a media agency) and Encyclomedia (a production and creative agency), and the areas covered were Andhra Pradesh (AP), Karnataka, and Tamil Nadu (TN). The brand used high impact billboard and bus shelters to wish people a happy and prosperous new beginning. To strike a chord with the residents directly, the agency used the regional languages on the creative displays. This effective and refreshing campaign had people sipping Maaza and having more fun.

Bright analogous colour scheme dominated by orange created the right mood of the festival. Interestingly, orange is also the colour of the Maaza product being advertised. As illustrated in Figure 21.15 (*see also Colour Plate 3*), the visual elements displayed are simple and directly related to Pongal celebrations. The Sun, worshiped for its rays, is responsible for life on earth. Pongal is the biggest harvest festival for paddy crops. The *ghara* (earthen pot) and the surface on which it is placed are decorated with Kolam using rice flour and red clay. The *ghara* is filled with rice pudding made from freshly harvested rice, milk, and jaggery. The local flavour of the message is also conveyed by the typography and language used. Strings of triangular flags at the corner added to the festive mood.

Humour in advertisements creates a big interest among the general public. They may or may not be interested in product benefit. The Gujarat Co-operative Milk Marketing Federation is known for adopting this approach to promote its brand Amul. It is one of the most memorable brands of India. Their advertising strategy is simple, and every time connects with the audience with messages that are from current news. They cover many activities including sports, politics, business, and even controversies. The ad agency associated with Amul, daCunha Associates, deserves credits for the punchy advertisements. They have not only kept the Amul brand alive in public memory but

Figure 21.16 Amul's humour advertisement

also entertained the viewers for over five decades.

Figure 21.16 shows an Amul advertisement depicting a Bollywood actor punching a film director. Another famous actor who hosted the party is shown standing behind. This advertisement was inspired by a high-profile controversy. Amul creatively utilized this episode using the slogan 'Please Maar Khan'. The humour is subtle, yet striking.

OUTDOOR DESIGN AS PUBLIC ART

The Indian urban experience is characterized by millions of people on the move. There is noise all around; people are talking loudly on their mobiles; drivers are honking to make their way out; and hawkers are shouting to sell their product. In these conditions, one should not expect aesthetics outside home.

The murals, photographs, paintings, and handicrafts at select public places available for the democratic community may be called public art. Some of the companies have showed their aesthetic vision by displaying their outdoor designs and public art at places where people must wait suspending their motion, even if it is short and brief. These outdoor designs are not merely meant for selling a product, but are primarily used for enhancing the aesthetic vision of the public who are otherwise tired of the noisy environment. The effort of some of the companies may be considered a well thought out experiment to make a large number of people to breathe in aesthetically pleasant surroundings.

As illustrated in Figure 21.17, the large signage at the petrol pump is simply a landscape, to identify its purpose. It is giving a personal touch to the business, and is distinctly different from art pieces that are possessed by an individual collector. It is art for the public. It also shows that the company dealing with gas products is concerned about green environment.

The commuters of metro rail often view public art while passing by a station or waiting for a train. Kolkata is known as the cultural hub of the country. The city has tried to maintain this impression at various public places despite the aggressive use of posters or graffiti.

Travel by metro in Kolkata and you will find how some of the outdoor panels at stations give the cultural theme of the area. Take for example the Mahanayak Uttam Kumar station of Kolkata Metro, previously named after Tollyganj, a south Kolkata area famous for film studios located there. The station houses a number of nostalgic photographic prints taken from some of the legendary actor Uttam Kumar's hit films. Move on to Kalighat station and you will find paintings on the wall representing Kalighat's well-known folk art. Figure 21.18 shows the paintings at Kalighat station what art lovers know it as *pot painting*.

Figure 21.17 Landscape billboard at a petrol pump

Figure 21.18 Pot painting at Kolkata's Kalighat metro station

Figure 21.19 shows the art pieces displayed at the Rabindra Sadan metro station illustrating the rich tradition of Tagore culture. Figure 21.20 shows the station Maidan, themed on sports and showcasing paintings of sporting activities.

The Delhi Metro Rail Corporation (DMRC) has developed various visual themes at its select stations. At its Kailash Colony station, paintings are displayed in frames along the railings as an effort to bring modern paintings out of the walls of dedicated exhibition halls and art galleries, as shown in Figure 21.21.

494 *Art and Print Production*

Figure 21.19 Tagore paintings at Kolkata's Rabindra Sadan metro station

Figure 21.20 Painting of sporting activities at Kolkata's Maidan metro station

Outdoor Design **495**

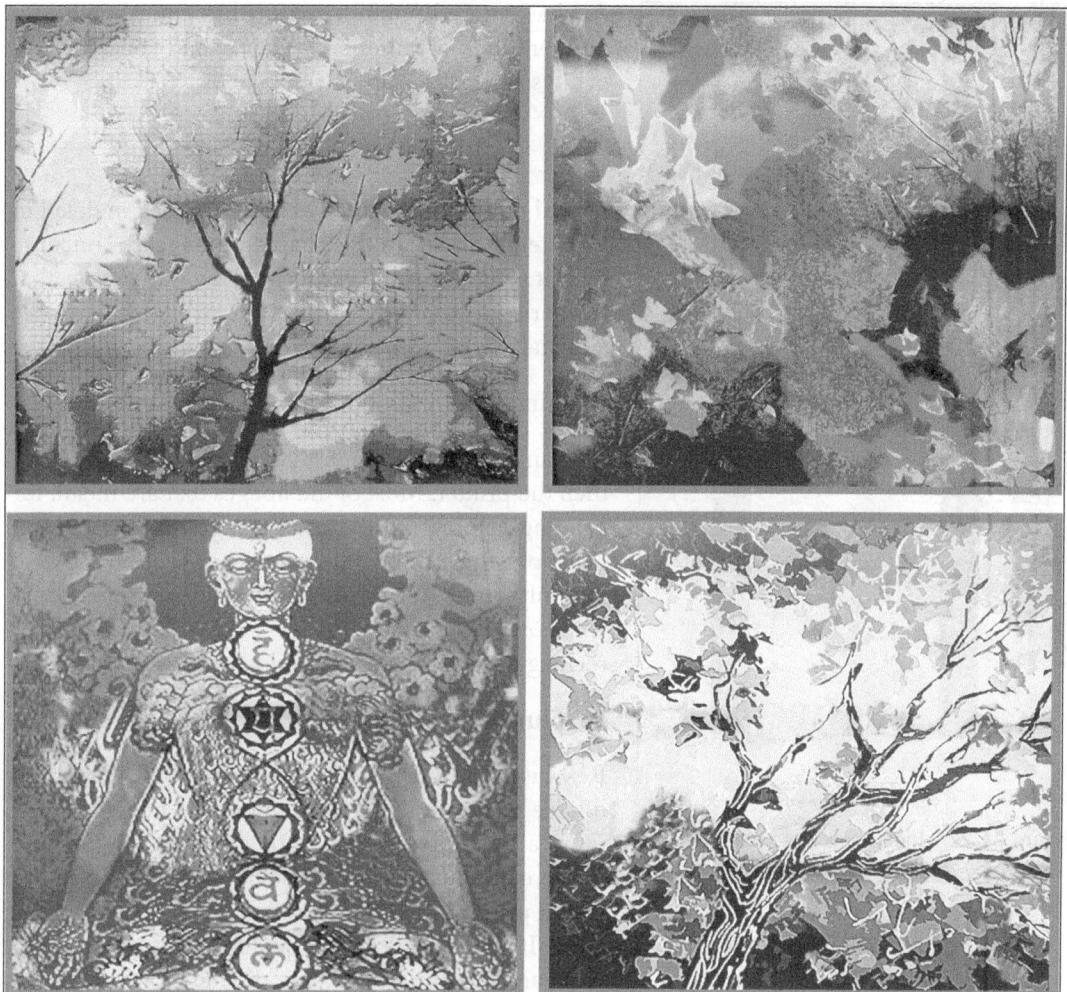

Figure 21.21 Art pieces displayed at DMRC's Kailash Colony metro station

Glimpses of the rich tradition of Indian art and craft are displayed at the INA metro station. These include *Mithila* paintings of Bihar, boat race of Kerala, and terracotta murals of Rajasthan. All these create a discourse of unity and diversity of the country. The Jawaharlal Nehru Stadium station is not themed on sports activities. As shown in Figure 21.22, the station has a big rectangular pillar with paintings on all sides depicting Indian women in folk style, which cannot escape attention of the metro riders.

A view of sensual India is shown in a large digital print of women in colourful jewellery and veils displayed at the Khan Market station.

These developments clearly reveal that art is no longer limited to certain groups of people who live within their personal taste for both creating and comprehending art.

Art has entered public space. It has contributed to a different look of commercialization and consumerism of cityscape.

DIGITAL ENVIRONMENT

Digital printing has already been discussed in detail in Chapters 8 and 9. In this chapter, the focus is on large format printing. The basic technology is the same, that is, a series of binary data drives a print engine to render a digital image on an output device.

Imaging

Like any other printing process, the image comes first, then the printer. Most of the images that are meant for printing are bitmap or raster images. In the current situation, the Adobe Photoshop application may be the only option for creating and editing an image. As we know, each bitmap image is a collection of pixels or rectangular dots and each dot describes its colour value.

Resolution

Resolution of an image is determined by its clarity or degree of details. Therefore, more the image quality, more are the pixels, and more space the file takes up in the computer. So what resolution should be set for digital printing? There is no standard rule of thumb in creating an image for digital printing. It all depends on the quality of output expected and the printer's resolution. This means the number of dots discharged through the print heads of a printer. Most of the large formats accept images that are rasterized at 360 dpi. However, it is always advisable to consult the output service provider before taking a decision on the resolution of the image.

Figure 21.22 Indian folk style painting at Delhi's Jawaharlal Nehru Stadium metro station

File Format

The next decision relates to the choice of file format for the image. A number of native formats, such as CDR (Corel Draw), AI (Adobe Illustrator), ID (InDesign), and PSD (Photoshop) are used to create an image. Each one has different features. In order to get the desired effect of an image, often the image of one file format is sent to another. It is converted or exported to a standard image format like EPS (encapsulated postscript). This file is then dropped into Adobe Acrobat Distiller to produce a PDF format, which is acceptable in most of the print houses including large format digital printing.

Digital Colour

Selecting colour is the next critical decision. The communicator and print service provider often face a problem of mismatch of colour between the computer screen and the output surfaces.

Monitor colour vs printer colour   Why does a printed image often look dull and appear different from the original? Since the computer monitor displays RGB colour and most commercial printers produce image on substrate using CMYK colour, there will always be a shift in colour from RGB to CMYK because they are physically different. RGB colours are the primary colours of light, which strike the eyes directly. On the other hand, CMYK is the colour of the physical object and is seen when light is reflected from the object. Also, RGB colours can display 16.7 million colours on computer screen, while the actual number of colours on printed surface using CMYK inks is significantly less than that of RGB colours.

What are the solutions to this problem? Fortunately, some software applications are able to indicate which colour of RGB mode cannot be converted into CMYK mode; in other words, cannot be printed by CMYK ink. This happens because those RGB colours are not of the range of CMYK colours. As per colour theory, it is called 'out of gamut colour'. However, simply indicating 'out of gamut' is not the solution. In some applications, there is an alert symbol by which one will be able to identify the RGB colour which will change when it is converted to CMYK. One can click on the alert symbol to switch to the closest colour that is within the CMYK gamut.

Colour conversion   Understanding monitor colour and converting it into printed colour is not enough. It is often difficult to handle individual colour to ensure its reproducible quality especially when it involves printing of a continuous tone image, such as photograph or painting. If one has to print a logo of a company or a brand of a product, such as the corporate colour red of Vodafone, or the greenish blue of IDBI bank, there will be very little provision of alternate colour. Inkjet printers hardly print spot colour (pre-mix colour) like other commercial printing processes.

Colour guide   Here, instead of relying on colour seen on the computer screen, one needs to get a colour guidebook developed by companies such as Pantone and Agfa. Colour guide will show you what the various process colours will look like when printed on a surface and will also give the CMYK values that create the colours. Here, value refers to various percentages of four colours that create the particular colour. For example, IDBI blue can be created by 80 per cent cyan, 22 per cent magenta, 65 per cent yellow, and 4 per cent black.

Rule of thumb

It is essential for you to remember some rules while selecting colour. You should (a) choose the required colour from the process colour guide; (b) note the colour value that will create the colour; and (c) enter those values in the colour picker page of the application. Even though the colours appearing on the screen may not be the same, it will, however, print just as one expected.

OUTPUTTING DEVICES

There are a number of outputting devices commonly used depending on the type and quality of print required. We will discuss some of them in this section.

Inkjet Printers

The most commonly used outputting device for outdoor design is inkjet printer. There is a wide variety of printers available in the market, which can be categorized in different ways. Printers can be classified on the basis of make: IRIS, HP, and Epson; on the basis of ink dispersing technology: continuous flow and drop-on demand; and on the basis of ink compatibility: dye-based, pigment-based, and resin-based solid ink. Within these categories there are two sub-groups: thermal and piezo. IRIS printers use continuous flow technology to produce dot free images like a photograph by dye-based ink. Technology used by HP is drop-on demand, where ink droplets form the image after heating the print head chamber and is thus called thermal inkjet process. Electric current utilized to shoot out tiny ink droplets on the substrate to form the image is called piezoelectric or piezo inkjet process. Epson is one such printer.

Inkjet technology This is the most commonly used printer technology—particularly at home or office. Graphic artists and designers favour this machine as it gives inexpensive and true layout prints. However, it is not popular as back-room office printing or at professional institutions as its typographical printing is not sharp and clean. This is because of its use of liquid ink that spreads a bit after printing and the colour image looks washed out with loss of details. Therefore, inkjet printer is a poor choice for printing long text documents.

Desktop inkjet printer Many individuals prefer this technology essentially for the low cost factor of the machine, instead of investing in the relatively costlier laser printer. Inkjet printers can be used for printing classroom projects of students, letters for correspondents, bills, etc. Since inkjet printers follow a non-impact process, they can print on any surface regardless of surface texture and pressure resistance. Sophisticated inkjet printers give very good reproduction of colours. One can choose these printers for printing charts, graphs, and illustrations with text. Even a photo quality image can be obtained using glossy paper specially made for this purpose. This printer is lightweight and can be carried in a briefcase.

In inkjet technology, digitized computer information directs the outputting device to spray tiny droplets of liquid ink through a nozzle onto the printing surface. The ink coming out of the nozzle is given an electrical charge to break the stream into tiny individual drops. Inkjet printers create colours on paper based on the same principle of process colour printing by four colours—cyan, magenta, yellow, and black. These colours are sprayed from the cartridge in various proportions to create different colours. Some printers use two cartridges—one with three colours of cyan, magenta and yellow, while the other is only black. Some printers have four separate cartridges of all process colours. This has extra advantage as it is easier to replace just one cartridge besides getting better print in black. Some inkjet printers use more than even four colour cartridges.

Outdoor Design **499**

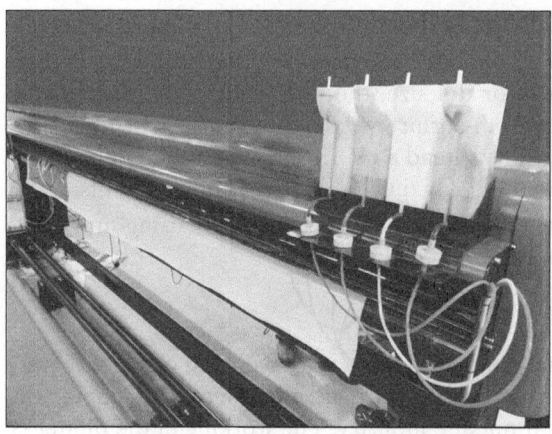

Figure 21.23 Wide-format printer with ink containers

Figure 21.24 Printing output showing a number of ups

These extra inks let the printer produce more subtle colours especially when blending from one colour to another.

Wide-format printers Printers used at home/office cannot print when the format is large. However, new age technology has invented wide-format printers. As illustrated in Figure 21.23, these printers can accept 24″ or wider formats and can print both sheets or roll media but at a slower speed.

Capability of printers Wide-format printers are designed for high-end production. Conventional print houses use these for high quality proofing. Outdoor signage makers utilize this format for quality output on various surfaces. Even art lovers, photographers, and painters prefer high quality prints (limited numbers) of their choicest work. In case of, say, one thousand prints, wide-format will be expensive. If one can plan the work imaginatively, a wide-format printer also can print a number of copies. Here, planning means how many ups can be printed on one sheet. Figure 21.24 shows a printing output with a number of ups. Remember that wide-format can print a smaller image but desktop normally cannot print a large one. Roll fed wide-format can print more than the size of the printer. If the output dimension is portrait, it means a 12′ wide printer can give an output of 12′ × 20′ or even larger.

Most desktop printers use four colours which are sufficient to obtain good quality prints. Since wide-format print heads travel a long distance and keep discharging ink per line, it is often difficult to maintain consistency of colour impression. Therefore, some extra print heads on these devices are used to double up the same basic colours and thus increase the print speed. It can also boost the colour gamut by adding extra ink such as orange and green.

Image and Print Quality

Image and print quality is the result of many factors. At least three quality features need attention while using a wide-format printer.

Resolution All wide-format printers have different resolution in terms of dpi (number of dots per square inch creating the image). It may be 2400×1200, 2880×720 or others.

For the general print buyer, it will hardly make any difference, because these dots are hardly discernible to the naked eye.

Ink droplet size The smaller the drop or dot size, the finer will be the details and smoother the colour variations, but slower the print speed. Some large dot printers also give good quality prints as these liquid dots spread a bit on surface and blend together and create a softer look. It also has an added advantage—it speeds up the prints.

Variable drop size Very advanced printers use these features for increasing fine highlight details and for optimizing continuous tone quality.

Cutting Plotter

It is a computer-driven die cutting machine, which has a role to play in outputting outdoor design. Traditional die cutter has already been discussed in detail in Chapter 18. The equipment is very useful in the sign-making industry. The working of the plotter is almost similar to wide-format printers and the look of the machine is also similar. The only difference is that printers print on various surfaces by inkjet technology, whereas plotters cut the desired shape in single colour line art.

Originally, a plotter was used in architectural drawing by attaching an ink pen to its print head. Modern cutting plotters replaced the ink pen with a sharp knife that could cut the shapes of the design. The plotter's knives are capable of cutting various materials, such as paper, card, vinyl, and film—anything that can be laid on the flat surface area of the plotter. The cutting plotter is equipped with computer software programs meant for cutting design or drawing. The plotter's knife is activated to produce the image correctly on giving necessary command to the software.

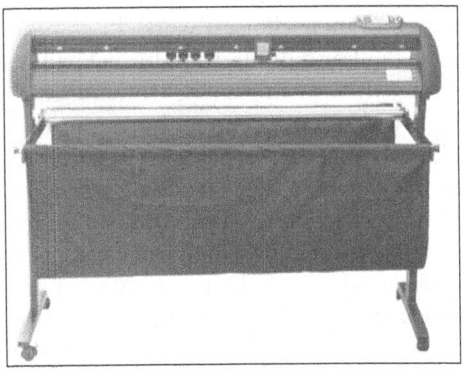

Figure 21.25 A vinyl cutting plotter machine

Vinyl cutter In sign making, it is popularly known as a vinyl cutter because of the versatile use of vinyl materials. Different materials need different pressure controls to determine how hard the knife should press into the substrate, to cut the design elements fully or partly. Since a plotter can cut design elements on a single sheet at a time, making multicolour designs with a plotter is complicated. In such a case, each coloured shape should be cut separately and then laid out as per the design plan, which is time consuming. Several design elements but in single colour can be handled by the plotter easily as it cuts through only the upper surface of the substrate, thus not allowing the back surface to be completely cut. These then can be easily pasted on the required surface. See Figure 21.25 for a vinyl cutting plotter machine.

Figure 21.26 A router

Router It is a cutting tool that hollows out or routs out an area of a hard surface, as shown in Figure 21.26. There are two kinds of routers: hand-held and computer numerical control (CNC). Both are commonly used in decorating a wood surface. In outdoor application, CNC router is used for cutting plastic, acrylic, aluminium, foam board, etc., besides wood decoration. Since the machine is computer operated, it can cut any intricate shape and also etch and curve the surface as per the desired design.

PRINT CONSUMABLES

Printing materials consumed during the printing process are of utmost importance. The two main consumables are ink and substrates.

Ink

It is basically a colour, which is composed of two components: colouring substance and vehicle. The vehicle may be aqueous or water-based and solvent or pigment-based.

Dye-based Most of us are familiar with the water-based ink, commonly known as dye, for colouring things like textiles. Colouring substance of dyes are minute molecules extracted from animals, plants, and minerals. On dissolving in water, it remains transparent and looks brilliant, and saturated. Thermal or piezo inkjet printers use this ink for various types of commercial and sign-making applications. Dye-based inks work well on uncoated paper that absorbs ink. The ink droplet also spreads a bit which is often advantageous for getting effect of continuous tone image. For outdoor images the colours fade fast and cannot stand humidity. Therefore, prints using dye ink must be protected by lamination.

Solvent-based Solvent is used to describe any ink that is a pigment and is not water-based. As the pigment particles are insoluble in water they must be carefully dispersed in a resinous vehicle that will deliver them on the substrate. Figure 21.27 shows some solvent-based ink containers.

Pigment inks are in general more stable than dyes. They are significantly more resistant to light and less sensitive to humidity and other environmental conditions. The resultant prints are waterproof. Pigment inks can be used to print on uncoated vinyl and other media as well as rigid substrates, such as foam, board, and PVC. However, the pigment particles are larger as compared to the dye particles due to which it scatters more light on the surface. This reduces the range of colours or colour gamut and makes some colours look weaker and dull. Pigment colours have a greater tendency of shifting colour under different types of lights. Glossy surface is not ideal for pigment colour as the image area looks dull as compared to the non-image area.

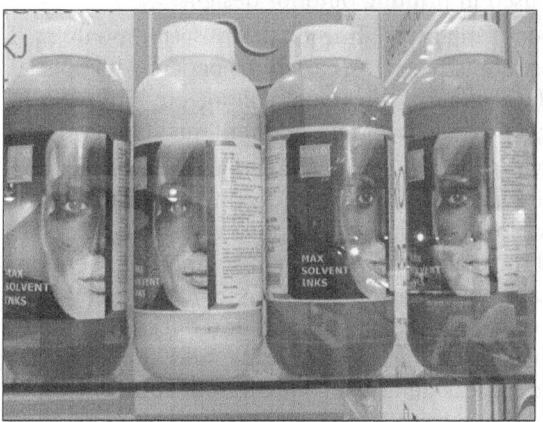

Figure 21.27 Solvent-based ink containers

In short, dye-based inks are more colourful on a wide range of media but are more prone to show colour changes on display, whereas pigment-based ink may offer less colour gamut but are more resistant to light and humidity and is also environment friendly. One solution to the above problem may be to mix dye and pigment together for a specific result. Another solution may involve UV curing after printing by any ink.

UV curing   Ultraviolet curing is commonly known as UV curing. It is basically a photochemical process in which high-intensity ultraviolet light is used to instantly cure or 'dry' printed inks, coatings, or adhesives. The resultant prints are waterproof, vibrant, and look embossed. UV curing offers many advantages over traditional drying methods. It increases production speed, reduces rejection rates, improves scratch and solvent resistance, and facilitates superior bonding. Any media material can be used in this technology; however, polymer-based media are the best. Some of the inkjet printers use UV curable ink for which no additional curing operation is required. Piezo inkjet is one such printer.

Fortunately, modern printing methods are improving. Ink manufacturers are continuously trying to come up with solutions to strike a balance between colour gamut and resistance to light.

OEM ink   Most of the inkjet printer manufacturers use inks commonly known as original equipment manufacturer (OEM) ink. However, a number of third-party inks are also available in the market nowadays. People use third-party ink because it is low cost, permanent, and has special uses. Before considering the third-party inks, one must check how close they are in terms of quality to the OEM inks and whether they are compatible with the printer. There is also the option of buying empty cartridges and filling them up with the ink of one's choice from the ink supplier. However, it is recommended to use only OEM ink for best results and trouble free life of a printer.

Substrates

They are the things used to print on, such as paper, vinyl, flex, etc. The substrates are available in the form of sheets as well as rolls. This chapter deals with substrates that are used in printing outdoor designs.

Paper   For any printing job the most commonly used substrate is paper. A variety of papers with special surface quality, thickness, colour, etc. are used in inkjet printing to obtain different quality images.

Vinyl   One of the primary media choices for signage is vinyl; technically called Polyvinyl Chloride (PVC). It is a low-cost plastic. It is, however, strong, durable, and moisture and humidity resistant. It is therefore suitable for various applications in outdoor signage. It is available in various colours and thickness, in both transparent and opaque forms, and can be single or double sided. The thickness of different vinyl may range from 150 to 350 gsm. Some vinyl rolls, as shown in Figure 21.28, are adhesive backed that

Figure 21.28   Vinyl rolls

facilitate pasting on various surfaces such as glass, acrylic, or wooden board. Images on hard transparent surfaces look brilliant when frontlit and backlit. Vinyl has a longer life when used for interior applications such as shopping malls, office interiors, etc., and has a shorter life if used for exterior applications. Images on polymer calendered vinyl surface gives photo quality effect, but is a bit costly because the ink required to achieve this effect is expensive.

Flex It is another media used to deliver high quality digital prints for outdoor hoardings and banners. Flex, which is ideal for front lit and backlit display, is widely used for large-sized printing. The fabricator and outdoor service provider improve the appearance of the printed materials by framing and appropriate lighting. The PVC coated flex provides anti-infiltration, good peel strength, and good tensile strength. It also gives better visual effect as compared to laminated flex. The surface coating optimizes ink adhesion and colour reproduction for long lasting brilliant prints. Some flex are also anti-flame and weather resistant. Frontlit flex are available in glossy and matte finish, suitable for all solvent-based inkjet systems.

Flex used for backlit signs and billboard are milky transparent. A light box is created at the back of a flex mounted frame; when the lights are illuminated, the image on the flex surface looks brilliant, especially at night. Backlit signs can also be used for indoor applications such as shop windows and store displays. The main advantage of backlit signs is that they stand out day and night. The light box for backlit signs can also be customized and adjusted to any shape. Even a single light box can be used on both sides of the display. One problem with a backlit display is that its one side is restricted by the width of the printer's output size, whereas a frontlit display's size can be increased by pasting two prints. Overlapping edges of two prints will be clearly visible in case of backlit signs, which gives it an unappealing finish.

Acrylic Another commonly used material in sign applications is acrylic. It is a highly durable plastic sheet available in a variety of colours—either milky or transparent. It comes in various thickness, ranging from 3 mm to 30 mm but easy to cut materials. The surface of most of the acrylic sheets are smooth and can be cut and bent to make the desired shape. Its natural glossy finish has high demand as display materials. These qualities of acrylic make it a perfect substrate for signs. Acrylic is ideal for indoor illuminated signs, directional signs at public transit places, wall displays at office receptions or restaurants, retail signs at malls and shops, menu boards at fast food outlets, and signs at various trade shows.

Images on acrylic can be obtained in various ways. Direct printing is possible by silk-screen printing methods or by fast drying inkjet printers. However, transfer sheet method is commonly used for printing an image on acrylic. It is like a sticker. Customized image is printed on a transfer sheet with an adhesive layer using a large format inkjet printer which is then pasted on acrylic. The backing sheet is then peeled off leaving only the printed image on the acrylic surface. Cutting out the image and pasting them on acrylic is another method. In this method, computer-driven cutting plotter is used to cut the image from self-coloured adhesive backed vinyl film that has a removable paper backing material.

A 3D look can be achieved on acrylic surface with cast and extruded. Cast acrylic is best suited for laser cutting. The edges of extruded acrylic, however, when cut, become rough and milky because of the stresses released. Acrylic sign letters are sharp and good to look at both in inside and outside applications and can be used in a variety of atmospheric conditions.

Low cost and versatility of acrylic are the greatest advantages for sign makers. The product can be cut into any shape because of computer-guided tools. It can be a logo of a company, type and design for a display banner, or any other design which has flat colours. Acrylic can be pigmented or painted with a long lasting durable baked enamel finish. Lineal bold face like Arial or Helvetica is preferable for acrylic signs. Fancy fonts are generally avoided for most acrylic surface. The signs can be illuminated with LED suitable for locations such as reception of a company or a window display of a shop. If you want a classy, effective, and clear looking sign that gets noticed, acrylic should be your choice.

Canvas Canvas is traditionally associated with an artist's painting medium. Besides being used as a painting surface, it is used as a utility media for making tents or bags, or covers of items that need environmental protection. Nowadays specially treated canvas has gained popularity among the printers and art lovers. The printed image on canvas gives a near original look to a painting. As a result one can buy a printed painting or print of a reputed work of art at an affordable price.

Large format inkjet printers are the best choice for printing on canvas. Canvas is available with different coatings, different weaves and textures, and are packaged as a roll for wide-format printers or cut sheets for desktop printing. It is a popular substrate for outdoor displays because of the sharp and vibrant image quality and its convenience to frame.

There are two kinds of canvas surfaces available—textured and stretchable. Textured canvas is similar to paper, which cannot be stretched or it might tear, while stretchable canvas can be placed on a traditional printer's frame, making a stretchable folding line. Textured/non-stretchable canvas gives a photo finish look but should be framed with a glass sheet to keep the canvas straight. Poly mix cotton makes the stretchable canvas strong and a protection coat makes its surface ideal for printing that has a long display life.

While choosing canvas as a medium for printing, one must keep in mind that unlike paper, canvas grains make the printed image a bit dull. It is therefore necessary to add some contrast and saturation to the image before printing. The best way to do this is to use the print profile in the computer for canvas and take a print on the desktop printer. Also remember that print meant for framing requires at least 2″ to 3″ space around the edge of the image to wrap the canvas around the frame attached to the back.

After printing, the canvas should be rolled and not folded until it is framed. This is because folding the canvas will make creasing marks which cannot be removed.

Aluminium Choice of aluminium for outdoor applications is due to its lightweight and rust-free characteristics. It is available in a variety of colours, some of which are fluorescent that glow at night, when light falls on it. It is sturdy yet easy to bend. Aluminium is the ideal choice for signage for real estate, traffic directions on highways, etc.

Corrugated plastic It is a lightweight versatile product used for short-term indoor and outdoor signage as it comes in a variety of colours to complement the sign message. It is a cost effective choice for special events, indoor point-of-purchase, trade shows, service companies, and temporary real-estate signage. Corrugated plastic can be cut to create collapsible signs. This product can be pre-cut into many shapes like the specialized golf ball shaped signs.

Expanded PVC Expanded PVC, also known as foam PVC, may be used indoors and outdoors for limited time. Its matte finish reduces glare and provides easy readability. Expanded PVC is lightweight, yet sturdy, and can be shaped into any form. It is an excellent product for trade shows' signage, menu boards, point-of-purchase displays, and architectural graphics. PVC is available in a variety of colours.

Foam core Foam core board is made up of two sheets of paper stuck to both sides of a foam core. It is lightweight but durable. Foam core board is easy to cut and customize, and is clay-coated for an extra smooth surface. Foam core accepts inkjet and full colour printing very well. Foam board comes in a variety of colours and is well suited for trade show applications and many other indoor uses. Standard foam core board is an economical product for temporary and short-term use.

SUMMARY

Outdoor design is synonymous with outdoor media. It has diversified forms and quite pervasive. Some of the forms are billboards, signs, banners, kiosks, and posters. It has many advantages including high impact of visuals which are seen from distance by the moving audience. Design plays a big role but does not have any set rules. Creativity of outdoor design depends on innovative ideas not only for selling a product but also to provide awareness and create an ambience. In advertising communication it is a support medium. Some forms of outdoor designs convey information, give direction, help in identification, and also give instructions. There are nevertheless some disadvantages. These include a brief message that often fails to register in the mind of the viewer; message loses effectiveness quickly due to high frequency of exposure; fabrication and technical support is expensive; and interspersed outdoor displays create visual pollution and often hinders public movement.

From design to production, outdoor media works in digital environment. The images meant for printing is bitmap. For quality output, image resolution and printer's resolution should be synchronized. Colour matching between computer images and printing image is another critical decision.

There are many outputting devices available for outdoor design. Most commonly used are large-format inkjet printers and cutting plotters. Both the devices get direction from computer to their printing heads. In inkjet, liquid ink is forced or sprayed through small air gap of print heads on a printing substrate, whereas in cutting plotter, a very sharp knife cuts each shape of design. Since inkjet printing is non-impact, it can print on different substrates such as vinyl, flex, acrylic, canvas, plastic, PVC, etc. Each one has distinctive characteristics and is suitable to particular types of outdoor design. Plotter's knives are capable of cutting different materials such as card, vinyl, or film that can be pasted on different flat surfaces as per the design requirement.

KEY TERMS

Acrylic Highly durable hard plastic that comes in various colours and thickness, either opaque or transparent. Materials can be cut easily and can be reasonably bent to give desired shape.

Aqueous Ink Colouring substance that dissolves in water. The ink works well with inkjet printers as it can spray ink through the small opening of the print head. Aqueous ink is brilliant but prone to damage fast.

Banner Large signage bearing a slogan or design either held in hand or hung in public places. It has multiple uses and may be in the form of a long strip of cloth, PVC, canvas, or flex material.

Billboards Large structured posters, also called hoarding or out-of-home (OOH) advertisement. Highly visible displays often found in high public transit areas that can be seen from a distance by the passing pedestrian and drivers.

Desktop Inkjet Printer A small portable, low cost printer ideal for home/office computer users. Technology works by spraying tiny droplets of ink on a page. The output is not very crisp and clear in comparison to other commercial printers.

Digital Colours Colours produced by digital devices—scanners, cameras, monitors, and printers. The first three devices use additive colours (RGB) system, whereas printers use subtractive colours (CYMK).

File Format A set of related data stored on a computer disk, which can be opened and transported in a specific application.

Flex A flexible roll or sheet of polythene available in various qualities. It is widely used to deliver high quality digital print for outdoor hoardings and banners and is mainly printed by wide-format digital printers.

Kiosk Small two- or three-dimensional structure that carries information in different forms of graphics for people walking or driving past.

LED Sign Light Emitting Diode, a semiconductor diode that emits light when a voltage is applied to it and that is used in an electronic display.

Neon Sign Images made out of hollowed glass tube that glows at appropriate temperature created by electric current.

Public Art Art pieces such as paintings, photographs, murals, and handicrafts that are displayed at public places for general viewing. These arts contribute to the aesthetics or mood of the environment.

Resolution Clarity of graphic image, which depends on several factors, such as the number of dots/pixels per inch, size and shape of dots, dot placement, type of substrate on which the image is printed, and printer driver setting.

Signage Visual graphics that represent a code is a signage. It is a form of finding information in public places for a particular audience.

Solvent Ink Colouring substances that are mixed with materials other than water, normally resinous vehicle, often called pigment ink. Pigment inks are in general far more stable than dyes.

UV Curing A photochemical process in which high-intensity ultraviolet light is used to instantly cure or 'dry' inks, coatings, or adhesives.

Viewing Distance The area that will provide optimum viewing of a display. More the distance, smaller will be the image and lesser details will be visible. If the viewing position is angular, the image will be vague and distorted.

Vinyl A form of low-cost plastic but strong and durable for outdoor utility. It is resistant to moisture, available in various colours and thickness, both in transparent and opaque form. It is one of the most common substrates for outdoor signage.

Wide-format Inkjet Printer Printing device that can handle sheets or reels of substrate equal to or greater than 24". It is useful for printing small run display jobs.

REFERENCES

- Gulati, Himani 2012, *Sign & P.O.P. World & Media 2000*, New Delhi.
- Jante, Vasant 2010–11, *Outdoor Asia*, V.J. Media Works Pvt. Ltd, Bangalore.
- Johnson, Harald 2005, *Mastering Digital Printing*, Muska & Lipman, Cincinnati, Ohio.
- O'Guinn, Thomas, Chris Allen, and Richard J. Semenik 2008, *Advertising and Integrated Brand Promotion*, South-Western College Publication.
- www.hippy.com, accessed in April 2012.

REVIEW QUESTIONS

1. Define outdoor design. Discuss the hand-painted era of outdoor design and its gradual demise.
2. Explain the characteristics of outdoor media in relation to graphic design.
3. Write in brief some important forms of outdoor designs and elaborate any three of them.
4. Why do people like outdoor designs? Answer the question mentioning the scope and challenges of outdoor creativity.
5. 'Despite the versatile forms of outdoor designs, some of the design rules are applicable at many situations in its design process.' Write the rules.
6. What do you understand by outdoor advertising and outdoor information graphics? Illustrate your answer with the help of appropriate examples.
7. Explain public art. Compare billboards and public arts, supported by suitable examples.
8. What is the role of digital technology in outdoor communication? Mention the points to be considered for digital imaging of outdoor design.
9. What are the most commonly used outputting devices of outdoor design? Identify one of them and discuss its working.
10. Explain dye-based and solvent-based ink. Mention their effect on outdoor images.
11. There are various substrates used for printing of outdoor designs. Mention as many as you can remember and elaborate two of them that are commonly used.

PROJECTS

1. Prepare a layout of a billboard for an airline company that is offering concessional airfare to see the Rio Olympics. Before jumping to a layout on the computer screen or paper, write down the following points and their details:
   (a) Target audience aimed at and their characteristics
   (b) Communication objective
   (c) Technical details which will include size, printing, substrate, and fabrication
   (d) Location and duration of display
   Now write some slogans and suggest a visual with each slogan. Select the best and develop on your computer screen. Take a printout and judge it as per the suggestions given in the text of this chapter and also see whether it is meeting the requirements of the points you have written down.
2. Take a day out of home with your digital camera or mobile phone with in-built camera. Keep on shooting the outdoor displays that come on your way. Transfer the images on your computer. Categorize the images as per the forms of outdoor you have learnt. Identify three of them which you like the most and discuss why you like them.
3. Take a desktop printout of your first project. Go to one of the digital printing houses of your locality. Discuss with them the printing feasibility of the layout and the costs involved. Write down the details of your discussion, starting from the type of artwork they need, substrate ink quality, and the number of prints to be supplied.
4. List three to four names of the companies that provide outdoor services in your town. They are available on the Internet, media directories, and also *Outdoor Asia*, a monthly journal on the subject. Visit them and take the rate of printing, substrate, and fabrication. Enquire the cost of site at different locations, maintenance of each site which will include illumination at night, and other special effects such as movement and glowing. Calculate the total cost and per unit cost. Give a presentation.
5. Collect the samples of substrates and printed samples of each kind of substrate of outdoor design. Take a folder containing the number of transparent plastic pockets. Insert a piece of substrate in the left pocket of the folder and the printed image in the right pocket. Write the details of the substrate and the printed image on a small sheet of paper and insert it in one of the pockets. Do this for all the samples you have collected. Title the project as 'Outdoor Samples'.

Index

A

absolute cost   399, 408
abstract association   356
accounts executive   282, 326
acrylic polymer   417
additive colour system   202
adhesive ink   184
Adobe FrameMaker   139
Adobe InCopy   139
Adobe InDesign   292
advertisement   299
   campaign   358
   classified   299
   comparative   326
   copy-heavy   299, 329
   display   299
   humour in   491
advertising
   agency   270
   campaign   316, 393
   creativity   321
   space   9
   strategy   491
Amul   491
analogous scheme   119, 491
antique finish   250
appeal   318
   direct sale   318
   emotional   319
   entertainment   319
   fear   319
   headline   329
   sex   319
Apple Macintosh   230
applied art   2
aqueous ink   506
arabesque figure   343, 364
Arabic numerals   461
arbitrary association   357
arbitrary mark   338
art and production   1
art director   326
art of printing   159
art paper   252, 453
art room   301, 311
artwork   173, 180, 206
aseptic packaging   430
'A' size paper   255
assembling   259
audio-visual system   359
authoritative approach   324
AutoCAD   430
automatic numbering   281

B

background elements   425
backlit display   503
backlit sign   503
back matter   462
balance   98, 99, 293
balanced lighting   56
banner   482, 506
   hand-painted   480
   bannerhead   307
   cloth   482, 489
bibliography   478
bilingual logo   345
billboard   406, 480, 491, 506
binary digit   194
binding   260
biological sign   357
bitmap image   60, 194
blanket-to-blanket printing
   press   177
bleed   210, 378, 403
   illustration   385
blind embossing   186
blind folio   461
block-out solution   182, 405
blue-line print   214
blurb   310, 379, 390, 474
bond paper   436
book   478
   binding   476
   jacket   474
   paper   251
   work   277
booklet   447

Brahmi script   16
brain-storming   327
brand
   identity   359, 423
   image   418
   name   340, 364, 422
broadsheet   254, 296, 386
   newspaper page   237
brochure   440, 456
bromide   331
   paper   406
'B' size paper   255
buckle folding   258
Buddhist philosophy   343
bullet   456, 467
bulletin board   481
business card   437, 456
business correspondence
   material   434
business process
   outsourcing   274

C

cable network   291
calendars   450
calendered finish   250
calendered vinyl   503
calibrate   202
calligraphic letterform   348, 472
calligraphy   17
camera-ready
   art   206
   artwork   279, 327
   copy   385, 478
captive audience   400, 408
carbon tissue   180
cardboard   426
case binding   261, 280
casebound book   476, 478
casting off   276
catalogue   456
centered   41
centrespread   382, 390
certification mark   340, 341

character kerning 227
Charles Wilkins 16
ChartWizard 64
chief sub-editor 290
chroma 113
chromoboard 333
chromo paper 396
circle 67
classical Roman faces 34
classical typefaces 24
clay craft 342
client brief 318
clip art 59
CMYK 152
coated finish 251
coated paper 257
cold typesetting 138
collage 55, 68, 304
collating 259
collective marks 340
colour
   additive 114
   and tint 106
   cartridges 498
   combination 118
   copy 151
   gamut 407, 501
   harmony 101
   in design 110
   luminous 113
   management 202
   page 311
   perspective 121
   picker 497
   primary 113
   reflective 112
   reproduction of 124
   scheme 118
   secondary 114
   separation 151, 203
   substractive 114, 204
   symbolism chart 344
   transmission 113
   transparency 405
   vision 112
   vivid 426
   wheel 119
coloured
   finish 251

pastel paper 282
column grid 293, 375, 380, 390
column width 310
comic book 467
communication
   art 3
   objectives 404
   technology 161
complementary scheme 119
comprehensive layout 84
compressed file format 198
compugraphic 348
computer-aided design
   (CAD) 227
computer-generated 53
   graphics 378
   illustrations 53
computer
   graphics 406
   imagery systems 384
   template 387
computer-to-plate 176
consumer profile 351
Consumer Protection Act 428
container 416, 430
contents page 378
continuous tone 173
   illustration 173
   image 54, 180
contrast 98, 102, 294
conventional artwork 86
conveyor belt 186
copy
   block 327, 331, 445
   chief 327
   editing 463, 478
   editor 132, 463
   estimation 302
   fitting 133
   marking 132
Copyright Act 429
copyright-free illustration 306
copyright
   infringement 429
   protection 350
copywriter 8, 318, 326, 446
CorelDraw 78, 84
corporate
   brochure 445

colour 497
   house 438, 449
   identity 362, 363, 364
   image 418
corrugated board 416, 430
costing 268
cover
   layout 77
   page 378
   paper 253
creasing or scoring 258
creative
   artist 322
   brief 281
   strategy 418
   team 318
credit line 390
crest 340, 341, 364
crop mark 210
cropping 68, 70, 143
crossover 211
Crown Sexto 257
crystallization 66
'C' size paper 255
cultural hub 492
customer benefit 420
cut-off rule 297
cutout halftone 67
cutout photo 310
cutting
   and trimming 260
   plotter 500, 503

D

dampening unit 172
dark scheme 121
data interfacing 138
David Ogilvy 267
deck 303
decorative
   element 425
   faces 28
   strokes 19
deep-etch plates 174, 279
Delhi Metro Rail
   Corporation 493
demi-official (DO) letter 456
demography 404, 408
Demy Quarto 375

design
  brief   281, 318, 419
  concept   419
  designer   8
  element   104, 299
  grid   206
  of a newspaper   292
  planning   375
  principles of   90
  software   106
  solving process   419
  studio   270, 274
  syntax   327
  work   270
desk calendar   451
desktop   498
  inkjet printer   498, 506
  inkjet printout   213
  proof   212
  publishing   161, 226
Devanagari   353
  letterform   345
  script   17
  style   472
diagonal line method   144
diaries   452
  executive   452
  illustrative   453
  non-executive   453
  pocket   452, 454, 464
  ready-made   452
die   186, 430
  stamping   186, 263
die-cutting   281
digital   164
  camera   200
  colour   506
  copy fitting   133
  file   206
  halftone   200
  image   59, 327
  imposition proof   222
  letterform   22
  outdoor   407
  page planning   86
  prepress   173
  printing   496
  proofing   427
  signboard   354

digitized typesetting   138, 161
direct association   355
direct interfacing   139
direct mailer   456
direct sale appeal   318
display
  faces   43
  types   136, 465
distribution   454
docket sheet   284
doctor blade   181
dot matrix printer   231
dots per linear inch   149
drop letters   132, 310, 382
drum scanner   199
dumb printer   231
dummy   76, 447
  book   463
  sheet   292, 299
duotone effect   67, 125
dye-based ink   501

E

ear pieces   297
economic liberalization   322, 394, 409
editorial
  page   309, 379
  planning   375
electronic
  page planning   333, 385
  pagination   306
  publishing   461
emblem   340, 341, 364
embossing   67
  hologram   187
emotional needs   420
end papers   476, 478
English finish   250
engraving   159, 169
envelope   439
  baronial   439
  booklet   440
  commercial   439
  metal clasp   439
  open-ended   439
ephemeral periodicals   367
EPS (encapsulated postscript)   496

file format   234
equipment   229
estimate form   275
estimating   269
excite curiosity   420
execution   8
exhibition design   281
external drum platesetters   219
eyelet punching   263
eye movement   296

F

face structure   18
face style   33
fake colour   125
fake duotone   67
feathering   68
feature article   310
file format   196, 496, 506
film   430
  lamination   416
  positive   174, 182
  separation proof   213
fine art   2
finished rough   81
finishing   262
five-star film   182
fixed cost   284
flap   474
flatbed
  cylinder letterpress   168
  platesetter   219
  scanner   199
flat lighting   56
flats   173
flexography   170
flickering effect   425
flyer   315, 456
folding   258
  carton   415, 430
folio   375, 461, 467
folk art   342
folk style painting   55
font   204
food package   426
footer   382, 448, 464
formal balance   99
format   464
four-colour   127

processing   311
process printing   204
Fournier–Didot   20
framer   106
free-hand graphic   227
freelance artist   270
French fold   443
front cover   472
frontispiece   461, 478
front page   306

G

galley   470
galley proof   78, 140, 381, 390
gate fold   443
gathering   259
generation loss   56
generic brand   430
generic name   423
geometrical centre   92
glass containers   416
global market   413
global networking   292
glossy raised image   186
gold leaf printing   187
grain direction   280
grained metal plates   172
grams per square metre   256
graphic
  art   4
  communication   5, 50
  design business   281
  designer   91
  journalist   290
  software   233, 234
graphics generation   227
gravure   180
greyscale image   194
grid and guidelines   104
grid sheet   375, 381
grid template   301
gross   255
gutter space   376, 381

H

half-line   67
half title   461, 478

halftone
  art   65, 600, 206
  film   200
  illustration   174, 181
  image   178
  reproduction   149
hand-cut stencil   183
hard copies   466
hardware   229
harmony   98, 101, 296
header   390, 448, 464
headline   302
hidden promise   424
hieroglyphics   14
hoarding   399, 409
hologram   478
  printing   187, 472
hot-foil stamping   187, 416
house style   364, 460, 463
hue   113
hygroscopic food   415, 430

I

IBM PC   230
Idea   490
identity manual   359, 364
identity mark   338
ideogram   338
illuminated sign   503
illustration   53
  computer-generated   53
  continuous-tone   173
  copyright-free   306
  editing of   68
  halftone   174, 181
  hand-drawn   53
  reverse line   63
  wood-cut   52
illustrator   78, 84
image
  assembly   179
  conversion   208
  cropping   304
  editing   227
  format   107
  integration   207
  resolution   195
  setter   223, 228, 470
imaginary line   93

imaginary point   91
imaging unit   218
impact printer   231
importing and linking   106
imposition   209, 218, 258
impression cylinder   173
impulse buying   423
in-built dictionary   227
indentation   132, 467
index   309
Indian
  motif   424
  ritual   343
  typefaces   30
indirect association   356
individual response   116
industrial designer   413
Indus Valley ideograms   16
informal balance   99
information technology   392
in-house
  designer   274, 463
  printing   388
ink density   215
ink flow identifiers   215
inkjet printer   408, 498
  piezo   501
inkjet printing   165
inkjet technology   498
ink viscosities   427, 430
insetting   259
insignia   340, 364
instant image   53, 58
intaglio   159
  printing   186
intangible
  attribute   324
  qualities   324
  value   420
intelligent printer   231
International Sizes (ISO)   255
intertype   137
introduction   390
ivory card   333

J

job work   277
Johann Gutenberg   16
jumps   309
justified   41

K

key communication
  message 318
kicker 303
kilograms (kg) for a ream 255
kiosk 399, 409, 481, 483, 506
  multimedia 483

L

label
  design 416
  printer 427
labour cost 269
lamination 262, 281, 408, 475
large format 484
  digital printing 484
  inkjet printer 408
  printer 409
laser
  printer 231
  printing 165
layout
  planner 76
  planning 76, 80
  program 470
  software 233, 237
  style 330
LCD monitor 202
lead story 302
leaflet 440, 446, 456
leaf printing 263
LED
  sign 483, 506
  signboard 484
left flushed 41
legibility 32
leisure reading periodical 367
letterhead 434, 456
letterpress 167
letter spacing 38
ligature 19
light box 487, 503
light-sensitive emulsion 182
limestone 172
lineal faces 31
line
  and halftone 61, 149
  and tint 149
  and tone image 61
  art 206
  image 54
  length 132
  negative 173
  reproduction 148, 181
  spacing 39
lines per inch 195
linguistic sign 338
linking image 208
linotype 137
  system 161
lithography 160, 172
  offset 160, 162
  process 392
logo 339, 364
logotype 355
long-run print 181
low-grade paper 396
'L' scale 69

M

machine proofs 214
magazine 374, 390
  aesthetic and culture 372
  editor 374
  format 375
  glamour 369
  news 368
  special interest 370
mailer 315
major printing 163
make-ready 179
make-up 78
  person 302
manual folding 258
manuscript 132, 462
Maqbool Fida Husain 481
market coverage 398, 409
marketing plan 281
marketing strategy 425, 472
mascot 340, 341, 364
master copy 228, 388
master page 107
masthead 297, 376
meaning 91
  primary 91
  secondary 91
media

planning 395
  space 76
memory (RAM) 230
memo sheet 434, 456
metal
  composing 161
  container 417
metallized film 187
mezzotint 67
micro-computer 230
Microsoft Excel 63
mini offset 166
Mithila painting 495
mock-up 78, 426
modular pattern 298
monochromatic scheme 121
monotone 121
monotype system 161
montage 68
motif 349, 365
movable type 16, 138, 159, 392, 459
  system 161
multi-bit scanner 233
multilingual society 423
multi-media environment 352

N

nameplate 306
national emblem 347
national flower 343
native format 196
natural environment 399
negative working plate 174
neon sign 482, 506
newsletter 385, 390
newspaper
  designing 290
  form 296
  format 297
  headline 302
  mainstream 292
  marketing 291
  picture 304
news photo 311
newsprint 252, 301, 384
news-stand 369, 390
non-impact printer 231
non-information-bearing

element 442
non-selective medium 398
non-verbal communication 337, 365, 459
non-verbal sign 338
notepad 434, 456
novelty calendar 451
numbering 263

O

object-oriented drawing program 235
OEM ink 502
offset printing 172
  plates 174
on-demand printing 163, 164
OOH 491
opacity 250
op art 52
OpenType 22, 205
opportunity-to-see (OTS) 399, 409
optical centre 92
optical character recognition 139, 233
original image 53
ornamental style 331
orphan line 467
outdoor
  advertising 481
  medium 399
  signage 499
outputting 227

P

package prototype 426
packaging media 413
  flexible 414
packaging technology 426
page
  layout 76, 206
  layout program 376
  make-up 463
PageMaker 85
paint program 236, 406
pamphlet 442, 447, 456
panchromatic plate 220
Pantone and Agfa 497
paparazzi 304

paperback 475, 476, 478
paper
  characteristic 249
  size 253
  stock 384
  varieties 251
paragraph spacing 40
paste-up 389
Patent Act 429
pattern 90, 187
patterned foil 188
PDF format 496
pencil sketch 55
perfect binding 261, 280, 476
perforating 451
periodical 367
  ephemeral 367
  leisure reading 367
  official 367
personal communication 441
photo editor 304
photographic stencil 182
photopolymer 220
  plate 298
Photoshop 84
phototypesetting 138, 162, 298
pica scale 21
pictograph 63
pictographic 348
pictorial style 354
picture libraries 304
pixel-based application 195
pixelization 66
placard 405
planography 171
plastic container 417
plate cylinder 174
platen letterpress 168
platen press 187
platesetter 218
plotter 427
pocketbook 375, 390
pointilizing 67
point of purchase (POP) 396, 409, 481
point of sale 454
political cartoon 309
pop art 52, 424
positive working plate 174

postal regulation 454
poster 409
posterization 62
PostScript 22, 195, 205
  fonts 23
pot painting 492
preface 478
preflight check 107, 212
preliminaries 448, 461, 478
prepress task 10
pre-sensitized plates 174, 179
press
  coverage 396
  layout 76
  proofs 215
  run 257, 390
pre-testing 395, 409
primary medium 393
print buyer 10, 275
printer 10, 231
printing 16, 107
  development 161
  processes 163
  registration 179
print line 390
print project 188
process
  camera 169, 333
  colour 114, 126, 152, 203
  colour guide 497
processing department 178
product
  design 418
  designer 421
production 10
  planning 384
progressive proof 279, 214
promotional folder 474
promotional literature 385, 440
proof 140
  checking 212
proofreading 140
  mark 467
proportion 98
prototype 358, 421
  container 427
psychographics 409
  psychological bridge 420
  psychophysical response 114

Index

psychography 404
public art 492, 506
public relation 385, 452
PVC coated flex 503
pyramid 303

Q

quad 254
QuarkXpress 78, 292
quartertone 62
quick print shop 388

R

radial balance 100
random access 230
rasterization 218
   raster image 60, 496
readability 32
ready-to-print 277
real or structural line 93
real or structural point 93
ream 255
recyclable material 416
redesigned logo 363
red triangle 357
regular fold 442
relief printing 167
remote interfacing 139
research bureau 282
resolution 496, 506
retail packaging 412
reverse line illustration 63
reverse type 42
RGB 113
RGB primaries 202
rhythm 98, 100, 293
rhythmic style 330
right angle fold 443
right ragged 41
Roman
   faces 24
   letterform 345
   styles 24
rotary letterpress 168
rotogravure process 180
rough layout 81
router 501
rubber blanket 172, 173, 179

rubber squeegee 182
running page 380

S

saddle stitching 476
satellite link 291
scaling 70, 143
   mathematical method 144
scanner 199, 232
   electronic 333
screen
   angle 201
   frequency 195, 201
   printing 181
section page 309
section sewn 382
selective medium 449
self-cover booklet 447
self-mailer 445, 454, 456
Semitic alphabet 15
service mark 340
sewn binding 261
sex appeal 319
shape harmony 101
sheet-fed presses 177
shipping packaging 412
short fold 443
short-run job 388
sidebar 478
side lighting 56
sign 338, 365
signage 492, 482, 506
signature 258, 448, 456, 476, 478
signographic letterform 348
signography 17
silent salesperson 420
silhouette
   image 63
   style 330
silk-screen printing 405
silver halide 220
simulated picture 446
simulated type 446
single-bit scanned image 233
sink 478
sizing and marking 146
skyline matter 307
soft-copy 466
soft scheme 120

software 229, 233
solarization effect 62
solar light 483
solvent-based ink 501, 506
souvenir item 449
specialized printing 163
special supplement 311
spine 478
   design 472
spiral/spico binding 262
split complementary
   scheme 120
spot colour 126, 151, 203
   printing 311
spreadsheet application 234
spreadsheet software 233
square serif 27
standard costing 269
standard image format 197
steel etch 67
stock photo 57
stock photographer 304
storyboard 79
stretch 250
stripping 173, 279
stroke 19
   curve 19
   decorative 19
   primary 19
structural line 93
structure 90
style and idea 354
style guide 465
substrate 187, 502
   acrylic 503, 505
   aluminium 504
   canvas 504
   corrugated plastic 505
   expanded PVC 505
   flex 503, 506
   foam core 505
   paper 502
   vinyl 502, 506
subtractive system 202
suitable grid 446
sunburst 446, 447
superimposing 304
swastika 338, 365
syllabary 14

Index 515

symbol   338, 365
symbolic response   116
syntax   98

T

tabloid   237, 296, 386
tag line   377
tantra art   365
tantric art   342
target market   351
terracotta mural   495
text
   fitting   133
   matter   33, 135
textured finish   251
texturizing   67
thermal-sensitive plate   220
thermography   184
   printing   263
three-dimensional
   illusion   188
   image   52
thumbnail   352
   sketch   80, 293, 404
TIFF format   208
tinplate   396, 417
tin rimming   451, 456
title page   478
tone   97
   harmony   102
tracing flap   282
trade association   275
trademark   339, 365
trade name   339, 365
traditional
   halftone   200
   packaging   414
   prepress   173
transparencies   468
transparent   503
trapping   209, 218
triad scheme   120
trimmed size   478
triotone effect   125
TrueType font   22, 23, 205
tusche glue   182
two-dimensional image   52
two-page grid sheet   381
type

body   18
composition   31
families   29
feature   18
legibility   404
measurement   20
size   37
typeface   18
   fancy   28
   handwritten   28
   lineal   26
   modern style Roman   26
   novelty   28
   old style Roman   26
typescript   132
typesetting   137
   typesetter   462, 465
typographical harmony   102
typographic letterforms   348
typography   17

U

ultraviolet coating   262
unity   98, 103, 296
ups   427
UV curing   502, 506

V

value-added packaging   417
variable cost   284
varnishing   262
vector
   based application   195
   image   60, 194
   object   194
   program   235
vedic tradition   365
verbal code   365
verbal copy   131
viewing distance   487, 506
vignette effect   68
vinyl   502, 506
   cutter   500
   sign   482
viscous ink   187
visual
   aesthetics   2
   art   1
   communication function   51

copy   143
image   50
literacy   3, 394
symbol   58
visualization   326
visualizer   327
vivid colour scheme   403
vocabulary   91
Vodafone campaign   486

W

wall calendar   450
wall newspaper   386
wash painting   55
water-based ink   501
web design   281
web-fed machine   375
web-fed press   177
web journalism   292
web-offset   280
weight and quantity   255
wide-format inkjet printer   506
wide-format printer   499
widow line   467, 478
Wilkins's types   16
window pack   421
wipe-on plate   179, 279
wipe-on solution   174
wire stitching   261
wood
   block printing   459
   carving   159, 180
   cut block   392
   cut illustration   52
Woodland   488
word processing software   233
word spacing   39
working rough   81, 404
wrapping material   415
writing and stationery
   paper   252
written statement   445

X

x-height   19

Z

zodiac   365